SELECTED STUDIES IN BIBLIOGRAPHY

Selected Studies in Bibliography

G. THOMAS TANSELLE

Published for the Bibliographical Society
of the University of Virginia
by the University Press of Virginia
Charlottesville

THE UNIVERSITY PRESS OF VIRGINIA
Copyright © 1979 by the Bibliographical Society of the
University of Virginia

First published 1979

Library of Congress Cataloging in Publication Data
Tanselle, George Thomas, 1934–
  Selected studies in bibliography.

  Reprinted from Studies in bibliography, 1967–79.
  1. Bibliography—Addresses, essays, lectures.
I. Virginia. University. Bibliographical Society.
Studies in bibliography. II. Title.
Z1005.T336 1979   011   79–12476
  ISBN 0–8139–0829–9

Printed in the United States of America

To

Fredson Bowers

Foreword

In 1963 Mr. Tanselle published a note in *Studies in Bibliography*, volume XVI, "An Unknown Early Appearance of 'The Raven,'" followed in the next year, volume XVII, with "Unsigned and Initialed Contributions to *The Freeman*." In the next volume, XVIII, of 1965, the article "The Historiography of American Literary Publishing" confirmed the appearance of a major talent in American bibliography, a scholar marked by extraordinary thoroughness and copiousness of investigation, the material ordered by a powerfully structured intelligence.

Sixteen years after 1963, his seventeenth *SB* article, "External Fact as an Editorial Problem," led off volume XXXII in 1979—a record of annual publication matched by no other contributor and one to be broken only by Mr. Tanselle himself. In addition, important contributions have appeared in *The Library* and in the *Papers of the Bibliographical Society of America*; but the *SB* articles as a group have had a major influence on the theory and practice of bibliography and textual criticism. The eleven most significant of these, of his own choice, have now been collected at the initiative of the Society and reproduced by offset as they were originally printed. These fall naturally into three divisions: (I) studies of the theory and tools of bibliography, chiefly descriptive; (II) analyses of the problems that occur in dealing with bindings and paper in descriptive bibliography; and (III) an important series on textual criticism and editing. Each of these articles has come to hold a place of authority in its specific area.

Mr. Tanselle has by no means had his final say on these and on a number of related topics, however. But his proposed revision of these pieces for a consolidated general survey, also to include matters not dealt with in his *SB* series, is still for the future. In the interval, the present collection will make this series more readily available for reference and close study by students and scholars in the field.

The Council of the
Bibliographical Society
of the University of Virginia

Contents

SELECTED STUDIES IN BIBLIOGRAPHY

Bibliography and Science

REVIEWER FOR THE *Times Literary Supplement*, COMMENTing in 1972 on two bibliographical annuals, remarked, "To argue about the scientific nature of bibliography now is surely to pursue a red herring."[1] I could not agree more. When I observed a few years ago, "All that 'scientific' can mean when applied to bibliographical analysis and textual study is 'systematic,' 'methodical,' and 'scholarly,' "[2] I was only repeating what a number of others have said and what many more must believe. It seems obvious that the word "scientific," when used to describe bibliography—as it has been off and on for more than a century—does not mean the same thing as when it is applied to physics, say, or chemistry. Apparently the issue cannot be dismissed so easily, however, for there have been several recent essays—notably those by D. F. McKenzie, James Thorpe, Peter Davison, and Morse Peckham[3]—which take up fundamental questions regarding the connections between science and bibliography. In a sense one must agree with the *TLS* that "it is perhaps a pity that he [McKenzie] revived the old argument about the scientific nature of bibliography"; at the same time, the existence of this group of essays suggests that the issue is not a dead one, and the *TLS* admits that the matter is "currently very much in the air."

Actually, of course, what is in the air is an attempt to clarify the nature of bibliography as a discipline, and what is a pity is that the focus on science may only serve to confuse the central question. Both "science" and "bibliography" have many different meanings, and, when

1. *TLS*, 2 June 1972, p. 640.

2. "Textual Study and Literary Judgment," *PBSA*, 65 (1971), 111.

3. McKenzie, "Printers of the Mind: Some Notes on Bibliographical Theories and Printing-House Practices," *SB*, 22 (1969), 1-75; Thorpe, "The Ideal of Textual Criticism," in *The Task of the Editor* (1969), pp. 1-32; Davison, "Science, Method, and the Textual Critic," *SB*, 25 (1972), 1-28; Peckham, "Reflections on the Foundations of Modern Textual Editing," *Proof*, 1 (1971), 122-55.

the two words are joined, the possibilities for confusion are multiplied. It is in this sense that the issue may be regarded as nonexistent, for "scientific bibliography" can mean almost anything, and arguments about it may amount to no more than knocking down straw men. Self-examination, though, is presumably a healthy thing, and bibliography will no doubt profit, as it has in the past, from soul-searching. It may be that bibliographers, at one stage, needed to overemphasize the scientific aspect of their work as a means of calling attention to, and insisting upon, its rigorous and scholarly nature, and that they have now reached a stage where they feel an urge to redress the balance. Bibliography—like many of the so-called "social sciences" (and I am not at this point claiming that it is a social science)—has been somewhat uneasy about its own identity, and it would not be surprising to find that attempts to define it have followed a pendulum-like course. Current discussion which questions in various ways the notion that bibliography is "scientific" may eventually lead—if a debate about "science" itself does not get in the way—to more fruitful analysis of the relations between one kind of bibliographical inquiry and another and of the procedures appropriate to each. In supposing that there is little to be gained by further discussion of how "scientific" bibliography is, I am not complaining about the general direction in which these recent articles are moving but about their circuitous path.

It is easy to understand why bibliographers have had a tendency to proclaim the scientific nature of what they were doing. For one thing, they have wanted, especially during the late nineteenth and early twentieth centuries, to demonstrate that bibliography is a scholarly pursuit, to be distinguished from a merely dilettante concern for book collecting. In their zeal to show the respectability of their relatively new discipline, bibliographers were naturally tempted to play up the aspects of their work that could be compared to science, for the spectacular accomplishments of the physical sciences made "science" glamorous and gave particular advertising value to the word. This temptation has been intensified by the fact that bibliography has been associated most closely with the study of literature and that bibliographers are frequently members of English departments who assume that, since much of their work seems more objective than literary criticism, it is somehow scientific. The misunderstanding which occasionally exists between bibliographers and other members of English departments seems to turn on the matter of "science": the bibliographer often makes extravagant claims for the definiteness of his conclusions and may feel flattered to think that he is a scientist of sorts;

certain literary scholars, on the other hand, believe that imagination and insight are unnecessary in the search for scientific facts and assume that bibliographical work is on a lower intellectual plane than literary criticism. Both are wrong in their understanding of science;[4] but the fact remains that it has become a cliché, in the context of literary studies, to regard bibliography as scientific in some way.

Any such tradition has a grain of truth at its center: obviously there is something more "factual" about bibliography than about literary criticism. But the usefulness of science *as an analogy* has led some people to take the claims for the scientific status of bibliography more literally or in a more precisely detailed sense than was originally intended. I think that a glance at the ways in which science has been linked with bibliography ("the scientific analogy")[5] over the years will reveal the shifting meanings of the two terms, the repetitiveness of the discussions, and the growing tendency to be critical of the comparison itself. And perhaps this kind of survey can provide a perspective from which to view the current situation.[6]

I

During much of the nineteenth century "bibliography" was understood to mean what we would now regard as "reference bibliography"[7] (or "enumerative bibliography")—that is, it was concerned with the intellectual content of books, with preparing lists of books on particular subjects, with the classification of knowledge and the arrangement of libraries.[8] Thomas Hartwell Horne, in *An Introduction to the*

4. F. H. Ludlam has commented, in another connection, on the failure of some scholars to recognize that "the aim of both artists and scientists is to communicate a new and valuable way of regarding the phenomena, an enterprise in which there can be no absolute and permanent correctness" ("The Meteorology of Shelley's Ode," *TLS*, 1 September 1972, p. 1015). Cf. A. E. Housman's classification of scholars as scientists (and his distinction between literary critics and scholars) in *The Confines of Criticism*, ed. John Carter (1969), pp. 26-34.

5. I shall use the term "scientific analogy" as a convenient shorthand to refer to any linking of "bibliography" (in any sense) with "science" (in any sense).

6. I have not attempted to provide an exhaustive history of the scientific analogy but rather a sketch which incorporates a representative sampling of relevant pronouncements over the years.

7. I am using the terms suggested by Lloyd Hibberd in "Physical and Reference Bibliography," *Library*, 5th ser., 20 (1965), 124-34.

8. The history of the word "bibliography" has been studied in great detail: one thorough survey is the opening section of David Murray's "Bibliography: Its Scope and Methods," *Records of the Glasgow Bibliographical Society*, 1 (1912-13), 1-105 (reprinted separately in 1917), which refers to bibliography as "one of the oldest, and yet one of the most modern of the sciences"

Study of Bibliography (1814), went somewhat further and included discussion of the materials of books and the history of printing; but when he referred, in his preface, to "the infant science of Bibliography," he obviously meant nothing more than "the classification of books as a field of knowledge."[9] The use of "science" in the general sense of "systematic knowledge" recurs in most of the nineteenth-century discussions. It is explicit, for example, in Reuben A. Guild's *The Librarian's Manual* (1858), which defined "bibliography" as "the Science or Knowledge of Books" (p. 3). That he equated this science primarily with checklists is evident when he went on to say, "In Great Britain Bibliography as a Science has received less Attention than upon the Continent, although valuable Works have been produced by HORNE and LOWNDES, DIBDIN and WATT" (p. 5). His view of bibliography as a "*practical* Science" (p. 5) was still essentially the same two decades later when he wrote an article entitled "Bibliography as a Science," in which "bibliography" really means "librarianship."[10] Similarly, E. Fairfax Taylor, in the ninth edition of the *Encyclopaedia Britannica* (1875), though he included some account of printing history under "Bibliography," defined his subject as "the science of books, having regard to their description and proper classification"—using "description," in the sense standard at the time, to mean a recording of the basic facts considered necessary to identify a book (those we would now think appropriate for a checklist).[11]

(p. 2); an even more extensive survey is Rudolf Blum's "Bibliographia: Eine wort- und begriffsgeschichtliche Untersuchung," *Archiv für Geschichte des Buchwesens*, 10 (1970), cols. 1010-1246. A convenient collection of quotations of definitions of bibliography appears in Percy Freer's *Bibliography and Modern Book Production* (1954), pp. 1-13.

9. Even at this early stage, however, the word "science" in this context did not go without criticism. Macvey Napier, writing the first full article on "Bibliography" for the *Encyclopaedia Britannica* (in the *Supplement* of 1816), complained about Horne's remark: "He seems to have allowed himself to be imposed upon, by the vague *verbiage* of those French Writers, who claim for this branch of knowledge a character of vastness which does not belong to it." In another criticism of the French view, he says that "some of her Biblio-

graphers have lately fallen into a very extravagant mode of describing the nature and rank of this branch of Learning. They go so far as to represent it as a Universal Science, in whose ample range all other sciences, and all other kinds of knowledge, are comprehended."

10. *Library Journal*, 1 (1876-77), 67-69. It is worth noting, however, that his inclusion among the bibliographer's concerns of "the materials of which books are composed" and the "external peculiarities or distinctions of an edition" foreshadows the later emphasis of physical bibliography.

11. He also referred to the development of "material" (or physical) bibliography as "due to the gradual formation of a technical science of books" and ended by saying that bibliographers should "recognise the chief value of their science as the handmaid of literature." Taylor's article

It is generally recognized that a new meaning for "bibliography" developed in the last third of the century from the work of William Blades, Henry Bradshaw, and Robert Proctor on incunabula. Blades's *The Life and Typography of William Caxton*, published in 1861-63, attempted to classify and date Caxton's books on the basis of a close examination of their typography; according to T. B. Reed, writing in 1891, this book "marked a new epoch in bibliography, and disposed finally of the lax methods of the old school."[12] Blades himself had commented a few years earlier on the achievement of Bradshaw, whose important classified indexes of incunabula began with his work on the de Meyer collection in 1869:

From an early period he perceived that to understand and master the internal evidences contained in every old book, the special peculiarities of their workmanship must be studied and classified, much in the same way as a botanist treats plants, or an entomologist insects. This he called "the natural-history system." . . . To make his work more effectual and scientific, he did that which many a bibliographer has to his great loss omitted to do—he made acquaintance with the technicalities of book-making.[13]

In remarks of this kind, both "bibliography" and "science" are obviously used in a different sense from the way in which Horne or Guild had understood them. "Bibliography" here means what we would now call "analytical bibliography," with the emphasis on physical evidence, and "science" refers not to systematic knowledge in general but to the examination of empirical data. The movement initiated by these men is what lies behind Henry Stevens's statement in 1877 that bibliography "is fast becoming an exact science, and not a whit too soon. It is high time to separate it from mere catalogue-making"[14]—a statement which was echoed in remarkably similar language by W. A. Copinger in his "Inaugural Address" before the newly formed Bibliographical Society fifteen years later.[15]

---

followed the same plan as Napier's 1816 article but was largely rewritten.

12. "Memoir of the Late William Blades," in Blades, *The Pentateuch of Printing* (1891), p. xii.

13. Quoted (from the *Printer's Register*, 6 March 1886) in G. W. Prothero, *A Memoir of Henry Bradshaw* (1888), p. 363. Reed called Bradshaw "the keenest of the new scientific school of bibliographers" (Blades, *Pentateuch*, p. xiii).

14. "Photo-Bibliography," *Library Journal*, 2 (1877-78), 172.

15. "There can be no doubt," Copinger said, "that Bibliography is now in process of development, and is fast becoming an exact science. It is high time, therefore, that it should be recognized as something very different from mere cataloguing." See *Transactions of the Bibliographical Society*, 1 (1892-93), 33. Henry Guppy, a few years later, said that "bibliography has, properly speaking, assumed the form of a science";

However inexact the term "exact science" might be, it served the rhetorical purpose these writers had in mind: an effort to contrast the methodical inspection of evidence found in books with the dilettante interest in old books merely as antiquarian objects. It is important to note that the putative inexactness which the new "exact science" would replace did not lie in the pursuit of enumerative bibliography but rather in the casual attitude of book collectors who—like the "new" bibliographers themselves—regarded books as physical objects. Since Stevens and Copinger both made a point of saying that bibliography—in their sense—was distinct from "mere" cataloguing, they may have given the impression that cataloguing was inexact work and that analytical bibliography was the exact work that had developed from it. But such an interpretation is actually an illogical mixture of two concepts which lie behind their statements: first, that "bibliography" in the sense of listing or cataloguing is a separate activity from "bibliography" in the sense of attention to books as physical objects; and, second, that the "exact" pursuit of the second kind of bibliography (examination of physical evidence) is replacing the "inexact" (vague dilettante interest). The first concept concerns definition of the field of activity; the second concerns the degree of seriousness with which the field is pursued. When the definition of an activity shifts in the middle of a discussion of a particular attribute of that activity, only confusion can result, and this kind of confusion could be regarded as the motif running through the whole history of attempts to link the words "science" and "bibliography." It is no wonder that Olphar Hamst, as early as 1880, felt that the word "bibliography" had so many meanings as to be useless for "any scientific purpose."[16] One further point may be noted about these early descriptions of analytical bibliography: the use of the phrase "natural-history method," like that of "exact science," was meant to be suggestive, not precise. Obviously Blades knew that books, being man-made objects, could not be studied in exactly the same way as plants or insects, but there was no reason for him to make that point, since he was concerned only with a general analogy between two examples of the use of empirical observation, in order to contrast that method with one which did not involve systematic observation at all.

In the years which followed, the Bibliographical Society and several younger bibliographical societies continued to advertise the "scientific"

see "The Science of Bibliography and What It Embraces," *Library Association Record*, 2 (1900), 173.

16. *Aggravating Ladies* (1880), p. 10.

nature of physical bibliography. The title of Falconer Madan's "On Method in Bibliography," read before the Bibliographical Society in 1893, is characteristic of the concern of these groups that their field should be systematic.[17] Speaking before the Edinburgh Bibliographical Society in 1899, John Ferguson said that bibliography "has nothing to do, in the first instance at least, with the contents. They may be good, bad, or indifferent, but they do not concern the bibliographer. If one may so say, he is not a book-ethicist, but a book-ethnologist."[18] Ferguson's choice of ethnology as his scientific analogy skillfully suggests that bibliography has both an objectivity of method and a concern with the human; even more revealingly he called bibliography "the biography of books" (p. 9). He did not develop the point, but his recognition that physical bibliography is a form of history probably accounts for his unwillingness to label bibliography flatly as a science; it is, he said, "the science or the art, or both, of book description" (p. 3). Although he went on to concern himself principally with the enumeration of books, his few comments on physical bibliography constitute an intelligent revision of the scientific analogy. Another speaker (J. Christian Bay) before another bibliographical society (the Bibliographical Society of America) observed in 1905, "Bibliography, as taught and practiced in the circle to which I address myself, ranks now equal to, if not among, the exact sciences"—phraseology which makes plain the metaphorical nature of the statement.[19] And Victor H. Paltsits at about the same time compared bibliography to anatomy in its concern with analyzing the "component parts" of a book.[20] Both writers, however, went on to confuse the issue somewhat by making the inevitable contrast with "library routine" and the compilation of lists. The whole tendency of this period to glorify the "scientific" aspects of bibliography, in contrast to what went before, is well summed up in James Duff Brown's *Manual of Practical Bibliography* (1906):

If once it is recognized that bibliography is really the index and guide to all past and existing knowledge, . . . then there will be some hope of the science being set in its proper place as a key to the knowledge stored, and

17. *Transactions of the Bibliographical Society*, 1 (1892-93), 91-106.

18. "Some Aspects of Bibliography," *Publications of the Edinburgh Bibliographical Society*, 4 (1899-1901), 2-3. Ferguson's monograph (amounting to 102 pages with its book list) was also issued separately in 1900.

19. "Contributions to the Theory and History of Botanical Bibliography," *PBSA*, 1 (1904-7), 75.

20. "A Plea for an Anatomical Method in Bibliography," *PBSA*, 1 (1904-7), 123-24.

too often hidden, in books. At present we cannot hope for this recognition. It has become crystallized in the public mind—if it ever considers the matter at all—as a dull, repulsive game for snuffy and cantankerous old men who spend most of their time buying books from ignorant booksellers at one twentieth part of their market value, in order to stow them away on musty bookshelves, there to accumulate a further value in the course of time. Book-hunting, indeed, has almost become synonymous with bibliography in the minds of a great many persons. But, luckily, a more advanced, more reasonable, and more scientific spirit is awakening, and many modern practical exponents of the new bibliography have completely repudiated the traditional view of the limits of the science. (pp. 19-20)

Brown's chief interest is obviously in reference bibliography, but his contrast of the scientific present with the dilettante past[21] is characteristic of the viewpoint lying behind the insistence on science in analytical bibliography as well.

By 1912 the tradition of comparing bibliography with science was well established, and W. W. Greg had given enough thought to the matter that he was ready to make what would be the first of an important series of statements on it. He recognized that a general analogy with science could be drawn, for bibliographers "are gradually evolving a rigorous method for the investigation and interpretation of fresh evidence."[22] But what distinguished his remarks from previous ones is that he turned the scientific analogy into a criticism, saying that bibliography was not yet a "satisfactory science":

In a sense every science is descriptive. But in so far as a science is merely descriptive it is sterile. You may dissect and you may describe, but until your anatomy becomes comparative you will never arrive at the principle of evolution. You may name and classify the colours of your sweet peas and produce nothing but a florist's catalogue; it is only when you begin grouping them according to their genetic origin that you will arrive at Mendel's formula. (pp. 40-41)

Like the writers before him, Greg contrasted enumerative and analytical approaches but, unlike them, did not feel that the analytical had developed far enough to provide cause for celebration; the scientific analogy, if it was useful at all, apparently could serve to stimulate bibliographers to greater activity. Still, Greg used the word "science"

---

21. Brown makes similar statements on pp. 8-9, 16-17; and the words "science" and "scientific" turn up repeatedly—e.g., see pp. 1, 3, 4, 15, 18, 157.

22. "What Is Bibliography?" *Transactions of the Bibliographical Society*, 12 (1911-13), 39.

in his own definition, which at the same time gave currency to another element that would complicate the issue. His chief interest in analytical bibliography, in contrast to that of Blades or Bradshaw, was the effect which its discoveries might have on the establishment of texts, and he defined bibliography (he called it "critical bibliography") as "the science of the material transmission of literary texts" (p. 48). In effect, his definition tended to make analytical bibliography the servant of literary study; and, while he did not say that the editorial process—choosing among variant readings and correcting mistakes—was a science, his statement did use the word "science" and did mention "literary texts." He had entered a fertile ground for misunderstanding, and it is not surprising that debates about the scientific nature of editing would occur, especially after others began to pronounce similar definitions.

Of course, one of the principal accomplishments of the Bibliographical Society in its early years—reflected in the emphasis of R. B. McKerrow's "Notes on Bibliographical Evidence for Literary Students and Editors . . ."[23]—was to demonstrate the bearing of analytical bibliography on literary matters; and it is understandable that A. W. Pollard, as he surveyed in 1913 the Society's first twenty-one years, should have defined bibliography as dealing with "the material mediums . . . through which the thoughts of authors reach those who will take the trouble to gain a knowledge of them."[24] George Watson Cole followed in 1916 with another statement stressing textual transmission—the "perpetuation of thought . . . by means of the printing-

23. *Transactions of the Bibliographical Society*, 12 (1911-13), 211-318. McKerrow recognized, however, that editing requires more than analytical bibliography by itself can provide: "The knowledge and literary training of a scholar like Dyce could and often did enable him better to represent his author's intention, than more 'scientific' methods in the hands of men unskilled to use them" (p. 219). In another comment in the "Notes" he expressed both the relative objectivity of analytical bibliography and its historical nature: analytical bibliography is "one of the most absorbing of all forms of historical enquiry," he said, in part because "such discoveries as we may make are real discoveries, not mere matters of opinion, but provable things that no amount of after-investigation can shake" (p. 221). His optimism about the possibility

of conclusive proof in analytical bibliography had not altered by the time he converted the "Notes" into *An Introduction to Bibliography for Literary Students* (1927), for this statement remains (p. 5).

24. "Our Twenty-First Birthday," *Transactions of the Bibliographical Society*, 13 (1913-15), 24. A few years earlier, in his article for the eleventh edition of the *Encyclopaedia Britannica* (1910), Pollard did not call bibliography the science but rather the "art of the examination, collation and description of books." Though he did not discuss the issue in *Shakespeare Folios and Quartos* (1909), one of the early monuments of the "new" bibliography, he did talk about establishing a "scientific hypothesis" to account for the 1619 quartos (p. 99).

press"—as the domain of bibliographical study.[25] And Falconer Madan, in his Presidential Address to the Bibliographical Society in 1920, saw bibliography as "the groundwork to which every literary researcher and writer will instinctively turn"; like Greg, but more elaborately, he had recourse to "science" in expressing the connection between bibliography and literary study: "It is not too much to say that our work bears, or ought to bear, the same sort of relation to literary subjects of research as mathematics bear to natural science."[26] By a curious shift, the natural-history analogy was now more indirect; bibliography was not compared to science directly but instead to mathematics, as a tool employed in the sciences, thus making bibliography a tool of literary study—a rather narrow view of both mathematics and bibliography. Whether this statement was intended as a summary of the current situation or as a recommendation for the future is not clear, but in any case its hint of some sort of exactness in bibliographical work is unusually vague. This tendency to increase the distance between analytical bibliography and science was furthered in Pollard's Presidential Address to the Edinburgh Bibliographical Society in 1923. Entitled "The Human Factor in Bibliography," it pointed out that, unlike botany and geology, bibliography deals with human productions, and any analogy between bibliography and science was therefore somewhat limited.[27] Pollard expressed a point of view which has been heard often since then, but one cannot help feeling that its target is a nonexistent argument, since surely no one who had called bibliography scientific had believed that its materials of study were of precisely the same order as those in the physical sciences. It was bibliographers like Greg and Pollard, interested in the literary application of analytical bibliography, who were finding increasing reason to suggest qualifications of the scientific analogy; but ironically their association of bibliography and literature helped give rise to the misconception that bibliographers were attempting to put literary criticism on a scientific footing.[28]

25. "Bibliographical Problems, with a Few Solutions," *PBSA*, 10 (1916), 124. In this essay he also described bibliography as "the comparative anatomy of the book" (p. 127). Four years later in "Bibliography —A Forecast," Cole asserted that bibliography could be regarded as a science in the light of the *Century Dictionary*'s general definition of "science" and again likened it to anatomy in its minute examination of books "to discover the relations that each part bears to the whole" (*PBSA*, 14 [1920], 10-11).

26. "Some Experiences of a Bibliographer," *Library*, 4th ser., 1 (1920-21), 139-40.

27. *Publications of the Edinburgh Bibliographical Society*, 12 (1921-25), 69-77.

28. One essay from the 1930s may be taken to show some of the problems that arise.

During the 1930s two bibliographers in particular—Greg and McKerrow—made comments about science which go to the heart of the matter. In each case they attempted to rectify certain fallacies which they believed the comparison with science had led to, and one begins to feel that they found the analogy more distracting than helpful. Greg, in his Presidential Address of 1930, recognized that bibliography is essentially a historical study; whether or not it is scientific thus turns into the question of whether historiography is a science, and Greg answered in the affirmative: "The knowledge of human events, and the methods by which that knowledge is pursued, have just as good a claim to be called a science as have any other body of facts and any other instruments of research."[29] Whereas he had believed earlier that bibliography was an immature science, he thought that it had now moved to a new stage, and he pointed out the meaninglessness of the often-used phrase "exact science":

Is not exactitude the aim of every science, which it approaches as it gains in mastery over its material? . . . I think that the real distinction is not between an exact science and any other, but between a mature science and one that is still groping after its foundations, or else merely between science and bunkum. (p. 256)

Although Greg was still calling bibliography a science, the implications were now different, since it had been equated with history. And as history it was an independent discipline, not "the slave of other

---

Hereward T. Price, in "Towards a Scientific Method of Textual Criticism for the Elizabethan Drama," *JEGP*, 36 (1937), 151-67, complained about what he called the "bibliographical school" of editing because he found its adherents guilty of "hasty generalization on insufficient data"; yet one of his chief examples was Dover Wilson, whose work would not be regarded by most analytical bibliographers as illustrating the way their discipline operates. (His criticism, however, is understandable, since Wilson himself spoke of bibliography as forming "the only secure and scientific basis for textual investigations"—see, e.g., *Library*, 3rd ser., 9 [1918], 153.) Price concluded by urging greater scientific rigor for "textual criticism": "Scholars think too much of an explanation which may be true and

not at all of an explanation which *must* be true. It rarely occurs to scholars that their business is not so much to find explanations for special cases, as to discover the explanation which fits all the cases of the same sort. This is a truism in the natural sciences; let us hope we can make it a truism in the science of textual criticism" (p. 167). It is not clear whether "textual criticism" here means the same as "analytical bibliography" or whether it includes editing as well; the statement would be more effective if it clearly distinguished between the two and recognized the possibility that different procedures might be appropriate to each.

29. "The Present Position of Bibliography," *Library*, 4th ser., 11 (1930-31), 258.

sciences" (p. 259).[30] If from the beginning analytical bibliography's subject had been described as (in Greg's words) "human events"— as opposed to "natural events"—there would perhaps have been less misunderstanding about it. By the end of the decade McKerrow seemed even more exasperated with the scientific analogy. In his *Prolegomena for the Oxford Shakespeare* (1939) he observed that the popular reputation of "science" caused people to wish "to bring within its scope, at least in name, many subjects which cannot properly be said to belong there" (p. vi). He admitted that science could be defined so as to include bibliography: "Truth is truth and logic is logic . . . and in a sense any honestly conducted enquiry may be termed scientific." But science as "usually understood," he asserted, involves demonstration by controlled experiment; in this sense the "textual critic"[31] cannot be scientific:

. . . for scientific proof of his theories he must substitute arguments based on what seems to him, from his "knowledge of human nature" and from what he can learn of the procedure and habits of early copyists, printers, and theatrical producers, most likely to have occurred, and which can seldom or never be more than *probably* correct, even though the probability may in some cases be of a high degree. (p. vii)

30. Greg apparently found it compatible to speak of bibliography as an independent subject and at the same time to define it in terms of literary study or as the "grammar of literary investigation." Of course, one of his reasons for stressing its independence was to oppose the notion of bibliography as a list-compiling service for other disciplines. In another address, a year and a half later, he emphatically stated that the "bibliography" he was talking about was "in no way particularly or prim. rily concerned with the enumeration or description of books—a belief which has done much in the past to reduce it to futility and retard the recognition of its real nature and importance." This kind of argument is merely an attempt to segregate analytical bibliography from what is regarded as "bibliography" in the popular mind; but he went on to explain once again that his kind of bibliography dealt with the "formal aspect," not the subject matter, of books, thus implicitly linking it with "exact" or "objective" studies. Indeed, he continued to define bibliography as "the science of the transmission of literary texts." See "Bibliography—An Apologia," *Library*, 4th ser., 13 (1932-33), 113-43. The same ideas also appeared in his address "The Function of Bibliography in Literary Criticism Illustrated in a Study of the Text of *King Lear*," *Neophilologus*, 18 (1933), 241-62: he praised critical insight but felt that the critic should accept bibliographical facts not with antagonism but "with the welcome accorded by the true scientific spirit, the spirit of intellectual integrity" (p. 244).

31. By "textual critic" McKerrow really meant "analytical bibliographer," since his (and Greg's) conception of bibliography stressed its relation to texts. But the possibility of interpreting "textual critic" to mean something roughly equivalent to "editor" may distract some readers from the main point of the argument. The issue McKerrow is discussing is not the scientific nature of the editorial process but rather— what had been repeatedly claimed—the scientific nature of the processes of analysis which form a foundation for the editorial process.

Taken together, these statements of Greg and McKerrow cover the crucial points: analytical bibliography is a form of historical investigation; its conclusions are on a lower plane of probability than the inductive generalizations of many sciences because of the impossibility in bibliography of repeating past events as experiments; it can be thought of as scientific only if "science" is taken in an extremely general sense. One wonders what more needed to be said on the subject.

The scientific analogy, however, having become established, continued to turn up. G. F. Barwick, sketching the history of the formation of the main bibliographical societies, used "scientific bibliography" to mean the examination of a book "as an entity" (as opposed to list-making) and commented on various societies in terms of their attention to "scientific bibliography."[32] Arundell Esdaile considered bibliography to consist both of enumeration and analysis, the first of these being an "art" and the second a "science."[33] And Stephen Gaselee, agreeing that both are legitimate aspects of bibliography, went farther than previous writers in finding that both could be called scientific in the same sense—"both are a part of science, at any rate of that natural science to which bibliography is ordinarily and reasonably compared."[34] In addition to comments of this kind, there was one event in the 1930s which gave new force to the scientific analogy: the publication of John Carter and Graham Pollard's *An Enquiry into the Nature of Certain Nineteenth Century Pamphlets* (1934). A spectacular instance of answering a bibliographical question by recourse to the laboratory was bound to become a classic illustration of "scientific bibliography." Yet no one would be likely to argue that the laboratory analysis of paper is a peculiarly bibliographical technique; it would be more accurate to say that it is a technique from a field other than bibliography which proved to be helpful in investigating a bibliographical problem. Microscopic analysis fits the popular conception of "science," but bibliography does not achieve scientific status merely through association with it. The way in which the *Enquiry* could legitimately be said to represent a "scientific" approach to bibliography

32. "Bibliographical Societies and Bibliography," *Library*, 4th ser., 11 (1930-31), 151-59.

33. *A Student's Manual of Bibliography* (1931), p. 13. His discussion of analytical bibliography begins, "In all sciences laboratory work on the specimen precedes classification" (p. 18); under "Historical Bibliography" he speaks of "anatomy" and the

"natural history method"—which he calls "Darwinism applied by analogy to a human activity" (pp. 20-21).

34. "The Aims of Bibliography," *Library*, 4th ser., 13 (1932-33), 228. Gaselee continued to use the analogy in describing Bradshaw's contribution as "a change of direction almost comparable to the work of Darwin or Mendel."

is in the frame of mind of its authors, whose objectivity in assessing physical evidence led them to see the necessity for turning to another discipline for assistance.[35] A carefully worded statement on the dust-jacket of their book clearly reflects this distinction, saying that the book "introduces scientific methods which have never before been applied to bibliographical problems of this period." But probably most people, when they call Carter and Pollard's work "scientific bibliography," are thinking of the microscope and do not reflect on the fact that they are thereby attaching an additional meaning to an already overburdened term.

Bibliography continued to be referred to as vaguely "scientific" through the 1940s,[36] though two important essays did appear—Madeleine Doran's "An Evaluation of Evidence in Shakespearean Textual Criticism" and R. C. Bald's "Evidence and Inference in Bibliography," both in the *English Institute Annual* of 1941. These essays constitute the most serious and extended treatment that had appeared of the implications of the scientific analogy, following the lines of Greg's and McKerrow's comments; more than that, they provided a direct examination of the nature of bibliographical reasoning and demonstration. Bald, agreeing with Greg, classified bibliography as history —or, more precisely, said that it belongs among those "organized human activities . . . loosely known as 'history and the social sciences' " (p. 162). Just as history studies "monuments" (material objects which survive) and "documents" (accounts of events, liable to human error), so bibliography, he reasoned, examines both books themselves, as physical objects, and external evidence bearing on their production and dis-

35. The same could be said of Allan Stevenson's use of beta-radiography for reproducing watermarks, as illustrated by *The Problem of the "Missale speciale"* (1967). Even if this technique becomes standard in bibliographical investigation of paper—as there is reason to believe it should—it is still a technique from outside the field of bibliography which has become useful in bibliographical work.

36. For example, Randolph G. Adams, in some "Remarks" before the Bibliographical Society of America in 1942, used the scientific analogy in recognizing the intrinsic interest of analytical bibliography, whether or not applied to a literary problem: "I often think of bibliography as akin to, or analogous to, pure science. The findings of pure scientists are not always applied in the lifetime of the discoverer" (*PBSA*, 36 [1942], 59). In the same year Rollo Silver, reviewing G. L. McKay's directory of the New York book-trade to 1820, declared, "In approach and method, bibliography is one more science," and compared McKay's accomplishment to that of "a chemist listing the components of a single compound" (*PBSA*, 36 [1942], 78-79). F. C. Francis, after surveying "Recent Bibliographical Work," concluded that it was characterized by the "careful amassing of all possible data before attempting to draw conclusions"; he had demonstrated, he believed, "that there is really scientific bibliographical work being done at the present time" (*Library*, 4th ser., 23 [1942-43], 126).

tribution. Because historical study involves human actions and because laboratory experiments cannot recreate the past, the method of "proving" a case in bibliography could be likened more appropriately to that followed in a court of law than to that employed in a scientific investigation.[37] "Bibliography," he summarized, "cannot claim for its conclusions the same universal validity as belongs to those of the exact sciences" (p. 162). Miss Doran, in her essay, provided a concise expression of this point of view:

> It should be clear that we are in a realm where demonstration, in the strict sense of the term, is impossible. For our method cannot be solely deductive; nor do our problems admit of controlled laboratory experiment. . . . The textual problem is always a historical one—an attempt at recovery of what actually did happen; demonstration, therefore, is always a matter of the establishment of probability. This is so great in some cases as to amount almost to certainty; in others, so slight as to be questionable.[38] (pp. 98-99)

It would be hard to find a more compact and penetrating statement of the case. Four years later the Bibliographical Society's commemorative volume, *Studies in Retrospect, 1892-1942* (1945), naturally gave some attention to the development of bibliography as a "scientific" pursuit,[39] but it included no comment which brings together all the central issues as this one does.

From this point forward the most prolific commentator on bibliographical theory has been Fredson Bowers, and his writings, as one would expect, repeatedly touch on the "scientific" question.[40] How-

---

37. A similar analogy was drawn by Henry Thomas, who maintained that "bibliography on its physical side is (or should be) at least as scientific as Scotland Yard" ("Watermarks," *Edinburgh Bibliographical Society Transactions*, 2 [1940-46], 450). This analogy has reappeared a number of times since then, as in Stevenson's *The Problem of the "Missale speciale,"* p. 69.

38. Her use of the word "textual" here as a virtual synonym for "bibliographical" shows that she (like Greg) was thinking of analytical bibliography in terms of its application to textual matters.

39. Greg, in his essay "Bibliography—A Retrospect," noted the movement of bibliography "from the dilettante stage to the technical. And it was the work of the incu-

nabulists," he continued, "and of those who followed their lead, that transformed bibliography from a study the main interest of which was artistic to one governed by the methods of scientific inquiry" (p. 27). Victor Scholderer said that the study of incunabula was put on "a truly scientific basis" (p. 32) during the early years of the Society and that Robert Proctor "found the history of early printing guesswork and left it a science" (p. 34). F. P. Wilson, in his remarkable chapter on "Shakespeare and the 'New Bibliography,'" wrote of Greg, "As do men of science, he has worked by analysis and synthesis" (p. 135). And Michael Sadleir referred to "the science of bibliography" (p. 146).

40. A glance at the writings of others during the 1950s and 1960s shows that the same variety of uses of the word "science"

ever, he uses the word "science" infrequently, and it is clear that he follows in the line of those writers who find the scientific analogy somewhat facile. His position, as set forth in "Some Relations of Bibliography to Editorial Problems,"[41] is that, although there has often been an "inferential identification of bibliography with textual criticism," the two are separate, and analytical bibliography can be pursued independently of any possible application to textual matters. Since analytical bibliography deals with physical evidence, it lends itself to logical, systematic procedures; "strictly bibliographical evidence," Bowers says, "crosses the line of probability into something close to the field which in science would be regarded as controlled experiment capable of being reproduced" (p. 58).[42] Textual criticism and editing,

---

continues. Stanley Morison called bibliography "essentially the same discipline as Palaeography," which he defined, in turn, as a "science . . . pursued primarily for the benefit of the efficient criticism of the physical means of the transmission of thought" ("The Bibliography of Newspapers and the Writing of History," *Library*, 5th ser., 9 [1954], 154). James G. McManaway asserted, "Pure bibliographical research may be defended in the same terms as pure scientific research. In fact, Bibliography is sometimes referred to as a science. Certainly its methods are scientific, and its purposes" ("Bibliography," in *Literature and Science* [1955], p. 27). F. N. L. Poynter believed that bibliography "is neither an art nor a science but may contain both," though the analytical methods developed by Pollard, McKerrow, and Greg "may justly be called 'scientific'" (*Bibliography: Some Achievements and Prospects* [1961], pp. 5, 6). Allan Stevenson considered bibliography "an art and a science, mixing the critical and creative with cool precision and method" (Hunt Library *Catalogue*, 2 [1961], cxlii) and later asked that watermarks be studied "as scientifically as we have studied types" (*The Problem of the "Missale speciale*," p. 69). William A. Jackson, on the other hand, avoided "science" in defining bibliography as "the art of looking at a book objectively, as a physical object" (*Bibliography and Literary Studies* [1962], p. 1); and Charlton Hinman did not use the word in distinguishing analytical bibliography from editing: "Bib-

liographical analysis can establish many facts about the printing-house history of a book. . . . It can provide all manner of general enlightenment. . . . Yet the final resolution of particular textual problems is ordinarily an editorial responsibility" (*The Printing and Proof-Reading of the First Folio of Shakespeare* [1963], 1: vii).

41. *SB*, 3 (1950-51), 37-62. An earlier remark on the "scientific" nature of descriptive bibliography occurs in *Principles of Bibliographical Description* (1949): "I do not see how one can escape the conviction that the 'scientific' is basic in true descriptive bibliography, and that no amount of other inquiry, no matter how valuable, can itself *substitute* for the analytical description of the book as a material object" (p. 34). But he adds that descriptive bibliographies need not be limited to "scientific description only": "I feel that strictly scientific bibliographers often unduly limit the more general value of their work to too few classes of readers."

42. He goes on to say that what this produces, rather than "high probability," is "practical demonstration on physical evidence of a mechanical nature, demonstrable by a mechanical process." Actually, of course, such "demonstration" is simply a higher level of probability, resulting from agreements within a body of inductive evidence which common sense tells one cannot be explained as mere coincidence.

on the other hand, require cirtical insight: "the great emendations have been inspired art and not systematic science" (p. 45);[43] evidence in this area "can seldom if ever afford more than a high degree of probability, and this is essentially different from positive demonstration" (p. 57). Bowers makes clear, both here and in succeeding essays, a point which some of the later writers on "science" in bibliography do not seem to recognize—that analytical bibliography, while it may at times invalidate a literary argument through a factual demonstration, cannot (and does not claim to) eliminate the need for judgment and critical acumen in editing. Indeed, Bowers repeatedly defends the authority of informed critical insight, when coupled with an understanding of the extent to which analytical bibliography can contribute to the solution of a given problem:

The scientific method should have its valued place in humane studies, but as a servant, not the master. The current exaltation of the scientist in other fields should not lead to his domination of the humanities. Yet the processes of logical and material demonstration which the more scientific bibliographical methods bring to literary studies cannot be idly surveyed from an ivory tower or they will eat away its foundations and topple it.[44]

In a concise statement of the point he says, "Bibliography endeavors to take as much guesswork as possible out of textual criticism, and the literary method endeavors to inform bibliography with value judgments as a check on mechanical probability."[45] Although Bowers does occasionally apply the word "scientific" to analytical bibliography,[46] therefore, he is careful not to use it to describe editing; and he has done more than any other bibliographer to give substance to the word, by examining at length—in his 1959 Lyell Lectures[47]—the nature of

43. Cf. his later comment, "I should prefer the taste and judgement of a Kittredge (wrong as he sometimes was), and of an Alexander, to the unskilled and therefore unscientific operation of a scientific method as if it were the whole answer" —in *Textual and Literary Criticism* (1959), p. 116. (And note the similarity to McKerrow's remark quoted in footnote 23 above.)

44. "Bibliography, Pure Bibliography, and Literary Studies," *PBSA*, 46 (1952), 208.

45. *On Editing Shakespeare and the Elizabethan Dramatists* (1955), p. 35.

46. For example, in *The Bibliographical Way* (1959), he calls it the "scientific

analysis of the physical evidence of the books themselves" (p. 8). Generally, however, he speaks of "laws of evidence" (p. 10) or "a logical method of analysis" (p. 34) without direct reference to science. Describing analytical bibliography in "The Function of Bibliography," he said, "The evidence utilized is circumstantial and physical, and the method, it may be said, is inductive" (*Library Trends*, 7 [1959], 498). And in the current *Encyclopaedia Britannica* article his analogy is not with science but with law: "The evidence utilized is circumstantial and physical, and would often be legally valid."

47. Published in 1964 as *Bibliography and Textual Criticism.*

the evidence which analytical bibliography produces and the soundness of the conclusions drawn from that evidence.

We shall have occasion shortly to return to those lectures. But, first, it is worth noting that the use of the word "science" in connection with analytical bibliography—as a brief historical sketch of this kind reveals—has developed in two phases. First came the enthusiastic phase, in which bibliographers found science a useful analogy to help them advertise the fact that their field was a serious and systematic study, not a dilettante pursuit. Exaggeration was probably inevitable;[48] but however strongly they claimed bibliography to be science, these bibliographers generally did not examine in detail the implications of such a comparison but instead used it in a vaguer way for its suggestive value.[49] The second—or critical—phase began when bibliographers, taking these scientific claims more literally, recognized that a comparison of bibliography with "science" (that is, in the usual sense of "physical science") involved pointing out many differences, perhaps as many differences as similarities. Leading bibliographers of the past fifty or sixty years have taken this second position and have stated over and over various distinctions between bibliography and "science." At the same time, through both phases, the issue has been complicated by shifting terms, with one person talking about a different kind of "bibliography" from another, or using "science" in a different sense. One begins to wonder whether the whole matter was not a red herring from the start. Presumably the point of the analogy is to define biblio-

48. The situation is not unlike that in which McKerrow found himself when he wished to counteract what he regarded as overly subjective and eclectic procedures in the editing of Shakespeare: in order to make his point, he went farther in the direction of rigidity than he would probably have gone if he had not been reacting against what seemed to him a lack of discipline. As Bowers sums up the matter, "it often appears that in his general editorial theory McKerrow's thinking was affected more by reaction to that of others than by positive theory of his own"; see "McKerrow's Editorial Principles for Shakespeare Reconsidered," SQ, 6 (1955), 309-24, which stresses McKerrow's reaction against Dover Wilson's use of supposedly "scientific" bibliographical methods. In this context Bowers sees a "pettishness" in McKerrow's comments on scientific method (quoted above)—though what "pettishness" there is may also reflect a more general impatience with the scientific analogy.

49. It is not surprising that recent efforts to introduce French-speaking scholars to analytical and descriptive bibliography should utilize the scientific analogy. See, for example, Roger Laufer, "Pour une description scientifique du livre en tant qu'objet matériel," Australian Journal of French Studies, 3 (1966), 252-72, and "La bibliographie matérielle dans ses rapports avec la critique textuelle, l'histoire littéraire et la formalisation," Revue d'histoire littéraire de la France, 70 (1970), 776-83—which speaks of analytical bibliography as "une discipline archéologique annexe de l'histoire" (p. 781), with problems similar to those posed by "la description des objets archéologiques" (p. 782). See also Wallace Kirsop's articles, such as "Vers une collaboration de la bibliographie matérielle et de la critique textuelle," Australian Journal of French Studies, 3 (1966), 227-51.

graphy, and definition by analogy can sometimes be illuminating, even when the supposed analogy serves as something to be reacted against. But when the comparison involves a concept as complex as "science," it may do more to confuse than to clarify. Whether bibliography can be defined as a "science" or as something else is of less importance than understanding, in a direct way, what in fact it does, what its methods of procedure are, what its strengths and weaknesses may be. More direct discussions of such matters might have promoted greater understanding than that which has resulted from the perennial concern with the "scientific" quality of bibliography. The course of these "scientific" comments over the years is not an inspiring one and appears to be leading nowhere; the last word on the subject would seem to have been said, and said repeatedly. But apparently Bradshaw's concept of a "natural-history method"—and all that follows from it—is so intriguing to bibliographers that they cannot let go of the analogy, for it remains a matter of discussion.

II

The recent essays on this subject continue the historical trend toward the criticism of the scientific analogy: they find fault, in one way or another, with the supposedly scientific pretensions of bibliography. Insofar as they touch on the nature of bibliographical evidence or the historical aspect of the field and fail to make distinctions between one kind of bibliography or one aspect of science and another, they repeat past history. In this sense the *TLS* is right in saying that they have "revived the old argument about the scientific nature of bibliography" (though apparently it was never dead). But in another sense they are pitched on a different level, for they offer extended discourses on the philosophic background, the methodology, and the logic of bibliographical demonstration. It does not matter if, for purposes of argument, they assume greater claims for the scientific rigor of bibliography than have normally been advanced; but they do little to alter one's feeling that the question of science in bibliography, initiated as a metaphor to help elucidate the nature of the subject, has developed into a verbal smog which threatens to hide it.

McKenzie's "Printers of the Mind"—the starting point for the current debate—is essentially a statement of the weaknesses of the inductive method.[50] Many of the conclusions reached through analytical bibliography, McKenzie shows, are unsound or less certain than

---

50. See footnote 3 above. McKenzie had made some of the same points earlier in the introductory remarks to *An Early Printing House at Work: Some Notes for Bibliographers* (1965).

they were thought to be, because in each case a generalization was based on an insufficient body of inductive evidence. The question which obviously follows is whether any body of inductive evidence can ever be large enough to support more than a reasonable guess. Although McKenzie is ostensibly criticizing bibliography for not being sufficiently "scientific," his discussion demonstrates that bibliography is like "science" in proceeding by empirical observation and that the problem of induction is therefore basic to both. Philosophers have never proposed a satisfactory solution to the problem of induction. Indeed, in the form in which it is often posed, there can be no solution: for if induction is by definition not a form of deduction, and if valid conclusions can result only from a deductive argument, then induction must be ruled out as a legitimate process of logical demonstration.

McKenzie's way of dealing with this dilemma is a standard one: to advocate the insertion of qualifications in any inductive generalization and thus the conversion of such generalizations into hypotheses to be tested deductively. In his words, "A franker acceptance of deductive procedures would bring a healthy critical spirit into the subject by insisting on the rigorous testing of hypotheses, and the prime method of falsification—adducing contrary particulars—would impose a sound curb on premature generalizations" (p. 61). This line of reasoning—given its classic statement in Karl Popper's *The Logic of Scientific Discovery* (trans. 1959)—rejects inductive generalizations in favor of unfalsified hypotheses; but it does not confront squarely the logical objection to inductive evidence, since any finite body of evidence which fails to provide falsification for a hypothesis would be open to the same kind of objection. There would seem to be little difference between a generalization held provisionally to be true on the basis of examined evidence and a hypothesis for which no falsifying evidence has yet been located. In either case, further investigation may overturn present judgments. This sort of argument, in other words, appears to make little distinction between induction and deduction, except for the supposed greater caution of the latter. But if the goal of observation is to find some kind of regularity that will be useful in making further observations, excessive qualification may almost negate the process. As Max Black says, "In converting a purportedly inductive argument into a valid deductive one, the very point of the original argument—that is, to risk a prediction concerning the yet unknown—seems to be destroyed."[51] One could perhaps restate McKenzie's observation, with-

51. "Induction," in *The Encyclopedia of Philosophy*, ed. Paul Edwards (1967), 4: 176.

out recourse to induction or deduction, simply by saying that bibliographers should be more careful in framing general statements and more thorough in surveying the relevant evidence. Clearly this is sound advice, and the most impressive part of McKenzie's essay is his effective account of instances in which bibliographers have jumped to conclusions that must be modified in the light of further evidence. McKenzie's article is important and timely: his work on the Cambridge University Press records has put him in a position to understand the value of knowing in detail the various jobs in progress in a printing shop at any one time, and one of the weaknesses of much bibliographical analysis in the past has been that the production of a single book was looked at in isolation, without sufficient regard for the total activity of a shop. The great value of McKenzie's essay, in other words, seems to me to lie in its challenge to widely held generalizations rather than in its theoretical discussions about the logic of bibliographical investigation.

Nevertheless, the objections to induction which McKenzie summarizes ought to be faced by bibliographers—anyone whose work involves argument from empirical observation should give some thought to the logical validity of what he is doing. The inconclusiveness of inductive reasoning cannot be denied, but it seems shortsighted to limit "scientific" argument to the deductive. Philosophers of science recognize that there is no such thing as "the" scientific method, except perhaps in the broadest characteristics.[52] One can say that "science" or "scientific method" involves scrupulous fidelity to evidence obtained empirically and a systematic means of handling that evidence. But the details of the procedure will vary from one kind of situation to another or from one area of endeavor to another. Inductive investigations can be "scientific" in this sense, and to deny their legitimacy is greatly to restrict the range of research. In justifying induction one must finally turn to the pragmatic or common-sense argument of common experience. Everyone, from birth, learns to get along through an inductive process. From time to time one's generalizations are proved incorrect, when the expected does not occur, and one makes adjustments in the generalizations; but the whole concept of "rationality" or "rational behavior" depends on expectations of regularity based on past experience. Perhaps there is no ultimate regularity in the universe; the point, however, is that the projection into the future of a seeming regularity from the past appears to be the only way of proceeding in

52. A convenient summary of points of view appears in Peter Caws's article on "Scientific Method" in *The Encyclopedia of Philosophy*, 7: 339-43.

the short run. If induction is denied, all human concepts would seem to be destroyed with it.[53] Furthermore, a deductive argument is conclusive only in terms of its premises, which may themselves be unrelated to the "real" world (that is to say, logical validity and truth are separate concepts). Therefore, to establish "truth"—that contact with the "real" or "objective" which is the aim of research—involves the testing of those premises by what amounts to an inductive procedure, even if it is expressed in terms of Popper's theory of falsification. In other words, one is driven to induction on pragmatic grounds, despite the unassailability of logical objections to it. I am making this amateurish summary of a familiar philosophical debate in order to suggest two points: first, bibliographers—though they should understand the implications of inductive reasoning—need not hesitate to proceed inductively, so long as they do so with care and responsibility; second, to collect and examine evidence with care and responsibility is by definition to be scientific, and discussions about whether or not bibliography resembles one particular scientific pursuit or another seem somewhat fruitless exercises (except perhaps to demonstrate the multiplicity of individual paths which scientific endeavor takes).

The more direct and positive approach to scientific method in bibliography is to accept induction openly and to set about examining what constitutes responsible handling of inductive evidence in this particular field, given the nature of the problems which bibliographers wish to solve. Fredson Bowers did exactly that fifteen years ago in his Lyell Lectures. After distinguishing analytical bibliography (con-

---

53. Something along these lines is what is sometimes known as the "linguistic" approach to the problem of induction; I quote again from Max Black, an advocate of this point of view: "The inductive concepts that we acquire by example and formal education and modify through our own experiences are not exempt even from drastic revision. . . . What is clearly impossible, however, is the sort of wholesale revolution that would be involved in wiping the inductive slate clean and trying to revert to the condition of some hypothetical Adam setting out to learn from experience without previous indoctrination in relevant rules of inductive procedure. This would be tantamount to attempting to destroy the language we now use to talk about the world and about ourselves and thereby to destroy the concepts embodied in that language. The idea of ceasing to be an inductive reasoner is a monstrosity. The task is not impossibly difficult; rather, its very formulation fails to make sense" (*Encyclopedia*, p. 179). The common-sense defense of induction does not of course answer the philosophical objections. As Black, in "The *Raison d'Etre* of Inductive Argument"—included in his *Margins of Precision* (1970)—says, "There is no way to cope with the 'problem' that, in my opinion, offers any prospect of satisfying those to whom its solution seems necessary except by patiently exposing the underlying confusions until the alleged problem withers away" (p. 177). He sees "no stultifying circularity" in holding that "there is indeed good inductive evidence for thinking that our universe is of such a character that continued trust in the inductive practice is reasonable."

cerned with books as "tangible objects") from textual bibliography
(in which analytical bibliography is applied to "internal form, or
contents" of books) and suggesting in general the relations of bibliographical research to editing, Bowers examines the nature of bibliographical evidence and states that one of the "laws" of bibliographical
procedure "requires us to reason inductively from specific, concrete
evidence in the text" rather than deductively from "our general ideas
about printing practice" (p. 36). Of course, if "our general ideas"
were adequately buttressed with evidence, there would be no problem,
but finding that evidence returns us to an inductive search—thus the
inductive process is basic, whatever it is called, and Bowers is not
interested in debating the terminology.[54] Instead, he proceeds to—what
is the heart of the matter—the question of the interpretation of inductive evidence, and he sets up "three orders of certainty":   the demonstrable, the probable, and the possible. Now to say that inductive evidence can ever lead to a "demonstrable" case (one in which physical
evidence "leaves no loophole for opinion") entails certain assumptions
—that all relevant evidence is known and has been examined[55] or that
extreme coincidences do not in fact take place. In other words, one has
to begin with some notion of the range of occurrences which it is reasonable to expect. Bowers calls this notion the "postulate of normality," which "depends on the working hypothesis that all we know at
any given time must be the truth, and therefore the details of the
printing process and their handling that have been recovered (when
tolerably full) must represent 'normality' unless we have stubbornly
inexplicable evidence to the contrary" (p. 72). The phrase "when
tolerably full" underscores the central problem, since one must have
surveyed a certain quantity of evidence in order to interpret a new
piece of evidence, and yet without that new evidence itself the inter-

54. "I am not happy," he says, "about
my need to use these terms ['inductive' and
'deductive'], and I hope they will be accepted in just the rough-and-ready, practical sense intended by Bacon" (p. 36).
Bowers has made some comments on
McKenzie's article in "Seven or More
Years?", *Shakespeare 1971*, ed. C. Leech and
J. M. R. Margeson (1972), pp. 50-51.

55. Elsewhere Bowers describes the search
for extant copies of a book in such a way
as to emphasize the open-ended quality of
inductive procedure: ". . . although no
way exists to protect oneself against the
unique copy of a variant in a private
collection, or in some out-of-the-way small
library which one would not ordinarily
consult, one's coverage should be so wide
as materially to reduce the odds that an
unknown variant will turn up later to dim
one's hopes for completeness. (The number
of variants I have already seen in unique
copies does not give me any great confidence, however, that an equal number still
does not lie in wait, unknown and unsung,
waiting for my book to be printed.)" See
"Bibliography and Restoration Drama," in
Bibliography (Clark Library, 1966), p. 4.

pretation may be faulty. Nevertheless, some assumption of normality is unavoidable:

> This hypothesis is necessary in some part because a confirmation of the validity of inductive bibliographical reasoning is that it leads us, by a series of tests of the evidence, to an explanation consistent with our knowledge of normality. (A different matter, incidentally, from deducing an explanation of evidence from this knowledge of normality.) Also, since certainty about every small detail in the operation is difficult to attain, it is essential whenever we can to assume that we know the general process of printing, for otherwise conjecture from evidence would be paralysed for lack of some standard for confirmation, or would have no bounds set to mere guesswork. (p. 72)

At this point McKenzie would say that we do not have a large enough body of evidence to define satisfactorily any kind of "normality."[56] Still, his description of a deductive process based on a recognition of "the partial and theoretic nature of bibliographical knowledge" is not, in practical terms, very different from Bowers's picture of an inductive procedure in which explanations "based on imperfect evidence" are modified or corrected by new evidence. Obviously we never know enough; but if we are to proceed, we have to assume that we know enough to get on with. Bowers's discussion, by providing numerous examples of what he regards as demonstrable, probable, and possible interpretations of bibliographical evidence, shifts the focus from the theoretical to the practical. He is not principally concerned with arguing the philosophical question of inductive versus deductive reasoning; the assumption lying behind his analysis seems to be that, since the demonstration of a "truth" finally rests on empirical observation, one might as well accept induction and proceed to confront and examine the evidence that turns up. As a result, his book is a more direct investigation of the "scientific" nature of bibliography than any other discussion, for, instead of concentrating on how well bibliography conforms to certain abstract qualities of "science," he looks at concrete examples of what bibliography in fact consists of, in order to see what particular brand of "scientific method" emerges as most appropriate for dealing with bibliographical evidence.

In the same year in which McKenzie's essay was published, James Thorpe delivered a paper entitled "The Ideal of Textual Criticism" at a Clark Library Seminar.[57] One section of this paper collects quota-

---

56. Indeed, he doubts that the concept of "normality" is meaningful "in any serious and extended sense" (see pp. 4-6).

57. See footnote 3 above; the essay is republished, in revised form, as a chapter in his book *Principles of Textual Criticism*

tions from several bibliographers—especially Greg and Bowers—which seem to assert the scientific nature of "textual criticism," and it cites a few instances of quantitative and mechanized approaches to textual problems. Thorpe then proceeds to conclude, "I can see nothing in the present or future of textual criticism, however it is carried on, which will make it answerable to the term 'science' or 'scientific'" (p. 68). Of course, if "science" is taken to mean "the physical sciences," it is easy to agree with him; but, since no analysis of the term or of the nature of textual criticism accompanies the statement, it has the effect of being simply an assertion, placed in opposition to a series of other assertions. The scientific analogy is worth analyzing if some illumination of the nature of the subject emerges, but little is gained by asserting its inadequacy or inappropriateness, particularly since leading bibliographers over the years have repeatedly made the same point. Although the bibliographers cited by Thorpe did make the comments he quotes, I hope that my earlier historical survey has shown the general drift of the major statements of the last half-century to be in the direction of finding fault with the scientific analogy and recognizing the important place which critical judgment occupies. The difficulty here—as in so many similar discussions in the past—is one of definition. Does "science" mean the same thing throughout all of Thorpe's quotations and in his own remarks as well? More to the point, does "bibliography" mean the same thing, and the same thing as "textual criticism"? Although Thorpe elsewhere discusses at length the relation of bibliography and textual criticism,[58] he does not at this point raise the issue of shifting definitions. His subject is specifically

(1972), pp. 50-79. The sentence from this paper quoted below is the same in both versions, and the citation is to the 1972 publication.

58. In the third chapter of *Principles of Textual Criticism*, pp. 80-104. It is his thesis in this chapter that bibliographers have attempted to "make textual criticism a branch of bibliography" (p. 101), and he provides a historical survey to exhibit "the process by which bibliography has taken over textual criticism" (p. 89). Although he says, "This development very closely parallels the twentieth-century association of science and bibliography," the survey of the scientific analogy which I presented earlier suggests that his view is somewhat overstated. He concludes that "textual criticism cannot properly have a single methodology" (p. 104), but it does not seem that the leading bibliographers ever suggested that it should. The issue is really whether or not the "bibliographical orientation" of textual criticism is excessive— a matter which cannot be decided on theoretical grounds. If analytical bibliographers can accept being plumbers rather than scientists, they would no doubt agree with Thorpe's final assessment: "The tools of one trade will not repair every breakdown, and the special expertise that the textual critic ought to possess is that of a skilled and knowledgeable handyman. He is not a plumber or an electrician, but he must know how to deal with pipes and wiring" (p. 104).

"textual criticism," yet the word "bibliography" is what apears in a number of his quotations; and it should be clear by now that the two terms have not normally been regarded as synonymous. (Even when "text" or "textual criticsm" appears, it is by no means certain that the writer is asserting the "scientific" nature of every step of the editorial process.) The trend in recent decades, as shown above, is to think of the techniques of analytical bibliography (analysis of physical evidence) as perhaps having certain "scientific" qualities but to regard textual criticism (often defined to include editing) as being—true to its name—*critical*. Thorpe may be concerned about the increasing amount of attention which an editor is expected to give to bibliographical information, but that is a different matter from suggesting that the editorial process itself is claimed to be mechanical (which is what "scientific" often means in this context). If Thorpe's conclusion is that editing involves critical judgment (or literary criticism), most people would undoubtedly agree, including those from whom he quotes. One can concur, in other words, with what Thorpe appears to be saying at the end and yet not see how he is led to that statement by quoting comments on "scientific" bibliography and textual criticism from various periods—especially without analyzing the sense in which each writer was using the key terms.

A similar problem emerges in Peter Davison's incisive discussion[59] of McKenzie's position, for Davison is chiefly interested in textual criticism, while McKenzie is concerned with analytical bibliography. In what is surely one of the most penetrating analyses of the nature of bibliography yet written, Davison argues persuasively that McKenzie's view of scientific method is oversimplified and that his view of bibliography as amenable to the "hypothetico-deductive method" is unrealistic. Nevertheless, Davison's examples are editorial problems, and he shows the shortcomings of the deductive method in terms of editing. He points out, for example, that editors "have to provide answers even if evidence is insufficient or contradictory" (p. 13); and he goes on to explain that the deductive method

cannot be more than a useful tool which may help us avoid the avoidable. Thus, in practice, one often has to choose between various courses, none wholly satisfactory, and the hypothetico-deductive method is a convenient means of testing the choices open to an editor, helping him to decide to which choice he should give preference. (pp. 13-14)

59. See footnote 3 above; Davison also offers in this essay a criticism of Thorpe's method of selecting quotations (pp. 5-6). He had presented some of the same points about McKenzie's paper earlier in "Marry, Sweet Wag," in *The Elizabethan Theatre II*, ed. David Galloway (1970), pp. 134-43.

All this seems reasonable, but it does not meet McKenzie on his own grounds, since McKenzie is talking about analytical bibliography. What starts out as a criticism of McKenzie's position—the advocacy of the deductive method for a particular purpose—turns into a criticism of the appropriateness of the deductive method for a different purpose. I do not believe that McKenzie would disagree with Davison's position in regard to editing: that an editor must frequently make decisions on the basis of his own interpretation and judgment (informed by whatever data are available) rather than on the basis of conclusively established facts. But McKenzie would still say that the deductive method should be followed in bibliographical analysis—in establishing, that is, the facts and hypotheses which may turn out to be of use in the process of editing. It is possible to meet this argument—as I tried to show earlier—by examining the general problem of induction; but Davison, though he makes an effective case against deduction, does not really speak directly to McKenzie's point, since he shifts the area of application to textual criticism. Once again, a debate about the scientific aspects of bibliography is rendered less clear than it might be through the failure to draw distinctions among different kinds of bibliography (or between "bibliography" and "textual criticism").

Davison's important essay takes up a still larger issue. The existence of essays like McKenzie's and Thorpe's, he believes, may suggest that bibliography is at a "moment of crisis," that it is engaged in what Thomas S. Kuhn calls "paradigm rejection"[60]—the replacing of one paradigm by another when the former is judged to be inadequate to handle the problems with which it is faced. He cites examples of dissatisfaction with the usual concepts of "author" and "text" and with the stemmatic approach to textual criticism. He then argues—in the most intriguing part of his discussion—that, just as a creative writer reflects the changing world-views that result from new scientific theories, so an editor (who responds to "the needs, general and scholarly, of his own society") should perhaps "take note of these changes in the physical explanation of our world and the response of creative writers thereto" (p. 27). The rise of the "new bibliography" is placed in this context:

It was the new awareness of science and man which developed in the nineteenth century (and which can be seen in the great creative writers as well as the scientists of the time) which came to be applied to textual

---

60. In *The Structure of Scientific Revolutions* (1962). Davison is aware of, and comments on, the fact that he is introducing another scientific analogy by referring to this concept.

studies in English literature from the time McKerrow and Greg met at Cambridge in the 1890s. (p. 26)

One illustration is the study of the history of textual transmission:

The response to the spirit motivating the understanding of man in society which influences the creative writing of, say, a Zola or a Shaw, or even a Lawrence or a Joyce, influences also that aspect of textual studies which seeks to discover what happened to texts in the societies which produced and transmitted them. (p. 26)

Insofar as this argument says that a man inevitably reflects the characteristic interests and approaches of his intellectual milieu, it is making a generalization about all men and not about bibliographers in particular. But in applying this observation to bibliographers, it has the merit of stressing the humanistic aspects of the field, of saying that bibliographers are like "creative writers," historians, and others who meditate on human behavior, in their reaction to scientific theories about the physical universe. By proposing a pervasive influence of science on bibliography, Davison is paradoxically setting the two apart, for he associates that influence not with specific methodological changes but with an altered outlook that bibliographers share with other thinking human beings. The result is to provide a strong affirmation of the creative in bibliography and to reject the idea that bibliography is like "science" (although the rejection is on a deeper level than is usually implied by the comparison).

The affirmation is salutary, and it gains weight from the thoughtful analysis lying behind it. But one is surprised to find the conclusion couched in language which seems to reopen the troublesome issue of "scientific bibliography." Davison is urging bibliographers to a renewed faith in intuition and subjective judgment:

What we *could* find is that the more precise techniques developed by "the school of Bowers and Hinman" (if I may use such an expression) are to us not unlike what Newtonian physics is to scientists, but that outside the usefulness of these methods (which are, after all, rather extensive) we ought not to be afraid of irrationality and infinite coincidence. Or, to put it more conventionally, imagination and taste. (pp. 27-28)

Here is the most sophisticated use yet made of the scientific analogy. But to claim that the recognition and acceptance of creativity in bibliography somehow involve modification of the bibliographical paradigm is to suggest that bibliography has been more rigidly mechanical than would appear to be the case, judging from the statements, and the work, of its practitioners. Even in the limited area of analytical bibliography—or in Newtonian physics—imagination plays its role (in recognizing significant evidence, in devising ways of arranging it, in making connections between related occurrences). Furthermore, if the bibliographical methods springing from McKerrow and Greg are regarded as the reflection, in the bibliographical area, of the nineteenth-century scientific revolution, it is hard to see the aptness of comparing a further development of those methods with Newtonian science. In any case, the emergence of ways of looking at the universe which go beyond Newtonian physics can indeed be said to require modification of a paradigm, since the Newtonian laws were thought to be universal; but the rules of procedure in analytical bibliography were never claimed to have the same kind of universal application throughout the whole realm of bibliographical pursuits. (Newtonian laws might be thought of as operating in all areas of one horizontal plane—which serves well enough to provide a perspective for everyday purposes—though we recognize the existence of other planes; in contrast, rules of analytical bibliography might be thought of as operating in the limited areas of several planes forming one vertical segment of the bibliographical whole, though we recognize that other segments— editing, for example—border on it.) Besides, to compare "Newtonian physics" and the "precise techniques" of analytical bibliography is seemingly to mix explanations with approaches, though both are called "methods." If the methods of the two areas are compared, it is true that both require care and accuracy, but so do all scholarly pursuits; if the discoveries of the two are compared, both share the ultimate inconclusiveness of all inductive generalizations, though one offers in support an incalculably greater body of evidence than the other. That bibliography and science can be compared in certain carefully defined respects and contrasted in others is not at issue. But Davison's closing comparison, like so many similar ones in the past, diverts attention from, rather than clarifies, his main point and therefore does less than justice to what he has to say.

Another essay which stresses the humanistic nature of bibliography appeared at about the same time as Davison's. Morse Peckham, in "Reflections on the Foundations of Modern Textual Editing," is chiefly concerned with examining the concepts of "text" and "author,"[61] but he begins by questioning the appropriateness of the words "mechanical" and "scientific" as descriptive of bibliography. To

61. See footnote 3 above. I do not propose here to go into this part of Peckham's paper; I believe it does no injustice to his argument to consider the first section (pp. 127-36) separately from the rest.

think of book production as a mechanical process in which the "human factor" must be adduced to explain anomalies is, he says, an inversion of the truth, since book production is essentially a form of human behavior, and its study is therefore a branch of historiography:

What the analytical bibliographer does, then, whether he realizes it or not, is, on the basis of certain artifacts which are the consequence or deposit of various behaviors, to make a theoretical reconstruction or construct of the behaviors responsible for the historical emergence of those artifacts. This is so obvious that it would scarcely need saying were it not for the constant appearance of the term "human factor" in both the theoretical and problem-directed discourse of analytical bibliography. The "human factor" is not something that occasionally enters into the bibliographer's thinking when he finds himself in a spot; it is almost exclusively all that he is concerned with. The analytical bibliographer is a historian, and he should not forget it for a moment. The object of his inquiry is not printed artifacts as physical objects but human behavior in the past, human behavior that no longer exists and cannot now be examined. (p. 131)

That bibliography is a historical study has been expressed before, by Greg and others, in less elaborate language, and Peckham is right in saying that it does not need to be repeated—except in the hope that one more repetition may convert those who apparently do not yet understand. But are there really any bibliographers who do not understand that they are dealing with human productions and human behavior? It seems unlikely, and yet the kind of terminology Peckham objects to undoubtedly persists. The problem, of course, is one of rhetoric. The old scientific analogy has become so entrenched as a cliché that it continually turns up in one form or another. While its history shows that it is productive of enough confusion that it might better be avoided, it obviously still serves a purpose for some writers. I do not believe that most bibliographers who use the term "human factor" would disagree with Peckham's statement that the term "actually explains nothing" and "only admits that the explanation has broken down." One impulse to use the scientific analogy comes from the need to explain just what approach the analytical bibliographer is taking toward human behavior; since he is dealing with an area which involves the use of mechanical instruments—pens, presses, type-formes, type matrices, paper moulds, and so on—his approach is to see how much can be explained by factoring out the "human" element and concentrating on those instruments. Obviously what he is trying to describe ultimately is a human action, but he wants to see how far he can go in that direction by examining the products of mechanical instruments. He can never go all the way, and sometimes he can hardly get started; when he resorts to a term like "human factor," he is admitting that his explanation can go no farther. Certainly the suggestion that his work is a "scientific" treatment of "mechanical" operations is an overstatement and a cliché, but the motivation for it is clear enough. The difficulty comes—as it has repeatedly—when people react to the rhetoric on a different level from the one intended, and Peckham's complaint about "human factor" is another instance.

Nevertheless, he usefully redirects our attention to the basically historical nature of bibliography and recognizes where that leaves the scientific question: "The scientific status of analytical bibliography is the scientific status of any historiographical construct" (p. 132). This, too, has of course been said before, but what Peckham adds that is new is his approach to the definition of historiography. Since statements about past events cannot be verified by empirical observation, he argues, their interior logic has no relation to any "truth" outside the historical account unless the historian, like the scientist, makes predictions about currently existing artifacts, which are thus subject to repeated direct observation. As he puts it in another essay, historical statements "cannot tell us how to locate the phenomenally perceptible, but only how to construct other statements that may, or may not, successfully instruct us how to locate something in the world before us."[62] In other words, the historian "predicts about where he is going to find documents and artifacts and what their attributes are going to be" (p. 133); and "like any scientist," Peckham says, the historian, after checking his prediction, may have to adjust the thinking that led to it. The question whether history is a science has been more widely debated than the question of bibliography's scientific status,[63] and what Peckham has done is to offer another explanation of the sense in which history does resemble science. His argument, though expressed in different terms, arrives at essentially the same point as McKenzie's: that analytical bibliography—or history—is scientific insofar as it continually

62. "Aestheticism to Modernism: Fulfillment or Revolution?" in *The Triumph of Romanticism* (1970), p. 204; the essay was originally published in 1967.

63. For a summary of some of the arguments, with a checklist for further reading, see Patrick Gardiner's "The Philosophy of History," in *International Encyclopedia of the Social Sciences*, ed. David L. Sills (1968), 6: 428-34, and his anthology *Theories of History* (1959); see also the chapters on the social sciences and history in Ernest Nagel, *The Structure of Science* (1961), pp. 447-606. A few theories of historiography are summarized in a bibliographical context by William H. Goetzmann in his contribution to a symposium on "The Interdependence of Rare Books and Manuscripts: The Scholar's View," published in *Serif*, 9 (Spring 1972), 10-18.

tests hypotheses against directly observable evidence, insofar as the "printers of the mind" move outside the mind.[64] In contrast to the natural sciences, however, with the large body of evidence which they have amassed, "analytical bibliography certainly is not a very highly developed science" (p. 134)[65]—a point which Greg made long ago. Peckham's analysis does not reach any new conclusions, but it goes farther than previous discussions in treating the relations of bibliography and science in the context of historiography.

The recognition that analytical bibliography is history should answer any questions about whether it is an independent pursuit or only the servant—"handmaid" is the favorite term[66]—of another pursuit. But the question has generated a considerable amount of heat, and recourse to the analogy of "pure" versus "applied" science has not helped to answer it.[67] When Copinger, and Greg after him, called bibliography the grammar of literary investigation,[68] they did not mean to imply that the grammar was of no interest in its own right. But the fact that analytical bibliography grew up in the hands of people who were concerned with literary texts led a number of literary scholars to believe that it existed only as an aid for establishing texts.[69]

64. McKenzie's point is specifically applied to history—theatrical history—by J. A. Lavin in "The Elizabethan Theatre and the Inductive Method," in *The Elizabethan Theatre II*, pp. 74-86.

65. The earlier part of this sentence reads, "Consequently the Bowers claim that analytical bibliography is a science is justifiable . . . ." I hope it is clear by this point that such a statement is an oversimplification and is characteristic of the kind of statements which have caused misunderstandings throughout the history of the scientific analogy.

66. See, for example, footnote 11 above; *Library Journal*, 1 (1876-77), 69; *Library Association Record*, 2 (1900), 174—these last two in almost identical wording.

67. J. D. Cowley, in *Bibliographical Description and Cataloguing* (1939), defined historical bibliography in such a way as to bring together the questions about its scientific and its independent status: historical bibliography (as opposed to subject bibliography and textual criticism), he

said, is "a science, if that term is used to mean any field of knowledge or knowing which is worth while approaching for its own sake" (p. 7).

68. See, among other places, *Transactions of the Bibliographical Society*, 1 (1892-93), 34; *Library*, 4th ser., 13 (1932-33), 113.

69. In the "Early Americana" section of *Standards of Bibliographical Description* (1949), Lawrence Wroth says that "bibliography is not an end but a means, a process in the study of the transmission of texts" (p. 105), and that unless it is regarded in this spirit it becomes "a species of research which closely approaches sterility" (p. 107). Curt Bühler, in the same volume, calls it "an ancillary investigation to the study of the text" (p. 8). E. E. Willoughby makes a similar comment in *The Uses of Bibliography to the Students of Literature and History* (1957): "Bibliography, in my opinion, is an ancillary science. It serves its true function when it is an efficient tool to solve problems in history, literature or some like subject" (p. 17).

As a result of this way of thinking, Bowers found himself in the position of insisting on the seemingly self-evident: that bibliography is "an independent discipline of scholarship and not merely an ancillary technique to literary investigation."[70] The possibility of understanding the word "bibliography" in various ways is again at the root of the matter, as it is when Thorpe returns to this issue. He quotes S. L. M. Barlow as saying, "It is none of the business of the bibliographer or the pure scientist what use is made of his findings";[71] and he objects by replying, "In my way of looking at textual criticism, its value derives only from serving the useful purpose of helping to present the text which the author intended" (p. 68). But "bibliographer" does not necessarily mean "textual critic"; it can mean "analytical bibliographer," whose field of interest—the printing practices of a given period or a given shop as revealed by physical evidence—is surely a legitimate subject of inquiry in its own right. If it had been as popular to call bibliography "history" as it has been to call it "science," these matters would probably have aroused less controversy; and Peckham's emphasis on the historical nature of analytical bibliography is therefore welcome.

Forty years ago Georg Schneider, in his book on reference bibliography, said, "It makes little difference whether bibliography is termed a science or an art, a technique or a skill, or even all of these together."[72] One is particularly ready at this point to apply the state-

70. "Purposes of Descriptive Bibliography, with Some Remarks on Methods," *Library*, 5th ser., 8 (1953), 22; though his article is specifically on descriptive bibliography, the comment quoted here refers to bibliography "in its several essential forms." This is only one of several similar statements Bowers has made; another was quoted above (and referred to in footnote 41). It is true that earlier, in the opening chapter of his *Principles of Bibliographical Description* (1949), he was more concerned with presenting descriptive bibliography as the "history of an author's book," not a mere guide to "points"; and in this context he quoted Wroth's comments as support (p. 9), called bibliography a "bridge" to textual criticism (pp. 9, 11), and said that "bibliography would be a limited science indeed if collection of external facts were its sole reason for existence" (p. 8). Some later writers have persisted in expressing doubt about the independent sta-

tus of bibliography. Roy Stokes, for example, in *The Function of Bibliography* (1969), claims, "Although bibliography is concerned with the physical problems and aspects of such material, there is little to be gained, apart from purely anitquarian pleasure, in unravelling such problems for their own sake. The major interest will always lie in some relationship to the text which is being transmitted" (p. 17). And E. W. Padwick, in the opening chapter of *Bibliographical Method* (1969), reports, as if it were a novel idea, that "contemporary leading exponents such as Professor Fredson Bowers wish to see it [bibliographical scholarship] accepted as an independent discipline no longer to be regarded solely as a handmaid of literature" (p. 12).

71. See the discussion in Randolph G. Adams, *Three Americanists* (1939), p. 9.

72. *Theory and History of Bibliography*,

ment to other areas of bibliography as well. The act of classifying a subject in terms of a larger framework ought to help clarify the nature of that subject, but the history of the association of bibliography with science shows that there are exceptions. Part of the trouble, it is evident, is that bibliography is not "a subject" but a related group of subjects that happen to be commonly referred to by the same term. There should be no problem in recognizing historical bibliography (the study of printing, publishing, and associated areas at particular times in the past) as history; nor is it hard to move from there to an understanding of analytical bibliography (the examination of the physical evidence in books as a clue to the processes of their production) as history. Descriptive bibliography again is history (the history of the forms in which a given group of books has appeared), drawing on both historical and analytical bibliography. It may have occasion, depending on the nature of the problems encountered and the level of detail contemplated, to utilize instruments or methods of measurement generally regarded as "scientific,"[73] but that fact does not make it a "science," except in the general sense that it is striving for accuracy; it may often take as its field of investigation the books written by a particular literary figure, but that fact does not make it a "literary" study. Textual criticism and scholarly editing,[74] however, though they draw on these three historical kinds of bibliography and though they aim at establishing the history of particular texts, deal with questions of meaning in texts which can frequently be resolved only by literary sensitivity, and they can reasonably be thought of as part of the field of literary criticism[75]—but they could also be defined as a form of history, and to debate the matter would be as fruitless as to debate whether they are a form of science. To regard bibliography as principally historical is not to settle anything, since the status of history is also in question;[76] but it places the debate about the scientific nature

trans. Ralph R. Shaw (1934), p. 24; other comments about science and bibliography appear on pp. 20-24.

73. I have touched on this question in more detail in "Tolerances in Bibliographical Description," Library, 5th ser., 23 (1968), 1-12.

74. As opposed to what may be called "creative editing"; I have made further comments on this distinction in PBSA, 65 (1971), 113-14.

75. The case is not altered, it seems to me, even when the text under consideration is one that would not conventionally be regarded as "literary"; obviously a knowledge of the subject matter taken up in the text is essential, but something beyond that is required.

76. The pointlessness of many of the discussions about whether one or another of the social sciences is really "scientific" is suggested by Ernest Nagel when he says that "the requirements for being a genuine

of bibliography in the context of a larger debate, about which much more has already been written, and it associates bibliography with other pursuits that concentrate on unique past events,[77] thus providing a more immediately acceptable analogue (if indeed it is not a tautology).

The impulse to use a scientific analogy is ultimately the natural human inclination to believe that what one is doing now is more rigorous and precise than what people were doing in the past. Speaking of textual criticism, Housman, in a well-known passage, says that "the most frivolous pretender has learnt to talk superciliously about 'the old unscientific days.' " But the truth is, he continues, "The old unscientific days are everlasting; they are here and now."[78] To talk about what one is doing can sometimes help one to proceed; but there are other times when it seems best to get on with the work and to define the work by doing it.[79]

---

science tacitly assumed in most of the challenges lead to the unenlightening result that apparently none but a few branches of physical inquiry merit the honorific designation" (*The Structure of Science*, p. 449).

77. That is to say, in more elaborate terms, pursuits which are not principally nomothetic.

78. "The Application of Thought to Textual Criticism," in *Selected Prose*, ed. John Carter (1961), p. 149.

79. David Shaw, in an extremely interesting article ("A Sampling Theory for Bibliographical Research," *Library*, 5th ser., 27 [1972], 310-19) published after the present article was written, comes to a similar conclusion. He works out a way of applying the sampling theory developed by statisticians to the bibliographical problem of determining how many copies of a book provide a significant body of evidence. At the end he recognizes that a "preoccupation with scientific method . . . is generally to be welcomed, provided that it leads to practical results and not solely to doctrinal disputes about the methodologies. My suggestion of a greater application of probability theory in fact favours a continuation of business as before, rather than a great upheaval in bibliographical method." Instead of arguing the advantages of induction or deduction, as he says earlier, his concern "is more simply cautionary. Whatever system of reasoning one uses or thinks one is using, due caution is a most scholarly virtue" (p. 316).

Descriptive Bibliography and
Library Cataloguing

IN A CELEBRATED ESSAY IN 1941 ON "THE CRISIS IN CATALOGING,"[1]
Andrew D. Osborn remarked, "The relationship between cataloging and bibliography has been a difficult one to define" (p. 400).
Indeed, anyone who has investigated the history of attempts to
define it will regard this comment as a considerable understatement:
the matter is intrinsically complex, but to make matters worse bibliographers and cataloguers have often been unsympathetic, or even
hostile, toward each other's practices and approaches. Yet descriptive
bibliography and cataloguing, as Osborn continues, "have many points
of contact and many elements in common. Their history has been
intertwined in many respects." The two are naturally related pursuits,
and the interests of all who are concerned with books are best served
by a spirit of cooperation between them; the split which threatens to
make them continually more incompatible does no one any good. Both
have become specialties, with the familiar result that communication
is hampered; and those working in each field go their own way, without being well informed about, or perhaps even interested in, what is
happening in the other. Bibliographers and cataloguers, and many
other people as well, constantly consult both catalogues and bibliographies; the two kinds of works are necessarily different, having different aims, but they are both parts of a larger undertaking—the recording of intellectual products and their physical embodiments. A user
of these works should ideally be impressed more by their compatibility

1. *Library Quarterly*, 11 (1941), 393-
411. The historical position of this essay is
commented upon in some of the works
mentioned in note 23 below, especially
those by Dunkin. Earlier Osborn had
touched on "the very important question
in cataloging theory as to the relation
between bibliography and cataloging" and
called for a "new theory of the dictionary
catalog," in "Cataloging Costs and a
Changing Conception of Cataloging," *Catalogers' and Classifiers' Yearbook*, 5 (1936),
45-54 (esp. 48-49).

than by their divergence, and anything which produces greater communication between bibliographers and cataloguers is a move in the right direction.

The present moment is particularly appropriate for an increased effort at mutual understanding. For their part, bibliographers have shown in recent years a renewed interest in the production of lists which do not entail full physical descriptions. D. F. McKenzie, for instance, has suggested that bibliography can perhaps best serve the study of history and literature "by returning . . . to the more directly useful, if less sophisticated, activity of enumerative 'bibliography.' "[2] And David F. Foxon has stated "the case for another species of bibliographer whose role lies somewhere between the enumerative and the descriptive";[3] after explaining the rationale of his own *English Verse, 1701-1750: A Catalogue,* he adds:

What I do feel very strongly is that work of this kind is as essential to scholarship as the full-scale descriptive bibliography; that if librarians are going to turn to computers and cooperative cataloguing, this is the sort of standard at which they should aim; and that bibliographers should be aware that this sort of drudgery is as rewarding, both to themselves and others, as its more fashionable manifestations. (p. 30)

Both writers allude to the accomplishments of Pollard, Redgrave, and Wing in producing "short-title catalogues" and comment on the need for an eighteenth-century STC; and the attention now being given to this need has provided the occasion for useful discussions about the nature and form of such works.[4] But the suggestion, in these two statements, that bibliographers must "return" from "sophisticated" or "fashionable" activity misleadingly implies that they have been irresponsible and have abandoned what is basic. There is no reason why these approaches have to be set in opposition to each other, for the pursuit of descriptive bibliography does not involve a disrespect for the making of outwardly simpler lists and catalogues. Fredson Bowers, on the opening page of his *Principles of Bibliographical Description* (1949), recognizes that catalogues "will always exist as one of the basic needs of scholarship." Whether or not this view may have been lost sight of by descriptive bibliographers, these recent statements are a

---

2. See p. 61 of his "Printers of the Mind: Some Notes on Bibliographical Theories and Printing-House Practices," *SB,* 22 (1969) , 1-75.

3. *Thoughts on the History and Future*

of Bibliographical Description (1970), p. 26.

4. See, for instance, the papers referred to at the end of note 85 below.

healthy reaffirmation of the value of catalogues and lists. To them should be added another obvious point: that bibliographers contemplating work on a short-title catalogue or list ought to be aware of standard library cataloguing practices, so that they are in a position to take advantage of any that seem useful for their purposes.

Conversely, cataloguers now more than ever need to examine descriptive bibliography for possible techniques or procedures that could be incorporated with advantage into their own work. Cataloguing in recent years has been at a critical juncture in its history, with the emergence of increasing possibilities for international standardization and cooperation as reflected in the extent of the agreement reached at the 1961 International Conference on Cataloguing Principles in Paris. The publication of the *Anglo-American Cataloging Rules* (1967), based on the Paris principles, and the development of the International Standard Bibliographic Description (1971), designed to make the elements of a catalogue description recognizable through punctuation, as well as the distribution of MARC (Machine Readable Cataloging) magnetic tapes,[5] have served to indicate the enormous influence which cataloguing procedures can have and to provide an occasion for rethinking those procedures. Although it is unfortunate that these standard codes were promulgated without consideration of the contributions which descriptive bibliography might make, it is not too late to incorporate alterations in them, if changes are found to be desirable. Relatively speaking, we are still at the beginning of the tenure of these rules; and, if further improvements can be made in them by drawing on the experience of descriptive bibliography, this is the time for effecting those changes.

Cooperation between bibliographers and cataloguers, however, can be significant only if the relations between their activities are clearly recognized. I should like to begin by looking into this relationship, attempting to define the position each occupies in the whole realm of bibliographical study. Then, on this tenth anniversary of the appearance of the *Anglo-American Cataloging Rules*, I propose to examine some of those rules from the point of view of the descriptive bibliographer. As a result, I hope that it will be possible to survey with understanding various suggestions for cataloguing "rare" books and to point out some ways in which the approach of bibliographers and that of cataloguers can be brought closer together without placing an unfair burden on cataloguers.

5. See *Information on the MARC System* (3rd ed., 1973), which includes a checklist of relevant items, pp. 37-44; for the International Standard Bibliographic Description, see note 26 below.

I

The distinction between catalogues and bibliographies is an elementary one; yet it is not always kept clearly in mind by those engaged in bibliographical activity. Of course, one person can call his work a "catalogue" and mean something entirely different from what someone else means by "catalogue." Neither person is necessarily confused in his thinking; each is merely using a different definition of "catalogue." Such differences are always possible where matters of definition are involved. But I am not speaking here of the definitions of particular terms; rather, I am concerned with two different concepts, regardless of what they are labeled. One kind of record of books[6]—which it is convenient to call a "catalogue"—is concerned with the particular copies of books that happen to be in a given collection (a private library, an institutional library or special collection within it, a dealer's stock, and the like) or that constitute a specifically defined assemblage (items brought together for an exhibition or an auction, for instance).[7] Another kind of record of books—which it is convenient to call a "bibliography"—is concerned with books which are related in some way, but not with specific copies of those books. In other words, an entry in a catalogue refers to a particular copy of a book; an entry in a bibliography refers to any copy of that book. This distinction can best be illustrated by noting that the goal of descriptive bibliography is the description of an "ideal copy" of each book, a term carefully defined by Fredson Bowers (*Principles*, pp. 113-123) to refer to the complete state that the printer or publisher "considered to represent the final and most perfect state of the book." An ideal copy is not necessarily free of textual errors, but it is free of those physical deficiencies which would prevent its representing a standard form of the book as published. It is therefore an abstraction, for conceivably all existing copies of a book might be defective in one way or another, but a description of an ideal copy could still be constructed by combining details observable in the defective copies. A description of an ideal copy sets a standard against which individual copies can be meas-

6   They can, for the moment, be called "books"; I shall take up below the significance of calling them that and the question whether they should at times be called something else.

7.   Although a list of books available from a publisher is often called a "catalogue,"

it is not a catalogue in the sense defined here; each entry in a publisher's list refers not to a specific copy but to any or all copies of the item in question. (The same might be said of a new-book dealer's "catalogue" listing books which the dealer can procure on demand but which are not actually in stock.)

ured; a catalogue entry describes or records an individual copy with all its peculiarities.[8]

Simple as this distinction essentially is, it raises some complicated questions which have been much discussed. Sometimes, there is a tendency to think that the amount of descriptive detail is a part of the distinction.[9] But it should be clear that both catalogues and bibliographies can run the gamut from the sparse to the elaborate. Some catalogues, like Allan Stevenson's volume of the Hunt catalogue (1961), include fuller physical descriptions than are found in a great many descriptive bibliographies. And some catalogues, like William A. Jackson's Pforzheimer catalogue (1940), involve comparisons between copies in the collection and other copies, so that the precise nature of the copies in the collection can be more clearly specified; in this way a catalogue can actually record the characteristics of an ideal copy, but so long as the object of description is one specific copy the work remains a catalogue. Naturally, as the quantity of detail declines, the differences between the entries for a given book in a catalogue and a bibliography are likely to become slighter—or nonexistent. If an entry consists of nothing more than a simple listing of author, title, and date, such an entry for a book in a catalogue could not be distinguished from the same style of entry for that book in a bibliography

8. Rolf Du Rietz has explored this distinction between catalogues and bibliographies in detail in the preface to his *Bibliotheca Polynesiana: A Catalogue of Some of the Books in the Polynesiana Collection Formed by the Late Bjarne Kroepelien and Now in the Oslo University Library* (1969), pp. xix-xxviii. The principal point I have been making is the one on which his discussion also is based: "the great difference between catalogues and bibliographies in respect of the Platonic 'idea' of the copy behind the description is . . . so obvious, so utterly significant, that it seems the only sound ground upon which to base a definition of the two terms" (p. xxiv). Fredson Bowers makes the same distinction more concisely in "The Function of Bibliography," *Library Trends*, 7 (1958-59), 497-510 (esp. 500-503).

9. For instance, Edward A. Petherick said in July 1897 that catalogues were becoming so full of details "that it is difficult to say where cataloguing ends and bibilogra-

phy begins" (p. 148), in "Theoretical and Practical Bibliography," *Transactions and Proceedings of the Second International Library Conference* (1898), pp. 148-149. A. W. Pollard, writing on "The Relations of Bibliography and Cataloguing" in the same volume, pp. 63-66, said that the librarian's work "necessarily becomes bibliographical" when his library has two editions of the same work, because he is "bound in some way to show how they differ" (p. 65). Georg Schneider, in *Theory and History of Bibliography* (trans. Ralph R. Shaw, 1934), where "bibliography" is used only in the sense of a reference list, states that "the entries in catalogs must be brief; entries in bibliographies must be accurate and complete, for they serve to supplement the former" (p. 51). See also Frank L. Tolman, "Bibliography and Cataloging: Some Affinities and Contrasts," *Public Libraries*, 10 (1905), 119-122; and Henry B. Van Hoesen, "Short Cataloging and Bibliographical Cataloging," *American Library Institute Papers and Proceedings* 1921, pp. 15-41.

(or "checklist"). But the indistinguishability of the two entries would not alter the fact that the purposes of the two lists, and thus the significance of the two entries, were different. In the first case, the entry refers to one specific copy of the book; in the second, it refers to any copy. A catalogue, then, is not merely a less detailed bibliography; the extent of detail is irrelevant to its classification as a catalogue. Furthermore, the account of an ideal copy in a descriptive bibliography, however much or little detail is given, requires a great deal more research (the examining of many copies) than is normally expended on a catalogue entry; but the catalogue entry can—within its limits (the description of a specific copy)—be equally authoritative. Of course, in describing a single copy without the benefit of a published bibliography or the examination of other copies, one cannot always know exactly which features may be of special significance; for this reason the entries in catalogues are in practice rarely as informative, even for the specific copy, as entries in bibliographies. Nevertheless, it is not the quantity of detail or the extent of research which distinguishes the two kinds of entry but solely the nature of the copy which each aims at recording.[10]

10. In "Bibliography Revisited," *Library*, 5th ser., 24 (1969), 89-128, reprinted in his *Essays in Bibliography, Text, and Editing* (1975), pp. 151-195, Bowers makes the same point: "The fullest description ever compiled would be a mere catalogue entry if based on the examination of only a single copy" (p. 194). When he goes on, however, to say, "It is the matter of standards of examination, quite apart from the differing forms of the entry, that distinguishes descriptive from enumerative bibliography," the issues become less clear, because "enumerative bibliography" is not synonymous with "cataloguing." Indeed, the preceding sentence has made clear that the form of the entry does not distinguish bibliographies and catalogues, and "enumerative bibliography" here must mean a listing with few details. In that case, one can see what Du Rietz objects to in Bowers's statement: "the very form of the entries," Du Rietz says, "is exactly what determines whether the list (bibliography or catalogue) is of the descriptive or of the enumerative (i.e. reference) kind, the standards of examination behind the form indicating solely the degree of quality of the list" (*Bibliotheca Polynesiana*, p. lix).

Certainly a cataloguer could set for himself as high a standard of examination of copies as a descriptive bibliographer, but the resulting work, containing descriptions of particular copies, would still be a catalogue. It is not the standards themselves which determine the genre of the work produced but the intent of the compiler as to the subject matter of the entries (that is, whether they refer to particular or ideal copies). When Du Rietz proceeds to point out that the "standards of examination are necessarily always more or less poor in entries for descriptive catalogues" and that such entries "must by their very nature always be more or less preliminary," he begins to blur the essential distinction, for it is not in the nature of a catalogue to be preliminary but simply to be a record of specific copies. (Cf. his comments on p. xxi.) If his phrases "necessarily always" and "by their very nature always" were each replaced with "usually" his statement would be a fair generalization about actual practice and would not imply that something in the very concept of a catalogue prevents it from representing more than a certain limited amount of research. (Whether or not Du Rietz should have

Another question which complicates one's thinking about catalogues and bibliographies is the determination of what is meant by "book"—of what, in fact, is being recorded. The word "book" is sometimes used to refer to a physical object (or a group of physical objects, such as all those comprising one edition); at other times it refers to the work (the verbal construction) embodied in the pages of the physical book. Clearly this distinction is basic, and the nature of a bibliographical record is determined by whether that record is principally concerned with *books* or with *works*. It might at first be supposed that a catalogue inevitably deals with books, not works, since it lists specific copies. Unquestionably a catalogue must involve this element; but many catalogues of *books* are used as guides to the *works* on a given subject, and their compilers sometimes have this function in mind and provide annotation which emphasizes it. Seymour Lubetzky, in *Principles of Cataloging* (1969), has offered a careful analysis of the book-vs.-work distinction in the context of library cataloguing (pp. 1-17).[11] First he sums up the perennial debate over whether a library catalogue should be a "finding list" or a "reference tool," whether it should merely locate certain books for its users or provide a guide to the works incorporated in those books.[12] Later he

equated "enumerative" and "reference" bibliography, as he does in the comment quoted earlier, is a separate question; the meaning of "reference" bibliography will be considered below.) In his *Principles*, Bowers suggests that the term "bibliographical catalogue" be used "when the high requirements of *bibliographies* have not been completely met either in the number of copies compared or in the method of examination" (p. 5). So long as this term is carefully defined as a technical expression, it can of course serve this purpose. But less confusion would be likely to result if "catalogue" were reserved strictly for works listing specific copies; to employ it in a phrase like "bibliographical catalogue" to designate a work which does not meet the requirements for a descriptive bibliography is to encourage the fallacy that a catalogue is simply an inferior bibliography, rather than a work with basically different aims. Cf. the similar objections raised by Lloyd Hibberd, *Library*, 5th ser., 20 (1965), 130, n. 5, and Du Rietz, p. xx, n. 3.

11. As he puts it, the modern concept of "bibliographic cataloging" reflects the recognition "that the *book* (i.e., the material record) and the *work* (i.e., the intellectual product embodied in it) are not coterminous" (p. 99). For Rolf Du Rietz's extended discussion of the same distinction, see his essay cited in note 15 below and "The Concept of 'Bibliotype,'" *Text*, 1 (1974), 78-92 (esp. 82-85). Various earlier writers have of course noted this distinction as well: e.g., see J. D. Cowley, *Bibliographical Description and Cataloguing* (1939), pp. 6-7; Thomas Franklin Currier, "What the Bibliographer Says to the Cataloger," *Catalogers' and Classifiers' Yearbook*, 9 (1941), 21-37 (p. 26: "In general it is safe to say that the cataloger should be more concerned with the substance and content of the book than with its physical form and make-up"); Pierce Butler, "The Cultural Function of the Library," *Library Quarterly*, 22 (1952), 79-91 (p. 88: a book as "so much matter" or as a "system of ideas").

12. A good historical survey of opinion

concisely states these two questions which are involved in cataloguing the "records of man's thought":

First, how are they, as concrete entities, to be individually identified and entered in a catalog so that they could readily be found when needed; and Second, how are they, as sources of information on various subjects, to be characterized and related so that they could be found by those in search of the information desired.[13]

It is obvious that a catalogue will be useful to more people if it performs both functions, and users of institutional libraries now regularly expect to find such catalogues of the holdings of those libraries. As a result, library cataloguing is generally divided into two activities, descriptive cataloguing (dealing with author or title entry and with the physical characteristics of the books) and subject cataloguing or classification (dealing with the content of the works). Lubetzky's principal point is that in neither activity has the distinction between book and work been clearly focused on in the past; therefore, he says, it has not been sufficiently understood that physical description is basic to all cataloguing, since works exist in a library only as embodied in individual books. If the record of particular copies in catalogues can thus serve to supply information about *works*, there is no question that bibliographies or checklists (recording ideal copies) can do so too. Indeed, the commonest form of checklist is that in which the primary emphasis is on the content of the works named. The border line separating details relating to the book from those relating to the work is not always sharp (some details serve both purposes), but one cannot think clearly about catalogues and bibliographies without keeping this division in mind and recognizing the extent of mixture of the two approaches in any given listing. Both catalogues and bibliographies can vary in the degree to which they lean toward providing information either on books or on works; but where they stand in that respect does not affect the crucial distinction between catalogues and bibliographies, based on the difference between specific and ideal copies.

The division between books and works is analogous to Lloyd Hibberd's separation of the field into "physical bibliography" and

---

on this question is provided by Raynard Swank in "Subject Catalogs, Classifications, or Bibliographies? A Review of Critical Discussions, 1876-1942," *Library Quarterly*, 14 (1944), 316-332.

13. From p. 97 of the concluding chapter, "Bibliographic Dimensions in Information Control," pp. 97-113, written in collaboration with Robert M. Hayes; this chapter was also published in *American Documentation*, 20 (1969), 247-252.

"reference bibliography."[14] His useful essay recognizes that the amount of detail which a bibliographical record contains is less significant for classifying it than whether it is concerned with the physical form or with the content of the items recorded. His survey of the confusing array of terms in use and his suggestions for terminology which more accurately shows the relationships among bibliographical activities have been generally well received; but Rolf Du Rietz in a thoughtful essay[15] recently complained that Hibberd's "well-meant" proposal "has unfortunately further contributed to separate the two supposedly widely different 'kinds' of bibliography from each other instead of bringing them closer together" (p. 22). According to Du Rietz, the belief that reference bibliography is concerned only with the content of books leads to such lax standards in the inevitable allusion to physical detail in reference bibliographies that physical bibliographers are bound to have a low opinion of it. His principal point is that all bibliographical lists are to some extent physical (e.g., pp. 15-16, 22), because lists referring only to works and not to the books embodying the works would simply have entries like "Hitler's *Mein Kampf*" and "do not deserve the name of bibliographies, since they do not list books at all" (p. 24); therefore, he says, reference bibliographers must have training in physical bibliography, so that their lists will offer responsible treatment of the physical details which they cannot avoid. This warning is salutary and, in noting the physical element in book lists, calls attention to a fact not sufficiently recognized. But Du Rietz goes too far, it seems to me, in the direction of blurring a useful distinction when he is led to conclude that there is "no such thing as 'a' physical bibliography, or 'a' reference bibliography" (p. 24). It is true that all bibliographies in one sense involve a mixture of both physical and reference elements, but that does not prevent the principal emphasis or concern of a given listing from being on one or the other. Reference lists, for instance, frequently cite the city, publisher, and date of the first printing of a work without implying that the reader is necessarily being directed to the first printing in preference to a later printing or edition. The facts of publication are offered as historical annotation, not as physical details, even though these same details would of course be a part of a physical bibliography as well. Such

14. "Physical and Reference Bibliography," *Library*, 5th ser., 20 (1965), 124-134. Hibberd conveniently brings together relevant comments from Fredson Bowers, Verner Clapp, Louise-Noëlle Malclès, and others.

15. "What Is Bibliography?", *Text*, 1 (1974), 6-40. Although the discussion which follows takes issue with Du Rietz occasionally, my conclusions have much in common with his. Cf. note 21 below.

listings are similar to references sometimes found in the body of a literary discussion: "*Moby-Dick* (New York: Harper, 1851)" may not mean anything more than "*Moby-Dick*," except that more historical details are provided; indeed, page references might be given to a later and more accessible edition—but again without any implication that the reader should not turn to still another edition, more convenient for him, to locate the cited passages. Even a catalogue can emphasize reference bibliography, if the interest is more in what works are represented by the books in a collection than in what particular books are there. To be sure, a catalogue cannot avoid physical implications, since it is based on a specific gathering of books; but the purpose of a catalogue can be, as its annotation would make clear, to show what *works* (regardless of edition) are available in that collection.[16]

Reference bibliography can simply be regarded as primarily concerned with works, physical bibliography as primarily concerned with books. The approach in each case will determine what details are reported and how they are treated; but it should not be surprising that some of the same details will turn up in both kinds of bibliographies, since the two approaches are complementary. I take it that Hibberd is making the same point when he says, "And though divergent in purpose and scope, the two divisions start from the common basis of systematic compilation and end in reciprocal fructification" (p. 133). Du Rietz, too, wishes to show the intimate relationship between the two, but in stressing the physical elements in reference bibliography he makes reference bibliography in effect a preliminary step leading toward, or a less thorough form of, physical bibliography.[17] He is unwilling to let the word "bibliography" move beyond its

16. Whether enough information is provided to identify *texts* is another question. The word "text" can have both a concrete and an abstract meaning: it can refer to the inked type-images in a given copy of a book, or it can signify a particular arrangement of words, abstracted from any particular physical embodiment. Du Rietz calls the first an "actual text" and the second an "ideal text," which can be either a "version" or a "work" (p. 11). What distinguishes a version from a work, however, is a difficult matter; see, for instance, G. T. Tanselle, "The Editorial Problem of Final Authorial Intention," *SB*, 29 (1976), 167-211.

17. He does not claim that it is necessarily less detailed, for he notes that the results of both kinds of bibliography can be recorded in lists (p. 23); he does, however, imply an ascending order, leading up from "humble" reference checklists to physical bibliography "on the highest level" (p. 26). He defines reference bibliography as "the activity of collecting, selecting, arranging, and sometimes also commenting upon information relating solely to the *existence* and *relevance* of such particular books as are united by a least common denominator selected as the basis for the bibliographer's work" (p. 23). But he goes on to say that the least common denominator is usually of a literary kind and that "the ultimate purpose is to list *works*." It

etymology and encompass a concern for works as well as for books; the result is that for him reference and physical bibliography together form one camp and "information science" the other. Although he is reluctant to link "the immensely powerful information science" with "the rather humble and unsophisticated kind of activity of reference bibliography," he admits that a bibliographical list could conceivably be regarded as involving both physical bibliography and information science (p. 26). The issue is thus a question of terminology, for the dichotomy in any case is between books and works. It makes little difference whether "reference bibliography" is salvaged as a term, so long as we know when we are thinking about works rather than books.

The relationships I am describing can perhaps be clarified by a diagram:

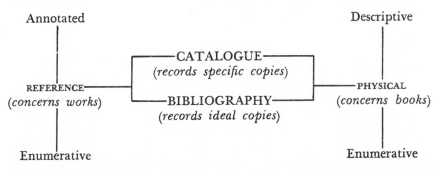

What this diagram attempts to suggest is, first, that there are two basic kinds of finished product resulting from bibliographical activity: the catalogue, dealing with specific copies, and the bibliography, concerned with ideal copies. The catalogue may refer to copies outside a given collection or to accounts of ideal copies, but its primary function is to refer to particular copies; the bibliography may cite the peculiarities of individual copies or offer a census of surviving copies, but its primary function is to refer to standard copies, free from the deficiencies which may happen to occur in any one copy. Both catalogues and bibliographies may take the form of essays rather than lists, but their essential function remains unchanged. Second, the arrangement of the diagram suggests that both catalogues and bibliographies partake of both reference bibliography, in which the subject matter is the works embodied in books, and physical bibliography, in which the subject matter is the books as physical objects. However, their interest in these

---

is difficult to see, therefore, how his definition would operate in practice to keep the focus of reference bibliography on books rather than works.

two approaches is rarely equal, and they may move in one direction or the other, stressing either reference bibliography or physical bibliography. Finally, both catalogues and bibliographies, whether emphasizing reference or physical bibliography, can present a great deal of detail or very little detail. If the emphasis is reference, that detail will take the form of annotation suggestive of the nature or value (or both) of the *works* included; if the emphasis is physical, that detail will take the form of description of the physical makeup of the *books* included.[18] As the detail in a reference or a physical bibliography becomes less, the entries in the two come to resemble each other more and more, and for that reason I have employed the same word, "enumerative," to refer to lack of detail in either case.[19] But the fact that the entries are stripped to the information basic to both approaches does not mean that the functions of reference and physical bibliography have become blurred; the entries may even be identical, but their significance is different depending on the context in which they occur. And the context is determined by two factors: whether the emphasis is on reference or physical bibliography and whether the product is a catalogue or a bibliography. For example, the city and year of publication reported in a catalogue entry are to some extent physical details because a particular copy is being referred to; yet the general approach, as revealed in a preface or in other notes attached to entries, may be to regard the listing as primarily useful for its record of works, not books, and in this case the city and year are not essentially physical details. The cataloguer has a right to take this approach if he wishes to; the trouble comes only if his practice in recording what are partly physical details is positively misleading to anyone familiar with the way the same details would be handled in a catalogue stressing physical bibliography. The problem arising from the fact that any catalogue or bibliography can move toward the physical or toward the reference end of the scale is not simply a matter

18. Hibberd makes the sensible suggestion that the word "description" should be reserved for "external description" and that "internal description" should be called "annotation" (see his discussion of these and the related terms "critical" and "analytical" on pp. 131-132). The ambiguous use of "description" in library cataloguing is commented on below.

19. Similarly, both catalogues and bibliographies which lack detail can be called "checklists" or "handlists," but their differing functions remain as before. Indeed, it would seem preferable to use "checklist" or "handlist" in such cases, so as to give the reader an indication of the amount of detail to be expected. But "bibliography" has been so widely used for so many years to signify an enumerative list as well as a detailed one that it seems futile at this late date to attempt to alter the usage. Careful writers, however, will continue to make the distinction.

of how many details are included but rather of how the included details are treated.[20]

There is no question that the differing approaches of reference and physical bibliography have frequently produced incompatible results in the past. Du Rietz has said that bibliography and information science are "notoriously at loggerheads in all matters terminological" and that "the libraries will apparently remain an unavoidable battle-field for the combatants until some *modus vivendi* may be achieved" (pp. 26-27). The libraries are at the center of this debate precisely because they attempt, through catalogues and indexes in whatever form, to offer a guide both to the books in their holdings and to the works contained in those books. Of course, any cataloguer or bibliographer confronts this issue to some degree in his own work, but institutional libraries, because they process large numbers of books, naturally become the most prominent illustration of the problem. The real point of contact between the two approaches (or the

20. A different sort of diagram, which makes some of the same points, appears in William J. Cameron, Brian J. McMullin, and Joginder K. Sood, *The HPB Project*: *Phase II* (1970), p. 3. It, like mine, attempts to show that both reference and physical bibliography can be undertaken at any level of detail, by equating the vertical axis with "elaborateness of description" and the horizontal with "the degree of attention to the *physical* character of the book on the one hand or to the *intellectual content* of the book on the other" (p. 2). However, I think that their diagram is somewhat misleading in marking off three levels of detail on the vertical axis, "identification," "description," and "analysis," with "analysis" at the top, because "analysis" is not a parallel concept and does not necessarily represent a greater elaboration of detail. In physical bibliography, analysis is a tool which plays a role in the production of a description; an analytical article may amount to a thorough physical description, or it may be only a partial description, less elaborate than a full-scale description, but in any case the fact that it is in essay form is beside the point. In reference bibliography, a book review—shown in their diagram as the counterpart of bibliographical analysis—is not the only

form of content analysis; one-word assessments, such as "important," "disappointing," and "basic," are often attached to the entries in a reference list and are examples of analysis, but they do not make those entries more elaborate than a standard library catalogue entry. Part of the problem, at least on the physical side, comes perhaps from the fact that the Cameron-McMullin-Sood diagram is not concerned with distinguishing between catalogues and bibliographies: it is possible for a physical description based on one copy to result from very little analysis (though some judgment is always involved), but a description of an ideal copy based on many actual copies inevitably results from analysis. Nevertheless, the accompanying discussion, "Principles of Short-Title Cataloguing" (pp. 1-19), offers a thoughtful consideration of certain basic issues, recognizing, for instance, that "bibliographical description pays some attention to the intellectual contents of a book, and descriptive cataloguing [i.e., reference bibliography] often pays attention to some aspects of the physical book" (p. 5). But it is not part of the purpose of the discussion to question the rationale behind present conventions of library cataloguing: "Adequate description of a book from the subject point of view is embodied in library cataloguing" (p. 4).

"battle-field" where one can see the conflict in progress) is in the pages or cards of bibliographies and catalogues. Certainly the concerns of information retrieval can lead one far from the physical book; but since information must be recorded in some concrete form and since different physical embodiments of the same work may contain variations in text which affect the "information" conveyed, the two approaches are ultimately inseparable. Physical and reference bibliography—or whatever we choose to call them—are tied together (as my diagram tries to show) in every catalogue or bibliography that is produced. Since they move in different directions, however, a catalogue or bibliography which is primarily concerned with reference bibliography may have only a small area which overlaps the concerns of the descriptive bibliographer, and vice versa—but they inevitably do overlap. It is in that overlapping area where the methods of the two approaches must be compatible; if they are not, catalogues and bibliographies will be less efficient tools, and scholarship will suffer. In preparing, using, and evaluating catalogues and bibliographies, one must keep firmly in mind the various relationships among the three sets of paired concepts discussed here: works vs. books, reference bibliography vs. physical bibliography, enumeration vs. detail. One will then realize that it is pointless to criticize a catalogue for being insufficiently descriptive of physical details, if it has set out to perform a different service; but one can legitimately complain if the physical details included are presented ambiguously or misleadingly or in a manner which is in actual conflict with the way those details would be presented in a catalogue stressing physical bibliography.[21]

---

21. Du Rietz makes a similar point: "What is important . . . is that information science must not be allowed to impose its descriptive standards (or rather, lack of such standards) upon the science of bibliography, or upon current and retrospective national bibliography" (p. 25). Because he believes it to be "quite unreasonable to demand" that information science should deal with *books* "in a scholarly way and with any pretensions to accuracy," one can understand why he places reference bibliography within the domain of physical bibliography. "The only result," he says, "of separating 'reference' and 'physical' bibliography from each other is that enumerative bibliography will continue to drift away from the only influences that could possibly save its scholarly standards in the long run, namely, the influences of 'physical' bibliography" (p. 22). But this approach only shifts the original problem from "reference bibliography" to "information science"—for one is still left with a field (though it has a different name) in which the overriding concern for *works* results in an unsatisfactory treatment of *books*. One can readily applaud Du Rietz's efforts to raise the standards of enumerative bibliography; but incorporating it into physical bibliography leaves one with the question of why inadequate references to books should be tolerated in "information science." Since an interest in works must entail some reference to the books in which they are found, information science (under whatever name) cannot be irresponsible in such

Reference bibliography and physical bibliography are complementary, and those who are seriously interested in contributing to either field must approach their individual task in a spirit of cooperation with those who are working in another branch of what is finally a single undertaking.

II

It is obvious that many more books are catalogued with fairly brief entries by librarians than are accorded detailed descriptions by bibliographers and that there are many more library cataloguers at work than there are descriptive bibliographers. It is not surprising, therefore, that more attention has been given over the years to the principles and practices of library cataloguing than to those of descriptive bibliography.[22] The present *Anglo-American Cataloging Rules* (*AACR*) have developed from a tradition that can be traced back to Panizzi's British Museum rules of 1841 and includes Charles A. Cutter's *Rules for a Printed Dictionary Catalogue* (1876), the American and British Library Associations' *Catalog Rules* of 1908, the "Preliminary American Second Edition" of those rules in 1941, the *Rules for Descriptive Cataloging in the Library of Congress* (1947, 1949), and the *A. L. A. Cataloging Rules for Author and Title Entries* (1949).[23]

references. Du Rietz is right, of course, to point out that essentially physical details form the link between information science and the recording of books; therefore—as both he and I are suggesting in somewhat different ways—those details, when they appear in a context stressing *works*, should be treated in a manner compatible with (but not necessarily identical with) the way they would be treated in a context stressing *books*.

22. Fredson Bowers's *Principles of Bibliographical Description* (1949), the culmination of the tradition of descriptive bibliography, does build on the work of several earlier scholars (see note 62 below); but the total number of methodological discussions in this field is relatively small, and the codifications are the products of individual scholars (not of committees and public conferences).

23. Paul S. Dunkin has provided several useful historical surveys of this tradition,

emphasizing the quarter-century preceding *AACR* (1967): "Criticisms of Current Cataloging Practice," *Library Quarterly*, 26 (1956), 286-302; "Cataloging and CCS [Cataloging and Classification Section of American Library Association]: 1957-1966," *Library Resources and Technical Services*, 11 (1967), 267-288; *Cataloging U.S.A.* (1969), pp. 1-22 *et passim*; "Two Decisive Decades: Cataloging & Classification—The Big IF," *American Libraries*, 3 (1972), 775-783; and "From Pig to Man," in *Toward a Theory of Librarianship: Papers in Honor of Jesse Hauk Shera*, ed. Conrad H. Rawski (1973), pp. 339-349. Other recent surveys include James A. Tait, *Authors and Titles* (1969); John Horner, *Cataloguing* (1970), pp. 25-87; P. K. Escreet, *Introduction to the Anglo-American Cataloguing Rules* (1971), pp. 17-36; and K. G. B. Bakewell, *A Manual of Cataloguing Practice* (1972), pp. 14-47. Many of the codes themselves (e.g., those of 1908, 1941, 1949) contain brief historical sketches, as do some of the reports of con-

At many stages along the way there have been formal discussions, committee meetings, investigative reports, and institutes to plan revisions and new developments in the code. In the fifteen years before the publication of *AACR* in 1967, Seymour Lubetzky prepared proposals for new rules (1953) and drafts of rules reflecting the work of the Code Revision Committee (1958, 1960); official institutes on revision of the code were held at Stanford (1958) and McGill (1960); other conferences on cataloguing took place at the University of Chicago (1956) and at St. Andrews, N. B. (1961); and an International Conference on Cataloguing Principles was held in Paris in 1961, with 53 countries and twelve international organizations represented.[24] Since then, dis-

ferences (see note 25 below). For broader background, see Dorothy May Norris, *A History of Cataloguing and Cataloguing Methods, 1100-1850* (1939); Ruth French Strout, "The Development of the Catalog and Cataloging Codes," *Library Quarterly*, 26 (1956), 254-275; John C. Olney, *Library Cataloging and Classification* (1963); and Eugene R. Hanson and Jay E. Daily, "Catalogs and Cataloging," in *Encyclopedia of Library and Information Science*, ed. Allen Kent and Harold Lancour, 4 (1970), 242-305. Among the relevant historical studies which focus on particular periods may be mentioned Jim Ranz, *The Printed Book Catalogue in American Libraries, 1723-1900* (1964); Nancy Brault, *The Great Debate on Panizzi's Rules in 1847-1849: The Issues Discussed* (1972); Charles Martel, "Cataloging 1876-1926," *Library Journal*, 51 (1926), 1065-69; Jens Nyholm, "The Code in the Light of the Critics," *College and Research Libraries*, 3 (1941-42), 139-149; Andrew D. Osborn, "Cataloging Developments in the United States, 1940-47," in *Actes du comité international des bibliothèques*, 13th session (1947), 68-72; Leonard Jolley, "Some Recent Developments in Cataloguing in the U.S.A.," *Journal of Documentation*, 6 (1950), 70-82; Seymour Lubetzky, "Development of Cataloging Rules," *Library Trends*, 2 (1953-54), 179-186; Henry A. Sharp, "Current Research in Cataloguing," in *Cataloguing Principles and Practice*, ed. Mary Piggott (1954), pp. 15-25; Mary Piggott, "Cataloguing," in *Five Years' Work in Librarianship, 1956-1960*, ed. P. H. Sewell (1963), pp. 225-236, and *1961-1965* (1968), pp. 420-

439; A. H. Chaplin, "Cataloguing Principles: Five Years after the Paris Conference," *UNESCO Bulletin for Libraries*, 21 (1968), 140-145, 149; and James A. Tait, "Cataloguing," in *British Librarianship and Information Science, 1966-1970* (1972), pp. 61-67. For comparisons between some major codes (often, however, emphasizing the rules for heading, not description), see J. C. M. Hanson, *A Comparative Study of Cataloguing Rules Based on the Anglo-American Code of 1908* (1939); Henry A. Sharp, *Cataloguing* (4th ed., 1948), pp. 284-310; S. R. Ranganathan, *Headings and Canons* (1955); F. Bernice Field, "The New Catalog Code: The General Principles and the Major Changes," *Library Resources and Technical Services*, 10 (1966), 421-436, and "Anglo-American Cataloging Rules [Chapters 1-4] Correlated with *A.L.A. Cataloging Rules*," in *New Rules for an Old Game* (see note 25 below), pp. 137-159; Claude-Lise Richer, *Étude comparative des codes de catalogage de 1967 et de 1949* (1968); and Donald J. Lehnus, *A Comparison of Panizzi's 91 Rules and the AACR of 1967* (1972). Lehnus has also studied the writings on cataloguing and constructed a basic list of those most often cited, in *Milestones in Cataloging: Famous Catalogers and Their Writings, 1835-1969* (1974). Other convenient checklists appear in Dunkin, *Cataloging U.S.A.*, pp. xv-xxii; Escreet, pp. 368-373; Bakewell, pp. 269-284; and in some of the proceedings of conferences (see note 25 below).

24. Lubetzky, *Cataloging Rules and Prin-*

cussion has continued, as at the conferences on *AACR* at the Universities of Toronto and British Columbia in 1967 and at the University of Nottingham in 1968,[25] and some further changes have been made in *AACR* (in a ten-page supplement added to the 1970 impression and in the version of Chapter 6 published separately in 1974).[26] As

ciples: A Critique of the A.L.A. Rules for Entry and a Proposed Design for Their Revision (1953); *Code of Cataloging Rules: Bibliographic Entry and Description, a Partial and Tentative Draft* (1958); *Code of Cataloging Rules: Author and Title Entry, an Unfinished Draft*, annotated by Paul Dunkin (1960). For both the Stanford and the McGill institutes, there are available a *Summary of Proceedings* (1958, 1960) and the *Working Papers* (1958, 1960), the latter containing in each case a general statement of philosophy and purpose by Wyllis E. Wright (and the McGill volume including Lubetzky on "Fundamentals of Cataloging"). The papers from the 1956 Chicago conference are published in *Library Quarterly*, 26 (1956), 251-366, and separately as *Toward a Better Cataloging Code*, ed. Ruth French Strout (1957); the St. Andrews volume is *Summary of Proceedings and Working Papers* (1961). The background of the Paris Conference is covered by Paul Poindron, "Preparation for the International Conference on the Principles of Cataloging, Paris, 1961" (trans. Richard H. Shoemaker), *Library Resources and Technical Services*, 5 (1961), 225-237; a general account is provided in the same journal by Katharine Ball, "The Paris Conference," 6 (1962), 172-175; the preliminary official report is in *Libri*, 12 (1962), 61-76; and a critique of the results is offered by Leonard Jolley, "International Conference on Cataloging Principles: II. Thoughts after Paris," *Journal of Documentation*, 19 (1963), 47-62. The working papers and summaries of the sessions are published in *International Conference on Cataloguing Principles . . . Report*, ed. A. H. Chaplin and Dorothy Anderson (1963); a provisional annotated edition of the Conference's *Statement of Principles* (annotated by A. H. Chaplin and Dorothy Anderson) appeared in 1966 and a final annotated edition (annotated by Eva Verona) in 1971, following a 1969

international conference in Copenhagen to examine the 1966 *Principles*—as reported in *Libri*, 20 (1970), 105-132.

25. *The Code and the Cataloguer*, ed. Katherine H. Packer, Delores Phillips, and Katharine L. Ball (1969); *New Rules for an Old Game*, ed. Thelma E. Allen and Daryl Ann Dickman (1967); *Seminar on the Anglo-American Cataloguing Rules*, ed. J. C. Downing and N. F. Sharp (1969). All three volumes, particularly the first (pp. 3-19) and third (pp. 1-5), contain some introductory historical material; and the checklists in the second (pp. 161-165) and third (pp. 92-95) provide good coverage of the most important publications of the period 1953-69. See also "The New Rules in Action: A Symposium," ed. C. Donald Cook, *Library Resources and Technical Services*, 13 (1969), 7-41; and *Cataloguing Standards: The Report of the Canadian Task Group on Cataloguing Standards* (1972).

26. Changes are also recorded in two series of bulletins: *Cataloging Rules: Additions and Changes* (for the North American Text) and *Anglo-American Cataloguing Rules Amendment Bulletin* (for the British Text). The occasion for the publication of a revised North American text of Chapter 6 was the necessity for incorporating into it the newly developed rules for International Standard Bibliographic Description (ISBD), although other changes were made in Chapter 6 at the same time. The purpose of ISBD is to provide standard punctuation in entries (such as an oblique line between the title and the author's name, a colon between the place of publication and the publisher's name, or a period-dash between the title-author statement and the imprint), so that the various elements of an entry can be identified regardless of language and so that the entries are therefore machine-

the product of so much deliberation, the *AACR* must be of interest to the descriptive bibliographer, both because any well-considered approach to the recording of books is relevant to his concerns and because this one in particular reflects the cumulative experience of several generations of cataloguers and will exert great influence. Michael Gorman has been quoted as saying, "This is not only the best cataloguing code we have, it is also the best we are likely to have for a very long time."[27] It is not unfair, therefore, to expect *AACR* to be based on a clear understanding of the kinds of relationships among bibliographical activities which were outlined above. And it is legitimate to scrutinize the extent to which the recording of physical details as directed by the rules is useful to descriptive bibliographers.

Chapter 6 of *AACR*, on the "descriptive cataloging" of separately published monographs, is naturally the focus of attention for the descriptive bibliographer. Perhaps the best way to begin an examination of its approach is to look at Rule 141, on "collation."[28] Traditionally what is called the "collation" in a library catalogue card or entry consists of three parts: pagination, illustrations, and size. The "preliminary note" to this rule emphasizes its concern with physical details: the "collation" is called "the cataloger's description of the

---

readable. For a good introduction, see C. Sumner Spalding, "ISBD: Its Origin, Rationale, and Implications," *Library Journal*, 98 (1973), 121-123 (cf. 124-130, 394-395, and 495-496); and George M. Sinkankas, "International Cataloging and International Standard Bibliographic Description," in *Encyclopedia of Library and Information Science*, ed. Allen Kent *et al.*, 12 (1974), 278-320. The first edition of the ISBD rules (1971) has now been replaced by a "First Standard Edition": *ISBD (M): International Standard Bibliographic Description for Monographic Publications* (1974). Historical background is provided in Dorothy Anderson, "International Standardization of Cataloguing and Bibliographical Records: The Work of the IFLA Committee on Cataloguing," *UNESCO Bulletin for Libraries*, 27 (1973), 66-71, 107, and in "IFLA Committee on Cataloguing, 1954-1974," *International Cataloguing*, 3. no. 1 (Jan./March 1974), 5-8.

27. Quoted from the jacket of the British Text by R. O. Linden in the Nottingham *Seminar* (see note 25 above), p. 45. Gorman

has also said that "these rules are undoubtedly correct in their general and in their basic conclusions" (p. 32) in his review in *Library Association Record*, 70 (1968), 27-32.

28. Except where otherwise indicated, the text cited and quoted here is the 1974 pamphlet version of the North American Text of Chapter 6 (redrafted by Paul W. Winkler). Certain differences between that version and the North American or British texts of 1967 will be commented on in footnotes; but I have made no attempt systematically to cover all the differences, which have been taken up by D. Whitney Coe in "A Cataloger's Guide to *AACR* Chapter 6, Separately Published Monographs, 1974," *Library Resources and Technical Services*, 19 (1975), 101-120. A number of discussions of the differences between the 1967 North American and British texts have been published; for Chapter 6 of *AACR*, see in particular R. O. Linden's analysis in the Nottingham *Seminar* (see note 25 above), pp. 45-54.

physical work" (p. 47), and one of the aims is "to present a picture of the physical characteristics of the work to the reader" (p. 48). But one should notice that "work" rather than "book" is the word chosen and that the physical characteristics are recorded in order to help the reader "both in identifying the work and telling him something of its nature." Furthermore, another aim is "to ensure that all those parts of the work are described which would be retained in the binding or rebinding of the work," implying that the emphasis is on the substance of the work and that other integral leaves, such as those containing advertisements, are unimportant. It is clear, even from this introductory statement, that the "collation" is to be principally concerned with an indication of the extent of the contents of the book and not with the book itself. There is no reason to object to this emphasis, except that the "collation" has been defined as the "description of the physical work." If "work" here means "book," the usage is imprecise and the statement untrue. If it is being used carefully, in distinction to "book," the inclusion of the word "physical" still causes a problem: since the work exists physically only as embodied in the book, the physical description can only be based on the book, which may contain elements (such as advertisements) which are not part of the *work*.

The rules for recording pagination (or foliation) reflect the same ambiguity. First one is told (141B1a) that the "extent of a work" is to be indicated in terms of pages, leaves, or columns, depending on the method followed in the book being catalogued. The implication is that the cataloguer is concerned with the characteristics of the physical book, since the method of numbering employed in a given book is not related to the extent of the work; if the sole interest were in indicating extent, all figures for all books could be converted to a single unit, such as pages. The same impression is conveyed by the further rule (141B1b) that arabic or roman numbers or letters are to be used, following the practice of the book. But this rule ends with the statement that "Pages or leaves numbered in words, or in characters other than Arabic or Roman, are designated in the collation in Arabic figures." Thus the emphasis has shifted to an indication of the extent of the work, eliminating a report of the actual system of numbering used. What is the rationale, one may ask, for allowing the nature of the characters employed in numbering the pages or leaves of a given book to determine whether the cataloguer reports in his entry a characteristic of the *book* (the actual system used) or a characteristic of the *work* (its extent, measured in convenient terms)?

If the numeration in a book is divided into two or more series, the

North American *AACR*—following a long-standing tradition in library cataloguing—requires the recording of the "last numbered page or leaf of each numbered section" (141B1c). In many books, of course, the last page of text is not numbered, and this rule clearly places the emphasis on recording a physical detail (which pages are in fact numbered) rather than on specifying with precision the extent of the work.[29] Yet the emphasis shifts the other way in the determination of what constitutes a section: "either a separately numbered group of pages, or leaves, or an unnumbered group which, because of its length (one fifth or more of the entire work), or its importance, should be mentioned."[30] When bulk or importance becomes a criterion for the inclusion of information, certainly no attempt is being made to provide an accurate accounting of the physical structure of the book. But, then, if a small or "unimportant" section of text can be omitted, the representation of the extent of the work is not entirely accurate, either. Indeed, the aim, as it emerges two paragraphs later (141B1e), is only to provide an approximate idea of the bulk of the work: one is told that a correction may be required if "the last numbered page or leaf does not represent the total number, or approximately the total number, of pages or leaves in the work or in the section."[31] The same mixture of aims appears in the instructions for recording the pagination: the figure representing a group of unnumbered pages is to be enclosed in brackets (141B1c), thus emphasizing a physical detail; but where the numbering changes from roman to arabic within a sequence (e.g., i-viii, 9-176), the whole sequence is to be represented by the arabic total (141B1e), thus emphasizing the extent of the section rather than the physical details of the numbering. Similarly, advertisements which constitute separate groups of pages (whether numbered or unnumbered) are to be disregarded (141B1c), placing the emphasis on the work, not the book; but if the advertising pages continue the page numbering of the text, the last page number in the

29. The 1967 British Text, in this respect, focuses more directly on content by requiring the last page of a section to be recorded (whether numbered or not) and by not requiring brackets for unnumbered pages: "a sequence consisting of the preface and list of contents on pages numbered i-ix, followed on the next recto by a list of tables extending over four unnumbered pages, is described in the collation as xiv p." (143B1c).

30. The 1967 British Text, again here, is more clearly concerned with content, for it does not make pagination in itself a sign of the importance of a section: it merely says that sequences, numbered or unnumbered, which consist of "inessential matter" are to be "disregarded" (143B1b).

31. The 1967 British Text does not need to say "approximately" because of its requirement of recording the unnumbered pages at the end of a sequence which are clearly a part of the sequence (143B1d; cf. note 29 above).

sequence is to be given, with a parenthetical indication of which pages the advertisements occupy (141B11), thus making the physical detail of pagination dominant over the content of the pages.[32] One of the awkward situations produced by these rules is illustrated at the end of rule 141B1c itself. Since the rules require that a note be provided to call attention to the presence and extent of a "bibliography" (that is, a reference list) in a book, and since such a "bibliography" might well occur on a final unnumbered page, provision must be made for referring to such a page in certain instances. The solution offered in this rule is illustrated by the pagination record "86, [1] p." and the note "Bibliography: p. [87]." Aside from the awkwardness of referring to the 87th page in two different ways, the basic difficulty is that the use of brackets implies a concern with the actual pagination, while the necessity for adding the "[1]" arises solely from the nature of the material printed on that page. There could be still more unnumbered pages, which would not be recorded because their content did not demand reporting. The principal interest, clearly, is in the content, and pagination references derived from physical description do not always serve that purpose efficiently; but, used in this way, they do not serve the purposes of the descriptive bibliographer either, because they do not necessarily form a complete record.

The handling of various special problems connected with pagination further reveals this awkward mixing of approaches. When there is no numbering in a book at all, the printed pages are counted and the number placed in brackets—or, if the figure is over 100, the number may be estimated (141B2). And when there are several (more than three) "numbered main sections," the numbers on the last numbered page of each section are added together and presented in the form "968 p. in various pagings" (141B3b). Both these rules obviously emphasize the work, not the book. Why, then, is the numbering of the individual main sections to be reported when there are no more than three of them, with other lesser sections recorded in the form of a total, as in "xiv, 226, [44] p." (141B3a)?[33] The fact that

32. The 1967 North American Text had made the inclusion of the pagination for advertisements in such cases optional: "the pagination may be presented in the following form: 124 p. (p. 119-124 advertisements) to alert the reader to the fact that this work might also be described as 118 p." (144A) .

33. Both 1967 texts specify only that "one or more" main sections are to be separately recorded, with a bracketed total for the remaining lesser ones (North American, 142A3; British, 143B3). This rule is somewhat more logical than the 1974 version because it merely differentiates principal from less important sections, rather than setting an arbitrary number of principal sections as the dividing line between two kinds of treatment.

there are fewer main sections does not alter the cataloguer's aim; and the resulting series of figures represents more than one system, since the bracketed figure here is a total of two or more sequences (it could also, in another situation, refer to a single unnumbered section). Furthermore, the bracketed figure itself could result from more than one system, if some of the sections it refers to are unnumbered and some numbered, since all printed pages are counted in unnumbered sections and only the last numbered page in numbered ones. If the primary interest is, as it would seem to be, in recording the extent of the work, what is the point of introducing an element of physical description which complicates that record and yet does not, because of its ambiguity, furnish an offsetting benefit to a descriptive bibliographer?

Two other rules about pagination deserve to be commented on. One describes the treatment of works in more than one volume (141C): when the pagination of the volumes is separate, only the number of volumes is to be recorded; but when the pagination is continuous, it is to be added in parentheses, as "2 v. (xxxi, 999 p.)." This rule is doubly peculiar. In the first place, it is difficult to understand why the physical division into two or more volumes renders a reference to pagination unnecessary, when pagination—rather than "1 v."—is considered the appropriate way to indicate the extent of a work in one volume. After all, some two-volume works are shorter than some one-volume works.[34] Second, it is not clear why the continuity of pagination is a reason for recording the paging; the pagination is either worth listing or not worth listing, but the fact that it starts over in the second volume does not make it irrelevant. The logic is even further confused in the statement that "Separately paged preliminary matter in volumes after the first is ignored unless it is important; if it is important, the work is not considered as being paged continuously"—in which case the pagination is not noted at all. One is left with the anomaly that the presence of "important" matter in a separately paged preliminary section in the second volume of a two-volume work is a reason for eliminating the record of pagination entirely.[35] Surely this is a prime example of the situation in which

34. The tradition of giving pagination only for books of one volume goes back at least as far as Charles C. Jewett's *Smithsonian Report on the Construction of Catalogues of Libraries* (1852, 1853).

35. The 1967 British Text handles this point more satisfactorily by simply saying that "separately paged sections of preliminary matter after the first volume may be ignored if not important" (143C3). If they are important, recording them poses no problem because the British Text allows for the recording of separate pagination for each volume ("the pagination of each volume may be given in parentheses after the number of volumes"), offering as an example "2 v. (xxxix, 429 p.; [4], 501 p.)" (143C2).

a physical detail of bookmaking is allowed to interfere with the effective indication of the extent of the work.[36]

The other pagination rule which requires particular comment deals with incomplete copies (141B12): "If the last part of a work is wanting, and the paging of a complete copy cannot be ascertained, paging is given in the form 179+ p., with note of the imperfection." Aside from the illogical reference to "the last part of a work," when a book can be defective in other places as well, the problem with this rule is its conception of the function of a catalogue listing. Whereas the rules previously discussed have shown some confusion about the distinction between books and works, this rule reveals some indecision about whether the undertaking is a catalogue or a bibliography. The implication here is that the pagination of a complete copy, when known, is recorded in the collation line (presumably with a note somewhere pointing out the defect in the copy under examination). But if these are catalogue rules—not rules for bibliographies, which refer to ideal copies—the basis for each entry must be the book present in the collection being catalogued.[37] The emphasis may be on the content of the book rather than on its physical features, but any physical features mentioned must conform to the characteristics of the specific copy at hand. Details about the characteristics of a complete copy may be useful, but they are strictly supplementary. Perhaps the role of the Library of Congress in supplying printed catalogue cards to other

36. There is further confusion here in the distinction between "bibliographical volumes" and "physical volumes" (141C1). "Bibliographical volumes" are apparently to be regarded as parts or divisions of a work, and they may or may not coincide with the physical volumes in which the sheets containing the work are bound. Thus the rule says to state the "bibliographical volumes" first, as "8 v. in 5"; but actually the physical element is basic in both numbers. A set originally containing eight physical volumes may later be rebound into five volumes, and this sort of notation may be helpful for identification; but if the division into eight means only that the work has eight sections or divisions, there would be no more reason to specify the number of "volumes" than to name the number of chapters. To put the point another way: a single volume may contain a work in which the text is divided into three "Volumes" or "Books"; it may also contain sheets which were printed in such a way as to indicate that they were intended to be bound in three physical volumes. While "3 v. in 1" might be an appropriate way of referring to the latter, it would seem pointless for the former; and this distinction is not conveyed by the concept of "bibliographical volume" in rule 141C1.

37. The same problem is presented by one of the statements in the "Principles of Descriptive Cataloging" at the beginning of Part II of the North American *AACR*: "An attempt is made to describe a physically complete copy" (p. 189). Such a statement is beside the point if the copy being catalogued happens not to be complete. The British Text at least recognizes this problem and attaches a second sentence: "When possible the description should be that of a perfect copy. Imperfections in a particular copy are indicated" (p. 159).

libraries has helped to weaken the concept of a catalogue entry as an
accounting of a specific copy; in any event, a code of cataloguing rules
should not contribute to the confusion by implying that a catalogue
card or entry refers to an ideal rather than an actual copy.[38]

The second element in the collation, following the designation of
the pagination or foliation or number of volumes, is a brief reference
to any illustrative matter in the book. It consists of nothing more than
the abbreviation "ill.", "unless particular types [of illustrations] in the
work are considered important enough to be specifically designated";
when that occurs there are several specific terms, like "diagrams,"
"maps," "music," or "portraits," to choose from (141D1a). As with
pagination, the intent is obviously to suggest something about the
content of the work, not to record the precise physical structure of
the book; but the emphasis here is on the nature of the illustrations,
not their extent. A later rule (141D4) does permit specifying the
number of illustrations, but only if they are numbered or "if the
number can readily be ascertained"; and any numbers given are to
be arabic and are not to appear in brackets even if the illustrations
themselves are unnumbered. This rule, unlike the rules for pagination, reveals no indecision regarding aims, for the focus is entirely
on content: such physical details as the manner of numbering the
illustrations are not allowed to intrude into a statement *about* the
illustrations. A problem arises, however, from the fact that the previous part of the collation, the pagination statement, may also refer to
plates (141B1d) and to music (141B10) when they occur in separately
paged or unpaged sections or on pages not otherwise covered by the

---

38. Still other pagination rules raise troublesome questions. The rules for treating
folded leaves, double leaves, duplicate paging, and two-way paging (141B4, 5, 6, 8)
require the mention of these features, as
if certain physical details are of particular
interest in their own right. Actually, the
first two—folded and double leaves—have
a bearing on an indication of the extent
of the work, since ten folded leaves can be
expected to contain more material than
ten ordinary leaves, and ten double leaves
will contain only half the material that
could ordinarily be printed on the same
amount of paper (twenty single leaves).
But when the foliation or pagination
(printed or inferred) in effect converts
such leaves to regular units—as when eighteen double leaves are referred to as "[36] p.

(on double leaves)"—the specification of
the nature of the leaves is superfluous,
except as a physical detail. But in a catalogue entry stressing the work, not the
book, what is the rationale for requiring
this detail in preference to others in those
cases where it does not contribute to an
understanding of the extent of the work?
The other two features—duplicate and two-
way paging—are only special cases of the
larger problem of separately numbered
sequences. It may be, as with other sequences, that it is easier to list the figures
separately than to add them together; but
the rules do not suggest that the practice
is merely one of expediency, not necessitated by the purposes which the entries are
intended to serve.

notation of pagination. Examples given are "xvi, 246 p., 24 leaves of plates" and "74 p., 15 p. of music." Apparently the rationale is that this part of the collation line indicates the "extent" of the work and would be misleading without the mention of these major elements; the second part then takes up the nature of the illustrative matter as a whole, whether it occurs on separate pages or on pages which are included in the numbering of major sequences.[39] This illustration statement thus becomes a commentary on one aspect of the content of the pages recorded in the pagination statement. Two questions immediately come to mind. First, if the extent of a work in numerical terms is to be supplemented by some comment on the manner of presentation of the material, why are illustrations singled out for comment? And why are illustrations defined to include genealogical tables and graphs (141D1a) and to exclude tables in general (141D1b)? Second, if other groups of pages need not be labeled in the pagination statement, why should those containing plates and music be named? Plates may be scattered through a volume, but as far as the measurement of the extent of the work is concerned they would seem to be no different from the "lesser variously numbered or unnumbered sections" (141B3a) for which a single unlabeled total is to be provided. The treatment of illustrations thus raises another question about the purposes of the pagination statement. As for the illustration statement itself, the problem is less one of aims than of consistency in carrying them out. One wonders whether the expression "ill." (or even one of the more precise terms) is informative enough to bother including; but the question clearly has to do with reference bibliography, not descriptive bibliography, for physical description is not intended.

The third part of the collation is an indication of size, consisting of the measurement in centimeters (rounded off to the next higher full centimeter) of the height of the binding (141E1). This measurement is of course a physical detail, but it is only one of several meas-

39. This point is further indicated by the fact that rule 141B1d says, "More than one illustration on a leaf, even if numbered by the printer, does not affect the numeration of the plates as such"—whereas it would obviously affect the numeration of the illustrations. No rule corresponding to 141B1d is present in the 1967 North American Text; the inclusion of this rule in 1974 is an improvement, bringing the North American Text closer to the British, where the distinction between plates and illustrations had been clearer from the beginning. The 1967 British Text defines "plate" as "a page containing illustrative matter" but not forming part of "either the preliminary or main sequence of pages" (143B1b); and it provides for recording the number of plates as part of the pagination statement (143B1b,c, 143B4, 143D1c). The illustration statement is therefore clearly concerned only with the nature of the illustrations, regardless of what pages they appear on, and it is "independent of the statement of pagination" (143D1a).

urements which would be of interest to the descriptive bibliographer. The purpose of including this one measurement in a catalogue entry generally stressing the content of works rather than the form of books is puzzling; and the four reasons furnished in a "Preliminary note" to this rule do nothing to suggest an answer.[40] First we are told, "The size of the work is included in the catalog entry as an aid in finding the work on the shelves." Of course "book" is meant instead of "work" in both instances, and this imprecision reflects a basic confusion as to the purpose of this information. The interest is unquestionably in the work, as stated, but the reason provided can only refer to the book; and locating a book by its size—even as a device to supplement other techniques—is certainly a primitive method of information retrieval.[41] The second stated reason for recording the height of a book is "as an aid to the user of the catalog in selecting a desirable edition." This preposterous point scarcely requires comment, for the correlation between the height of a binding and the desirability of the edition it covers would be relevant (if at all) only to the choice of books for reading in bed or for packing in luggage. The other two reasons are that the height "serves the reader who wishes to borrow the work through interlibrary loan or who wishes to order a photocopy of the work or a part of it." Again, "book" is meant; and the person who would be influenced by the height of the book in his request for a loan or a photocopy cannot be very seriously interested in the work it contains. The only justifiable reason for including the height of a binding in an entry oriented toward the content of the book is one that is not mentioned: the height could be regarded as a supplement to the pagination details, further indicating the extent of the work by suggesting the size of the pages. But this function—indicating "the space occupied by the work"—would be served still better by the specification of two or three dimensions, as required for broadsides (141E3) and "unusual formats" such as "boxes or cans" (141E6). The discussion of "size" (that is, height), as it stands, is not well thought through and provides no sensible reason for the inclusion of that detail; if no better reasons are to be offered, the requirement of specifying height is a flagrant example of the insistence on a physical detail which is unnecessary in relation to the emphasis of the entry and inadequate to serve as an aid to the physical bibliographer.[42]

40. This unsatisfactory note, repeated verbatim from the 1967 North American Text and the 1949 LC *Rules*, does not appear in the British Text at all.

41. Books may of course be shelved according to their size, but their call numbers or shelf marks—not their dimensions—would serve to locate them.

42. The practice, which has been followed in certain catalogues, of using for-

The rules for description in the North American Text of *AACR* developed from—and remained close to—those in the 1949 *Rules for Descriptive Cataloging in the Library of Congress*. And both these codes represent a considerable simplification of what had been proposed in 1941 in the "Preliminary American Second Edition" of the *A. L. A. Catalog Rules*. The pagination rules set forth there result in such illustrations as "xii p., 5 l., [3], 219 p." and "v, 365, [3] p., 2 l."—which suggest careful attention to physical details but are nevertheless intended to indicate the extent of the work, not of the book. One rule, for instance, states that "Blank leaves at the beginning of a book are not counted even if they have apparently been included in the paging"; and another requires that intermediate unpaged matter be reported as leaves "when some or all of the leaves are blank on one side, except that unpaged matter continuing the text from a preceding numbered page is given as a page, even if printed on a leaf one side of which is blank" (rules 271-272). Despite the elaboration of rules such as these,[43] the system does not manage unambiguously to convey just which pages contain printed matter (the number of blank *pages* in the groups designated as leaves in the illustrations cited above is not determinable from the formulas)[44]—and it certainly does not provide a register of all the pages in a book. Dissatisfaction with these proposed rules was fortunately widespread and began even before their publication, for a note facing the title page of the 1941 volume

mat designation (like "4o" and "8o") vaguely to suggest shape is even less defensible than the *AACR* requirement because it misuses a notation with a long-established meaning in physical bibliography and thereby increases the possibilities for confusion. *The Prussian Instructions* (trans. Andrew Osborn, 1938) are guilty in this respect, for they recommend that "4o," for instance, be used to refer to a height of 25-35 cm. (p. 13). An example of the difficulties which such usage can cause is illustrated by John R. Hetherington in "Signatures and Sizes," *TLS*, 14 October 1965, p. 928; he summarizes his experiences in one project by saying, "Thus in a field restricted to two titles, books reported to me as sixteenth and seventeenth-century quartos have included folios, octavos, 12mos, and 16mos." A fourth element sometimes required in the collation is taken up in rule 141F: the mention of "accompanying materials," such as a teach-er's manual or materials placed in a pocket inside the cover of a book. The logic of attaching this information to the height is not clear, nor is the reason for regarding some items in pockets as illustrations (141D5) and others as "accompanying materials."

43. Another perplexing rule shows that even fidelity to the printed numbers is not an absolute requirement: in the preliminaries, a single numbered recto (but not verso) which does not match the actual count is to be disregarded (271).

44. The "5 l." means that "some or all of the leaves are blank on one side" (272); and the "2 l." at the end may mean two printed rectos (the number of leaves is given "instead of several groups of pages in brackets separated by commas") or else three or four printed pages which do not continue the main text (273).

acknowledges that there had been "considerable disagreement as between some catalogers and some administrators." But the complaints and the ensuing discussions too often resulted merely in requests for simplification, without a reexamination of the underlying function of the catalogue entry—without, that is, exploring why the elaboration of detail did not further the aims of the entry.[45] The rules had indeed become too complex, but not in any absolute sense. They had become inappropriately complex because the complexity arose from the notation of physical details, when the function of the pagination record was to suggest the extent of the work and was not primarily concerned with the physical book. The resulting formula was bound to be an inefficient and finally unsuccessful instrument for conveying information about either the work or the book. It was more dramatically unsuccessful than the present rules; but they still suffer from the same confusion. Even the British Text of *AACR*, which is more logical in its presentation of rules for description and its requirements than the North American,[46] falters from indecision regarding the purpose of including physical details. The *AACR* treatment of pagination may look good in comparison with that in the complex 1941 rules; but the act of simplifying the rules has not altered the underlying problem which made those earlier rules unsatisfactory.

Cataloguers and librarians themselves have been uneasily aware that the collation statement is a trouble spot, the treatment of which has never been satisfying. Herman H. Henkle, in the *Studies of Descriptive Cataloging* (1946) which formed part of the deliberation leading up to the 1949 Library of Congress *Rules*, summed up the problem:

The question of the collation statement—whether its principal function is to characterize the contents of the book by describing its significant physical features, or whether it is to account in detail for the completeness of the volume—continues in a stalemate condition. Those who favor detailed collation maintain that it eliminates the exercise of judgment on the part of the cataloger; insures uniformity of result; assists in the identification of

45. For some reactions to the 1941 rules, see the four papers gathered under the title "Scholarly Libraries and the New Cataloging Rules," *College and Research Libraries*, 3 (1941-42), 117-138.

46. See, for instance, notes 29, 30, 31, 35, 37, 39, and 40 above. Seymour Lubetzky speaks of the "noxious compromises" in the North American Text, says that the British

"could not bring themselves to go along with the more glaringly aberrant compromises," and urges a revision of the North American Text to "heal the fissure"; see "1976 Minus 6 . . . 5 . . . ," *Library Journal*, 96 (1971), 450-451. Although he is referring principally to the rules for entry and headings, the North American Text is inferior in the rules for description also.

an edition, issue, or copy, and in the detection of an imperfect copy; and obviates any confusion to the inquirer checking in the catalog a reference containing the pages not shown in the collation of the entry. Those who favor brief collation do not think that these ends justify the means; they point to the collation of works in more than one volume as an indication that detailed collation is unnecessary; and they regard detailed collation as a dissipation of cataloging energy on the production of a result which is unintelligible to many users of the catalog. Comments and advice on this question are especially needed. (pp. 29-30)

This passage is instructive: Henkle's opening statement accurately sets forth the issue; but his summary of the arguments on both sides shows how the discussion generally focuses on the amount of detail involved rather than on the alternative functions of the collation as expressed in his earlier comment. (Certainly the arguments of those favoring "brief collation," as recorded here, are extremely weak; but that does not mean that theirs is necessarily the weaker position, for their arguments simply do not touch the basic question.)[47] Some years after the Library of Congress *Rules* appeared, Leonard Jolley described Library of Congress cataloguing as "still avowedly bibliographical"[48] and questioned the value of including the collation at all, since without an identification of type sizes and layout the number of pages does not very accurately denote the size of the work and since the details provided "do not produce a statement of pagination upon which a bibliographer can rely in all cases" (p. 132). Like Henkle, he saw the central issue, and he stated it even more trenchantly:

The weakness of the Library of Congress *Rules* is that they do not recognize sufficiently bluntly the essentially approximate nature of the information which is added to a catalogue entry not really because it helps identify a book but because it conveys some information of value about the book. As a result of this failure practices are sometimes prescribed which are not elaborate enough to provide a full bibliographical description and yet more elaborate than the ends they can achieve warrant.   (pp. 133-134)

47. Seymour Lubetzky, in Appendix E to the same booklet, criticizes "our elaborate collation statement in which we undertake to give an accounting of every page and detail, whereas its real function is only to give a physical characterization of the work" (p. 43). Henkle had earlier reported on the "Library of Congress Conferences on Cataloging, October 18 - November 19, 1943," in *Catalogers' and Classifiers' Year-* *book*, 11 (1945), 68-84, where he says that "librarians have appeared to be excessively preoccupied with the problems of collation" (p. 73).

48. He explained, "That is to say it sets out to provide a description of a book which can be used as a standard of a perfect copy, by readers far removed from the library." See his *The Principles of Cataloguing* (1960), p. 133.

With this kind of statement before them, the planners of *AACR* should have been able to confront the real problem and produce a set of rules for collation firmly based on a well-defined view of its purpose. Instead, it was decided that the discussions preceding the 1949 *Rules* constituted a largely sufficient basic reconsideration of the rules for description and that the rules for entry and heading were the ones which now demanded full-scale rethinking;[49] as a result the *AACR* rules for description are disappointingly similar, in their confused underlying principles, to what had existed before. This fact has not gone unobserved. Andrew Osborn has said, "I am much concerned because in the AA code the rules for descriptive detail are not in the same class as the rules for entry and heading."[50] And R. O. Linden has pointed out in *AACR* "a confusion in general between the bibliographical, and what might be termed the evaluative function of collation."[51] In his discussion of the rule regarding the date of a volume, he makes a comment about the meaning of "edition" which again would apply to other rules for description: "Two approaches appear possible—one, a definition that gives emphasis to the bibliographical character of the work, the second, a definition that is based on the intellectual content. Two values appear to be confused here" (p. 50).

---

49. This concentration on rules for entry is also a reflection of the fact that the library cataloguer is primarily concerned with the contents of books. Lubetzky has called description "the simpler aspect of cataloging" and the rules for entry "the most critical and complex aspect" (*Principles of Cataloging*, pp. iv, 18; see also his "Some Observations on the Revision of the Cataloging Code," *Library Quarterly*, 26 [1966], 362-366). Bakewell asserts, "The collation is certainly the most expendable part of the entry" (*A Manual of Cataloguing Practice*, p. 4).

50. "Summary of Proceedings," in *The Code and the Cataloguer* (see note 25 above), pp. 91-101 (quotation from p. 94). Jack R. Nelson, in his review of the North American *AACR*, states, "It is this section of the new code, in fact, with which I am least happy. . . . it is very regrettable that in this problem area the new code is so disappointing" (*Australian Library Journal*, 16 [1967], 119-123).

51. In his paper on Chapter 6 of *AACR* in *Seminar on the Anglo-American Cataloguing Rules* (see note 25 above), pp. 45-54 (quotation from p. 46). He elaborates on the confusion in this way: "pagination and the statement of the number of volumes is a bibliographic statement, the illustration statement is an evaluative statement, and finally size is a bibliographic statement, but different from pagination" (p. 46). But the first and last, as they are set up, are not really "bibliographic"; they are made to serve an "evaluative" function (to use these terms), so the confusion between the two exists within the individual elements of the collation line. Linden, in some of his other comments, seems to imply that physical description ought to be the goal. Thus he says that the listing of the total of unnumbered plates is "a good move in the direction of a true collation statement" (p. 50), whereas a recording of the number of illustrations would give "a false impression of physical make-up" (p. 51). Similarly he comments, "Size has always been something of a dubious item in cataloguing. Quite often it is not strictly a bibliographical statement at all" (p. 51).

It is clear that this confusion has been recognized not only by descriptive bibliographers but by those within the library profession as well.

Of course, as these comments suggest, it is not merely the collation line which reveals a confusion between books and works. I have concentrated on that part of the entry, particularly the pagination statement, as a telling illustration of the problem; but the problem is not confined to that element. For instance, the treatment of the title pages of books bears some awkward traces of a concern with physical detail. The basic rule for the "transcription" of titles makes clear that a literal transcription is not intended, for exactness is required only "as to order, wording, spelling, accentuation, and other diacritical marks" but "not necessarily as to punctuation and capitalization." Furthermore, if "diacritical marks are omitted from the title page, they are added in conformity with the usage in the text" (134B1). The emphasis is clearly on the content of the title, not on its formal presentation or typographic layout. Yet when long titles are abridged (as they are "if this can be done without loss of essential information"), three dots are required to mark the ellipsis (134B2). This requirement is understandable when part of the title quoted follows the omission, for not to indicate the omission in such instances would simply be irresponsible quotation; but when the omission occurs at the end of the quoted part of the title, one could argue, as with ordinary quotations within a text, that the ellipsis dots are unnecessary. The recording of the title is admittedly a special type of quotation, since punctuation and capitalization need not be followed; but it nevertheless is a quotation (concerned with words and the accompanying marks conventional to the language), not quasi-facsimile transcription (concerned with the typography and layout in which those words and marks are presented).[52] Other recorded details, aside from titles (main titles, subtitles, series titles, and so on), need not be regarded as quotations, however, but as reports of information. Therefore, when the author's name is provided as the heading for the entry, it seems unnecessary to repeat the name following the title, as the basic rule requires (134D1).[53] The concern of this rule is obviously not with the physical form of the title page, because it recognizes that the

52. Thus the reproduction of an error and its correction in brackets (133A2) is proper—and is not an example of an inappropriate concern for a physical detail—because the meaning of the quoted words is involved.

53. There has been much discussion of this point, resulting—in the 1974 version of Chapter 6—in an "alternative" rule 134D1 presented as a footnote. This new alternative rule says that the author statement may be omitted "unless the form of name in the heading is not recognizably the same as that in the book" or unless certain other conditions obtain—almost the

author's name may have to be taken from a different position on the
title page or even from somewhere else in the volume; but there is a
lingering sense that the exact form in which an author's name appears
in a book must be recorded, even when fuller information about him
(his complete name and perhaps his dates) is already provided in the
heading. In regard both to the ellipsis dots and to the repetition of
the author's name, one could argue that in some cases their presence
might suggest or convey important information (as when the form
of the author's name on the title page is considerably different from
his established name cited in the heading), and in these cases their
inclusion would be justified, since the goal is to be informative regarding substantive, not formal, matters. But the criterion for inclusion,
given the emphasis of the entry as a whole, must turn on the relevance
of the detail as information about the work or author, not on an
assumption that the mere physical presence of the detail in a particular
form is relevant in itself.

The treatment of some parts of the title page reflects this principle
more firmly than that of other parts. If a subtitle, for example, is
printed at the head of the title page, above the title, it is silently
transposed to a position following the title in the entry (134C4b).[54]
And the imprint is regularized into the order place-publisher-year,
regardless of the order on the title page, and neither this rearrange-
ment nor omissions of words need be specified (136A, 136C1, 138A).[55]

---

same as the basic rule in the 1967 British
Text (there labeled 134A). The 1967 North
American Text was somewhat more strict
in that the names had to be identical, not
just "recognizably the same," before the
author statement could be eliminated; but
at least provision for eliminating the repetition was a part of the basic rule (134A).
By relegating this kind of rule to a footnote and making it an alternative to a
more rigid rule, the 1974 version has taken
a step backward; the acceptance of the
British model is sensible, but the resulting
rule should have been incorporated into
the main text.

54 In the 1941 proposed code, rule 226
required ellipsis dots to show the omission
of words at the head of the title page;
and if the omitted material were relevant,
it was to be reported in a note, following
the body of the entry, beginning with the
words "At head of title." Even an author's

name appearing at the head of the title in
exactly the same form as the one used for
the heading of the entry was to be repeated
in such a note. This rule clearly shows an
exaggerated attention to the form of the
title page, since there is no intention of
producing an exact transcription in any
case. The North American Text of *AACR*
still contains a provision for "At head of
title" notes (145 in 1967, 144 in 1974); but
the ellipsis dots are not required, and the
note is only for relevant information "not
transposed to another position in the catalog entry" and thus "not provided for by
the general pattern of the catalog entry"
(cf. the brief treatment in the 1967 British
Text, 145C2).

55. An illustration of the way in which
the imprint statement can be regarded
from the point of view of reference, rather
than physical, bibliography is provided by
Henkle, who refers to the "premise that

The inconsistency in the handling of different parts of the title page is strikingly shown by the fact that data for the imprint statement can be taken from elsewhere in the book and recorded without brackets,[56] whereas the author's name must appear in brackets if it is taken from somewhere in the book other than the title page (132B, 134D1).[57] Few people, I think, would question the propriety of the rearrange-

---

the principal value of the publisher statement is its contribution to the characterization of the quality, authenticity, or bias of the book" (*Studies of Descriptive Cataloging*, p. 9).

56. Indeed, the basic rule for "Date" (139A) requires that precedence be given to the "year of publication of the first impression of the edition," even if the year of a later printing appears on the title page (the example given is "1970, t.p. 1973"). It is proper that entries in a library catalogue should indicate the date of the *work* (or *text*); and the rule is in this respect an improvement over the corresponding rule (141A) in the 1967 North American Text, which emphasizes the imprint date and makes no provision for indicating the date of original publication of the edition (the revised rule comes closer to what the British Text recommended from the beginning in its 142A: "The date to be given is the date of the edition, which may be followed by the date of the imprint where the difference is important"). But the date of the impression which the library holds should also invariably be recorded—and not be regarded as an optional item when it does not appear on the title page, to be noted only "if it is important to identify a later impression as such, e.g. because it contains textual variations." (Cf. 135A: "Statements relating to the impression or printing are included only in the case of items having particular bibliographical importance or when the impression or printing has been corrected or otherwise revised.") In most cases one cannot know, without a great deal of work, just what differences may exist between two impressions; therefore, calling attention to the particular impression in a library catalogue entry is appropriate not merely because the busi-

ness of any catalogue entry is to report on the copy at hand but also because the indication of the impression can always turn out to be important to those who are primarily concerned with the content of the book. For a criticism of the 1967 form of the rule in the North American Text and an argument that library cataloguers should be capable of recognizing a reprint even when not labeled and establishing the date of original publication of the edition, see Robert N. Broadus, "The Problem of Dates in Bibliographic Citations," *College and Research Libraries*, 29 (1968), 387-392. Ronald Hagler, speaking of the 1967 rule, comments, "I think that, as cataloguers, we continue to suffer from ambivalence about whether we really want to describe the dating of the material or the dating of the particular physical book which we have" (*New Rules for an Old Game* [see note 25 above], p. 92).

57. The 1967 North American Text requires brackets around any information within the body of the entry which does not come from the title page (132A1); the alterations in 1974 are a move in the right direction but have not been made consistently. In the British Text, the requirement was never as rigid as that in the North American but does involve inconsistency: the edition statement, the imprint, and the series statement "may be taken from other places in the book without the use of square brackets," but information for the title and author statements may not (132A1). Clearly the title, in this respect, does fall in a different category from the other details, so long as the title is defined (for those books with title pages) as that form of the title which appears on the title page; but the reason for placing the author's name in the same category is not apparent.

ment of the material so as to produce relatively uniform catalogue entries, and the fact that this approach is so widely accepted suggests a broad understanding—whether consciously expressed or not—that library catalogue entries serve largely a reference function. Even the descriptive bibliographer generally assigns a standardized title to each of his descriptions to aid the reader in locating them; his focus is of course on physical description, but that aspect of his work which involves reference bibliography entails standardization for efficiency of reference. The library cataloguer, unlike the descriptive bibliographer, is primarily concerned with reference bibliography, and thus the body of each of his entries can be expected to be a standardized presentation of facts, not a transcription of forms. In the *AACR* treatment of title-page information, those few rules which imply some obligation to offer physical description stand out, against this background, as incongruous and, indeed, confused.[58]

It should come as no surprise that the emphasis of library cataloguing, as reflected in *AACR*, is on what may be called reference bibliography, where the primary concern is the intellectual content of books. Of the two conventional divisions of library cataloguing, subject cataloguing—or classification—obviously deals with content; what may be less clear at first is that the other division, so-called descriptive cataloguing, does so as well.[59] Because descriptive *bibliography* treats of books as physical objects, some confusion may be caused by the use of the term "descriptive cataloguing" to denote an activity which does not. The difficulty, however, is not entirely one of terminology. The present cataloguing code, *AACR*, in all its versions, states that "The collation is the cataloger's description of the physical work and is limited to standard bibliographical terminology" (132A; 1967 texts, 131).[60] Yet, as this examination of the rules for collation indicates,

58. Seymour Lubetzky said in 1946 that cataloguing "practice represents the result of an effort to preserve the integrity of the title-page and an inability to do so. . . . the aim of the cataloger should be not to point out the differences of the title-pages but the identity of the books under them" (in Appendix E of Henkle, *Studies of Descriptive Cataloging*, pp. 44-45).

59. In the 1949 Library of Congress *Rules*, the opening section on the "Definition of Descriptive Cataloging" points out that there is "some ambiguity in the use of the term," because the "determination of the form of the headings" is sometimes

regarded as a separate activity from "the description of an item" (as in the 1941 preliminary second edition of the *A.L.A. Catalog Rules*), whereas both are "commonly understood" to comprise "descriptive cataloging" (the whole being distinct from subject cataloguing). This ambiguity, involving the way the divisions of a single professional field are labeled, is in addition to the one I am talking about, which results from the use of the same term in two fields with differing aims.

60. Statements of this kind are made repeatedly in writings and textbooks on library cataloguing. Cf. Wyllis E. Wright,

attention is not given to physical details for their own sake but as clues suggestive of the extent or nature of the work contained in the book being catalogued. The descriptive cataloguer's job, as set forth in these rules, has a basically different aim from that of the descriptive bibliographer, and the "standard bibliographical terminology" employed is not that which is standard in the field of descriptive bibliography.[61] What the library cataloguer normally means by "descriptive" is "annotated with certain largely physical details which help to characterize the content of a book." The objection to the cataloguer's practice, as codified in *AACR*, is not that he gives too much attention to the work and neglects the book: it is entirely proper that he should emphasize the work. The flaw in the *AACR* is that some of its recommendations for handling physical details reflect a failure to keep this goal firmly in mind and to recognize the relationships between reference and physical bibliography. The result is a lack of decisiveness and singleness of purpose in a number of rules, producing in turn certain data in a form not entirely appropriate to either interest. Descriptive bibliographers should have no quarrel with reference bibliography; but their respect for it is not likely to increase so long as it can appear at times as merely a less precise form of descriptive bibliography. Part II of the *Anglo-American Cataloging Rules*, as a product of great deliberation and a document destined to have wide influence, is disappointing in that it is not able clearly to place its subject in relation to descriptive and reference bibliography and thus to offer rules informed by a well-defined point of view.

"Some Fundamental Principles in Cataloging," *Catalogers' and Classifiers' Yearbook*, 7 (1938), 26-39: "The collation attempts to give, in brief form, a physical description of the volume" (p. 36).

61. *AACR* provides a brief glossary (North American, pp. 343-347; British, pp. 266-269), but it does not contain such crucial terms as "edition," "impression," or "issue." For terms not listed, one is referred to the outdated *A.L.A. Glossary of Library Terms*, ed. Elizabeth H. Thompson (1943), where "edition," for instance, after being defined properly as all impressions from one setting of type, is said to be dependent on format as well. Under "impression," one reads, "If, however, the pages are reimposed to produce a different format, the resultant impression should be considered a different edition." And the confusion is further compounded under "edition": "A facsimile reproduction constitutes a different edition." A catalogue code which assents to such definitions is built on a weak foundation. By "bibliographical terminology" *AACR* also perhaps means the form for the recording of pagination and size; but to call the recommendations in those areas "standard" is to beg the question, since they do not conform with the practices of those whose principal field of interest is physical description.

III

How to reconcile the practices of descriptive bibliography and library cataloguing in the area where the two fields overlap is a problem which has exercised many people over the years. If the Anglo-American code reflects little awareness of the issue, there has nevertheless been a succession of librarians who have touched on the matter, generally in connection with the cataloguing of rare books. Whereas one tradition of bibliographical writing, developing through Pollard, Greg, McKerrow, and Bowers,[62] has taken up the problems of description for those concerned with the physical book (and the use of physical evidence in historical and literary studies), another tradition has consisted of librarians writing for other librarians about the physical details appropriate for inclusion in the catalogue entries for certain classes of material. The two traditions intertwine occasionally, and such men as Esdaile, Cowley, Dunkin, Alden, and Bennett, addressing themselves to library cataloguers, are fully aware of the other tradition of writing about the description of books. Their discussions are worth surveying, as significant attempts to bring the two approaches together, even though their attention is primarily directed toward rare books and special collections, not toward the larger problem of general cataloguing.

Arundell Esdaile, in *A Student's Manual of Bibliography* (1931), one of a series originally called "The Library Manuals," does attempt to encompass all kinds of cataloguing and begins his chapter on description with this statement: "Every catalogue-entry is a description of the book catalogued; but according to the purpose of the catalogue is the degree of elaboration of the description" (p. 248). What this pronouncement overlooks is the fact that a given purpose may be served by differing degrees of detail. By stating that "purpose" and "degree of elaboration" fluctuate together, it postulates a situation in which a shift in the aim of an entry entails a quantitative, rather than qualitative, shift in the annotation. Esdaile's four levels of description reflect the difficulties of this position. His "minimum entry" consists of nothing but title and author's name and is thus an

62. In such works as A. W. Pollard and W. W. Greg, "Some Points in Bibliographical Descriptions," *Transactions of the Bibliographical Society*, 9 (1906-8), 31-52; Pollard, "The Objects and Methods of Bibliographical Collations and Descriptions," *Library*, 2nd ser., 8 (1907), 193-217; R. B. McKerrow, *An Introduction to Bibliography for Literary Students* (1927), pp. 145-163; Greg, "A Formulary of Collation," *Library*, 4th ser., 14 (1933-34), 365-382; Fredson Bowers, *Principles of Bibliographical Description* (1949), and "Bibliography Revisited," *Library*, 5th ser., 24 (1969), 89-128.

entry for a *work*, even though the work must necessarily be represented in the library being catalogued by a particular copy. The next
higher level, called "short-entry" (p. 249), records place and date, but
the intention is not so much to identify a book as to specify a *text* of
the work. Esdaile's illustration includes the symbol "12°," though he
admits that such notation, as well as a statement of pagination, "serves
little purpose here"—except that pagination would "distinguish a
pamphlet from a substantial work." And he adds that size notation
"seems to be entirely useless." The concern of the entry, in other
words, is still with a *work*; the increased detail does not stem from a
different aim, though of course it allows the aim to be pursued with
greater sophistication. The interest, clearly, is not in physical characteristics for their own sake. Esdaile's third level, the "short standard
description," represents ,a "minimum standard" for all entries, since
one "cannot be sure what book will become important, or what book
will become rare" (p. 250). The entry now contains a quotation of the
title with omissions noted and a record of format, signatures, pagination, and plates. Its emphasis is beginning to shift toward the physical
and, one should observe, away from the individual copy, for the entry
describes ";firstly all copies, and secondly, the one copy" (p. 252). The
highest level, the "full standard description," requires, among other
things, quasi-facsimile transcription of the title page, a pagination
statement showing which pages are numbered, information on type,
and a detailed record of the contents (p. 253). It is designed to "anticipate as far as possible questions which may be asked about a book's
physical and intellectual composition" (p. 250), yet the emphasis is
definitely now on the side of the physical. Few people today would
defend Esdaile's scheme,[63] largely because his inclusion of signature
collation in a minimum entry is not a feasible requirement for routine
library cataloguing. But a more basic weakness is theoretical: by
shifting his emphasis as he moves to higher levels of detail, he is

63. Roy Stokes, in his 1967 revision of
Esdaile, abandons "the older tradition of
descriptive work" characterized by "distinct stages such as Short description or
Short standard description" and says, "The
description should be as detailed as the
purpose of the listing demands, and no
longer" (p. 256). In proceeding to point
out that an antiquarian bookseller would
be likely to emphasize different facts from
a bibliographer preparing a subject list,
he touches on an important concept that
could profitably have been elaborated.

(Cutter's 1876 *Rules* represent the "older
tradition" Stokes refers to, for Cutter sets
up requirements for "Short, Medium, and
Full" entries [p. 9]. Cf. also the work of
Pollard mentioned in note 62 above, and
the well-known article of Falconer Madan
on "Degressive Bibliography," *Transactions of the Bibliographical Society*, 9
[1906-8], 53-65. Abandoning such precisely
defined steps, however, as Stokes realizes,
does not mean that the level of detail
cannot be varied under differing circumstances.)

blurring the distinction between quantity of information (from simple enumeration to great detail) and orientation of approach (toward the work or the book). Nevertheless, he at least is confronting the problem of defining a framework which will embrace both a brief reference entry and an elaborate physical description.[64]

Eight years later, J. D. Cowley addressed another book, *Bibliographical Description and Cataloguing*, to library-school students, setting out specifically to help them "distinguish sufficiently between what is appropriate to cataloguing and what is suitable in a published bibliography" (p. v). In a carefully considered introductory chapter, he segregates, much more successfully than Esdaile, the aims, and resulting methods, of physical and subject bibliography. Recognizing that differing aims dictate the nature of the details to be included in an entry, not their quantity, he says, "Minute description of the physical form of the material is therefore out of place" in a subject listing; "Description of physical features need only be sufficient to secure identification of the work or the edition which is described" (pp. 6-7). That is, the number of physical details can be reduced not because a subject list is a less detailed descriptive bibliography but because it is not concerned with physical books, except as necessary to locate the physical embodiments of works; if annotation is to be provided, it should be of a different kind.[65] Having laid this admirable foundation, Cowley is disappointing in his ensuing recommendations, as they relate to the stated problem of "what is appropriate to cataloguing and what is suitable in a published bibliography." His real interest is in the latter, and virtually his whole work is devoted to detailed descriptive bibliography (it is the most thorough pre-Bowers exposition of the subject). As far as library cataloguing is concerned, he is content to accept uncritically the Anglo-American code then in effect. At the start, he says that for subject bibliography "a simple catalogue entry, constructed according to one of the recognized codes of rules, is the best form of description" (p. 7). And in his chapter on format and collation, after eighteen pages on a method of format designation and a formulary for the recording of pagination and signatures, he appends four lines: "In short entries or entries for subject bibliographies the

---

64. The integrative direction of his effort is suggested by this expression in his chapter on collation: "The bibliographer, who includes the cataloguing l i b r a r i a n" (p. 215).

65. Cowley goes too far in asserting that these different approaches "must not be mixed" and that they "cannot be combined in one piece of work" (p. 9). But perhaps his extreme position is the effect of a salutary reaction against the much more common error of mixing them indiscriminately and carelessly—without, indeed, realizing that any mixing is taking place.

technical note should be reduced to the form adopted in the Anglo-American code, e.g. viii, 182, [10] p., illus., 10 plates, diagrs., 20 x 15 cm." (p. 106). It is clear that he equates library cataloguing in general with subject bibliography; but why the details for library cataloguing prescribed in the Anglo-American rules are appropriate for subject bibliography as defined in his opening chapter is never explored. Although his work makes a contribution to descriptive bibliography and offers a helpful theoretical distinction between that field and library cataloguing, he leaves the break between the two as ill-defined in practice as he found it.

In 1951 Paul S. Dunkin's booklet on *How to Catalog a Rare Book* was published by the American Library Association. Like Cowley, Dunkin does not attempt to correlate reference and physical bibliography. Routine cataloguing has to do with subject matter: "People want to find an ordinary book because they want to read it. Simplified cataloging serves well enough for such a book because it gives a call number and tells what the book is about" (p. 1). A rare book, on the other hand, is of interest as a physical object: "If people wanted only to read it, a microfilm or reprint would do. The fact that the rare book is valued as a material object must be the keynote of any useful approach to rare book cataloging." The booklet proceeds to offer an introduction to title-page transcription, determination of format, and the recording of signatures and pagination—the "cataloging problems peculiar to rare books" (p. 2)—without further considering what rationale underlies the segregating of certain books for this treatment.[66] Indeed, the cataloguer is not supposed to think about this question: "it is not," he says, "the cataloger's job to decide if a book is rare; that has been decided before the book reached his desk." But someone had to make a decision, for the dividing line between "rare books" and others is not self-evident, nor therefore is the division between books of interest for their content and books of interest as physical objects. Obviously any book can be of interest for either reason; but despite the title of his opening chapter, "Whys and Wherefores," Dunkin does not conceive of his task as involving any examination of such matters. Instead, he concentrates on particulars of form and is at pains to show that the recording of physical details need not

66. Except for repetition of the initial distinction: on p. 59 the reader is again told that "the prospective user" of "an ordinary book" wants to know "only what it is about and how much there is of it for him to read," so collation of pagination is sufficient; but a rare book is "valuable chiefly, if not only, as a physical entity," and therefore "the description of a rare book must make the book's physical structure perfectly clear."

be complex, as in his recommendation for "collation by gatherings in simple language" (p. 82). He insists that what he is talking about is "simplified cataloging," not descriptive bibliography of the kind treated in Bowers's *Principles*.[67] "A cataloger," he adds, "tells only what a rare book looks like; a bibliographer tells how it came to look that way" (p. 1). In taking this position he is creating a false opposition, implying first that the difference between a catalogue and a bibliography lies in the amount of detail and then, rather confusingly, suggesting that the difference results from the presence or absence of analysis.[68] His later writings continue to make these points and show an increasing irritation with the practices of descriptive bibliographers. In the preface to the 1973 revised edition of this booklet he expresses "surprise" at the wide acceptance of Bowers's "highly complicated collation formula" and hopes that "catalogers will never . . . use the Bowers formula in their entries."[69] The new edition "tries to make the Bowers formula easy for catalogers to understand" only because they may have to consult printed bibliographies which employ it. Yet his comparison of Bowers's system and his own "simpler" one (in a section entitled "Collation: Cataloger and Bibliographer," pp. 94-97) succeeds only in demonstrating the superiority of Bowers's formula, not merely in consciseness but in clarity as well,[70] and in showing that the rumors of its difficulty had been greatly exaggerated.[71] More

67. The paragraph which contains this statement and concludes with the sentence I quote next was dropped in his 1973 revision, apparently because the point was largely covered in his new preface; in any case, his later writing shows that his deletion does not mean that he had changed his mind.

68. Dunkin had earlier expressed the view that cataloguers do not interpret evidence (and voiced his dissatisfaction with Bowers's definitions of "issue" and "state") in "The State of the Issue," *PBSA*, 42 (1948), 239-255. I have commented on his argument in "The Bibliographical Concepts of *Issue* and *State*," *PBSA*, 69 (1975), 54, n. 41. The 1973 revision of his booklet includes a new section (called "Distinctions: Cataloger and Bibliographer," pp. 14-15) summarizing his position regarding "issue" and "state." (On cataloguers as analysts, see also note 92 below.)

69. And in his checklist, Bowers's *Princi-*

ples is described as an "elaborate and arbitrary codification" (p. 7). In an earlier treatment of some of the same material, "On the Catalog Card for a Rare Book," *Library Quarterly*, 16 (1946), 50-56, he praises the collation formula of Greg and McKerrow (adding that a catalogue card should use words instead).

70. It is difficult to see, for instance, why Dunkin's "[A]^2 A-Y^4" is simpler than Bowers's "π^2 A-Y^4"; but it is clear that Bowers's form gives rise to less ambiguity.

71. The other major addition to the revised edition is a simplified method of title-page transcription, which he calls "calculated-risk transcription," resembling the quotation of titles in routine library cataloguing (pp. 36-40). If this method sometimes fails to identify "an edition or issue," the risk is worth taking because "it is not unlikely that the scholar wanting to use the book would insist on making his own judgment about its edition and issue

recently, in *Bibliography: Tiger or Fat Cat?* (1975), he has repeated his attacks on Bowers's system, concluding that "the space saved by shorthand notation is more apparent than real" (p. 28)—as if conciseness were the only reason for it. He also dismisses the descriptive bibliographer's definitions of "issue" and "state" as "jargon," though "harmless" (p. 18)—as if the lack of careful definitions would not lead to sloppy thinking. His resentment emerges in irony at times, as when he labels the cataloguer a "Country Cousin" and says, "In the hierarchy of Bibliography the cataloger stands lowest of the low" (p. 29). It is unfortunate that he chooses to pursue this unconstructive approach, which can do nothing to promote greater understanding and cooperation between cataloguers and bibliographers.

In contrast, John E. Alden, in his excellent essay on "Cataloging and Classification" for the Association of College and Research Libraries' *Rare Book Collections* (1965),[72] stresses the mutually fruitful relationship that can exist between the two groups. He calls rare-book cataloguing "bibliographical cataloging" (p. 68) and sees the cataloguer as a person with "a great opportunity to render a particular, not to say unique, service to the scholar—the opportunity to describe individual books analytically and to achieve significant patterns either by the correlation of these descriptions or, by means of classification, by the correlation of the books themselves" (p. 65).[73] But in order to play this creative role, Alden believes, the cataloguer must also learn from the scholar and keep abreast of developments in analytical bibliography and textual study. To say that the rare-book cataloguer can ignore those developments or that he can follow the standard catalogu-

anyhow." This line of argument, of course, could lead to doing nothing; the real question is not whether a user will uncritically accept the information but whether that information is relevant to the purposes of the entry and also falls within the level of detail established for it.

72. ACRL Monograph No. 27, ed. H. Richard Archer, pp. 65-73. Alden had earlier written the introduction to the 1946-47 Rosenbach Lectures, *Standards of Bibliographical Description* (1949), pointing out the revolutionary impact of McKerrow's *Introduction* and the need for agreement on "acceptable minimum standards" for bibliographical description. Although the volume is not primarily concerned with library cataloguing, Lawrence C. Wroth's essay on "Early Americana" does set forth "an intermediate form of entry" (p. 104) more appropriate for a library catalogue than a "full-dress bibliography"; his position is that considerations of time and money demand "brevity and simplicity" in a library catalogue. He is of course principally speaking about degrees of detail in the recording of physical data, but he believes that a full-scale description should also give proportionate attention to the text and its history (p. 106).

73. Or as he puts it in another place, speaking as a rare-book cataloguer: "we can, in the course of describing what we possess in a significant fashion, provide signposts and achieve a high bibliographical standard" (p. 69).

ing codes is "a counsel of despair": "The more productive view is certainly that the 'new bibliography' is the province not only of the avowed bibliographer but also of the rare book cataloger, who in the course of his day-to-day activity has occasion to contribute to knowledge and to scholarship by his own discoveries or by making possible discoveries at the hands of others" (p. 67). Although Alden does make some specific recommendations, he places his emphasis "on ends rather than on means," feeling that cataloguers have given too little attention to "what purpose cataloging served"; formal matters will be handled imaginatively, in response to a given situation, by the cataloguer who is "a humanist before he is a technician" (p. 73). Alden does not therefore address himself to the evaluation of particular systems for recording details in physical and in reference bibliography; but his view that the card catalogue "is adaptable enough to serve the objectives of both rare book cataloging and general cataloging" (p. 68) presupposes a basic compatibility among entries prepared with different aims in mind.[74] The world of cataloguing which emerges from Alden's pages is far removed from the one Dunkin writes about; it is surely the more rewarding one to inhabit.

The approach which Alden describes in general terms is the one which underlies the detailed specifications set forth by Josiah Q. Bennett in his impressive booklet on *The Cataloguing Requirements of the Book Division of a Rare Book Library* (1969).[75] Bennett's thorough treatment of the form and nature of the elements required in an adequate catalogue entry for a "rare book" is concerned both with upholding scholarly standards and with recognizing practical realities. It is grounded in the belief, first, that library cataloguing of rare books—which necessarily emphasizes physical details—need provide only enough information for identification, not the greater quantity required for true description (e.g., pp. 8, 29); second, that careful initial cataloguing is more economical than the repeated investigation which would otherwise be necessary to answer inquiries or check

74. Similarly, Andrew Osborn writes, "At its best that process [rare-book cataloguing] is a skilful blending of the general techniques of cataloguing and the insights of critical bibliography. Rare-book cataloguing is thus a borderline discipline; if at any time the cataloguing or the bibliographical insights and skills are absent or weak, the results are bound to leave a great deal to be desired." See pp. 126-127 of "Relation between Cataloguing Principles and Principles Applicable to Other Forms of Bibliographical Work," in the *Report* (1963) of the 1961 Paris Conference, pp. 125-137.

75. A "revised and corrected" printing appeared in 1972, but the passages quoted below were not affected; however, some of the citations of pages would be slightly different if keyed to the 1972 impression (the references to pp. 41-42, 19-20, 18-19, 46, and 45-46 would become, respectively, 42, 20, 19, 47, and 46).

dealers' catalogues (p. 10); and, third, that standard Library of Congress entries can be converted, with a minimum of adjustment, to serve as informative basic entries for rare books, leaving plenty of space on the cards, in most cases, for the additional required data (e.g., pp. 41-42). His recommendations on particulars, therefore, naturally throw into relief the differences between ordinary LC entries and bibliographical cataloguing. For example, he underscores the absolute necessity of recording the characteristics of the actual copy at hand, not the ideal copy (pp. 19-20); he explains the usefulness of noting format, even for modern books; he rejects the measurement of the spine to the nearest centimeter in favor of measuring the sheets to the nearest millimeter (pp. 21-22); and he denounces the policy of confining "the page collation to the mere recording of the last page number found," which "has absolutely no place in rare book or special collections cataloguing" because it fails to take account of initial and terminal blanks or advertisements (pp. 18-19). Although he is making these criticisms of conventional library practice only in regard to rare-book cataloguing, his comments suggest the further question whether that practice is really appropriate to any cataloguing. A hint of this question comes to the surface when he speaks of "the decision to 'short catalogue,' not in the sense of eliminating detail unnecessary to the service of any particular type of library but in the sense of *requiring* inaccuracy for a presumed (one wonders if an actual) saving of time, as in 'last numbered page' collation and inaccurate measurement" (p. 45).[76]

It is beyond the scope of his essay to pursue the implications of this remark outside the rare-book field—that is, outside the area where interest in the physical book predominates. But his underlying concern with the split between the two ways of looking at books permeates his discussion, and the general problem is treated with understanding and insight in his opening section, on the "Rationale" of rare-book cataloguing, and in his closing section, on "The Indicated Symbiosis." The two groups that must learn to be symbiotic are of course those persons interested in information and text retrieval on the one hand and those interested in "bibliographical data retrieval," as Bennett puts it, on the other. The average library cataloguer holds a belief—

76. He makes similar criticisms of the size and pagination rules in "Some Thoughts on the Card Catalogue Description of Incunables," *Serif*, 10, no. 2 (Summer 1973), 10-18. On the LC page collation: "I still think of it in the old New England phrase—neither fish, nor flesh, nor good red herring. Even its main attraction, brevity, is not always apparent; and when brevity is brought in by the neck, it is often at such a gross expenditure of accuracy that the line might better be left empty" (p. 13).

fostered by library schools[77] because of the "overwhelming preponderancy and influence of the informational library" (p. 46)—that "the basic purpose of cataloguing is simply the identification of a text in an informational series *to the exclusion of all other factors*" (p. 44). Bennett realizes that "serial identification" is also part of the task of the rare-book cataloguer, and thus the symbiosis between "serial" and "bibliographical" identification begins with the card entries prepared for the former purpose:

while these entries may not be sufficient in depth for bibliographical purposes, they are sufficient to the serial identificational process for rare books if the cataloguer is allowed to develop the entries to the limits of accuracy of which they are reasonably and practically capable. Therefore, let these entries be made in this manner for this specific purpose. Beginning with the note, let the necessary entries for bibliographical identification and physical description be made as efficiently as possible for these specific purposes. The realities of space and time should be considered, and one card made to serve where possible, but the rigors of bibliographical accuracy must be maintained. There is space for both identifications, and such space is essentially provided by the semantic division of the card between serial formula and note. The two identifications can be made on the same card, and are not in any sense exclusive of each other. A symbiosis is not only possible and necessary but also may be achieved without difficulty under the present system.   (pp. 45-46)

This solution is not simply determined by the exigencies of economics; the basic card entry makes a positive contribution to the final expanded entry. The symbiosis, in practical terms, is feasible; what is more difficult to achieve is mutual understanding among persons

77. Further comment on the need for more bibliographical training in library schools can be found in Fredson Bowers, *Bibliography and Modern Librarianship* (1966), reprinted in his *Essays in Bibliography, Text, and Editing* (1975), pp. 75-93. For related comments, see Randolph G. Adams, "Librarians as Enemies of Books," *Library Quarterly*, 7 (1937), 317-331; Frederick B. Adams, Jr., "Long Live the Bibliophile!", *College and Research Libraries*, 16 (1955), 344-346; Cecil K. Byrd, "Rare Books in University Libraries," *Library Trends*, 5 (1956-57), 441-450; Rollo G. Silver, "The Training of Rare Book Librarians," *Library Trends*, 9 (1960-61), 446-452; Gordon N. Ray, "The Changing World of Rare Books," *PBSA*, 59 (1965), esp. 117-124; and David C. Weber, "Bibliographical Blessings," *PBSA*, 61 (1967), 307-314. Roy Stokes is thinking more of deficiencies in bibliographical training than in the cataloguing codes when he says, "In view of the number of years during which we have had cataloging codes, or have been working towards new ones, it is disheartening to think that there are comparatively few libraries which have catalogs of which they might justly be proud"; and he suggests that in certain areas "an acute understanding of bibliography and its problems is essential if anything worth-while is to be accomplished" (p. 585 of "The Teaching of Bibliography," *Library Trends*, 7 [1958-59], 582-591).

with differing habits of thought. As Bennett points out, the rare-book cataloguer must have "a habit of mind flexible enough to approach each book brought before it as an entity in itself" (p. 42), not merely as a unit in a series. The development of this habit of mind is crucial to the symbiosis, and one of the merits of Bennett's treatment is that he recognizes questions of personality as well as of bibliographical theory.[77a]

It is natural that discussions of the relation between reference and physical bibliography have generally addressed themselves to problems of rare books and special collections. Cataloguing codes from Cutter to *AACR* have generally included a section on incunabula,[78] thus tacitly admitting to any user of the codes that certain situations demand fuller attention to physical details than the basic rules allow for. But since no clear dividing line separates "rare books" from other books, the thoughtful reader of these codes will be moved to reexamine those basic rules. Bennett has shown what can be done with a minimum of effort to convert a standard entry into a satisfactory entry for a "rare book"—a book, that is, the physical features of which are, or can be anticipated to be, of interest because it falls into a category of books frequently approached in that way. Any book, however, no matter how unlikely the choice, may be studied as a physical object, the product of a certain moment in printing and publishing history.

77a. More recently Roderick Cave, in his book on *Rare Book Librarianship* (1976), has included a chapter on "Processing, Cataloguing and Classification" (pp. 67-82), but it does not contain any detailed consideration of the relationship between standard and rare-book cataloguing. Recognizing that the rare-book department is concerned "with the book as artifact and not just as vehicle for the text" (p. 68), Cave generalizes that "the librarian charged with the responsibility of developing catalogues of a special collection needs to approach his material more in the manner of a bibliographer than of the librarian applying the standard techniques and codes of his profession" (pp. 70-71). It is not the purpose of his discussion, however, to examine what this difference of approach consists of or to question the practices of standard cataloguing. He finds "routine cataloguing" appropriate as the basic cataloguing for a rare-book collection, to be supplemented by special catalogues of definable units within it. These catalogues may sometimes require detailed attention to physical features, but, he says, "The rigour of descriptive bibliography will naturally be the exception and employed normally only in those libraries pre-eminent in a particular field and in which catalogue descriptions serve as a substitute for a formal bibliography" (p. 72). His comments seem designed as an introductory survey of presently accepted practices, not as an inquiry into the rationale for those practices. Yet his chapter does convey, however indirectly, a sense of the awkwardness of the split between "routine cataloguing" and the "rigour of descriptive bibliography."

78. It is interesting that Cutter's rules of 1876 refer to a wider range of rare books than incunabula (p. 80), whereas the 1941 and 1949 codes and *AACR* have a section specifically restricted to incunabula.

But if the conversion of a typical card entry into one appropriate for physical study entails the addition of several pieces of information, it is obviously unrealistic to ask that all books be catalogued as if they were "rare books." What can be done is to look at the matter from the other direction: instead of examining what needs to be added to a routine entry for the purposes of physical bibliography, one can ask to what extent the elements present in the routine entry are useful to the physical bibliographer. In other words, recognizing that for practical reasons the majority of books will be catalogued with a minimum of elaboration and that some essentially physical details will be included even in catalogue entries primarily intended to serve a reference function, one can ask whether those physical details are presented in a form which seems sensible—or at least is not misleading—to the physical bibliographer. To ask this is to ask whether it is not possible to refer to physical details unambiguously in all entries.

I should like to suggest a way of answering this question, taking the statement of pagination as my illustration—both because I concentrated on pagination in my comments on the Anglo-American rules and because the record of pagination is (among the elements included in an LC entry) of particular interest to physical bibliographers. Some of the problems involved in integrating the approaches of reference and physical bibliography toward pagination can be suggested by the practices of two bibliographers, one attempting to incorporate into a descriptive bibliography the pagination formula employed on LC cards and the other trying to devise a formula for brief catalogue entries that would have the precision expected by descriptive bibliographers. Donald Gallup, in his bibliographies of T. S. Eliot and Ezra Pound, gives pagination in a system adapted from the 1949 Library of Congress *Rules*. He says, "I have modified the system, which ignores blanks and leaves containing only advertisements, in order to account for all leaves, although blank pages are not mentioned."[79] When the preliminary pages add up to the total implied by the first numbered page, they are not specified; but when there would be a discrepancy in the numbering, the preliminaries are specified in leaves, with an indication of which are blank: "1 blank leaf, 3 leaves, 9-29 pp." At the end of a volume, a single blank verso is not mentioned ("29 pp." implies that page 30 is blank), but a single unnumbered verso with printed matter is indicated ("29, [1] pp."). When more leaves follow, the number is recorded, with those blank on both sides being labeled

<hr>

79. Quotations and examples from Gallup are taken from *A Bibliography of Ezra Pound* (1963), pp. 9-10; but the same discussion can be found in *T. S. Eliot: A Bibliography* (rev. 1969), pp. 11-12.

"blank." Thus the notation "29 pp., 1 leaf" means, in Gallup's explanation, that "the text ends on page 29 and that additional material not a continuation of the text appears on a final unnumbered leaf, either recto or verso or both being printed." Because Gallup's system is intended for descriptive bibliography, it properly emphasizes physical details, recognizing that all leaves which form part of the printed gatherings must be recorded. But in two respects, influenced by the LC rules, it does not consistently stress physical form. First, the decision not to indicate which preliminary pages are unnumbered when their total matches the sequence established by the first numbered page means that the physical detail of printed page numbers is regarded as of secondary importance at the front of a book (whereas a notation like "29, [1] pp." suggests that it is primary at the end of a book, since no pagination is inferred there). Second, the distinction between "29 pp." and "29, [1] pp." reflects a concern with the content of a page (since the thirtieth page exists physically in either case), whereas for the later leaves or the preliminaries the only concern is with knowing the number of physical leaves, not which individual pages among those leaves are blank.[80] Gallup's experiment is interesting, but there remains in his formula a conflict between those details of physical and those of reference emphasis. The context is one of physical bibliography, and the intrusion of elements relating more to content than to form lessens the value of the formula as a physical record.

Rolf Du Rietz's experiment, in his *Bibliotheca Polynesiana*, illustrates a somewhat different problem. His goal is to work out a pagination formula for reference bibliography—not, like Gallup, for physical bibliography. Yet he believes, with Gallup, that all leaves must be accounted for; he believes, in other words, that a pagination statement for reference bibliography must be more than an approximate indication of the extent of a work—it must be an accurate representation of the physical book in terms of pagination. "One of the aims of a page formula," he says, "must always be that of making possible references to any pages in the unit described, and to meet this and the other purposes of a page formula, it is absolutely necessary to assume a purely analytical approach to the problem of collational formulas for the purposes and needs of reference bibliography" (p. xli). The formula he proposes (and uses in his catalogue) is made up of two ele-

---

80. Of course, the specification of which entire leaves are blank—as in "1 blank leaf, 3 leaves, 9-29 pp."—also shows a concern with content, a concern not carried on into the "3 leaves."

ments: a listing of the total number of pages in each sequence of pagination (inferring page numbers wherever possible), in the form "xii + 268 pp."; and parenthetical indications of which leaves are blank or devoted to advertisements, using a set of abbreviations, such as "BL" for "blank leaf (or leaves)," "FLA" for "first leaf (leaves) advertisements," "LLBA" for "last leaves blank (one or more) and advertisements (one or more)," and so on. A hypothetical collation which Du Rietz offers as an illustration takes this form: "[πIV] (BL) + xii (FLA) + 268 + 369-800 (3 LLB) + ²32 (FLB, 2 LLA) + ³98 (3 FLBA, 4 LLBA) + XVI + (8) pp." Of course, most actual books are not likely to be so complicated: entry 168, for instance, reads "xx + 344 (LLB) pp.," and entry 15 reads "280 (2 FLB, LLB) pp." The trouble with this system is that its complications arise from the inclusion of information not directly relevant to the reference function of the entries, yet not really sufficient for physical bibliography either. For reference purposes, the extent of the work is the central fact to be communicated by the pagination statement; therefore Du Rietz's inclusion in the record of all the leaves (except binder's leaves) in the physical book necessitates his insertion of explanatory parentheses to account for those leaves which are not part of the *work*.[81] But this elaboration of statement does not turn the record into one appropriate for physical bibliography, as Du Rietz recognizes: "a page-collation formula in reference bibliography is normally not concerned with the individual numbering of each page" (it records "*sequences* of pagination") and "should thus not be confused with pagination statements (or formulas) of the kind given in descriptive bibliography" (p. xliii). One of the principal expressions of his rationale illustrates the essential problem:

It seems to me that the very concept of collation implies completeness, and I can see no real reason why a page-collation system should not aim at completeness to exactly the same extent as the analytical system employed by descriptive bibliography. If a page collation serves any real purpose at all (more than that of giving the reader a very rough notion of the bulk of the work described, a purpose which may be achieved by far less expensive and less complicated methods than those commonly employed today), it has to aim at completeness and at being able to serve as the page-collation equivalent of a full analytical formula. This cannot, as a rule, be achieved

81. The parenthetical abbreviations are supplying some of the information which would be presented in a contents paragraph in a physical description: "reference bibliography, which usually need not give collational lists of contents in the entries, has to add some brief information about the existence of blank leaves and advertisement leaves at the beginning and end of each pagination sequence" (p. xlii).

without basing the collation on some elementary kind of analytical investigation of the unit involved (even though the page formula itself does not necessarily reflect the physical structure of the unit—the actual pagination frequently does not).   (p. xl)

As this passage reveals, his system falls between two stools: the extent or bulk of a work could be indicated much more simply, and in order to be a "real analytical formula" (p. xliv) still more information would have to be given.[82]

Du Rietz is right to observe that the pagination formulas in library catalogue entries frequently do not reflect any clear understanding of the purposes they are to serve.[83] But his own proposal seems to me, both on theoretical and on practical grounds, not to provide the answer. The theoretical problem results from his unwillingness to let the pagination formula in reference bibliography refer solely to the extent of the work. So long as one insists that the formula have a physical orientation, even in a reference context, and yet does not require it to conform to the practices of descriptive bibliography, the purposes of the formula are bound to be somewhat confused. Du Rietz asserts, "Since hardly any of the thousands of page collations for reference bibliographical purposes that are every week constructed all over the world are analytically conceived, it follows that they might as well have been left unwritten and that they mean a tremendous waste of time, labour and money" (p. xl). Then he adds, "I do not say that a page-collation formula in reference bibliography should conform to the standards required for the pagination formulas supplementing the analytical formulas in descriptive bibliography." Why not? Is it not also a waste of time to have people learn an intermediate system, when an unambiguous system already exists for recording pagination from a physical point of view? The theoretical consideration is thus linked to the practical one: any solution to the problem of appropriate pagination formulas must be based on a realistic assessment of the feasibility of its adoption. The farther it departs from standard practices, already widely understood, the less its chances of ready acceptance, unless what it proposes is so obviously necessary that no resis-

82. "A page formula," he says, "can never be analytical, and need not be so, but nevertheless has to be based upon some kind of analytical investigation, in order to make it quantitatively equal to a real analytical formula" (p. xliv).

83. At one point he says, more emphatically, that "the collational systems hitherto employed in reference bibliography and library cataloguing do not really serve the purposes they have been supposed to serve," and he doubts whether in some cases "there has been any real awareness of purposes at all" (p. xli).

tance is conceivable. Du Rietz realizes that his system will require additional "training in analytical and descriptive bibliography" for cataloguers (p. xl), but he regards that fact as an advantage, since such training would help to promote rigorous standards in the field.[84] Of course, bibliographical training is an asset; but requiring an analytical approach to the pagination of every book and a special system (different from that in descriptive bibliography) for recording pagination is bound to work against the acceptability of the system. "I am aware," Du Rietz remarks, "that what has been said above may not be altogether agreeable to many librarians and reference bibliographers, but I assure them that there really is no choice" (p. xli). My belief is that a choice does exist, but Du Rietz's discussion is valuable in raising the issues and in pointing the way toward a more workable solution.[85]

Let us postulate a book which would have the following pagination formula in a descriptive bibliography (following Bowers's *Principles*): pp. [i-v] vi-viii [ix] x-xi [xii-xiii] xiv-xvii [xviii-xx], [1] 2-275 [276-277]

84. On this point, he says, "It is a truism, that as long as reference bibliographers remain bibliographically ignorant, their bibliographies and catalogues will be bibliographically worthless, and their collations and classifications useless and unreliable" (pp. xl-xli). He also discusses this matter in *PBSA*, 64 (1970), 242-250.

85. Another recent proposal, not concerned directly with pagination, is relevant here as further illustrating the attempt to work out a scheme for concisely including more physical information in a brief catalogue entry. J. W. Jolliffe, in *Computers and Early Books: Report of the LOC Project* (1974), describes a method for "fingerprinting" books, devised in connection with Project LOC, a project for "investigating means of compiling a machine-readable union catalogue of pre-1801 books in Oxford, Cambridge and the British Museum" (to quote the title page of the report). The "fingerprint" consists of the characters which appear at specified positions on several specified pages in a given book (according to the standard proposed on pp. 95-99, it would contain sixteen symbols, being the last two or first two characters—for rectos and versos respectively—in each of the last two lines on four precisely specified pages). It is intended as an identifier (easily constructed by a person without bibliographical training) which would be useful in computer sorting, but its supporters see a broader usefulness for it: "it seems clear that the fingerprint may also be of use, in descriptive cataloguing and other library activities in which it will be established by fully trained professional librarians" (p. 95), and "it is to be hoped that it or something like it will become a part of regular descriptive bibliography" (p. 8). Whether such an identifier offers a practical approach for linking entries in library catalogues and in bibliographies is doubtful. One immediately apparent limitation, admitted by its supporters, is that it cannot by itself distinguish among impressions from a single setting of type or line-for-line resettings. Jolliffe has made further comments on Project LOC and on an eighteenth-century STC in his contribution to *Eighteenth-Century English Books Considered by Librarians and Booksellers, Bibliographers and Collectors* (1976). For some criticisms of the "fingerprint" system, see Donald D. Eddy's comments in that volume. Another approach to computerized short-title cataloguing, the HPB Project, is described by its director, William J. Cameron, in the same volume (cf. note 20 above).

278-283 [284-288].[86] If one is interested in a physical record of pagination, it would be hard to improve on this approach. The great advantages of this formula are that it is readily understandable and that its construction does not require subjective or time-consuming decisions. Indeed, there are no special rules to be learned, except for an agreement never to link with a hyphen an inferred and a printed page number. When, in a reference bibliography, one wishes to pay particular attention to physical details, it seems pointless to construct a new system when an established one of such simplicity and clarity exists. This kind of formula may be somewhat longer for most books than the kind traditionally required for library catalogues, but whether its construction in most cases would take much (if any) longer is doubtful. And the reader who wishes to know only the extent of the work can tell from this formula just as readily as from "xvii, 283 p." what the approximate length is. Of course, the formula does not indicate the contents of any page, because in a descriptive bibliography a contents paragraph would follow; if this formula were used in a reference bibliography, the bibliographer might wish sometimes to specify separately the contents of certain pages, as "Checklist, pp. [277-284]; advertisements, pp. [285-286]; blank, pp. [i-ii], [287-288]."[87] Du Rietz's system, which would produce "xx (FLB) + 288 (2 LLBA) pp." is undeniably more concise, but it is far from self-explanatory and much less informative—for (like Gallup's system) it does not specify blank pages but only whole blank leaves,[88] and it does not attempt to show which pages are numbered. If the pagination record is going to be of use to physical bibliographers, the longer formula is so much more straightforward and precise as to outweigh whatever slight saving of time or space an abbreviated formula effects.[89] After all, the reason for complicating the pagination state-

86. Inferred page numbers may be more conveniently printed in italics than enclosed in brackets. But I have used brackets here, since they are a more widely recognized convention.

87. It would actually appear to be unnecessary in this statement to specify which numbers are inferred, since the pagination formula provides a full record of that information.

88. Whether there were two or three blank pages in the group 285-288—that is, whether there were two pages, or only one page, of advertisements—the notation would remain "2 LLBA," and it would not in any case indicate which of the two leaves contained advertising.

89. One possible exception is the abbreviated version of this descriptive formula which Bowers makes a part of his formulary (p. 462). The system is the same as for the full formula, except that unnumbered pages within a sequence are not noted. Thus the short form for the book postulated earlier would be as follows: pp. [i-v] vi-xvii [xviii-xx], [1] 2-283 [284-288]. Without an accompanying contents note, of course, this form is not entirely unambiguous as a physical record.

ment in the first place is to provide physical information, and it does not seem worthwhile to introduce complications without going far enough to achieve an unambiguous physical record.

I am not suggesting, however, that a full pagination formula of the kind employed in descriptive bibliography is appropriate for the majority of entries in a library catalogue or a checklist at the end of a book or any other bibliographical work emphasizing reference bibliography.[90] My point is that whenever a library cataloguer or reference bibliographer wishes (for whatever reason he finds persuasive) to include information about the physical details of pagination, he would be better advised to adopt the formula of descriptive bibliography than to settle for some intermediate scheme which only partially accomplishes his purpose. But the corollary is that in most instances, when he is concerned solely with reference bibliography, he need not complicate his statement at all with physical details. For the hypothetical book under discussion, why could he not simply say "xvii, 284 pp." (or, adding the two figures, "301 pp.")?[91] According to the Anglo-American rules he would have to say "xvii, 283 [1] p.," including the "[1]" only because the 284th page, containing part of a checklist, would be referred to in a note. Or if the printed matter in the preliminaries extended to page [xix], why should he not say "xix, 284 pp." (or "303 pp.")? If reference bibliography is a legitimate pursuit, as it plainly is, there is no reason to insist that entries devised for reference purposes should satisfy the demands of physical bibliography. Where library cataloguing rules for pagination have generally gone astray is in paying too much attention to the physical details of pagination when the interest of the entry is in the extent of the work. Why should a work be labeled as "283 p." merely because the last page number is "283," when the last page of printed matter is actually the 284th page? If the concern is with the extent of the work, that extent might as well be recorded as accurately as possible, especially since the presence or absence of a printed page number is a detail of

90. It must be remembered that citations in footnotes and in lists at the ends of articles, chapters, and books constitute one of the commonest types of reference bibliography, and any realistic proposal about the form which reference entries should take must involve an awareness of what can reasonably be expected in such cases. Of course, reference bibliography can operate on different levels of detail, and a library catalogue entry may sometimes be more, and sometimes less, detailed than

an entry in a checklist; but the realities of the various situations in which reference bibliography is employed must be recognized in any attempt to develop a workable approach to the whole field.

91. One could argue that the division into roman and arabic figures is a physical detail which need not be perpetuated in a reference entry; on the other hand, one could say that it reveals more accurately the extent of the main body of the work.

typographic design irrelevant in this context.[92] Or why should the work be listed as "283, [1] p.," giving the impression of a fidelity to physical detail which is not only beside the point but in fact not true? I do not see why a descriptive bibliographer should be bothered by an entry in a reference bibliography which simply records the total number of pages occupied by a work in a given embodiment. What is objectionable is a reference entry which appears to be concerned with the physical details of pagination but in fact is not fully committed to recording them and is therefore misleading and inaccurate. Either a pagination statement should aim solely at indicating the extent of a *work*, ignoring both the typographic form of the pagination and such nontextual features as blank pages, advertisements, and colophons (but not appendixes or indexes); or else it should offer a full and dependable accounting of all the pages in a *book*, showing exactly which ones are numbered and in what form. A simple convention would serve to distinguish the two: the former would follow the pattern "284 p." or "284 pp.," in which the abbreviation for "pages" follows a numerical total; the latter would take the form "pp. [1] 2-283 [284-288]," in which the abbreviation for "pages" precedes an indication of numerical sequence(s). Both systems are easy for the bibliographer to employ and easy for the user of a catalogue or bibliography to understand; each is appropriate in different situations and is recognizable for what it is. Neither reflects an indecisiveness as to its purpose: each is efficiently constructed in accordance with the aims of one branch of bibliography.

It is true, as Du Rietz says, that "One of the most urgent needs of reference bibliography is the working out of adequate rules for page collations" (p. xl). What I have tried to suggest here is that a sensible solution can only flow from a clear understanding of the aims of and relations between reference and physical bibliography. Pagination is not the only problem, and I hope that what I have said offers an approach, a way of thinking, which can be applied to other elements of an entry, such as the recording of dimensions or the quoting of

92. The amount of judgment involved in putting down a number other than the last printed one would surely take no more time and be subject to no more errors than is the case in following the present rules. Sometimes the recording of the last printed page numbers has been justified on the grounds that it does not involve the cataloguer's judgment; but, as Henkle points out in his 1945 article (see note 47 above), "It would hardly seem to follow that a principle of book description which requires the least exercise of judgment on the part of catalogers necessarily results in the most intelligible entries" (p. 81). Margaret Mann gives the first chapter of her *Introduction to Cataloging and the Classification of Books* (2nd ed., 1943) the title "The Cataloger as an Interpreter of Books."

titles. The work of reference and physical bibliographers inevitably overlaps, and fruitful cooperation between them must rest on mutual respect and a recognition that each will need to draw on the expertise of the other. A physical bibliographer, in the aspects of his work which touch reference bibliography (such as establishing headings or classifications, indexing, citing particular libraries, and the like), should be glad to avail himself of the established practices which result from the accumulated experience of workers specializing in that field. Similarly, a reference bibliographer, in the parts of his work which impinge on physical bibliography (such as recording certain basically physical details like pagination), should turn for advice to those who specialize in studying the physical book and who have developed conventions for expressing their findings about physical form. In neither situation is it necessary to import a highly technical approach from the other field if it would be excessive in the context; but whatever is adopted should seem sensible to the specialists in the other field and be compatible with their approach. Library cataloguers, for instance, need not employ the full pagination formulas of descriptive bibliography; but their formulas should then be unambiguously focused on the content of the books, so that no one will mistake them for attempts to record physical facts. And when a need does arise for paying more attention to the physical book, they have the descriptive bibliographer's system to turn to.[93]

Much has been made of the difficulty of the formulas and terminology employed in descriptive bibliography and of the fact that a library cataloguer cannot speak to the user of the catalogue through a preface explaining his system.[94] But the standard formulas of descrip-

---

93. A library cataloguer obviously is restricted in the amount of time that can be spent on an entry; but abbreviating the examination of a book and shortening the resulting entry are not synonymous with abandoning careful distinctions or lowering standards of definition. Paul S. Dunkin has repeatedly argued that, because many more books are recorded in catalogues than in descriptive bibliographies, cross-reference between entries for a given book would be facilitated if the definitions employed were "based on easily recognized physical differences" (that is, rather than on an analytical approach). See the practically identical wording in *How to Catalog a Rare Book* (rev. 1973), p. 15, and *Bibliography: Tiger or Fat Cat?*, p. 15;

see also my comment in *PBSA*, 69 (1975), 54, n. 41. Of course, the fact that reference bibliographers outnumber descriptive bibliographers in defining a term like "edition" in a given way does not alter the fact that the subject is one in which the descriptive bibliographer is the specialist.

94. Dunkin in particular has emphasized these points: see, for instance, "The State of the Issue" (see note 68 above), pp. 252-255; and *Bibliography: Tiger or Fat Cat?*, pp. 29-33, ending with the statement, "He [the cataloguer] serves everyman; therefore he must use the tongue of everyman." Cf. Foxon, *Thoughts* (see note 3 above), pp. 22-23.

tive bibliography are not complex, except in the case of complicated books which would be likely to require more complex formulas under any system. An unfamiliar convention often appears to be more difficult than it really is, but the presence of a full descriptive pagination formula on a library card—without explanation—could not possibly prevent anyone unacquainted with the system from extracting the information he wished about the length of the work. To some extent a conflict is unavoidable between what A. Hugh Chaplin calls "tradition" and "principle."[95] The traditional practices of a field may restrict its receptivity to new approaches which are possibly more logical; yet tradition is important in maintaining stability and uniformity. Chaplin urges cataloguers—in their role as reference bibliographers—to be responsive to the requests for information from those who use their entries. He says that revisers of cataloguing codes "must adapt their rules to development and change in the user's tradition, the expectations of people using the catalogue, and where this would be hindered by their own habits, their own tradition, the cataloguer's tradition must be disregarded" (p. 11). But, as he recognizes, "The difficulty is that the expectations of the users of catalogues are inconsistent and variable, while the rules must conform to a system. The solution is to make general rules, which conform to generally prevalent expectations." When physical details are incorporated in a reference entry, the professional approach is to attempt to satisfy the prevalent expectations of physical bibliographers. And in the reverse situation, the physical bibliographer should of course meet the expectations of reference bibliographers. A century ago Charles A. Cutter concisely described the attitude which stands in the way of this kind of cooperation when he said, speaking of the reaction of catalogue-users to schemes of subject classification, "The reader at first glance is frightened by the appearance of a system to be learned and perversely regards it as a hinderance instead of an assistance."[96] All fields probably have some needless jargon; but for precise and efficient communication they must also have technical vocabularies and conventional forms. It is perhaps natural to be apprehensive about unfamiliar

---

95. *Tradition and Principle in Library Cataloguing* (1966). On tradition in cataloguing, see also Pierce Butler, "The Bibliographical Function of the Library," *Journal of Cataloging and Classification*, 9 (1953), 3-11. Ann F. Painter says, in *Reader in Classification and Descriptive Cataloging* (1972), "Probably more than with classification, descriptive cataloging suffers from the secure attitude of 'we've always done it this way and it works'" (p. 155).

96. *Rules for a Printed Dictionary Catalogue* (1876), p. 75. My attention was called to this comment by J. C. M. Hanson's reference to it on p. 19 of "Revision of A.L.A. Catalog Rules," *Catalogers' and Classifiers' Yearbook*, 3 (1932), 7-19.

systems. But if we can learn to approach fields related to our own in an open-minded and positive spirit, assuming that they have some-ing to teach us which will be helpful in our own field, we will be well on the way toward achieving the advances which cooperation naturally produces.

Copyright Records and the Bibliographer

I N A COUNTRY WHICH PROVIDES COPYRIGHT PROTECTION BY STATUTE or which requires the deposit of works for the benefit of one or more of its libraries, the operation of the law will usually produce a body of documents relating to the literary and artistic output of that country. The exact nature of such material will vary according to the requirements of the statute, but one may expect it to contain information of bibliographical significance which would be difficult (and in some cases impossible) to locate elsewhere. For example, if the law defines the term of copyright for any work as dating from its publication, the records may include publication dates; if there is a manufacturing clause in the law, certain facts about the printing and binding of individual books may be given; if there is provision for the deposit of copies, the recorded deposit dates will furnish proof of the existence of particular books. Thus the bibliographer who knows what copyright records survive for the period and country with which he is concerned, and who possesses enough historical understanding of the copyright law to interpret them, has at his command a valuable tool for research.

In the case of England and the United States, not only are the extant copyright records extensive; in addition, because of the unusual situation in which two countries with important literatures speak the same language, the copyright laws of each country have had an effect on the original publication of the literature of the other, so that bibliographers of authors writing in English must be aware of the

*Among the many persons to whom I am indebted for assistance, I wish particularly to express my gratitude to Joseph W. Rogers for his generous interest and encouragement over several years; he and Waldo H. Moore have demonstrated that the United States Copyright Office is a place which welcomes scholarly researchers with courtesy and understanding. For a careful reading of the manuscript, I am grateful not only to Mr. Rogers and Mr. Moore but also to Elizabeth K. Dunne and Benjamin W. Rudd of the Copyright Office; for additional help, I wish to thank Frederick R. Goff and Roger J. Trienens of the Library of Congress and Donald W. Krummel and Richard Colles Johnson of The Newberry Library.

copyright records of both countries. The English copyright law required registration of copyrighted works between 1710 and 1912, and there are also some records of registered books before and after this period. The United States, from the time of its first federal copyright law in 1790, has always included a provision for registration in its copyright legislation. For obvious reasons these records, even when they survive intact, do not constitute national bibliographies — some works may be copyrighted but never published, and many others may be published but never copyrighted. They do, however, provide a preliminary basis for a record of the two nations' literary output.

Whenever a bibliographer finds information of interest to him in copyright records, he is making a secondary use of those records; he is finding them helpful in ways other than those for which they were designed, just as he may profitably consult a publisher's files which are no longer useful to the publisher in carrying on his business. Quite understandably and properly, the officials in charge of such records have normally been more concerned with maintaining whatever records are required for current purposes than with servicing archives of older material. In the United States, such men as William Elliot and Thorvald Solberg did recognize some of the bibliographical uses of the copyright records, but their hopes for a national bibliography based on them were not realized until 1891, and then only in part — a story which has been admirably set forth by Joseph W. Rogers in *U. S. National Bibliography and the Copyright Law* (1960). Since that time such men as Verner W. Clapp, former Chief Assistant Librarian of Congress, Joseph W. Rogers of the Copyright Office, and Frederick R. Goff of the Library's Rare Book Division have been particularly concerned with the historical importance of the old records. But the general indifference to this material, on the part of officials and scholars alike, has not yet disappeared, and bibliographers have remained peculiarly unaware of its potentialities.

Although an enormous literature of copyright exists,[1] practically

---

1. The fullest listing is Henriette Mertz, *Copyright Bibliography* (1950); the earlier standard list (still useful) is Thorvald Solberg's "A Bibliography of Literary Property" in R. R. Bowker's *Copyright: Its Law and Its Literature* (1886). Since June 1953 a current bibliography has appeared in each issue of the *Bulletin of the Copyright Society of the U. S. A.* Among the prominent earlier writers on copyright were Augustine Birrell, William Morris Colles, George Ticknor Curtis, F. S. Drone, E. J. Macgillivray, George Haven Putnam, and Thorvald Solberg (specific titles can be checked in the Mertz bibliography); more recent treatments include such books as R. R. Shaw's *Literary Property in the United States* (1950) and Benjamin Kaplan's *An Unhurried View of Copyright* (1967). Two standard works, continually revised, are W. A. Copinger, *Copyright*, ed. F. E. and E. P. Skone James (10th ed., 1965), and Melville B. Nimmer, *Nimmer on Copyright* (loose leaf, 1963-   ).

nothing has been written about the secondary use of copyright material by literary scholars and bibliographers. Walter Pforzheimer, in his well-known essay on "Copyright and Scholarship" in the *English Institute Annual 1940* (1941), outlined the essentials of English and American copyright history for the use of scholars (pp. 164-99) but said little about the ways in which the records could be employed. In connection with the American records, only two writers have gone very far in discussing the specifically bibliographical significance of such material. On 30 December 1937, Martin A. Roberts of the Library of Congress read a paper before a joint session of the American Historical Association and the Bibliographical Society of America describing the pre-1870 records and urging their publication as a "national heritage."[2] Seven years later Ruth Shaw Leonard intensively studied the Massachusetts records of the period 1800-09 for her Master's thesis at Columbia and summed up her findings in 1946 in an essay entitled "The Bibliographical Importance of Copyright Records."[3]

At that time the American copyright records had been used by only a few bibliographers. Charles Evans, in the 1910's, had taken advantage of some of the early district court records to add titles and deposit dates to his *American Bibliography* for the last decade of his coverage (1790-1800). And Miss Leonard, with Harry C. Bentley, had conscientiously read through the records in preparing the *Bibliography of Works on Accounting by American Authors* (2 vols., 1934-35) — which also contained an introductory chapter entitled "Copyright Laws and Administration — Their Significance to Bibliographers" (I, xi-xxi). In 1940 Louis C. Karpinski published his *Bibliography of Mathematical Works Printed in America through 1850*, which made effective use of the copyright records to establish the publication of many titles no longer extant, just as Lyle Wright's *American Fiction, 1744-1850* (1939) included some otherwise unknown titles discovered in a search through the collection of deposited title pages, and Marcus McCorison's *Vermont Imprints 1778-1820* (1963) contained some

2. This paper has been printed three times, under slightly different titles: as "Records in the Copyright Office of the Library of Congress Deposited by the United States District Courts, 1790-1870," in *PBSA*, XXXI (1937), 81-101; as *Records in the Copyright Office Deposited by the United States District Courts Covering the Period 1790-1870* (Government Printing Office, 1939); and as "Records of the United States District Courts, 1790-1870, Deposited in the Copyright Office of the Library of Congress," *Annual Report of the American Historical Association for the Year 1937* (1939), pp. 93-106.

3. *College and Research Libraries*, VII (1946), 34-40, 44. Hellmut Lehmann-Haupt, in *The Book in America* (2nd ed., 1951), also recognized the copyright records as "bibliographical source material of first-rate importance" (p. 202).

unlocated titles taken from district court copyright records. Sidney Kramer, one of the pioneers in the use of copyright records for bibliographical purposes, included deposit dates in his *A History of Stone & Kimball and Herbert S. Stone & Company* (1939), and this practice of giving deposit dates in descriptive bibliographies has been used occasionally since then, notably in Jacob Blanck's *Bibliography of American Literature* (1955-   ). For a more recent period, the published copyright catalogues were diligently searched by Wynot Irish for *The Modern American Muse* (1950), a list of American poetry between 1900 and 1925. Beyond these few works, American copyright records have rarely been drawn upon by bibliographers.

The English records have been used more extensively. The registers of the Stationers' Company between 1554 and 1708 have been regularly employed for decades by bibliographers of Elizabethan and Jacobean literature, and such literary and bibliographical scholars as A. W. Pollard, W. W. Greg, R. C. Bald, Giles Dawson, C. J. Sisson, and Leo Kirschbaum have turned their attention to the whole question of copyright in England in the sixteenth and seventeenth centuries. Pollard and Redgrave, of course, included references to the Stationers' Company registers in the *Short Title Catalogue* (1926) of pre-1640 books, and both Greg and W. A. Jackson edited parts of the Stationers' court records (1930, 1957). For the eighteenth, nineteenth, and twentieth centuries, the English copyright materials are perhaps lesser known; but the increasing recognition of the textual importance of overseas editions of both English and American authors is drawing more attention to the copyright records of both countries, especially to the way in which the copyright laws of each affected the literary properties of the residents of the other. I. R. Brussel, in his pioneer bibliographical work on trans-Atlantic literary publications, the two-volume *Anglo-American First Editions* (1935-36), understood the indispensability of copyright records, and Graham Pollard contributed to the first volume a thoughtful discussion of the bibliographical implications of the Anglo-American copyright situation. More recently Simon Nowell-Smith has gone into the question of nineteenth-century international copyright from a bibliographer's point of view.[4] And James J. Fuld's *The Book of World-Famous Music* (1966) illustrates some of the bibliographical uses of copyright data on a world-wide scale.

Copyright records have thus not been totally ignored by bibliographers, but they have not been drawn upon as frequently as one

---

4. In the Lyell Lectures for 1966; see his "Firma Tauchnitz 1837-1900," *Book Collector*, XV (1966), 423-36. Matthew J. Bruccoli spoke on "Transatlantic Texts" before the Bibliographical Society on 15 March 1966.

might expect, considering the obviousness of the uses to which they can be put. They can help to establish publication dates; they are a source of information about anonymous and pseudonymous works; they can supply publication details for individual author-bibliographies and titles for comprehensive imprint lists. It is not too much to say that a check of the relevant copyright records should be a routine part of any bibliographer's investigations; and no bibliography can be considered definitive or thorough which does not utilize them.

Their precise bibliographical usefulness, however, depends on the provisions of the copyright laws at any particular time and place; in order to know how to interpret the records — or, indeed, what records to look for — the bibliographer must have some understanding of the copyright laws of the country and period with which he is concerned. It is with this in mind that I have drawn together a few suggestions for extracting from such records the bibliographical information they can yield. Since the American records are perhaps more complex and certainly less well-known than the English, the emphasis will be on them; and they can most conveniently be taken up in four groups: 1783-90, 1790-1870, 1870-1909, 1909-present. Following these four discussions are some briefer notes on the English records and some general considerations.

I.   1783-1790

Although the Massachusetts Bay Colony passed a law on 15 May 1672 prohibiting any printer from printing more copies of a book than its author had agreed to,[5] and although occasional *ad hoc* copyright acts were passed in the colonies upon the petition of particular individuals, there was no general copyright act in any of the states until Connecticut instituted one in January 1783. Massachusetts and Maryland followed in March and April, and on 2 May 1783 the Continental Congress passed a resolution recommending that each of the states work out a copyright law. Between that time and 1790, when the first federal law was enacted, all the other states except Delaware passed copyright laws, in several cases through the energetic sponsorship of Noah Webster.[6]

5. This act was in response to a petition by John Usher; see Evans 168 and *Copyright Enactments* (1963), p. 140. For a Massachusetts bill exactly one century later, see Rollo G. Silver, "Prologue to Copyright in America," *Studies in Bibliography*, XI (1958), 259-62.

6. Webster described his efforts to promote copyright laws in the various states in "Origin of the Copy-right Laws in the United States," in *A Collection of Papers on Political, Literary and Moral Subjects* (1843), pp. 173-78; see also Harry Warfel, *Noah Webster: Schoolmaster to America* (1936), pp. 54-60.

Of particular interest to bibliographers in these twelve laws are any provisions they contain for registration or deposit. Whenever copyrighted works were to be registered, some sort of ledger or record book for that purpose must have existed at one time and might be extant today; whenever copyrighted works were to be deposited, the deposit copies might still survive, or at least a record of the deposits to prove that certain books once existed. The list below sums up these features of the state laws:[7]

	Date of Law		Term of Copyright (years)	Renewal Period (years)	Registration Required	Deposit Required
Connecticut	8 Jan.	1783	14	14	yes	no
Massachusetts	17 March	1783	21	—	no	yes
Maryland	21 April	1783	14	14	yes	no
New Jersey	27 May	1783	14	14	yes	no
New Hampshire	7 Nov.	1783	20	—	no	no
Rhode Island	Dec.	1783	21	—	no	no
Pennsylvania	15 March	1784	14	14	yes	no
South Carolina	26 March	1784	14	14	yes	no
Virginia	Oct.	1785	21	—	yes	no
North Carolina	19 Nov.	1785	14	—	yes	yes
Georgia	3 Feb.	1786	14	14	yes	no
New York	29 April	1786	14	14	yes	no

In addition, seven states (Conn., Mass., N. H., R. I., N. C., Ga., N. Y.) specifically included a provision extending copyright privileges to citizens of other states only if the states involved had similar laws. And in five states (Conn., S. C., N. C., Ga., N. Y.), an author who did not allow a sufficient quantity of his books to be printed or charged an excessive price for them could be required to have more printed or lower the price; if he failed to comply, the state could authorize the complaining party to print additional copies.

It can be seen from the list that nine states made the registration of titles a requirement for copyright. In six (Conn., N. J., S. C., N. C., Ga., N. Y.), registration was to be made with the Secretary of State; in Maryland it was to be handled by the "clerk of the general court," in

7. The full texts of these laws, as well as all the later federal copyright laws, are conveniently brought together in *Copyright Enactments: Laws Passed in the United States since 1783 Relating to Copyright* (Copyright Office Bulletin No. 3, 1900; revised 1963). The original printings of these state laws are listed there, following the text of each act; many of the laws have been reprinted in later compilations of state documents, where additional related material is sometimes available. The state copyright acts of Georgia, North and South Carolina, and Virginia are also reprinted in *A Documentary History of Education in the South before 1860*, ed. Edgar Wallace Knight, II (1950), 52-63. A general survey of the provisions of the state laws is Karl Fenning's "Copyright before the Constitution," *Publishers' Weekly*, CXIV (1928), 1336-38, reprinted in the *Journal of the Patent Office Society*, XVII (1935), 379-85.

Pennsylvania by the "prothonotary's office in the city of Philadelphia," and in Virginia by the "clerk of the council." Two of the laws (Md., S. C.) specifically mentioned the "register" into which the titles were to be entered. Two of the states (Md., Pa.) with registration requirements, however, had the further clause that the law was not to go into effect until such time as "all and every" of the states had enacted similar laws; since Delaware never passed a copyright law, the state copyright laws did not go into effect in Maryland or Pennsylvania either, and the number of possible record books is therefore presumably reduced by two (although, as it turns out, copyright entries were made in both states). As for the deposit of copies, only two states had such a clause — Massachusetts and North Carolina. In Massachusetts, two copies of each work were to be presented to "the library of the University of Cambridge [Harvard], for the use of the said university"; in North Carolina (the only state to require both registration and deposit), one copy of each work was to go — before publication — to the Secretary of State "for the use of the executive of the State."

Of the nine possible sets of records and the two groups of deposit copies, the records for Connecticut, Maryland, and South Carolina have been located among state archives and the copies for Massachusetts have been traced in the Harvard library:

Connecticut, 1783-89: Connecticut Archives (Colleges and Schools), 1st ser., II, 154-55, 159-61, 165-68. Published in *The Public Records of the State of Connecticut*, ed. Leonard W. Labaree, V (1943), 245-46, 459; VII (1948), 87. See also James Hammond Trumbull, *List of Books Printed in Connecticut, 1709-1800* (1904), items 308, 954, 998. [5 entries]

Maryland, 1786: Maryland Provincial Court Deeds, Liber T. B. H. No. 1, f. 532. Published in Irving Lowens, "Copyright and Andrew Law," *PBSA*, LIII (1959), 152-53. [8 entries]

Massachusetts, 1783-90: Deposit copies in the Harvard Library. Published in Earle E. Coleman, "Copyright Deposit at Harvard," *Harvard Library Bulletin*, X (1956), 135-41. [11 entries]

South Carolina, 1785-88: Georgia Grants Ledger, pp. 1-4, in the office of the Secretary of State. Published in "Copyrights and Patents Granted by South Carolina," *South Carolina Historical and Genealogical Magazine*, IX (1908), 56-58. [6 entries for books]

The located Connecticut records show only three entries (for Robert Ross, Joel Barlow, and William Blodget) under the 1783 act; but Trumbull, in his list of Connecticut imprints, supplies the registration dates of two more (for Andrew Law and John Lewis).[8] In addition, the Connecticut General Assembly granted Andrew Law a five-year

8. Since these dates do not appear in the books themselves and since the Law and Lewis works are not among the indexed copyrights in the Connecticut Archives, I have been unable to discover Trumbull's source for this information.

copyright ("patent") for certain pieces of music in October 1781, fourteen months before the state passed its general law.[9] The eight Maryland entries of 7 January 1786 (for works by four men — Webster, Dwight, Barlow, and Law) were published in an article by Irving Lowens, whose thorough research has impressively demonstrated the bibliographical value of copyright records. The other most important investigation into pre-1790 copyright is Earle Coleman's essay, which records eleven Harvard deposit copies with the deposit dates for each (works by Barlow, Belknap, Billings, Bingham, French, Law, Webster, and Wood); undoubtedly other volumes were deposited which cannot now be located. The six South Carolina entries, published as long ago as 1908, are for books by David Ramsay, Henry Osborne, Noah Webster, Robert Squibb, Nicolas Pike, and John F. Grimke.

Another aspect of copyright legislation in which bibliographers are interested is whether or not printed notices of copyright were required in copyrighted books. Only one of the state laws — in Pennsylvania — had such a clause; but, since Pennsylvania's law was not to become effective until all the other states had copyright laws, one should not expect to find printed notices even in Pennsylvania books. Nevertheless, such notices do appear, and a list of books with these notices forms at least a partial record of Pennsylvania pre-1790 copyrights. Charles Evans, working on the sixth and seventh volumes of his *American Bibliography* (1910, 1912), located fourteen works with these printed notices and recorded the copyright dates given in twelve of them. These references constitute in effect another published copyright record:

Pennsylvania, 1784-89: Evans 18883 (Wharton); 19628 (Lutheran Church); 20471 (M'Culloch); 20481 (Markoe); 20632 (Lloyd); 20862, 20869 (Webster); 20889 (Wilson); 21081 (Falconer); 21365, 21371 (Lloyd); 21568 (Wall); 21651 (American Philosophical Society); 21745 (*Columbian Magazine*). [14 entries]

Of the two books for which Evans did not give the date of copyright entry, one, Henry Wharton's *Letter to the Roman Catholics* (Evans 18883), contains only the statement (at the foot of the last page), "Entered according to Act of Assembly";[10] but the other, the second edition of the opening volume of the *Transactions* of the American

---

9. *The Public Records of the State of Connecticut*, ed. Charles J. Hoadly, III (1922), 537-38. See Irving Lowens, "Copyright and Andrew Law," *PBSA*, LIII (1959), 150-59; "Andrew Law and the Pirates," *Journal of the American Musicological Society*, XIII (1960), 206-23, reprinted in his *Music and Musicians in*

Early America (1964).

10. Charles R. Hildeburn, in *The Issues of the Press of Pennsylvania* (1885-86), lists this work (entry 4591) and states that it is the earliest example of American copyright he has encountered.

Philosophical Society (Evans 21651), does carry the entry date of 29 April 1789. When Roger Bristol's list of additions to Evans is completed, it is possible that more books with Pennsylvania copyright notices can be traced.

Apparently none of the copyright records of the other five states with requirements for registration are in existence, for officials in those states have not been able to turn up any copyright material for this period.[11] It is occasionally possible, however, to learn something of the copyright registrations in these states through secondary documents — such as the 1842 letter from Stephen Dodd to George Hood, in the Boston Public Library, which gives the Pennsylvania (1784) and New York (1786) registration dates for Andrew Law's music books.[12] Judging from the located records, the number of registrations in each state was probably quite small, and the information could have been entered in ledgers mainly devoted to something else — just as the South Carolina entries are found on the opening pages of a volume labeled "Georgia Grants," recording plats of land granted by Georgia authorities. Such records are naturally difficult to locate, and it is not impossible that more of them will eventually come to light. In the meantime, bibliographers must be content with copyright information concerning fewer than forty American books before 1790.

II. 1790-1870

Since the United States Constitution (17 September 1787) gave Congress the power to grant copyrights, several authors in 1789 petitioned the federal government (rather than the states) for copyrights to their works — David Ramsay on 15 April, Jedidiah Morse on 12 May, Nicholas Pike on 8 June, and Hannah Adams on 22 July; and in granting copyrights to David Ramsay on 20 April 1789 for two of his books, Congress was making its first use of the copyright provision of the Constitution.[13] Noah Webster, at the same time, was drafting *A Bill to Promote the Progress of Science and Useful Arts*, printed in

11. I wrote to officials in each of the states involved on 30 January 1967 and received replies in each case to the effect that no pre-1790 state copyright materials were now known to exist in their archives. J. H. Whitty reported as long ago as 1911, in his *Record of Virginia Copyright Entries (1790-1844)*, that "No records have been discovered of State copyright entries in Virginia" (p. 5). The *Catalogue of Records of the Office of the Secretary of State* for New York (1898) mentions some miscellaneous papers relating to copyrights by the Secretary of State (p. 133), which may have been the pre-1790 records, but these papers apparently no longer survive.

12. Cited by Irving Lowens, *PBSA*, LIII (1959), 153.

13. See *Copyright in Congress 1789-1904*, ed. Thorvald Solberg (1905), pp. 112-15. Cf. Evans 21394, 21978, 22090, and 22192.

New York on 23 June 1789, which led to the passage, on 31 May 1790, of the first federal copyright law in the United States (1 Stat. 124).

This law required three steps for the securing of a copyright. First, a printed copy of the title page of any work proposed for copyright was to be deposited before publication with the clerk of the district court for the district in which the author (or copyright proprietor) lived, and the clerk was to record this deposit in a ledger which he kept for that purpose. Second, the text of the clerk's registration was to be inserted, within two months, in at least one United States newspaper, where it was to run for a period of four weeks. Third, within six months of the publication of the work, a copy was to be deposited in the office of the Secretary of State. The term of copyright was fourteen years, renewable for another fourteen years if this same procedure were repeated within six months of the expiration of the first term.

Although later revisions of the law before 1870 modified the details somewhat, the basic procedures remained the same throughout this period, and each of them has important implications for the bibliographer who wishes to use the copyright records:

(1) *Title Pages and Record Books.* Since title pages were to be deposited in advance of publication, many title pages were deposited (or entries recorded) for works which never actually got printed and published, and the amassed collection of title pages and record books thus serves in part as an account of unfulfilled projects — occasionally of great historic or literary importance. At the same time, certain works known to have been printed no longer survive, so it cannot be assumed that all title pages or entries for works no longer in existence necessarily represent books which were never printed, and the title pages or record books may therefore supply titles, not otherwise known, for inclusion in bibliographies or imprint lists. Because loose title pages are more easily lost than large record books, the record books are more complete and are the basic tool for research; but since the title-deposit dates were written on the title pages, it is conceivable (though not likely) that certain title pages might turn up for periods in which there is a gap in the record books for a particular district and thus supplement the record books. In any case, the title pages have an interest of their own for students of printing; especially after 1 January 1803, when prints and commercial labels were also included in the copyright law, these deposits form an enormously important collection of printed ephemera, sometimes containing examples of the earliest printing in various territories and states. Anyone interested in the records from this point of view should remember that the clerks

of some district courts regularly pasted the title pages and labels into the record books rather than filing them in a separate place.[14] These materials have not been exploited by bibliographers and historians of printing as they should have been, though Frederick Goff has called attention to the importance of the title-page collection, and Roger Trienens has demonstrated the usefulness of the title pages in supplementing published bibliographies.[15] Lyle Wright, in compiling his three-volume bibliography of *American Fiction* (1939, 1957, 1966), used the title pages both as a source for additional entries and as a means of ascertaining the authorship of many anonymously published works (since the district-court clerks often wrote the names of the proprietors — who could also be the authors — on the title pages).[16] One should always keep in mind that items may not have been entered in the district which at first seems most likely, for the title could be entered by either the author or the proprietor,[17] who would not necessarily have lived in the same district. The most obvious bibliographical use of the record books (or the title pages) is to establish the date of title-page deposit; and since the title-page deposit was to be made before publication, this date provides a *terminus a quo* for the publication date.[18] The chief difficulty in using these records is that they are not adequately indexed. There is no general index to them all (since they were produced in various district court offices); while many of the individual volumes (but by no means all of them) do have

14. The loose title pages are now housed in 92 boxes (in the Rare Book Division of the Library of Congress), arranged chronologically and then alphabetically within the year. But a number of them, especially for well-known authors, have been removed from their proper place and put in a single miscellaneous box; in addition, two boxes and one folder of title pages are shelved with the record books, and some title pages can be found among the correspondence.

15. Goff, "Almost Books," *New Colophon*, I (1948), part 2, pp. 125-33; Trienens, "Copyright Deposit Title Pages of American Medical Books, 1790-1820," *Journal of the History of Medicine and Allied Sciences*, XX (1965), 59-62, which supplements Robert B. Austin's *Early American Medical Imprints 1668-1820* (1961).

16. This information is also available in the record books, of course. Wright com-

ments on his use of copyright evidence in "In Pursuit of American Fiction," in *Bibliography: Papers Read at a Clark Library Seminar, May 7, 1966* (1966), pp. 41-45, as well as in *American Fiction 1774-1850* (rev., 1948), p. x. Louis C. Karpinski, in his *Bibliography of Mathematical Works Printed in America through 1850* (1940), includes a separate section of 105 "entry titles" known only through the copyright records (pp. 551-64).

17. The copyright proprietor, if not the author himself, was generally the publisher but could also be the printer or someone else acting on behalf of the author.

18. That is, the announced date on which a work was to be made available to the public, which is not synonymous with the date of completion of printing, though occasionally the two may in fact be identical.

indexes, they vary greatly in their comprehensiveness (some including titles and authors as well as proprietors, but most of them listing only proprietors), although they are usually accurate as far as they go.

(2) *Newspaper Notices.* The requirement that each copyright proprietor insert a copy of the clerk's certificate of title-page deposit in a newspaper for a period of four weeks amounts in fact to a publication of the entire copyright record (until 1831) — but in a form which by its nature is difficult to consult. The scarcity of early newspapers is not the principal handicap, since each notice was to run for four weeks (making scattered missing issues not of crucial importance) ; the real difficulty is in guessing just which newspaper a particular proprietor would choose. These newspaper notices, therefore, are of little practical usefulness to the bibliographer, unless someone should undertake the unenviable task of indexing them. But whenever a gap exists in the surviving district court record books, the bibliographer will find it worthwhile to search the newspapers of that area for the appropriate period. Filling in such gaps (even if only in part) constitutes the chief bibliographical value of the newspaper notices.

(3) *Deposit Copies.* Since published works were to be deposited within six months of publication, knowledge of the deposit date provides a *terminus ante quem* for the publication date: if the law were properly followed, the publication date could not have been more than six months before the deposit date. Taking the deposit date in conjunction with the date of title entry, one can usually narrow the time span during which publication took place: since the title was to be entered before publication, if the date of title entry is less than six months earlier than the date of deposit, the period in which publication occurred is correspondingly shortened. Deposit dates were written into the copies, and the Secretary of State also kept a record book for these deposits; even when certain deposit copies can no longer be found, therefore, it is often possible to ascertain the deposit dates from the Secretary of State's record books, which survive from 1796. The dates given are those on which the works were received in the Secretary of State's office, and they may be considerably later than the dates on which the works were dispatched by the proprietor or author (if such dates could be known). Bibliographers should not conclude that titles entered in the district court record books which do not reappear in the record books of deposits received by the Secretary of State were never printed or published. Inevitably some proprietors failed to comply with the deposit requirement, even though they had begun properly by entering the title; and, just as inevitably, certain

deposit copies, duly posted by the proprietors, never reached their destination.

(4) *Renewal Records.* Because a copyright proprietor was required to go through the same steps for renewal as for the original copyright, title pages had to be deposited again and a new entry made by the clerk of the district court. For this reason, copyright renewals furnish another way of filling some gaps in the records; if one is looking for the entry of a book published in a year for which the records of the appropriate district court are not extant, one may try the records fourteen years later, if they exist, or search the newspapers and find the renewal entry. Since the renewal was to be made within the last six months of the original term, one then has some idea of the time when the original copyright was entered (the copyright term ran from the date of title entry, not copy deposit). In the same way, if no deposit for a given book was recorded by the Secretary of State in the year of its known publication, a check of the deposit record fourteen years later may at least reveal the date of the renewal deposit.

The amendments and revisions which followed are of interest to bibliographers in terms of the changes they brought about in the form of the records. The act of 29 April 1802 (2 Stat. 171, effective 1 January 1803) is significant from a bibliographical point of view only because it required all copyrighted works to carry a printed notice of the date of title entry, either on the title page itself or on one of the two pages immediately following (usually the verso of the title page),[19] a provision which has continued in effect to the present. On 3 February 1831 was passed the first general revision of the copyright law (4 Stat. 436), which as of that date superseded the 1790 act. It contained four important revisions: (1) the copyright term was henceforth to be twenty-eight years (instead of fourteen), renewable for fourteen; (2) the newspaper notice was required only for renewals; (3) copies of published works were to be deposited with the clerk of the district court (not the Secretary of State) within three (not six) months of publication; (4) the clerks of the district courts were to send these deposit copies and certified lists of all titles recorded, at least once each year, to the Secretary of State. In most other respects, the law remained as before.

19. Although the notice was not legally required until 1 January 1803, a number of books published between 1790 and 1802 included such a notice, since it was to the proprietor's advantage to announce his copyright. For example, Elihu Hubbard Smith's anthology *American Poems, Selected and Original* (1793) carried a line on its title page which read, "The Copyright secured as the Act directs"; and Hannah Foster's *The Coquette* (1797) included a notice similar to the kind that was later required, with the precise date of copyright entry.

One result of these changes was that clerks of some district courts began entering the deposit date for each work on the same page of the ledger which recorded that work's title entry. Another result was that the records were kept in duplicate, so that one set could be furnished to the Secretary of State. This system normally provides the bibliographer with more than one source for the dates of registration and deposit. Since the original record books and the duplicate set were kept in different places before 1870, it is unlikely that the same portions of each set would be lost or destroyed; thus the so-called "duplicates" can be used to fill in many gaps which now exist in the original records. Similarly, in cases where the deposit copies themselves are no longer available, the deposit dates can often be located in the record books (usually the original set only) — a fact not generally recognized by bibliographers, even those who utilize deposit dates. Although neither copy of Melville's *White-Jacket* in the Library of Congress, for example, has a deposit date written in it, the deposit date (26 March 1850) may be ascertained from the record books of the Southern District of New York; the Library of Congress copy of his *Piazza Tales* contains a note specifically pointing out that the present copy is a replacement of the deposit copy, but again the deposit date (20 May 1856) may be found in the district court ledger. Whenever both sources of information exist for a deposit date (both the copy itself and the record book) — or for a registration date (the two sets of record books) — some discrepancy is possible, particularly since these are handwritten records (another reason why the "duplicates" are not really duplicates). In such cases, for the registration date precedence should be given to the original record over the "duplicate," and for deposit dates to the actual copy of the work[20] over the record book. One should also remember that, after 1831, a publication date can be gauged with somewhat more accuracy than in the 1790-1831 period, since it can be no more than three months prior to the deposit date. But the most important point, worth repeating, is that there are few published and copyrighted American works, especially after 1831, for which the deposit dates cannot be ascertained, even if the deposit copies are no longer in existence.

The amendments to the 1831 revision have principally to do with the places where copies were to be deposited and the number of deposit copies required. The act of 10 August 1846 (9 Stat. 106, establishing

20. That is, if the copy is the one originally deposited with the district court. Later provisions, explained below, required additional deposits, and there is no reason why the deposit date in a copy originally deposited in the Library of Congress has to match the date on which another copy was deposited at the district court.

the Smithsonian Institution) provided that one copy of every copyrighted work be deposited — for use rather than record — in the Smithsonian and one in the Library of Congress (in addition, of course, to
the essential copy of record deposited with the district court for transmittal to the Secretary of State). The copyright amendment of 5
February 1859 (11 Stat. 380), which repealed these deposit regulations
in regard to the two libraries, transferred the copyright duties from
the Secretary of State to the Department of the Interior: previous
records and deposits were moved, and all future ones were to be sent
there. Finally, on 3 March 1865, another amendment (13 Stat. 540)
again required that a second deposit copy be sent to the Library of
Congress — and within *one* month of publication. The various changes
in deposit requirements[21] should perhaps be summarized:

1790-1831: One copy to Secretary of State within six months of publication.
1831-1846: One copy to district court (for transmittal to Secretary of State) within
            three months of publication.
1846-1859: Three copies: one to district court (for transmittal to Secretary of State)
            within three months of publication; one to Smithsonian Institution; one
            to Library of Congress.
1859-1865: One copy to district court (for transmittal to Department of Interior)
            within three months of publication.
1865-1870: Two copies: one to district court (for transmittal to Department of
            Interior) within three months of publication; one to Library of Congress
            within one month of publication.

One must keep these changes in mind when using the surviving deposit
ledgers in order to interpret the dates properly. The district court
deposit dates are usually preferable, when available, because in most
cases the deposit copies had to travel a shorter distance to reach the
clerk's office than to reach Washington and thus arrived sooner; on
the other hand, for the five years after 1865, the law did not insist
that copies be sent to the district courts as quickly as to the Library
of Congress. A further complication is that many publishers did not
comply with the deposit requirement, forcing Congress to make
special provisions (in the acts of 3 March 1865 and 18 February 1867
[14 Stat. 395]) to penalize proprietors who failed to comply; so the
recorded deposit dates for some works (particularly those of the
smaller publishers) may not provide a reliable basis for estimating
publication dates, since they may be late deposit dates resulting from
a demand for compliance issued by the Librarian of Congress.

The records of the receipt of deposit copies by the various depository agencies in Washington are now available for reference in the

21. On the deposit requirements for this   of Copyrighted Works," *Copyright Law*
period, see Elizabeth K. Dunne, "Deposit   *Revision Studies*, No. 20 (1960), pp. 11-13.

Rare Book Division of the Library of Congress and are complete except for a few gaps, as noted:

> State Department: 2 January 1796-29 May 1841 (11 vols.) [1841-59 not located]
> Department of Interior (Patent Office):   28 April 1859-5 July 1870 (3 vols.)
> Smithsonian Institution: 18 June 1852-1856 (unbound, in envelope 326); 29 February 1856-6 October 1858 (1 vol.) [1846-52 not located]
> Library of Congress: 1 December 1848-29 November 1852 (1 vol.); 31 March 1865-3 December 1886 (1 vol.) [1846-48 and 1853-58 not located]

None of these is indexed, and the titles in each are arranged according to the order in which they were received; usually only the year of publication of each book is given, along with the precise day of receipt (but the Smithsonian sheets from 1852 to 1856 list only the year of publication, and its ledger from 1856 to 1858 adds only the date the entry was made). Finding a particular title can be a time-consuming process, but if one already knows the district court deposit date, the search is facilitated. Melville's *Mardi*, which was deposited at the district court on 17 April 1849, was received by the Library of Congress on 19 April; his *Battle Pieces*, deposited at the court on 17 August 1866, was received by the Library on 20 August. These facts suggest that bibliographers should always check the district court record books for deposit dates (at least after 1846) even when deposit copies are still on the shelves of the Library of Congress, for those deposit copies may not contain the earliest deposit dates. The district court deposit copies, forwarded to the State Department and then to the Department of the Interior,[22] should have been turned over to the Library of Congress in 1870; but copies in the Library may also be those originally sent to the Library in the periods 1846-59 and 1865-70. Two copies presently in the Library may contain different dates, one of them the date of receipt by the clerk of the district court, the other the date of receipt by the Library. So the deposit ledgers of the various agencies are helpful in understanding these discrepancies and in locating the earliest deposit dates.

In addition, these registers of deposits received may be supplemented by certain published lists, for three attempts[23] were made

22. Deposit copies do still turn up, on rare occasions, in the libraries of these two Departments, but the bulk of them was transferred according to law. On 1 March 1967 I checked the stacks of the State Department library and could find no deposit copies; the small size of the American literature section indicates in itself that the deposits, in this area at least, are no longer there, and the few pre-1870

volumes of literary interest show no signs of being deposit copies. The printed *Catalogue of the Library of the Department of State* (1825; rev., 1830) undoubtedly includes books received as copyright deposits, but the sources of the books are not indicated.

23. These three works have been discussed by Joseph W. Rogers in *U.S. National*

during this period to provide a published account of copyright deposits:

William Elliot, *A List of Patents Granted by the United States* (1822, 1823, 1824, 1825, 1826). [Supplements in these volumes list all deposits received by the State Department between 1796 and May 1825. The supplements in the 1822 volume cover 1796-1821, and the succeeding volumes contain annual supplements through May 1825.]

Charles Coffin Jewett, "Copy-right Publications," in the *Fifth Annual Report of the Board of Regents of the Smithsonian Institution for the Year 1850* (1851), pp. 146-325. [Two supplements list all deposits received by the Smithsonian between 10 August 1846 and the end of 1850 (the first, pp. 146-236, covers 1846-49; the second, pp. 236-325, covers 1850).]

Catalogue of the Library of Congress (1849, 1861); *Supplement* (1846-60). [The *Supplements* from 1846 through 1856 contain separate sections listing copyright deposits; the four *Supplements* for 1857 through 1860, as well as the two complete catalogues of 1849 and 1861, do not list deposits separately but mark them with a double dagger wherever they occur in the main alphabet. Together these *Catalogues* and *Supplements* entirely cover the Library's first period as a depository, from 10 August 1846 to 5 February 1859.]

These published listings fill some of the gaps in the manuscript ledgers presently located: the Jewett list, covering 1846-50, reduces the gap in the Smithsonian ledgers to a year and a half, since those now available begin with 18 June 1852; and the Library of Congress *Catalogues* and *Supplements* completely fill the gaps in the located Library ledgers. The Library lists and the Jewett list for 1846-49 are the least useful of the published lists, however, because they do not give the dates of receipt, as both the Elliot and the 1850 Jewett lists do. The places to look for deposit dates, therefore, other than in copies of the works themselves, may be summarized in this way:

1796-1831: in the registers of copyrights received by the State Department (or, through May 1825, in Elliot's published version of these registers).

1831-1841: in the district court record books for certain states; and in the registers of copyrights received by the State Department.

1841-1846: in the district court record books for certain states.

1846-1859: in the district court record books for certain states; in Jewett's list of Smithsonian deposits and the handwritten registers of copyrights received by the Smithsonian; in the registers of copyrights received by the Library of Congress, supplemented (without dates) by the Library's published *Catalogues* and *Supplements*.

1859-1865: in the district court record books for certain states; and in the registers of copyrights received by the Department of Interior (Patent Office).

1865-1870: in the district court record books for certain states; in the registers of copyrights received by the Department of Interior (Patent Office); and in the registers of copyrights received by the Library of Congress.

Bibliography and the Copyright Law (1960), pp. 11-29; and more briefly by Elizabeth K. Dunne and Rogers in "The Catalog of Copyright Entries," *Copyright Law Revision Studies*, No. 21 (1960), pp. 55-57.

It is clear from this summary that the most important tool for research into deposit dates after 1831 is the long series of record books kept by the clerks of the district courts. Because they record the dates of original title entries (the "copyright" dates) and because they cover the entire period 1790-1870, they are obviously basic to any kind of copyright research for these years and constitute what is usually thought of as the "copyright records" before 1870. The copyright law of 1870 required that all the previous district court records be sent to the Library of Congress in Washington, and when those ledgers (dating from 1790) were added to the "duplicates" already there (dating from 1831), the result was a collection of over 600 large volumes and many additional bundles of loose papers (containing approximately 150,000 entries from 35 states). All this material (including 92 boxes of title pages) is now shelved in the Rare Book Division of the Library of Congress and constitutes a largely untapped bibliographical storehouse. Any bibliographer of nineteenth-century American literature should be intimately acquainted with the characteristics and contents of these records.

The difficulties in using these volumes are a result of the lack of centralization in the administration of the copyright law before 1870, since complete uniformity would be impossible in records kept at scattered offices throughout the country. Most of the books contain only one entry per page, consisting of the formal phraseology required by law, the date of entry, and the exact wording of the title page; they may be entirely handwritten (as the majority were in the earlier years), or they may be made up of printed forms, filled in as required. But they vary in several respects: some include the actual printed title pages, and others give only a handwritten title; some have single-volume or multi-volume indexes (by title or proprietor or both), and others are not indexed at all; some report the dates of deposit of published copies (after 1831), and others do not. In addition, not all the district courts sent their records to Washington, or some were lost en route, for the "duplicates" sometimes cover periods missing from the original volumes, and gaps still remain. (An inventory of these records is provided below in Appendix A.) [24]

24. Roberts gives a similar list (*PBSA*, XXXI, 97-101), but I have felt it useful to go over this ground again because additional material has turned up since the time of his article. In particular, an examination of the miscellaneous bundles furnishes a surprising amount of new material — for example, Roberts's list gives 1845 as the beginning date for the Savannah records, but one of the miscellaneous binders contains the entries for 1800-44. Anyone wishing to refer to the unbound sheets may have a difficult time locating certain of the years as specified in Appendix A because the sheets for a particular district may turn up among the loose papers in several dif-

One of the problems in using these records in their present form is that a bibliographer can never be sure that he has checked all the relevant material. This uncertainty is compounded by the inevitable feeling that the missing records may still exist in the states, not having been sent to Washington in 1870. A check of other repositories reveals that certain pre-1870 copyright records (for nine states and the District of Columbia) do indeed exist outside the Library of Congress — in the National Archives, the Seattle Federal Records Center, the South Carolina Library, the Texas State Library, the Virginia Historical Society, and the federal archives in Kentucky, Maryland, Ohio, and Rhode Island. (A list of these materials is given in Appendix B.)[25] Out of this entire group of pre-1870 records, only a few have been published or transcribed. Most of these publications consist of small groups of entries taken from the record books in the Rare Book Division of the Library of Congress; but four of them — for Kentucky, Rhode Island, Texas, and Virginia (Richmond, 1864-65) — draw on the material housed in other locations, and one (for Richmond, 1790-1844) preserves the content of a record apparently now lost.[26] (See Appendix C.)

The collection of copyright materials in the Rare Book Division of the Library of Congress also contains, in addition to the district court record books, the boxes of title pages, and the registers of deposits received by the four Washington deposit libraries, a small number of miscellaneous papers: (1) *Letters* — Library of Congress correspondence, both incoming and outgoing, on copyright matters (particularly acknowledgments of deposit copies) between 1852 and 1855, a letter

---

ferent binders or envelopes. Since the records are not catalogued, it is impossible to make specific citations; some of the binders and envelopes have a pencilled number on the outside but no identification numbers for the sheets enclosed; others have no identification of any sort.

25. See also Richard S. MacCarteney, "Some Records Dealing with or Related to Copyright, Located Outside the Copyright Office" [1963], a 10-page memorandum in the Copyright Office Library.

26. The Richmond entries for 1790-1844 were transcribed by James H. Whitty from a group of title pages then in the possession of Judge Robert W. Hughes. Whitty's transcription appeared in 1911 in two sep-

arate editions (see Appendix C); therefore, since it was set in type twice, there may be some discrepancies between the two editions (though a spot check has revealed none), and both should always be consulted. H. R. McIlwaine, then the State Librarian, prefaced Whitty's work by saying, "Undoubtedly, some errors have crept in in the copy made by Mr. Whitty, and the absence of the original records has made it impossible to correct them." For discussion of a Confederate copyright trial, see Thomas Conn Bryan, "General William J. Hardee and Confederate Publication Rights," *Journal of Southern History*, XII (1946), 263-74. Entry dates for individual authors have sometimes been cited, as Charles Feinberg does for Whitman in *PBSA*, LII (1958), 91.

book of the Commissioner of Patents, 1859-70, and some miscellaneous letters in Box 308; (2) *Ledgers* — a volume marked "Maps Labels &c." (1849-58), with some music entries (1849-51) at the beginning; a volume listing the returns made by the clerks of the district courts for the Department of State, 1853-68; three unidentified indexes; and a volume containing (pp. 3-6) a list of the district court records received by the Library of Congress in 1870 (the list which formed the basis for the one Roberts published in 1939). This last ledger is of further interest because it contains (pp. 540 ff.) lists of books by twenty-six selected authors,[27] with the date of title entry for each work and often a reference to the volume and page of the original entry in the district court record books; it was evidently an attempt by someone in the Library of Congress, after the records were received in 1870, to furnish a convenient index for the most popular authors. Even though it omits a number of books, it can still serve today as a short-cut to locating the original title entries for these authors.

The fact that such a list, incomplete as it is, can be useful suggests the complex nature of the records for this period. Until all the pre-1870 entries are published, with a complete index, no bibliographer can feel certain that he has found everything relevant to his subject. If the desired information happens to be in one of the indexed bound volumes, it can be found easily; but if it involves a district for which there is no index or for which the only surviving records are scattered loose sheets, the search can be time-consuming. The lack of centralization in the administration of the copyright law before 1870 made complicated records inevitable, and a consolidated index is essential if they are to be an effective tool for research. But the bibliographer who understands the changing provisions of the law which produced those records can find in them, even as they stand, a large amount of information not elsewhere available about the publications of many of the major writers of nineteenth-century America.

III.   1870-1909

The copyright act of 8 July 1870 (16 Stat. 212), the first general revision of the copyright law after 1831, is a landmark in American copyright legislation. Its significance lies not in any altered conception

---

27. The authors covered are T. B. Aldrich, J. S. C. Abbott, Boucicault, G. W. Curtis, Emerson, Stephen Foster, G. S. Hilliard, Hawthorne, Holmes, J. G. Holland, Irving, J. H. Ingraham, Longfellow, Lowell, D. G. Mitchell, Motley, Parkman, E. S. Phelps, H. B. Stowe, J. G. Saxe, E. C. Stedman, Bayard Taylor, Whittier, A. D. T. Whitney, and Susan and Anna Warner; also there was a page for the Webster dictionaries and one for the ninth edition of the *Encyclopaedia Britannica*.

of the nature of copyright but rather in a change of administrative procedure, for all copyright business was henceforth to be centralized in the Library of Congress. Title pages and copies were to be deposited with the Librarian of Congress, not the clerks of the district courts; and all previous records, from the various district court offices and the Department of the Interior, were to be transferred to the Library of Congress. It is impossible to overemphasize the importance of this centralization: the year 1870 is a dividing line which marks the end of fragmentary and inconsistent copyright records and the beginning of records that are complete and uniform.

The basic requirements of the law were scarcely changed: the term of copyright was 28 years, renewable (within six months of expiration) for 14 more; the newspaper notice was for renewal only (to be printed for a period of four weeks, within two months of the date of renewal); a printed title page was to be deposited before publication; and two copies of the work were to be deposited after publication (mailed within ten days of publication). The bibliographer can use these dates to establish the approximate time of publication in exactly the same way as for the preceding period, since the publication date should fall, according to law, in the interval between the date of title entry and the date of copy deposit. This interval will generally be smaller (and its usefulness for determining a publication date presumably greater) than for the preceding period, since the deposit copies were supposed to be put in the mails no later than ten days after publication. From the bibliographer's point of view, therefore, the records for the period 1870-1909 are different from the earlier ones not in the kind of information they provide but in their completeness and greater ease of reference.

Between 1870 and 1909 the various amendments and revisions of the copyright law generally had no effect on these provisions for title entry and deposit of copies. The revision of 1 December 1873 (Rev. Stat. 957) retained them as they were set forth in 1870; and the only change in them effected by the act of 3 March 1891 (26 Stat. 1106) was that copies be deposited (or placed in the mails for deposit) no later than the day of publication, thus reducing still further the legal interval between the date of title entry (which could be as late as the day of publication) and the date of copy deposit. Books were not always deposited as promptly as the law stipulated, however, and the act of 3 March 1893 (27 Stat. 743) specifically granted copyright privileges to works, however belatedly deposited, that had been received before 1 March 1893. Of the other amendments, those of interest to bibliographers are the act of 18 June 1874 (18 Stat. 78), which transferred one category of printed material — commercial prints and labels — to the jurisdiction of the Patent Office; the act of 19 February 1897 (29 Stat. 545), which established the position of Register of Copyrights; and the act of 7 January 1904 (33 Stat. 4), which described a special two-year copyright privilege for foreign works that were to be exhibited at the Louisiana Purchase Exposition.

The act of 1891, if it made only one small change in the deposit regulations, was nevertheless of the greatest importance in other ways, for it inaugurated certain features which have caused American copyright records to be of particular usefulness to bibliographers. For one thing, it provided for the granting of copyright protection to citizens of foreign countries, if those countries gave reciprocal protection to United States citizens — of bibliographical significance because of the publication data about foreign works which were thus inserted into the American record books. Along with this provision came the much-discussed requirement of American manufacture (the books deposited for copyright "shall be printed from type set within the limits of the United States, or from plates made therefrom"). Although the name and address of the printer were not entered into the record before 1909, it was this manufacturing clause which resulted, after 1909, in a large quantity of information of bibliographical interest. Finally, the 1891 act required the Librarian of Congress to report title entries of all works received to the Secretary of the Treasury, who in turn was "directed to prepare and print, at intervals of not more than a week, catalogues of such title-entries for distribution to the collectors of customs of the United States and to the postmasters of all post-offices receiving foreign mails." While the purpose of this provision was to facilitate the enforcement of the manufacturing clause, the more important result was the complete publication of the American copyright record (for deposited works) from 1891 forward.

The record materials which have accumulated since 1870 under the centralized administration of the copyright acts (with a few exceptions) are now housed in the Copyright Office of the Library of Congress and are available there for reference. After 1891 the published records make a great deal of the copyright data readily accessible without a trip to the Copyright Office, but even for that period there is no substitute for the indexes and other resources to be found in the Office itself. For the years between 1870 and 1891, since there are no published records except for drama, most copyright information can be obtained only in the Copyright Office records; bibliographers dealing with this period should search these records in person whenever possible, even though the Office provides, for a fee, an excellent search service. To the uninitiated, the stacks and indexes at the Copyright Office may appear bewildering, but they actually are not difficult to use and are far less confusing than the pre-1870 records. For the period 1870-1909, the bibliographer should know in particular about three kinds of materials: the record books, the card indexes, and the published records.

(1) *Record Books.* For the entire period 1870-1909, the record books are uniform in the kind of information they contain: the date of entry of a printed title page on or before the day of publication, a transcription of the title page, the name of the claimant, and the date of deposit of two copies on or after the day of publication. As before 1870, some titles were entered for works never finally published, and copies were sometimes not deposited for works that did get published. In a few cases the copies were received, but the date was not posted onto the record (in some of these instances the Library still has one or both of the copies bearing the copyright deposit date or stamp) ; in other cases the copies probably meant for deposit were received by the Library but not by the proper office and were therefore not recorded. The only changes in the record books during this period are changes of form, not of content. Between 1870 and the end of 1897, when application for copyright was made by letter, the record books have four printed forms per page for the insertion of information regarding four applications; each entry has a serial number, and there is a separate sequence of numbers for each year, with an attached letter designating the year, from A through C^2. From 1898 through 30 June 1909 application was made on printed forms; and on 2 January 1900 a new series of volume numbers began, since in that year copyrights were divided into separate classes (for books, periodicals, and so on), with separate series of volumes for each class (but the volumes for drama, Class D, did not begin until 1901). For book applications there was now only one printed form per page (500 per volume), and the new sequence of serial numbers was prefixed with "XXc" (for "twentieth century"), running continuously from year to year; by 30 June 1909, volume 488 and XXc 243564 had been reached. For Class D (drama), the number of record books by 1909 amounted to seventeen (with four applications per page). Record books before 1900 are at present housed in closed stacks and may be requested by searchers; those from 1900 onward are shelved in open stacks.

Assignments and renewals were handled in different ways. All assignments were entered in a separate series of record books, beginning on 25 July 1870 and continuing in an unbroken sequence throughout this period. These records are an unparalleled source of information, especially for bibliographers interested in the history of publishing firms, because it is possible here to trace mass transfers of titles and establish the line of succession of various firms. Renewals, on the other hand, do not form a separate category of records. Since the law required that copyright proprietors comply with the same requirements for renewal as for original registration, renewal entries are like the entries for original copyright and occur in the same sequence of serial numbers.[28] The deposit requirement of two copies also applied to renewals, and some publishers, such as Houghton Mifflin, occasionally printed cancel title pages bearing the renewal date for insertion into the deposit copies; this production of bibliographical oddities was by no means widespread, however, and was certainly not required.[29]

The changes of form in the records are of little practical significance to most searchers, who will come to the books with a list of particular serial numbers they wish to look up. The important point is that these volumes constitute the basic copyright record for the period and that they are complete. The printed title pages and the applications for these years are stored in the Federal Records Center in Alexandria, Virginia; although they are available upon request, the completeness of the record books makes them of less significance than in the pre-1870 period, for there are no gaps in the records which they might fill and no information in them not included in the record books.[30] The deposit copies themselves no longer form a part of the

28. Renewal entries can occasionally be located for works originally registered in a district court office for which the records no longer survive; on the other hand, one sometimes finds renewal entries quite close to the original entries, in cases where a proprietor (who had printed a copyright notice in his book) had failed to register or deposit his work until the time for renewal had almost arrived.

29. Kenneth E. Carpenter, in "Copyriyht Renewal Deposit Copies," *PBSA*, LX (1966), 473-74, discusses seventeen such items produced by Houghton Mifflin (for books by William Dean Howells) and cites further examples of this practice by Henry Holt & Co. The regulations for renewing copyrights at this time are thoroughly explained by Thorvald Solberg in *Directions for Securing Copyrights* (Copyright Office Bulletin No. 2, 1899).

30. Students of typography would be interested in the title-page collection, but less so than in the preceding period, partly because it contains few examples of early printing in various localities and partly because commercial prints and labels form no part of it after 1874. Between 1874 and 1940, commercial prints and labels were deposited and registered in the Patent Office; in 1940 the registration of these works was transferred to the Copyright Office, where it has since remained. When the transfer of function was made in 1940, a transfer of the complete Patent Office files of these materials, including the deposit copies, also took place. Following the transfer, the Copyright Office continued the Patent Office's methods of handling such materials until April 1947. The Copyright Office continues to preserve these files; consequently a substantially complete collection of original deposit copies of commer-

records of the Copyright Office, but many of them are on the shelves of the Library of Congress, and others may turn up almost anywhere. The 1909 act empowered the Librarian to make requisitions for the second deposit copies of any previously deposited works which he considered desirable for the Library to possess in more than one copy; in this way both deposit copies of certain works by a number of major writers have been preserved.

(2) *Card Indexes.* Because the entries were made in the record books in chronological order, some kind of index is essential for locating particular items with any efficiency. The years from 1870 through 1897 are covered in one card index, affectionately referred to by the Copyright Office staff as "Old High." This index consists of handwritten cards and slips of various sizes: some cards contain many entries, others only one; some were written at the time of registration, others much later in an attempt to improve the index; some are Library of Congress requisitions for second deposit copies, and others have printed strips mounted on them. Entries are under copyright claimants, authors, and titles. The claimant entries are supposed to be complete, but the entries for authors and titles were not consistently made throughout the period. As a result, the index is not entirely complete; in addition, cards may sometimes be misfiled, since they are not held in the drawers by rods and since there have been various attempts to improve the index by adding cards. Despite its deficiencies, the index generally provides the desired reference, especially if one knows the name of the copyright claimant and can check under it. These cards do not normally give the dates of registration and deposit but only the registration serial numbers, which can then be looked up in the proper record book. The card for Herman Melville, for example, lists beside the title *Clarel* simply the number G7090; one then locates this entry in the 1876 (G) record books and finds that the title for *Clarel* was entered on 8 June 1876 and the copies deposited the following day — information not available, incidentally, in the deposit copy in the Library of Congress.

The remainder of this pre-1909 period is included in a card index which covers the years 1898 to 1937. This index is divided according to the various classes of copyrightable material, but the index for books is usually the only one bibliographers will need to consult. The book index for 1898-1937 consists of two alphabets, one of claimants and

cial prints and labels registered in the Patent Office or Copyright Office between 1874 and April 1947 is available. Since 1947 this material has been subject to the disposal routines mentioned below.

one of authors (and some titles). For the years 1898 to 1909 the claimant entries are on printed "proprietor cards" which record the dates of title entry and copy deposit, transcribed from the original applications, along with the registration serial number. It is not necessary, therefore, to consult the record books themselves during this period, except for the purpose of double-checking (and the information in the record books is also a transcription from the applications). The author index is complete for copyrighted books represented by Library of Congress cards, but its completeness in regard to the authors of works not so represented cannot be assumed. Claimant indexes are always the basic and most thorough ones for copyright purposes, a fact which bibliographers, generally accustomed to searching by authors, should keep in mind (and this very fact is what makes copyright records so useful for research into the history of publishing firms). To sum up, the entire 1870-1909 period is adequately (if not quite completely) indexed in two basic card catalogues: a claimant-author-title catalogue covering 1870-97, and separate claimant and author files covering 1898-1937. Books falling near the dividing line (that is, in 1897 or 1898) could conceivably turn up in either index and should be checked in both.[31]

(3) *Published Records.* The copyright records for this period have been partially published, in two publications, one covering all entries for drama and the other containing deposits of all classes beginning with 1891. Both publications should be basic tools for all bibliographers of American literature, but they are not as well known as they deserve to be. While they are not a substitute for the materials in the Copyright Office, they are in some respects easier to use, and they at least provide the basic data about many works from this period without the trouble of a trip to the Copyright Office or correspondence with a member of the search staff.

In 1916 and 1918 the basic tool for copyright research in the field of drama during this period was published:

Dramatic Compositions Copyrighted in the United States, 1870 to 1916. 2 vols. Washington: Government Printing Office, 1916-18.

The arrangement is by title, with an index of authors and claimants; for each title are given the dates of registration and deposit and the registration serial number. It is important to note that this work lists

---

31. A useful survey of the card indexes is Dorothy Arbaugh's "The Card Files Comprising the Copyright Card Catalog," a mimeographed paper (dated January 1962) for the use of the Copyright Office staff.

all titles of dramatic compositions registered, not just those that were eventually deposited, and consequently is a substitute for the record books as far as drama is concerned. The thoroughness of the work and its indexing also make it a more dependable guide than the sometimes erratic card catalogue for 1870-97. Anyone seeking copyright information about drama during this period should consult this work first and will probably have no reason to check further in the Copyright Office itself.[32]

The other work, authorized by the act of 1891, is surely one of the most important bibliographical tools in existence, at least in the form which it eventually assumed. The 1891 law provided for the publication of all title entries for which copyright had been completed by the deposit of two copies, and the *Catalogue* thus started has continued to the present, with one change of title:

> *Catalogue of Title-Entries.* 47 vols. 1 July 1891-June 1906.
> *Catalogue of Copyright Entries.* July 1906-

During its early years the *Catalogue* was not an effective instrument for research, both because it did not contain sufficient information and because the information it did contain was not conveniently arranged. For the first 227 weekly issues, the titles were listed in one column and the names of proprietors in another, but in no particular order and with no index and no specific dates (although one could conclude that the works had been deposited during the week covered by the issue). These early issues do serve as a record of all works deposited, but they can be used for reference only by running through the entire list of titles. Gradual improvements occurred in the following stages:

No. 228 (11-16 Nov. 1895): books arranged alphabetically by proprietors in each issue.
No. 323 (6-11 Sept. 1897): specific date of receipt of deposit copies recorded.
No. 327 (4- 9 Oct. 1897): books arranged alphabetically by authors, followed by index of proprietors.
No. 340 (3- 8 Jan. 1898): registration number as well as deposit date recorded.
No. 348 (28 Feb.-5 March 1898): specific date of title entry as well as registration number and deposit date recorded.

32. The deposit of unpublished typescripts of dramatic works, one of the most interesting features of the period after 1901, is commented on below in connection with deposit copies. One other cumulative catalogue of copyrights has been published for this period, Howard Lamarr Walls's *Motion Pictures 1894-1912* (1953), but its subject matter limits its usefulness for bibliographers. Three more volumes have appeared, covering 1912-39 (1951), 1940-49 (1953), and 1950-59 (1960). One use of *Dramatic Compositions* is illustrated by Paul T. Nolan's "Alabama Drama, 1870-1916: A Check List," *Alabama Review*, XVIII (1965), 65-72; and by Edgar Heyl's "Plays by Marylanders, 1870-1916," beginning in *Maryland Historical Magazine*, LXII (1967), 438-47.

It was not until nearly seven years after the start of the *Catalogue*, with No. 348, that the entries contained the information one would expect — registration number and dates of registration and deposit — and even then the only indexes were weekly. With volume 26, for the first three months of 1901, appeared the first index for an entire volume (giving the names of proprietors and authors and the titles of plays and periodicals). When the new series began on 1 July 1906, the *Catalogue* was divided into four parts, for books, periodicals, musical compositions, and fine arts. The successive sections of Part I (Books) were cumulated into semi-annual volumes with excellent author-proprietor indexes, so that from the middle of 1906 there are only two indexes per year (for books).

The *Catalogue* is essentially a twentieth-century tool, therefore, because its indexing is inadequate before 1901 and the information it contains not sufficiently detailed before 1898. For the years before 1901 the card indexes in the Copyright Office are much simpler to use than the published *Catalogue*, although before 1898 they may be somewhat less dependable; even after 1901 they may be more convenient for certain kinds of research, since they bring together entries from large spans of years and obviate the drudgery of going through numerous annual indexes. And for information about titles which were never deposited, the Copyright Office card indexes are essential, since this information is not included in the published catalogues (except the cumulated one for drama). The *Catalogue* does not supersede the Copyright Office files, but it does make possible extensive copyright research, at least from 1901, without recourse to those files.[33]

This period may be divided into three segments, according to the kind of indexing available (aside from the published index for drama):

1870-1891: card index, not entirely complete, containing references to record books.
1891-1897: card index, not entirely complete, containing references to record books; complete published record of deposits, lacking important information and index.
1898 and after: complete card indexes, duplicating information in record books; complete published record of deposits, with basic copyright data and indexes (cumulated volume-indexes beginning in 1901).

These changes are evidence of the fact that the period was a transitional one, in which the newly centralized Copyright Office was gradually developing the efficient techniques which would characterize it in the twentieth century.

33. For a further description of the *Catalogue of Copyright Entries* during this period, see Rogers, pp. 47-70; Dunne and Rogers, pp. 57-58.

IV. 1909 — present

Whereas the 1870 law represented a change in administrative procedure rather than in definition of the term of copyright, the act of 4 March 1909 (35 Stat. 1075, effective 1 July 1909) made fundamental changes in the procedures required for securing copyright, the first such changes since the original law of 1790. From 1790 to 1909, the term of copyright had dated from the deposit of a printed title page prior to publication, in order to protect a work during the course of publication; the 1909 statute eliminated entirely the necessity of registering title pages in advance of publication and designated the term of copyright to begin with the date of publication. (The term was still 28 years, but renewable for another 28, rather than 14 — without inserting a notice in a newspaper.) Henceforth the "copyright date," by legal definition, was to be synonymous with the publication date; and as a result bibliographers have at their fingertips, in the copyright records and the published *Catalogue*, the official publication dates of all copyrighted works for which registration has been made in the United States since the middle of 1909. To be sure, the actual publication date (or date of release to the general public) may in some cases be different; but deciding what constitutes an "actual publication date" is an arbitrary matter anyway, and the fact remains that the date in the copyright records is the one reported by the publisher (or author, or whoever was the copyright proprietor) as the publication date (and therefore the date on which he wished his copyright protection to begin). So, in the post-1909 records, there are no title registration dates and no collection of title pages, but only the dates of publication — and, as before, the dates of deposit of two copies, important for the bibliographer as proof that physical copies of the books existed on those dates.

The other most important feature of the 1909 law, from the bibliographer's point of view, has to do with the requirement of American manufacture, initiated in the 1891 act. Whatever its merits (or demerits) from other points of view, it became a great boon to the bibliographer in 1909, for the new statute required, as part of each application for copyright, an affidavit giving the names of the printer and binder and the date of the completion of printing. Since the printer was not obliged, as in England, to place his name on the printed matter itself,[34] this manufacturing information for American books is

34. For a discussion of the bibliographical usefulness of this British regulation, instituted in the act of 12 July 1799, see William B. Todd, "London Printers' Imprints, 1800-1840," *Library*, 5th ser., XXI (1966), 46-59 (with an appendix, pp. 60-62, by Paul Morgan, on provincial imprints, 1799-1869).

usually not elsewhere available, unless the printers' or publishers' files exist and are accessible. Descriptive bibliographers generally record the names of printers when they are provided in a colophon or printer's imprint and sometimes go to elaborate lengths to consult publishers' records. While there is no doubt that publishers' records are valuable (in furnishing facts about sizes and dates of impressions, for example), the point here is that those records are not the most convenient source for the names of the printers and binders of all copyrighted American books after 1909. The copyright records, open to public inspection, contain them, and often in addition the officially sworn date of the completion of printing for each book (but the presence of this date depends on the form of affidavit in use at any given time). One can easily discover that Henry James's *Gabrielle de Bergerac* was printed and bound by J. J. Little and Ives (completed on 12 November 1918) and that Sherwood Anderson's *Winesburg, Ohio* was printed by the Van Rees Press (finished 28 April 1919) and bound by the H. Wolff Estate — information not provided in the standard bibliographies of these authors.

One other provision of the 1909 law will serve to suggest the bibliographical usefulness of twentieth-century American copyright records even for students of English and foreign literatures. Sections 21 and 22 of the act provided for "ad interim copyrights" of works in the English language first published abroad. Depositing one copy of any such work in the Copyright Office within thirty days after publication would secure to the author (or proprietor) an American copyright to last for a period of thirty days; if during that period the author (or proprietor) arranged to have an American edition of the work printed and deposited, he could secure a regular 28-year copyright. Although the lengths of these periods have varied in the years since 1909, the application for an ad interim copyright has always necessitated a statement of the original date of publication of the foreign edition; the ad interim record books (which begin with 16 July 1909) therefore contain the English publication dates of a great many works of twentieth-century English literature. The works entered naturally represent only an erratic sampling of all English books published (amounting to something more than 29,000 entries by the end of 1945); but for the works included, this source of information about publication dates is frequently a more convenient and accessible one than any which exists in England. From the ad interim record books one can learn that Norman Douglas's *South Wind* was published on 5 June 1917 and D. H. Lawrence's *Pansies* on 4 July 1929, facts which are not recorded in the standard Soho bibliographies of these authors. A similar statutory arrangement in regard to works first published abroad in a language other than English had existed from 3 March 1905 (33 Stat. 1000) until 1 July 1909, when a provision went into effect, as a part of the general revision of that year, specifying that a full-term copyright could be secured for works of foreign origin in a language other than English whether or not such works or translations of them were manufactured in the United States; the resulting "Class A Foreign" record books contain the original publication dates for a large number of foreign works (over 3000 entries between 22 March 1905 and 1 July 1909, and over 85,000 more by 1945).

The copyright records for the post-1909 period are not strikingly different from those for the preceding period, except for the kinds of dates they include, but certain points about them are worth noting:

(1) *Record Books and Card Indexes.* During the years from 1870 to 1909 both the record books and the card indexes contained information that had been transcribed from the claimants' original applications (which were then tied into bundles and are now stored in Alexandria). From 1909 on, the actual application forms were brought together to constitute these records, first as the card index and later as the record books. On 1 July 1909 a card form of application was introduced; each card (for books), when folded once, was the size of the proprietor cards which had been filed since 1898 and could be interfiled with them. These card applications continued in use for books until early March 1948 (for other classes the date varied between 1946 and 1948); they were filed alphabetically by claimants through 6 November 1937 and by registration number thereafter. Thus between 1909 and 1937 the claimant cards in the card index are the actual applications, not transcriptions of them; between 1937 and 1946 the card index may be used to supply registration numbers, which are then checked in the separate application card file. The publication date, the date of receipt of deposit copies, the date of the affidavit of American manufacture, and the XXc registration number are visible on each card without unfolding it; to learn the names of the printer and binder and the date of completion of printing, one must unfold the card (which of course necessitates pulling the rod from the card drawer). The record books for this period are correspondingly less useful, for three reasons: the entries in them are arranged by registration number, so that one must first ascertain the number in the card index anyway (or in the published catalogue); they contain no information not on the application cards (except, in some cases, that taken from the book itself); they are transcriptions, not original documents. From 1909 to late 1940 (for books) these

record books contain handwritten entries on large pages; from October 1940 through early 1946 they consist of carbon copies of the certificates of copyright registration sent to claimants.

Beginning with May 1946 (for books) a new page form of application came into use (although the old card form continued to be accepted until early 1948, so that original applications for book registrations during these years may be found either in the application card file or in the record books). The new applications were simply bound together in registration number sequence (thus in the approximate order of receipt) to constitute the record books. But after May 1946 the relationship between the record books and the card indexes is reversed, since the cards for the card indexes again became transcriptions of information contained in both the works and the applications. One must use the card index (or published catalogues) to ascertain the registration number; but if one wishes to check the application itself, one must look up the number in the record books. Though all the record books are official documents and the published catalogues prima facie evidence of the information they contain (by the law of 1909), historical scholars are always alert to the possibility of mistranscription and will find 1946 and 1948 the most important dates to remember in using the records, since that two-year period forms the dividing line between original applications as cards in drawers and original applications as pages in record books.[35]

In addition to these basic indexes and record books, the Copyright Office contains a number of other files and records, some of which should be mentioned for their potential bibliographical usefulness. (a) The assignment card indexes, with entries under assignor, assignee, and (from 1927) titles, serve as a guide to the series of assignment record books; both the indexes and the record books provide information about the transfer of titles and are an essential source for publishing history and for author-bibliographies that take later editions and impressions into account. (b) The renewal record books (a separate series after 1909, with their own XXc numbers) are indexed (by claimants, authors, and some titles) in separate card indexes between 1909 and 1937, and in the general card indexes thereafter; whenever a renewal card for a given book is not present, one should check the original registration number in the appropriate record book, for the

35. The fact that the card catalogues are arranged in sequences of years which overlap these changes of form causes no difficulty when one is using them. There are the separate claimant and author files for each class between 1898 and 1937, followed by general claimant-author-title alphabets for 1938-45, for 1946-54, and for 1955 to the present. These indexes are described by Dorothy Arbaugh in the mimeographed paper cited above.

renewal registration numbers have consistently (since 1898) been posted at the point of original entry in the record books. (c) The pseudonym card file consists of twenty drawers covering the years before 1938 and forms a useful supplement to the record of pseudonyms in the Library of Congress catalogues of printed cards. (d) The "bio-biblio" file of material in vertical folders contains many bibliographical lists which have resulted from previous searches and dust jackets which include biographical information. (e) The correspondence and remitter indexes contain summaries of copyright correspondence and names of the actual remitters of copyright fees; these indexes, not open to public inspection, contain little of bibliographical significance but could occasionally furnish details for biographical studies of authors or publishers. Correspondence directly relating to completed registrations is, however, available for public inspection and copying if the request identifies the work either by registration number or in sufficient detail to allow the registration to be found.

(2) *Deposit Copies.* Because of limitations of space, the Copyright Office in the twentieth century has employed the policy of keeping deposits only for a limited time (normally three or five years) and then transferring them to the Library of Congress for disposal, with the result that there is no complete set of copyright deposits in existence. The only exceptions are certain categories of unpublished materials, particularly music and drama; since unpublished typescripts of plays are accepted for copyright, it was felt that all the typescripts should be retained. These plays, dating from the creation of Class D in 1901, are now housed in the Library of Congress (where they form a largely untapped body of material for the history of American drama and a substantially neglected source of unpublished titles for bibliographies of American dramatists).[36] The general policy of disposing of deposits was changed in 1959, however, and from that date forward single copies of deposits were to be kept by the Copyright Office as a permanent record (except those that were transferred to the stacks of the Library of Congress). The only deposits, therefore, which are available for examination in the Copyright Office are those from 1959 to the present (they can be recalled, upon request, from storage in Alexandria).

The point of interest in this situation is the whereabouts of the earlier deposit copies. Even though a deposit copy may not always

---

36. The titles of these works through 1916 are of course included in *Dramatic* *Compositions Copyrighted . . . 1870 to 1916* (1916-18), discussed above.

represent the earliest form of a book in every respect, it is an interesting bibliographical object simply by virtue of its being an official copy of record. Since the Copyright Office stamps deposits as they are received, deposit copies can almost always be identified; the question is where to look for them. The Library of Congress has on its shelves most of the kinds of deposits with which bibliographers are concerned: in some cases it has both deposit copies, in other cases only one copy, and sometimes neither one. Copies which the Library does not choose for its permanent collections are available to other governmental libraries and to other institutions, according to a general scheme of priorities established by the Exchange and Gift Division of the Library. The result is that copyright deposit copies can turn up anywhere, even in secondhand book stores. Obviously such scattered copies are of no value for general reference because one would never know where to look for any particular work. But large or regular transfers of deposits are worth knowing about, since the receiving institutions became in effect small depository libraries for given fields or periods. One of the most important of these arrangements provided for the transfer to the library of Brown University, over a period of nearly thirty years, one of the two deposit copies of every volume of American poetry and drama copyrighted during that time; between 1909 and 1922 alone this transfer amounted to 15,556 volumes.[37] The excellent collection of poetry at Brown thus gains an added dimension as a place where deposit copies can often be found, and it is possible that deposit copies exist there for works no longer present (at least in the form of the original deposit copy) on the shelves of the Library of Congress. Other similar arrangements have prevailed at various periods — certain scientific books were regularly sent to the John Crerar Library, children's books to the University of Illinois, and foreign books to the District of Columbia Public Library; during the first world war many thousands of deposits went to the War Service Library; and in 1930 over 1300 city directories were transferred to the American Antiquarian Society. A complete list of such mass transfers would perhaps be impossible to compile, but bibliographers should at least realize that the Library of Congress is not the only place where deposit copies may be examined.[38]

37. *Report of the Librarian of Congress for . . . 1923*, p. 151. See also the 1930 *Report*, p. 61, and the 1936 *Report*, p. 29; general comments about transfers occur in most of the annual *Reports*.

38. The most thorough discussion of American deposits, with a brief survey of foreign systems, is Elizabeth K. Dunne, "Deposit of Copyrighted Works," *Copyright Law Revision Studies*, No. 20 (1960), pp. 1-40.

(3) *Published Records.* The published *Catalogue of Copyright Entries* (spelled "Catalog" as of 1934) extends throughout this period, and the entire copyright record is available in any good research library. Before 1909 part of the record was excluded from the printed version, since only deposited works were included and not registered titles for which no completed works had been deposited. After 1909, when title registrations were abolished, the record of deposits became at the same time a complete record of copyright entries. It is as simple a matter to look up the publication date, deposit date, or affidavit date for any work copyrighted in the United States since 1909 in the *CCE* as it is to look the work up in the *CBI* or the Library of Congress catalogue or any other standard source; why the *CCE* is used so infrequently by bibliographers is a mystery. From a bibliographical point of view, the only weakness of the *CCE* is that it does not include the names of the printer and binder of each book, nor the date of completion of printing; this information can be found only in the applications filed in the Copyright Office. Everything else is found in the printed record, including the claimant's name and the registration number.

In the second series of *CCE* (1906-46), bibliographers will generally need to refer only to Part I (Books) and Part II (Periodicals). Beginning with 1909, however, pamphlet and dramatic material was designated as Group 2 of Part I, listed in separate volumes with separate annual indexes; since some works could be classified either way, it is generally wise to check the annual indexes for both Groups 1 and 2. A Group 3, for dramatic compositions, was added in 1928; again, published drama could appear in Groups 1, 2, or 3, and all are worth checking. The annual indexes, by claimant and author, are excellent through 1938, but from 1939 through 1946 they contain only the names of authors, not of claimants, making the *CCE* less useful during this period for work on publishing history.[39] The war also necessitated certain abbreviations in the scope of each entry: from 1938 through 1945 some of the information available on Library of Congress cards (such as the total pagination) was eliminated, and from 1940 through 1946 the publication date alone (and not the deposit date) was given. In the third series of *CCE* (1947-   ), bibliographers may be interested in Parts 1A (Books), 1B (Pamphlets and Contributions to Periodicals), 2 (Periodicals), 3/4 (Drama and Works for Oral Delivery), and possibly 5 (Music) and 6 (Maps and

39. The use of the claimant entries in the indexes to *CCE* for research into the history of individual publishing firms is further discussed in G. T. Tanselle, "The Historiography of American Literary Publishing," *SB*, XVIII (1965), esp. pp. 17-21.

Atlases). The entries for Part 1 are now arranged alphabetically by authors, obviating an author index, but with two alphabets per year (since there are two semi-annual issues); not until 1951 and 1952 are there claimant indexes, and beginning with 1953 there are cross references, in the same alphabet, from the names of claimants. Only publication dates and registration numbers are given in the third series. Despite a few deficiencies between 1938 and 1951, the *CCE* is a remarkable work of reference that can serve many bibliographical uses for which it was not originally designed.[40] Bibliographers working in the period after 1909 will find that the American copyright records contain more information of the kind they are seeking than has been preserved in the official records of any other nation.

V. *A Note on English Copyright Records*

England was the first country to institute statutory copyright, in the famous Statute of Anne of 4 April 1710 (8 Anne, ch. 19). Before that time the closest counterpart to copyright was the control which the Stationers' Company exercised over the printing of books by its members, but this regulation did not resemble the modern concept of copyright, since it was designed as protection for the printer rather than the author. Nevertheless, the requirement of entering titles in an official register maintained by the Stationers' Company has resulted in records of great bibliographical value similar to those which are produced by a system of copyright registration. The registers covering the years 1554 through 1708 were transcribed and published many years ago[41] and are well known to bibliographers, as are the published records of the Court of the Stationers' Company between 1576 and 1640.[42] The bibliographical importance of these materials has long been recognized, and extracts from them were published by J. P. Collier as early as 1853;[43] since that time several important biblio-

40. On the *CCE* for this period, see Rogers, pp. 71-96; Dunne and Rogers, pp. 58-72. On the legal status of *CCE* and other "records," see Benjamin W. Rudd, "Facts Needed for Registration Records" [1955], a 15-page memorandum in the Copyright Office Library. An essay which takes up the usefulness of both deposits and records is M. William Krasilovsky, "Observations on Public Domain," *Bulletin of the Copyright Society of the U.S.A.*, XIV (1966-67), 205-29.

41. Edward Arber, *A Transcript of the Register of the Company of Stationers of London, 1554-1640* (5 vols.; 1875-77); G. E. B. Eyre and C. R. Rivington, *A Transcript of the Registers of the Worshipful Company of Stationers from 1640-1708* (3 vols.; 1913-14).

42. W. W. Greg and E. Boswell, *Records of the Court of the Stationers' Company, 1576 to 1602 — from Register B* (1930); W. A. Jackson, *Records of the Court of the Stationers' Company, 1602 to 1640* (1957).

43. Collier, *Extracts from the Registers of the Stationers' Company from 1557 to 1587* (1853).

graphical publications relating to the period before 1710, by such scholars as Rollins, Greg, and McKenzie, have been based on records at Stationers' Hall.[44] Anyone interested in pursuing the complications of sixteenth- and seventeenth-century English copyright should acquaint himself with the papers available in Stationers' Hall, as listed in the *Library*, 4th ser., VI (1925-26), 349-57,[45] as well as with certain basic work in this area: Harry Ransom has recounted, in historical terms, the operation of English copyright before the act of 1710;[46] Leo Kirschbaum has described "The Stationers' Company in Operation" and has helped to clarify the difficult relationship of registration to both license and copyright;[47] and W. W. Greg has taken up in detail the bibliographical implications of the records of the Stationers' Company.[48] Although problems remain to be solved, it is clear that the essential researches of these and a few other scholars[49] have provided a

44. Hyder E. Rollins, *An Analytical Index to the Ballad-Entries (1557-1709) in the Registers of the Company of Stationers of London* (1924); W. W. Greg, *The Decrees and Ordinances of the Stationers' Company, 1576-1602* (1928); Greg, *Licensers for the Press, &c to 1640* (1962); Greg (with C. P. Blagden and I. G. Philip), *A Companion to Arber* (1967); D. F. McKenzie, *Stationers' Company Apprentices, 1605-1640* (1961). See also such works as Philip Lee Phillips, "List of Books Relating to America in the Register of the London Company of Stationers, from 1562 to 1638," *Annual Report* of the American Historical Association for 1896 (1897), I, 1249-61; Fred S. Siebert, "Regulation of the Press in the Seventeenth Century: Excerpts from the Records of the Court of the Stationers' Company," *Journalism Quarterly*, XIII (1936), 381-93. Graham Pollard is editing *Liber A of the Stationers' Company* for the Bibliographical Society.

45. With an introductory note by A. W. Pollard, "The Stationers' Company Records," p. 348. The list covers materials through 1799.

46. Ransom, *The First Copyright Statute* (1956); a useful "Short Calendar of English Literary Property, 1476-1710" appears on pp. 119-34, and "Leading Cases before 1710" on pp. 135-36.

47. Kirschbaum, *Shakespeare and the Stationers* (1955), esp. pp. 25-86; "The Copyright of Elizabethan Plays," *Library*, 5th ser., XIV (1959), 231-50; "Author's Copyright in England before 1640," *PBSA*, XL (1946), 43-80.

48. Greg, *Some Aspects and Problems of London Publishing between 1550 and 1650* (1956); see esp. "The Stationers' Records," pp. 21-40, and "Entrance and Copyright," pp. 63-81.

49. E. M. Albright, *Dramatic Publication in England, 1580-1640* (1927); W. J. Couper, "Copyright in Scotland before 1709," *Records of the Glasgow Bibliographical Society*, IX (1931), 42-57; Graham Pollard, "The Company of Stationers before 1557," and "The Early Constitution of the Stationers' Company," *Library*, 4th ser., XVIII (1937-38), 1-38, 235-60; R. C. Bald, "Early Copyright Litigation and Its Bibliographical Interest," *PBSA*, XXXVI (1942), 81-96; Percy Simpson, "Literary Piracies in the Elizabethan Age," *Oxford Bibliographical Society Publications*, n.s. I (1947), 1-23; Giles E. Dawson, "Copyright of Plays in the Early Seventeenth Century," *English Institute Annual 1947* (1948), pp. 169-92; C. J. Sisson, "The Laws of Elizabethan Copyright: The Stationers' View," *Library*, 5th ser., XV (1960), 8-20; Cyprian Blagden, *The Stationers' Company: A History, 1403-1959* (1960).

fuller treatment, from a bibliographical and literary point of view, of this period than of any other in Anglo-American copyright history.

The act of 1710 is the principal dividing line in the story of English copyright: it provided for a copyright term of fourteen years, renewable for 14 more (but not clearly established as author's, rather than printer's, copyright until 1769 in *Millar* v. *Taylor*); it made prepublication title entry in the register of the Stationers' Company a statutory requirement; and it stipulated that nine deposit copies be furnished upon demand (for the Royal Library [later the British Museum], the university libraries at Oxford, Cambridge, Edinburgh, Glasgow, and St. Andrews, the Library of the King's and Marischal Colleges Aberdeen, Sion College London, and the library of the Faculty of Advocates in Edinburgh). Although the force of the Stationers' Company declined after the lapsing of the Printing (or Licensing) Act in 1695,[50] the stationers continued, even after the 1710 act, to turn copyright to their own advantage, through trade boycotts and court injunctions. Their contention that common-law copyright still obtained for any work after the expiration of its term of statutory protection was finally invalidated in the case of *Donaldson* v. *Becket* (1774), and a stream of cheap reprints followed.[51] The upshot of this situation for bibliographers in search of records is that the "Entry Books of Copies" at Stationers' Hall for the eighteenth century[52] (with a printed index 1710-73, a manuscript index thereafter) are even less full than those for the earlier years: stationers before 1774 considered their copyrights perpetual by common law; after 1798 (*Beckford* v. *Hood*) they saw that failure to register prevented only suits for the statutory penalties, not the more important suits for damages; and, in addition, they felt that by not registering they were not obligated to provide copies for the depository libraries, even though the Universities Copyright Act of 1775 (15 Geo. III, ch. 53) emphasized the requirement of prepublication registration and deposit. The records at Stationers' Hall from 1814 through 1841 have a slightly different

50. The period between this event and 1710 has been called the "years of confusion" by A. W. Pollard, in "Some Notes on the History of Copyright in England, 1662-1774," *Library*, 4th ser., III (1922-23), 97-114.

51. See John W. Draper, "Queen Anne's Act: A Note on English Copyright," *Modern Language Notes*, XXXVI (1921), 146-54; A. S. Collins, "Some Aspects of Copyright from 1700-1780," *Library*, 4th ser.,

VII (1926-27), 67-81; Ransom, pp. 94-117; Cyprian Blagden, "The Stationers' Company in the Eighteenth Century," *Guildhall Miscellany*, I, no. 10 (1959), pp. 36-53; F. C. Avis, "The First English Copyright Act," *Gutenberg Jahrbuch 1961*, pp. 182-84.

52. David Foxon is editing *The Stationers' Register, 1710-46* for the Bibliographical Society.

significance for bibliographers: because the 1814 amendment to the copyright law (54 Geo. III, ch. 156) required that entry be made within one month after publication (rather than before publication), only works actually published are listed during this time.

The next major revision of the copyright law, the act of 1842 (5 & 6 Vict., ch. 45), made the copyright term 42 years (or the life of the author plus seven years, whichever was longer), and it reenforced the requirement of registration at Stationers' Hall. The copyright registers and related documents which accumulated in the administration of this act, covering the period 1842-1923, are now in the Public Record Office, not Stationers' Hall. The entries in them fall far short of constituting a national bibliography, for understandably many publishers still did not bother with registration; it was not a condition of copyright, and, in case of a suit for infringement, it need be performed only before the actual court proceedings. But the records are worth checking, for American as well as English books, if one keeps in mind the fact that the entry may occur long after the date of publication. Indexes exist for the entire period, in seven segments, giving the date of entry and the date of publication for each work registered. The first five volumes, covering 1842-1907, have been published as the *Index of Entries* (1896-1907) and are available in many reference libraries; the remaining years, 1907-23, are covered in six unpublished manuscript volumes in the Public Record Office. All eleven are listed here with the index numbers assigned them by the Public Record Office:

    1842-1884 (literary): Ind 16908 (titles)
    1842-1884 (commercial): Ind 16915 (titles)
    1884-1897: Ind 16909 (titles, with author-publisher index)
    1897-1902: Ind 16910 (titles, with author-publisher index)
    1902-1907: Ind 16911 (titles, with author-publisher index)
    1907-1911: Ind 16912 (titles), 16913 (authors), 16914 (publishers)
    1911-1923: Ind 20293 (titles), 20294 (authors), 20295 (publishers)

These indexes furnish the same information that is available in the original registers; but if one wishes to check the original entries, the next step is to ask at the Assistant's desk in the Long Room for the typewritten *Guide to the Records of the Copyright Office* (classified as ff. 78), which indicates the dates covered by each of the registers (Ind 5791 through 5869).[53] It is also possible to send for the original copyright entry forms, stored at Ashridge (classified as Copyright 1/567

53. There is also a series of manuscript indexes of the registers: the first 28 volumes of registers (Ind 5791-5818), for example, are indexed by Ind 5996-6004. But the published indexes usually make it unnecessary to consult these manuscript volumes.

through 887, and designated by year in the *Guide*.) After 2 July 1883 copyright assignments are entered separately (Ind 5870-5872, indexed by Ind 6005-6007), as are certain foreign entries after 1854.[54] Other materials from this period in the Public Record Office, particularly papers relating to copyright suits, can furnish publication data of value to bibliographers. By checking the bills of complaint (in C.14) and the cause books (C.32) — as well as the depositions (C.24) and affidavits (C.31) at Ashridge — one can discover, for example, the publication dates of the Routledge piracies of Melville and Irving.

The act of 1911 (1 & 2 Geo. V, ch. 46), which made the term of copyright (for unpublished as well as published works) the lifetime of the author plus fifty years, abolished the statutory requirement for registration, although this requirement remained in force in some parts of the United Kingdom (e.g., Canada) through 1923. Voluntary registration was still possible, however, and entries made on this basis since 1 January 1924 are in registers at Stationers' Hall. But the new law retained a provision for deposit, emphasizing the split between registration and deposit which had prevailed throughout English copyright history. A sort of deposit system had existed as early as 1610 in an arrangement Thomas Bodley had made with the Stationers' Company, and the Printing Act of 1662 had required the deposit of three copies (for the Royal Library and the universities at Oxford and Cambridge). The list of nine copies established by the 1710 act was increased by two in 1801 (41 Geo. III, ch. 107), with the addition of Trinity College and the Society of the King's Inns, Dublin; then in 1836 (6 & 7 Will. IV, ch. 110) the four Scottish universities were removed from the list; and in 1842 (followed by the 1911 act) only six depository libraries were designated: the British Museum, Oxford, Cambridge, Trinity College Dublin, the Library of the Faculty of Advocates in Edinburgh (after 1925 the National Library of Scotland), and the National Library of Wales. The number of places to look for deposit copies thus varies with the period and, in addition, with the requirements of particular libraries, since copies were to be deposited upon request by the libraries. The necessity of depositing on demand, however, was not limited to registered books; after 1812 the interpretation of the law was that the deposit provision applied to

54. From 1847 to 1854 foreign entries are in the general registers (Ind 5794-5797) but indexed separately (Ind 6012-6015). From 1854 to 1891 there are separate foreign registers (to 1883, Ind 5876-5889, indexed by Ind 6016-6029; from 1883 to 1891 for books, Ind 5890-5894, indexed by Ind 6030-6034; from 1883 to 1890 for foreign assignments, Ind 5899, indexed by Ind 6039); and after 1891 the foreign entries are again in the general registers, except for foreign dramatic and musical entries, 1883-1912 (Ind 5873-5875, 5900-5901, indexed by Ind 6008-6011, 6040-6041).

all books published in England, whether or not they were entered at Stationers' Hall.[55] Libraries often mark the date of receipt in books; the British Museum began this practice in 1833 (the exact day from 1837 forward), stamping copyright deposit copies in blue and colonial copyright deposits in black.[56] Since dated deposit copies may exist for books which were never registered, both sources — official registers and depository libraries — should always be checked. English copyright records, at least after 1710, are not particularly complex and for much of the period are conveniently indexed in printed form; at the same time they are not especially full and represent an unpredictable sampling of the national literary output.

VI. *Some General Considerations*

Although copyright records are national documents, the operation of a national copyright law can at times produce records of interest to students of another country. Even when the records themselves do not contain information about the publication of foreign works, the international copyright situation is always a principal factor in publishing history. Whenever two countries employ the same language, authors in one country sometimes deliberately publish their works first in the other, in an effort to forestall unauthorized (or "pirated") editions. In regard to English-speaking countries, this situation existed between England and Ireland in the eighteenth century (since the English copyright law did not extend to Ireland until 1801) and between England and the United States in the nineteenth (since the American law did not include English works until 1891). Many famous English books of the nineteenth century were first published in America because, even though the works could not be copyrighted in the United States, the authors could at least gain something from the

55. 104 Eng. Rep. 1109. A convenient summary of English registration and deposit provisions is in Benjamin Kaplan, "The Registration of Copyright," *Copyright Law Revision Studies*, No. 17 (1960), pp. 1-9; a fuller study is S. A. Olevson's in *Copyright Law Symposium*, No. 10 (1959), pp. 1-74.

56. Red denoted purchased copies, and green or yellow indicated donations. These practices, as well as the deposit provisions and the use of deposit copies for bibliographical purposes, are summarized by James J. Fuld in *The Book of World-Famous Music* (1966), pp. 16-18. A survey of English deposit practices from the time of Bodley is Robert Partridge's "The History of the Copyright Privilege in England," *Library Association Record*, 3rd ser., II (1932), 41-48, 73-83, and *The History of the Legal Deposit of Books throughout the British Empire* (1938); see also J. C. T. Oates, "The Deposit of Books at Cambridge under the Licensing Acts, 1662-79, 1685-95," *Transactions of the Cambridge Bibliographical Society*, II (1957), 290-304; and Philip Ardagh, "St. Andrews University Library and the Copyright Acts," *Edinburgh Bibliographical Society Transactions*, III (1956), 179-211.

American market by selling advance sheets to an American publisher; many famous American books were first published in England because American authors could secure English copyrights during most of this period only if they published their works first in England or were residents of England.[57] A great deal of bibliographical and literary research has been directed toward this aspect of copyright history — from I. R. Brussel's *Anglo-American First Editions* (1935-36) to individual studies of the trans-Atlantic publication of Scott, Marryat, Cooper, Irving, Dickens, Tennyson, Longfellow, and Mark Twain,[58] among others. But copyright records are not involved, except when a country allows foreign works to be registered or deposited. American titles do appear in the nineteenth-century British records; but foreign titles are listed in the American records (under authority of the 1891 act) beginning at different times for different countries: copyright privileges were extended to some countries (e.g., France and England in 1891, Germany and Italy in 1892) by individual Presidential proclamations, to others (China, Hungary, Thailand) by bilateral treaties, and to still others through the Mexico City Convention (after 1908), the Buenos Aires Convention (after 1914), and the Universal Copyright Convention (after 1955).[59]

57. Since the English law was not specific about foreign works, the interpretation of the law by the courts varied throughout the century. Although British publishers were often willing to pay for advance sheets of American works (just as American publishers did for English books), the legal status of any copyright claim thus secured was not at all clear. The English law of 1838 granted copyright protection to foreign works only on a reciprocal basis, and, since the United States did not provide for copyright of English works, copyrighting an American work in England appeared to be technically impossible. Sir Frederick Pollock reaffirmed this view in *Boosey* v. *Purday* (5 June 1849), opening the way for the Routledge piracies of 1850. In 1854 prior publication was regarded as a means of securing English copyright only if the author was present in the United Kingdom at the time of publication (the reason for certain American authors' "Canadian copyrights" later in the century).

58. David A. Randall, "Waverley in America," *Colophon*, n.s. I (1935), 39-55;

Arno L. Bader, "Captain Marryat and the American Pirates," *Library*, 4th ser., XVI (1935), 327-36; Robert E. Spiller, "War with the Book Pirates," *Publishers' Weekly*, CXXXII (1937), 1736-38; Lawrence H. Houtchens, "Charles Dickens and International Copyright," *American Literature*, XIII (1941), 18-28; W. S. Tryon, "Nationalism and International Copyright: Tennyson and Longfellow in America," *American Literature*, XXIV (1952), 301-09; Herbert Feinstein, "Mark Twain and the Copyright Pirates," *Twainiana*, XXI (1962), 1-3 (May), 1-4 (July), 1-4 (Sept.), 3-4 (Nov.). See also George T. Goodspeed, "Wiley and Putnam's *Library of American Books*: Notes on International Copyright," *PBSA*, XLII (1948), 110-18; and Clarence Gohdes, *American Literature in Nineteenth-Century England* (1944).

59. See Arpad Bogsch, "Protection of Works of Foreign Origin," *Copyright Law Revision Studies*, No. 32 (1961), esp. pp. 1-8. The literature dealing with the international copyright relations between the United States and England is particularly large. Some of the relevant documents are

Despite the differences between the English and American copyright laws and records, the two countries have held the same basic traditions of copyright. The English concept of perpetual common-law copyright in unpublished work and limited statutory copyright in published work (implying that copyright is not a natural right of authorship), established in *Donaldson* v. *Becket* (1774), formed the tradition inherited by the United States and supported judicially in *Wheaton* v. *Peters* (1834). The philosophy of copyright which exists in any country naturally affects the kinds of records that accumulate, but not their thoroughness, for compulsory registration and deposit are not necessarily tied to statutory provisions for limited-term copyright. Furthermore, official copyright information not found elsewhere may be embodied in court decisions; thus the judicial process by which a national attitude toward copyright is evolved serves at the same time to record specific facts about the individual books which occasioned the decisions. Changes in the law or its interpretation may not always result in changes, from a practical point of view, in the bibliographer's approach to the records; but since the records are a creation of the law, shifts in policy will usually alter the theoretical significance of particular inclusions or omissions.

The most striking conceptual change, since the Statute of Anne, was effected in the 1911 British act by removing unpublished works from the realm of common law; a similar provision has been proposed in the copyright revision bill in the United States (H.R. 2512, S. 597, 90th Congress, 1st session).[60] If this bill is passed as presently written,

---

reprinted in " 'Bookaneering' or Fair Play?", *History Reference Bulletin*, X (1937), 113-28. See also Albert J. Clark, *The Movement for International Copyright in Nineteenth Century America* (1960); Gohdes, pp. 14-46; Harry G. Henn, "The Quest for International Copyright Protection [1837-1953]," *Cornell Law Quarterly*, XXXIX (1953), 43-73; Joseph V. Hoffman, "The Position of the United States in Relation to International Copyright Protection of Literary Works [1891-1953]," *University of Cincinnati Law Review*, XXII (1953), 415-61; and some of the works listed in the Mertz bibliography under such authors as A. L. Bader, A. J. Eaton, F. Freidel, H. A. Howell, M. M. Kampelman, J. A. Rawley, and T. Solberg.

60. The Celler copyright revision bill (introduced in July 1964) was preceded, in 1960 and 1961, by an important and scholarly series of 34 *Copyright Law Revision Studies*, prepared by various authorities for the Subcommittee on Patents, Trademarks, and Copyrights of the Committee on the Judiciary; most of the studies have historical sections, and a consolidated subject index for the whole series has been issued. A thorough explanation of the 1967 form of the bill is Report No. 83 (254 pp.) of the 90th Congress, 1st Session; Benjamin Kaplan discusses the bill in *An Unhurried View of Copyright* (1967), pp. 79-128; and Henry B. Cox takes up "The Impact of the Proposed Copyright Law upon Scholars and Custodians" in *American Archivist*, XXIX (1966), 217-27. See also the six parts of the *Copyright Law Revision Reports* (1961-65) and the three parts of *Hearings* (1966). The bill, passed by the House, is still pending in the Senate as of 1968.

all works, unpublished as well as published, come within the scope of statutory protection, and the term of copyright is the same for both — the life of the author plus fifty years. Bringing unpublished works under the statute and basing the term of protection on the author's lifetime will result in the recording of useful biographical information for literary historians. Both registration and deposit, however, are specifically stated not to be conditions of copyright protection. Registration is permissive rather than compulsory and may be performed at any time during the term of copyright (though it is a prerequisite for a suit for infringement); deposit of two copies within three months of publication is requested for the Library of Congress (enforceable upon the Register's demand). Under these regulations, most copyright holders will see the value of prompt registration and deposit, and the bibliographer will find no great change in the information he can derive from the records. At the same time, the view that copyright protection is not dependent upon any administrative technicalities of registration — with the consequent permissive nature of the registration procedure — means that the records which the bibliographer searches fall short, by legal definition, of constituting a list of all copyrighted works.

Bibliographers and literary historians do not often have the opportunity to document their research with sworn testimony, and evidence from copyright records therefore comes to the scholar with a kind of guarantee he rarely encounters. Information in the American *Catalogue of Copyright Entries*, for example, can be presented as prima facie evidence in a court of law; thus when a currently unlocated book is recorded as having been deposited on a particular day, the bibliographer, even though he may wish he personally could see the book, has the strongest assurance that it did actually exist at that time. No materials except official documents can carry such authority, and for this reason copyright records are a uniquely important source for the bibliographer. The English and American records, as described here, vary from period to period in their completeness, but it is evident that copyright registration has been carried out more punctiliously and in greater detail in the United States than in England and that the American records, especially after 1870, constitute an unparalleled storehouse of bibliographical facts. The Copyright Office of the Library of Congress should be familiar territory to every bibliographer; as a center for bibliographical research into American books (and many foreign ones after 1891), there is no other place equal to it.[61]

61. For a description, see "The Copyright Office" in the *Report of the Librarian of* *Congress for . . . 1901*, pp. 278-91; William D. Johnston, *History of the Library of*

The convenience of using the English and American copyright records has been greatly increased by the publication of substantial portions of them. Even when published indexes do not carry the official sanction which the *Catalogue of Copyright Entries* does, they serve a useful purpose. It is to be hoped, therefore, that the remaining sections of these records can be published, either as official governmental projects or as separate volumes prepared by individual scholars. For English copyright, the Bibliographical Society has undertaken to publish part of the remaining records, beginning with David Foxon's edition of the *Register* for 1710-46; for the rest of the period before 1842 and after 1907, at least the kind of index which has been published to cover the years from 1842 through 1907 should be made generally available. As for the American records, the two unpublished segments present different problems. The record books from 1870 to 1891, which are complete and orderly, offer little difficulty; the essential facts in each entry could be transcribed and indexed (perhaps in a form similar to *Dramatic Compositions*) , and the resulting volumes could be issued *seriatim*. But for the district court records, from 1790 to 1870, all.the surviving documents (including the title pages) should be thoroughly indexed on cards before any volumes are published, since the nature and physical arrangement of these materials are such that information relevant to one period and state can turn up at a number of places. The published entries could then be arranged chronologically by states, with one master-index, or else the master-index itself could be constructed to contain the information from the entries: the most important requirement is that all titles registered in any given period, regardless of the state in which the registration took place, eventually be brought together in one alphabet. Such projects, though expensive and time-consuming, are justifiable and desirable. The publication of these entries would facilitate and stimulate bibliographical and historical research into the Anglo-American cultural heritage; it would also insure the preservation of the most detailed official record ever produced of a nation's literary and artistic product.

Congress (1904), esp. pp. 439-50; David C. Mearns, *The Story Up to Now* (1947) , esp. pp. 90-94; and Barbara A. Ringer, "No Place for Poetic License: The Copyright Office at LC," *Library Journal*, XC (1965) , 2958-63.

Appendix

UNITED STATES DISTRICT COURT COPYRIGHT
RECORDS, 1790-1870

A. *Records in the Library of Congress*

The following inventory of the records now located in the Rare Book Division of the Library of Congress has been prepared as an aid to bibliographers who wish to check the copyright facts about a particular book but have no idea what sort of record exists for the period and district involved. Dates given by month or day below refer to the original entry books; those given only by years are the "duplicates" (often submitted in yearly batches), which may consist of full copies of the original entries, or of abbreviated lists, or of both. Records of copyright assignments, when kept in separate volumes from the title entries, are indicated by "A." The approximate size of each record is suggested by the number of volumes, but considerable quantities of material remain as unbound sheets (indicated by "u"). For the original volumes the presence (+) or absence (—) of three characteristics is recorded: whether they usually contain copy-deposit dates after 1831 (D) in addition to title-entry dates; whether they occasionally have printed title pages and labels pasted in (T); and whether they are indexed (I) by names of proprietors and/or authors (n) or by titles (t). The "duplicates" usually lack all three of these features, and exceptions may occasionally be found in the original volumes to the general attributes assigned them here:

Alabama (Mobile): 1837, 1839, 1858-59 (u).
Alabama (Montgomery): 1850-51, 1855, 1857-58 (u).
Arkansas: 1837-70 (u).
California: 23 July 1851-9 July 1870 (2 vols; —D, +T, —I); 1865-66 (u). A 12 Sept. 1854-19 July 1870.
Colorado: 14 Oct. 1864-6 May 1870 (1 vol; —D, +T, —I).
Connecticut: 10 Sept. 1804-9 July 1870 (4 vols; —D, +T, +In); 1831-53 (3 vols + u). A 29 March 1837-2 Sept. 1868 (1 vol).
Delaware: 1849-54, 1855-56, 1865 (u).
District of Columbia: 16 April 1829 (u), 8 Aug. 1845-6 July 1870 (2 vols; +D, +T, +In); 1818-45, 1848-53, 1855, 1858-64, 1866-67, 1869-70 (u).
Georgia (Atlanta): 23 Feb. 1849-20 June 1870 (1 vol; —D, +T, —I).
Georgia (Savannah): 30 Dec. 1800-10 July 1870 (4 vols + u; —D, +T, —I); 1856-59 (u).
Illinois (Chicago): 24 Aug. 1821-7 July 1870 (7 vols; +D, +T, +In); 1861-63, 1865-69 (u).
Illinois (Springfield): 9 July 1855-12 July 1870 (1 vol; +D, —T, +In); 1864-69 (u).
Indiana: Oct. 1822-24 June 1870 (3 vols; +D, —T, +In); 1853-60, 1866-67 (u).
Iowa: 20 May 1868-6 July 1870 (1 vol; —D, +T, —I).
Kansas: 1865-69 (u).
Kentucky: 22 Nov. 1860-8 July 1870 (1 vol; —D, +T, +Int); 1807-45, 1849-55, 1857-70 (u).
Louisiana: 14 Nov. 1833 (u), 25 March 1835, 17 Nov. 1851-23 Sept. 1856, 13 Aug. 1863-17 June 1870 (3 vols; +D, +T, —I); 1832, 1838-44 (u).
Maine: 14 Aug. 1790-1 July 1870 (2 vols; +D, —T, +In); 1792, 1819-28, 1832-55, 1857-69 (2 vols + u).
Maryland: 24 Feb. 1831-5 July 1870 (6 vols; +D, —T, +In); 1831-55, 1867-69 (2 vols + u).
Massachusetts: 10 July 1790-18 June 1870 (45 vols; +D, —T, +In except Feb. 1804-July 1806, April 1814-1825, 1829-30); 1831-70 (13 vols + u). A 1834-70 (4 vols).
Michigan (Detroit): 5 May 1824-9 July 1870 (5 vols; +D, +T, —I); 1833-70 (5 vols + u).
Michigan (Grand Rapids): 23 Sept. 1863-18 June 1870 (2 vols; —D, +T, —I); 1863-66 (u).
Minnesota: 20 July 1858-4 June 1870 (2 vols; +D, +T, +In after 24 Sept. 1866); 1858-62 (u).

A System of Color Identification for Bibliographical Description

THE INTRODUCTION OF PUBLISHERS' CLOTH IN THE 1820's WAS an unfortunate day for bibliographers, since the description of bindings has turned out to be perhaps the most troublesome aspect of the description of nineteenth- and twentieth-century books. Other parts of the description, which generally apply to earlier books as well, have become by now reasonably standardized. The bindings on earlier books, since they are products distinct from the process of publication, are not ordinarily the concern of the descriptive bibliographer; and specialists in the history of bookbinding have developed a vocabulary for dealing with them.[1] Even publishers' "bindings" (or casings), of course, are not bibliographical objects, strictly speaking, since they are not part of the letterpress. However, aside from the fact that binding variants can sometimes help to determine the priority of an issue,[2] the cloth is part of the dress in which an author's words are presented to the public, and its appearance therefore deserves to be recorded by the historian of such matters, the descriptive bibliographer.

To frame in words an adequate description of a cloth binding requires essentially some kind of notation of the texture, or "grain," of the cloth and some indication of its color. The first of these problems, though by no means solved, has received a great deal more attention than the second and is much nearer solution. Michael Sadleir, in his

---

1. Occasionally a bibliographer describing pre-nineteenth-century books will include information on bindings, especially if he is describing the particular copies in a given collection; see, for example, Allan Stevenson's discussion in his introduction to the eighteenth-century volume of the *Hunt Botanical Catalogue*, II (1961), clxxxiii-clxxxvi.

2. Cf. Fredson Bowers, "Purposes of Descriptive Bibliography, with Some Remarks on Methods," *Library*, 5th ser., VIII (1953), 4. Bowers further points out that identifying binding states may aid in detecting concealed impressions. His general discussion of the description of publishers' cloth is in *Principles of Bibliographical Description* (1949), pp. 446-450.

pioneering *Trollope: A Bibliography* (1928), used such terms as "silk-grained" or "morocco-grained" to describe binding cloth, a gain in precision over "grained cloth" or simply "cloth," if one could visualize what the words implied; and two years later, in *The Evolution of Publishers' Binding Styles, 1770-1900*, he furnished photographs of four common cloth grains (facing p. 46). Then John Carter, the other pioneer historian of edition binding, made the next step forward in *Binding Variants in English Publishing, 1820-1900* (1932), with his preliminary section on "Terminology of Grains and Designs" (pp. xvi-xviii). Here he supplied a plate illustrating twelve grains and provided a table of equivalences between descriptive terms like Sadleir's and the letter designations in use by Winterbottom's, the principal supplier of book cloth.

This table suggests the inevitable dichotomy in the verbal presentation of visual data: one may either use a precise, technical term, which often has little immediate meaning for the uninitiated reader, or else a more readily visualized term, which often is less exact and which breaks down when fine discriminations are needed. Carter declared his preference for the Sadleir terms — that is, "diaper" instead of "H" cloth, "sand-grain" instead of "C", and so on — but not all bibliographers have agreed with him. The two most important recent sources for photographic identifications of cloth grains represent these two approaches. Sadleir, at the end of the first volume of his great catalogue, *XIX Century Fiction* (1951), includes four plates showing twenty-four grains and giving them descriptive names; Jacob Blanck, at the front of each volume of the *Bibliography of American Literature* (1955-   ), illustrates twenty-eight grains, assigning them the letter symbols used in the trade.[3] Either of these sets of photographs provides a basis for standardization of nomenclature, if followed scrupulously by bibliographers. Perhaps a chart should be issued making these standards more readily accessible, and perhaps bibliographers should, for precision, use both terms — such as "bold-ribbed (T) cloth."[4]

When one turns to the other basic ingredient of the description of cloth, the indication of color, one is surprised to find that practically no attention has been given to the matter. In the *Bibliography of*

3. In some cases, if the finish is no longer being produced, "arbitrary symbols" have been assigned (I, xxxi). All the symbols are of course arbitrary, but some of the combinations are meaningful, given the original symbol: thus HT combines the characteristics of H ("diaper") and T ("ribbed").

4. This double system of nomenclature, combining a readily understood term with a more precise technical one, is parallel to the method recommended later in this article for the designation of color.

American Literature, for example, the careful specification of cloth grains is in sharp contrast to this comment about color: "No attempt has been made to give other than a brief statement regarding color, and commonly accepted designations are used; variations in tone are recorded" (I, xxxiii).[5] One does not expect bibliographers who strive for precision in most respects to emphasize the casualness of their approach to color, as in these remarks:

> . . . where colour is concerned, we have hesitated to accept such British exoticisms as "Auricula Purple" and "Cossack Green" and have quite simply described the colours as they appeared to us in broad daylight. *Rust red, olive brown, salmon pink* may not stand all tests, but they function adequately for such readers as are not wholly colour-blind. When we encountered variant bindings of the same basic colour, but with differences in shading, we on occasion appealed for help to the sex which daily distinguishes colour-variations in clothing, jewellery and household goods.[6]

One is not surprised, however, given the subjective nature of color descriptions produced in this casual way, to find that any two bibliographers in the past, treating the same book, have been likely to come up with two different designations of the cloth color. Thus T. J. Wise, in his Browning bibliography (1897), describes the wrappers of *Pippa Passes* (1841) as "yellow" (p. 7), though he explains that they are sometimes "pale cream" or "light brown"; the Broughton-Northup-Pearsall bibliography (1953), on the other hand, calls these wrappers "light apple-green" (p. 4). Similarly, J. W. Robertson (1934) sees the covers of Poe's *Al Aaraaf, Tamerlane, and Minor Poems* (1829) as "purple" (p. 38), while for Heartman-Canny (1943) they are "grey-blue" (p. 23). Sometimes the difference is a matter of emphasis, as when Duval (1939) designates the cloth of Aldous Huxley's *On the Margin* (1923) "blue-green" (p. 28) and Muir-van Thal (1927) finds it "greenish-blue" (p. 20); or when McDonald (1925) considers D. H. Lawrence's *The Widowing of Mrs. Holroyd* (1914) to be "red" (p. 32) and *The Prussian Officer* (1914) to be "dark blue" (p. 35), while Roberts (1963) finds them, conversely, "dark red" (p. 24) and "blue" (p. 25). Even the relative proportions are not constant, for Hogan (1936) labels Edwin Arlington Robinson's *The Man Against the Sky* (1916) and *Merlin* (1917) equally as "maroon" (pp. 11-12), while

5. Jacob Blanck, in "A Calendar of Bibliographical Difficulties," *PBSA*, XLIX (1955), 1-18, reported that he had considered, for use in the BAL descriptions, both Robert Ridgway's color chart and the spectrophotometer, but he rejected both and in the end had his own eyes examined (pp. 4-6).

6 Leon Edel and Dan H. Laurence, *A Bibliography of Henry James* (1958; rev. 1961), pp. 18-19.

Beebe and Bulkley (1931) say that the first is "dark maroon" and the second plain "maroon" (pp. 14-15). For Currie (1932), Booth Tarkington's *In the Arena* (1905) is "dark olive" (p. 53), but for Russo and Sullivan (1949) it is "sage-green" (p. 14); for Williams and Starrett (1948), Stephen Crane's *The Red Badge of Courage* (1895) is "tan" (p. 18), but for H. F. West (in the Dartmouth catalogue, 1948) it is "yellow" (p. 5); for Parker (1948), Joyce's *Dubliners* (1914) is "plum" (p. 22), but for Slocum and Cahoon (1953) it is "dark red" (p. 12); both Stewart (1959) and Livingston (1927) agree that Kipling's *The Seven Seas* (1896) is "red" (pp. 136, 160), but for Martindell (1923) it is "maroon" (p. 53); for Sadleir (volume 12 of the Constable edition, 1923), Melville's *Typee* (1846) is "fawn" (p. 341) and *Mardi* (1849) is "dark green" (p. 348), but for Minnigerode (1922) the first is "yellow" (p. 102) and the second "dark brown" (p. 135).

Such a list could be extended indefinitely, but the process would be pointless, since confusion of this kind is to be expected when color names are chosen on the basis of personal preference, without recourse to any set of standards. There have been only a few signs in recent years that bibliographers are beginning to be concerned about the problem. John Carter, in his *ABC for Book-Collectors* (1952), understated the case when he said, "There has never been much precision or uniformity in describing the colours of cloth"; but he went on to make a specific suggestion: "until we all agree to use the official *Dictionary of Colour Standards*, this imprecision will no doubt persist" (p. 55). The following year Patrick Cahill, in *The English First Editions of Hilaire Belloc*, adopted standard 381c of the British Standards Institution, *Colours for Ready Mixed Paints* (1948; 3rd impression, 1951), and thus described his bindings with such terms as "dove-grey" or "deep buff" or "pale-crimson." Then in 1956 Raymond Toole Stott took up Carter's recommendation in his bibliography of Somerset Maugham and used one of the British Colour Council's publications — the *Dictionary of Colours for Interior Decoration* (1949). Though it may seem strange to read of "hay" or "biscuit" endpapers, the experiment was, as Stott recognized, "at least a step on the way to the systematized description of colours of binding cloth" (p. 8). And it was undoubtedly more efficient and precise than the method used by Frederick T. Bason in his earlier (1931) Maugham bibliography: the binding of *Of Human Bondage* (1915), labeled "petrol blue" by Stott

(p. 35), had been described by Bason as "dark sea-green cloth (a more distinct green than *The Casuarina Tree*)" (p. 33).[7]

These worthy efforts, however, did not convert other bibliographers from their subjective ways. Anthony Rota, reviewing Keynes' bibliography of Siegfried Sassoon (1962), remarked that "Sir Geoffrey's treatment of colours again points the need for the adoption of a common standard for defining binding shades"; and he quoted Keynes' description of *The Old Hunstman* (1917) as "drab or grey-blue" (with its ambiguous *or*, since the two colors do not seem synonymous) and of *The Daffodil Murderer* (1913) as "orange" (when to Rota's eyes it is yellow).[8] That this kind of confusion has not prodded bibliographers long before now to attack the problem of color designation is remarkable. On the other hand, this neglect can perhaps partly be explained by the fact that significant nineteenth-century binding variants generally do not depend on color differences alone; books were frequently issued in several colors simultaneously, and later bindings often involved a different cloth texture as well as color.[9] But in the twentieth century color variants may be more meaningful, since the simultaneous issue of multiple colors has not been customary. In any event, there should be a precise method for describing the color of a given binding whether or not the priority of an issue depends on its specification. No bibliographer would estimate the dimensions of a leaf without using a ruler; in the same way no bibliographer should make his own subjective estimate of a color without turning to a color chart, which ought to be an equally essential part of his equipment. The point is self-evident; there should be general agreement, in the words of the reviewer of Cahill's bibliography, that "it would be a great relief to all concerned if *some* standard scale could be adopted."[10]

The question then becomes the determination of the particular system best suited to the requirements of bibliographical description. And this decision is not to be lightly made; for any kind of standard, to serve its purpose, must be capable of wide acceptance and future

7. Another bibliography which uses a comparative method for gaining greater precision in its careful attention to color is R. L. Purdy's of Hardy (1954): after *The Return of the Native* is described as "brown," the secondary binding can be called "a slightly redder shade of brown" (p. 24).

8. *Library*, 5th ser., XVIII (1963), 243-245. Rota also refers to the Cahill and Stott bibliographies and remarks that B. J. Kirkpatrick's bibliography of Virginia Woolf (1957) employs terms for nine shades of green, without referring the reader to any chart or standard.

9. Cf. Carter, *Binding Variants in English Publishing*, p. 82.

10. *TLS*, 23 January 1953, p. 64.

applicability. At the outset, it should be possible to agree that any system selected for bibliography must meet certain minimum conditions: (1) it must contain color chips or samples which can be compared easily with book covers; (2) it must include a sufficient number of different colors to be compatible with the degree of precision required in making the kinds of distinctions between bindings that are likely to be significant under varying circumstances; (3) it must assign to each color a name (not simply a number or symbol), avoiding names so fanciful as to carry no immediate connotation; (4) it must be compact in physical form and easily portable, so that the bibliographer can conveniently carry the standards with him to the libraries in which he is working; (5) it must be inexpensive enough that it can become a standard tool in every bibliographer's possession (for it is too much to expect, even for an accepted standard, that each collection in which one works will have a copy at hand); (6) it must provide strong assurance of continued availability in the future. The number of color systems which have devised since the time of Isaac Newton is vast,[11] and it is necessary to know something about the currently available ones in order to make an intelligent choice.

I

The fundamental scientific method for measuring or specifying a particular color was established in 1931 by the Commission Internationale de l'Eclairage (CIE).[12] In this system, the proportions of red, green, and blue light required to match a given color are measured with a colorimeter, and the *chromaticity coordinates* of the color are thus established. The Commission also defined the characteristics of the *standard observer* and the properties of three *standard illuminants*. The usual notation of a color consists of two of the chromaticity coordinates plus the luminance value as established by spectrophotometer; these *tristimulus values* represent dominant wave length, purity, and reflectance. For example, the color of a tomato might be expressed as follows: $x = .622$; $y = .350$; $Y = 10.2\%$.[13] However basic this

11. A sketch of the history of color systems can be found, among other places, in Faber Birren, *Color Dimensions* (1934), pp. 4-9, and Aloys Maerz and M. Rea Paul, *Dictionary of Color* (2nd ed., 1950), pp. 137-144.

12. Also referred to as the ICI (International Commission on Illumination).

13. This system is discussed in all basic books on color and in many articles in the *Journal of the Optical Society of America* (*JOSA*). References to such discussions, both for the CIE system and for the other systems referred to below, will be found in the appended "Note on the Literature."

system is for scientific measurement, its disadvantages for bibliographical description are obvious. To demand that bibliographers acquire the necessary knowledge of optics would decimate their already small ranks; and the prospect of setting up shop, with delicate and expensive instruments, in each rare book room would eliminate the few that remained — if, indeed, the librarians had not already resigned. Not only is this method impractical for bibliographical purposes; it is undesirable. For the degree of accuracy attainable with a spectrophotometer is not required in a bibliographical description (and is thus wasteful of effort); in addition, it could often be actually misleading, since it would continually reveal variants, most of which (depending on the tolerances established by the manufacturer of the cloth or the dye) would have no significance to the bibliographer. To put the matter another way, if the bibliographer makes finer distinctions than those required by the adopted tolerances of the manufacturer, he may find himself recording as variants bindings which came from the same bolt of material or consecutive ones.[14] Furthermore, the notation in tristimulus terms is not one which could be readily comprehended by the readers of a descriptive bibliography.

If the CIE system is not feasible for bibliographical work, the next question to ask is whether or not another more appropriate system exists which is at the same time scientifically accurate and respectable. The alternative to spectrophotometric measurement is visual comparision with material standards, such as a set of color chips (sometimes known as the "ratio method"). Depending on the selection and production of the colors represented in any given set of material standards,

---

14. Of course, one might argue that if two bindings do in fact vary, even if they came from bolts which the manufacturer or the binder considered identical, the variations should be recorded, whether or not any question of priority is involved. And if the notion of a descriptive bibliographer's duties is extended to its ultimate limits, the argument cannot be denied. However, in practical terms it is impossible for a bibliographer to record every physical (and chemical) fact about a book; those facts must therefore be selected which have some meaning or usefulness to the persons for whom the information is being assembled. In the case of binding color, even if it were possible to determine that certain copies of a given impression of a book were bound earlier than other copies from the same bolt of material, the fact would be of no significance to the bibliographer — or the sane book-collector. On the other hand, if a slight variation in binding furnishes a clue to an interruption in the binding process that produced two binding "issues" (which may or may not coincide with two states or issues of the sheets), the fact may turn out to have bibliographical significance. The bibliographer will have to explore each case on an individual basis to determine his own tolerance limits — to determine, that is, the degree of precision beyond which he need not go in order to make meaningful discriminations.

this approach to color specification can be very precise and is scientifically valid. Although individual perception of a color is subjective, the act of matching a color with a carefully produced standard (which can then be referred to by other persons) reduces to a minimum the effects of subjectivity. And if the color chips have been chosen to represent particular CIE specifications that will result in a systematic sampling of color space, the whole process rests on a sound scientific foundation.[15] Aside from the danger of fading, an unavoidable problem in any material standard, the principal limitation of such systems is the necessity of interpolation. Since the eye can distinguish about ten million colors and since there are theoretically an infinite number of colors in three-dimensional color space, any color atlas or set of standards must represent a selection based on some principle of organization (hence the generic term "color-order systems"); therefore, depending on the number of colors selected and the accuracy of specification required, it is sometimes necessary to estimate the relation of a given color to two of the colors in the standard. This sort of interpolation, though it can be performed skillfully with practice, remains of course a subjective matter. A material color standard for bibliography should contain enough colors that, within the limits of accuracy desired, interpolation would seldom be required; on the other hand, it should not include so many colors that the process of matching becomes time-consuming and indecisive.

Color-order systems fall into three groups: (a) color-mixture (or additive) systems contain copies of colors established by mixing colored lights in particular proportions with a tristimulus colorimeter; (b) colorant-mixture (or subtractive) systems contain colors produced by mixing colorants (pigments, dyes) in various proportions; (c) color-appearance systems contain colors arrived at by means of psychological

15. Cf. W. D. Wright, *The Measurement of Colour* (3rd ed., 1964), p. 161, in which he describes how the CIE system "can, and should, be related to subjective descriptions of colour." An early statement of the ratio method is Lewis F. Richardson, "Quantitative Mental Estimates of Light and Colour," *British Journal of Psychology*, XX (1929), 27-37; see also *Tentative Recommended Practice for Visual Evaluation of Color Differences of Opaque Materials* (American Society for Testing and Materials, Method D1729-60T, 1960). Another approach, developed in the nineteenth century by James Clerk Maxwell, is to take a few basic material standards in the form of disks and spin them in various combinations until a match is attained; the proportions may be expressed in CIE terms, as Dorothy Nickerson explains in "Disk Colorimetry," *JOSA*, XXV (1935), 253-257. A disk-spinning motor and other equipment for disk colorimetry are available from the Munsell Color Company; but the process is too cumbersome and time-consuming to be appropriate for bibliographical purposes.

perceptions of color differences and spacing. Some systems, such as atlases printed by a screen-plate process, are intermediate, partaking of the characteristics of both the color- and colorant-mixture types.[16] The methods by which the colors are produced, however, will be of less concern to the bibliographer than the physical features and range of the resulting standards; and the three most promising systems are surveyed here with the needs of the bibliographer in mind:

(1) *The Munsell System* — In 1905 Albert H. Munsell, a Boston artist and teacher, published a little book called *A Color Notation*, which he later supplemented with a *Color Atlas* (1915). This notation, with the system which lies behind it, is perhaps the most widely used of the color-order systems. It is readily applicable to diverse fields, and scientists often convert color information to Munsell terms; it is the system described in the *Encyclopaedia Britannica's* current article on "Colour" (by A. C. Hardy) and officially recommended in 1942 by the American Standards Association, and it is particularly useful for educational purposes.[17] The notation for any color contains three terms, since the eye detects three characteristics of color — hue, brightness, and saturation (parallel to the CIE tristimulus values for dominant wave length, reflectance, and purity); in the Munsell system these qualities are referred to as *hue, value,* and *chroma.* With these three "dimensions," a color solid, representing color space, can be envisioned as an irregular sphere: the axis corresponds to the *value* scale, from black at the south pole to white at the north; perpendicular distances from this axis indicate *chroma,* from gray near the axis to the pure, fully saturated color at the surface of the sphere; and planes perpendicular to the equator, passing through the axis, represent *hue.*[18] Ten hue segments (made up of five basic hue names) are marked off around

16. See Donald R. Dohner and Carl E. Foss, "Color-Mixing Systems: Color vs. Colorant Mixture," *JOSA*, XXXII (1942), 702-708; Carl E. Foss, "Color-Order Systems," *Journal of the Society of Motion Picture Engineers*, LII (1949), 184-196; and Deane B. Judd and Günter Wyszecki, *Color in Business, Science, and Industry* (2nd ed., 1963), pp. 202ff.

17. Adrian Bernard Klein, in "The Munsell Colour System and the Need for a Standardisation of Colours," *Penrose's Annual*, XXIX (1927), 57-63, makes the point that no system which requires spectrophotometric equipment can be commonly accepted: "A yard-stick is not a fine micrometer, but it serves the practical purpose of measuring a piece of cloth accurately enough for ordinary use" (p. 59).

18. The solid would be irregularly shaped because the point of saturation for certain coloring materials at certain value levels is farther from the axis than for other materials. At the same time, the problem of the spacing of material standards is further complicated by the fact that equal perceptual differences in color do not correspond to equal distances in Euclidian space.

the circumference of the equator plane: red, yellow-red, yellow, green-yellow, green, blue-green, blue, purple-blue, purple, red-purple. The axis is divided into ten steps from black to white, and the number of possible chroma steps varies with the hue and value. Any color can then be referred to in a form such as "R 4/8," in which R signifies "red," 4 means the fourth step up from black toward white along the axis, and 8 indicates the eighth step perpendicular to the axis on that value level. R 4/12 would be more fully saturated and R 4/6 less; R 5/8 would be lighter and R 3/8 darker. Each hue segment may be subdivided into ten numbered planes so that, for example, 7R 4/8 would be a yellower red than 5R 4/8, and 3R 4/8 would be more purple. This system of notation is flexible enough to accommodate theoretically an infinite number of colors (by using decimals, as in 3.7RP 8.4/3.3) but is simple enough to be immediately comprehended (without reference to a table) by anyone acquainted with it.

Another advantage is that the Munsell Color Company of Baltimore publishes a wide variety of excellent color charts and atlases based on this system,[19] and the continued availability of the material is assured by the existence of a nonprofit Munsell Color Foundation, established in 1942.[20] The basic publication is the *Munsell Book of Color* (1929-43, and later editions), issued in both a library and a pocket edition; it is a loose-leaf book, each leaf representing a constant hue plane, with small chips illustrating the possible chroma steps on a number of value levels. The current (1960) pocket edition (7" x 4½") contains 1000 samples of a matte finish, each ⅝" x ½", and costs $90; it is more suitable for bibliographical work than the library edition, which is not so easily portable and contains glossy chips. However, the chips of the library edition are removable, which is a great advantage; and even the matte chips of the pocket edition are not so satisfactory as cloth samples would be for matching binding colors, and the price is another hindrance to the widespread adoption of either edition for bibliographical work. The same considerations would apply to the Opposite Hues Edition of 1950 ($100) and the Neighboring Hues Edition of the same year ($155), both with glossy chips. Of the many special Munsell charts (*Standards for Plastic*

19. A booklet describing all the materials available may be obtained from the Munsell Color Company, 2441 North Calvert Street, Baltimore 21218.

20. This foundation, in the words of the Company's literature, exists to "further the scientific and practical advancement of color knowledge, and in particular, knowledge relating to standardization, nomenclature and specification of color; and to promote the practical application of these results to color problems arising in science, art and industry."

Insulated Wire and Cable; Plant Tissue Color Charts; Soil Color Charts; Rock Color Charts for the Geological Society of America; *Value Scales for Judging Reflectance*), each representing a selection from the *Munsell Book of Color*, there is one which offers possibilities for bibliographical description — the *Color Fan* developed by Dorothy Nickerson for use in horticulture.[21] Convenient in size (7¾" x 1⅞"), each of the 40 hue leaves of the fan displays six or seven value steps, and the samples (1⅞" x ⅞") fill the entire width of each leaf, avoiding the usual disadvantage of nonremovable samples and greatly facilitating comparison with a binding; there are 262 colors shown and the price is $7.50. The limitation of the published *Fan* is that it illustrates only maximum chroma (other fans are planned to sample the sphere in other ways), so that one would be dealing only with colors on the surface of the sphere. All in all, the Munsell system has, from the bibliographer's point of view, the advantages of continued availability, wide acceptance and respect, an easily learned and comprehensive notation, excellently produced charts, convenient size, and (in the case of the Nickerson *Color Fan*) a feasible price; its only real limitation for the description of bindings is the discrepancy in surface texture between the color chips and cloth.

(2) *The Ostwald System* — The other most widely known system is the one developed by Wilhelm Ostwald, 1909 Nobel laureate in chemistry. His theories of color appeared in a long succession of works following *Die Farbenfibel* (1916) and were translated by J. Scott Taylor in 1931 as *Colour Science*. The Ostwald solid is a double cone with a vertical black-white axis; thus any hue plane, up to the axis, may be pictured as an equilateral triangle, with its three angles at the points of black, white, and the pure color. There are eight steps from white to black, lettered *a, c, e, g, i, l, n, p*; from each of these points lines are drawn parallel to the other two sides of the triangle and each intersection is labeled by the letters of the two lines which meet there. Thus the points where the line from *e* meets the other two sides of the triangle would be *ea* and *pe*; and the point of saturation would be *pa*. The equator of the double cone is divided into twenty-four hue steps, each assigned a number; in this way a color can be specified as *8pa* or *10nc*, and so on. The system is ingenious and has been widely used in solving problems of decoration and color harmony, but two defects

21. See Dorothy Nickerson, "Modern Color Science Is the Background for a New and Useful Color Chart for Horticulture," *Proceedings of the Eleventh Annual American Horticultural Congress* (October 1956), pp. 3-11. The *Color Fan* is distributed by the American Orchid Society, the American Horticultural Council, and the Munsell Color Company.

are immediately apparent — one of theoretical, and the other of practical, importance. Because the point of highest saturation for any given hue falls at the apex of a triangle which contains the other shades and tints of that hue, no provision is made for the irregularities in the surface of the solid resulting from the divergences in saturation attainable by different coloring materials; so the system is inflexible, and the development of new methods for producing greater saturation in a given hue necessitates readjusting the entire triangle. On the practical level, the method of notation is much more difficult to learn and remember than the Munsell notation.

Between 1932 and 1935 J. Scott Taylor arranged *The Ostwald Colour Album*, which contained twelve plates in a box and displayed about 1400 colors. But the most widely used collection of color chips based on the Ostwald system is the Container Corporation of America's *Color Harmony Manual* (1942; 2nd ed., 1946; 3rd ed., 1948) by Egbert Jacobson, Walter C. Granville, and Carl E. Foss. The latest edition contains 949 removable hexagonal chips (one side glossy and the other matte) on loose leaf charts in a zippered portfolio. These features make it extremely convenient, but its price of $150 militates against its choice by bibliographers. In 1950 Helen D. Taylor, Lucille Knoche, and Walter C. Granville published a *Descriptive Color Names Dictionary* as a supplement to the third edition of the *Manual*. The color names were selected after a survey of previous dictionaries and of the terms used commercially by various companies; by means of this dictionary the Ostwald symbols may be translated into verbal expressions — *10pl* is "deep eggplant" and *16ne* is "peacock blue." However, such terms are somewhat too fanciful to give a clear idea of the color to a reader of a descriptive bibliography who does not happen to have the *Manual* at hand. In short, the *Color Harmony Manual* is an admirably produced tool, but the Ostwald system on which it is based is not so suitable a standard for bibliography as is the Munsell system.

(3) *British Colour Council Dictionary of Colour Standards* — The color standard officially adopted by the British Standards Institution (Standard 543-1934) is the *Dictionary of Colour Standards* (1934; 2nd ed., 1951) issued by the British Colour Council. The second edition displays 240 colors (twenty more than the first edition), produced on silk ribbons, each divided into smooth and ribbed surfaces and fastened as a loop so that the sample may be lifted enough to insert the item to be matched beneath. The *Dictionary* takes the form of two volumes in a portfolio: one volume (57 pp.) is a list of the colors, with their BCC numbers and the origin of the name; the other is a folding chart exhibiting the colored ribbons, each sample numbered consecutively

and assigned a name and a code reference. The fact that the *Dictionary* is an officially adopted standard and the fact that it consists of cloth samples are enormous advantages, which no doubt lie behind John Carter's choice of this *Dictionary* for bibliographical purposes, but its nomenclature is not so appropriate as might be desired. In the first place, the identifying numbers (from BCC 1 to BCC 240), unlike the Munsell notation, give no indication of the position of the color in color space. On top of that, the names, however conventional some of them may be in certain fields, have often been chosen for industrial uses and are not always clear to the general reader — for instance, BCC 71 is "Garter Blue," BCC 235 "Crayon Blue," BCC 239 "Gloucestershire Green," BCC 142 "Corn Husk," and BCC 170 "Natal Brown." The colors have usually been matched to the object named, as the description of the origin of "Peacock Blue" (BCC 120) illustrates: "A very old colour name. The colour here given was matched to peacock feathers, and is a general representation of samples submitted by textile and other colour using industries." The arrangement of the samples is also less meaningful than might be hoped: thus "Brick Red" (BCC 125) and "Guardsman Red" (BCC 126) are separated by several leaves from the related "Signal Red," "Post Office Red," and "Union Jack Red" (BCC 208-210).

Of the other publications of the British Colour Council, two should be mentioned. In 1938 the Council issued (in collaboration with the Royal Horticultural Society) the first volume of a *Horticultural Colour Chart*, also called the *Wilson Colour Chart* after Robert F. Wilson, the active and prominent general manager of the Council at that time. It consists of a portfolio containing 100 loose plates of printed color samples (not affixed chips). Each leaf lists foreign synonyms of the color name and the equivalents in four other systems (BCC *Dictionary*, Ridgway, Oberthür-Dauthenay, Ostwald); it also indicates a special notation for the color, in which the last two digits stand for one of 64 hues and the preceding digit represents lighter tints (600's and below) and darker shades (700's and above) — thus "Rose Bengal" is 25 and "Phlox Pink" is 625 — with prefixed zeros for steps of graying. In 1941 a second volume of 100 more plates was published. These two volumes, with their somewhat awkward notation and nomenclature and their rather inconvenient physical form, would not be successful for bibliographical description. The other publication is the one used by Stott in his Maugham bibliography, the *Dictionary of Colours for Interior Decoration* (1949), with 378 colors (labeled CC1-CC378) displayed in silk samples in three volumes. The Council's regular *Dictionary of Colour Standards* contains cross references to this chart, but the names do not always match — BCC47, "Victrix Blue," for example, is the same as CC287, "Ming Blue." This situation does not seem conducive to standardization of terminology, particularly when the terms are not self-explanatory. Stott, after using this *Dictionary*, reported that "many book cloths defy even the 378 examples shown on the chart" (p. 8) ; and a reviewer of his bibliography questioned the BCC nomenclature by asking whether the gain in accuracy was "worth achieving at the cost of superficial confusion in the minds of those who are more familiar with *The Library* than with *Vogue*."[22] Another disadvantage of all three publications was expressed by Cahill when asked why he adopted a paint standard instead of the British Colour Council's *Dictionary*:   "its bulk and price make it an impossible tool for the Belloc collectors, enthusiasts and booksellers for whom my book is mainly intended."[23]

The bibliographer should be aware of the features of certain other systems, though none of them would serve as a practical choice for a bibliographical standard: (1) the *Standard Color Card of America* (9th ed., 1941), with 216 silk swatches, used mainly by the textile industry, employs rather bizarre nomenclature and is an unsystematic sampling of color space; (2) the *DIN-Farbenkarte* (1953), with samples representing equal psychological steps, is the official German standard, not very widely known in England and America; (3) the great *Villalobos Colour Atlas* (1947), probably the most extensive guide available, shows 7279 samples, each with a hole in the center to facilitate matching; (4) the *Dictionary of Color* (1930; 2nd ed., 1950) by Aloys J. Maerz and M. Rea Paul is the standard work on color nomenclature, with 7056 colors on 56 plates, and it is no criticism of the work's great authority to say that the small size of the color squares (usually 144 to the page, with no holes for comparison) and the historical purpose of the work (with some colors assigned no name at all) make it inappropriate as a standard for bibliography; (5) the *Plochere Color System* (1948) by Gladys and Gustave Plochere, with 1248 colors on 3" x 5" cards (or smaller mounted rectangles) , is basically a guide for interior decorators; (6) *Federal Standard No. 595* (1956), with 358 color chips, is not a systematic sampling and is mainly intended for the specification of paint colors in use by the United States government; (7) Robert Ridgway's *Color Standards and Color Nomenclature* (1912), with 1115 colors and names, was long a standard for naturalists but is now out of print; (8) the *Nu-Hue Color Coordinator* (1949, 1952), prepared by Carl E. Foss for the Martin-Senour Company, is

22. *TLS*, 25 January 1957, p. 56.   23. *Notes and Queries*, CXCVIII (1953), 452 (cf. p. 365) .

perhaps the most ambitious and elaborately produced of the colorant-mixture systems developed by paint manufacturers; (9) the 1962 *Reinhold Color Atlas* (in England the *Methuen Handbook of Colour*), by A. Kornerup and J.H.Wanscher, displays 1266 colors in extremely (perhaps overly) compact form. These systems are of course only a few out of a possible list of seventy-five or more; but the bibliographer cannot seriously consider the great majority of color charts, devised specifically for stamp collectors, horticulturists, interior decorators, paint dealers, textile dyers, or ornithologists.

Clearly the various attempts at color standardization have not in the past led to any general system which encompasses or coordinates a large number of them, and the bibliographer is faced with a multiplicity of systems, none of which precisely suits his needs. The choice of one with the fewest disadvantages becomes a matter of deciding which of the desired features are most important — whether it is better to have a standard with a large number of colors, or a satisfactory nomenclature, or a low price, or something else. There is no doubt that the problem of nomenclature is extremely important for bibliographical description, because the reader of a bibliography should not be required to consult a color chart except when a question arises. He should not be confronted with "8pa" or "13432," unaccompanied by a commonly understood color expression; yet the common expression must be firmly attached to a precise area in color space so that it will hold the same meaning for each user. Fortunately, such a system is now available.

II

In 1931 the Inter-Society Color Council was formed as an organization of national societies whose work involved color; it was not only to be a clearinghouse for color problems and research but more specifically was to assist in revising the color names used in the U. S. Pharmacopoeia.[24] E. N. Gathercoal, the ISCC's first chairman, was a member of the Pharmacopoeial Revision Committee, and he had arranged a symposium on color names at the 1930 Pharmacopoeial Convention in Washington. His goal was a color nomenclature "sufficiently standardized as to be acceptable to science, sufficiently broad to be appreci-

24. Dorothy Nickerson, "Inter-Society Color Council," *JOSA*, XXVIII (1938), 357-359; H. P. Gage, "Color Theories and the Inter-Society Color Council," *Journal of the Society of Motion Picture Engineers*, XXXV (1940), 361-387; William J. Kiernan, "A Story About the Inter-Society Color Council," *ISCC News Letter*, No. 173 (September-December 1964). The ISCC may be addressed in care of its present secretary, Mr. Ralph M. Evans, at the Photographic Technology Division, Building 65, Eastman Kodak Company, Rochester 14650.

ated and usable by science, art, and industry, and sufficiently common-place to be understood, at least in a general way, by the whole public." By 1933 I. H. Godlove had sketched out the foundation for such a system; by 1936 Kenneth L. Kelly of the National Bureau of Standards was working on the task of assigning boundaries to the suggested color designations; and in 1939 Deane B. Judd and Kelly published Research Paper 1239, "Method of Designating Colors," in which common color names were defined in terms of specific areas of the Munsell color solid.[25] This ISCC-NBS method, as it was called, was an enormous step forward, but by 1949 a committee of the ISCC had revised the color boundaries in response to certain criticisms which some users had made. Finally, in 1955, Kelly and Judd published the revised version of their 1939 work, which now also contained a dictionary relating the ISCC-NBS names to those in other systems. This remarkable book, *The ISCC-NBS Method of Designating Colors and a Dictionary of Color Names*, is NBS Circular 553, available from the Superintendent of Documents, U. S. Government Printing Office, at $2, and should certainly be a part of every bibliographer's equipment.

In the history of color nomenclature, the work is epoch-making in at least two ways. First, instead of assigning names to particular color chips, it proceeds in the other direction, setting up a system of easily understood names and then mapping out the entire color solid for the first time into segments which define the precise limits of each name. The system of names — which takes into account the three attributes of color — is a simple one based on ten hue names, three neutrals, their modifying forms, and ten other modifiers, as follows:

	Hues			Value Modifiers	(Lightness)
B	blue	b	bluish	d.	dark
Br	brown	br	brownish	l.	light
G	green	g	greenish	med.	medium
O	orange			v.	very
Ol	olive				
P	purple	p	purplish	Chroma Modifiers	(Saturation)
Pk	pink	pk	pinkish	gy.	grayish
R	red	r	reddish	m.	moderate
V	violet			s.	strong
Y	yellow	y	yellowish	v.	vivid

	Neutrals			Value and Chroma Combinations		
Black	black	blackish	blackish	brill.	brilliant	[light, strong]
Gy	gray	gy.	grayish	deep	deep	[dark, strong]
White	white			p.	pale	[light, grayish]

25. *Journal of Research of the National Bureau of Standards*, XXIII (1939), 355-385. Cf. Dorothy Nickerson, "Standardiza-tion of Color Names: The ISCC-NBS Method," *American Dyestuff Reporter*, XXIX (1940), 392-396.

The abbreviations provide a concise notation (as "v.d.pR" for "very dark purplish red") but of course are not essential. The point is that there are no "post office reds," nor "puces," nor even "garnets" here, but only combinations which — however complicated, as "dark grayish olive green" — at least give a suggestion of the particular color to any reader. The color solid is then divided into 267 named segments, and the boundaries of each are plotted on 31 charts representing ranges of Munsell hue. Thus, for example, both Munsell renotation 4R 3/6 and 3R 2.5/5 fall within the area designated as "dark red." Since colorimetric measurements have been made of the colors of Munsell renotation,[26] even a color identified in CIE terms could be converted to an ISCC-NBS name.

The second important feature of the work — the second part, added in 1955 — is the dictionary, which makes it equally easy to convert to these names from a number of systems other than Munsell. This dictionary is a compilation of the names used in fourteen previous charts or atlases: Maerz-Paul, Plochere, Ridgway, Federal Specification TT-C-595, Wilson's *Horticultural Colour Chart*, the *Color Card of America*, Taylor-Knoche-Granville (supplement to the *Color Harmony Manual*), the American Association of Textile Chemists and Colorists and the Society of Dyers and Colourists' standard, Commercial Standards CS147-47 (Urea Plastics) and CS156-49 (Polystyrene Plastics), the National Research Council's *Rock-Color Chart*, the Department of Agriculture's *Soil Color Chart*, H. A. Dade's *Color Terminology in Biology*, and W. H. Beck's *Postage-Stamp Color Names*. First comes a list (pp. 35-82) of the 267 ISCC-NBS names with the synonyms from these systems listed under each name. Then follows the dictionary proper (pp. 83-158), which lists alphabetically all the names from these fourteen systems (about 7500 names), giving for each the source and the ISCC-NBS designation (and serial number). Previous dictionaries drawing names together from various sources have not subordinated them to a new terminology nor attempted to provide names to cover the entire color solid systematically; the ISCC-NBS method is thus a kind of master-system, furnishing a common ground to coordinate earlier systems. If one person, using Maerz-Paul, describes a color as "Rhodonite Pink" and another, using Plochere, refers to "Orchid Mauve," both can consult the ISCC-NBS dictionary and discover that they are dealing with the same color, "dark purplish pink" (no. 251).

---

26. "Renotation" refers to the adjustments made in 1943 in the original Munsell specifications. See the "Note on the Literature" below.

The advantages of this system for bibliographers (or for anyone else) are immediately apparent. It provides a consistent, standard, easily understood nomenclature for color, regardless of the particular set of color chips employed for matching. If one bibliographer prefers for some reason to use the Plochere system but hesitates to describe the color of a certain binding cloth as "Best Effort" (or as 1224 YYg 3-h), he can look that name up in the ISCC-NBS dictionary and find that it corresponds to ISCC-NBS 121, "pale yellow green." Then if another bibliographer, who wishes to check this color himself, has only a copy of Ridgway at hand, he may make the comparison, find that Ridgway's "Glaucous" is the one that matches, and check the dictionary to see that "Glaucous" is also within the area defined by "pale yellow green." The same would be true of a third bibliographer or collector who had identified the binding as "Rhone" (Maerz-Paul 18 B 3). In this way uniformity results in the final bibliographical description, despite the multiplicity of systems which may have been used by individual bibliographers. Even if a bibliographer buys for himself a copy of the *Munsell Book of Color*, for example, he may not always have it with him; if he finds himself in a library which has only a copy of Maerz-Paul, he may proceed with his description of the binding and later convert the Maerz-Paul term by using the ISCC-NBS dictionary. For accuracy and for general scholarly indication of sources, the ISCC-NBS name should be accompanied by a reference in parentheses to the actual color sample used — as "dark red (Maerz-Paul 6 L 11)," or "dark red (Plochere 353 R 3-a)," or "dark red (TCCA 65020)," or "dark red (Munsell 2.5R 3/7)." The Nickerson *Color Fan* is particularly convenient (aside from its price, size, and arrangement) because it designates on each sample both the Munsell notation and the ISCC-NBS name (thus obviating any reference to the dictionary itself after the process of matching). In any case, two points are essential: that bibliographers agree to compare binding colors with *some* collection of color samples and that they convert the identifications into ISCC-NBS names.[27]

The only real limitation of the ISCC-NBS system as published in 1955 was that it contained no actual color chips to illustrate the names.

27. Of course, only the first is truly essential; for if a color is specified in terms of any published color sample, one can always refer to the sample when it becomes necessary to see precisely what color the bibliographer had in mind. The conversion to ISCC-NBS names is, from this point of view, merely a convenience to readers; but that convenience is of great importance, for a really meaningful and efficient standardization of color names cannot be achieved until all bibliographers use the same name for the same color.

However, by 1958 Kenneth L. Kelly had worked out the Munsell renotations for the center of gravity of each of the 267 ISCC-NBS color-name blocks,[28] and handmade charts illustrating these centroid colors were produced as an aid to ISCC-NBS Subcommittee on Problem 23, the Historical Expression of Color Usage, as explained in its *Interim Report* of 20 November 1960. The NBS then began preparing such charts for general distribution as a supplement to Circular 553, and they became available in February 1965 from the Standard Reference Materials Office at the National Bureau of Standards, as Standard Sample No. 2106, for $3 per set.[29] The *ISCC-NBS Centroid Color Charts* complete the system, and for a total of $5 the bibliographer can now equip himself with both the dictionary and the charts, which together comprise the most efficient method of color naming yet devised and the one most likely to become a general standard accepted by all fields. The charts alone are all that the bibliographer need carry with him, and they are convenient in size. There are twenty leaves, 10½" x 8", of which the first two contain a table giving the Munsell renotation for each centroid sample and the other eighteen are hue charts illustrating 251 of the 267 ISCC-NBS names in glossy chips 1" square. The chips are arranged on each sheet as they would appear on a Munsell hue plane (that is, with the grays at the left, the highly saturated colors at the right, the lighter colors at the top, and the darker ones at the bottom), against a neutral background of about their own value level; beneath each chip is the identifying number of that color-name block and the abbreviation of its color name. Using these charts the bibliographer will not have to make any conversions from one color name to another; he can simply find the chip which most nearly matches his binding and record it as "deep bluish green (Centroid 161)" or "vivid orange (Centroid 48)" or "dark grayish yellowish brown (Centroid 81)."

The first question which bibliographers are likely to raise is whether a system with 267 colors (and 251 chips) can be sufficiently accurate, particularly in view of Stott's comment, in his Maugham

28. Kelly, "Central Notations for the Revised ISCC-NBS Color-Name Blocks," *Journal of Research of the National Bureau of Standards,* LXI (1958), 427-431. Cf. the previous calculations in Dorothy Nickerson and Sidney M. Newhall, "Central Notations for ISCC-NBS Color Names," *JOSA,* XXXI (1941), 587-591; and Dorothy Nickerson, "ISCC-NBS Color Names," *Bulletin of the American Ceramic Society,* XXII (1943), 306-310.

29. Kenneth L. Kelly, "The ISCC-NBS Centroid Color Charts," *ISCC News Letter,* No. 175 (March-April 1965), pp. 7-8. The Munsell Color Company has prepared for sale large samples of the centroid colors, in 9" x 12" sheets.

bibliography, that the 378 samples in the BCC's *Dictionary of Colours for Interior Decoration* were not sufficient. The question may be answered in two ways. First, one must consider the principle of selection of the 267 colors. Though not a great number, they represent blocks which, taken together, comprise the entire color solid; the chips, in turn, represent the center of 251 of these blocks. In contrast to other systems, then, each chip illustrates a color *characteristic* of a well-defined area. When one decides that a particular binding color does not match precisely any of the centroid chips but comes closest to matching Centroid 16, one can be sure that the block of the solid labeled "dark red" contains the particular color, and "dark red" is thus an accurate term, even though the match with the color chip was not exact. To this degree, the system is capable of complete accuracy, whereas in other systems the fact that one chip is closer than another to the color in question has little significance for naming, since the boundaries of the color-name have not been defined.

Second, since the ISCC-NBS dictionary encompasses fourteen other systems (plus the Munsell name charts), it is always possible, when finer discriminations are required, to utilize a system with more chips and yet remain within the framework of the ISCC-NBS method. Indeed, Kelly has explained six levels of accuracy in color description attainable within this method.[30] In the first the color solid is divided into only 13 sections, corresponding to the ten hue names and the three neutrals; for some purposes it is enough to distinguish "pink" from "red," or "yellow" from "orange." The second level works with 29 name-blocks, consisting of all the hue terms — such as "olive brown," "greenish yellow," "yellowish brown," or "olive green." The 267 names produced by adding the modifiers descriptive of value and chroma, as in the ISCC-NBS dictionary and centroid charts, constitute the third level of refinement, the one on which bibliographers may normally find themselves. But many distinguishable colors naturally fall within each of these name-blocks, and it may be that certain binding variants are not distinguishable in terms of the centroid colors alone. One may then move to the fourth level, which involves consulting an appropriate color-order system — Munsell if possible, but, if not, perhaps Plochere, with 1248 colors, or Maerz-Paul, with 7056.[31] If an exact

30. Kenneth L. Kelly, "Some Problems of Color Identification," *Journal of the American Institute of Architects*, XXXVII (1962), 80-82; Kelly, *Coordinated Color Identifications for Industry* (National Bureau of Standards Technical Note 152, November 1962); Kelly, "A Universal Color Language," *Color Engineering*, III (March-April 1965), 2-7.

31. Even a system not represented in the ISCC-NBS dictionary may be used, for the

match is not found, the next step (the fifth level) is to make a visual interpolation from the *Munsell Book of Color*. Because the Munsell system is based on psychological spacing (a color-appearance system) and because the Munsell notation is conveniently manipulated to reflect changes in any of the three attributes, a person with some experience can accurately indicate about 100,000 colors by such interpolation. The sixth and highest level of accuracy is of course the CIE method of spectrophotometric measurement, capable of dividing the color solid into about five million parts. Bibliographers will need to leave the third level only rarely, but the accuracy required at certain times[32] may necessitate moving to the fourth or fifth levels. In any event, the ISCC-NBS system adequately takes into account the fact that varying degrees of accuracy are desirable under varying circumstances.

Another problem arises from the fact that the centroid color chips are glossy and book cloth is not. Since the ideal system for bibliography is undoubtedly one with cloth samples, there is no answer to this objection, except to say that the system offers so many other advantages that it is still the best one to choose. Besides, the importance of the surface texture of the sample in any given case is a function of the accuracy required. In some instances, then, the bibliographer may wish to turn to the textile *Color Card* — so long as he realizes that its sampling of the color solid is not systematic — or to the British Colour Council's *Dictionary*. The difference in appearance between a glossy chip and a cloth swatch of the same color is also to some degree a function of the viewing conditions. It is normally recommended, in most systems of color identification, that the matching be done in natural light, preferably northern light and certainly not direct sunlight; the light should strike the surfaces to be matched at an angle of 45°, and the surfaces should be viewed from 90°. Some sets of chips include masks which can be used to block out the colors on the chart surrounding the chip being matched. Although the ISCC-NBS charts do not contain masks, it is a good idea to prepare a few of them by making a hole 1" square in a stiff piece of gray paper or cardboard.

Still another of the bibliographer's questions will concern notation — what form the color information is to take in a bibliographical description. The ISCC-NBS abbreviations — as "d.gy.G" — should

color name may still be obtained from an approximate match in the centroid charts and the more precise designation then read from the samples in the other system.

32. See above, footnote 14. Interpolations may also be made by spinning Maxwell disks of Munsell standard paper; see footnote 15 above.

probably not be used, for they give essentially common terms an esoteric appearance; "dark grayish green" does not take up too much space. The centroid number can conveniently be inserted in parentheses following the name, just as the letter identifying a cloth grain can be placed after the verbal description of it. Thus what formerly might have been referred to as "dark green ribbed cloth" may now appear as follows:

> dark grayish green (Centroid 151) bold-ribbed (T) cloth
> *or* bold-ribbed (T) cloth, dark grayish green (Centroid 151)

The length of the color expression, including its parenthesis, may be clearer and less awkward if it follows, rather than precedes, the designation of grain. A further convention may perhaps be agreed upon: the presence of a centroid number suggests only that the color falls within that color-name block and does not necessarily imply an exact match with the centroid color; however, if another set of chips is referred to as the standard for the identification, the match may be inferred as exact, unless the abbreviation "cf." precedes the notation. To illustrate:

dark grayish green (Centroid 151) [indicates the color-name block]
dark grayish green (Nickerson 10 GY 3/2) [indicates precise match]
dark grayish green (cf. Nickerson 10 GY 3/2) [indicates approximate match]

Obviously the last of these represents an extension of the fourth level of accuracy; it stops short of the fifth level because an interpolation has not been suggested. When an interpolation is made, the notation should be enclosed in brackets:

> dark grayish green [Munsell 10 GY 3.2/1.75]

In this system the color of Waldo Frank's *Time Exposures* (Boni & Liveright, 1926) is "brilliant yellow (Centroid 83)," of Vachel Lindsay's *Adventures While Preaching the Gospel of Beauty* (Kennerley, 1914) "very deep red (Centroid 14)," of Sherwood Anderson's *Horses and Men* (Huebsch, 1923) "strong reddish orange (Centroid 35)"; and a complete description — of Eunice Tietjens' *Jake* (Boni & Liveright, 1921) — would go something like this:

Binding: linen (B) cloth, strong red (cf. Nickerson 5R 4/12); blocked in brilliant orange yellow (Centroid 67). Front: 'JAKE | [design] | *BY* EUNICE | TIETJENS'. Spine: '[thick-thin rule] | JAKE | [design] | EUNICE | TIETJENS | BONI AND | LIVERIGHT | [thin-thick rule]'. Back: blank. Stiff wove endpapers, strong red (cf. Nickerson 2.5R 5/12). All edges trimmed; top edge stained as endpapers.

In this instance the slight difference in color between the cloth and the endpapers could not be indicated by reference to Centroid 12, so approximations to two colors in the Nickerson *Color Fan* were used.

However, it should be emphasized here that, despite an occasional example of this kind, the bibliographer generally need feel no urge to go beyond the centroid charts. Given the nature of book cloth and of material standards, the majority of matches are going to be only approximate; and in any case the purposes of most bibliographical descriptions would not be further served by a more precise match. For these reasons the centroid colors, which are simply the *representative* colors of particular color-blocks, constitute an ideal frame of reference. If a bibliographer goes outside this system, one must assume either (1) that another system was the only one at hand when the comparison was made (with the result later converted to the corresponding centroid name) or (2) that greater accuracy was required — and obtained — by specification in terms of another system. It would be a mistake to overuse the "cf." designation, for, if the match is only approximate anyway, nothing is gained in precision over the simple reference to the centroid color.

Because of the advantages of the Munsell notation, it may be that some bibliographers, if they have had to turn to another set of chips for an exact match, will want to indicate the equivalent Munsell notation or renotation as a convenience to their readers. The Munsell equivalents of the most commonly used systems have been tabulated, and it may prove helpful to bring together the principal references to these conversion tables:

Color Harmony Manual	Walter C. Granville, "Munsell Renotations of *Color Harmony Manual Chips* (Third Edition) from Spectrophotometric Measurements," available from Container Corporation of America, Color Standards Department, 38 South Dearborn Street, Chicago 60603.[33]
DIN-Farbenkarte	W. Budde, H. E. Kundt, and Günter Wyszecki, "Überführung der Farbmasszahlen nach dem Farbsystem DIN 6164 in Munsell-Masszahlen und umgekehrt," *Farbe*, IV (1955), 83-88.
Horticultural Colour Chart	Dorothy Nickerson, "*Horticultural Colour Chart* Names with Munsell Key," *JOSA*, XLVII (1957), 619-621.

33. Cf. Walter C. Granville and Egbert Jacobson, "Colorimetric Specification of the *Color Harmony Manual* from Spectrophotometric Measurements," *JOSA*, XXXIV (1944), 382-395; Granville, Carl E. Foss, and I. H. Godlove, "*Color Harmony Manual*: Colorimetric Analysis of Third Edition," *JOSA*, XL (1950), 265 (summary).

Maerz-Paul	Dorothy Nickerson, "Interrelation of Color Specifications," *Paper Trade Journal*, CXXV (1947), TS219-237.
Plochere	W. E. Knowles Middleton, "The Plochere Color System: A Descriptive Analysis," *Canadian Journal of Research*, XXVII (1949), F1-21.
Ridgway	D. H. Hamly, "Ridgway Color Standards with a Munsell Notation Key," *JOSA*, XXXIX (1949) 592-599.
Standard Color Card	Genevieve Reimann, Deane B. Judd, and Harry J. Keegan, "Spectrophotometric and Colorimetric Determination of the Colors of the TCCA Standard Color Cards," *JOSA*, XXXVI (1946), 128-159; or *Journal of Research of the National Bureau of Standards*, XXXVI (1946), 209-247.

Whether the original match was exact or approximate, an equals sign may be used to indicate the Munsell equivalent; but if one wishes to give only the centroid number, the symbol for "approximately equals" ($\cong$) should be used:

grayish purplish red (*Standard Color Card* 70189 = Munsell 6RP 5.1/5.7)
grayish purplish red (cf. *Standard Color Card* 70189 = Munsell 6RP 5.1/5.7)
grayish purplish red (*Standard Color Card* 70189 $\cong$ Centroid 262)
grayish purplish red (cf. *Standard Color Card* 70189 $\cong$ Centroid 262)

If Munsell renotation is employed, it should be so specified:

grayish purplish red (*Standard Color Card* 70189 = Munsell renotation 5.5RP 5.2/5.9)

The Munsell renotations of the centroid colors are provided in the table accompanying the centroid charts; if a binding happens by chance to match exactly a centroid chip, the coincidence may be indicated by including the renotation figure:

grayish purplish red (Centroid 262 = Munsell renotation 7RP 4.5/5.1)

These equivalences are of course simply additional information which may be furnished for the convenience of the reader in making his own further comparisons; they are by no means required. But knowledge of the existence of these conversion tables may be useful to the reader of a bibliography which does not provide the equivalences.

Another question — and one of the most troublesome — is the problem of fading, both of the color samples and of the bindings. As far as the samples are concerned, one should not expose them to light except when they are being used; and after extended use one should perhaps compare them with a new copy to see whether they have yet faded. A consideration of faded bindings is tied up with the whole matter of the degree of accuracy required, for in some cases it may be necessary to determine whether a given binding is variant or merely faded. But in most instances the determination of a secondary binding will not turn solely on color discrimination, and, since a bibliographical description records the characteristics of an "ideal copy,"[34] the general rule is to include in the binding description a notation of the brightest copy examined. Then, if one wishes to provide the color-matching data for the other copies, the paragraph listing "Copies Examined" is the proper place for the information. In the case of certain scarce books, all copies may appear faded, even on the covers (as well as the spine, where fading is to be expected). If there is no small patch or strip of brighter color (as on the inside edge of a cover) to serve as a basis for the color identification, one may have to describe the color as it appears and append a note explaining one's hunch that the color is probably faded. A descriptive catalogue of the books in a particular collection, however, is obligated to describe a binding in whatever faded state it is found in that collection; but an energetic cataloguer will go further (by examining other copies or consulting a published bibliography) and indicate the extent of the fading, either through an exact match or through interpolation.

moderate red (Centroid 15), faded from strong red (Centroid 12)

moderate red (Munsell renotation [3.8R 3.9/8.75], faded from 3.8R 4.4/9.1 = Centroid 15)

moderate red (Munsell renotation 3.8R 4.4/9.1 = Centroid 15, faded from [3.8R 4.4/9.75])

Dorothy Nickerson has worked out a formula for an Index of Fading, whereby the amount of fading can be indicated in a single figure. Though the formula is not a complicated one, the single-figure index is more meaningful for expressing tolerances in the textile industry than for describing the fading of bindings, since the single figure (consolidating the differences in hue, value, and chroma) does not enable one to visualize the changes in the three attributes.

A final consideration has to do with the fact that colors in books are not limited to bindings. There are colored sheets, inks, dust jackets, and endpapers; and the ISCC-NBS names are appropriate for describing them all. In fact, Deane Judd has specifically commented on the applicability of these names for the paper industry and has shown some of the equivalents between the ISCC-NBS names and those in the Grading Committee of the Groundwood Paper Manufacturers' Asso-

34. Cf. Bowers, *Principles*, pp. 113-123.

ciation's "Blue Book," *Standard Color Nomenclature System and Manual* (1936).[35] The methods developed for measuring the whiteness of paper, however useful for specification and standardization in the paper industry, go beyond the degree of accuracy required in the bibliographical description of white papers. Colors of printing inks may also be specified in ISCC-NBS terms; in 1935 the International Printing Ink Corporation issued *A Series of Monographs on Color*, which included a description of the advantages of the Munsell system. But the many atlases and sets of color chips circulated by both paper and ink companies are not convenient as general standards. Not a great deal of attention has been given to the description of dust jackets,[36] but the main problem is simply a question of the completeness of the description rather than of method; and the ISCC-NBS names should make such descriptions more accurate. Another kind of paper, however, causes greater trouble — the marbled papers sometimes used as end-papers or binding papers. The difficulty in describing them is analogous to that in specifying cloth grains and is not essentially a color problem. It would be very helpful, therefore, to have a chart illustrating such marbling patterns as "gold vein" or "nonpareil" — the same sort of chart (but on a more elaborate scale) that Bernard C. Middleton furnishes as the frontispiece to his *A History of English Craft Bookbinding Technique* (1963), where twelve common kinds of decorated papers are displayed.[37]

In 1953 Fredson Bowers remarked, "As a matter of fact, when the technicians really get to work on the problems of machine-printing, I rather suspect that the general reader and the bibliographer who has catered to him are due to suffer a shock."[38] Whether or not the method of color description outlined here will offer a shock to those bibliographers who fondly remember the good old days when it was possible to speak of "puce" or "Eureka" or "Victoria Lake," depending on one's mood, the fact remains that a move in this direction is inevitable. The ISCC-NBS system can be as simple or as complex as is required under different circumstances, and its use is no more difficult, and only slightly more time-consuming, than the measurement of leaves

35. Judd, "Systematic Color Designations for Paper," *Paper Trade Journal*, CXI (17 October 1940), TS201-206.

36. Cf. Charles Rosner, *The Growth of the Book-Jacket* (1954).

37. Rosamond B. Loring, in *Decorated Book Papers* (1942; 2nd ed., edited by Philip Hofer, 1952), includes a chapter on nineteenth-century endpapers (pp. 71-80) and one on publishers' endpapers (pp. 81-90).

38. *Library*, 5th ser., VIII (1953), 22.

with a ruler. The color names should shock no one, and the whole method seems ideally suited to descriptive bibliography — with the exception of the glossy chips. Perhaps a handbook can some day be produced which will contain illustrations and names of binding grains and decorative papers along with the centroid colors in cloth samples. In the meantime it is not asking too much that bibliographers compare each binding cloth with the centroid chips or some other collection of samples and express the color name in ISCC-NBS terms. Maerz and Paul, at the beginning of their *Dictionary of Color*, observe that, "while standardization has been arrived at in practically all other fields, in the use of color names for identifying color sensations a condition prevails that is usually characterized as chaotic." Bibliographers can ill afford to perpetuate chaos in any of their endeavors, if their general concern with order and accuracy is to be meaningful.[39]

A Note on the Literature

The bibliographer who wishes to pursue further the problems of color specification and nomenclature and is generally unacquainted with the technical literature of the field discovers few places to turn for help except several alphabetical checklists in the basic books on color and I.H.Godlove's *Bibliography on Color* (Inter-Society Color Council, 1957). The present list groups the significant literature by topic or system, with the interests of the bibliographer in mind, and is intended also to record the material which served as the basis for the somewhat perfunctory dismissal of a large number of color systems in the text.

The principal general surveys of color systems, which vary in the number of systems covered and in the thoroughness of their comment, are as follows: Ralph M. Evans, *An Introduction to Color* (1948), pp. 205-234; Optical Society of America Committee on Colorimetry, *The Science of Color* (1953), pp. 317-340; Robert W. Burnham, Randall M. Hanes, and C. James Bartleson, *Color: A Guide to Basic Facts and Concepts* (1963), pp. 163-172; Deane B. Judd and Günter Wyszecki, *Color in Business, Science, and Industry* (2nd ed., 1963), pp. 202-264; W.D.Wright, *The Measurement of Colour* (3rd ed., 1964), pp. 161-192; *Symposium on Color — Its Specification and Use in Evaluating the Appearance of Materials* (American Society for Testing Materials, 1941), pp. 37-44; Arthur G. Abbott, *The Color of Life* (1947), pp. 141-163; Sterling B. McDonald, *Color Harmony* (1949), pp. 111-118; *Color Charts: A Descriptive List* (Letter Circular 986, National Bureau of Standards, 1950); H. D. Murray (ed.), *Colour in Theory and Practice* (1939; rev. ed., 1952), pp. 143-158; Frederick M. Crewdson, *Color in Decoration and Design* (1953), pp. 90-108; A. Ames, Jr., "Systems of Color Standards," *JOSA*, V (1921), 160-170; K. S. Gibson, "The Analysis and Specification of Color," *Journal of the Society of Motion Picture Engineers*, XXVIII (1937), 388-410; Morton C. Bradley, "Systems of Color Classification," *Technical Studies*

39. For their helpful letters and advice, I wish to thank Mrs. Blanche R. Bellamy, of the Munsell Color Company; Mr. Ralph M. Evans, Secretary of the Inter-Society Color Council; Mr. V. G. Grey, Secretary of Sectional Committee Z55, American Standards Association; Mr. Kenneth L. Kelly, of the National Bureau of Standards; Mr. W. J. Kiernan, Chairman of Committee E-12, American Society for Testing and Materials; Mr. Paul J. Smith, of the American Society for Testing and Materials.

in the Field of the Fine Arts, VI (1937-38), 240-275; Forrest L. Dimmick, "Color Nomenclature and Specification," *Psychological Bulletin,* XXXV (1938), 473-486; Deane B. Judd, "Color Systems and Their Inter-relation," *Illuminating Engineering,* XXXVI (1941), 336-369; Carl E. Foss, "Color-Order Systems," *Journal of the Society of Motion Picture Engineers,* LII (1949), 184-196.

CIE SYSTEM. A helpful elementary discussion is G. J. Chamberlin, *The C.I.E. International Colour System Explained* (1951), a pamphlet published by The Tintometer, Ltd. Any basic book on color, of course, contains a detailed explanation; see, for example, Evans, pp. 205ff.; *The Science of Color* (1953), pp. 254-334; Burnham, Hanes, and Bartleson, pp. 123-150; Wright pp. 96-160. Also see such articles as Deane B. Judd, "1931 I.C.I. Standard Observer and Coordinate System for Colorimetry," *Journal of the Optical Society of America [JOSA],* XXIII (1933), 359-374. The American Standards Association *Methods of Measuring and Specifying Colors* (in CIE terms), Standard Z58.7 (1951), is reprinted in *JOSA,* XLI (1951), 431-439. For information on the equipment, see Arthur C. Hardy, "A Recording Photoelectric Color Analyser," *JOSA,* XVIII (1929), 96-117, "A New Recording Spectrophotometer," *JOSA,* XXV (1935), 305-311, and *Handbook of Colorimetry* (1936); E. J. King and D. S. Robdell, "An Experimental Color Comparator," *JOSA,* XLI (1951), 830-835; Richard S. Hunter, "Color Difference Meters for Precision and Accuracy," *Farbe,* X (1961), 173-192; J. M. Adams and S. Bergling, "A Comparison of Colorimeters," *Printing Technology,* VIII (1964), 16-27. For modifications in the system, see David L. MacAdam, "Projective Transformations of I.C.I. Color Specifications," *JOSA,* XXVII (1937), 294-299; and Günter Wyszecki, "Proposal for a New Color Difference Formula," *JOSA,* LIII (1963), 1318-1319 (cf. LIII, 1012).

MUNSELL. Dorothy Nickerson, "History of the Munsell Color System and Its Scientific Application," *JOSA,* XXX (1940), 575-586; John E. Tyler and Arthur C. Hardy, "An Analysis of the Original Munsell Color System," *JOSA,* XXX (1940), 587-590; Dorothy Nickerson, "The Munsell Color System," *Illuminating Engineering,* XLI (1946), 549-560 ("the most widely known and useful of color order systems"); Maitland Graves, *Color Fundamentals* (1952), pp. 134-151; *Method of Specifying Color by the Munsell System* (American Society for Testing and Materials, Method D1535-58T, 1958). In 1921 the Strathmore Paper Company issued a handsome book, *A Grammar of Color,* in which the colors of the paper samples were specified in Munsell terms; in the same volume T. M. Cleland published "A Practical Description of the Munsell Color System" (pp. 13-26). Another early discussion is Irwin G. Priest, K. S. Gibson, and H. J. McNichols, *An Examination of the Munsell Color System* (Technologic Papers of the Bureau of Standards, No. 167, 30 September 1920). Norman Macbeth, in "Munsell Value Scales for Judging Reflectance," *Illuminating Engineering,* XLIV (1949), 106-108, discusses one of the special Munsell charts. Measurements in CIE terms are reported in J. J. Glenn and J. T. Killian, "Trichromatic Analysis of the *Munsell Book of Color,*" *JOSA,* XXX (1940), 609-616; Kenneth L. Kelly, Kasson S. Gibson, and Dorothy Nickerson, "Tristimulus Specification of the *Munsell Book of Color* from Spectrophotometric Measurements," *JOSA,* XXXIII (1943), 355-376, or *Journal of Research of the National Bureau of Standards,* XXXI (1943), 55-76; Walter C. Granville, Dorothy Nickerson, and Carl E. Foss, "Trichromatic Specifications for Intermediate and Special Colors of the Munsell System," *JOSA,* XXXIII (1943), 376-385; Josephine G. Brennan and Sidney M. Newhall, "ICI Specifications of Difference Limens for Munsell Hue, Value, and Chroma," *JOSA,* XXXVIII (1948), 696-702; Dorothy Nickerson and Davis H. Wilson, "Munsell Reference Colors Now Specified for Nine Illuminants," *Illuminating Engineering,* XLV (1950), 507-517 (cf. XL, 159-171).

On the problem of color spacing and equal psychological steps, expressed generally in Munsell terms, see Dorothy Nickerson, "Color Measurements in Psychological Terms," *JOSA*, XXI (1931), 643-650; Sidney M. Newhall, "The Ratio Method in the Review of the Munsell Colors," *American Journal of Psychology*, LII (1939), 394-405; Domina Eberle Spencer, "A Metric for Color Space," *JOSA*, XXXII (1942), 744 (summary); Parry Moon and D. E. Spencer, "Geometric Formulation of Classical Color Harmony,"*JOSA*, XXXIV (1944), 46-59; Arthur Pope, "Notes on the Problem of Color Harmony and the Geometry of Color Space," *JOSA*, XXXIV (1944), 759-765. In 1943 some of the original specifications in the *Munsell Book of Color* were modified in terms of the CIE coordinate system and standard observer, and the results are referred to as the "Munsell renotation system" (as opposed to "book notation"): see Sidney M. Newhall, Dorothy Nickerson, and Deane B. Judd, "Final Report of the OSA Subcommittee on the Spacing of the Munsell Colors," *JOSA*, XXXIII (1943), 385-418 (cf. XXX, 617-645); Dorothy Nickerson and Sidney M. Newhall, "A Psychological Color Solid," *JOSA*, XXXIII (1943), 419-422; Dorothy Nickerson, "Spacing of the Munsell Colors," *Illuminating Engineering*, XL (1945), 373-386; Dorothy Nickerson, Josephine T. Tomaszewski, and Thomas F. Boyd, "Colorimetric Specifications of Munsell Repaints," *JOSA*, XLIII (1953), 163-171; Deane B. Judd and Günter Wyszecki, "Extension of the Munsell Renotation System to Very Dark Colors," *JOSA*, XLVI (1956), 281-284; Werner C. Rheinboldt and John P. Menard, "Mechanized Conversion of Colorimetric Data to Munsell Renotations," *JOSA*, L (1960), 802-807. A limited edition of a *Munsell Renotation Color Book* is announced in *JOSA*, LIV (1964), 851. The basis for a set of chips, systematically sampling the color solid and truly representing equal perceptual differences, is set forth by Günter Wyszecki, "A Regular Rhombohedral Lattice Sampling of Munsell Renotation Space," *JOSA*, XLIV (1954), 725-734; the Committee on Uniform Color Scales of the Optical Society of America is working on the preparation of such a system.

OSTWALD. J. Scott Taylor, *A Simple Explanation of the Ostwald Colour System* (1935); Herman Zeishold, "Philosophy of the Ostwald Color System," *JOSA*, XXXIV (1944), 355-360; Carl E. Foss, Dorothy Nickerson, and Walter C. Granville, "Analysis of the Ostwald Color System," *JOSA*, XXXIV (1944), 361-381;. Egbert Jacobson, *Basic Color: An Interpretation of the Ostwald Color System* (1948). For a comparison of the merits of the two systems, see Milton E. Bond and Dorothy Nickerson, "Color-Order Systems, Munsell and Ostwald," *JOSA*, XXXII (1942), 709-719. The Ostwald system has had a number of enthusiastic supporters who have developed their own applications of it, notably Faber Birren in his many books. In *Color Dimensions* (1934), after praising Ostwald as the "greatest scientist ever to devote a large portion of time and energy to color harmony" (p. 35) and after pointing out that "the vast majority of systems so far invented are utterly spurious and impractical" (p. 4), Birren presents his own version of Ostwald, the Color Equation (based on the spinning of Maxwell disks — cf. footnote 15 above), and declares that with it "the problem of color standardization — so long a complex affair — has been adequately solved" (p. 57). Hilaire Hiler, in *Color Harmony and Pigments* (1942), expresses his admiration of Ostwald before explaining his own Color Circle, Color Piano, and cylindrical Color Solid; J. A. V. Judson bases his textbook, *A Handbook of Colour* (1935; rev. ed., 1938), on Ostwald; *The Color Helm* (1932, 1940), designed by J. P. Gangler for Fiatelle, Inc., uses the Ostwald system; and *The New Color Culler* (1951, 1960) of the Desarco Corporation contains eleven Ostwald triangles.

BRITISH COLOUR COUNCIL. See Robert F. Wilson, "Colour and Colour Nomenclature," *Journal of the Royal Society of Arts*, LXXXIII (1934-35), 307-323, for a sketch of the Council's history, activities, and *Dictionary*.

OTHER SYSTEMS. (1) *Color Card Association.* Margaret Hayden Rorke, "The Work of the Textile Color Card Association," *JOSA,* XXI (1931), 651-653. (2) *DIN-Farbenkarte.* Manfred Richter, "Das System der DIN-Farbenkarte," *Farbe,* I (1952-53), 85-98; Hellmut Goeroldt, "Die Herstellung des Entwurfs der DIN-Farbenkarte," *Farbe,* I (1952-53), 128-134; "Normblatt-Entwurf DIN 6164: DIN-Farbenkarte," *Farbe,* I (1952-53), 147-158; Richter, "The Official German Standard Color Chart," *JOSA,* XLV (1955), 223-226; H. E. Kundt and Günter Wyszecki, "Zusammenhang zwischen Munsell und DIN-System," *Farbe,* IV (1955), 289-293; Richter, "Die Beziehung zwischen den Farbmasszahlen nach DIN 6164 und den Ostwald-Masszahlen," *Farbe,* VI (1957), 49-62. (3) *Villalobos Colour Atlas.* Cf. Carl E. Foss's review in the *Inter-Society Color Council News Letter,* No. 82 (May 1949), p. 8. (4) *Maerz-Paul.* M. Rea Paul describes the work in "Dictionary of Color," *JOSA,* XXI (1931), 358-360. (5) *Plochere.* Before their *Plochere Color System,* Gladys and Gustave Plochere had produced the *Plochere Color Guide* (1940) and *Color and Color Names* (1946). (6) *Federal Standards.* See "New Federal Standard on Colors," *JOSA,* XLVII (1957), 330-334; examples of other governmental standards are the National Bureau of Standards chart of colors for kitchen and bathroom accessories, the Army's color card for sewing threads, the Bureau of Federal Supply's samples of colors for upholstery leather, the Maritime Commission's standard colors for flags and for paint, the Bureau of Ships' standards for electrical insulation, and so forth. Cf. British Standard 2660, *Colours for Building and Decorative Paints* (British Standards Institution, 1955); RAL-Farbtonregister 840R (Muster-Schmidt KG, Göttingen). Standards and specifications are also published by the American Standards Association (10 East 40th Street, New York City 10016) and the American Society for Testing and Materials (1916 Race Street, Philadelphia 19103). The former, in its Standard Z44-1942, *Specification and Description of Color,* recommended the Munsell system. The latter, in its catalogue of publications, lists some sixty pamphlets on color tests and measurement, dealing with dyes, acids, plastics, varnishes, petroleum products, etc. It has also published an extension of the three-attribute system of color description to take into account the total appearance of engineering materials: *Visual Appearance: A Five-Attribute System of Describing* (STP 297; 1961). (7) *Ridgway.* Before his famous 1912 work, Ridgway had published *A Nomenclature of Colors for Naturalists* (1886), with 186 samples. See D.H.Hamly, "Robert Ridgway's Color Standards," *Science,* CIX (1949), 605-608. (8) *Other Special Charts.* A bibliographer wishing to survey even more widely among the alternative systems might glance at the following: the National Philatelical Society's *Color Chart* of 1884 or B.W.Warhurst's *Color Dictionary* of 1899 (now Stanley Gibbons' *Colour Guide for Stamp Collectors,* with 75 colors); René Oberthür and Henri Dauthenay's *Répertoire de couleurs pour aider à la determination des couleurs des fleurs, des feuillages et des fruits* for the Société francaise des chrysanthémistes in 1905, with 1356 colors, or the *Fischer Color Chart* of the New England Gladiolus Society, revised in 1944, with 108 colors on a circular board (recommended also for geneticists in 1933 by Edgar Anderson, in *Science,* LXXVIII, 150-151); *The Colorizer* (1947) showing paint proportions for 1298 colors, or Pratt & Lambert's *DeLuxe Color Book* (1954?); C.J.Jorgensen's *The Mastery of Color* (1906) or Sterling B. McDonald's *Color Harmony with the McDonald Calibrator* (1949); E.A.Séguy's *Code universel des couleurs* (1936), with 720 colors on 55 printed plates, or the *Cheskin Color System* (Color Research Institute of America, 1949), with 4800 colors on 48 printed hue charts;*Hesselgren's Color Atlas* (1955); the *Colour Index* of the Society of Dyers and Colourists (2nd ed., 4 vols., 1956); Ralph S. Palmer and E.M.Reilly's *Concise Color Standard* for the American Ornithologists' Union (1956); Faber Birren's *The American Colorist* (1939); Edward Friel's *The Friel System: A Language of Color* (1961); and even musical systems of color

— with scales, keyboards, and the like — such as *The Taylor System of Color Harmony* (1921) and Maud Miles' *A Suggested Plan for a National Color Standard* (1922).

NOMENCLATURE. There is a historical account of the development of color nomenclature at the beginning of the Maerz-Paul *Dictionary*. Further discussions of nomenclature include Milton Bradley's pamphlet *Some Criticisms of Popular Color Definitions and Suggestions for a Better Color Nomenclature* (n.d.); M. Luckiesh, *The Language of Color* (1918); "Report of the Committee on Colorimetry for 1920-21," *JOSA*, VI (1922), 527-596 (section II on nomenclature); "Report of the Committee on Color Terminology Questionnaire," *JOSA*, XIII (1926), 43-57; Loyd A. Jones, "Colorimetry: Preliminary Draft of a Report on Nomenclature and Definitions," *JOSA*, XXVII (1937), 207-213; Colour Group of the Physical Society, *Report on Colour Terminology* (1948); Arthur Pope, *The Language of Drawing and Painting* (1929; rev. ed., 1949), esp. pp. 3-34. The question of color terminology in relation to theater gelatins has been taken up in "Names for Colors," *Theatre Arts Monthly*, XVI (July 1932), 604, 604a, 604b; and by Deane B. Judd in *A System for Specifying Theater Gelatins* (Report to ISCC, February 1938). Kenneth L. Kelly, in "Color Designations for Lights," *Journal of Research of the National Bureau of Standards*, XXXI (1943), 271-278, shows the applicability of the ISCC-NBS system to self-luminous sources and gives a good historical checklist. A later effort to define the boundaries of colors is the dictionary part of Kornerup and Wanscher's *Reinhold Color Atlas* (1962).

TOLERANCES. The Nickerson formula for the Index of Fading is as follows: (average chroma / 5) x (difference in hue / 3) + (difference in chroma / 2) + difference in value. For an explanation of the basis for the formula, see Dorothy Nickerson, "The Specification of Color Tolerances," *Textile Research*, VI (1936), 505-514; and "How Can Results of Fading Tests Be Expressed?", in *ASTM Standards on Textile Materials* (October 1936), pp. 238-241. Cf. "The Inter-Society Color Council Symposium on Color Tolerance," *American Journal of Psychology*, LII (1939), 383-448; F. Scofield, "A Method of Representing Color," *ASTM Bulletin*, No. 102 (January 1940), pp. 11-12; Dorothy Nickerson and Keith F. Stultz, "Color Tolerance Specification," *JOSA*, XXXIV (1944), 550-570; and "Interim Method of Measuring and Specifying Color Rendering of Light Sources," *Illuminating Engineering*, LVII (1962), 471-495.

COLORS OF PAPERS AND INKS. Federal Specification 9310, *Paper Specification Standards* (No. 4, 1 May 1965), includes (as Part 3) samples of eight colored papers for government use and describes briefly (in Part 2) the methods of color measurement by visual comparison (ASTM D1729-60T) and by spectral reflectivity. The annual *Bibliography of Papermaking and U.S. Patents*, published by TAPPI (Technical Association of the Pulp and Paper Industry), contains a section on color. Cf. W. B. Van Arsdel, "Color Specification in the Pulp and Paper Industry," *JOSA*, XXI (1931), 347-357; F. A. Steele, "The Optical Characteristics of Paper," *Paper Trade Journal*, C (21 March 1935), TS151-156; CI (24 October 1935), TS245-249; CIV (25 February 1937), TS129-130; Institute of Paper Chemistry, "Color and Color Measurements," *Paper Trade Journal*, CV (1937), TS285-306; and the Strathmore Paper Company's *A Grammar of Color* (see under Munsell above). On "whiteness": D. L. MacAdam, "The Specification of Whiteness," *JOSA*, XXIV (1934), 188-191; Deane B. Judd, "A Method for Determining Whiteness of Paper," *Paper Trade Journal*, C (23 May 1935), TS266-268; CIII (20 August 1936), TS154-160; V. G. W. Harrison, *The Measurement of "Shades" of "White" Papers* (PATRA Reports Nos. 2-3, 1938-39). Some of the atlases issued by the paper and the ink trades are Charles J. Schott's *Modifications of Pigment*

Colors as Used in Printing Inks (1929), with 502 cards; IPI *Simplified Color Matching Chart* (1935), with 90 printed color samples; *Colors for Paper* (Calco Chemical Company, Heller & Merz Division, 1938); John Henry Graff, *A Color Atlas for Fiber Identification* (Institute of Paper Chemistry, 1940); *Cheskin Color System* (1949); Jack W. White, *The Lithographic Technical Foundation Color Chart* (1957); *ROP Color Ink Book* (ANPA Institute, 1963), with mixing ratios for newspaper inks.

The Bibliographical Description of Patterns

THE BASIC TECHNICAL PROBLEM OF BIBLIOGRAPHICAL DESCRIPtion arises from the difficulty of expressing the visual in verbal terms. Parts of a description like the collation and contents paragraphs, which are condensed statements of sequential arrangement, can be handled easily enough in words or formulas; but the title-page transcription and the paragraphs on binding, paper, and typography present the same challenge that one meets in the attempt to frame an exact (not impressionistic) description of any physical object, whether it be a tree or a sculpture. Books are not exempt from the human urge to decorate empty spaces, and the descriptive bibliographer is faced with a wide array of patterns and designs (as in binding cloths and endpapers) which he must somehow record in a fashion precise enough to serve as an identification.

Among the decorative elements of a book, patterns and illustrations can be usefully distinguished. A *pattern* results when a figure (or combination of figures) is repeated (either exactly or approximately) at regular (or irregular) intervals or in a systematic arrangement; if a figure (or combination of figures) appears only once, the result is an *illustration*. While illustrations are frequently representational and patterns abstract, these qualities do not serve to distinguish the two, since a representational figure can be repeated as the motif in a pattern and an abstract figure can be used by itself as a single decoration. Repetition — whether precisely detailed or suggestively vague — of a basic unit is the essential feature of a pattern, and it provides a means for classifying the pattern. Although the number of possible patterns is infinite, individual patterns bear structural relationships to one another and can be grouped into a limited number of families. Whenever such a framework can be established as a standard of reference, verbal descriptions can become both more concise and more exact. Illustrations, by their nature, are less readily amenable to identification on the basis of a structural classification (though they can be classified by technique of reproduction) and therefore present a separate problem. Pragmatically, from the bibliographer's point of view, illustrations can best be handled, as they come up, on an individual basis; but patterns, which occur in some form in nearly every book, can often be treated most meaningfully and efficiently in terms of a classification scheme.

There are three ways in which patterns can be recorded in a bibliography — in pictures, in words, or in a combination of the two. The first is the most straightforward and explicit method and at the same time the most objectionable — and not simply on the grounds of expense. To rely exclusively on photographs of patterns is to abandon description in favor of reproduction. The task of a description is to provide a verbal identification which can be quoted in contexts where pictures are inappropriate. Pictures may of course be useful supplements to a description, but they are not substitutes for any part of it. The opposite extreme, of describing patterns exclusively in words, can be successful and precise only if an adequate vocabulary has evolved. In heraldry, for example, the technique of blazoning utilizes a special vocabulary and syntax which make the resulting descriptions both concise and unambiguous. The bibliographer has no such established terminology to draw on in describing patterns, except perhaps in the case of marbled papers. As a result, bibliographical descriptions of patterns must use some kind of combination of words and pictures. That is, the description itself will contain only words (preferably a standardized wording which will convey the same meaning to a large number of readers), but part of that verbal description will be a reference to a readily accessible illustration; in this way any reader who cannot visualize the pattern from the verbal description clearly enough for his purposes can look up the illustration which serves as a standard of reference.

The two essentials, then, in the bibliographical description of patterns are a standard terminology and a visual standard of reference. In a few areas, bibliographers already have such references at their disposal — R. B. McKerrow and F. S. Ferguson's *Title-page Borders Used in England and Scotland, 1485-1640* (1932) is a good example — but for the most part no accepted standards exist. Enough research has taken place in certain areas, however, that it would not be premature to attempt to codify a standard of reference for those areas, particularly if it is set up in an expandable fashion, so that additions can be made in the future without affecting the basic classification. Patterns in books generally appear in one of three media: in binding cloths, both as a grain and as a stamping upon the grain; in decorated papers, whether used as endpapers or as a covering for boards; and in sheets of letterpress, either as borders or as divisional indicators. Each of these areas involves special problems and should be considered separately.

I. BINDING CLOTHS

Before the introduction of edition binding in the 1820's, the binding of a book generally had no connection with the publisher and was not part of the book as it was issued to the public. The description of such bindings, executed individually for owners of books, is thus outside the scope of the descriptive bibliographer's task and constitutes a separate field of investigation.[1] The only exceptions are the temporary coverings in which books were sometimes issued to serve as a protection until the books could be properly bound;[2] these covers usually consisted of plain boards with printed paper labels, and they offer little difficulty for the descriptive bibliographer. From the 1820's on, however, most books have been issued in bindings or casings by their publishers, and these coverings must be described in bibliographical descriptions. The most common material for publishers' bindings has been cloth, and the history of publishers' cloth has been traced by several bibliographers — notably Michael Sadleir, John Carter, and Joseph W. Rogers.[3]

1. The standard treatment of binding description, upon which the present discussion is based, is Fredson Bowers's *Principles of Bibliographical Description* (1949), pp. 376-78, 446-50.

2. Some canvas bindings were used in this transition period (from about 1770 until the early 1800's) and are discussed by Douglas Leighton in "Canvas and Bookcloth: An Essay on Beginnings," *Library*, 5th ser., III (1948-49), 39-49. This period is also treated in Charles M. Adams, "Illustrated Publishers' Bindings," *BNYPL*, XLI (1937), 607-11 (cf. Davidson Cook, "Illustrations on Bindings," *TLS*, 17 April 1937, p. 296, and the letter from John Carter, 12 June 1937, p. 452). A survey of the binding terms used in catalogues in this period is R. A. Peddie's "Publishers' Bindings, 1762-1850: A List of Terms," *Library World*, XLVI (1943-44), 20-21. For background, see also Graham Pollard, "Changes in the Style of Bookbinding, 1550-1830," *Library*,

5th ser., XI (1956), 71-94; and Ellic Howe "London Bookbinders: Masters and Men, 1780-1840," *Library*, 5th ser., I (1946-47), 28-38.

3. Sadleir, *The Evolution of Publishers' Binding Styles, 1770-1900* (1930); Carter, *Binding Variants in English Publishing, 1820-1900* (1932), and *Publisher's Cloth: An Outline History of Publisher's Binding in England, 1820-1900* (1935) — also published in *Publishers' Weekly*, CXXVII (1935), 807-09, 901-04, 1006-08, 1085-87, 1167-69; Rogers, "The Industrialization of American Bookbinding," *Gutenberg Jahrbuch 1938*, pp. 243-52, and "The Rise of American Edition Binding," in *Bookbinding in America*, ed. Hellmut Lehmann-Haupt (1941, 1967), pp. 129-85. In 1931-32 a series of letters in *Publishers' Circular* discussed the origins of publishers' cloth, following an article by A. Whitaker Ridler, "The Earliest Cloth Binding," *Publishers' Circular*, CXXXV (1931), 763-64; the

The historical investigation of publishers' cloth, while it provides a perspective for viewing specific cloths, does not in itself furnish the framework for classifying them. Sadleir's book of 1930 took the first step by including four photographs of cloths, showing their distinctive textures or "grains"; Carter's of 1932 (which displayed twelve photographs) discussed the problem in "A Note on Terminology" (pp. xv-xviii) and worked out the equivalences between Sadleir's descriptive terms and the letter designations used by the Winterbottom Book Cloth Co. Ltd., the chief manufacturer of book cloth; and Rogers's 1941 essay furnished illustrations of eleven cloths, labeled with the Sadleir-Carter terms (Plates 30-40). It was not until 1951, however, that a collection of photographs of cloth grains was published which could serve as a comprehensive standard of reference. In that year Michael Sadleir included, at the end of the first volume of his *XIX Century Fiction*, illustrations of twenty-four cloth grains, labeled with descriptive names such as "sand grain," "hexagon grain," and "dotted-line-ribbed." Although the photographs were based on the Sadleir collection, that collection was extensive, and the photographs could be taken to represent most of the grains in common use in the nineteenth century;[4] but the photographs were not arranged in terms of any overall system of classification, and their physical location in a large two-volume reference work, which could not always be at hand when a bibliographer needed to identify a cloth, limited their influence as a standard.[5] Four years later, in 1955, appeared a second large collection of photographs. Jacob Blanck, at the beginning of the first volume of his *Bibliography of American Literature*,[6] provided illustrations of

letters, from John Carter, Joseph Pennell, Douglas Leighton, R. A. Peddie, and others, appeared in CXXXV (1931), 781; CXXXVI (1932), 12-13, 28-29. 47, 66. A more recent specialized essay is Sybille Pantazzi, "Four Designers of English Publishers' Bindings, 1850-1880, and Their Signatures," *PBSA*, LV (1961), 88-99. See also George A. Stephen, *Machine Book-sewing, with Remarks on Publishers' Binding* (1908); Douglas Leighton, *Modern Bookbinding: A Survey and a Prospect* (1935); *The Andrus Bindery: A History of the Shop, 1831-1838*, ed. Newton C. Brainard (1940); Edith Diehl, *Bookbinding: Its Background and Technique* (1946), I, 40-42, 70-78; and Lionel S. Darley, *Bookbinding Then and Now: A Survey of the First Hundred and Seventy-Eight Years of James*

Burn & Company (1959). A standard account of the present technology of edition binding is in Victor Strauss's *The Printing Industry* (1967), pp. 617-716.

4. Rogers shows that "English book cloth was the standard article in use in America throughout the century" (p. 163).

5. Sadleir's photographs were reprinted in the *Book Collector* two years later "in order that they may reach the widest possible public and so encourage the use in catalogues and bibliographies of a potentially standard vocabulary." See "The Nomenclature of Nineteenth-Century Cloth Grains," *Book Collector*, II (1953), 54-58.

6. These photographs have been repeated

twenty-eight grains, identified by letter designations (based on the system used in the cloth trade), such as "T" (for ribbed cloth) and "Z" (for what Sadleir calls "honeycomb"). Blanck's selection, with four more photographs than Sadleir's, covered nine grains not present in Sadleir and omitted five which Sadleir included.[7] The fact that a large and important reference work like the *BAL* keyed binding descriptions to photographs by means of letters was bound to be influential, and some bibliographers now refer to "T-cloth," for instance, without finding it necessary to explain the term or provide a reference; yet the system has the same disadvantages as Sadleir's — and in addition utilizes terms which convey no meaning except to the initiated.

Both systems have had a beneficial effect to the extent that they have called attention to the necessity of photographic samples as standards for verbal descriptions. At the same time, the two systems have dramatized the essential split between the two kinds of verbal descriptions: those which employ ordinary words and convey a meaning to every reader, and those which use technical symbols and convey a meaning only to those who have been introduced to the symbols. Both are based on photographs, but the selections are different, and neither suggests a systematic classification. Here the matter rested until 1967, when Martha Hartzog worked out, for the first time, an outline which shows relationships among types of cloth grains.[8] What was needed, as she recognized, was "an overall organizing principle which is consistent and logical, involving a symbol system which is concise and meaningful" (p. 115). She set up seven basic categories of grains, using terms largely derived from Sadleir — Morocco, Pebbly, Beaded, Geometric, Rippled, Striped, Woven — and designated the initial letter of each category as its symbol. Distinct patterns falling within these groups were then numbered — "Sandy," for example, as the second style in the "Pebbly" category, was "P2." Varieties of patterns could be indicated by modifying adjectives, so that "Coarse sandy" became "coarse P2." In Miss Hartzog's words, the system indicates "differences of degree by an adjective and quality by a separate variant number" (p. 118). Although she did not provide photographs, her chart indicated the correspondences between her terms and the illustrations of Sadleir, Blanck, and Carter.[9]

---

at the front of each succeeding volume of *BAL*.

7. For a list showing the equivalences between Sadleir and Blanck, see my note on "The Specification of Binding Cloth," *Li-brary*, 5th ser., XXI (1966), 246-47.

8. "Nineteenth-Century Cloth Bindings," *PBSA*, LXI (1967), 114-19.

9. She also listed the equivalent symbols of Winterbottom, as recorded by Carter.

The Hartzog system is important as the first attempt to provide "a coherent organizational framework within which all cloth bindings can be fitted" (p. 118), and the nature of the system is a revealing indication of the kinds of problems involved. The choice of the seven main divisions, for example, is not self-evident. Since "Geometric" is an inclusive term which subsumes many patterns of geometric regularity, perhaps "Beaded" would more properly be classified as a variety of "Geometric" than as a separate division parallel to it. On the other hand, if the main divisions are to have more specific headings like "Rippled" and "Striped," then perhaps some of the varieties of "Geometric" — like "bead & line" or "herringbone" — deserve to be elevated to the status of generic divisions. The difficulty in formulating a classification of patterns is that there is no natural spectrum on which to base it. In the study of color, one begins with the concept of a spectrum or a solid representing the range of all possible color, and each of the infinite varieties of color has its unalterable place in the scheme. But cloth patterns are artistic, not natural, products, and no natural continuum encompasses them. Is "Striped" a development of "Rippled"? Is "Woven" closer to "Striped" than it is to "Pebbly"? One could construct an argument for various kinds of relationships, but each would be subjective and none would be definitive.[10]

The symbols employed in the Hartzog system further reveal this problem, for such symbols as "P2" and "G7" combine two principles of notation. The letters are intended to be mnemonic — "P" for "Pebbly" and "G" for "Geometric" — and not to show relationships, for alphabetical order cannot be expected to coincide with structural evolution. The numbers, on the other hand, have no mnemonic value but imply a fixed order within each lettered division; yet there is no reason that the patterns must be arranged in this order. Thus the numbers are merely arbitrary index figures, while the letters are suggestive; and the modifying adjectives — as in "coarse P2" — carry the symbols farther in the direction of rational content.[11] Another comparison with the field of color terminology may be helpful. In the ISCC-NBS *Cen-*

10. An example of a thorough and complex scheme of classification in this area is Law Voge and F. R. Blaylock, "Tentative Expanded Classification of Bookbinding Techniques," *Share Your Knowledge Review*, XX (May 1939), 12-21. This outline, intended as a subject guide for a card index of current literature, is not appropriate for the present purpose but does illustrate some of the complications involved in attempting to construct a comprehensive classification in this field.

11. Since there are only five adjectives employed in the Hartzog system ("fine," "smooth," "coarse," "diagonal," "reverse"), they could easily be abbreviated with small letters to render the symbols more concise — thus "coarse P2" could become "P2c."

troid Color Charts (1965) the letter symbols — such as "d.yG" for "dark yellowish green" — are intended to serve only as easily recognizable abbreviations (to be used when it is inconvenient to spell out complete words), not as reference notations. For purposes of reference the centroid colors are numbered consecutively from 1 to 267, and any given centroid color may be referred to by its number ("d.yG" is 137). A single consecutive sequence of figures is feasible in the case of color because the spectrum of possible colors defines the scope of the classification. If the entire range of color is divided into 267 segments, those segments can be definitively numbered, because it is logically impossible for anyone to discover a new segment which should be inserted, say, between segments 137 and 138. In the classification of patterns, however, subdivisions can never be definitively established, since (in the absence of a spectrum) the possibility will always remain that another pattern may be discovered or a new pattern devised. An outline, with provision for expansion at any point, is therefore the most workable form of classification for material which, like patterns, does not fall into a continuous series. The Hartzog system recognizes this fact; while the numbered series of species under each major division (or genus) does not represent any necessary sequence, it at least provides for the indefinite expansion of that division, and the modifying adjectives allow for variations within the species.

The outline and illustrations offered below as a standard for the classification and nomenclature of binding-cloth grains are therefore derived from the Hartzog system, but with a number of modifications based on the rationale just presented. In the first place, it is imperative that the divisions in a classification in outline form be not only parallel but mutually exclusive. The seven divisions in the Hartzog system do not fulfill this condition, for such terms as "Pebbly" and "Beaded" are too precise to be parallel to inclusive terms like "Geometric" and "Woven"; neither are they mutually exclusive, for "bead & line," included under "Geometric" (G7), could have been placed under "Beaded," since "pebble & line" is listed under "Pebbly" (P5). The first mutually exclusive division which suggests itself is one which distinguishes those patterns that are regular from those that are irregular: regular patterns reproduce themselves precisely, while irregular ones repeat themselves only in general effect but not in exact detail. Regular patterns, in turn, may be divided into those which are lineal in their symmetry and those which are radial; both "Rippled" and "Striped," among the Hartzog terms, are lineal, while both "Beaded" and "Geometric" are radial. Irregular patterns divide themselves into those which resemble fabric threads and those which resemble leather grains; the Hartzog heading "Woven" corresponds roughly to the former, but the latter comprises both "Morocco" and "Pebbly." Beyond these four divisions, mutually exclusive categories are increasingly difficult to formulate and cumbersome to employ, and it seems most sensible simply to list the basic patterns under them. In the numbering system suggested here, the four divisions are assigned to the hundreds-digit, and the two succeeding digits signify the particular pattern.[12] Since any pattern can be made more coarse or fine, and since most patterns can be given a watered effect or a diagonal arrangement, these variations do not properly constitute separate patterns and are indicated here by letters which can be used to form subdivisions of any of the numbered patterns.

CLOTH PATTERNS

REGULAR		IRREGULAR	
100	*Lineal*	300	*Fibrous*
2	Rib	2	Calico
4	Ripple	4	Linen
6	Wave	6	Cord
8	Dotted-line		
10	Dot-and-line		
12	Dot-and-ribbon		
14	Beaded-line		
16	Weave	400	*Coriaceous*
18	Net	2	Morocco
20	Crisscross	4	Straight-grain morocco
22	Checkerboard	6	Pebble
24	Diaper	8	Sand
		10	Patterned sand
200	*Radial*	12	Whorl
2	Bead		
4	Bubble		
6	Hexagon		
8	Honeycomb		
10	Pansy		

Modifiers

(a)	(regular)	d	moiré
b	fine	e	diagonal
c	coarse	f	moiré diagonal

Thus "rib-cloth" is 102, "fine rib-cloth" 102b, and "diagonal fine rib-cloth" 102be. Additional patterns can be accommodated by inserting

12. Logically, the thousands-digit should be employed to make the primary distinction between "Regular" and "Irregular" patterns; but in order to keep the figures more conveniently manageable, the two major divisions under "Regular" and the two under "Irregular" are assigned to four consecutive hundreds.

numbers between those given (only even numbers are used here to allow for this possibility) or by extending any of the series of numbers.

It should be understood that these numbers and letters are only reference figures and not substitutes for pattern names. They have no significance in themselves, but they serve two functions: they provide index figures for referring to photographs; and they make possible a meaningful arrangement of photographs, in which related patterns are grouped together. In a bibliographical description, both the name of the cloth pattern and its reference figure should always be given (followed by a designation of the color of the cloth), as in these examples:

> moiré fine rib-cloth (102bd), deep brown (Centroid 56) [13]
> coarse diaper-cloth (124c), very dark red (17)
> diagonal dot-and-line-cloth (110ae), strong yellowish green (131)
> fine pebble-cloth (406b), grayish blue (186)

The verbal description enables the reader to visualize the cloth — exactly enough for many purposes — without reference to any illustration; but if he needs to know more precisely the details of the pattern described, he can use the reference number to locate the illustration in the accompanying set of photographs (or in any future set based on this system). When he does so, he finds related patterns close together; but if the cloth on the copy he is checking turns out to be a variety not illustrated, this system provides for interpolation. If, for example, it is bead-cloth of a coarser texture than that illustrated as 202, he can label it "coarse bead-cloth (202c)," even though no illustration for 202c is available. The importance of a standardized terminology cannot be overemphasized: a name, when defined by reference to an illustration, can be precise only if it is used exclusively for that pattern and if the pattern is always referred to by that name. Since the terms employed by Sadleir and Carter have achieved fairly wide acceptance and utilize commonly understood words, they form the natural basis for any standard terminology. The descriptive names assigned here are essentially theirs, though for parallelism all are listed in noun forms; for bibliographical descriptions, the names of the patterns should probably be attached with a hyphen to the word "cloth" (as "bead-cloth"). Modifying adjectives are reserved for indicating variations of a pattern: "fine" or "coarse" immediately precede the name of the pattern, but,

13. This parallel system of referring to colors by the names and reference numbers established in the ISCC-NBS dictionary (1955) and color charts (1965) is described in my "A System of Color Indentification for Bibliographical Description," *SB*, XX (1967), 203-34.

when a pattern corresponds to the norm between the two, no adjective is required; adjectives for other qualities (like "moiré"), when needed, precede the indication of coarseness ("moiré fine rib-cloth," not "fine moiré rib-cloth"). When the letters standing for these adjectives are appended to the reference figures in alphabetical order,[14] the resulting arrangement of photographs preserves the basic grouping of variations according to coarseness.[15]

Since the illustrations in Blanck's *Bibliography of American Literature* and in Sadleir's *XIX Century Fiction* have been consulted by many bibliographers in recent years and since some bibliographical descriptions refer to one or the other, it may be convenient to have a table of equivalences. The list below records the reference figure in the present system which corresponds to each of the photographs in *BAL* and Sadleir (and in the three previous showings of grains):[16]

EQUIVALENCES

BAL

A	306	CM	408c	LG	404b	T	102
AA	102bd	EC	122	LI	402	TB	118
AR	306c	FL	108	P	406	TR	106
B	304	H	124b	PD	112ae	TZ	106ae
BD	202	HC	206	PR	412	V	302
BF	202b	HT	110	RH	210	YR	304c
C	408	L	404	S	102be	Z	208

Sadleir (*1951*)

i	402b	vii	102be	xiii	106ae	xix	118
ii	402	viii	102bd	xiv	104	xx	116
iii	124b	ix	202	xv	108c	xxi	406
iv	124c	x	202b	xvi	108	xxii	208
v	408	xi	106	xvii	110	xxiii	210
vi	410	xii	204	xviii	120	xxiv	206

14. Just as the adjective "regular" need not be used for patterns representing the norm, so the letter "a" need not be attached to the number when there is no other modfier. But whenever a regular grain is moiré or diagonal, the "a" should be inserted before "d," "e," or "f" in order to keep the regular grains grouped together. Thus "102" would be followed by "102ad" and "102ae" and then by "102b."

15. The adjective "reverse" (included in the Hartzog system) is not listed here among the basic adjectives which are assigned letters in the classification because it seems superfluous to provide photographs of reversed patterns. Sometimes binders do use cloth with the reverse side out, how-ever, and in these cases the verbal description can include the word "reversed."

16. The 1953 printing of the Sadleir photographs in the *Book Collector* (II, 54-58) shows the grains in the same order (and with the same names) as in *XIX Century Fiction* but without the accompanying roman numerals. The "ribbon-embossed" cloths depicted by Sadleir (Plate IVb, 1931), Carter (Photograph *e*), and Rogers (Plate 33) are here classed as "pebble-cloth" because the background corresponds to pebble-cloth; the embossed ribbon pattern is the kind of ornamentation which — as explained below — must be taken up separately for each book.

Sadleir (1930)

| IVa | 402 | IVb | 406 | IVc | 102 | IVd | 202 |

Carter   *Rogers*

a	302	g	106be	30	402	36	404
b	402b	h	106	31	102af	37	202
c	102bf	i	202	32	124c	38	106
d	124	j	114ce	33	406	39	408
e	406	k	408	34	102	40	110
f	102	l	110	35	102b		

This table facilitates cross-references among the systems. If a bibliographer, checking a previously published description which utilizes Blanck's letters, finds it more convenient to look at the photograph of the cloth in the chart presented here, he can easily make the conversion to the proper reference figure. Similarly, if a bibliographer is examining a book but has only Sadleir readily available, he can match the cloth with a Sadleir photograph and later convert the description to the name and figure suggested here. What is important is not the particular photograph used but its relation to one central system with fixed terminology.

How exact the match between a cloth and a photograph should be is part of the general question of tolerances[17] and must necessarily vary with different circumstances. The dividing lines between "fine," "regular," and "coarse" — like those between "condensed" and "expanded" in regard to type faces — are not precise, and the decision to call a cloth "coarse" rather than "regular," when it falls between the illustrations of the two, will sometimes be subjective. Whether or not this imprecision takes on practical importance depends on the degree of accuracy required in a particular instance. If two states of the binding of a given book are too similar to be distinguished by means of a standard set of photographs, the bibliographer may find it necessary to include in his bibliography special illustrations of the two varieties. The standard provides a frame of reference but cannot eliminate entirely the need for individual photographs; in most cases, however, such fine distinctions in the specification of cloth grains are not necessary. Only the bibliographer who has examined a great number of copies of a book is in a position to decide the degree of precision desirable in any instance.

Since various levels of accuracy and detail are appropriate in different situations, it is helpful to think in terms of a standard series of

17. For a general statement on this subject, see my "Tolerances in Bibliographical Description," *Library*, 5th ser., XXIII (1968), 1-12.

graduated levels.[18] On the first and least detailed level, only the distinction among basic binding materials is made — leather, vellum, cloth, or paper. Many early bibliographies, even those which give careful attention to such details as line-endings in title-page transcriptions, represent this level; but it is now generally agreed that publishers' bindings require fuller description than the simple designation of "cloth" or "paper." The next step, if the material is cloth, is to classify the design in terms of one of the four major divisions (e.g., "a lineal-pattern cloth," "a fibrous-pattern cloth," and so on). This level, like the previous one, is not sufficiently detailed for most bibliographical work. In general, descriptive bibliographies can be expected to conform to one of the next two levels: the third, involving the designation of specific patterns ("rib-cloth," "pebble-cloth," etc.); or the fourth, adding the adjectives which distinguish varieties of each pattern (as "coarse diaper-cloth" or "diagonal rib-cloth"). If further refinement is necessary in a particular case, one can move to a fifth level and specify divergences within the standard modified terms. Instead of piling on additional adjectives, one can use the phrase "a variety of"; the reference is then either to a special photograph (if an exact representation is required) or to the standard photograph, with the index figure preceded by "cf." (if an approximate match is adequate):

> a variety of fine bead-cloth (see Plate 00)
> *or* a variety of fine bead-cloth (cf. 202b)

It should be understood that "cf." is used only to indicate variations between cloths covered by the same name — between, for example, "fine bead-cloth (202b) " and "a variety of fine bead-cloth (cf. 202b) ." Generally speaking, if such distinctions are required, it is also necessary to provide individual photographs of the specific cloths involved. The absence of "cf." in a given case does not imply that the match is exact but only that the fourth level is adequate. Finally, one can attain a sixth level in some instances, if the proper documents survive and the effort is worth making, by tracing a cloth to a specimen book of a particular manufacturer; but the standard pattern names employed on the preceding levels are still required to complete the verbal description.

Once the specification of the cloth grain on one of these levels is completed, there remains the problem of describing the pattern or

18. This concept was suggested by Kenneth L. Kelly's system of levels for specifying colors in "A Universal Color Language," *Color Engineering*, III (March- April 1965), 2-7; its application to descriptive bibliography is more fully discussed in the essay on "Tolerances" cited above.

decoration stamped into the cloth for the edition casing of a particular book. Sometimes such patterns resemble those found on leather bindings and could be referred to by the names employed for them by the historians of the art of bookbinding decoration — such names as "Harleian" or "Grolier," "fanfare" or "cottage." But the historical associations of such terms, as well as their established use in connection with hand-tooled leather bindings, make unwise any attempt to apply them to the mass-produced designs of publishers' cloth casings. Instead, terms more immediately descriptive, like those adopted for cloth grains, seem more appropriate. Some of the phrases used in the description of leather bindings, of course, are of this sort — such as "center and corner piece" or "interlacing strapwork" — and they can equally well be applied to the stampings in cloth bindings; but normally terms must be devised to meet specific situations. Any such *ad hoc* description should be kept as simple as possible and be accompanied by a reference to a photograph of the design. The number of binding designs employed by publishers over the years is naturally so much greater than the number of cloth grains that it would not be feasible to attempt the compilation of a comprehensive and classified set of photographs; rather, those designs which need to be referred to in a given bibliography should be illustrated by plates within that bibliography.[19] Such a requirement does not necessitate showing every individual binding, for the principle of illustration can still be generic rather than specific: one design, used on several different books, need be illustrated only once. Since publishers frequently have employed the same binding design, as a kind of trade-mark, on successive volumes by the same author, the number of patterns which require reproduction in any single author-bibliography should not be excessively large. This system combines — as in the designation of cloth grains — a readily understood general description with a specific reference to an illustration and at the same time emphasizes, by the use of generic illustrations, the relationships among binding designs.

As an example of a complete binding (or casing) description, the

---

19. Pictures blocked into or pasted onto the binding cloth are a different matter, of course, since they are not "designs" or "patterns" as those terms are used here. A bibliographer may choose, for various reasons, to reproduce such pictures; but their inclusion in a bibliography is less important than the inclusion of patterns, for patterns often recur on other books (whether by the same author or other authors) issued by the same publisher. Reproducing these patterns thus enhances the value of the bibliography as a contribution to the history of the book trade and will ultimately facilitate the comprehensive study of publishing practices in a given period.

following represents the paragraph on casing from a description of the 1855 Harper impression of Melville's *Typee*:

CASING. *Material*: diagonal wave-cloth (106ae), brownish black (Centroid 65). *Front*: blind-stamped decorative-rule frame, 16 mm. wide (Harper 4, Plate 00). *Spine*: stamped in strong orange (50), '[quadruple rule (thin-thick-thin-decorative)] | TYPEE: | OR | FOUR MONTHS | IN THE | MARQUESAS. | NEW-YORK. | HARPER & BROTHERS. | [quadruple rule (decorative-thin-thick-thin)]'. *Back*: same as front. *Edges*: cut, undecorated. *Endpapers*: pale greenish yellow (104) surface paper.

Such a description is understandable without reference to any illustrations and allows any reader to visualize the casing. If a reader is in doubt about the meaning of a patricular term or if he thinks he has discovered a variant but is not sure on the basis of the verbal description, he can turn to the references indicated and find visual specimens. For the cloth grain and the colors, he is referred to a comprehensive generic standard; for the ornamentation of the cloth he is provided with a plate in this particular bibliography. But in every case a commonly understood term is reinforced by the citation of a specific standard. Only in this way can the terms become standardized and take on an exact significance.

II. DECORATED PAPERS

Paper, decorated by various processes, was used in connection with bookbinding long before the introduction of publishers' casings, and it remains today an important resource for the designers of bindings. In both hand- and machine-bound volumes, endpapers are often decorated in one fashion or another, and the boards forming the front and back covers are frequently adorned with decorated papers (in conjunction with cloth or leather spines, and sometimes corners as well).[20] Despite the widespread use of decorated paper as a binding material, little historical study of it has been made, and virtually no discussion treats it from the viewpoint of the descriptive bibliographer; the literature of the subject, though extensive, concentrates more on the methods of producing the patterns than on the history of the art. One exception is Rosamond B. Loring's classic *Decorated Book Papers* (1942, 1952),[21]

20. See Hellmut Lehmann-Haupt, "The Use of Paper as a Cover Material," in *Bookbinding in America* (1941, 1967), pp. 211-18 (cf. pp. 269-72).

21. The second edition of the book (1952), edited by Philip Hofer, contains an essay by Dard Hunter on "Rosamond Loring's Place in the Study and Making of Decorated Papers," pp. xxvii-xxxii. Another comprehensive work is Albert Haemmerle and Olga Hirsch, *Buntpapier: Herkommen, Geschichte, Techniken, Beziehungen zur Kunst* (1961), which includes an

a pioneer work based on the study and classification of the Loring collection (now at Harvard); it should be the starting point for any bibliographical investigation of the subject.

What the bibliographer requires, in this area as in any other involving patterns, is a system of classification and a standardized terminology. Since the characteristics of patterns are determined, to a large extent, by the methods used to produce the patterns, the most meaningful basic scheme for classifying decorated papers groups them according to the processes of production. The conventional system, as it emerges from the work of Loring and other writers,[22] has four divisions into which the majority of decorated papers fall:

> Marbled
> Printed
> Embossed
> Paste

In most cases a bibliographer will wish to include somewhat more detail than the simple indication of "decorated paper"; his next step, then, is to place the paper in one of these categories. Marbled papers are produced by bringing the paper into contact with colors which are floating on the surface of a gelatinous solution; the designs frequently resemble the veined patterns of marble but, if the colors are combed, may take on more regular forms. The term "printed paper" encompasses all papers produced by the transfer of a design from a carved wood-block, an engraved plate, and the like. Embossed papers have raised patterns; and paste papers, produced by manipulating a flour-and-water mixture on their surfaces, can be recognized by the blurred and cloudy effect of their designs. Technological developments have tended to make these divisions less distinct by introducing different methods for reproducing characteristic designs. Marbled and paste patterns, for example, can be reproduced and printed photolithographically, and it would be inexact to refer to the result as "marbled paper" or "paste paper." What the bibliographer should do in such cases is to

---

extensive bibliography (pp. 183-95). Other historical studies are Bertrand Guégan, "History and Manufacture of End-Papers" (trans. Katherine Knight), *Publishers' Weekly*, CXVI (1929), 1755-57, 1759; Edith Diehl, *Bookbinding: Its Background and Technique* (1946), I, 182-89; and Charles M. Adams, "Some Notes on the Art of Marbling Paper in the Seventeenth Century," *BNYPL*, LI (1947), 411-22.

22. See, for example, Enid Marx, "Pattern Papers," *Penrose Annual*, XLIV (1950), 51-53; and Olga Hirsch, "Decorated Papers," *Penrose Annual*, LI (1957), 48-53. For further samples, see *A Specimen Book of Pattern Papers, Designed for and in Use at the Curwen Press* (1928).

speak of "marbled-pattern paper" or "paste-pattern paper"; if he can determine the method of reproduction he can add that information: "paste-pattern paper, photolithographically printed." This usage avoids the ambiguity which arises when the basic terms are allowed to refer at times to the patterns as distinct from the processes and at other times to the patterns as the result of the processes.

Classifying a paper under one of these headings does not yet provide the reader of a bibliography with a very precise idea of the pattern, and most bibliographers will move to a third level of detail, which involves describing the main features of the particular pattern. A standard set of photographs would of course be helpful for this purpose, if one could be produced; but the last three divisions listed above — "Printed," "Embossed," and "Paste" — offer the same difficulties as those presented by the patterns stamped into cloth for the casings of particular books. So many variations are possible in these categories that no chart could be devised which would do more than illustrate characteristic specimens; it could not, in other words, be used as a standard for matching and identification. Under such circumstances, the most efficient and exact method is to frame in words a simple description of the prominent features of the pattern and then provide a reference to an accompanying plate in which the particular pattern is illustrated. Indication of the principal colors is also a necessary part of the verbal description, as in these examples:

printed paper, with medium olive brown (Centroid 95) birds and scroll-work on a deep green (142) background (see Plate oo)

embossed paper, with silver flowers on a dark blue (183) background (see Plate oo)

paste paper, grayish reddish orange (39), with horses and trees stamped alternately (see Plate oo)

paste-pattern paper, photolithographically printed in grayish reddish orange (39), with lozenges stamped on a brushed background (see Plate oo)

Standardization of terminology, beyond the names of the basic kinds of paper and the colors, is not possible in this situation; what can be achieved is standardization of approach.

The remaining category, "Marbled," can be handled somewhat differently. Because of the nature of the marbling process, the number of types of pattern is more restricted; every specimen, though unique, corresponds in its general outlines to one of a relatively small number of kinds of pattern. Specifying marbled papers[23] is thus analogous to identifying binding-cloth grains, and, as with grains, a set of photographs showing the principal patterns is feasible. Although much has been written on the subject of marbling,[24] there has been almost no attention given to the problem of classifying the various patterns. The two major books in English on marbling — those by Woolnough and Halfer[25] — are comprehensive enough, however, both in their discussions of methods and in their inclusion of actual samples, to provide a useful starting point for surveying the range of possible patterns. But they would not be practical choices as standards of reference because they are not at present widely available and because their emphasis is on the techniques of production rather than on classification. What is needed, from the point of view of the descriptive bibliographer, is a set of photographs of basic patterns, each illustration accompanied by a standard name and reference figure.

The outline below is an attempt to extract from the literature of marbling a meaningful and comprehensive scheme of classification. All marbled patterns fall into one of two categories, according to whether or not the colors are drawn after they are dropped onto the solution. If they are not touched, the resulting patterns (here called "Whisked") consist of irregular spots separated by veins and resemble real marble; if the colors are manipulated by a stylus, comb, or other utensil, the resulting patterns (here called "Combed") contain more regular lines, swirls, or loops and generally do not suggest actual marble. Traditional names for the individual patterns have emerged over the years (marbling dates from the sixteenth century); even though some of these names are not in themselves descriptive, they have become so well

23. The marbling process can be applied to cloth as well as paper, and marbled cloth has occasionally been used as a binding material; see Bernard C. Middleton, *A Manual of the Art of Bookbinding Technique* (1963).

24. See Dard Hunter, "A Bibliography of Marbled Paper," *Paper Trade Journal*, LXXII (28 April 1921), 52, 54, 56, 58.

25. C. W. Woolnough, *The Whole Art of Marbling* (1853, 1881); Josef Halfer, *The Progress of the Marbling Art* (1884; trans. Herman Dieck, 1893). Other prominent treatments of marbling, with a number of samples, are M. Fichtenberg's *Nouveau*

Manuel Complet du Fabricant de Papiers de Fantasie (1852); James B. Nicholson's *A Manual of the Art of Bookbinding* (1856), pp. 82-130, 246-56; and Rosamond B. Loring's *Marbled Papers* (1933). A more recent display of marbling patterns is the frontispiece to Bernard C. Middleton's *A History of English Craft Bookbinding Technique* (1963). Verbal descriptions of the standard patterns are given in E. J. Labarre's *Dictionary and Encyclopaedia of Paper and Paper-Making* (1952), pp. 155-58. The best places to examine samples, of course, are in such outstanding collections as that of Olga Hirsch (British Museum) — see Printing Historical Society *Newsletter*, No. 12, Feb. 1969.

established that it would be impractical at this point to introduce a new set of terms. Alternate names exist for several patterns, and they are recorded in parentheses in this outline, with the preference in each case given to the more descriptive one.

MARBLED PATTERNS

1100	*Whisked*	1200	*Combed*
2	German	2	Nonpareil
4	Hair-Vein (Italian)	4	Dutch
6	Stormont	6	Antique Spot
8	Gloster	8	Curl (Snail)
10	Shell (French)	10	Peacock
12	Smooth Body	12	Bouquet
	(1112d = Spanish)		

Modifiers

(a)	(regular)	d	moiré
b	fine	g	drag
c	coarse	h	moiré drag

This classification follows the same plan as the one for cloth grains and allows for expansion in the same way. The index numbers facilitate reference to standard illustrations; and the accompanying set of photographs, showing the basic patterns, can perhaps serve as the first step toward such a standard. It is printed in black and white because its function is to display patterns, not colors. Although some of the patterns are traditionally associated with certain colors, there is no necessary connection, and it is best to keep the specification of color a distinct process from the specification of pattern.

Given the nature of these names, one can learn their significance most readily by studying the photographs, but it may be helpful to point out verbally some of the characteristics of the patterns. "German" consists simply of small spots and, unlike the other whisked patterns, does not have veins. "Hair-Vein" (often called "Italian"), has, as the name suggests, a fine network of thin hair-like veins. In "Stormont" the presence of turpentine creates many small dots which give the pattern a lacy effect; "Gloster" also has fine dots on the body color, but its veins are thick and multi-colored, in contrast to the thin veins of "Stormont." The "Shell," or "French Shell," pattern displays light shell-like rings on the body color, produced by the addition of olive oil. If a pattern has veins of medium thickness and a body color not mottled with dots or rings, it may be given the name "Smooth Body," as here. The most common variety of this pattern, called "Spanish," is characterized by diagonal streaks traversing the basic pattern, giving it a moiré effect.[26] Among the combed patterns, "Nonpareil," easily recognizable by its horizontal parallel lines, has been perhaps the most widely used. "Dutch" is similar, except that the colors follow one another in an exact sequence and can come together in an occasional curl. If the colors are drawn along an irregular path, rather than in straight lines, and spots of a lighter color are then dropped on, the result is another pattern encountered frequently, "Antique" or "Antique Spot." "Curl," "French Curl," or "Snail," as the name implies, involves the use of a frame which can produce a series of rotary movements and thus a pattern consisting of rows of coiled colors. Similarly, "Peacock" and "Bouquet" require equipment which can produce fan-shaped designs reminiscent of peacock feathers or sprays of flowers.[27]

If the bibliographer finds it desirable to move one step farther, he can add modifying adjectives to these names, as in the designation of cloth grains. The relative terms "fine" and "coarse" are more frequently applied to the combed patterns to indicate the nature of the comb, but they can also be used with the whisked patterns to suggest the relative distances between the veins. When it is necessary for the bibliographer to make distinctions on this basis among examples of the same basic pattern, he can take the illustrations presented here as "regular." The other adjectives, "moiré" and "drag," are more commonly used for the whisked patterns. In this connection, "drag" refers to the elongated spots produced when the paper is dragged along the surface of the size.

Whenever the addition of these adjectives does not provide a

26. Because a watered effect can be produced on other patterns as well, "moiré" must be used as a modifying adjective which can be attached to any pattern name; therefore "Spanish," though a prominent pattern, cannot logically be listed as one of the basic unmodified patterns, since the moiré effect is an essential part of what the name traditionally implies.

27. Detailed descriptions of the methods of producing the various patterns are found in the books by Woolnough, Halfer, Nicholson, and Loring. Among other treatments are Sydney M. Cockerell, *Marbling Paper as a School Subject* (1934); J. Halliday's essay in *How to Make Hand Decorated Patterned Papers for Book Craft* (2nd ed., 1934), pp. 36-42; Franz Weisse, *Die Kunst des Marmorierens* (1940); Tim Thrift, *Modern Methods in Marbling Paper* (1945); Morris S. Kantrowitz and Ernest W. Spencer, *Process of Marbling Paper* (GPO-PIA Joint Research Bulletin B-1, 1947); "Marbling Magic," *Inland Printer*, CXXII (Jan. 1949) 48-49; G. Bernard Hughes, "English Marbled Papers," *Country Life*, CXII (1952), 2100-01; William Bond Wheelwright, "How Marbled Papers Are Made," *Paper Maker*, XXII, no. 2 (Sept. 1953), 1-5; and "The Neglected Art of Paper Marbling: A Detailed Survey of Current American Techniques and Materials," *British Printer*, LXVII (March-April 1955), 36-41. Cf. Kiyofusa Narita, "Suminagashi," *Paper Maker*, XXIV, no. 1 (Feb. 1955), 27-31.

precise enough reference, the bibliographer can go on to a fifth level
(as with cloth) and note variations within patterns by the phrase "a
variety of" (and "cf." before the index figure); he may also find it
necessary to include specific photographs of the papers involved. The
fact that only a small number of adjectives are listed in the outline
should not prevent the bibliographer working on this level from
employing additional ones when the occasion arises. Those listed represent the standard ways of modifying a pattern and are theoretically
applicable to all patterns; but, particularly in the case of the combed
patterns, the unlimited variations cannot always be accurately designated without recourse to other descriptive words or phrases (such as
"crosswise nonpareil," meaning nonpareil produced by drawing the
comb crosswise). When such additional terms are employed, they
should be accompanied by a reference to an illustration of the particular pattern.

Specification of the colors in marbled patterns is best handled in
two different ways, depending on the nature of the pattern. For
whisked patterns the most prominent color (the "body color") should
be given first, followed by the colors of the veins; for combed patterns
it is generally sufficient simply to list the colors included:

shell marbled paper (1110), with medium orange (Centroid 53) body and
    veins of dark blue (183)

nonpareil marbled paper (1202), in very deep red (14), dark blue (183),
    brilliant yellow (83), and white

In binding descriptions, "paper" should be taken to mean "paper-
covered boards," in the same way that "cloth" means "cloth-covered
boards"; if the paper is used by itself, the term "wrappers" should be
included or the paragraph should be headed "Wrappers." The following examples of openings of possible paragraphs on publishers' casings
will illustrate the usage:

CASING. *Material*: sides of drag Spanish marbled paper (1112h), with dark
gray (Centroid 266) body and veins of medium blue (182), strong reddish
orange (35), medium orange yellow (71), black, and white; spine and
corners of coarse calico-cloth (302c), brilliant blue (177) . . . .

CASING. *Material*: sides of printed paper, with light olive brown (94) fleurs-
de-lys on a pale yellow (89) background (see Plate 00); spine of fine rib-
cloth (102b), very dark red (17) . . . .

WRAPPERS. *Material*: Dutch marbled paper (1204), in dark red (16), deep
orange yellow (69), yellowish white (92), and light blue (181) . . . .

Decorated papers can thus be dealt with in the same fashion as publishers' cloth, by making reference to standard illustrations for a limited number of basic patterns and to special photographs for the numerous other patterns which may arise.

III. LETTERPRESS SHEETS

Patterns may also appear in the sheets of a book, on the same pages as letterpress. The most common location for such decoration is the title page, where there may be a border or a design separating the major elements of the page; but patterns occur frequently in other places, such as the beginnings and endings of chapters or principal divisions. They may be reproduced by means of wood-blocks, typographical ornaments, or various other processes.[28] The nature of these patterns, therefore, is not similar to that of cloth grains or marbled papers, with their relatively small number of standard designs; obviously, from the point of view of the difficulty of classification, patterns in letterpress sheets are analogous to those of cloth ornamentation or of printed, embossed, or paste papers. A publisher can use a different border on every title page if he chooses, and no limited selection of illustrations of these borders could do more than offer characteristic examples; it could not serve as a guide to the identification and description of any given border. Generally, then, verbal descriptions of patterns in letterpress sheets must be keyed to specific illustrations of individual patterns.

There are exceptions, however. Whereas binding cloths and decorated papers are of interest to the descriptive bibliographer chiefly in the period since the advent of publishers' bindings, when the output of books has been enormous, the patterns in letterpress sheets are the descriptive bibliographer's concern in all books since the beginning of printing. For the earlier periods, when the number of books was smaller, the supply of types and woodcuts more restricted, and the technology less advanced, the task of cataloguing all the patterns in particular categories, though not an easy one, is at least feasible. As a result, a few excellent reference works of this kind exist, particularly those issued by the Bibliographical Society in its series of "Illustrated Monographs" and "Facsimiles and Illustrations." R. B. McKerrow and F. S. Ferguson's *Title-page Borders Used in England and Scotland,*

---

28. Engraved title pages, though produced separately and not part of the sheets, are also covered by this discussion. For terminology to employ in describing typographical ornaments, Franz Sales Meyer's *A Handbook of Ornament* (trans. Hugh Stannus, 1894) is sometimes helpful.

1485-1640 (1932)[29] provides a model of a pattern-reference which bibliographers can hope may eventually be repeated in other areas. Within its self-imposed limits (borders designed specifically as borders, not those made up of typographical ornaments), it illustrates each border and records the books in which each appeared. When a bibliographer is describing a book that includes one of these borders, he can identify the border precisely by simply appending to his brief verbal description the appropriate McKerrow-Ferguson number. Besides serving as a standard of visual reference, the McKerrow-Ferguson work, in listing all the occurrences of a border, provides in effect a history of each pattern; this information about the course of a pattern through the hands of several printers may be important for the bibliographer's analysis of the dating and printing of a particular work. A. F. Johnson's *German Renaissance Title-Borders* (1929) and *A Catalogue of Engraved and Etched English Title-Pages down to . . . 1691* (1934) are other examples of title-page reference works for the same period.

Woodcut illustrations are frequently not "patterns" in the sense employed here, but some patterns are woodcuts, and any reference book which comprehensively catalogues the woodcuts of a period should be consulted in connection with the identification of patterns; for early English books, the chief work is Edward Hodnett's *English Woodcuts, 1480-1535* (1935). Publishers' devices constitute a similar category: not patterns themselves, they can form the basis of patterns and are repeated from one book to another. Verbal descriptions of devices in early English books should be keyed to R. B. McKerrow's *Printers' & Publishers' Devices in England & Scotland, 1485-1640* (1913).[30] While it is possible to survey all the borders, woodcuts, and devices used in particular countries during the first two or three centuries of printing and produce catalogues for precise identification, it is clearly impossible to attain such comprehensiveness for later periods, when the output of the press reached staggering proportions.

A workable approach for later periods is to organize the study of patterns by publisher. The task of recording the borders and other patterns (and devices) used by a particular publisher, even a prolific one of the nineteenth or twentieth century, is manageable; indeed, it should be a regular part of any full-scale study of a publishing house. Publishing histories could then become the standard reference works

29. See also F. S. Ferguson, "Additions to *Title-page Borders, 1485-1640*," *Library*, 4th ser., XVII (1936-37), 264-311.

30. See also W. Craig Ferguson, "Some Additions to McKerrow's *Printers' and Publishers' Devices*," *Library*, 5th ser., XIII (1958), 201-03; and J. A. Lavin. "Additions to McKerrow's *Devices*," *Library*, 5th ser., XXIII (1968), 191-205.

for the descriptive bibliographer in his specification of the patterns in letterpress sheets. Some histories of publishers already exist which serve this function in regard to devices. Geoffrey Keynes's *William Pickering Publisher* (1924) and Sidney Kramer's *A History of Stone & Kimball and Herbert S. Stone & Company* (1940) bring together at one place reproductions of all the devices used by these firms; each is numbered and can be referred to by number in the description of any title page (or spine) bearing it. A Coleridge bibliographer, when he comes to the 1844 Pickering *Poems*, can thus refer in his title-page transcription to "[dolphin and anchor device within oval scrollwork frame (Keynes ix)]." As more studies of major publishers become available, recording not only devices but all patterns used by these publishers, the task of specifying such patterns in bibliographies will become increasingly more simple and more exact. In the meantime, most descriptions of patterns occurring in letterpress sheets will have to be accompanied by specific illustrations.

Greater standardization in the specification of patterns in descriptive bibliographies is desirable in order to make verbal descriptions more precise. After all, any rendering in words of visual characteristics depends for its meaning on conventions, and the more detailed the conventions the more exact the verbal reference can be. Standardization should not, however, be carried to the point where it restricts rather than facilitates; and the infinite variety of possible patterns in books raises this problem in an acute form. In the case of certain patterns — cloth grains and marbled designs — a comprehensive standard and generic scheme of classification can be devised without becoming so involved or cumbersome as to defeat the purpose; and other patterns which by their nature must be illustrated specifically rather than generically can still be covered comprehensively for certain periods without becoming unmanageable. But in some cases the attempt to bring together all patterns falling within a given category (such as all stamped patterns on nineteenth-century publishers' casings) might not be worth the effort, if the result was so unwieldy that reference to it was more time-consuming and less meaningful than reference to a limited set of illustrations provided for the specific purposes of one bibliography.

Whenever a comprehensive standard set of photographs is possible, it is to be preferred to separate photographs in individual bibliographies, for two reasons: since terms become precise to the extent that everyone uses them to refer to the same things, widespread reference to a single set of photographs serves to encourage this precision;

in addition, reference to a standard more comprehensive than is possible on the basis of a single author-bibliography places the individual pattern in a larger context and provides a more meaningful form of description. Whether or not a comprehensive standard is possible — or presently available — in a given area, the general principle is the same: a bibliographical description must remain a verbal construction, but its descriptive phrases can have exact meanings only if they are supported by reference to pictorial representations. This double approach lays the groundwork for a generally understood terminology and therefore, however clumsily, bridges the gap between the verbal and the visual.

Sources of Photographs

In order not to multiply unnecessarily the number of individual photographs of grains and patterns in print, the photographs presented here have been selected from those previously published (and therefore already used by a number of people). The following seventeen are reprinted, by kind permission of Yale University Press, from Jacob Blanck's *Bibliography of American Literature* (1955-): 102, 110, 112ae, 118, 122, 202, 202b, 302, 304, 304c, 306, 306c, 402, 404, 404b, 408c, 412. From Michael Sadleir's *XIX Century Fiction* (1951), by kind permission of the University of California Press, come the following nineteen: 102bd, 102be, 104, 106, 106ae, 108, 108c, 116, 120, 124b, 124c, 204, 206, 208, 210, 402b, 406, 408, 410. Those reprinted from Bernard C. Middleton's *A History of English Craft Bookbinding Technique* (1963), by kind permission of Mr. Middleton and Hafner Publishing Company, Ltd., are as follows: 1102, 1106, 1108, 1204. From Josef Halfer's *The Progress of the Marbling Art* (1893) are taken 1202, 1210, and 1212; and from James B. Nicholson's *A Manual of the Art of Bookbinding* (1856) come 1104, 1110, 1112ad, 1206, and 1208.

102   rib

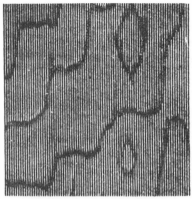

102bd   moiré fine rib

102be   diagonal fine rib

104   ripple

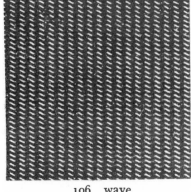

106   wave

106ae   diagonal wave

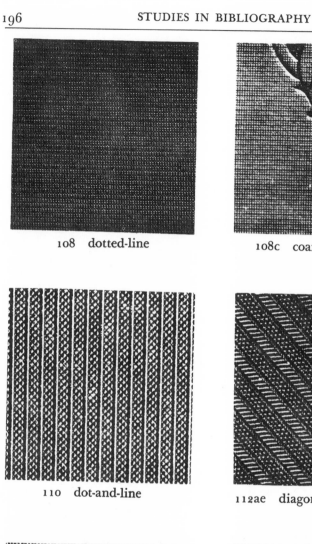

108   dotted-line

108c   coarse dotted-line

112ae   diagonal dot-and-ribbon

110   dot-and-line

116   weave

118   net

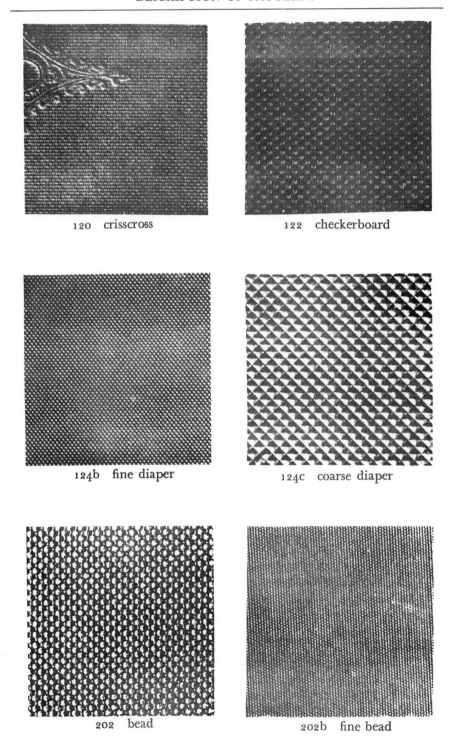

120   crisscross

122   checkerboard

124b   fine diaper

124c   coarse diaper

202   bead

202b   fine bead

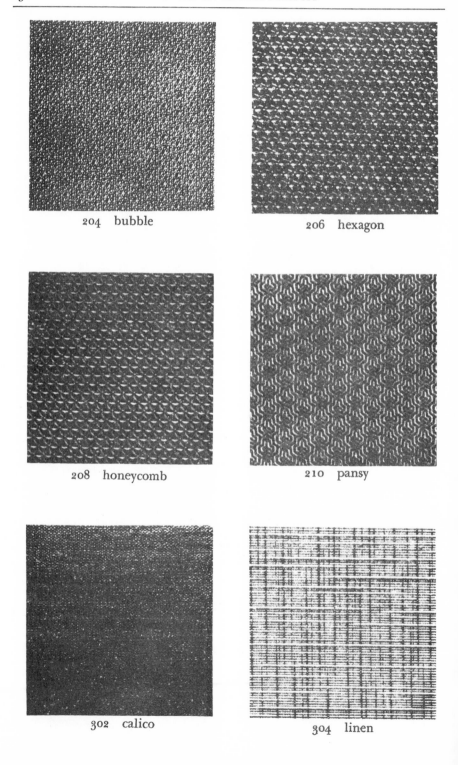

204 bubble

206 hexagon

208 honeycomb

210 pansy

302 calico

304 linen

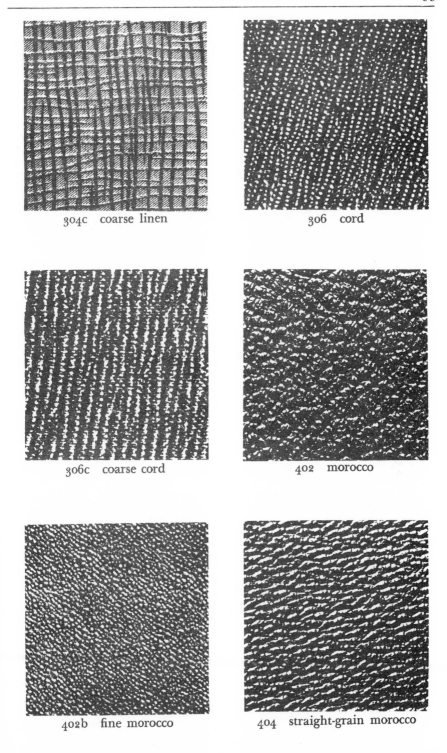

304c   coarse linen

306   cord

306c   coarse cord

402   morocco

402b   fine morocco

404   straight-grain morocco

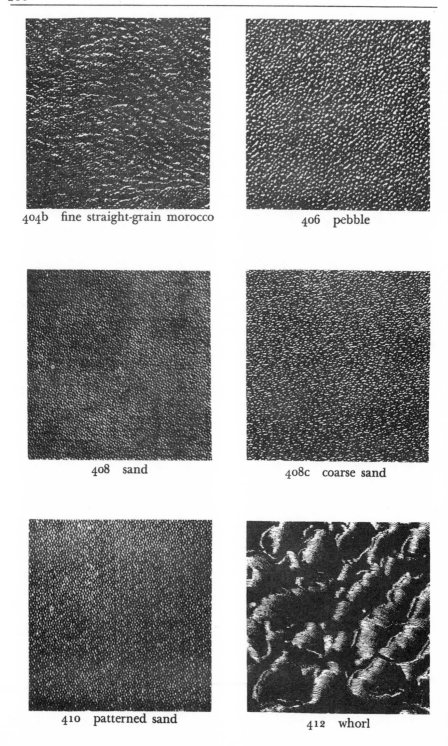

404b　fine straight-grain morocco

406　pebble

408　sand

408c　coarse sand

410　patterned sand

412　whorl

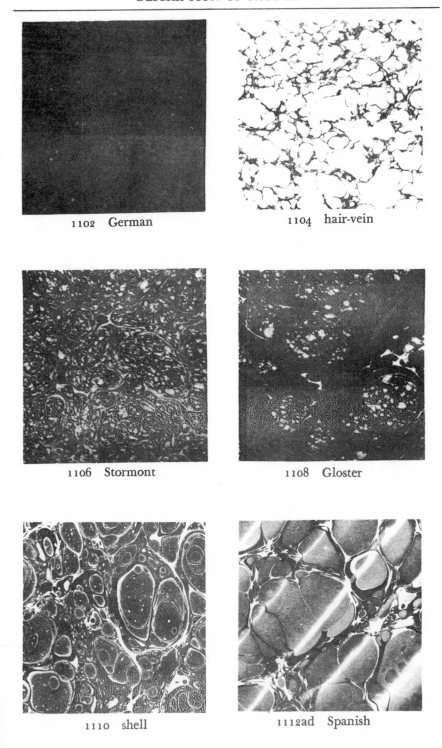

1102   German

1104   hair-vein

1106   Stormont

1108   Gloster

1110   shell

1112ad   Spanish

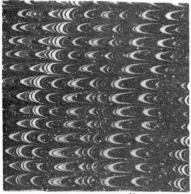

1202 nonpareil

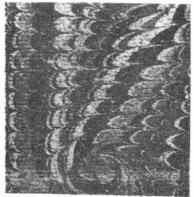

1204 Dutch

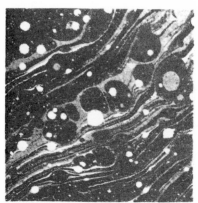

1206 antique spot

1208 curl

1210 peacock

1212 bouquet

The Bibliographical Description of Paper

ONE OF THE PECULIARITIES IN THE HISTORICAL DEVELOPMENT of descriptive bibliography has been the small attention paid to paper. Since paper and inked type-impressions are the two principal physical ingredients of a book and since paper is the one which gives a book its most obvious physical characteristics (shape, size, weight, bulk), it would seem natural for a description of paper to occupy a prominent position in any description of a book. Yet the majority of descriptive bibilographies of the past make no mention of paper, except the indirect references afforded by an indication of format or leaf measurement. Those that do include some description of paper generally provide no more than a few words, such as "Wove paper, unwatermarked" or "Printed on white wove paper."[1] Some, like Fred H. Higginson's *A Bibliography of the Works of Robert Graves* (1966), offer bulk measurements and careful descriptions of watermarks. And occasionally a bibliography which does not give particular attention to paper recognizes its usefulness for analysis and identification, as when Karl Yost distinguishes the first printing of Millay's *Renascence* by the "AGM Glaslan" watermark[2] or when Donald Gallup says of Eliot's *The Dry Salvages*, "Late copies of the first impression are printed on slightly thicker paper without the watermark ADELPHI."[3] But it is safe to say that most descriptive bibliographies — including many classic ones — make no attempt to record the nature of the paper used in the books under examination.

1. These quotations happen to have been taken from, respectively, Alfred P. Lee's *A Bibliography of Christopher Morley* (1935), p. 31, and Dorothy R. Russo and Thelma L. Sullivan's *A Bibliography of Booth Tarkington* (1949), p. 36. But similar phrases are found in a number of other bibliographies.

2. Yost, *A Bibliography of the Works of Edna St. Vincent Millay* (1937), entry 3.

3. Gallup, *T. S. Eliot: A Bibliography* (1952), entry A39.

There are several reasons for this situation. In the first place, the bibliographical interest in type-impressions has tended to deflect bibliographers' attention from the paper on which those impressions appear. It was natural that early bibliographers should have regarded type-impressions as the more promising field for analysis, since there are many immediately apparent impressions on every page and since the possibilities for variation in their arrangement, in the design of individual letters, and in the damage suffered by individual types are infinite. Because the nineteenth-century incunabulists found the analysis of type faces to be an effective tool in the identification of printers and the classification of editions, a concise description of type faces became a standard part of their descriptions of the books. Following in this tradition, bibliographers of Renaissance books have discovered important information about the printing of the books through elaborate analysis of typography and damaged types — information which, in turn, has a bearing on the establishment of texts. Furthermore, the natural interest in the text of a book serves in itself to call attention to typographical features, for the eye in reading observes the type-impressions more directly than the paper. As a result, misprints, broken types, or other typographical peculiarities which may serve to distinguish issues, states, or impressions are noticed and reported more frequently than the distinguishing features of paper. Given the historical evolution of analytical bibliography, descriptive bibliography, and editing, it is not difficult to see why typographical evidence has entered into descriptive bibliographies to a larger extent than have details about paper.[4]

Another factor is the tradition of book collecting out of which descriptive bibliography grew. Some descriptive bibliographies—aimed primarily at collectors — have concentrated on those points which distinguish first impressions (or states or issues of first impressions). In the case of books issued in publishers' bindings or casings, one result has been an emphasis on the description of bindings and endpapers. Since publishers frequently do not bind all copies of an impression at one time but instead bind small batches as required, variant states of bindings are common occurrences, especially on nineteenth-century books; when priority can be established, collectors are often concerned with knowing the characteristics by which the earliest copies can be identified. The upshot is the absurd — but extremely common — situation in which a bibliographer describes the endpapers of a book, the

---

4. Although actual descriptions of type are not common in bibliographies of post-incunabular books.

binders' leaves, or the inserted advertisements in great detail, without ever mentioning the sheets on which the main text of the book is printed.

In addition to these reasons for the neglect of paper, there is the simple one of ignorance: bibliographers have not known what to say about paper. They have generally been able, of course, to distinguish between laid and wove, to use the direction of the chainlines for assistance in determining format, and to compare the general characteristics of each leaf for identifying cancels.[5] But when it came to a description of paper in its own right, they could produce little more than a three-word phrase such as "white laid unwatermarked" — and even that, when included at all, was often inserted in a mechanical fashion, with seemingly little notion of the reasons for doing so. Papermaking is a complex field with an immense technical literature,[6] and any bibliographer who is not also a specialist in the study of paper may be expected to feel somewhat uncomfortable in confronting the task of describing it. The situation is analogous to that faced by the bibliographer in describing typography: he may be able to utilize evidence from type for analysis without being able to say much directly about the type, owing to a lack of technical knowledge and vocabulary. But, since bibliographers historically have examined type faces more often than paper, their knowledge of types, however fragmentary, is generally greater than their knowledge of paper.

Nevertheless, many bibliographers have harbored a lingering uneasiness over this neglect, for in the back of their minds are always the classic examples of the use of paper evidence. As early as 1908, W. W. Greg discovered the false dating of the Pavier quartos of Shakespeare through a study of their watermarks;[7] in 1934 John Carter and Graham Pollard exposed the Wise forgeries by analyzing the ingredi-

5. The classic discussion of cancels is R. W. Chapman's *Cancels* (1930).

6. The principal guide to the technical literature is *Pulp and Paper Manufacture: Bibliography and Patents* (edited, under various titles, first by Clarence J. West and then by Jack Weiner), which covers the period 1900-55 in five volumes and the years since 1955 in annual volumes; it includes — especially under the headings "History" and "Watermarks" — material of interest to bibliographers which is not always reported in the checklists that bibliographers more frequently consult. An-

other basic guide to this field is the *Abstract Bulletin of the Institute of Paper Chemistry* (1930-   ); a useful shorter collection of abstracts is Jack Weiner and Lillian Roth, *Paper and Its Relation to Printing* (Institute of Paper Chemistry Bibliographic Series No. 164; 2nd ed., 1962). A helpful selective checklist appears at the front of E. J. Labarre's *Dictionary and Encyclopaedia of Paper and Paper-Making* (2nd ed., 1952), pp. xi-xx.

7. Greg, "On Certain False Dates in Shakespearian Quartos," *Library*, 2nd ser., IX (1908), 113-131, 381-409.

ents of the paper;[8] and, most recently, Allan Stevenson has conclusively dated the so-called "Constance Missal" by comparing the states of the watermarks in it with occurrences of those watermarks in other books.[9] These are the spectacular achievements, but during the last thirty years there have also been several encouraging indications that increasing attention is being directed toward the description of paper as a routine part of bibliographical investigation. In 1942 A. T. Hazen said, in his introduction to *A Bibliography of the Strawberry Hill Press*, "I have paid special attention to the paper on which the books and Detached Pieces are printed; possibly to some people the development of this method will be the most interesting part of the book" (p. 10); and he proceeded, in the first entry, to prove that the thick-paper copies of Gray's *Odes* (1757) were printed in 1790 or later (pp. 24-29). Then in 1949 Fredson Bowers, in his *Principles of Bibliographical Description*, recommended that a paragraph on "Typography and Paper" be a standard part of a description (pp. 444-446);[10] a decade later two outstanding bibliographies appeared which included separate paragraphs on paper in each entry — Philip Gaskell's *John Baskerville: A Bibliography* (1959) and Allan Stevenson's *Catalogue of Botanical Books in the Collection of Rachel McMasters Miller Hunt*, Volume II (1961). And during the last two decades Stevenson, in many essays, has singlehandedly evolved a methodology for the bibliographical analysis of paper and has demonstrated the uses to which that analysis can be put.

There can by this time be no doubt that a bibliographer's routine examination of a book is deficient if it does not include an analysis of paper as well as of type-impressions. The descriptive bibliographer is then faced with the question of how much of the information turned up in such analysis ought to be recorded in a descriptive bibliography. If a bibliography is regarded simply as a handbook for the identification of particular impressions or states, then only those facts would be reported which serve to distinguish impressions or states — the usual practice in the past. But if a bibliography is to take on its proper

8. Carter and Pollard, *An Enquiry into the Nature of Certain Nineteenth-Century Pamphlets* (1934), esp. pp. 42-55 ("The Analysis of the Paper").

9. Stevenson, *The Problem of the Missale speciale* (1967).

10. Also, at roughly this time, Henry Thomas expressed the need for a "hand-book" of paper study, particularly the use of watermarks in bibliographical analysis; see "Watermarks," *Edinburgh Bibliographical Society Transactions*, II (1938-45), 449-450. And James G. McManaway, in his contribution to *Standards of Bibliographical Description* (1949), commented on the neglect which paper study had suffered (p. 68).

function and serve as a history of the forms in which an author's works have appeared and thus as a partial history of the book trade, details about paper become an important part of the descriptions, whether or not they furnish "points" for the recognition of impressions or states. The usefulness of paper evidence and the description of paper, though separate matters, are obviously related. As more descriptive bibliographers take seriously the responsibility of furnishing careful descriptions of paper, the store of information amassed in this way will become correspondingly more valuable as an aid to further investigation; conversely, progress in the bibliographical analysis of paper can only be slow if bibliographers, whenever they examine a book, do not contribute to that store of information by recording the characteristics of the paper as they observe them.

It should go without saying, in other words, that a descriptive bibliography, if it is adequately to describe certain books as physical objects, is obligated to include some description of the paper used in those books. But bibliographers have no place to turn for detailed instructions about which features to record, how to present them, and how to vary the treatment so as to preserve the overall proportions of the description. A standard procedure for these matters is desirable, both to insure balanced coverage in the recording of information and to facilitate later reference to the information. The present state of research on paper — though much work remains to be done — is sufficiently advanced that it does not seem premature to begin thinking about such a procedure. I shall attempt, in the pages that follow, to draw together some of the previously formulated techniques for the description of paper and to make a few preliminary suggestions for presenting the material in a descriptive bibliography.

I

One of the basic physical attributes of any object is its size, and the dimensions of the sheets of paper used in the production of a book naturally constitute one of the most important characteristics of that paper. Obviously the bibliographer, in order to determine those dimensions, cannot simply measure the sheet directly, since in most cases he has before him a copy of a finished book, in which the dimensions of the sheet have been obscured through folding and perhaps trimming. Specifying the dimensions of the original sheet can come only through the process of analyzing the evidence present in the finished book; even if the bibliographer has access to external documents (such as printers' or publishers' records) which list the size of the paper, he must still check the accuracy of the documents by examining the physical evidence.

A consideration of the sizes of paper used in books therefore necessarily involves the question of format.[11] As a concept, of course, format has nothing directly to do with size, for it is merely an indication of the number of leaves which result from the folding of a sheet, whatever the size of the sheet. Quarto format means that a sheet has been folded twice to produce four leaves, but the term implies nothing about the dimensions of the sheet or the resulting leaves.[12] The designation of format in a bibliographical description, according to the Greg-Bowers formulary, is the first element in the collation line, not part of the description of paper: format is not one of the properties of paper but represents something done to the paper. However, since the bibliographer can measure directly only the dimensions of a leaf, he must know the format if he is to arrive at the size of the unfolded sheet. There will be many instances in which he has insufficient evidence to establish the format, and in these cases all he can give is the leaf measurement; but whenever the format can be discovered, he should provide an indication of the sheet, as well as the leaf, measurement.

The use of certain characteristics of paper, such as chainlines and watermarks, to assist in determining the format of a book was one of the earliest techniques of bibliographical analysis. William Blades explained the method in the *Library* in 1889,[13] and further instructions appear in any of the introductory manuals of bibliography, such as those of McKerrow and Esdaile.[14] Many people, even with only a

11. An important treatment of the general subject is Graham Pollard, "Notes on the Size of the Sheet," *Library*, 4th ser., XXII (1941-42), 105-137. See also Lawrence Wroth, "Formats and Sizes," *Dolphin*, I (1933), 81-95; and David Foxon, "Some Notes on Agenda Format," *Library*, 5th ser., VIII (1953), 163-173.

12. Nor about the number of leaves in a gathering, for a gathering can consist of half a sheet or of several sheets and still represent the same format (the same number of leaves per full sheet). For some discussion of the distinctions among format, signature, gathering, and size, see John R. Hetherington, "Signatures and Sizes," *Times Literary Supplement*, 14 October 1965, p. 928; and G. T. Tanselle, "The

Sizes of Books," *AB Bookman's Weekly*, XXXIX (5-12 June 1967), 2330, 2332. Methods of analysis for detecting half-sheet gatherings are taken up in William H. Bond, "Imposition by Half-Sheets," *Library*, 4th ser., XXII (1941-42), 163-167; Luella F. Norwood, "Imposition of a Half-Sheet in Duodecimo," *Library*, 5th ser., I (1946-47), 242-244; and Kenneth Povey, "On the Diagnosis of Half-Sheet Impositions," *Library*, 5th ser., XI (1956), 268-272.

13. Blades, "On Paper and Paper-Marks," *Library*, 1st ser., I (1889), 217-223.

14. R. B. McKerrow, *An Introduction to Bibliography for Literary Students* (1927), pp. 164-174; *Esdaile's Manual of Bibliog-*

slight knowledge of bibliography, are acquainted with the well-established rules: vertical chainlines, watermark in the center of the leaf, and large rectangular shape signify folio; horizontal chainlines, watermark centered at the gutter in two leaves, and squarish shape signify quarto; vertical chainlines, watermark at the top edge of the gutter in four leaves, and rectangular shape signify octavo; and so on. It is true that this system will serve to identify the format of the large majority of books printed before the nineteenth century,[15] but there are instances in which it does not apply. For one thing, the procedure assumes that chainlines always run parallel to the shorter dimension of the original sheet and that the principal watermark is placed in the center of one half of the sheet. Actually, it is more accurate to say that chainlines run parallel to the shorter dimension of the *mould*; sometimes large moulds were used to produce either double-size paper or two sheets side by side, with the result that the half-sheets or individual sheets — though the size of ordinary sheets — had chainlines running in the opposite direction from those in ordinary sheets.[16] Examples of these "turned chainlines," as they have been called, are not uncommon from the late seventeenth century onward, and bibliographers must keep the possibility in mind when determining format. But even though one recognizes turned chainlines, one cannot always be sure whether the original sheet was one of double size (cut in two before printing) or one of two separate sheets produced in the same mould. The pattern of deckle edges would of course settle the question, but for books of this period — before the introduction of publishers' binding — one rarely encounters copies which have not been trimmed down in the course of binding and rebinding, thus destroying the evidence which the deckle edge could provide.[17] When the

raphy, rev. Roy Stokes (4th ed., 1967), pp. 237-244; Paul S. Dunkin, *How to Catalog a Rare Book* (1951), pp. 31-56.

15. In rare cases additional kinds of evidence may turn up, such as the printed lines which showed the binder where to make the cut-off in duodecimo; see Giles E. Dawson, "Guide-Lines in Small Formats (About 1600)," *SB*, XIV (1961), 206-208.

16. See A. T. Hazen, "Eighteenth-Century Quartos with Vertical Chain-Lines," *Library*, 4th ser., XVI (1935-36), 337-342; and Kenneth Povey and I. J. C. Foster,

"Turned Chain-Lines," *Library*, 5th ser., V (1950-51), 184-200. Several books from the fifteenth century have been noted in which some leaves appear to represent different formats from other leaves, as a result of certain sheets having been cut in half (or quartered) before printing; see Curt F. Bühler, "Chainlines versus Imposition in Incunabula," *SB*, XXIII (1970), 141-145.

17. If one could count on the presence of a single main watermark in the center of one half of every sheet, whether a double sheet or one of the companion

matter cannot be settled conclusively, the clearest course is to follow Bowers's recommended procedure and use such a phrase as " $(4^\circ$-forme) 8°" — meaning that the book has most of the characteristics of a quarto but is octavo in the sense that the amount of paper for eight of its leaves was in the mould at one time.[18] As for watermarks, their positions, too, can sometimes vary from the normal;[19] if, therefore, all the evidence except the watermark points to a particular format, the position of the watermark does not necessarily disprove it. Finally, the usual method presupposes the presence of chainlines and watermarks, but some books printed in the late eighteenth century, when the use of wove paper was increasing, do not offer these aids to bibliographers.

In the case of later books, it is not the frequent absence of chainlines and watermarks which causes the chief difficulty in determining format but rather the widespread use of machine-made papers. Before the introduction of paper-making machines early in the nineteenth century, the size of sheets was limited to the size of the mould which one man could pick up; but after the technological revolution, which produced presses that could print larger sheets and machines that could manufacture them, the sizes of sheets used for books showed much greater variety. In addition, any chainlines present in machine-made paper are of no use for analysis since they are not a natural result of the manufacturing process but merely a design impressed upon the paper. Of course, whenever nineteenth- and twentieth-century books have been printed on handmade paper with chainlines, the standard method of analysis can be used just as effectively as for pre-1800 books;[20] but the point is that for the majority of books of these two centuries the traditional procedure is of no help. A modern book, for example, may have the same general shape as an old octavo and may even be gathered in eights, but it may well have been printed on quad sheets, each of which furnished four eight-leaf gatherings, so that the format is 32°. Although the number of leaves in a gathering cannot be taken in the books of any period as an indication

---

sheets from a double mould, one could use watermarks as a guide; but the lack of regularity in the placing of watermarks makes this test unreliable.

18. Bowers's discussion of turned chainlines is in *Principles*, pp. 193-195. A related example is taken up in Richard J. Wolfe, "*Parthenia In-Violata*: A Seventeenth-Century Folio-form Quarto," *BNYPL*, LXV (1961), 347-364.

19. See Edward Heawood, "The Position on the Sheet of Early Watermarks," *Library*, 4th ser., IX (1928-29), 38-47.

20. Although handmade papers can be made in unusually large sizes by having more than one man manipulate the mould.

of format, the two figures correspond far less often in post-1800 books than in earlier ones. It has long been recognized that the format of machine-printed books can frequently (perhaps usually) not be determined from physical evidence,[21] and bibliographers from McKerrow to Bowers have recommended that, for modern books, the dimensions of a leaf be substituted in the collation line for a designation of format.[22]

As bibliographers begin to turn their attention to problems of machine-printed books, various new techniques for ascertaining format may be developed. But at present one of the few techniques available is the analysis of the edges of leaves, a technique which presupposes the existence of an untrimmed copy — indeed, an unopened copy, or at least one opened in such a way that it is still possible to tell which leaves were originally joined at the edges. Such conditions, while not common, are more easily found in nineteenth- and twentieth-century books than in earlier ones, since most modern books have been issued in publishers' bindings and, if issued untrimmed, may still remain so. In the case of an untrimmed — and, preferably, unopened — machine-printed book, one can sometimes work out the format by observing the pattern of joined leaves, or of rough edges where joined leaves have been opened. Using this method Oliver L. Steele has shown that the first edition of *The Scarlet Letter* was printed on double-size sheets, each of which formed two of the eight-leaf quires;[23] the format of the book could thus be described as octavo-form sextodecimo, and the size of the sheet could easily be calculated by multiplying both dimensions of the leaf by four. Steele has also detected in this way the 32° format of Cabell's *Jurgen* and the 64° format of Cabell's *Gallantry* and has recorded the patterns of the edges which can be used to recognize half-sheet imposition of eight-leaf quires in these two common formats.[24] One is often not so fortunate, however, in finding untrimmed copies and in working out the format,

21. Charles Evans in 1876 considered it "practically impossible at the present time to correctly define the size of a modern book in the old manner"; see "The Sizes of Printed Books," *Library Journal*, I (1876-77), 58-61.

22. McKerrow, p. 164n.; Bowers, pp. 429-430.

23. Steele, "On the Imposition of the First Edition of Hawthorne's *The Scarlet Letter*," *Library*, 5th ser., XVII (1962), 250-255. He further demonstrates that the book was printed by half-sheet imposition, with each forme containing the inner and outer sub-formes of a single quire.

24. Steele, "Half-Sheet Imposition of Eight-Leaf Quires in Formes of Thirty-Two and Sixty-Four Pages," *SB*, XV (1962), 274-278.

even with the aid of imposition diagrams in printers' manuals.[25] When this approach is not successful, one must search for errors or damage which can reveal format. For instance, if the leading and following edges of a forme receive most stress, examination of the locations of in-press type or plate damage may disclose the imposition and thus the format; Steele has used this technique to demonstrate that Glasgow's *The Wheel of Life* is 32°, with each sheet furnishing two copies of two consecutive eight-leaf gatherings.[26] In addition, such rare occurrences as errors in folding the sheets, creases which marred the sheets before folding, and failure to eliminate imposition figures can serve, when available, to help determine format.[27] But in many cases the format cannot be established, and the bibliographer must then of necessity allow a leaf measurement to stand as a substitute for an indication of format.

For books of all periods, once a format has been determined, the bibliographer is ready to supply the first element in a description of paper — the specification of the size of the sheet. He simply multiplies the dimensions of the leaf the proper number of times to correspond with the format[28] and checks to see whether the resulting dimensions approximate one of the sheet sizes known to have been standard, or at least common, during the period in question. The match can rarely be more than a rough approximation for two reasons: the dimensions of the original sheet can be expected often to be larger than those obtained by multiplying the dimensions of the leaf, since the sheet

25. Practically all of the many printers' manuals published during the nineteenth and twentieth centuries contain imposition diagrams applicable to machine printing; a convenient one for reference is Theodore Low DeVinne's *Modern Methods of Book Composition* (1904), or his *Book Composition*, ed. J. W. Bothwell (1918).

26. Steele, "Evidence of Plate Damage as Applied to the First Impressions of Ellen Glasgow's *The Wheel of Life* (1906)," *SB*, XVI (1963), 223-231; part of his study also consists of an effective statistical analysis of the reliability of the sample of 150 copies which he examined. For some comment on the "leading edge" in modern half-sheet imposition, see Oliver L. Steele, "A Note on Half-Sheet Imposition in Nineteenth and Twentieth Century Books," *Gutenberg Jahrhuch 1962*, pp. 545-547.

27. J. D. Thomas, in "A Modern Instance," *PBSA*, L (1956), 302-304, describes this kind of error in the folding of a sheet in the second edition of Besterman's *World Bibliography of Bibliographies*; and Matthew J. Bruccoli and Charles A. Rheault, in "Imposition Figures and Plate Gangs in *The Rescue*," *SB*, XIV (1961), 258-262, demonstrate the intended 64° format of the second impression of the second edition of Conrad's *The Rescue* through an analysis of the surviving imposition figures which identify the four-page plate gangs.

28. For folio, the shorter dimension of the leaf would be doubled; for quarto, both dimensions would be doubled; for octavo, the shorter would be quadrupled, the longer doubled; and so on.

may have been trimmed in binding (and, in the case of repeatedly rebound older books, trimmed several times) ; and paper sizes in use at any time have always exhibited numerous variations from the norms, while the norms themselves have shifted from period to period. Nevertheless, the bibliographer, in his role as historian, should attempt to make some correlation between the size he has calculated and one of the sizes actually available at the time.

Despite the considerable amount of historical research on paper,[29] information about paper sizes in different periods is not easy to come by. The English paper trade, from at least some time in the seventeenth century,[30] has employed a series of names — ranging from "Post" through "Crown" and "Demy" to "Royal" and "Imperial" — to designate sheet sizes, and these names were also common in America[31] until the twentieth century. Apparently some of the names originally referred to watermarks but gradually came to stand for certain relative sizes of sheets, regardless of what watermarks they bore. Although a great many names have been used at various times, there are only seven of primary importance in connection with paper for printing: Foolscap, Post, Crown, Demy, Medium, Royal, and Imperial. However, with the addition of such adjectives as "Super," "Large," "Double," "Extra," and the like, a bewildering array of individual designations has been constructed. While the relation of all these names to each other has remained virtually unchanged over the years, the specific measurements attached to each have varied considerably, and the standard sizes adopted by law or agreement in one period are not always retained unaltered by a later generation.

The whole matter is extremely complex, and it seems unrealistic to require of descriptive bibliographers any great precision in the naming of these sizes. Sometimes the differences between two standard

29. The standard general history is Dard Hunter, *Papermaking: The History and Technique of an Ancient Craft* (1943), which includes a highly selective checklist of other historical treatments. Some additional checklists, which can serve as partial guides to the mass of historical research, are mentioned in footnotes 6 and 59; items before 1800 are described in Dard Hunter, *The Literature of Papermaking, 1390-1800* (1925); and work since 1949 can be located through the annual *SB* checklists.

30. See R. W. Chapman, "An Inventory of Paper, 1674," *Library*, 4th ser., VII (1926-27), 402-408; cf. Chapman, "Notes on Eighteenth-Century Bookbuilding," IV (1923-24), 175-177 esp. Allen T. Hazen, in "Eustace Burnaby's Manufacture of White Paper in England," *PBSA*, XLVIII (1954), 315-333, reproduces a 1691 announcement of a paper auction, showing many names (but not dimensions) of paper sizes.

31. See the examples from 1821 reported by Lyman Horace Weeks in *A History of Paper-Manufacturing in the United States, 1690-1916* (1916), pp. 119-120.

sizes are small enough that the bibliographer, unsure how much paper has been trimmed off in the copies he has examined, will have no basis for choosing between them; in any case, he cannot always know with certainty the exact dimensions of the sizes available. What seems more reasonable, therefore, is to expect him only to name the general size class to which the sheets he is describing probably belong. It is more meaningful historically to refer to the sheets of a given post-seventeenth-century book as "Crown," if they seem to fall within the range of the sizes which at one time or another have been labeled "Crown," than to attempt to infer the exact measurements of the sheets used, since these inferred measurements may not in fact have been the actual ones. Although many books provide short lists of these English size names, the most useful source for the bibliographer is E. J. Labarre's *Dictionary and Encyclopaedia of Paper and Paper-Making* (2nd ed., 1952), which contains a long table of names (pp. 252-267), arranged alphabetically and giving the various dimensions which have been attached to each name.[32] For quick reference, the following brief list may prove convenient. It shows the modern standard and the customary range of variation for the seven basic names, as extracted from Labarre's table and his individual entries for these words; the first figures are inches, those in parentheses millimeters:

	Standard	*Variation*
Foolscap	17 x 13.5 (431.8 x 342.9)	15 x 12.75 / 18.5 x 14.5 (381 x 323.85 / 469.9 x 368.3)
Post	19 x 15 (482.6 x 381)	18.75 x 15.25 / 20 x 16 (476.25 x 387.35 / 508 x 406.4)
Crown	20 x 15 (508 x 381)	19 x 15 / 20 x 16.5 (482.6 x 381 / 508 x 419.1)
Demy	22.5 x 17.5 (571.5 x 444.5)	18 x 14.5 / 23 x 18 (457.2 x 368.3 / 584.2 x 457.2)
Medium	23 x 18 (584.2 x 457.2)	21 x 16.5 / 24 x 19 (533.4 x 419.1 / 609.6 x 482.6)

32. Bibliographers who consult Labarre's *Dictionary* should also be acquainted with Allan Stevenson's review of it in the *Library*, 5th ser., IX (1954), 59-63, which makes comments on some size-names not included in Labarre. See also E. J. La-barre, "The Sizes of Paper, Their Names, Origin and History," in *Buch und Papier*, ed. Horst Kunze (1949), pp. 35-54; and E. G. Loeber's *Supplement* (1967) to Labarre's *Dictionary*.

Royal	25 x 20	22.25 x 18 / 26 x 20
	(635 x 508)	(565.15 x 457.2 / 660.4 x 508)
Imperial	30 x 22	28 x 20.5 / 36 x 24
	(762 x 558.8)	(711.2 x 520.7 / 914.4 x 609.6)

A companion table in Labarre, which may be of even greater initial use to bibliographers, arranges the names in the order of the sizes (pp. 268-272). All the sizes of printing papers recorded in his table are listed below (along with the millimeter equivalents in parentheses) :

15 x 12.5 (381 x 317.5)	Pott
17 x 13.25 (431.8 x 336.55)	Foolscap
17 x 13.5 (431.8 x 342.9)	Large Foolscap
18.5 x 14.5 (469.9 x 368.3)	Small (or Pinched) Post
19 x 15 (482.6 x 381)	Post
20 x 15 (508 x 381)	Crown
20 x 16 (508 x 406.4)	Copy; Tea Copy
20.75 x 14.375 (527.05 x 365.13)	Music Demy; Short
21 x 14 (533.4 x 355.6)	Large Half Royal
21 x 16.5 (533.4 x 419.1)	Large Post
22.5 x 17.5 (571.5 x 444.5)	Demy
23 x 18 (584.2 x 457.2)	Medium
23.5 x 19.5 (596.9 x 495.3)	Sheet-and-a-half Post
24 x 19 (609.6 x 482.6)	Small Royal
25 x 15 (635 x 381)	Double Pott
25 x 20 (635 x 508)	Royal
26.5 x 16.5 (673.1 x 419.1)	Double Foolscap
26.5 x 22.5 (673.1 x 571.5)	Sheet-and-a-half Demy Square
27.5 x 20.5 (698.5 x 520.7)	Super Royal
28 x 21 (711.2 x 533.4)	Double Music
28 x 23 (711.2 x 584.2)	Elephant
29 x 19 (736.6 x 482.6)	Small Double Post
30 x 20 (762 x 508)	Double Crown
30 x 22 (762 x 558.8)	Imperial
30 x 25 (762 x 635)	Quad Pott
30 x 30 (762 x 762)	Sheet-and-a-half Demy Double Crown
30.5 x 19 (774.7 x 482.6)	Double Post
33 x 17.75 (838.2 x 450.85)	Sheet-and-a-half Demy Usual
33 x 21 (838.2 x 533.4)	Double Large Post

33 x 22 (838.2 x 558.8)	Large News
34 x 27 (863.6 x 685.8)	Quad Foolscap
35 x 22.5 (889 x 571.5)	Double Demy
36 x 23 (914.4 x 584.2)	Double Medium
38 x 28 (965.2 x 711.2)	Double Globe
40 x 25 (1016 x 635)	Double Royal
40 x 27 (1016 x 685.8)	Double Elephant
40 x 30 (1016 x 762)	Quad Crown
40 x 32 (1016 x 812.8)	Quad Post
41 x 27.5 (1041.4 x 698.5)	Double Super Royal
44 x 30 (1117.6 x 762)	Double Imperial
45 x 35 (1143 x 889)	Quad Demy
50 x 40 (1270 x 1016)	Quad Royal
55 x 31.5 (1397 x 800.1)	Double Atlas
56 x 38 (1422.4 x 965.2)	Quad Globe

The bibliographer who has reason to feel confident that he has deter-mined the exact dimensions of a sheet can, by checking this list, cite a precise name (a basic name with its modifying adjectives).

Although these lists will serve to identify in general terms the sheet sizes of the majority of English and American books since the seventeenth century, they can profitably be supplemented by other tables or sources of information for particular periods. A bibliographer dealing with eighteenth-century books should certainly take advan-tage of the research of Philip Gaskell and Allan Stevenson, both of whom have worked out tables for that period.[33] At other times one can utilize specimen books which reflect the standard practices of a period. For instance, the book of paper samples issued in 1855 by T. H. Saunders of London gives 151 specimen sheets of handmade, machine-made, and special papers, along with a table of contents pro-viding the name for the size of each sample.[34] Modern American paper, following the standardization codified in 1923 by the National Bureau of Standards (and revised in 1932), is not referred to by the traditional English names but simply by the dimensions of the stand-

33. Gaskell, "Notes on Eighteenth Century British Paper," *Library*, 5th ser., XII (1957), 34-42, and *John Baskerville: A Bib-liography* (1959), p. xvi; Stevenson, *Cata-logue of Botanical Books in the Collection of Rachel McMasters Miller Hunt*, II (1961), ccxxvii. Cf. D. C. Coleman, *The British Paper Industry, 1495-1860* (1958), p. 351.

34. A copy of this book, *Illustrations of the British Paper Manufacture*, can be found in the Wing Foundation of The Newberry Library.

ard sheets (millimeters are given here in parentheses):

29 x 26 (736.6 x 660.4)	44 x 33 (1117.6 x 838.2)
32 x 22 (812.8 x 558.8)	44 x 34 (1117.6 x 863.6)
35 x 22.5 (889 x 571.5)	45 x 35 (1143 x 889)
36 x 24 (914.4 x 609.6)	46 x 33 (1168.4 x 838.2)
38 x 25 (965.2 x 635)	48 x 36 (1219.2 x 914.4)
39 x 26 (990.6 x 660.4)	50 x 38 (1270 x 965.2)
40 x 26 (1016 x 660.4)	51 x 41 (1295.4 x 1041.4)
41 x 30.5 (1041.4 x 774.7)	52 x 29 (1320.8 x 736.6)
42 x 28 (1066.8 x 711.2)	56 x 42 (1422.4 x 1066.8)
44 x 28 (1117.6 x 711.2)	56 x 44 (1422.4 x 1117.6)
44 x 32 (1117.6 x 812.8)	64 x 44 (1625.6 x 1117.6)

Foreign paper sizes, though different from the English and American in dimensions and names, are roughly parallel to them, and introductory information on the foreign systems is available in Labarre (pp. 251-252, 282-290) and in Stevenson's table. For books issued during the first two centuries of printing, when paper sizes were less standardized and names had not become attached to particular sizes, the bibliographer can do little more in describing a given book than report the inferred sheet-dimensions of the largest copy known; but in addition he may wish to survey other bibliographies and bibliographical studies [35] in order to gain some idea of the sizes prevalent at the time and make some comparative comment. Sometimes an estimate of a sheet size can be made on the basis of the size of the type page and the inner margin[36] or on the basis of the location of the tranchefiles, which often appear as chainlines traversing a sheet of paper roughly six or seven millimeters from each end. Regardless of the period, the lengths to which the bibliographer is obliged to go in attempting to establish actual sheet sizes depends on the individual situation — the condition of the books he is describing (whether or not they are uncut or are thought to be only slightly trimmed), taken in conjunction with the characteristics of the period involved (wheth-

35. Such as, for the sizes of fifteenth-century printing paper, Conrad Haebler's *The Study of Incunabula*, trans. Lucy E. Osborne (1933), pp. 49-54.

36. For an illustration of the method, see Curt F. Bühler, "The Margins in Mediaeval Books," *PBSA*, XL (1946), 34-42. Bühler mentions two sizes of medieval paper, 43 x 32 and 45 x 30 cm.; and he estimates that the average type page was 68% x 45% of the total height of the paper, that the inner margin was 8-10% of it, and that the height of the type page was equal to the breadth of the leaf. Cf. A. W. Pollard, "Margins," *Printing Art*, X (1907-8), 17-24; and "Margins," *Dolphin*, I (1933), 67-80.

er or not paper sizes were standardized or at least fairly regular).
When these factors allow the possibility of accuracy in naming the
sheet size, the bibliographer ought to do whatever research is necessary to achieve that accuracy; but when, as is more often the case,
these factors permit only a rough approximation in specifying the
sheet size, the bibliographer can simply refer to such lists as those
provided here.

Once the original sheet size is ascertained, either precisely or approximately, the bibliographer has to decide how to enter the information in his description. Since minimum sheet-dimensions can be calculated on the basis of direct measurement of the leaves and since any
indication of the original name or size of a sheet is generally an
inference based on that direct measurement, the description should
emphasize the former (which constitutes demonstrable evidence) rather
than the latter (which usually constitutes speculation). An economical
way of achieving this emphasis is to begin the description with the
demonstrable measurement (the longer dimension preceding the shorter), followed in parentheses by the speculated name or dimensions of
the original sheet. When an uncut copy is available for examination,
the calculated dimensions and the original dimensions coincide, and
the figures can be given without qualification; but when trimmed, or
possibly trimmed, copies are the only ones available, the measurements based on the largest examined copy must be prefixed with "at
least," or some equivalent phrase, and the inferred name or size with
"probably":

> 25 x 20 (Royal) . . .
> 24.5 x 19.5 (a variety of Royal) . . .
> at least 24.5 x 19.5 (probably Royal) . . .
> at least 24.5 x 19.5 (probably Royal, 25 x 20) . . .
> at least 26 x 19.75 (probably a variety of Royal, 26 x 20) . . .
> at least 31 x 21.75 (probably 32 x 22) . . .

Thus the first two examples are based on uncut copies, and the figures
can be taken as proved facts; in the first instance the dimensions are
exactly those of the standard Royal sheet, but in the second — as the
phrase "a variety of Royal" makes clear — they fall within the range
historically covered by the name "Royal." The third example, based
on a trimmed copy, gives the minimum sheet-dimensions (signaled by
"at least"), based on the maximum known leaf-dimensions; since these
figures come close to the standard for Royal, one can then add the
speculation "probably Royal." If there is additional evidence for judg-

ing the amount cut off, one may wish to include a specific estimate of the dimensions, as in the next two examples. The last illustration represents a trimmed modern American book, with the probable standard sheet size given only in figures and not named. This arrangement of the information not only emphasizes what is factual and subordinates what is conjectural but also provides a standardized form applicable to all circumstances — for whenever a regular or probable size cannot be postulated, as often with early books, the parenthetical comment can simply be eliminated. It goes without saying that, when format itself cannot be established and the leaf-measurement replaces the format abbreviation in the collation line, nothing need be said about size in the paragraph on paper.

Two further problems in the specification of size should be commented on: the degree of accuracy required and the system of measurement to be employed. Questions of accuracy are part of the whole matter of tolerances,[37] but in general it can be said that one should follow Bowers's recommendation of measuring leaves to the nearest thirty-second of an inch (*Principles*, p. 431) — or, in the metric system, to the nearest millimeter. In practice, however, only the bibliographer who is intimately acquainted with a particular situation can say just what tolerance is meaningful or appropriate. The presence of deckle edges in an untrimmed copy of a given book may render ridiculous the idea of measuring to the nearest millimeter, though one should attempt, as Bowers suggests, to measure to an imaginary line drawn through the base of the deckle (checking the measurement in several leaves). On the other hand, a situation may arise, in connection with a machine-trimmed book, which requires the bibliographer to take readings to the nearest half-millimeter if he is adequately to distinguish certain states, issues, or impressions.

The question of what system of measurement to use — inches or millimeters — has been discussed in the past[38] with inconclusive results. Although the theoretical advantages of the metric system are obvious, English and American bibliographers are accustomed to measuring in inches, and paper sizes in both countries have traditionally been expressed this way. Despite the weight of tradition, it seems desirable to utilize the same system of measurement throughout a bibliographical description, and the metric system has already become established for certain measurements, particularly those relating to

37. For general comments on this subject, see G. T. Tanselle, "Tolerances in Bibliographical Description," *Library*, 5th ser., XXIII (1968), 1-12.

38. Cf. Bowers, *Principles*, pp. 308, 430.

typography in incunabula (the dimensions of the type page and the size of the type face as reflected in the measurement of twenty lines). Furthermore, it has been recommended for the typography of all periods,[39] and whatever system is adopted for type measurements should certainly be employed for paper measurements also, to facilitate the comparison of type-page size with leaf size. The DIN system of standardized paper sizes, based on the metric system, has been adopted by many countries, and in 1959 the British Standards Institution endorsed it as an alternative to the traditional British system.[40] There is no question but that, in the field of paper as in most other fields, the general trend in measurement is increasingly toward the metric system. In the light of these considerations, as well as of the inherent convenience of the millimeter as a unit, the bibliographer would be well advised to adopt the metric system.[41] For this reason, the lists given above provide metric equivalents for the usual inch-sizes of paper ($1'' = 25.4$ mm.); if the bibliographer feels awkward in mixing the traditional names with millimeters, he can always include both sets of figures:

> 635 x 508 (Royal)
> *or* 635 x 508 (Royal; i.e., 25″ x 20″)

> at least 622 x 495 (probably Royal, 635 x 508)
> *or* at least 622 x 495 (probably Royal, 635 x 508 [= 25″ x 20″])

39. See G. T. Tanselle, "The Identification of Type Faces in Bibliographical Description," *PBSA*, LX (1966), 185-202. The British Federation of Master Printers has officially adopted the metric system; cf. Eugene M. Ettenberg, "Is Type Measurement Overdue for Change to the Metric System?", *Inland Printer/American Lithographer*, CLXII (January 1969), 48.

40. See British Standard 3176: 1959. Cf. "The DIN System of International Paper Sizes," *British Printer*, LXXI (December 1958), 70-71; "International Standard Paper Sizes — Pipe Dream or Tangible Reality?", *British Printer*, LXXV (June 1962), 107-111; John Tomkins, "DIN — A New, Old Cause," *Typographica*, n.s., no. 5 (June 1962); Labarre, *Dictionary*, pp. 286-287; W. C. Kenneison and A. J. B. Spilman, *Dictionary of Printing, Papermaking and Bookbinding* (1963), pp. 211-213. In the DIN system, the basic sheet has an area of one square meter, and its dimensions are in the ratio of the side to the diagonal of a square ($1:\sqrt{2}$) — i.e., 1189 x 841 mm. Such a sheet is referred to as "A0"; "A1" is the sheet resulting from a halving of the longer dimension (841 x 594); "A2" from another halving (594 x 420), and so on. A "B" series (based on a 1414 x 1000 sheet) establishes intermediate sizes between those of the "A" series; long sizes may be specified in terms of a fraction of a standard size, as "¼ A4" (210 x 74).

41. The printed catalogue cards prepared by the Library of Congress express the height of books and the dimensions of broadsides in centimeters, and these practices are recommended in the *Anglo-American Cataloging Rules* (North American Text, 1967), pp. 210-211.

Inserting the inch measurements should eliminate any objection to the historical inappropriateness of associating the metric system with the size names; and the slight inconvenience of making the adjustment is far outweighed by the advantages gained in the ease with which the figures can be manipulated and compared with others in the description.

II

After the specification of the size of the sheet, the next fact to be recorded in a description of paper is an indication of the markings in the sheet — chainlines and watermarks. An adequate accounting of these features involves (1) stating whether the paper is laid or wove and, if laid, measuring the distance between the chainlines;[42] and (2) describing any marks present (watermarks or countermarks), identifying them if possible. All paper before approximately 1756 was "laid" — that is, made in moulds, the bottoms of which consisted of wires parallel to the longer dimension and crossed perpendicularly at wider intervals by heavier chains. After that date, with the introduction of moulds containing a finely woven wire mesh, "wove" paper (which bears no easily discernible crossing lines) was possible, though it did not come into wide use until near the end of the century.[43] Nineteenth- and twentieth-century machine-made paper can also be classified as "laid" or "wove," but the terms in this connection refer only to patterns impressed on the paper, since those patterns are not the result of anything functional in the manufacturing process. In the bibliographical description of pre-1800 books, therefore, it is unnecessary to specify the paper as "laid": any paper not specifically labeled can be assumed to be laid, and those late eighteenth-century instances of wove paper can be explicitly marked "wove." Strictly speaking, the mention of "laid" is superfluous even for later paper, since the indication of the distance betwen the chainlines makes clear the fact that the paper has a laid pattern; nevertheless, since the laid pattern is no longer predominant, it is probably more sensible in post-1800 books to specify "laid" or "wove" in each instance. For

42. The direction of the chainlines in the sheet need not be mentioned unless it is unusual; the direction of the chainlines in the leaf — like other facts about the folded form of the sheets — should be recorded later, at the end of the paragraph on paper.

43. See A. T. Hazen, "Baskerville and James Whatman," *SB*, V (1952-53), 187-189; and Thomas Balston, *William Balston, Paper Maker, 1759-1849* (1954), *James Whatman, Father and Son* (1957), and "Whatman Paper in a Book Dated 1757," *Book Collector*, VIII (1959), 306-308.

books of all periods, if there is no watermark, this part of the description is quite simple: it consists either of the single word "wove" or of a phrase such as "laid, chainlines 18 mm. apart."[44] Of course, "unwatermarked" is understood in each case, but it does no harm to add the word "unwatermarked" (or "unmarked") after the words "wove" and "laid."

When a watermark is present, it is the bibliographer's duty to provide as accurate a description of it as possible, following the general procedure which he would use in describing any other kind of pattern[45] — that is, a combination of a verbal statement with a reference to a visual standard. The verbal statement may be expanded or contracted according to the relative accuracy and accessibility of the illustration cited as a standard, but certain minimum information should always be included: a brief indication of the general form of the mark (as "crown" or "bull's head") and a measurement of the maximum height and width of the mark (with the height preceding the width).[46] Allan Stevenson has suggested a convenient system for recording such measurements so that they reveal, at the same time, the distance between the chainlines and the position of the watermark in relation to the chainlines.[47] In this system, whichever dimension of the watermark crosses the chainlines is recorded in brackets, with the distance to the nearest chainline on either side entered on each side of the brackets. Thus the notation "6[28]4" would mean that the mark is 28 mm. wide at its widest point, with one chainline running 6 mm. to the left and another 4 mm. to the right, when the mark is viewed "right side up" and from the mould side of the sheet (the side with the indentations from the chains and wires); and the chainlines would be 38 mm. apart. If a chainline cuts through the watermark, the bracketed measurement can be divided with a vertical stroke at the proper place: thus in "6[13|15]4," the chainlines are 19 mm. apart, and one of them runs through the watermark 13 mm. from one side and 15 mm. from the opposite side. It is frequently unneces-

44. The importance of chainlines for bibliographical analysis in tests for cancels and conjugacy — not simply their distance apart but also the leaf-patterns of mould- and felt-sides as revealed by the indentations of chainlines — is discussed by Allan Stevenson in "Chain-Indentations in Paper as Evidence," *SB*, VI (1954), 181-195.

45. See G. T. Tanselle, "The Bibliographical Description of Patterns," *SB*, XXIII

(1970), 71-102.

46. "Height" and "width" here refer to the mark itself; for some marks, therefore, the larger figure will appear second.

47. "Paper as Bibliographical Evidence," *Library*, 5th ser., XVII (1962), 200. An example of the use of chainspace measurements is Stevenson's "Tudor Roses from John Tate," *SB*, XX (1967), 15-34.

sary, therefore, to specify separately the distance between chainlines, since this system of watermark measurement includes that information and, in addition, shows the relationship between the two measurements:

laid, with bull's head tau mark, 49 x 4[13|10]7

In this example the chainlines are 17 mm. apart, and it would be superfluous to add a phrase explicitly saying so. For machine-made papers, however, the relationship between the laid pattern and the watermark is less important, and it may seem more sensible in some instances — particularly when the watermark appears several times in a sheet in different positions relative to the chainlines — to give the measurements separately:

laid, with mark reading 'WARREN'S | OLDE STYLE',
40 x 8[16|24|24|20]4
or laid, chainlines 24 mm. apart, with mark reading 'WARREN'S | OLDE STYLE', 40 x 84

In handmade papers, on the other hand, any difference in the position of a watermark relative to the adjacent chainlines provides significant evidence for bibliographical analysis, and the variation should always be noted:[48]

bull's head tau mark, 49 x 5[28]5/4[28]6

It is also a good idea, for purposes of documentation, to cite after every measurement a leaf (or leaves) which provides an example of the watermark with the specified measurements:

bull's head tau mark, 49 x 5[28]5 (B4)/4[28]6 (G4)

Watermarks obviously will be easier to measure in some formats than in others — indeed, when handmade papers are involved, folio is generally the only format in which one can measure the entire watermark at one time. Nevertheless, it is often possible to construct an accurate measurement by piecing together the measurements of the portions of the watermark visible in various leaves; but when too much of the watermark is hidden in the gutter of a tightly bound volume or has been trimmed off in the process of binding, an ap-

---

48. Since moulds were regularly used in pairs (see below, note 51), the presence of companion watermarks need not be specifically mentioned; however, a difference between the two can be conveniently recorded in this fashion: "bull's head tau mark, (I) 49 x 5[28]5, (II) 49 x 4[28]6."

proximate measurement must be given, preceded by some such notation as "at least" or "about."

Following the verbal description of the watermark should come a parenthetical reference to an illustration of that mark. Such a reference is an important part of the bibliographer's responsibility: it helpfully supplements the verbal description, since some users of a bibliography may require, in particular instances, a more precise idea of the design than can manageably be expressed in words and figures; and it places the mark in a larger historical context through associating it with a published illustration which has been (or can be) cited by other bibliographers under similar circumstances. A number of large compilations of tracings of watermarks have been published; when the bibliographer locates in one of them a tracing which is identical with (or closely resembles) the mark in question, he can enter the name of the work and the tracing number in his description. If no standard collection of tracings seems to include the mark, the bibliographer can provide an illustration in his own section of illustrations (and the parenthetical reference would then be simply to this illustration in the same volume). It is usually preferable in descriptive bibliography, when one is dealing with designs or patterns, to cite whenever possible a separately published standard rather than an illustration provided for the particular occasion. With watermarks, however, the situation is different. Since tracings are inadequate for modern bibliographical analysis of watermarks, a reference to a tracing is less helpful than a reproduction of a good photograph of a watermark. If large collections of photographs of watermarks were available in published form, it would often be unnecessary to provide individual photographs; but since no such reference works exist at present, a bibliographer who furnishes photographs of watermarks, far from creating an unnecessary proliferation, is usefully contributing to the meager published supply. These considerations are not meant to suggest that there is no point in referring to the standard collections of tracings, for they have their uses: they assist in classifying watermarks; they provide approximate representations of a large number of marks; and they furnish leads for additional research. Citations of published tracings are, therefore, still appropriate; but, ideally, reference should also be made to photographs.

To understand why tracings are inadequate — in fact, to make any positive identification of a watermark at all — the descriptive bibliographer must be familiar with the revolutionary techniques which Allan Stevenson has developed for analyzing watermarks. In a series of brilliant articles beginning in the late 1940's, he demonstrated some of the ways, unrecognized before, in which watermarks can furnish evidence for bibliographical analysis;[49] the monument of the method, his book on *The Problem of the Missale speciale* (1967), draws all these techniques together and uses them to solve a celebrated problem.[50] As a result of his work, analysis of watermarks is now an established bibliographical tool, and no bibliographer can be said to have examined a book properly without giving its paper the same careful attention which has long been accorded to typographic matters. Stevenson's method stems from the basic discovery that individual watermarks can be positively identified by their "sewing dots." In the mould, the watermark pieces were attached to the wires and chains by means of thin wire thread; at each of the points where the watermark was fastened, this thread formed a small lump which left its mark in the finished paper as if it were part of the design itself. Since only a remote coincidence could result in any two watermarks of the same design being attached to the wires and chains at exactly the same spots with the same relative amounts of thread, examination of the patterns of sewing dots can provide conclusive identification of the mould in which a given piece of paper was produced. Moulds were regularly used in pairs with supposedly identical watermarks,[51] and many pairs, unrelated to each other, contain quite similar designs; but analysis of the sewing dots can distinguish between individual moulds in every instance. Tracings are not detailed enough for this kind of research, whereas photographs[52] — or, preferably, beta-radiographs[53] which reproduce watermarks without reproducing the inked

49. See especially *Observations on Paper as Evidence* (1961), and "Paper as Bibliographical Evidence," *Library*, 5th ser., XVII (1962), 197-212; for a brief statement, see "The Natural History of Watermarks," in C. M. Briquet, *Les Filigranes*, ed. Stevenson (1968), pp. *20-23. In one of his earlier articles, he demonstrated how watermarks can be useful in the detection and analysis of press variants, the sequence of formes through the press, and related problems: "New Uses of Watermarks as Bibliographical Evidence," *SB*, I (1948-49), 151-182. For his discussion of chainlines, see above, note 44.

50. A condensed version of the argument appears in his "Paper Evidence and the *Missale speciale*," *Gutenberg Jahrbuch*

1962, pp. 93-105.

51. Stevenson, "Watermarks Are Twins," *SB*, IV (1951-52), 57-91.

52. See T. Gerardy, "Die Fotografische Registrierung von Wasserzeichen," *Papiergeschichte*, XVI (December 1966), 22-25. The use of sensitized paper to make direct photographs of watermarks was suggested at least as early as 1904 by Gilbert R. Redgrave, in "The Water-Marks in Paper," *Library*, 2nd ser., V (1904), 91-92.

53. See J. S. G. Simmons, "The Leningrad Method of Watermark Reproduction," *Book Collector*, X (1961), 329-330, which describes the method first announced in 1960 by D. P. Erastov and also used in J.

type-impressions over them — can be better for study than the paper itself. Indeed, the future of watermark study lies in radiography, and the student of paper will need to carry with him a Carbon 14 source.

Stevenson has further shown how variant states of individual watermarks can be recognized and employed for such purposes as dating. As a mould was used, some of the threads would loosen or break and allow the watermark to slip or to bend out of shape; and periodically, as this deterioration was noticed, it would be repaired, but the repaired state would not be identical with the original state. Therefore, by examining sewing dots, one can not only identify a watermark but also place any state of it chronologically in relation to another state of the same watermark; in other words, one can distinguish variations which signify separate watermarks from those which merely constitute states of a single watermark. Since the life of a mould in normal use was about a year, and since long runs of paper in a book are more significant for dating than stray remnants which the printer may have had on hand for a considerable time, one is sometimes able, by combining all the evidence, to date a book with remarkable precision — just as Stevenson assigns the *Missale* to 1473, probably between February and October.

The descriptive bibliographer cannot be expected to consider an extensive investigation of watermarks — of the kind Stevenson performed for the *Missale* — a routine part of his description of every book. What should be expected is that he be aware of the techniques at his disposal; that he employ them whenever necessary to establish, or assist in establishing, basic facts in the printing and publishing history of a book; and that in every case his ordinary description of paper reveal his awareness of the needs of bibliographers who employ these techniques. For example, providing the measurements of a watermark in addition to a brief verbal description helps in itself to distinguish among similar watermark designs; but if the bibliographer also includes in his figures the relation of the watermark to the chainlines, he is, in brief space and with little additional effort, offering a fact of great potential usefulness to those engaged in paper study.

L. Putman's *Isotopes* (1960); O. K. Nordstrand, "Beta-Radiographie von Wasserzeichen," *Papiergeschichte*, XVII (1967), 25-28; Stevenson, *Problem*, pp. 66-68; Stevenson, "Beta-Radiography and Paper Research," in *VII International Congress of Paper Historians Communications* (1967), pp. 159-168; Stevenson, "Watermark Beta-Radiographs," in his edition of C. M. Briquet's *Les Filigranes* (1968), following p. *36; *Papermaking: Art and Craft* (Library of Congress, 1968), pp. 72-77; and J. S. G. Simmons, "The Delft Method of Watermark Reproduction," *Book Collector*, XVIII (1969), 514-515.

Since the watermark ordinarily slipped to the right in the mould (to the left on the sheet, viewed from the mould side), observation of the shifting distances between the watermark and the adjacent chainlines can help to establish a sequence of successive states of the watermark.[54] Such evidence must eventually be used in conjunction with that from sewing dots; but since the precise locations of sewing dots cannot be indicated conveniently or accurately in words or numbers and since the locations of the chainlines in relation to the watermarks can be so indicated, the descriptive bibliographer is in a position to supply at least this much initial data about watermark states. The fact that he does not find it necessary, in terms of the book he is describing, to pursue the investigation of the watermark further does not mean that another bibliographer, dealing with a different book which may have been printed on the same paper, will not be greatly assisted by the information. The second bibliographer will no doubt have to look at the paper himself, but the point is that the first man's bibliography served as a guide telling him where he could go to find some paper relevant to his own study. As more bibliographies include this kind of information, the mass of accumulated data will become increasingly useful, and bibliographies will be fulfilling all the more successfully their role as storehouses of information on the bookmaking practices of a given period.

The identification of a watermark, as Stevenson has revealed, involves more than the location of a similar mark in one of the published collections of tracings. But the bibliographer who understands the limitations of such collections will also know how to utilize them intelligently, and providing references to these collections must remain a requirement of any description of a watermark. Stevenson has offered good instruction in this area by explaining how to use Briquet's *Les Filigranes* in his introduction to the Paper Publications Society's magnificent edition of that work (1968).[55] The bibliographer cannot claim to have done his basic research if he has not attempted to locate any watermark he describes in the relevant published collections. The largest and most famous is Charles M. Briquet's *Les Filigranes* (1907), with its 16,112 tracings; but since it does not extend beyond 1600 and does not cover Spain, Portugal, Scandinavia, and Britain, the bibliographer must expect to turn to other collections as well and should be familiar with the most important ones. The Paper

54. Stevenson, *Problem*, pp. 248-252.

55. See also his essay on "Briquet and the Future of Paper Studies," in Briquet's *Opuscula* (1955), pp. xv-l.

Publications Society, founded in Hilversum, Holland, in 1948 by E. J. Labarre, has performed an invaluable service both in fostering the production of new works on watermarks and in reprinting older ones with masterful commentary and annotation. Its edition of Briquet, for example, contains 151 large pages of supplementary material, including many pages of addenda and corrigenda; and the wealth of information available in its main series of volumes, the "Monumenta Chartae Papyraceae Historiam Illustrantia," should not be overlooked by any descriptive bibliographer. Students of English books should in particular know the following works, two of which were issued by the Paper Publications Society (PPS):

Edward Heawood, "Sources of Early English Paper-Supply," *Library*, 4th ser., X (1929-30), 282-307, 427-454; "Papers Used in England after 1600," XI (1930-31), 263-299, 466-498; "Further Notes on Paper Used in England after 1600," 5th ser., II (1947-48), 119-149; III (1948-49), 141-142. [567 tracings][56]

W. A. Churchill, *Watermarks in Paper in Holland, England, France, etc., in the XVII and XVIII Centuries and Their Interconnection* (1935). [578 tracings]

Edward Heawood, *Watermarks, Mainly of the 17th and 18th Centuries* (PPS, 1950). [4078 tracings][57]

Alfred H. Shorter, *Paper Mills and Paper Makers in England, 1495-1800* (PPS, 1957). [217 tracings]

But since a large proportion of English books before the seventeenth century were printed on imported papers, the bibliographer of these books must also be acquainted with Briquet; and bibliographers in general should also know the principal foreign collections, at least the ones brought out by the Paper Publications Society — those by Zonghi, Eineder, Uchastkina, Lindt, Tromonin, Bofarull y Sans, and Voorn, and *The Nostitz Papers* — and a few others such as Midoux-Matton, LeClert, Nicolaï, Piekosinski, Klepikov, and Likhachev.[58] When it is

---

56. Heawood's article on "Watermarks," in Labarre's *Dictionary*, pp. 328-360, is a useful introductory survey, but its tracings are less appropriate for bibliographical citation.

57. In using this work, one should consult Allan Stevenson, "A Critical Study of Hea-

wood's *Watermarks, Mainly of the 17th and 18th Centuries*," *PBSA*, XLV (1951), 23-36.

58. At the back of Dard Hunter's *Papermaking in Pioneer America* (1952) are some good photographs of early American marks.

necessary to go beyond these works, a convenient list to consult is E. J. Labarre's *A Short Guide to Books on Watermarks* (1955),[59] which describes 82 titles.

A bibliographer, finding in one of these books a tracing which corresponds to the watermark in question, enters the name of the author and the serial number of the tracing in his description; if he provides a photograph of his own, his primary reference is to that photograph, with an added note asking the reader to compare certain published tracings:

> dolphin mark (Briquet 5873), 35 x 1[23]1 (C4)
> *or* dolphin mark (Plate 7; cf. Briquet 5873), 35 x 1[23]1 (C4)

Since tracings are never exact reproductions, it is unnecessary to use "cf." when the only reference is to one tracing (though it may be prudent to do so).[60] When the match is so inexact that nothing more specific than a whole class of marks can be cited, the "cf." can conveniently be used with the inclusive numbers referring to that class; it can also be employed when two or more individual tracings are cited, as a way of indicating the less exact of them. The brevity and wording of the verbal description are to some extent determined by the citations. If there are no citations of published tracings — either because the watermark is in modern machine-made paper or because, even though earlier, it does not correspond with any located tracing — the verbal description must be more ample than would otherwise be necessary; but if a tracing is cited or a specific photograph is provided, the verbal description can be quite brief. The form of the wording, however, should in all cases conform as much as possible to an accepted standard, so that the same figures will not be called different names by different bibliographers. A. F. Gasparinetti has suggested, to bring about this uniformity, that Briquet's terms (or their equivalents in other languages) be used, even when one is

59. Reprinted in *The Nostitz Papers* (1956), pp. xxxvii-xlii, and in *Philobiblon*, I (1957), 237-251. Another important list of material, limited to the period before 1600, is in C. M. Briquet, *Les Filigranes*, ed. Stevenson (1968), pp. *37-53; an earlier list is Dard Hunter, *Handmade Paper and Its Watermarks: A Bibliography* (1916). See also E. J. Labarre, "The Study of Watermarks in Great Britain," in *The Briquet Album* (1952), pp. 97-106.

60. Stevenson, in the Hunt *Catalogue*, uses "cf." and also explains concisely its significance: "The references to Heawood, Churchill, Voorn, Nicolaï, and others are not to marks from the same moulds (which are difficult to be sure of from tracings) but to sufficiently similar marks for the reader's understanding" (p. clxxix).

referring to other works.[61] The proposal is sensible, since Briquet's collection is the largest and since the equivalents of his French terms have been provided in several languages both in *The Briquet Album* and in the 1968 edition of *Les Filigranes*.[62] Longer verbal descriptions, when required to compensate for the lack of citations, need not be elaborate but should always include quasi-facsimile transcriptions of words or numbers; when the situation warrants, of course, more detailed treatment can be furnished, either as an appendage to the paragraph on paper or in the "Notes" section. Any countermarks or subsidiary marks can be recorded in exactly the same way as the main marks. Stevenson, in the Hunt *Catalogue*, employs a long equals sign between the description of a main mark and that of a countermark;[63] the device is convenient, but, if one wishes to use words instead, one can simply insert "countermark" ("cornermark," "edgemark") or "countermark reading":

dolphin mark (Briquet 5873), 35 x 1[23]1 (C4) = 'IV', 10 x 6[13]6 (C1)

or dolphin mark (Briquet 5873), 35 x 1[23]1 (C4), and countermark 'IV', 10 x 6[13]6 (C1)

This treatment of watermarks, countermarks, and chainlines is not time-consuming and requires little space in the final description; yet it provides essential information for an identification of paper and records facts of potential significance for further bibliographical analysis.

III

In addition to the dimensions and the markings, there are many other characteristics of paper which the bibliographer could conceivably take into account. The paper industry has developed a wide range of procedures and machines for testing various properties of paper in order to maintain standards and to identify precisely the features of any given sample. Although these tests are usually applied to modern machine-made paper, they could be employed to ascertain the characteristics of earlier papers as well. Some of them are not

---

61. Gasparinetti, "On the Adoption of a Universal Terminology for Watermarks," in *The Briquet Album*, pp. 122-124.

62. *The Briquet Album*, pp. 125-154 (English, German, Italian); *Les Filigranes*, pp. *109-131 (French, English, German).

63. Gaskell, in the Baskerville bibliography, uses an oblique line for this purpose; oblique lines have been suggested above, however, as separators for variant measurements.

appropriate for bibliographical work, but the bibliographer should be aware of the general range of physical, chemical, and optical characteristics which are mechanically testable. The physical characteristics can be subdivided into five categories: (1) substance, involving such matters as basis weight, thickness, bulk, and bulking thickness; (2) strength, as revealed by tests for tensile strength (e.g., Schopper static tester, Van der Korput dynamic tester), bursting tests (Mullen, Schopper-Dalen), tearing tests (Elmendorf), and folding tests (Schopper); (3) permeability and absorbency (as tested by the Gurley densometer, the Potts permeability apparatus, the Cobb method, the Currier apparatus, and so on); (4) formation (as indicated by the degree of uniformity of transmitted light); and (5) smoothness (judged by microscopic or photographic techniques or by the flow of air between the paper and a standard surface). The chemical characteristics can be determined by tests for (1) the fiber and mineral constituents of a furnish; (2) the sizing agents (gelatin, rosin, casein); and (3) acidity and alkalinity (both colorimetric and electrometric tests). Finally, the optical properties fall into three groups: (1) color (tested against a standard or by spectrophotometer) and whiteness (tested by the Zeiss Leukometer); (2) gloss (surface reflectance measured by such instruments as the Ingersol Glarimeter or the Sheen Gloss meter) and brightness (General Electric Brightness meter or Institute for Paper Chemistry Automatic Color and Brightness Tester); and (3) opacity (measured by a photometer).[64]

Some of these tests can be ruled out immediately for bibliographical purposes because they entail destruction or mutilation of the

64. The basic tests for paper are outlined in any of the standard works on paper manufacture. See, for example, Julius Grant, *A Laboratory Handbook of Pulp and Paper Manufacture* (1942), pp. 179-297 (which includes a good analysis of the appearance of fibers, pp. 251-258); Robert H. Clapperton, *Modern Paper-Making* (3rd ed., 1952), pp. 450-464; J. Newell Stephenson (ed.), *Manufacture and Testing of Paper and Board* (1953); C. Earl Libby (ed.), *Pulp and Paper Science and Technology* (1962), II, 373-398; Robert R. A. Higham, *A Handbook of Papermaking* (1963), pp. 72-86; and Victor Strauss, *The Printing Industry* (1967), pp. 577-580. An important introduction to the subject of paper testing is *Paper and Paperboard: Characteristics, Nomenclature and Significance of Tests* (ASTM Special Technical Publication No. 60-B; 3rd ed., 1963); it provides, at the beginning, a list showing the correspondences between the two sets of test standards, those of the American Society for Testing and Materials (ASTM) and those of the Technical Association of the Pulp and Paper Industry (TAPPI). The ASTM standards are set forth in Part 15 of the *Book of ASTM Standards*, issued annually; the TAPPI *Standard Testing Procedures* are available in two loose-leaf volumes, revised continually. A *Bibliography of Paper Testing* appears in the Institute of Paper Chemistry Bibliographic Series as Nos. 154-156 (2nd ed., 1954, with supplements in 1960 and 1965) and Nos. 157-159 (2nd ed., 1960).

paper (all the tests for strength fall into this category). Others, though they do not damage the paper, are impractical for a bibliographer to undertake because they involve precision instruments which are not easily portable and are not available in libraries (many of the optical tests fall into this category). In any case, the details established by most of these tests are not of primary relevance to bibliographical studies. Since a verbal description of a physical object necessarily represents a selection of details out of an infinite number of possible details, an intelligent description depends on a systematic selection of details made in the light of the purposes for which the description is intended. The elaborate tests performed in the paper industry do not provide exhaustive coverage of every conceivable property of paper, but they furnish those details necessary for the efficient operation of the industry. Similarly, the description of paper in a bibliography should record only those characteristics which are of primary interest to the persons for whom the bibliography is prepared—in general, students of literature, of history, and of printing and publishing. One cannot, of course, say that such details as the tensile strength or the chemical composition or the opacity of paper are necessarily irrelevant to historical study; the student of book production in a particular period would doubtless be happy to have a large body of such information available for his use in author-bibliographies. But one can say that these kinds of detail are not of primary importance to the majority of users of a bibliography and that the practical difficulties they involve outweigh their usefulness for this audience. If, in certain instances, some of these details do turn out to be of significance in establishing the printing history of a book, they can then be recorded — the classic case is Carter and Pollard's use of evidence regarding the composition of paper in detecting the Wise forgeries. Only the bibliographer who has a detailed knowledge of a particular situation will be in a position to decide whether or not some of these tests are likely to be fruitful for his purposes; when he thinks they may be, he can turn for assistance to an appropriate laboratory, but it would be absurd to require him to go to such lengths as part of the ordinary routine of bibliographical description.[65] In the light of these considerations, only two of the tests employed in the paper trade — those for thickness and color — seem appropriate for bibliographical use, while a third group of the tested characteristics — those relating to finish — can be treated bibliographically in a less precise fashion.

65. Cf. Tanselle, "Tolerances," pp. 5-6.

(1) *Thickness.* The measurement of paper thickness is one of several related measurements of primary importance in the paper industry. Of these, the basic measurement is that of the "substance" of paper, generally expressed in terms of "basis weight" — that is, the weight per standard unit area (usually, per ream of specified dimensions).[66] Thus the designation "35 x 45, 100 lbs., 516's" describes a paper of which a 516-sheet ream, with each sheet measuring 35 x 45 inches, weighs 100 pounds. A more convenient method of indicating substance, based on the metric system, is to specify grams per square meter; in this way only one figure need be given, since it is not dependent on the size of the sheet. Instead of saying "35 x 45, 100 lbs., 516's," one can simply say "87 g.s.m."[67] Although the substance of paper is one of its most prominent characteristics, measurement of substance cannot normally be performed in bibliographical work, since the bibliographer is not usually in a position to weigh the sheets of a book separately from the binding, endpapers, and inserted plates. If he cannot make this measurement, then he cannot present other figures based on it, such as "bulk," the ratio of the thickness of a sheet to its substance.[68] The thickness of a sheet, on the other hand, is not obscured when the sheet is folded and bound into a book; it is thus available for direct measurement by the bibliographer, and it should be reported in his description of paper.

Measurement of the thickness of a single sheet of paper is performed with a micrometer caliper. Many styles of micrometers are available (both spring-actuated and dead-weight-actuated), and most of them can be used for measuring paper thickness; since suitable pocket models can be purchased for about $30, every bibliographer should have one as part of his standard equipment.[69] They are manufactured with dials graduated in fractions of inches or in fractions of millimeters, and the bibliographer should choose one with a dial corresponding to whichever system is being used for other measure-

66. See TAPPI Method T410-os and ASTM Method D646.

67. Tables of equivalences, for converting pounds per ream to grams per square meter, are available; see, for example, Clapperton, *Modern Paper-Making*, pp. 496-497.

68. The term "bulk" is also used to mean the total thickness of a given number of sheets, and it is in this sense that the word may appear later in a bibliographical description of paper to indicate the combined thickness of the folded sheets in a finished book.

69. Micrometers for official paper testing must conform with TAPPI Method 7411-m44 and ASTM Method D645-64T and have .0001" graduation; but most dial micrometers with .001" graduation are adequate for bibliographical work.

ments.[70] The sheets of a given book may vary in thickness, according to the micrometer readings, and the significance of such variation may differ according to the period and type of paper. In handmade paper, if the chainlines and watermark suggest that all the sheets were intended to be "the same paper," certain variations in thickness may be of no importance, and one can report either an average reading or the range of readings; but in machine-made paper a slight difference in thickness between two sheets can indicate that two stocks of paper were used and may even be important in distinguishing between two impressions.[71] Therefore, one should normally take a micrometer reading on one leaf in every sheet (if not on every leaf, as a test for cancels). When a representative reading for each paper is arrived at, one simply records the reading in the description, along with the citation of a specific leaf which yields that reading, in some such form as the following: "thickness .003 in. (B3)," or "thickness .076 mm. (B3)," or "thickness 76μ (B3)."[72]

Some bibliographers in the past have reported the thickness of all the sheets of a book taken together, in such a form as "sheets bulk 1 7/16 in." This kind of measurement is useful in enabling a reader to visualize the thickness of a book and serves as a guide to the "bulking thickness" of the paper. When the figure for the total thickness of the leaves of a book is divided by the number of leaves, the resulting figure is nearly always larger than that representing the thickness of a single sheet as measured with a micrometer; this larger figure is known as the "bulking thickness" and is an important characteristic of paper. For these reasons the bibliographer should continue to record the total bulk of the sheets (and perhaps the calculated bulking thickness of a single sheet), even though a micrometer reading of the paper thickness is given also. Such a measurement, however, is often not very precise because it can vary with the amount of pressure applied to the sheets when the measurement is taken and with the

---

70. A convenient pocket micrometer, satisfactory for bibliographical purposes, is the Ames Thickness Measure No. 25 (with .001″ graduation) or No. 25M (with .01 mm. graduation), manufactured by the B. C. Ames Co., Waltham, Massachusetts 02154; or the Cady Pocket Micrometer, Model CPM (with .001″ graduation), manufactured by E. J. Cady & Co., Chicago 60635.

71. Few bibliographers in the past have

utilized micrometer measurements of thickness to distinguish impressions. For an exception, see Matthew J. Bruccoli and Joseph Katz, "Scholarship and Mere Artifacts: The British and Empire Publications of Stephen Crane," *SB*, XXII (1969), 277-287 (esp. p. 278).

72. A micron (μ) is equal to one thousandth of a millimeter and is an appropriate unit for expressing the thickness of paper.

particular place on the edge of the book chosen for measurement. The center of the top edge is usually the best place to measure if a ruler is used, but calipers that reach in to the center of the leaves provide a more dependable reading; whichever method is employed, only those leaves comprising the sheets that went through the press are to be measured, excluding any endpapers and binder's leaves.[73]

Even with these precautions, the measurement is not dependable enough to be relied upon in bibliographical analysis whenever much precision is required. If, for example, some copies of a particular book are printed on uniform paper throughout and other copies include one gathering made up of heavier paper, the variation in total bulk between copies of each kind may be so slight as to seem insignificant to the bibliographer; he may dismiss the variation (especially if he does not have copies yielding the two readings side by side) as due simply to the ways in which he held the copies when taking the measurements. But if he had taken micrometer readings of each sheet, he would have known that the variation resulted from the presence of a heavier sheet in some copies. Of course, chainlines and watermarks also serve to distinguish between papers in some books; but, for books printed on wove unwatermarked paper, micrometer measurement may be the only easy way of detecting mixed papers — and thus of locating what may be called "sheet-cancels" (substituted sheets rather than single leaves), not uncommon in machine-produced books.[74] Whenever a book does contain mixed papers, the figure for bulking thickness (as opposed to total bulk), if it is to have meaning, must be given separately for each different paper and must be based on the bulk of particular sections of the book; in such cases, dividing the total bulk of the entire book by the number of leaves gives only an average and tells one nothing about the bulking thickness of the individual papers involved. For this reason, figures for bulking thickness — when they are deemed significant enough to report — should be associated not with the figure for total bulk but with the other characteristics of the individual papers. A convenient way to put the figures for bulking thickness in proper perspective is to place them

73. See Bowers, *Principles*, p. 446.

74. Obviously leaf-cancels can often be located by micrometer measurements also, and one can argue for this reason that micrometer readings should be taken on every leaf of a book, not just on every sheet. One cannot rely on the detection of stubs as the sole method for finding cancels, and chainlines and watermarks are not always present; micrometer measurements are therefore an invaluable aid in approaching the problem of cancels in machine-produced books printed on **wove** paper — a problem set forth by John Carter in "Some Bibliographical Agenda," in *Nineteenth-Century English Books* (1952), pp. 68-70.

immediately after the figures for the thickness of single sheets (with a parenthetical indication of the section of the book which served as the basis for the calculation): "thickness .076 mm. (B3), bulking .079 mm. (B-G)." The one figure for total bulk of the sheets should come later in the description, since it is a feature of the finished book, not a characteristic of any of the papers involved.

(2) *Color.* The most precise way of specifying color, in paper as in other objects, is in terms of spectrophotometric measurement; but a simpler — yet reliable and scientific — method, also used when appropriate in the paper industry, is visual comparison against a standard. Since the Centroid Color Chart worked out by the Inter-Society Color Council and the National Bureau of Standards has been recommended for other instances of color specification in bibliographical description,[75] it is an appropriate choice for the reporting of color in paper also. Certainly the same system of referring to color should be used throughout a bibliography, and the ISCC-NBS dictionary offers a convenient way of converting all specifications to the ISCC-NBS system regardless of the color chart originally employed. Furthermore, Deane B. Judd, writing in the *Paper Trade Journal*, has specifically shown the applicability of the ISCC-NBS names to the description of paper.[76] The advantages of the system, in terms of general acceptance and convenience, outweigh its two chief disadvantages: the glossiness of the centroid color chips and the limited distinctions the centroid chart makes among the common colors of printing papers. The two are related, for the less fine the discrimination required in specifying color, the less important the distortion created by surface texture. Of the 267 ISCC-NBS color-name blocks, only seven are of much use in describing the papers generally employed for printing books: white (Centroid 263), pinkish white (9), yellowish white (92), greenish white (153), bluish white (189), purplish white (231), and light gray (264). The colors of the majority of book papers, in fact, fall nearer the centroid chip for "white" than any of the other chips. Several methods of measuring and specifying more accurately the various degrees of whiteness in paper have been developed in the paper industry,[77] but under most circumstances the bibliographical significance of the precise color of paper is not great enough to war-

75. See G. T. Tanselle, "A System of Color Identification for Bibliographical Description," *SB*, XX (1967), 203-234.

76. Judd, "Systematic Color Designations for Paper," *Paper Trade Journal*, CXI (17 October 1940), TS201-TS206.

77. For a brief list of works on this subject, see *SB*, XX (1967), 233.

rant the use of spectrophotometers and other elaborate equipment. In unusual instances the bibliographer may find it necessary to turn to these methods; but he need not make them part of his standard routine, for the information they yield would often prove more distracting than helpful to the readers of descriptive bibliographies. Ordinarily, therefore, the distinctions among near-whites provided by the ISCC-NBS centroid chips, though not subtle, are adequate for bibliographical purposes. Indeed, since the nearest match will usually be "white," a bibliographer may wish to establish the convention within an individual bibliography that all papers described are white unless otherwise specified; on the other hand, it does no harm to repeat "white" in each instance, since the word takes little space and emphasizes the fact that the color of the paper has been taken into account. It is perhaps unnecessary to cite the centroid number for white, but for other colors a parenthetical reference to a visual standard should always be provided. If a bibliographer describes a paper as "yellowish white (Centroid 92)," the reader knows that the color of the paper, though not necessarily an exact match, falls within that color-name block of which centroid chip 92 is representative.

(3) *Finish.* The finish of paper is one of its most prominent characteristics, involving such related properties as gloss, brightness, and smoothness. Since the general roughness or glossiness of a piece of paper immediately catches the eye, it is reasonable to expect that a description of paper should take this quality into account. The only accurate way of measuring gloss, however, is in terms of the surface reflectance of light, and the test for smoothness is in terms of the surface flow of air; these procedures again involve instruments which make finer discriminations than are generally usable or meaningful in a bibliography. What will usually suffice, for bibliographical purposes, is a simple verbal description of gloss and smoothness, preferably in the form of a single adjective (since the two qualities, except when measured by instruments, are difficult to separate). Although a standard series of adjectives exists in the paper trade — "antique," "eggshell," "vellum," "machine," and "English" (for uncoated papers), or "dull," "semidull," and "glossy" (for coated papers) [78] — any attempt to employ these terms without reference to a visual standard or recourse to numerical measurement would tend to accentuate the problem of subjectivity. Other similar series could be formulated — such as "very rough," "rough," "medium," "smooth,"

78. Definitions of these terms can be found in *The Dictionary of Paper* (3rd ed., 1965).

and "extra glossy"[79] — without reducing the difficulty of deciding where the lines between the categories should be drawn. Besides, would any two bibliographers agree on these lines, and could even a single bibliographer observe them consistently? Such considerations render impractical the attempt to establish on this level any multi-term sequence. Yet it is usually not difficult to secure agreement that certain papers are "rough" and others are "glossy." The most sensible course of action, therefore, is to use "rough" to describe uncoated papers which have a pronounced roughness and "glossy" to describe coated papers which have an unquestionably shiny surface; for all papers in between, whether coated or uncoated, one can use "smooth," or possibly no adjective at all, implying that only wide variations from the norm need be specified. Such a tripartite scheme does not eliminate subjective judgment but merely reduces the number of dividing lines where it must operate. When instruments or visual standards are not to be employed, it is futile to attempt subdividing a continuum into more than a few large sections if the results are to convey the same meaning to different people. For bibliographical purposes, distinguishing "rough" and "glossy" papers from the broad range in between is usually adequate and comprehensible; if a bibliographer needs on occasion to employ greater precision, he should turn to the appropriate instruments rather than increase his stock of adjectives and intensifying adverbs, which are more likely to confuse than to refine his description.[80]

The specification of finish, like that of color and thickness, tends to have greater significance in connection with machine-made and wove papers than with handmade and laid papers. Variations in these characteristics in hand-produced paper, given the nature of the process, may be of little importance in distinguishing separate runs, whereas such variations in machine-made paper, with its greater regularity, may be of more consequence for identification; similarly, precise notation of these properties in laid (and particularly watermarked) paper may not be especially helpful, since the chainlines and watermarks generally provide sufficient identification, whereas such notation for wove (and particularly unwatermarked) paper may be quite useful,

79. This series is suggested by William Bond Wheelwright in "Identification of Paper Samples," *Paper & Printing Digest*, V (September 1939), 3-9.

80. Among the twentieth-century specimen books which offer samples of various finish-

es, two comprehensive ones are *A Book of Samples of Paper* (Champion Paper Co., 1922) and, especially, *Paper for Books: A Comprehensive Survey of the Various Types of Paper Used in Book Production* (Robert Horne & Co., 1953, 1961).

since there is little else to rely on. Thus the advantages of having detailed information about these characteristics rarely outweigh the difficulties of obtaining and utilizing it when the paper under examination is handmade, laid, or watermarked; for these papers the unsophisticated approach described here is often adequate. On the other hand, the usefulness of precise data about these matters may well justify the efforts entailed when the paper being analyzed is machine-made, wove, or unwatermarked; for these papers significant differences may be overlooked if precision instruments are not employed. All one can say is that any bibliographical description of paper should be expected to take some account of thickness, color, and finish. For the most part, the techniques used can be quite simple; but, when the occasion warrants, the bibliographer — aware of the more elaborate methods available to him — should not hesitate to turn to the laboratory for aid.

IV

All of these characteristics, which constitute the main part of a bibliographical description of paper, have to do with the *sheet*, not the *leaf* — that is, they are characteristics of the paper itself, not of the paper as it happens to be folded in a particular book (though some of them obviously must be inferred from the paper as folded). But at the end of the description two characteristics of the *leaf* — or the paper as it appears in the finished book — ought to be appended: the dimensions of the leaf[81] and the total bulk of the leaves.[82] These figures are important, first of all, because they represent direct measurements and thus serve as documentation for some of the inferences presented earlier in the description. In addition, being directly observable, they are sometimes of more immediate assistance to users of a bibliography than such figures as those for the dimensions and thickness of the sheet. Even for a book published before the time of edition binding, every copy of which may exhibit a different leaf size, a report of the leaf dimensions of the largest known copy is helpful, both to support the inference about sheet size and to serve as a conveniently usable standard of comparison. As for bulk, even though

81. Of course, if the format of a book cannot be determined and the dimensions of the leaf are given in the collation paragraph, they need not be repeated here.

82. The treatment of the edges (stained, rough-trimmed, and so on) is more appropriately specified in the paragraph on binding, since it is not a characteristic of the paper but represents something done to the paper in the process of binding.

it is difficult to obtain precise figures, sometimes two issues of a book differ so greatly in bulk that even approximate figures are adequate to distinguish them. For example, two issues of the first printing of O'Neill's *The Moon of the Caribbees and Six Other Plays of the Sea* (1919) can be distinguished by the paper: one bulks 18 mm. and the other 24 mm. The difference is pronounced enough that, even though the figures are not really precise, one has no difficulty in determining to which issue a particular copy belongs.[83] In this case the figures for total bulk are more immediately useful for identification than the information that the thickness of each sheet of one issue is .160 mm. and of the other .216 mm. Furthermore, if the bulking thickness were reported as .165 mm. for the first and .220 for the second, the figures for total bulk would be necessary to indicate the basis of the calculation. Leaf dimensions and total bulk, therefore, though not actually characteristics of paper itself, serve an important function in a bibliographical description of paper. Also, it is useful to record at this point, for laid paper, the direction of the chainlines in relation to the leaf.

The kinds of detail and the accuracy of measurement suggested here represent a somewhat fuller description of paper than is often found in bibliographies but clearly not the most elaborate description possible. Indeed, the procedure recommended here is intended to occupy a middle ground — detailed enough to provide information for identification and for historical study, and yet not so burdensome as to be self-defeating. It may be helpful to think of this procedure as occupying the middle stages in a series of graduated levels.[84] The lowest level, frequently employed in bibliographies in the past, is the simple designation of paper as either laid or wove. A second level, only slightly more detailed, includes a brief indication of any watermarks and perhaps a reference to color and finish. Although there will continue to be situations in which this brief sort of description is

---

83. Bulk measurements which include the covers and endpapers are cited for this book in Merle Johnson, *American First Editions*, ed. Jacob Blanck (4th ed., 1942), p. 401. Higginson's Graves bibliography reports two figures for bulk (as "1.8/2.3 cm."), one for the sheets and endpapers and another for the sheets, endpapers, and covers. However, bulk measurements should properly include only the sheets; if in rare instances a variation in the thickness of the covers is significant, the information can be recorded in the paragraph on binding.

84. The idea of a series of levels to represent the spectrum of possible details for investigation was suggested by Kenneth L. Kelly's use of this device in "A Universal Color Language," *Color Engineering*, III (March-April 1965), 2-7; further comments on its usefulness in descriptive bibliography are found in the essay on "Tolerances" cited above (note 37).

sufficient, it cannot now be considered appropriate for a full-scale descriptive bibliography. Instead, the descriptive bibliographer will operate on one of the next two levels: the third, which entails direct measurements with a ruler (distances between chainlines, dimensions of watermarks, and total bulk and dimensions of the leaves) ; and the fourth, which involves inferences (to establish the dimensions of the sheets), recourse to reference works (to identify the watermarks) , and use of a micrometer (to measure the thickness of individual sheets) .[85] Beyond this level, two more may be postulated, but the bibliographer will move to them only in unusual cases: the fifth, in which the paper is subjected to one or more laboratory tests; and the sixth, in which the paper, on the basis of these tests, or reference to specimen books, or other research, is traced to an individual manufacturer or mill. The bibliographer who has examined a large number of copies of a given book will be best able to judge whether or not laboratory tests are worth investigating in that particular instance; though bibliographers in the past have been excessively reluctant to avail themselves of such assistance, it would be equally foolish to overestimate the value of laboratory tests for bibliographical work. As a general rule — subject to exceptions in special cases — what one can reasonably expect of a bibliographer in his description of paper is a level of detail equivalent to the fourth level described here.

After these characteristics of paper have been ascertained, there remains the problem of how best to record them in a descriptive bibliography. Since so little attention has been given to paper in the past, no accepted practice in this regard has become established. The only tradition which can be said to exist derives from the two major bibliographies which include paragraphs on paper, Gaskell's *Baskerville* and Stevenson's Hunt catalogue; their record of paper takes the following forms:[86]

PAPER: Brownish, poor quality *Large Printing Demy* laid, watermark fleur-de-lys / IV, size of sheet 21 x 17¼ in.

PAPER: Crown, Genoese, with double chains, countermarked IV and

---

85. The degree of accuracy of measurements is a separate question from the quantity of detail. Generally speaking, dimensions of sheets and leaves, as well as total bulk, should be reported to the nearest millimeter (or the nearest thirty-second of an inch) and thicknesses of paper to the nearest thousandth of a millimeter (or of an inch).

86. The first of these descriptions is from Philip Gaskell, *John Baskerville: A Bibliography* (1959), entry 37; the second is from Allan Stevenson, *Catalogue of Botanical Books in the Collection of Rachel McMasters Miller Hunt*, II (1961), entry 466.

corner OO. Plates in text: same paper. Frontispiece: thick paper with single chains, countermarked IV. Leaf 13.1 x 8.6″ = sheet [14 x 18″].

This pattern — the size-name of the paper, followed by a designation of chainlines and marks, with the leaf measurement at the end — is the basis for the sample forms presented below. They are purely hypothetical examples, designed to suggest ways of handling a variety of situations:

PAPER. *Sheets*: at least 500 x 376 mm. (probably Crown, 508 x 381) ; laid, with dolphin mark (Briquet 5873), 35 x 1[23]1 (B4) / 0[23]2 (G3), and countermark 'IV', 10 x 6[13]6 (B1) ; thickness .244 (B4), bulking .250 (B-P); light gray (Centroid 264). *Plates*: laid, chainlines 22 mm. apart; thickness .272; light gray. *Leaves*: at least 376 x 250 (B4) ; chainlines vertical; total bulk 14 mm.

PAPER. *Sheets (A-D, I-M)* : wove, unwatermarked; thickness .203 mm. (I1), bulking .207 (I-M); bluish white (Centroid 189) ; glossy. *Sheets (E-H)*: wove, unwatermarked; thickness .221 (E1), bulking .227; white (263) ; glossy. *Frontispiece*: wove, unwatermarked; thickness .279; bluish white; glossy. *Leaves*: total bulk 20.5 mm.

The first represents a book which is printed on laid watermarked paper and for which the format can be determined; the second represents one which is printed on two kinds of wove unwatermarked paper and for which the format is not known. Various modifications will naturally suggest themselves in particular instances. It is more important, of course, to be concise, unambiguous, and consistent within a given bibliography than to follow uncritically a form prescribed in advance; on the other hand, in the absence of special difficulties, a prescribed form is to be preferred over individual variations, since it leads to greater uniformity among bibliographies in general and thus to greater ease of reference.

The approach to the description of paper suggested here would not, in most cases, involve a great investment of time, nor would the resulting paragraph occupy much space on the printed page. Yet the information amassed in this way — particularly after a large number of bibliographies had recorded such details — would be of incalculable value to the historian of paper and of book production; and a descriptive bibliography cannot be said to have fulfilled its function unless it provides this kind of historical data. In any event, paper is a major ingredient of the printed book, and it is only common sense to expect a description of a book to include some comments on paper. There are signs that more bibliographical attention is now beginning to turn in this direction. Even the technical research into paper deterioration has given some impetus to the historical study of nineteenth-century paper[87] and has caused certain present-day publishers to include in their colophons the results of various paper tests.[88] And Allan Stevenson's work has dramatically demonstrated to bibliographers that the investigation of paper can play a significant role in bibliographical analysis. A bibliographer cannot know just what aspects of paper are going to take on greater importance for analysis in the future but by recording certain basic facts about size, watermarks, thickness, and the like he can help to accumulate the data upon which new discoveries will rest. The descriptive bibliographer is a historian, and one measure of his success is the extent to which he gives paper — like any other element of the book — its rightful place in the total picture.[89]

87. See, for example, *Strength and Other Characteristics of Book Papers, 1800-1899* (1967), Publication No. 5 in the series on *Permanence/Durability of the Book* (1963-), issued by the W. J. Barrow Research Laboratory of Richmond, Va.

88. A recent example occurs in *The National Union Catalog: Pre-1956 Imprints* (1968-), where the paper on which the work is printed is described in this fashion: "Substance 89 gsm / pH cold extract 9.4 / Fold endurance (MIT ½ kg. tension) 1200 / Tear resistance (Elmendorf) 73 (or 67 x 3) / Opacity 90.3%."

89. I am grateful to the late Allan Stevenson and to Dr. Philip Gaskell for their generosity in taking time to read a manuscript version of this article.

Greg's Theory of Copy-Text
and the Editing of American Literature

LTHOUGH THE EDITING OF LITERARY TEXTS HAS LONG BEEN regarded as one of the basic tasks of literary scholars, I think it can be said that in the last fifteen years an unusual amount of scholarly attention has been directed toward editing and editorial theory. The situation is particularly striking in the field of American literature, for these years have witnessed the development of a coordinated effort—on a scale rare in scholarly endeavor generally and unparalleled in the editing of literature in English—to produce full-scale editions of most of the major (and several other important) nineteenth-century American writers. The need for reliable editions of the principal American figures had been given official recognition much earlier, when the American Literature Group of the Modern Language Association of America established—in 1947-48—a Committee on Definitive Editions, with Willard Thorp as chairman. Although that committee was unsuccessful in securing financial support for such editions, it laid the groundwork for continued discussion, which, after two conferences in 1962, resulted in the establishment in 1963 of the Center for Editions of American Authors. Since that time the Center has coordinated the work on fourteen editions[1] and since 1966 has allocated funds amounting to more than one and a half million dollars, provided by the National Endowment for the Humanities of the National Foundation on the Arts and Humanities. (In addition, many universities and university presses, as well as the Office of Education of the Department of Health, Education, and Welfare, have helped with individual editions.) As a result, more than one

---

1. Presenting the work of twelve authors: Cooper, Stephen Crane, John Dewey, Emerson, Hawthorne, Howells, Irving, Melville, Simms, Thoreau, Mark Twain, and Whitman.

hundred volumes have now been completed, and others are in various stages of preparation.[2]

The fact that an accomplishment of such magnitude, involving the cooperation of more than two hundred scholars, could be produced in little more than a decade of concentrated work—to say nothing of the existence of the Center as an official committee of the MLA or of its support by public funds—suggests a widespread recognition of the importance of the whole undertaking. This is not to say, however, that there is any unanimity of opinion as to the precise editorial principles which ought to be followed, and the CEAA editions have been the subject of a considerable number of critical attacks, directed both to particular editions and to general matters of policy. Now one of the unusual features of the CEAA as a scholarly coordinating committee is that it has insisted, from the beginning, that certain editorial principles be followed in any edition that is to be associated with it and receive its approval. To this end, it has established a seal to be printed in every volume which meets the requirements, certifying that the text is "An Approved Text" of the CEAA. The administration of this plan obviously involves the pre-publication inspection of each text by an examiner appointed by the Center, and the result is that any reader who sees the CEAA seal on a volume knows that its text has been prepared in conformity with a set of carefully defined guidelines, relating not only to editorial theory but to the practicalities of setting forth evidence and of proofreading as well. In essence, the editorial principles of the CEAA—set forth in its *Statement of Editorial Principles and Procedures* (originally published in 1967 and revised in 1972) —are those enunciated by W. W. Greg in his famous paper for the 1949 English Institute, "The Rationale of Copy-Text." Although he was talking specifically about English dramatic literature of the Renaissance, his discussion raised basic questions applicable to editorial theory in general, and his "rationale" has since been adopted by

2. A more detailed account of the history of the CEAA can be found in William M. Gibson's "The Center for Editions of American Authors" and in John H. Fisher's "The MLA Editions of Major American Authors" (and the chronology which follows it) in *Professional Standards and American Editions: A Response to Edmund Wilson* (Modern Language Association, 1969), pp. 1-6, 20-28. A survey of editions in progress and proposed editions at the time of the inception of the CEAA (and based on the 1962 discussions) is provided by William M. Gibson and Edwin H. Cady in "Editions of American Writers, 1963: A Preliminary Survey," *PMLA*, 78 (September 1963, part 2), 1-8 (reprinted in an MLA pamphlet, *The Situation of English, 1963*); another essay useful for background relating to the inception of the CEAA is Willard Thorp's "Exodus: Four Decades of American Literary Scholarship," *MLQ*, 26 (1965), 40-61.

various editors working in later periods of English literature as well as in American literature. But some scholars have questioned the applicability of Greg's principles to later literature and have thus questioned the wisdom of the CEAA requirements descended from Greg.

The time now seems appropriate—since both the CEAA and its critics have a substantial amount of material in print—to review the phenomenon of this debate.[3] Certainly the existence and the accomplishment of the CEAA as an institution constitute a phenomenon unique in the history of literary scholarship in English; but the response to the CEAA also is phenomenal in the amount of critical notice which it has bestowed on editorial and textual concerns. The controversy has doubtless caused people who normally pay little attention to editing to focus on some of the problems involved in editorial work, and as a result editing may have moved somewhat nearer to being a matter of vital concern to the scholarly literary world at large. Even if the tone of some of the discussion has served as a poor introduction to scholarly debate in this area, the fact remains that a number of respected figures have raised objections on matters of principle, and their criticisms deserve to be given serious attention. Sometimes, as it happens, their comments prove to be beside the point because of a misconception as to the nature of Greg's rationale or of its use by the CEAA; but some legitimate issues, worthy of continuing scrutiny, are raised in the process. An analysis of these discussions, it seems to me, must begin with a re-examination of Greg's seminal essay. By this time, that essay has reached the status of a classic; and, like any classic statement, it has so frequently been adduced to support or refute particular arguments that renewed exegesis of the document itself seems called for periodically. An understanding of exactly what Greg said is a prerequisite for examining, first, what application of his principles the CEAA stands for and, second, what criticisms of his and the CEAA's position have been put forth. In such an examination, it is important always to distinguish between theoretical and practical concerns. Criticisms on either level demand careful attention, but it is no aid to orderly thinking to treat purely practical questions as if they involved theoretical issues. I hope that these notes can begin to clarify the context within which each of the arguments must be judged and can thus help to provide a perspective from which the whole controversy can profitably be viewed.

3. A convenient record of the books and articles related to CEAA editorial theory and practice is provided as an appendix (entitled "Relevant Textual Scholarship") to the CEAA *Statement* (2nd ed., 1972), pp. 17-25.

I

Greg's contribution to the 1949 session of the English Institute, "The Rationale of Copy-Text"—read for Greg by J. M. Osborn on 8 September 1949—was first published in the third (1950-51) volume of *Studies in Bibliography* (pp. 19-36). (There is a certain appropriateness, therefore, in re-examining the essay, on the twenty-fifth anniversary of its original appearance, in the pages of the same journal.) Since that time it has been republished in the posthumous volume of Greg's *Collected Papers* (1966), edited by J. C. Maxwell, who incorporated into its text a few minor revisions and a new footnote, as indicated by Greg in his working papers.[4] The essay is not long or complicated and is expressed with Greg's usual clarity. That such an essay should have given rise to so much discussion, and even controversy, is not surprising, however, for it has the kind of simplicity frequently characteristic of great concepts—a sweeping simplicity that results from having penetrated beyond peripheral complexities and arrived at the heart of a problem. Just as it is not easy to achieve such simplicity, neither is it always easy for others to follow or accept it.

Greg begins by referring to the first use of the term "copy-text"—by R. B. McKerrow in 1904 in his edition of Nashe—and sketches the history of the idea of "the most authoritative text"; it is evident, from this kind of beginning and from later references to McKerrow's and his own changes of position, that he is presenting his ideas on copy-text as the outgrowth of an evolving train of thought extending back over many years. Indeed, his opening paragraph says nothing about putting forth a new theory but only that he wishes to consider the "conception" and "implications" of a change in McKerrow's position. Although he soon admits (p. 377) that he is drawing a distinction which "has not been generally recognized," his emphasis is not on the

---

4. The added footnote, enclosed in brackets on p. 382 of *The Collected Papers*, is the one which attributes the phrase "the tyranny of the copy-text" to Paul Maas. (He used it in his review of Greg's *The Editorial Problem in Shakespeare*, *RES*, 20 [1944], 76; Greg's reaction appears on pp. 159-160 of the same volume.) The 1966 text also adds the second "are" to "what readings are possible and what are not" at 381.31; it inserts the comma in "In the folio, revision and reproduction are so blended" at 390.32; and it adds the clause set off by commas in the statement that "the quartos contain, it is generally assumed, only reported texts" at 391.19. Another difference in the 1966 text is an error: in the quotation from McKerrow's *Prolegomena* at 380.32, "what we call inner harmony" ought to read "what we may call inner harmony," as it did in the original *SB* printing. As one would expect, the essay has been included in anthologies: *Bibliography and Textual Criticism*, ed. O M Brack, Jr., and Warner Barnes (1969), pp. 41-58; *Art and Error*, ed. Ronald Gottesman and Scott Bennett (1970), pp. 17-36. Both of these anthologies reprint the *SB* text rather than the text from *The Collected Papers*.

novelty of his contribution but rather on the way in which it seems but a natural step in the line of thinking already pursued both by him and by McKerrow. In effect he is saying that he has finally come to recognize something which he had overlooked earlier and something toward which McKerrow had gradually been moving.

It is important to notice the historical framework of Greg's essay: for Greg, stepping into the discussion at a particular point in its development, accepts without further analysis certain ideas about scholarly editing—two in particular—which he feels have already been adequately established. First, he makes clear that he rejects "purely eclectic methods," in which an editor has no restraints placed on his freedom to choose among variant readings on the basis of his subjective judgments of their aesthetic appropriateness; the "genealogical method," developed by Lachmann and his successors in the nineteenth century, was, he says, "the greatest advance ever made in this field," because it provided a more objective basis for preferring one text over another. McKerrow's concept of "copy-text"—taking the term to mean, in Greg's words, "that early text of a work which an editor selected as the basis of his own"—is clearly placed in the context of the genealogical method, for it implies that an editor has determined, through genealogical analysis, the "most authoritative text" and therefore the one to which his own text should adhere. By introducing Housman's criticism of the mechanical application of this procedure (the fallacy of believing that the readings of the "authoritative text" which are not manifestly impossible are in fact correct), Greg suggests the direction in which his argument is to move. But he sees no necessity to argue the general superiority of genealogical methods over eclectic ones; at mid-twentieth century this superiority can simply be asserted. A second assumption is that one can reject without discussion the notion of choosing the last edition published during the author's lifetime as the most authoritative. Placing his comment in a footnote—and in the past tense—to suggest how little attention the idea deserves, Greg says, "I have above ignored the practice of some eccentric editors who took as copy-text for a work the latest edition printed in the author's lifetime, on the assumption, presumably, that he revised each edition as it appeared. The textual results were naturally deplorable" (p. 378). Obviously Greg is not saying that one should ignore late revisions which one has reason to think are authorial; but, he is implying, it is no longer necessary to bother refuting the assumption that the last edition in the author's lifetime is automatically the most authoritative.

Without going over ground which he regards as already established,

then, Greg begins to reflect on current editorial practice and observes
that the situation facing editors of English texts is different from that
facing editors of classical texts, since the preference for "old-spelling"
editions is now "prevalent among English scholars," whereas editors
of classical texts normalize the spelling. Greg explicitly says that he
does not wish to argue the virtues of old-spelling editions but accepts
this "prevalent" view—that is to say, he accepts the view that editions
of English works for scholars' use should not involve normalized or
modernized spelling and punctuation. It should be clear, therefore,
that his essay deals with one particular, if basic, kind of edition and
implies nothing about the relative merits of modernized editions for
other purposes—a point sometimes overlooked. If the editor of English
texts properly follows the general tradition of the genealogical method
inaugurated by classical editors, and if he must be concerned with the
spelling and punctuation of his text in a way different from classical
editors, it follows that his conception of copy-text must contain an
additional element. In fact, viewed in this way, as Greg says, "the
classical theory of the 'best' or 'most authoritative' manuscript . . . has
really nothing to do with the English theory of 'copy-text' at all"
(p. 375)—because, under the classical theory, the spelling and punctuation are not involved in selecting the copy-text.

By the beginning of the fourth paragraph of his essay, Greg has led
the reader, with astonishing ease, to see the current situation in English
editing against the background of its development and to anticipate
the distinction he is about to set forth between, on the one hand,
spelling and punctuation, and, on the other, the words themselves. The
rhetorical strategy of the essay demands proceeding explicitly to make
this distinction before returning to an examination of McKerrow's
changing position (which thereby takes on a new dimension), and
this remarkable fourth paragraph (pp. 375-377) contains the essence of
what is now referred to as "Greg's theory of copy-text." First of all, it
makes the point that an old-spelling edition must rely on some contemporary document, for the "philological difficulties" of attempting to
recreate or establish spellings for a particular author at a particular
time and place are overwhelming. Second, in view of this practical
necessity, it says, one must distinguish between the actual words of a
text and their spelling and punctuation:

. . . we need to draw a distinction between the significant, or as I shall
call them "substantive", readings of the text, those namely that affect the
author's meaning or the essence of his expression, and others, such in
general as spelling, punctuation, word-division, and the like, affecting

mainly its formal presentation, which may be regarded as the accidents, or as I shall call them "accidentals", of the text. (p. 376)

The explicit separation of these classes for separate editorial treatment is one of Greg's key contributions; the third major point of the paragraph is what that separate treatment amounts to. Separate treatment is justified, the argument goes, because copyists and compositors are known to treat the two categories differently; since they generally attempt to reproduce accurately the substantives of their copy but frequently are guided by their own preferences in matters of accidentals, it follows that later transcripts of a work may depart considerably from earlier ones in accidentals and at the same time be very close to them in substantives. What an editor should do, therefore, as a practical routine, is first to determine the early text which is to be his copy-text; then, Greg says,

I suggest that it is only in the matter of accidentals that we are bound (within reason) to follow it, and that in respect of substantive readings we have exactly the same liberty (and obligation) of choice as has a classical editor, or as we should have were it a modernized text that we were preparing.   (p. 377)

In other words, because a copyist or a compositor reproduces substantives more faithfully than accidentals, substantive variants in later transcripts or editions are more likely to be worth editorial consideration as possible authorial revisions than are variants in accidentals.

Now a few observations are worth making in regard to what Greg does and does not say in this statement of his "theory"—particularly as an anticipation of some of the points which, as we shall see, have been raised in recent years. To begin with, while the terms "substantive" and "accidental" are not very happy choices,[5] what is crucial to

5. Greg himself calls attention in a footnote (p. 378) to the fact that McKerrow used the word "substantive" to refer to "an edition that is not a reprint of any other," and he adds, "I do not think that there should be any danger of confusion between 'substantive editions' and 'substantive readings.'" Nevertheless, it is unfortunate that the word should be given two special meanings in editorial discourse. The awkwardness of "accidental" (when it is not used as a plural noun, "accidentals") is obvious and is in fact demonstrated by Greg's own prose a few lines after his introduction of the term: "As regards substantive readings . . . they will doubtless sometimes depart from them accidentally and may even . . . do so intentionally: as regards accidentals, they will normally follow their own habits . . ." (pp. 376-377). Furthermore, since both terms are used by grammarians, one might at first suppose that editors, also concerned with language, might use them in the same way; but "substantive" in grammar means "noun" (which is a less inclusive concept than Greg's "substantive"), while "accident" (or "accidence") refers to inflection for case, number, tense, and so on (which is not "accidental" alteration in Greg's sense but

the theory is the distinction itself, and one should not be distracted from it by other associations which these words have. The terms have by now become so well established in editorial commentary that it would be foolish to attempt to change them, even though their use tends unfortunately to give the impression to the general reader that editing involves an arcane vocabulary and mysterious concepts. The situation is ironic because Greg did not pretend to be dealing with any abstruse concepts: he merely hoped that these two words could serve as a shorthand means for making a distinction between what are popularly regarded as content and form in verbal expression, a distinction with which everyone, in one way or another, has come in contact. Indeed, he goes out of his way to emphasize the fact that he is not setting forth a philosophical theory about the nature of language but is only drawing a practical distinction for use in the business of editing.[6] Naturally he is aware that content and form are never completely separable and that the line separating meaning and formal presentation in written language is not distinct (and philosophically raises complex issues); but for his purposes it is enough to append a footnote (p. 376) acknowledging "an intermediate class of word-forms about the assignment of which opinions may differ and which may have to be treated differently in dealing with the work of different scribes." Since the purpose of the substantive-accidental division is to assist the editor in deciding what variants in a text can reasonably be attributed to the copyist or compositor rather than the author, the focus is pragmatic—on the habits of individuals—and Greg is therefore more concerned with providing a suggestive approach, which can be used with flexibility to meet various situations, than in defining as philosophic concepts two mutually exclusive terms. The procedural recommendation which concludes Greg's paragraph is similarly couched in practical, and flexible, terms: the reason for selecting a copy-text in the first place is the limited nature of historical knowledge about accidentals (the copy-text is selected "on grounds of expediency, and in con-

---

rather falls within the scope of "substantive" changes). Perhaps the closest parallel is the use of "substance" and "accident" in philosophy to signify the essential and the nonessential; yet Greg insists, rightly, that his concern is not with a philosophical distinction. (Greg had used the word "accidents" in 1942 in The Editorial Problem in Shakespeare, where one section is entitled, "Note on Accidental Characteristics of the Text," pp. l-lv; but instead of "sub-stantives" the term "essentials of reading" is employed.)

6. After defining the two terms (p. 376), he says in the body of his text, "The distinction is not arbitrary or theoretical, but has an immediate bearing on textual criticism"; and in a footnote to the definitions he emphasizes, "The distinction I am trying to draw is practical, not philosophic." See also footnote 12 below.

sequence either of philological ignorance or of linguistic circumstances"), and therefore one should follow the copy-text in regard to
accidentals—but "within reason." This last phrase underscores Greg's
approach: one follows the "theory" when there is no persuasive reason for doing otherwise, but when one has reason to depart from it, a
rigid application of it would be foolish. Because the editor generally
has fewer means for rationally determining authorial readings in accidentals than in substantives, he generally follows the copy-text in
accidentals; but Greg is not asking him to fly in the face of reason by
adhering to this procedure in situations which are exceptions to the
generalization. Nowhere does Greg claim that following his rationale
will invariably produce "correct" readings; what he suggests is that it
offers the safest approach when one has otherwise no particular reason
for choosing one reading over another as authorial. The theory clearly
is one of expediency.

The skillful organization of Greg's essay is nowhere better exempli-
fied than in his return to the subject of McKerrow in the pages following this basic exposition of his theory. The rigidity of McKerrow's
approach is the more evident in contrast, and the reader is now in a
position to see its limitations; at the same time he recognizes how
Greg's ideas developed from McKerrow's and how McKerrow was on
the verge of the same insight as Greg. In the 1904 Nashe (which Greg
quotes), McKerrow had held firmly to the view that an editor should
take as his copy-text the latest edition which could convincingly be
shown to contain authorial revisions; so long as some of the variants
in that edition were authorial, all its readings should be accepted
(since conceivably they could all be authorial), except when they were
obviously impossible. McKerrow allowed for some editorial discretion
in the determination of what was obviously impossible, but in general
he was determined to preserve the "integrity" of individual texts. But
by 1939, when he published his *Prolegomena for the Oxford Shakespeare*, he had come to believe that a later edition, even one with
authorial revisions, should not serve as copy-text, for—with the exception of those revisions—it would be less likely to reflect the author's
manuscript than an earlier edition, which stood that much closer to
the manuscript. He thus understood, without explicitly stating, something very close to the distinction between substantives and accidentals,
since he now believed that the edition closest to the manuscript preserved the general texture of the work better than later editions and
that authorial revisions should be incorporated into the text of that
edition. Although this position represented a considerable move away

from his earlier fear of eclecticism,[7] he was still not ready to allow an editor to combine readings from more than two editions. When the editor believed a particular edition to contain authorial revisions, he said, all the variants in that edition "which could not reasonably be attributed to an ordinary press-corrector" (that is, in general, all the substantive variants) must be accepted into the copy-text. By the time of his death, therefore, McKerrow was well on his way to the position finally advanced by Greg,[8] the essential difference between the two being in the amount of responsibility given to editorial judgment. For McKerrow, the editor uses his judgment in determining what edition should be copy-text, what edition, if any, contains authorial revisions, and what readings are impossible, but he cannot go further and reject some of the variants in that authorially revised edition as not authorial.[9] For Greg, the editor who has already made certain basic decisions should be allowed to go on and choose among the possibly authorial variants. The effort to eliminate as much editorial decision as possible, he believes, is misguided:

7. Although Greg does not say so here, McKerrow's attitude doubtless sprang from his overreacting against the abuses of some nineteenth-century editors, who felt free to choose among variant readings without adequate study of the nature and origin of the editions in which those variants appeared. Later Greg does make a similar point in general terms: "The attitude may be explained historically as a natural and largely salutary reaction against the methods of earlier editors. Dissatisfied with the results of eclectic freedom and reliance on personal taste, critics sought to establish some sort of mechanical apparatus for dealing with textual problems . . ." (p. 383). For a development of this point, see Fredson Bowers, "McKerrow's Editorial Principles for Shakespeare Reconsidered," *SQ*, 6 (1955), 309-324; and "Multiple Authority: New Problems and Concepts of Copy-Text," *Library*, 5th ser., 27 (1972), esp. 90-91.

8. Greg did not move all at once to his final position. In "McKerrow's Prolegomena Reconsidered," *RES*, 17 (1941), 139-149, and, more fully, in the Prolegomena to *The Editorial Problem in Shakespeare* (1942), he recognized the unnecessary rigidity of McKerrow's insistence on adopting all the substantive variants from an edition which contains some authorial revisions, but he followed McKerrow's inclusion of "wording" as one of the criteria for choosing a copy-text. By the end of the decade, however, in this "Rationale," he had developed his distinction between substantives and accidentals and therefore admitted in a footnote, "There is a good deal in my Prolegomena that I should now express differently, and on this particular point I have definitely changed my opinion. I should now say that the choice of the copy-text depends solely on its formal features (accidentals) " (p. 386). In making revisions in 1950 of *The Editorial Problem*, he added a new preface repeating this point and referring to the "Rationale" essay.

9. More than once Greg calls attention to McKerrow's use of the word "reprint" for "critical edition" (e.g., pp. 379, 380). "Reprint," of course, implies complete absence of editorial interference; but while McKerrow expects an editor to use critical judgment in correcting obviously impossible readings he does not conceive of the result as a "critical edition." Greg calls this confusion "symptomatic"—that is, of McKerrow's pervasive reluctance to give rein to individual judgment.

Uniformity of result at the hands of different editors is worth little if it means only uniformity in error; and it may not be too optimistic a belief that the judgement of an editor, fallible as it must necessarily be, is likely to bring us closer to what the author wrote than the enforcement of an arbitrary rule.   (p. 381)

Again Greg's emphasis is on the use of reason and discretion, as it is in the brief summary which follows immediately: "the copy-text should govern (generally) in the matter of accidentals, but . . . the choice between substantive readings belongs to the general theory of textual criticism and lies altogether beyond the narrow principle of the copy-text" (pp. 381-382). Greg is careful here to insert a qualifying adverb even in the first part of his statement, which deals with accidentals and thus the more mechanical part of his theory; but in the second part he makes clear that the handling of substantive variants is a matter of critical judgment and cannot be regarded as mechanical in any sense. Not to recognize that substantives and accidentals must be treated in different ways, he points out, has led in the past to a "tyranny of the copy-text"—a tyranny because its readings were thrust on the editor, without the benefit of his critical thinking about their merits.

The remainder of Greg's essay, amounting to about half of it, consists of illustrative examples and discussions of particular problems in the application of the theory but does not add any essential point to the basic idea set forth economically in the first half. After citing examples from F. S. Boas's edition (1932) of Marlowe's *Doctor Faustus* and Percy Simpson's edition (1941) of Jonson's *The Gipsies Metamorphosed* to show the operation of the "tyranny of the copy-text,"[10] Greg provides a second brief recapitulation of his rationale (pp. 384-385), reiterating the limitations of mechanical rules and concentrating on the nature of the editorial judgment required for dealing with substantive variants. That judgment depends partly on an evaluation of the circumstances of the production of the editions in which those variants appear and partly on the relative reliability of those editions

10. The examples are effective in demonstrating not only undue reliance on the copy-text but also the self-confidence required to alter the copy-text, and in both instances Greg perhaps overstates the obviousness of the emendations he proposes. His arguments for emending the copy-text in each case are persuasive; but the larger argument of his essay does not require him to assert that these emendations are in fact correct but only to show that an editor ought not to be prevented from seriously considering them by too rigid an adherence to the copy-text. It is one thing to say that Boas and Simpson might have adopted his emendations if they had not been under the tyranny of the copy-text, but quite another to imply that they certainly would have done so.

as suggested by the number of "manifest errors" in them; but the heart of the matter is the editor's evaluation of particular variants in terms of "the likelihood of their being what the author wrote rather than their appeal to the individual taste of the editor" (p. 385). Then, to provide more practical help, Greg expands on three points already introduced. First, he suggests that an editor may legitimately decide to alter some of the accidentals of the copy-text and thus provides a gloss on the expressions "within reason" and "generally" which he had inserted parenthetically in his earlier statements about following the accidentals of the copy-text. Spelling or punctuation known to be at variance with the author's can be altered, for instance, and, when substantive emendations are made on the basis of later texts, the spelling of such words can be made to conform with the habitual spelling (if there is one) of the copy-text. Second, he restates in somewhat more detail his belief that an editor should not accept from an authorially revised edition any substantive variant that seems obviously incorrect, that seems not to be a reading which the author would have inserted, or that seems completely indifferent. The latter point illustrates once again the expedient nature of what Greg is proposing: if a variant appears so indifferent to the editor that he has no basis for arguing either for or against its adoption, then he simply follows the copy-text reading as a practical means for deciding what to do. "In such a case," Greg points out, "while there can be no logical reason for giving preference to the copy-text, in practice, if there is no reason for altering its reading, the obvious thing seems to be to let it stand" (p. 386). Third, he makes explicit (pp. 389-390) what was only implied before, that the choice of copy-text itself varies with circumstances and that situations arise in which one must choose a revised edition as copy-text, as when an author is thought to have overseen a revised edition so carefully that its accidentals as well as its substantives must be taken to carry his approval, or when revision is so complex or pervasive that it is not meaningful to think in terms of emending the unrevised text with later readings (*Every Man in His Humour*, *Richard III*, and *King Lear* are cited).

In connection with all three of these points Greg again defends the use of editorial judgment. When discussing the first he says, "These [decisions to alter accidentals], however, are all matters within the discretion of an editor: I am only concerned to uphold his liberty of judgement" (p. 386). In his discussion of substantives he repeats the view emphatically:

I do not, of course, pretend that my procedure will lead to consistently correct results, but I think that the results, if less uniform, will be on the whole preferable to those achieved through following any mechanical rule. I am, no doubt, presupposing an editor of reasonable competence; but if an editor is really incompetent, I doubt whether it much matters what procedure he adopts: he may indeed do less harm with some than with others, he will do little good with any. And in any case, I consider that it would be disastrous to curb the liberty of competent editors in the hope of preventing fools from behaving after their kind.   (p. 388)

And in the third instance, dealing with the choice of copy-text, he states that no "hard and fast rule" can be laid down but that, whatever text is chosen, the editor "cannot escape the responsibility of distinguishing to the best of his ability" between authorial revision and "unauthorized variation": "No juggling with copy-text will relieve him of the duty and necessity of exercising his own judgement" (p. 390). This sentiment is clearly the dominant motif of the essay; if McKerrow had been reacting against nineteenth-century eclecticism in restricting the role of editorial judgment, Greg is here turning toward more reliance on judgment, but within a framework that does not encourage undisciplined eclecticism. It is in keeping with his approach throughout that Greg ends by saying, "My desire is rather to provoke discussion than to lay down the law."

I hope that my account of Greg's essay, by its very repetitiousness, has shown that the essay itself consists of repeated statements of a simple idea. Three times he presents a concise summary of his theory followed by a discussion of particular points implied by it, as if he were turning over an object in his hand, focusing his attention alternately on the piece as a whole and on certain of its details. The simplicity of his proposal is certainly one of its most remarkable features and is a natural result of the emphasis on individual judgment, for a methodology inevitably becomes more complicated the more one tries to substitute rules for judgment in the handling of the various situations that may arise. In somewhat blunt language, Greg's theory amounts to this: it tells the editor what to do when he otherwise does not know what to do. If he does know otherwise—that is, if his analysis of all available external and internal evidence (including, of course, his own intimate knowledge of the author and the period) convinces him that a particular text comes closest in all respects to the author's wishes or that a particular variant is the author's revision—then he does not need further guidance. But when there remains a doubt in his mind, after thorough analysis, about whether, for example, the author gave close attention to the punctuation of a revised edition or whether a particular altered wording, in a text which contains many clearly authorial revisions, was the author's, the editor does need further help, since he has gone as far as reasoning can take him and the results are inconclusive. All that Greg suggests, in effect, is that the editor can most sensibly extricate himself from this situation by keeping two points in mind: (1) successive editions based on earlier editions become increasingly divergent from the earliest edition in the sequence, particularly in such matters as punctuation and spelling, not merely through carelessness but through the natural tendency of compositors to utilize their own habitual forms; (2) when an author makes revisions in a later edition, he may be likely to give considerably less attention to spelling and punctuation than to the words themselves, and even some of the differences in wording in a revised edition may in fact result from the process of resetting rather than from the author's revision. It follows that the editor who chooses the edition closest to the author's manuscript as his copy-text when he does not have strong reason for choosing a later one, and who follows the readings of that copy-text when he does not have strong reason to believe them erroneous or to believe that a later variant in wording (or, more rarely, in punctuation or spelling) is the author's—that such an editor is maximizing his chances of incorporating the author's intended readings in his text. No one would claim—and Greg specifically does not—that this procedure always results in the correct choices, but it tells an editor how to proceed when he most needs such advice (when he has exhausted the available evidence without reaching a decision) and it is more satisfying than tossing a coin (since there is at least a rationale involved, based on a generalization about the incidence of human error and the behavior of human beings in dealing with written language). The fundamental common sense of this approach can be seen foreshadowed in Samuel Johnson's comments on the editing of Shakespeare, when he says that "though much credit is not due to the fidelity, nor any to the judgement of the first publishers, yet they who had the copy before their eyes were more likely to read it right, than we who read it only by imagination."[11] The probabilities favor the correctness of the first edition, and it makes sense to rely on that edition except when there is compelling evidence for not doing so.

Expressed in this way—which emphasizes the flexibility and lack of dogmatism basic to Greg's position—this "rationale of copy-text" would seem to apply to all situations. But it is important to raise the

11. *Johnson on Shakespeare*, ed. Arthur Sherbo (1968), I, 106.

question of its universality, for Greg's primary interest, after all, was in the printed drama of the English Renaissance, and all his illustrations are taken from that literature. Did he believe that his rationale was more widely applicable? He was dealing with a period from which relatively few manuscripts have survived, but can the same procedure be applied to texts for which manuscripts do survive? He was working with a period in which greater variations in spelling were tolerable than in later times and in which any editorial supervision of a printed text normally occurred in the printing shop rather than, as later, in the publisher's office with its more highly developed editorial routine; but can Greg's rationale be applied to the products which emerged from the very different publishing circumstances of later periods? Greg's own answer to these questions, I think it can be plainly inferred from his essay, would be Yes. It is true that he limits himself in his illustrations to the field he knows best and limits his more abstract discussion for the most part to printed books, but there are indications that he is thinking in broader terms. For example, in that crucial fourth paragraph, distinguishing substantives and accidentals, he twice refers to "scribes" and "compositors" simultaneously, suggesting that the way human beings react to the two categories is the same regardless of whether they are copying by hand or setting type. He goes on, in the paragraph which follows, to restrict himself to printed books for the historical reason that "the idea of copy-text originated and has generally been applied in connexion with the editing of printed books" (p. 378). The focus of the essay, it must be remembered, is historical: a new approach to editing is set forth as a corrective to what had been developing over the previous century. Since the principal developments in editorial theory had taken place in connection with the editing of Elizabethan and Jacobean drama, it was natural that he should set forth his criticisms of current procedure with reference to the same field—and convenient, also, since that was his own area of competence. But he clearly implies that he is dealing with a larger principle that could be illustrated in other ways than the one he has chosen. Indeed, he suggests that the editors he is criticizing might have taken a different approach if they had been more familiar with the problems of variation in works transmitted in manuscript. And then he adds:

For although the underlying principles of textual criticism are, of course, the same in the case of works transmitted in manuscripts and in print, particular circumstances differ, and certain aspects of the common principles may emerge more clearly in the one case than in the other.   (p. 378)

The implication certainly is that he is concerned with a basic concept[12] which might not be clear to one who has dealt only with a particular class of problems. And while his illustrations come from Renaissance drama, some of them do involve authorial proof-correction (*Every Man in His Humour*) and revised editions incorporating corrections derived from authorial manuscript (*Richard III* and *King Lear*). In any event, his whole approach, stressing expediency and judgment, suggests that he thinks of his procedure as one capable of fitting widely varied situations. When an editor judges that he has sufficient evidence for proceeding in a particular way, he has no need for a plan of expediency; but a lack of sufficient evidence is a common occurrence in dealing with works of every period, and Greg's rationale commands respect in such situations because it is based on what observation shows to be characteristic human behavior. If I have set forth accurately here what Greg says, then it would appear to be a self-evident proposition that his recommended procedure would serve in handling editorial problems involving manuscripts as well as printed books, arising in twentieth-century literature as well as sixteenth.

There is one kind of editorial problem, however, which clearly lies outside the scope of Greg's essay. To place presumptive authority for accidentals, as a general rule, in the edition closest to the author's manuscript presupposes an ancestral series, in which the line of editions—with each edition based (for the most part, at least) on preceding ones—leads back to the manuscript. Although some of Greg's examples involve complicated variations (such as the revisions incorporated in the folio text of *Every Man in His Humour*), in which a later edition is chosen as copy-text because of the extent and nature of fresh authority (authorial revision or recourse to authorial manuscripts), those examples do not include situations in which two or more texts stand in exactly the same genealogical relationship to a lost ancestor, with no earlier texts surviving. In such a case, Greg's approach offers no help in selecting a copy-text, for no one of these texts is nearer the manuscript (or the antecedent text) than any other. The inapplicability of Greg's rationale to this kind of situation is obvious,

---

12. It should be clear that there is no contradiction involved between the assertion that Greg is dealing with a concept and his own repeated emphasis on the practical rather than the theoretical. Obviously, as the word "rationale" in his title suggests, his argument is conceptual and theoretical, since it attempts to formulate a general statement which can be illustrated by reference to specific situations. But the theory itself is proposed as a matter of expediency, as a workable practical solution to a problem, rather than as a philosophic truth. One can say that it is a theory suggesting how best to accommodate one's ignorance but not that it is a theory leading to a reduction of that ignorance.

once it is pointed out, but it has only recently been examined in detail. Fredson Bowers was confronted with the problem in editing Stephen Crane's syndicated newspaper pieces: the variant texts of a given piece, as they appeared in various newspapers, are all equidistant from the syndicate's proofs which had been sent to those newspapers; in the absence of the proofs, the editor is faced with several texts, any one of which could be chosen as copy-text under Greg's rationale. The solution, as Bowers sets it forth in "Multiple Authority: New Problems and Concepts of Copy-Text,"[13] is to combine the features of these "radiating texts," as he calls them, through a statistical and critical analysis of the variants. In effect, one has to construct a copy-text, and the more surviving texts there are the more accurately can the common ancestor (the lost syndicate proof) be reconstructed. From that point on, naturally, Greg's rationale takes over, and the text thus constructed may be emended with variants from later printings, as may happen with an ordinary copy-text. The essential difference is that, in the case of radiating texts, no one document can serve as copy-text, for no one of the radiating texts can be presumed to have reproduced the accidentals of the syndicate proof more accurately than another. Bowers's detailed exposition of his solution therefore becomes a major supplement to Greg; his essay—which incidentally offers an extremely useful statement of Greg's position—deserves to be taken as a companion piece to Greg's "Rationale," and the two essays together provide a comprehensive editorial theory.

Bowers's discussion of radiating texts, in other words, does not invalidate Greg's theory in any sense, but it does show one respect in which that theory is not all-encompassing. No comparable supplement to Greg's theory has been made in the twenty-five years since its first

---

13. *Library*, 5th ser., 27 (1972), 81-115. His later article, "Remarks on Eclectic Texts," in *Proof*, 4 (1974), furthers the discussion by elaborating upon and providing numerous examples to illustrate the distinction between single-authority and multiple-authority situations. There are, of course, many instances of multiple authority in which the earliest surviving texts (earliest in each line) are not equidistant from the lost common ancestor. But Greg's theory operates in such cases, because—in the absence of contrary evidence—one can presume the text nearest the lost ancestor to be the most reliable in accidentals. At times, as in any other copy-text situation, an editor may have reason to believe that some text other than the nearest one is the most reliable, and he would then select it as copy-text; otherwise he would select the nearest one. Unlike a situation of equidistant radiating texts, the editor in these instances has a presumptive authority to fall back on when there is no other means for reaching a decision. In other words, it is the existence of authoritative texts that are equidistant from a lost ancestor, not simply the existence of texts representing independent lines of descent from that ancestor, which poses a problem for the application of Greg's approach.

appearance, though many questions have been raised. But these questions (such as the extent to which the idiosyncrasies of nineteenth- or twentieth-century authors' manuscripts should be preserved in print), often interesting in themselves, involve matters of editorial judgment, not the basic theory. It is unfortunately true that such questions have frequently been posed as an attack on the theory; and the failure to distinguish between the theory itself and the individual decisions of editors who are following the theory has rendered much of the discussion less useful than it might have been, if not wholly beside the point. My own summary of Greg in these pages has tried to emphasize those elements of his essay which anticipate the later criticisms. Seemingly it takes many words to explain something which is simple and many assertions to proclaim lack of dogmatism; but the simplicity and lack of dogmatism of Greg's rationale have apparently not been perceived by a number of people, for many of their criticisms are undercut by a recognition of those qualities. A renewed close examination of Greg's essay does not suggest to me any reason to question Bowers's description of its thesis as "the great contribution of this century to textual criticism."[14]

II

In the years since Greg's "Rationale" appeared, the person who has done most to make Greg's theory widely known and to demonstrate its broad applicability is Fredson Bowers. His contributions have been of two kinds: (1) general discussions of editing, which call attention to and recapitulate Greg's ideas and which sometimes specifically take up the question of applying his rationale to areas other than Renaissance drama; (2) actual editions based on Greg's rationale, not only showing its workability on a large scale but also developing an appropriate apparatus to accompany texts edited in that way.

Bowers began his commentary on Greg's essay, even before it appeared in print, in his 1950 article on "Current Theories of Copy-Text, with an Illustration from Dryden."[15] To use several examples from *The Indian Emperour* to support the rightness of Greg's approach obviously suggests its usefulness for Restoration, as well as Renaissance, drama; but, more important, Bowers anticipates three objections which he thinks may be raised. One is that editors, afraid of the greater role given to editorial judgment, will complain that too much weight has been given to it; but the reply is that, if an editor is preparing a *critical* text, "editorial responsibility cannot be disengaged

14. "Multiple Authority," p. 91.   15. *MP*, 48 (1950-51), 12-20.

from the duty to judge the validity of altered readings in a revised edition" (p. 13). A second objection is that the result will be a conflated or eclectic text; but, again, a *critical* text, as opposed to a reprint, is by definition eclectic, and there is no reason to fear eclecticism for its own sake but only irresponsible eclecticism. It is in connection with the third objection, however, that Bowers most usefully expands on Greg's remarks—the objection that even an editor who accepts the responsibility of judging between authorial and nonauthorial substantive readings may hesitate to judge the authority of accidentals and may feel that the accidentals of a revised edition at least possibly preserve some authorial alterations. Bowers's reply calls attention to a point which Greg had not perhaps sufficiently made clear: it is precisely because an editor has less evidence for judging accidentals that he should normally fall back on the first-edition copy-text for them, since one of the few generalizations that can be made about accidentals is their gradual corruption from edition to edition and the unlikelihood of close authorial attention to accidentals in revised editions. If an editor chooses a revised edition for copy-text, as Bowers succinctly puts the matter, "in order to preserve a single accidentals variant which *may* have been the author's, he is introducing a very considerable number of other alterations which under no circumstances could possibly have been authorial" (p. 16). Bowers preserves Greg's emphasis on the expedient by repeatedly using an expression which helpfully captures the spirit of the procedure: he speaks of the "odds" favoring the readings of the first edition and of the editor "playing the correct odds" in retaining those readings.[16]

This first apologia for Greg's theory was promptly buttressed when, only three years later, the first volume of Bowers's edition of Dekker appeared, inaugurating the first full-scale edition to be produced according to Greg's rationale. Besides making that rationale more widely known and demonstrating its use in handling the problems of an actual edition (as opposed to isolated examples of textual problems), the Dekker introduced a form of apparatus which broke with tradition and which was particularly appropriate for reflecting the central ideas of Greg's approach. The traditional apparatus, which

16. Bowers calls it "one of Greg's three criteria for determining the authority of variants that when a choice seems indifferent, the odds are in favor of the specific authority of the original reading" (p. 15). Actually Greg does not make this one of the three criteria (as stated on p. 385 of *Collected Papers* and summarized above, p. 177, in the sentence beginning "That judgment depends partly") but rather a procedure to follow when use of these criteria proves inconclusive (for if they were not inconclusive, the choice would not be indifferent).

McKerrow still supported in his 1939 *Prolegomena*, was to have two sets of notes, one for recording variant readings and one for making more discursive comment on any matter which the editor wished to address; and the first of these kinds of notes, though not always the second, was placed at the foot of each page of text. The departure of the Dekker edition from this plan is two-fold: it divides the record of variants into several categories (editorial alterations of substantives in the copy-text, editorial alterations of accidentals in the copy-text, press-variants, and substantive variants in pre-1700 editions) and it relegates part of that record to an appendix (all but the first category). The result is to dramatize the differing status of the copy-text from that of later texts by segregating the record of its readings and by specifying every change—in accidentals as well as in substantives— which the editor has made in it. Given Greg's reasoning about the accidentals of the copy-text, it is important for the reader to know where the editor has altered them, so a full record is provided; but it is of no importance, in most cases, for the reader to know the thousands of variants in accidentals which entered the text in later editions, so only the substantive variants in those editions are listed. There is a clear distinction between the record of editorial decisions to emend the copy-text and the historical record of substantive variants in later editions. This apparatus, while it does not clutter the reading page with any but the most significant category of editorial decisions,[17] does enable the reader easily to focus on all the editor's decisions— which is especially important in view of the prominence given to editorial judgment in Greg's rationale.

Bowers continued through the 1950s to keep Greg's theory before the scholarly public, in the successive volumes of the Dekker and in various theoretical discussions.[18] But as his work on Dekker neared completion and he turned his attention to the editing of Hawthorne, he produced the first detailed illustration of the application of the theory to the period of machine printing and highly developed publishing firms. His 1962 paper, "Some Principles for Scholarly Editions of Nineteenth-Century American Authors,"[19] is the principal docu-

17. This streamlining of the apparatus extends also to the simplification of the symbols employed, utilizing considerably fewer than were envisaged by McKerrow in his *Prolegomena*.

18. Such as that in *On Editing Shakespeare and the Elizabethan Dramatists* (1955), pp. 71-83; "Old-Spelling Editions of Dramatic Texts," in *Studies in Honor of T. W. Baldwin*, ed. D. C. Allen (1958), pp. 11-12; and *Textual and Literary Criticism* (1959), pp. 141-142.

19. Read before the American Literature section of the South Atlantic Modern Language Association on 22 November 1962 and published in *SB*, 17 (1964), 223-228.

ment which stands between Greg's "Rationale" and the large series of CEAA editions currently in progress. This paper begins by establishing two crucial points which underlie all the others: that a scholarly text must be unmodernized[20] (recognizing this as an issue even for nineteenth-century works) [21] and that it must be critical[22] (recognizing that probably "no nineteenth-century text of any length exists that is not in need of some correction").[23] Bowers, like Greg, and like the CEAA editors to follow, is concerned with *unmodernized critical texts*, presenting "classic texts in as close a form as possible to the authors' intentions"; the fact cannot be overemphasized, in the light of later events, that these editors are not attempting to lay down rules for all kinds of editions for all purposes but are concerned with one particular kind of edition.[24] After summarizing Greg's rationale for an audi-

20. The term often used in connection with Renaissance texts is "old-spelling"; but "unmodernized" is probably better, since it more clearly suggests that the modernizing of accidentals in general, not just spelling, is the point at issue.

21. The fact that nineteenth-century accidentals are nearer our own than those of the sixteenth century means that the general reader or the classroom student has less difficulty in using an unmodernized text for this period; but it has nothing to do with the fact that a scholar requires a text representing as accurately as possible the author's own accidentals, regardless of the ease or difficulty with which that text can now be read. There are, in fact, a considerable number of differences between nineteenth- and twentieth-century accidentals, particularly punctuation; but, as Bowers says, "one may flatly assert that any text that is modernized can never pretend to be scholarly, no matter at what audience it is aimed" (p. 223). Obviously, if accidentals form part of an author's expression of meaning, one cannot modernize and still have what the author wrote and meant. One can always argue that the authors themselves would not want their punctuation and spelling to be preserved at the cost of not being read; but such an argument has no bearing on the needs of scholars to have before them, insofar as it is possible, exactly what the author wrote. Modernized editions can then follow, when

they seem necessary, though they must inevitably be a compromise. Some of the issues involved in the question of modernizing are discussed in John Russell Brown, "The Rationale of Old-Spelling Editions of the Plays of Shakespeare and His Contemporaries," *SB*, 13 (1960), 49-67; Arthur Brown, "The Rationale of Old-Spelling Editions . . . A Rejoinder," *SB*, 13 (1960), 69-76; and Jürgen Schäfer, "The Orthography of Proper Names in Modern-Spelling Editions of Shakespeare," *SB*, 23 (1970), 1-19. See also footnotes 93, 98, and 99 below.

22. That is, it must result from editorial decisions and not be simply a reprint of one particular text. It could, of course, in rare instances be such a reprint—but only because the editor judged no emendations to be necessary, not because he was committed to reproducing a single document without alteration.

23. He continued to demonstrate the bibliographical and textual problems raised by nineteenth-century works in "Old Wine in New Bottles: Problems of Machine Printing," in *Editing Nineteenth-Century Texts*, ed. John M. Robson (1967), pp. 9-36.

24. But one which, it seems reasonable to assume, is basic, since it can provide the details necessary for use in preparing other kinds of editions.

ence which at that time was not likely to have been particularly familiar with it, Bowers proceeds to show how Greg's approach accommodates the two principal differences in the kinds of materials with which the editor of a nineteenth-century work is likely to deal: (1) the fact that nineteenth-century American books were normally plated does not mean that alterations do not appear in later printings, and examples from Hawthorne illustrate the necessity for making machine collations[25] of copies of the first printing from a set of plates against copies of the last printing; (2) the fact that authors' fair-copy manuscripts frequently survive from this period means that in such cases the editor will generally find himself employing a manuscript, rather than a first printing, as copy-text, for what Greg said about the usual degeneration of the accidentals from edition to edition applies also to the initial step from manuscript to print. In making the latter point, Bowers clearly restates the view of accidentals which is basic to Greg's whole theory: "if an author's habits of expression go beyond words and into the forms that these take, together with the punctuation that helps to shape the relationships of these words, then one is foolish to prefer a printing-house style to the author's style" (p. 226).[26] The other concern of Bowers's paper is an appropriate apparatus for the kind of edition he is describing, and he lists five classes of material which scholars should expect to find recorded: (1) variants among copies of a single edition, revealed by machine collation of multiple copies; (2) emendations made by the editor in the copy-text (along with discussions of any problematical readings); (3) substantive differences in editions published during the author's lifetime[27] and in

25. The use of the Hinman Collator, developed by Charlton Hinman for the detection of variant formes in the Shakespeare first folio, to make collations of copies of machine-printed books from the same typesetting or plates is another instance of the application to later books of methods conceived in connection with earlier ones. For a list of articles dealing with mechanized collation, see the CEAA *Statement* (2nd ed., 1972), pp. 19-20.

26. He also emphasizes, like Greg, the practical side of the point: "This distinction," he says, "is not theory, but fact." Obviously the "fact" is not that the editor can always distinguish correctly between the author's and others'. changes but that Hawthorne's manuscripts do exhibit many

differences from their first printings and that unauthorized changes are likely to enter a text every time it is set in type.

27. Bowers, using the example of Hawthorne, speaks of reporting all the editions during the author's lifetime. But since the reason for choosing that period is to cover any editions which might incorporate authorial changes, one can infer that any pirated edition—which can be established as pirated and thus as having no connection with the author—can be excluded from the listing. A collation of such an edition, however, is naturally still called for, so that the editor can be sure that the variant readings in it do not suggest authorial revision in spite of the external evidence.

any posthumous editions that the editor judges to be of sufficient interest; (4) "all the rejected readings and revisions during the process of inscription" of the manuscript, when a manuscript exists—in other words, the pre-copy-text variants; (5) compound words hyphenated at the ends of lines in the copy-text (and thus requiring editorial judgment to determine how they should be printed in the critical text),[28] along with the copy-text forms of words which are divided at line-end in the critical text. This list is obviously an adaptation of the Dekker apparatus to a situation in which a manuscript may be available, and it also recognizes for the first time the editorial problems which line-end hyphens produce. Acknowledging the amount of effort involved in preparing such an edition, Bowers ends with an explicit reference to the continuity of editorial problems by calling on scholars of American literature to "bring to their task the careful effort that has been established as necessary for English Renaissance texts."

In the same year the first volume of the Ohio State ("Centenary") edition of Hawthorne (*The Scarlet Letter*, 1962) was illustrating in detail the points made in this paper and was exhibiting the kind of apparatus advocated there. By providing a comprehensive essay analyzing the textual history of the work and the editorial procedures employed and by keeping the pages of the text entirely free of apparatus (unlike the Dekker, all emendations were listed at the end), the Hawthorne edition was to furnish a practical model for the later CEAA editions. Influential as Bowers's work on this edition was, his exposition of Greg which was perhaps of the greatest potential influence came the next year. In 1963 the MLA published a pamphlet, edited by James Thorpe, on *The Aims and Methods of Scholarship in Modern Languages and Literatures*;[29] consisting of four essays, on linguistics, textual criticism, literary history, and literary criticism, it was intended, according to Thorpe's introduction, to offer a "review

---

28. This point again reflects Greg's rationale in its focus on the accidentals of the copy-text. Once the importance of preserving the accidentals of the copy-text is established, the importance of deciding when to retain, and when to omit, copy-text line-end hyphens becomes evident—as well as the importance of informing the reader in this respect, as in others, of exactly what occurs in the copy-text.

29. The history of the pamphlet is sketched by Thorpe in his introduction.

The MLA's Committee on Research Activities had earlier presented a report (edited by Helmut Rehder) entitled "The Aims, Methods, and Materials of Research in the Modern Languages and Literatures," published in *PMLA* (67, no. 6 [October 1952], 3-37) and as a pamphlet. The section of that report on "Editing and Textual Criticism" (pp. 15-19), written by Lawton P. G. Peckham, does not mention Greg's rationale and sets forth the idea that "the last edition revised by an author, or published in his lifetime with his consent, is most likely to satisfy literary needs" (p. 16).

of some current ideas" for "any members of the scholarly community," particularly those "into whose hands the future of American scholarship will in due course fall." Such a pamphlet, circulated by the MLA— even though it was not claimed to be "an official statement" of the organization—was bound to be widely read and referred to, and Bowers's essay on "Textual Criticism,"[30] being concise, up-to-date, and readily accessible, became the most convenient source of information on editing literary texts. In his essay Bowers not only suggests[31] the wide applicability of Greg's rationale, by citing illustrations from Shakespeare, Dekker, Dryden, Fielding, Sheridan, Shelley, Hawthorne, Whitman, F. Scott Fitzgerald, and Sinclair Lewis, among others, but also sets forth a practical routine to be followed in the process of collating and emending and some considerations to keep in mind in constructing an apparatus and a textual introduction. Because the only editions at that time which illustrated the use of Greg's rationale —and of apparatus which separates the listing of emendations from the historical record of variants—were those with which Bowers himself was associated, he cites the Dekker and the Hawthorne (along with the forthcoming Beaumont-Fletcher and Fielding), thus bringing to those editions the attention of a wider audience than might otherwise have been expected to examine them.

When, that same year, the Center for Editions of American Authors was established as an official committee of the MLA, it had available, in Bowers's work, the reasoned and detailed application of Greg's theory to nineteenth-century American literature. And when its *Statement of Editorial Principles* emerged in 1967, several drafts having been previously circulated for criticism among interested scholars, the principles were those of Greg and the categories of apparatus were those of Bowers's 1962 paper and thus of the Hawthorne edition. It was necessary, of course, for the CEAA to have a public statement outlining its standards, if it was to award a seal (and dispense funds) to individual editions on the basis of adherence to those standards. But the pamphlet has served a larger function, for its practical recommendations of procedure are more detailed than any available in the earlier discussions of editing in the light of Greg's "Rationale." As

---

30. The essay appears on pp. 23-42 of the original edition. In 1970 a revised edition was published; Bowers's essay, on pp. 29-54, was enlarged chiefly by the insertion of illustrations from the writings of Stephen Crane (the longest such insertion occurs on pp. 51-52).

31. In addition to covering, as one would expect, such matters as whether a text is to be critical, whether it is to be modernized, and what role analytical bibliography plays in editing.

indicated by its subtitle, "A Working Manual for Editing Nineteenth Century American Texts," the pamphlet concentrates on a step-by-step explanation of the processes of bringing together the "authentic forms" of a text, selecting the copy-text, performing collations (by machine and by "sight"—that is, without a machine), presenting the evidence, writings notes and introductions, and proofreading. It thus attempts to set forth the principles behind this kind of editing as well as to offer practical advice on how to proceed; while addressed specifically to editors who seek CEAA support and approval, it functions also as a way of informing a larger audience, wishing to keep abreast of developments in the scholarship of American literature, of what is involved in these editions. Two features of the *Statement* deserve particular notice. One is its emphatic recognition of the importance of proofreading in the production of a reliable edition; it sets a minimum of five proofreadings against copy as a requirement for any edition applying for the CEAA seal (p. 11). Second is its provision for the dissemination of these editions by attaching certain conditions to the seal: the editors of editions which received public funds are to forgo royalties, and the publishers of those editions are to make the texts (not necessarily the apparatuses) "available to reprinting publishers no longer than two years after the date of original publication for reasonable royalties or fees" (p. 14). These provisions remain as important parts of the CEAA requirements in the revised edition of the *Statement* published in 1972,[32] although the new edition makes clearer the fact that the seal is available to any edition which meets the standards, whether or not it has been funded through the Center, and that in such cases no stipulations can be made about royalties or the availability of a text for reprinting. The CEAA, as its *Statement* indicates, is concerned not only with the production of sound texts and informative apparatuses but also with the practical problems of fostering a general demand for reliable editions and of encouraging their widespread distribution.[33]

---

32. Under the revised title *Statement of Editorial Principles and Procedures*. The revised discussion of proofreading adds a further requirement, based on the experience of several editions: that a final check be made to determine whether printers' errors have entered after the final proofs, by performing a machine collation of the unbound printed gatherings against the last set of proofs.

33. The seal itself was of course devised as a shorthand way of informing the reader or buyer that certain standards had been met and of promoting a broader general awareness of the need for reliable texts— with the potential result that readers would begin to demand, and publishers to seek, texts which qualified for the seal.

It should be clear that the CEAA's endorsement of Greg's theory and its requirement of a particular kind of apparatus are separate matters. Greg says nothing about apparatus in his "Rationale,"[34] and his approach entails no specific form of apparatus; obviously one can edit a text according to Greg's principles without supplying the reader any apparatus at all. The position of the CEAA on the two must be examined separately. As to its choice of Greg's theory, it could not responsibly have chosen any other. Greg was building on the experience of McKerrow and thus represented the main line of bibliographical development of this century; his theory not only emerged from long experience but had a compelling internal logic of its own. Since, by 1963, Bowers had amply demonstrated—what Greg himself had implied—that this approach was not limited to Renaissance literature, the CEAA was fortunate, at the time of its organization, in having readily available a theoretical position that it could scarcely ignore if it was to promote unmodernized critical texts. Clearly, one might wish to argue that it ought to have decided to promote some other kind of text in the first place; but, aside from the fact that the MLA, as a learned society, has a responsibility to support scholarly work, any text which is modernized or in some other way prepared for the "general reader" must, if it is to be reliable, first entail the research involved in producing a scholarly (that is, unmodernized and critical) text. The CEAA decision, therefore, makes practical sense, particularly if the results of that research are made available, so that editors who wish to produce different kinds of editions can take the evidence already amassed and reinterpret it according to different principles. Here is where the CEAA requirements for apparatus come in. The Center was again fortunate, at its inception, in having previous work to turn to, for the Hawthorne edition provided the obvious example—the work of a nineteenth-century American figure, edited according to

34. Except for one footnote, which suggests that the "graphic peculiarities of particular texts" should probably not be recorded in the "general apparatus" but "may appropriately form the subject of an appendix" (p. 386). Apparently the "general apparatus" Greg has in mind consists of footnotes; and, since he believes that "in this respect the copy-text is only one among others," he is expressing the view that emendations of accidentals in the copy-text should "probably" not be listed at the foot of the page but rather at the end of the volume—the practice which Bowers adopts in the Dekker. As early as 1760 Edward Capell, in his *Prolusions*, employed a similar system, in which one category of readings is listed at the foot of the page, and at the end come "all the other rejected readings of the editions made use of" (p. iii). Capell saw the value of making a specific text the "ground-work" of his own and of recording all departures from it as well as variant readings from other editions, so that the reader would have "all the materials that can be procur'd for him," in order to re-examine the editor's decisions.

Greg, and supplied with an appendix containing a list of editorial decisions as well as a historical record of substantive variants. Recognizing that the precise form in which this material is to be laid out need not follow that of the Hawthorne, the CEAA has never prescribed the physical arrangement of the data; but it has always insisted on the presence of the same categories of information as are found there, because those categories are essential for any reader who wishes to reconstruct the copy-text with which the editor worked and to examine the evidence on which the editor's decisions were based.[35] Inevitably the Hawthorne has served as an influential model in formal matters,[36] but there is no uniformity among CEAA editions in the exact forms employed—only in the kinds of material included.[37] The practice of the Hawthorne in presenting so-called "clear text"—pages of text entirely free of editorial apparatus—has been of particular importance. While the CEAA *Statement* does not insist on clear text, it strongly urges the use of clear text whenever feasible (there are some kinds of material—especially those not intended for publication, such as letters or journals—for which clear text may be impractical or even misleading);[38] and most of the CEAA volumes have in fact presented clear text. The decisions of the CEAA, in regard to editorial theory

35. The only way in which adherence to Greg's theory affects the content of the usual CEAA apparatus is that the historical record of variants normally lists only substantives, not accidentals. There would obviously be no objection to the inclusion of the accidentals as well, but in most cases the number involved would be so great that the effort and expense of listing them would not seem to be justified, in view of the lack of importance attaching to accidentals in later editions under Greg's theory. If someone disagrees with the editor's choice of copy-text, therefore, and wishes to re-edit the work using a different copy-text, he cannot reconstruct the accidentals of that text from the usual CEAA historical collation. Nevertheless, the editor of a CEAA edition explains his choice of copy-text in his textual essay, citing not only external evidence but illustrative readings from the texts; he generally provides enough evidence so that a reader will have an adequate basis for agreeing or disagreeing with his choice. Naturally a person who decides to re-edit the text employing a different copy-text will have to turn to a copy of the edition containing that copy-text; but he should be able to rethink the question of copy-text in the first place on the basis of what is included within the CEAA volume.

36. Obviously it makes sense to follow established forms whenever there is no particular reason for not following them, so that readers will have fewer adjustments to make as they turn from one edition to another.

37. For an examination of the variations in apparatus among CEAA volumes and of certain considerations to keep in mind in choosing among them, see G. T. Tanselle, "Some Principles for Editorial Apparatus," *SB*, 25 (1972), 41-88; and "Editorial Apparatus for Radiating Texts," forthcoming in the *Library*.

38. For some discussion, see William H. Gilman, "How Should Journals Be Edited?", *Early American Literature*, 6 (1971), 73-83.

and to apparatus, were prudent ones, both in the historical sense that they took advantage of the most advanced current thinking and in the more practical sense that they allowed for maximum future use of the material—since they resulted in basic scholar's editions, which at the same time contained easily readable texts that could be reproduced photographically in paperback and other editions and which offered the evidence that could be utilized by other editors in re-editing the text along different lines.

What emerges from all this is the fact that the CEAA does not regard the editions it approves as the only respectable or desirable editions of those works that are possible. After all, its seal reads "An Approved Text," not "The Approved Text"—which can be taken as implying two possibilities: first, since emendations are based on the editor's judgment, another editor, still aiming at an unmodernized critical text and following Greg's theory, may arrive at different judgments and may therefore conceivably produce another "approved text," even under the same general guidelines; second, since a CEAA text is one particular kind of text, the existence of a CEAA text of a work does not preclude the possibility that another kind of text might be worthy of approval for other purposes.[39] What is now referred to as a "CEAA edition," then, is the specific combination of two elements—a text edited according to Greg's theory, combined with an apparatus providing the essential evidence for examining the editor's decisions.[40] In a paper presented in 1968 on the occasion of

39. The CEAA has recently begun to offer a seal for "An Approved Facsimile." The first facsimile to be published under this plan is that of the manuscript of *The Red Badge of Courage*, edited by Fredson Bowers with extensive introductory material and appendixes and published in two volumes in 1973 by Microcard Editions Books. The next two such facsimiles are to be those of F. Scott Fitzgerald's *Ledger* and of the manuscript of *The Great Gatsby*, edited by Matthew J. Bruccoli.

40. The CEAA seal, reading "An Approved Text," is awarded only to editions which contain these two elements. However, when a CEAA text is leased by a reprinting publisher, the "An Approved Text" seal remains on the new volume, so long as the text is faithfully reproduced, even if the apparatus is not also reprinted. Perhaps logically the original CEAA edi-

tion should contain a seal for "An Approved Apparatus" as well as for "An Approved Text," when it appears in the originating edition, covers more than the text. Such a seal—reading "An Approved Apparatus"—already exists for a different purpose: it is available to editors who have gone through precisely the same CEAA editorial process but find that publication of the actual text is not feasible (because of copyright restrictions, for example, or lack of interest on the part of a publisher). In these cases the apparatus is keyed by page-line references to the copy-text edition, and a reader, entering the listed emendations on a copy of that edition, can bring its text into conformity with the critical text established (but not published) by the editor. The first apparatus of the CEAA pattern to be published separately from a text was Matthew J. Bruccoli's "Material for a Cen-

the publication of *The Marble Faun* in the Hawthorne edition, Bowers undertook to define the relationship between a "CEAA edition" and the kinds of editions commonly encountered in classroom use.[41] The first he called a "definitive edition," which "establishes with absolute accuracy the exact documentary forms of all authoritative early texts of the work being edited" (p. 52), presents in lists "the concrete evidence on which the establishment of the text has rested" (p. 54), and offers a text reflecting "the author's final intentions insofar as these can be recovered by systematic, principled selection from among the variants of different authoritative forms of the text, supplemented by editorial emendation" (p. 54). The research required for this kind of edition is time-consuming and is carried through without regard for financial return, whereas the editions usually circulated among students and the general public are commercial products, in the preparation of which the factor of expense has to be taken into account. The latter are "practical editions," which "present to a broad audience as sound a text (usually modernized and at a minimum price) as is consistent with information that may be procurable through normal scholarly channels and thus without more special

---

tenary Edition of *Tender is the Night*," *SB*, 17 (1964), 177-193; the advantages of and appropriate occasions for such an approach are discussed in James B. Meriwether's "A Proposal for a CEAA Edition of William Faulkner," in *Editing Twentieth-Century Texts*, ed. Francess G. Halpenny (1972), pp. 12-27. Bruccoli has recently prepared the first separate apparatus to receive the CEAA seal and to be issued as an independent publication (*The Great Gatsby*, University of South Carolina Press); see his discussion of it and the proposed series of which it is to be a part, in "The SCADE Series: Apparatus for Definitive Editions," *PBSA*, 67 (1973), 431-435.

41. "Practical Texts and Definitive Editions," delivered on 16 February 1968 and published, along with a paper by Charlton Hinman, in *Two Lectures on Editing: Shakespeare and Hawthorne* (1969), pp. 21-70. Bowers's essay includes (footnotes 8, 9, 11, 16, 17, on pp. 36-39, 42, 46-48) some comments on Richard H. Fogle's unfavorable review of the Hawthorne edition in *American Notes & Queries*, 1 [1962-63], 159-260); and "The Ecology of American Literary Texts," *Scholarly Publishing*, 4 (1972-73), 133-140. Joseph Katz discusses the shortcomings of certain practical editions in "Practical Editions: A Bad Resource for American Literary Study," *Resources for American Literary Study*, 3 (1973), 221-229 (which includes references to the *Proof* articles surveying the practical editions of individual works).

American Literary Scholarship: An Annual, 1965, ed. James Woodress (1967), pp. 21-27; Fogle's comparison of the Ohio State edition of *The House of the Seven Gables* with a classroom edition (Riverside) prompted Bowers's decision to elaborate on the differences between the two kinds of editions: "without the stimulation of his confusion of the true issues it is unlikely that this paper would ever have been written" (p. 38). Bowers has continued to discuss the differences in later articles, such as "The New Look in Editing," *South Atlantic Bulletin*, 35 (1970), 3-10 (which also comments on Jesse H. Shera's review of the Hawthorne edition

research than is economically feasible" (p. 26). Practical editions, while useful in the absence of more scholarly editions, clearly represent a compromise, and better practical editions can come only as more "definitive editions" are produced to serve as the source of information for them. The CEAA, it is true, is supporting work principally on only one carefully defined kind of edition—but one that provides the materials basic to other kinds of editions, if they are to be reliable. By focusing on these basic editions and at the same time encouraging the use of clear text and the photographic reproduction of these texts by other publishers, the CEAA is accommodating both the needs of scholars and the long-range interests of the general reading public.

Of course, some people may feel that it is proper for the CEAA to support basic scholarly editions without believing that Greg's theory (or, perhaps, any other single theory) ought to be the required approach, and they may be inclined to think that such a requirement contradicts the freedom from dogmatism which Greg himself emphasized. This position, however, involves several confusions. To begin with, any standard against which performance is measured must inevitably be dogmatic to the extent that it asserts a particular position, and the CEAA cannot avoid taking a position if it is to attempt to control the quality of work performed under its auspices or published with its endorsement. But that kind of dogmatism, if it can be called such, is an entirely different matter from the dogmatism, or lack of dogmatism, of the position actually taken. Since Greg's approach allows for the operation of individual judgment (providing a dogmatic, or arbitrary, rule only when there is no basis for rational judgment) and since the CEAA has adopted Greg's approach, it follows that the CEAA's dogmatism amounts only to insisting on an approach which in itself minimizes the role of mechanical rules and maximizes that of critical judgment.

Furthermore, whatever rigidity there is in the adoption of a single approach is reduced by the inclusion, in CEAA editions, of the materials out of which texts based on other approaches can be prepared. To call these editions "definitive" may sound dogmatic, but Bowers's definition makes clear that "definitive edition" has come to be a technical term, referring to an edition which includes a text prepared in a particular way along with an apparatus containing certain information. The word "definitive" has undoubtedly been used too freely and unthinkingly and may even at times have been applied loosely, though still incorrectly, to a *critical text* rather than an *edition*. If a critical text depends on editorial judgment and critical perception, it cannot be definitive in itself, for judgments and perceptions are always, at least to some extent, arguable. But such a text can be based on a definitive assemblage of relevant material, on painstaking research which, if done properly, does not have to be repeated.[42] No serious student of literature would wish to put a stop to the endless process of rethinking the nuances of a text; but none would desire to repeat the process of accumulating the factual evidence necessary as background for informed judgment if that process had already been satisfactorily completed. A so-called "definitive edition" thus achieves its status through the inclusion of a definitive apparatus; the text presented in such an edition commands respect, because of the thoroughness of the research involved, but it cannot be regarded as the element of the edition which justifies the appellation "definitive." Confusion has arisen because the word "edition" sometimes is used to mean simply "a text" and sometimes refers to a text and its appurtenances. The CEAA, with its dual focus on a rationale for editing and a rationale for presenting evidence, has clearly been aware of these problems and has obviously recognized in its requirements the desirability of encouraging critical thinking about a text by providing the reader with the basic factual information necessary for such thinking. The CEAA's use of Greg's theory, therefore, has perpetuated Greg's recognition of editing as an activity of informed criticism.

III

When one understands Greg's theory and the CEAA's implementation of it, one cannot help regarding many of the recent discussions (both favorable and unfavorable) of this joint subject as naïve and parochial, and frequently as uninformed or misinformed.[43] A few,

42. This point has been well put by Leon Howard in his review of the Hawthorne edition in *NCF*, 22 (1967-68), 191-195, when he remarks that, "even though textual theory might change, the work has been done and the information made available for every serious student of American literature" (p. 193). Of course, new information can turn up later, as Bowers recognizes when he says that "definitive" is "only a comparative term, since we must always believe that from time to time the accumulation of scholarship will enable an editor to improve on the work of his predecessors" ("Old-Spelling Editions of Dramatic Texts" [cited in footnote 18

above], p. 13). Similarly, he begins his discussion of "Established Texts and Definitive Editions," *PQ*, 41 (1962), 1-17, by noting, "Nothing but confusion can result from the popular assumption that only one form of an established text can ever exist, and hence that a definitive edition of a single form of a literary work is invariably possible."

43. Although I shall be commenting here principally on essays which take an adverse view of Greg's theory and the CEAA (since they naturally bring into sharpest focus the issues involved), it is clear that some of the reviewers who have written favor-

however, do raise important issues, and it is regrettable that a survey of these discussions must begin with one of so little substance as that of Edmund Wilson. In a two-part article entitled "The Fruits of the MLA," published in the *New York Review of Books* on 26 September and 10 October 1968, Wilson offered what can only be called an ill-tempered and incoherent attack on the CEAA editions, making references to six volumes ostensibly under review;[44] in December of that year the article, with a postscript commenting on some of the correspondence provoked by it,[45] was published in pamphlet form as "A New York Review Book," and in 1973 it was collected into the posthumous volume *The Devils and Canon Barham* (pp. 154-202), edited by Leon Edel.[46] Because of Wilson's stature, this article has received

---

able, but often perfunctory, notices of CEAA volumes have no real conception of the aims of those editions. References to some of the more significant reviews are made in the CEAA *Statement* (2nd ed., 1972), p. 23; a number of other reviews, principally from 1969, are listed (along with other CEAA publicity) in *CEAA Newsletter*, No. 3 (June 1970), pp. 36-38. Although a few of these reviews, and some others, are referred to in these pages, I do not take up individual reviews in any detail, since the questions they raise usually involve judgment of particular cases rather than general principles and procedures.

44. In the 26 September installment (pp. 7-10), headed "Their Wedding Journey," he comments not only on this volume of the Indiana Howells edition but also on *Typee* in the Northwestern-Newberry Melville and *The Marble Faun* in the Ohio State Hawthorne; on 10 October (pp. 6, 8, 10, 12, 14) he limits himself to "Mark Twain," taking up three volumes of the California edition of Mark Twain papers—*Satires and Burlesques, Letters to His Publishers*, and *Which Was the Dream?*

45. The *New York Review of Books* for 19 December 1968, pp. 36-38, contained letters from William H. Y. Hackett, Jr., and Theodore Besterman, which Wilson prints in his postscript; letters from George B. Alexander, Ronald Gottesman, and Paul Baender, which Wilson refers to; and letters from Frederick Buechner and Frank J. Donner, which Wilson does not mention

(but whose correction of "Albert Payson Terhune's" to "Albert Bigelow Paine's" is incorporated in the text at 189.6).

46. As Wilson notes in the 1968 pamphlet, the article had originally appeared "in a slightly different form." For pamphlet publication a number of stylistic revisions were made (e.g., "persistent" for "acute" at 179.21 [all page references are to the 1973 volume, as the most accessible text]), some errors were corrected (e.g., the comments on the Constable Melville and the Russell & Russell reprint at 191.6-9), some additions were incorporated (e.g., the parenthetical sentence at 172.8-11), and five footnotes were added (those on pp. 164, 166, 182, and 186, and one not retained in the 1973 book: attached to the sentence ending at 156.4, it read, "These volumes now range in price here from $10 to $14"). Three of those footnotes cite information supplied by correspondents (those on pp. 164 and 166 based on Gottesman's published letter, and that on p. 186 credited to Alexander's published letter). As Wilson points out in his postscript, other revisions were based on comments in letters, particularly Gottesman's (though in describing one of the corrections—"Reedy" to "Rudy" at 164.5—he reverses the two words); but some corrections available to him in letters were not in fact utilized (see footnote 49 below). The 1973 volume incorporates a few more corrections (e.g., "Newberry" for "Newbury" at 163.22) and omits one footnote (as noted above).

a considerable amount of attention and will continue to have an audience in the future as part of his collected essays; if it had been written
by a lesser figure, however, its obvious motivation and manifest confusion would have prevented its being taken seriously. Wilson makes
transparent his motive for discrediting the CEAA editions by quoting,
at the start, a letter he had written to Jason Epstein in 1962 setting
forth the idea of "bringing out in a complete and compact form the
principal American classics," based on "the example of the Editions
de la Pléiade" (pp. 155-156); this undertaking he had hoped would
be supported by the National Endowment for the Humanities, but
the MLA, he says, "had a project of its own for reprinting the American classics and had apparently had ours suppressed" (p. 159).[47]
Thus determined to find fault with the results of the MLA project,
Wilson never addresses himself to the basic editorial rationale (that is,
to Greg's theory) but instead is content to ridicule such matters as the
laboriousness of the research involved, the extent of the apparatus,
and the physical size of the volumes. The article is, uncharacteristi-
cally, full of confusions, if not inconsistencies,[48] the most egregious
perhaps being his professed admiration for a "sound and full text"
(p. 157) combined with his view that collation is unrewarding if it
does not uncover "serious suppressions and distortions" (p. 161) or

47. Epstein and John Thompson submitted a proposal—for a series of editions
of the kind Wilson desired—to various
foundations and eventually to the National Endowment; in 1966, at the time of the
initial award of $300,000 to the MLA,
$50,000 was to be made available for the
Wilson plan whenever facilities for admin-
istering it were developed (they never
were). The *New York Review of Books*,
edited by Epstein's wife, had included,
eight months before Wilson's article, another review critical of a CEAA edition—
Lewis Mumford's "Emerson Behind Barbed
Wire" (18 January 1968, pp. 3-5). Mumford objected to the Harvard edition of
*The Journals and Miscellaneous Notebooks
of Ralph Waldo Emerson* because of its
inclusion of material discarded by Emerson
and its use of editorial symbols within the
text to record Emerson's revisions. The
Mumford piece provoked considerable correspondence, including a letter from Wilson criticizing the MLA "stupid academic
editions" and describing his Pléiade idea.

The issue of 14 March 1968 (pp. 35-36)
contained letters from (besides Wilson)
Lewis Leary, William M. Gibson, and
G. S. Rousseau, and a reply from Mumford;
another letter, from M. H. Abrams and
Morton W. Bloomfield, along with another
reply from Mumford, appeared in the
issue of 23 May (p. 43). Mumford's review,
of course, does not touch on the subject
of Greg's rationale, since the choice of
copy-text is not an issue in connection
with Emerson's manuscript journals.

48. For example, he approves the inclusion in the Pléiade Proust of "an omitted
episode" and the restoration in the Soviet
editions of Pushkin and Tolstoy of "cut or
altered passages," and he looks forward to
a complete edition of Mark Twain's *Autobiography*, since "we have never had the
whole of this work"; yet he believes that
one of the pieces included in *Which Was
the Dream?* ("Three Thousand Years
among the Microbes") "might well be
omitted from the canon" because "it turns
out to be disappointing" (p. 178).

interesting variants ("the scrutinizing of variants may, in some cases, be of interest," p. 172). What Wilson is unwilling to acknowledge is that the CEAA's concern extends beyond a scholarly audience to the general public: the CEAA, he says, is "directing a republication of our classics which is not only, for the most part, ill-judged and quite sterile in itself but even obstructive to their republication in any other form" (p. 190). He fails to note that the pages of text, unencumbered in most cases by editorial intrusions, are suitable for photographic reproduction in volumes more convenient to hold and that the apparatus (which, admittedly, helps to make some of the volumes cumbersome), rather than being "sterile," may serve to generate other editions, based on differing evaluations of the evidence—or at least to encourage analysis of the editor's judgments. Wilson's piece scarcely demands any reply, but the celebrity it achieved caused the MLA to feel that some sort of official notice was appropriate, and in March of 1969 the MLA published a pamphlet entitled *Professional Standards and American Editions: A Response to Edmund Wilson*, containing two accounts of the history and aims of the CEAA, by William M. Gibson and John H. Fisher, along with letters from five scholars enumerating errors or confusions in Wilson's remarks.[49] Actually, all that was necessary, if a reply was to be made, was Gordon Ray's brief comment which stands as the epigraph to the pamphlet. Recognizing that "this attack derives in part from the alarm of amateurs at seeing rigorous professional standards applied to a subject in which they have a vested interest" (and thus recognizing the attraction which Wilson's position had for a number of people one might have expected to see through it),[50] Ray observes, "As the American learned world has come

49. Gibson's essay, "The Center for Editions of American Authors" (pp. 1-6), was reprinted from *Scholarly Books in America*, 10 (January 1969), 7-11. Two of the letters (pp. 7-12), by Ronald Gottesman and Paul Baender, had previously been published in the *New York Review of Books* (19 December 1968); two others (pp. 13, 17-19), by Frederick Anderson and Oscar Cargill, also addressed to the *New York Review*, had not been published before; and a fifth (pp. 14-16), by John C. Gerber, had been sent directly to Wilson and had not been published. (A footnote to Gerber's letter points out that Wilson did not correct in the pamphlet his misstatements about the Mark Twain *Papers* and *Works* noted here.) Fisher's essay, "The MLA Editions of Major American Authors" (pp. 20-26), besides providing a historical account which includes information about Wilson's "Pléiade" plan, makes some response to Wilson's articles. The pamphlet ends with "A Calendar" (pp. 27-28), listing relevant events back to 1947. Bowers's comments on Wilson's articles appear in *Two Lectures on Editing*, pp. 23-25 (footnote 2) and p. 70 (footnote 30). Benjamin DeMott's "The Battle of the Books," in the *New York Times Book Review*, 17 October 1971, pp. 70-72, offers a journalistic account of the controversy.

50. It is symptomatic that Wilson, and Mumford before him, both try to divorce these editions from humanistic learning.

to full maturity since the second World War, a similar animus has shown itself and been discredited in field after field from botany to folklore. In the long run professional standards always prevail."

In contrast to Wilson's article, which makes no reference to Greg's theory, two brief essays which appeared soon after it—the work of Paul Baender and Donald Pizer—do raise questions directly about the applicability and usefulness of Greg's "Rationale." Although each of these essays is weakened by a partial misunderstanding of Greg, they at least raise issues the discussion of which may serve to clarify certain points in some people's minds. Baender, an editor associated with a CEAA edition, published in 1969 a note entitled "The Meaning of Copy-Text,"[51] which asserts that the term has become "ambiguous and misleading," principally for two reasons: first, that it is a "banner word" which "tends toward the superlative" and which thus implies "authority beyond its denotation, as though the term itself ratified an editor's choice of text"; second, that it is "not suited to the full range and complexity of editorial problems" (p. 312). The first point has nothing to do with the word "copy-text" or the concept but only with unscholarly reactions to it—unscholarly because they depend on the "prestige" (as Baender calls it) of the term rather than the arguments lying behind it. The second is of more consequence but is based on an oversimplification and distortion of Greg's position. If it were accurate to say flatly that Greg's theory is eclectic with respect to substantives but maintains "a single-text criterion" with respect to accidentals (p. 314), or if it were fair to suggest that its application to situations involving prepublication texts results in "another stage for a retrogressive pursuit of copy-text" (p. 316), then one would have grounds for claiming that it is "not suited to the full range and complexity of editorial problems." But nothing in Greg's theory, as we have seen, prohibits the emendation of accidentals in the copy-text when one has grounds for doing so; nor is it consistent with his theory to assume that a surviving manuscript must necessarily—regardless of its nature— become copy-text, since he allowed for the possibility that in some

---

Mumford says that the culprit behind the Emerson edition is the "Academic Establishment," fostering "the preconceptions and the mock-scientific assumptions governing the pursuit of the humanities today" (p. 4). Wilson makes disparaging remarks about editors who are not interested in literature (p. 170), exaggerates the technical language employed (p. 169), and prints with obvious delight a letter from

W. H. Y. Hackett, Jr., ridiculing, among other things, the Hinman Collator (pp. 198-99). Ray's comment, though printed without a citation of source, is taken from his "Foreword" to *The American Writer in England: An Exhibition Arranged in Honor of the Sesquicentennial of the University of Virginia* (1969), p. viii.

51. *SB*, 22 (1969), 311-318.

cases a later, rather than an earlier, text is the appropriate choice. One of Baender's illustrations[52] rests on a basic confusion (of which Baender is not alone guilty) between "copy-text" and "printer's copy." Baender cites a situation in which the number of authorial alterations in a later printing makes it more convenient for the editor to use a reproduction of that later printing as the basis for his text, entering onto it the readings of the first printing wherever the later readings are not judged to be authorial. Such a procedure, of course, does not violate Greg's theory (however risky it may be in practical terms, since one is increasing the probability that nonauthorial readings may inadvertently be allowed to remain in the text); but Baender's feeling that one follows the procedure "despite this convention of copy-text" makes clear that he is not focusing on the distinction between "text," meaning a particular arrangement and formal presentation of a group of words, and "printer's copy," meaning a specific physical copy of a text furnished to the printer. Greg's "copy-text" is a "text"—which can exist in more than one physical embodiment (for example, the individual copies of an edition)—and Greg did not comment on the manner in which that text should be reproduced for the use of the compositor who is setting type for the editor's new edition. The CEAA *Statement* does go on to recommend, for obvious practical reasons, the use of a photographic reproduction of the copy-text as printer's copy; but not to follow this course, whether for convincing or questionable reasons, does not in itself contradict Greg's theory, since no theoretical matter is at issue.[53]

Two years later Donald Pizer raised again,[54] but in broader terms, the question of the applicability of Greg's theory to recent literature

52. The other of his principal illustrations deals with collateral texts, deriving independently from a lost common ancestor; in these situations he believes that it would be "misleading" to denominate one of the collateral texts a "copy-text." An editor's statement, however, ought to make clear the reasons for selecting a particular text as the basic one, so that the reader will not find the label "misleading." If the collateral texts are equidistant in descent from the lost common ancestor, of course, it is true that there may be no basis for selecting one over another, and the editor must then construct a copy-text on the basis of all these texts, as Bowers has explained in his discussion of "radiating texts," referred to above (footnote

13); but from that point on Greg's theory of copy-text applies as usual. And if the collateral texts are not equidistant from the lost common ancestor, the editor is able to follow Greg's rationale directly, by selecting the one nearest the ancestor unless he has strong evidence pointing toward another choice.

53. My views on Baender's argument are set forth in greater detail in "The Meaning of Copy-Text: A Further Note," *SB*, 23 (1970), 191-196. See also Bowers's comment in "Multiple Authority" (cited in footnote 13 above), p. 82 (footnote 1).

54. "On the Editing of Modern American Texts," *BNYPL*, 75 (1971), 147-153.

by enumerating five ways "in which copy-text theory is unresponsive to the distinctive qualities of [that is, the historical circumstances lying behind] modern American texts" (p. 148).[55] Although Pizer calls attention to some issues that deserve careful consideration, his article is ineffective as an argument against the general usefulness of Greg's rationale because it fails to distinguish between theoretical and practical concerns and to recognize fully the lack of dogmatism in Greg's approach. The last three of his points are irrelevant to an analysis of Greg's theory—what they are relevant to is a consideration of the particular kind of edition (in the sense of text plus apparatus or other commentary) appropriate for modern (nineteenth- and twentieth-century) American literature. While this subject is of course a legitimate matter for debate, the issue is only confused by the implication that the adoption of Greg's theory determines the nature of the apparatus (or whatever accompanies the text) as well as of the text itself. Thus his third point—that the multiplicity of manuscripts, typescripts, and proofs which survive for some modern works makes the task of recording all variant readings excessively onerous[56]—presupposes that something in that theory of copy-text necessitates a complete record of variants, for he concludes: "the theory of copy-text either hinders the preparation of critical editions or encourages the production, at immense expense, of unusable editions" (p. 151). But whether or not one wishes to follow the practice of CEAA editions in recording variants (and the CEAA does not require as an absolute rule that all pre-copy-text variants be noted in print) has nothing to do with whether or not one edits a text in accordance with Greg's theory; and naturally the job of editing a reliable text is complicated by the survival of numerous documents, for the variants in them must be examined carefully regardless of whether a listing is to be published. Pizer's fifth point is a related one, dealing also with apparatus: he objects to clear text in a "critical edition" because turning to the back of a book to consult the apparatus is more difficult than looking at the foot of a page, and he disapproves specifically of the sections of apparatus which the reader of a CEAA edition must "juggle" (p. 152). The

---

55. Although Pizer continually refers to "the" theory of copy-text, it is obviously Greg's theory which he is discussing. One should understand, however, that an editor necessarily has a "copy-text," whatever he may call it, and that Greg's is only one among many conceivable rationales for selecting a copy-text.

56. That the result might be "complex and bulky" is undeniable; that it is therefore "all but unusable" does not follow. Anyone who wishes to comprehend a complex textual history would presumably not expect to find the evidence as easy to follow as it might be in less complicated situations.

possibility that a more efficient apparatus can be devised is always
open; but the plan of the apparatus does not alter the editorial procedure, and a dislike of "the tendency toward clear-text publication"
cannot through any argument become an "objection to copy-text
theory."[57] The fourth of Pizer's observations amounts to nothing more
than the recognition that some editors may choose to edit works which
some readers deem unworthy of the effort expended. He speaks of "the
absolutism of copy-text procedures"—meaning the uniform treatment
of major and minor works—without acknowledging that the decision
to edit is a critical evaluation in itself. Not all the CEAA editions are
"complete" editions, and those that are reflect—rather than any
requirement of Greg's theory—the critical belief that the stature of
the authors involved demands full-scale investigation of even their
lesser pieces.[58] Very few people (and certainly not the CEAA) would
dissent from the view that—since time and money are not unlimited—
"practical editions" must suffice for many literary works; but there
will never be complete agreement on exactly what works those are.

Pizer's first two objections, in contrast, do raise questions about
theory, but not, as he implies, solely about Greg's theory; they are
serious questions which any editor must face, whether in the context
of Greg's rationale or not. It is Pizer's contention that Greg's theory,
by leading an editor normally to adopt the accidentals of a manuscript
in preference to those of a first printing, ignores the fact that modern
authors sometimes "rely on the taste" of particular publishing-house

57. Pizer is particularly worried about
the future republication of CEAA clear
texts without accompanying apparatus:
"It is a nice point," he believes, "whether
a clear-text critical edition sans apparatus
is any different from an unedited text"—
because "in either case the reader must go
to considerable effort to check the evidence" (p. 152). A critical text exists to
present an informed reconstruction of an
author's intended text, based on an examination of all known evidence and on critical insight into the author's aims and
methods; a text which is "unedited" (presumably edited only by the original publisher's editor or reproduced from a contemporary printing by a later editor) does
not purport to serve this purpose. There is
nothing similar about the two except that
they are texts of the same piece of writing
and that they are texts as opposed to ap-

paratuses. If a reader wishes to consult the
documentation which an apparatus provides and finds no apparatus accompanying
his text, he may be somewhat inconvenienced by having to go to a library to
examine a CEAA edition (text plus apparatus), but surely less so than if he had
to collect the evidence himself with which
to judge an "unedited" text.

58. If Pizer is concerned (as he seems to
be in his proposal of "textual organicism,"
pp. 152-153) to preserve as a respectable
possibility the idea of a collected set which
includes some "definitive editions" along
with some "practical editions" (to use
Bowers's terms), all one can say is that
there is no theoretical objection to it, so
long as each text is clearly labeled for
what it is.

editors, who thus "have increasingly participated in the creative process of their authors." He argues, in other words, that an author who expects or encourages certain kinds of alterations to be made in the publisher's offices must be said to prefer or "intend" the resulting text. "If an author," as Pizer concisely puts it, "within such a relationship and for whatever motives, accepts an editorial change or suggestion, his acceptance is the equivalent of a creative act, even though the act is the initial responsibility of an editor" (p. 148). The aim of Greg's theory, with which no scholarly editor would quarrel, is to establish the text which the author intended; and by concentrating on unmodernized texts it aims to establish the author's intended text in respect to accidentals as well as substantives. What constitutes the author's "intention" is of course the crucial question, and in answering it the editor must always depend, to a greater or lesser degree, on his critical insight. It is axiomatic that an author's own statements of his intention, when they exist, do not, for a variety of reasons, necessarily coincide with his actual intention—the only guide to which is the work itself. An author may acquiesce in his publisher's decisions and then rationalize his behavior; or he may genuinely be grateful for changes which make his work, in one way or another, more acceptable (and salable) to the public; or he may approve of alterations in many other kinds of situations—without truly believing that the result quite represents his own style or approach. What appears in a prepublication form of a text is normally a better representation of the author's habits than what appears in a first printing, and the text of a fair-copy manuscript or typescript reflects the author's intention, whether or not it turns out to be his final intention in every respect. It is true, as Pizer says, that choosing "an early copy-text encourages a frame of mind which requires later variants to 'prove themselves' as authorial rather than as editorial or printer's variants" (p. 149); but such would seem to be the safest course in most instances, since the author's responsibility for a later reading—especially in accidentals—is normally less certain than his responsibility for an early one.[59] Of course, such editorial caution may occasionally produce a text reflecting "an author's dis-

---

59. Pizer, in his footnote 5 (p. 148), gives the impression that he has not fully grasped Greg's central insight: that there is no reason to expect authority in substantives and authority in accidentals to reside in the same text. What Pizer says is that the "suspicion of later texts . . . affects the entire matter of the choice of copy-text while receiving explicit expression primarily in relation to accidentals." That is of course just the point: the potential authority of a later text in respect to substantives is in no way affected by the choice of an early text as the authority in accidentals.

carded rather than final intentions," but at least it reflects his, rather than someone else's, intentions. The editor's critical judgment—his literary taste exercised in the light of his intimate knowledge of the author and all known relevant external evidence—must finally determine the case; and there is nothing in Greg's theory to prevent him, on this basis, from deciding that the later variants have indeed "proved themselves." If, however, he starts from the assumption that the author and the publisher's editor are creative collaborators, he will, to be sure, produce an unmodernized text—in the sense that it reflects the author's period—but it may be far from the text which the author wished (finally, or at any other time).[60]

This question leads to a consideration of eclecticism, and Pizer's second point is that an eclectic text, incorporating later substantive readings into an earlier copy-text, violates the integrity (or "imaginative 'feel,'" as he calls it) of individual stages of an author's work. The result, which "may incorporate changes made by the author over many years," is, he says, "a text which never existed and which has little or no critical interest" (p. 150). Certainly it never existed, for a critical text by definition differs from any single extant documentary form of the text; but whether it is of critical interest depends on how well the editor has performed his task, for his aim is to produce a text which accords with the author's intention more fully than that of any given extant document or printing. The fact that an author may make alterations in a work over a long period of years does not necessarily mean that they reflect different conceptions of that work; when they do, then of course each version should be edited separately as a work in its own right (following the theory of copy-text with regard to each). But surely it blurs a critical distinction to insist that every revision "constitutes a distinctive work with its own aesthetic individuality and character" (p. 149).[61] What this argument leads toward, obviously, is the abandonment of the editor's critical function and the restriction of editing to the production of accurate facsimiles. It is somewhat puzzling that Pizer is reluctant to allow the scholarly editor to attempt

60. Pizer's sixth footnote (p. 148) recognizes this fact and is a more trenchant discussion of the issue than what appears in the body of his article: "I should note my awareness of the great range of variation possible within the publisher-author relationship and of the consequent need for editorial knowledge and discretion in determining the degree of authorial acceptance of a publisher's changes."

61. While it is possible to argue that the change of even a single word in a text produces a new work, critical discrimination has not advanced very far which makes no attempt to locate that point along the spectrum of revision where alterations to improve the expression of one conception give way to alterations that shift the conception itself.

a historical reconstruction of the author's intended text, when he is quite ready to believe that contributions of the original publisher's editor were accepted by the author as furthering his intentions. And it is paradoxical that a person who objects to the uniform editing of major and minor works for its failure to make "critical distinctions" ("which is what the study of literature is all about for most scholars and students") should disapprove of texts that involve an editor's critical judgment and should hesitate to offer to the public clear-text editions without apparatus, since they constitute "only the editor's beliefs about the author's final intentions" (p. 152). If, as he recognizes, editing is "in varying degrees an aesthetic enterprise," the "editor's beliefs" command respect to the extent that the editor is at once a careful historian and a sensitive critic; and the existence of insensitive editors casts no more doubt on the undertaking as a whole than the existence of obtuse literary critics does on the activity of literary analysis. When Pizer calls Greg's theory of copy-text "'scientific' in its central impulse" because it "establishes a principle (albeit a flexible one) that is supposed to work in every instance" (p. 153), he disregards the fact that the principle is "flexible" for the very reason that it places no restriction on the operation of informed judgment.

In the months following the appearance of Pizer's article, several communications stimulated by it were published in the pages of the same journal. Norman Grabo, in April 1971, and Hershel Parker, at greater length in October, criticized Pizer's position.[62] Then in November John Freehafer, applauding Pizer, set forth what he considered to be three additional "major deficiencies of the CEAA editions."[63] It is significant that the deficiencies are said to be "of the CEAA editions" and not of Greg's theory, for what Freehafer objects to is not Greg's approach but the way it has been put into practice in CEAA editions, along with the decisions reflected in those editions about the kinds of material to be presented. His first two points are patently argumentative: the CEAA editions, he believes, exhibit "a failure to learn from the best editorial practice of the past," because the history of Shakespearean scholarship has shown that the "empty boasts" of an editor like Theobald prove in the long run to be of little substance

62. Grabo, "Pizer vs Copy-Text," BNYPL, 75 (1971), 171-173; Parker, "In Defense of 'Copy-Text Editing,'" 337-344. Bowers makes a few remarks on Pizer's article in "Multiple Authority" (cited in footnote 13 above), pp. 86-87 (footnote 11).

63. "How Not to Edit American Authors: Some Shortcomings of the CEAA Editions," BNYPL, 75 (1971), 419-423.

(whereas critical discussions, like Johnson's, are often of lasting value); and they demonstrate "a failure to present literary works as such" by not providing critical analyses[64] and explanatory notes, by being "almost totally concerned with bibliographical questions." The first point springs from the CEAA use of the word "definitive." As I have said before, this word was an ill-advised choice and has been too freely used; nevertheless, it should be clear to any reader of a CEAA apparatus, from its discussion of various problematical points, that CEAA editors are not claiming (nor did Greg expect editors following his rationale to be able to claim) that they have made all the right decisions and thus produced a "definitive" text; all they can aim for as a goal is to provide a definitive apparatus, recognizing that it is at least possible sometimes to establish facts. The decision to emphasize the history of the text (including the history of critical reaction to it) in CEAA introductions and afterwords is obviously related to this point, for those essays constitute another part of the apparatus, directed toward laying out what historical facts can be established.[65] That these editions are historically oriented, however, does not mean that they fail "to present literary works as such" but simply that they do not present literary works accompanied by any one critical interpretation.[66]

Freehafer's third point, however, raises an issue which deserves to be commented upon, even though what must be said is implicit in Greg's theory and will therefore seem redundant to some readers. He

64. Because Freehafer cites Hershel Parker's reply to Pizer in connection with this discussion, Parker makes a further brief comment in "Historical Introductions vs Personal Interpretations," *BNYPL*, 76 (1972), 19. Freehafer's statement that "those who cannot successfully criticize an author ought not to edit him" (p. 420) seems not to recognize editing as a critical activity itself; what constitutes "successful" criticism is of course an open question.

65. As for explanatory notes, the CEAA editions have not by any means uniformly excluded them, and the CEAA *Statement* encourages them for certain kinds of works. In any case, Freehafer's belief that an editor who does not provide explanatory notes will be less likely to detect, for example, errors in the spelling of proper names is merely questioning editorial competence in general; any responsible editor investigates the spelling of names of per-

sons and places as a routine part of his job, and, if he makes a mistake in a given instance, the fault surely cannot be traced to the fact that he was not obliged to write explanatory notes.

66. The view that the CEAA editions "will probably be looked upon in the future as a monument to a temporary overemphasis on an imperfectly borrowed and excessively bibliographical style of editing" (p. 421) is puzzling. The "bibliographical" emphasis is an emphasis on establishing the history of each text, and the CEAA editors could be charged with "excess" in this regard if they claimed that all future editions of these works should have the same emphasis; but it is odd to regard as "temporary overemphasis" the effort to put on record information which will be useful in the future for producing different kinds of editions with texts based on other principles.

complains that the CEAA editions have failed "to use Greg's theory of copy-text with sufficient boldness and imagination to reconstruct ideal authorial texts of many of the works being edited" (p. 419). In support of this proposition he cites the differences in the texture of accidentals between *The Scarlet Letter* and *The House of the Seven Gables* in the Ohio State edition, resulting from the fact that copy-text for the former is a first printing (the manuscript not having survived) and for the latter is a manuscript; these differences, he says, can be regarded as "valid reconstructions of the author's intentions . . . only on the incredible supposition that within a year Hawthorne turned from a passionate devotion to house-styling to a passionate rejection of it" (p. 422). What this argument fails to notice is that Greg's theory, as a scholarly procedure, must operate on the basis of the available materials for a given text and aims at reconstructing the author's intention insofar as surviving evidence permits. One can well believe, with Freehafer, that Hawthorne's preferences did not shift so drastically within a year. But can one therefore say that the features of one known manuscript would also have been those of another, now missing, manuscript from approximately the same time, and that an editor would on that basis know how to set about inserting those features into the text for which no manuscript survives? Answering No could perhaps be called unimaginative, but one should then add that to be more "imaginative" would be inconsistent with the scholarly goal of exercising critical judgment within the bounds set by ascertainable fact and documentary evidence. The belief that the accidentals in one CEAA text should be identical to those in another contemporary text by the same author stems from an assumption that the CEAA goal is to reconstruct the author's "intention" in an absolute sense, rather than in the more realistic sense of that intention for which there is documentary evidence for a particular work. Naturally the editor's knowledge of the author's practice in other works, for which a different range of documents exists, ought to play a role in any decision he makes; but it would be a rare instance indeed in which such knowledge was so certain and comprehensive that the editor could feel confident in his ability to repunctuate or respell for the author without introducing far more readings that never existed than those that did. Anyone who wishes to take a more "imaginative" approach and to interpolate the habits of one manuscript or a group of manuscripts into the texts of other works would of course be able to examine and utilize the evidence present in the texts and apparatuses of the relevant CEAA volumes. A second illustration of Freehafer's is again indicative of a fundamental misunderstanding of what kind of text the CEAA is attempting to provide. Turning to a different period, he cites two recent editions of Dryden's *The Indian Emperour* (one in the University of California Press *Works*, 1966, and the other in the University of Chicago *Four Tragedies*, 1967) and observes that, by selecting two different copy-texts, these editions present, even after editing, two very different texts. Since both attempt to reconstruct the author's intention, both should theoretically, he says, "have arrived at identical texts" which "agree word for word, letter for letter, comma for comma" (p. 422); that they do not so agree he attributes to an unimaginative use of Greg's theory, to "tyranny of the copy-text." But Greg, precisely because he recognized the role of imagination and judgment, would never have expected two editors to make all the same choices and emerge with identical texts. What the scholarly editor is striving to do is to put his critical judgment at the service of recognizing what the author intended, and no one, including the CEAA editors, would claim that any one attempt at this is the final or "definitive" one. Freehafer's urging of a more imaginative use of Greg's rationale to produce an "author's ideal text" seems rather at odds with his criticism of the Ohio State Hawthorne, both here and in an earlier detailed discussion of *The Marble Faun*,[67] for making too many emendations; the existence of arguable emendations and variants suggests the impossibility of universal agreement on critical issues, and a more imaginative approach would not be likely to lessen the range of disagreement. Several times Freehafer speaks of "definitive texts"— not "definitive editions"—and in that earlier essay says that how definitive the Hawthorne edition is "largely depends upon how the editors

---

67. "*The Marble Faun* and the Editing of Nineteenth-Century Texts," *Studies in the Novel*, 2 (1970), 487-503. This article is a detailed review of the Ohio State edition of *The Marble Faun* and makes fewer general observations than the title might suggest. It represents the kind of close examination of a CEAA volume which has been all too infrequent, but for the most part it is concerned with the evaluation of particular emendations rather than with questions involving the use of Greg's rationale. One paragraph (pp. 498-499), however, does say that, because Greg's theory seems to work in connection with *The Marble Faun* manuscript, it does not follow that the theory can be applied "to all fair-copy manuscripts of the nineteenth century," since certain authors (several are cited) are known not to have punctuated their manuscripts for publication and others (Henry James) are known to have carefully revised their punctuation for later editions. It should not be necessary to repeat that Greg's theory does not demand the use of manuscript as copy-text when there is convincing evidence favoring another course. Freehafer makes some of the same criticisms of the Hawthorne edition, especially in regard to emendations resulting from a policy of "normalization," in his reviews of Hawthorne scholarship in *Jahrbuch für Amerikastudien*, 15 (1970), 293-294, and 16 (1971), 268-269.

have used their collations, concordances, and other data in establishing Hawthorne's texts" (p. 487); however, the distinction between a "critical" *text* and a "definitive" *edition* (which embodies such a text along with other information) cannot be overlooked if debates about these matters are to get anywhere. Pizer, too, in his response in December 1971 to Grabo and Parker,[68] reiterated the need for "flexibility" and for resistance to "the tidy and neat," apparently without recognizing that CEAA critical texts and their apparatuses reflect those qualities.

The same month saw the appearance of the first volume of *Proof*, which contained a long essay by Morse Peckham, "Reflections on the Foundations of Modern Textual Editing."[69] Peckham is the only critic of Greg's theory thus far to explain his criticisms in the context of a thoughtfully developed analysis of the nature of human communication. Most of the previous comments, as we have noticed, either arose from a misunderstanding of Greg or dealt with largely superficial matters; Peckham, on the other hand, attacks Greg's central assumptions by setting forth a view of human behavior incompatible with them. Although I shall try to show why his argument does not seem

68. " 'On the Editing of Modern American Texts': A Final Comment," *BNYPL*, 75 (1971), 504-505. Pizer has published remarks on CEAA editions or on Greg's theory in a number of other places. For example, he has commented unfavorably on the Crane edition in a review in *MP*, 68 (1970-71), 212-214, and in his survey of Crane scholarship in *Fifteen American Authors before 1900*, ed. R. A. Rees and E. N. Harbert (1971), p. 100 (the edition reflects "the present emphasis on critical texts and common sense be damned"). And his Rosenbach lecture, "Dreiser's Novels: The Editorial Problem" (published in *Theodore Dreiser Centenary*, 1971), asserts that Greg's theory, by causing editors to focus on that prepublication state which is "at once chronologically closest to the printed book and still completely sanctioned by the author" (p. 10), results in neglect of earlier prepublication states. A twentieth-century author, he says, "was more apt than his fellow novelist of a hundred years earlier to find that what appeared in a first edition was indeed what he wanted to appear in that edition" (p. 11); as a result, the real editorial problem becomes—for Dreiser, at any rate—"not

to determine his final intention but to use the material at hand to demonstrate how he reached that intention" (p. 12). Most editors, however, unless they have decided to edit a particular early version of a work, are inevitably concerned with "final intentions"; but that concern does not mean that their editions cannot include data relevant to a genetic study of the prepublication stages of the work, and indeed the CEAA *Statement* urges editors to include a record of at least the substantive precopy-text variants. (The principal difference between the two approaches is that Pizer prefers printing selected passages from earlier states as footnotes to the main text, whereas the CEAA *Statement* recommends a discussion, illustrated by quotations, of the nature of the various stages of prepublication revision.)

69. *Proof*, 1 (1971), 122-155. Peckham's ideas had earlier appeared, in compressed form, in the discussion of "General Textual Principles" in the first and second volumes of the Ohio University edition of Robert Browning (1969, 1970), pp. vii-ix; beginning with the third volume (1971) this section is somewhat expanded (pp. vii-xiii) and contains a reference to this *Proof* essay.

to me to invalidate Greg's rationale, I hope it will be clear, at the same time, that Peckham is raising the kind of fundamental questions that have been too little discussed. His essay—aside from its examination of whether analytical bibliography can be regarded as "scientific"[70]—attacks Greg's theory in two respects: (1) it denies that substantives and accidentals can be meaningfully segregated; (2) it denies that the reconstruction of a text representing the author's intention is a meaningful (or attainable) goal. Although the argument supporting the first can be seen as consistent with and deriving from the larger propositions underlying the second, the first point can be taken up separately and is discussed first by Peckham.

The distinction between substantives and accidentals, Peckham says, was necessary to Greg because of the nature of the material he was dealing with: "the sparse and inconsistent punctuation in [Renaissance] dramatic manuscripts *that have survived*" (p. 124).[71] But, he adds, the distinction "is useless outside of his very special class of texts" (p. 125), because most later authors (and some Elizabethans as well) were aware that punctuation affects meaning and were not helpless victims of a house-style imposed by their publishers. Punctuation, he argues, does more than affect meaning, for, without punctuation, "it is frequently impossible to decide on that meaning":

Punctuation is not a form or dress of substantives, something different from words. It is part of speech. Juncture, pitch, and stress are inseparable components in the semantic continuum of the spoken language. Their signs are punctuation. (p. 124)

Thus "an educated author produces his punctuation as he produces his words; together they make up an unbroken semantic continuum." Clearly Peckham is correct in believing that no fixed line separates punctuation (or other "accidentals") from wording in the expression of meaning; and I am not aware of any editor who accepts Greg that would take issue with this point. But it does not therefore follow that

70. I have discussed this part of his essay in "Bibliography and Science," *SB*, 27 (1974), 55-89.

71. It is not clear, however, why "sparse and inconsistent" punctuation in itself justifies the separate treatment of substantives and accidentals. Similarly, Peckham states in the next paragraph, "Greg's distinction rests upon the fact . . . that nobody but Ben Jonson [among Renaissance dramatists]

took writing for the public theater seriously" (p. 125). Does this imply that later writers of "serious" literature normally managed to exert careful control over the printed forms of their work? And does it imply that for works of later periods editing usually involves only the correction of obvious errors in a text which otherwise embodies the author's final wishes in every respect?

no practical distinction can be made between them. Greg, of course, insisted that he was concerned with a "practical," not a "philosophic," distinction; but Peckham finds illogical (because it does seem to claim a "philosophic" basis for the distinction) Greg's footnote in the "Rationale" which asserts that punctuation "remains properly a matter of presentation," despite the fact that it can affect meaning. Now that footnote, it must be admitted, is not written with Greg's characteristic clarity, but the point he was getting at (as the drift of his whole essay suggests) is not, in my opinion, illogical. A paraphrase might go something like this: "Although punctuation and spelling are, from a theoretical (or 'philosophic') point of view, inseparable from words in the written expression of meaning, in practice people (i.e., scribes, compositors, and even authors at times) do react to them as if they were somehow less significant." What Greg meant by a "practical" distinction is one which, however mistaken it may be, has in fact operated to govern human behavior; and, since the editor is concerned with analyzing the behavior of certain individuals, such a distinction may be useful to him. It is certainly true, as Peckham later points out (p. 145), that Elizabethan compositors felt freer to depart from the punctuation and spelling of their copy than later compositors. But does not a modern publisher's editor generally feel less compunction about inserting a comma than altering a word? Does not the author who acquiesces to a suggested change of punctuation more readily than to one of wording, or who believes that his punctuation but not his diction actually demands revision, feel that there is some sort of distinction? So long as one can say, "I think my quotation is accurate, though it may differ in a mark of punctuation here and there," and not be regarded by most people as uttering nonsense, one can believe that a "practical" distinction between the two does widely exist in people's minds. To the extent that punctuation and spelling are popularly regarded as distinct from what is being said—and it scarcely requires demonstration that they are, and have been, so regarded—the transmission of texts is correspondingly affected. However much an editor may deplore the confusion behind this attitude (analogous to the popular oversimplification of the relation between form and content), it is his business to take into account, as realistically as he can, the factors that influence textual transmission. (Of course, some accidentals do have less effect upon meaning than others: a comma marking a phrase-ending that would be recognized even without the comma serves less purpose than one which marks the beginning of a nonrestrictive clause. But no definite line separates this second type of accidental, sometimes called "semi-substantives," from the first, which also, though more subtly, may affect the sense.) What I take Greg to be saying, then, is that the editor distinguishes substantives and accidentals not because he believes that he is making a valid conceptual distinction between two elements in written language but because the distinction is one which is likely to have been made by the persons who have been involved in the transmission of any given text (and which therefore may be useful in segregating different features of that text which may have been accorded different treatment).

Obviously Greg does not expect an editor to be bound by this distinction in his own thinking, for he makes no requirement that the editor always accept the accidentals of a first edition or that he always accept all the accidentals of whatever text he selects as copy-text. He merely observes that, given the popular tendency to be less careful with accidentals than with substantives, more of the author's accidentals are likely to be present in a first edition than in later editions. And, of course, the whole point of attempting to recover the author's accidentals is that they do indeed constitute an important part of his expression. The distinction between substantives and accidentals has no influence on what an editor decides to do when he believes that he has convincing reasons for doing a particular thing,[72] but when he does not have such reasons, the distinction enables him to make a decision in accord with what common experience shows to be a widespread attitude (one which is thus likely to have been operative in any given instance).[73] Although English spelling has become more fixed over the centuries and styles of punctuation have altered, I see no evidence that the popular conception of spelling and punctuation as the accouterments of words has shifted[74]—or any reason, therefore, not to find

---

72. When Peckham says that "what to do about punctuation is an empirical matter, not a theoretical matter, not a matter of editorial principles or rules" (p. 126), he is actually agreeing with Greg's position that each situation must be examined on its own terms; Greg was providing a "rule" only for those situations in which empirical evidence does not convincingly settle the question.

73. Of course, errors are made in the transmission of substantives as well as accidentals. David J. Nordloh, in "Substantives and Accidentals vs. New Evidence: Another Strike in the Game of Distinc-

tions," *CEAA Newsletter*, No. 3 (June 1970), pp. 12-13, cites an instance in which a substantive variant between a manuscript and a magazine text can be shown to have resulted from a typist's error in the intervening typescript. It may be that without the typescript an editor would have taken the magazine reading as the one intended by the author; but the existence of such instances does not affect the general proposition that substantives as a class have normally received more careful treatment in transmission than accidentals.

74. Peckham's recollection of having heard, as a boy, stories about the serious

Greg's approach applicable to later writings. Greg's choice of the terms "substantive" and "accidental" was, as I have said before, unfortunate, and the fun which Peckham has with them, calling them "strangely medieval," is deserved; there would have been fewer misunderstandings (and certainly fewer complaints about unnecessary jargon) if, as Peckham suggests, plain terms like "words," "punctuation," and "spelling" had been employed. But surely the point Greg was getting at is not completely hidden behind the terms he chose.[75]

Peckham's principal argument, however, deals not with accidentals but with the concepts of "text" and "author." He believes that many literary scholars—including Greg and his followers, who attempt to establish the author's intended text—are guilty of literary hagiolatry, exalting the ideas of "author" and "work of art" in ways not consistent with the nature of human communication. An author, he says, is simply an organism which produces utterances, not as a result of any special inspiration but as a result of being human:

A writer produces utterances because he is a human being. It is a condition of being human. We do not know why human beings produce utterances, nor even how. It is a primitive, or surd, with which we begin and, to make matters worse, within which we must operate. To talk about self-expression, or projections, or mental ideas being expressed in language, is at worst to cover up our ignorance with pseudo-explanations, and at best to use a

consequences of incorrect punctuation in government documents (p. 125) does not really illustrate any common awareness "that punctuation cannot be separated from words," for the point of telling such stories is that the situations involved are exceptional and contradict everyday experience. Similarly, the "shift from rhetorical to syntactical punctuation in the first half of the nineteenth century" is not convincing evidence of such an awareness; both approaches support Peckham's view that punctuation consists of written signs for juncture, pitch, and stress and thus is part of the meaning, but he does not make clear why the *shift* from one to the other reflects a general awareness of this point.

75. One further observation of Peckham's on accidentals deserves notice. A logical consequence of his view that accidentals and substantives are inseparable is to deplore the absence of accidentals variants

in the historical collations in CEAA volumes. The CEAA *Statement* naturally does not prohibit their inclusion; but it is undeniable that their absence springs not merely from the great expense that would be incurred in most cases by listing them but also from the emphasis of Greg's theory itself on the lack of significance of post-copy-text accidentals. As Peckham points out, a record of variants in accidentals would be important for the historical study of punctuation, and in addition, of course, it would give the reader a still fuller picture of the evidence which the editor had at his disposal. My own view is that variants in accidentals ought to be included whenever feasible (and particularly when the copy-text is a manuscript); but the time and money involved may in many—perhaps most—instances seem out of proportion to the amount of use that would be made of such information. See also footnote 35 above.

verbal category to subsume the production of language and the production of nonverbal behavior.   (p. 139)

But the author is different from other utterers in that he assembles a series of utterances into what "he judges to be a discourse" and makes this series available to others, proposing "that they too judge it to be a discourse" (p. 138). The development of the discourse up to that point has involved a combination of producing utterances and changing (or revising) them;[76] thus the author, even before his work becomes public, has already been in the position of looking back over something previously written, reacting to it as a reader, since he is not at that moment the producer. This process, Peckham argues, continues indefinitely: sometimes other human beings (such as publishers' editors) react to and change the discourse, and sometimes the author continues to change it. Each is responding to a particular version, and each "can make a change acceptable to the author or to anyone else involved" (p. 141). The "textual editor" is but one more human organism in this sequence, producing one more version of "a *postulated* work, that is, of a construct" (p. 128). Whether a valid distinction can be made between changes by the author and by others, therefore, turns on

the question of whether the author is an organism engaged in the production of utterances, an activity which as a human organism he cannot avoid, even when alone and engaged in covert utterance, or whether he is an individual. So far there have appeared no grounds, save linguistic hypostatization and literary hagiolatry, for considering him an individual. The notion to be understood here is that he is but an organism and not an individual or monad or entity which can be differentiated from other similar entities.   (p. 143)

As a result, one cannot speak meaningfully of a single ideal "text" of a work; if the development of the concept of individuality ("self-mediated divergence from a cultural norm") had not caused the editor to confer "sainthood" on the supposed "author" and exalt certain works as canonical (p. 149), he would realize that he is "simply continuing an activity initiated by the author" (p. 144).

Although this is a greatly simplified summary of Peckham's analysis, I think that it does not distort the main outlines of his position. But one does not have to disagree with this general position in order to

76. Peckham uses the word "change" as more neutral than "revise," for he is under the impression that " 'revise' now generally means to change for the better" (pp. 138-139).

believe that such editors as those of the CEAA volumes are pursuing a sensible, meaningful, and useful goal. The "textual editor" whom Peckham describes—he defines the term as subsuming "both analytical bibliographer and textual critic" (p. 141)—is naturally, in Peckham's general terms, just another person making changes in a text; but it would seem to be more illuminating to go on and note how he is to be distinguished from others who do that. For persons who make changes in pieces of writing—and are admittedly engaging in basically similar actions—fall into two groups, those performing scholarly editing and those performing what may be called "creative editing."[77] There is no reason why one cannot regard a piece of writing as the common product of all beings who have come in contact with it and reacted to it; when it is viewed in this way, any change, made at any time, whether by the original publisher's editor, by the author, or by a later "editor," has the same status and may be judged to have improved the work, harmed it, or left it the same. From this point of view a critic is not performing his function conscientiously if he does not alter the work to make it, according to his standards, more satisfying than it has ever been before. There is, as I say, no objection to this procedure—so long as one's goal is critically rather than historically oriented. But the scholar sets a goal of historical reconstruction.[78] That the "author" has some individuality is suggested, even in Peckham's approach, by the recognition that he *initiated* the discourse, which is then operated upon by himself and others. If that discourse is of sufficient interest, a historical interest may also attach to the initiator; and if the same being initiates a number of such discourses, the interest may be correspondingly greater. What the scholarly editor attempts—recognizing the difficulty of the task and even the impossibility of its absolute achievement—is to remove from the discourse those features for which the initiator was not responsible.[79] The result is not neces-

77. As I called it in "Textual Study and Literary Judgment," *PBSA*, 65 (1971), esp. 113-114. I do not mean that "scholarly" editing is not also creative in a general sense but am using "creative editing" as a shorthand way of referring to editing which has a different aim from that of historical reconstruction. Lewis Leary, who uses the term in "Troubles with Mark Twain," *Studies in American Fiction*, 2 (1974), does not, in my view, sufficiently distinguish between the editor who adopts a reading which seems "best" to him and the editor who selects what he thinks would have been regarded as "best" by the author.

78. In the section of his essay on analytical bibliography and science (pp. 129-136), Peckham recognizes that the analytical bibliographer is a historian; see Tanselle, "Bibliography and Science" (cited in footnote 70 above), pp. 83-87.

79. Whether one is attempting to reconstruct his first, or last, or some other, intention is an important matter but is beside the point until one grants the goal

sarily what the editor himself prefers but what he believes to be the
author's contribution to a given discourse. The scholarly editor is thus
a different kind of responder from the others in the chain Peckham
is talking about; it may be that the editor, if he lives in the mid-
twentieth century, cannot avoid reacting in part in mid-twentieth-
century terms, but his aim is to use his critical faculties[80] to place
himself in the frame of reference of the author and the author's
environment. That such an aim is impossible of full attainment does
not invalidate it as a guideline for a direction in which to move,
despite Peckham's labeling of this attitude as "pure hagiolatry"
(p. 138).[81]

The difficulty with accepting Peckham's statement of the case is
evident when he remarks that the concepts of "text" and "author"
require the "textual editor" to "produce a definitive edition, which
he cannot do, instead of producing a new version more satisfactory
for some specific purpose than any existing version, which he can do"
(p. 151). What Peckham says the editor can do is in fact what CEAA
editors do (and realize they are doing): they produce a critical (not
definitive) text which they believe to be more satisfactory for the
purpose of the historical study of literature than any previous text,

---

of reconstructing authorial intention of
some sort. The question of "original" versus "final" intentions is helpfully illustrated by examples from Melville in
Hershel Parker's "Melville and the Concept of 'Author's Final Intentions,'" *Proof*,
1 (1971), 156-168.

80. When Peckham says that "textual
editing" is "logically independent of problems of aesthetics" (p. 136), he means that
the artistic status of a work (whether or
not it is generally considered to be an
effective work of art) has nothing to do
with the process of editing the work. But
that does not mean that critical or aesthetic
judgment is not involved in the editor's
assessment of the evidence. At another
point (p. 151) Peckham states, "The no-
tions of text and author have been responsible for the fact that a discipline which
came into existence as a reaction against
textual eclecticism has returned to textual
eclecticism"; but the more likely explanation would seem to be simply the growing
recognition that it is foolish to attempt

to eliminate critical judgment from historical research.

81. Let me repeat: I recognize that Peckham is asserting the essential identity of
all "editorial" actions and that the scholarly editor I am speaking of cannot avoid,
in Peckham's terms, producing his own version of a work. I am not disagreeing with
Peckham on this point but am trying to
show that there are valid discriminations to
be made nevertheless among the versions
produced and that it is not meaningless to
regard some as approaching more closely
than others to an "authorial" version, even
if what is "authorial" must be to some
extent a subjective judgment. (A "critical"
edition, of course, by definition involves an
editor's inferences about authorial intention, as Bowers makes clear by using the
word "inferential" in his description of an
editor's aim as "an attempt to approximate
as nearly as possible an inferential authorial fair copy"—in "Textual Criticism" [cited
in footnote 30 above], p. 33.)

and they regard the edition embodying that text as "definitive" only in its recording of certain classes of data. Part of the problem, throughout the essay, is Peckham's interchangeable use of "text" and "edition" and his belief that CEAA editors really think they are producing definitive *texts*.[82] Perhaps, indeed, this is the fundamental problem, for his concluding section (pp. 153-155), recognizing that the "textual editor" may decide to produce a text representing any given stage in the history of a work, goes on to assert, "No misplaced confidence in inadequately based theory can justify his evasion of the problems of an empirical situation." But when one observes that Greg's approach is an attempt to confront the empirical realities involved in the reconstruction of a particular stage in the history of a work and that it does not proclaim the result to be the only useful text of the work (even for historical study), the issue Peckham raises is no longer an issue. It seems to me that Peckham's final description of "the task of the textual editor" is—after one has penetrated the vocabulary—accurate:

to produce a new version from a series of a postulated text by a postulated author by making up for the policing, validating, and changing deficiencies in the long, complex, and interlocking series of behaviors the consequence of which was the production of that series.   (p. 155)

But when he proceeds to say that there is no definitive version to be arrived at and "no one set of instructions" to follow, he is responding to a nonexistent argument. Much of Peckham's essay helpfully focuses on the nature of written language, and his suggestion that editors ought to be aware of the nonliterary uses to which their apparatuses can be put (as in a study of human behavior) is worth serious consideration; but as a critique of Greg's "Rationale" and the CEAA editions, it misses the mark.

During the following year (1972) there appeared two books with general-sounding, but somewhat misleading, titles, James Thorpe's *Principles of Textual Criticism* and Philip Gaskell's *A New Introduction to Bibliography*. Each raises some questions, either explicitly or implicitly, about the validity of CEAA procedures—questions which, by this time, seem very familar. Thorpe's most direct comment on the CEAA—a brief discussion of its *Statement*—is related to his underlying belief that textual criticism has become too bibliographical in approach and that bibliographers are trying to make textual criticism

---

82. Their whole approach shows their recognition of the impossibility of a defini-tive *text*, even though they, too, sometimes contribute to the confusion by an imprecise use of the words "text" and "edition."

a "science." Despite his assemblage of quotations intended to serve as background, these issues are in fact illusory: for the leading bibliographers over the years have recognized that textual criticism can never be mechanical and that bibliography is simply one tool among several useful in dealing with textual problems.[83] Thorpe paints a picture of bibliographers greedy to annex the whole "province of textual criticism," as he calls it; but whether the present emphasis of textual criticism is excessively bibliographical is a question that cannot be approached in general or theoretical terms but only in relation to the details of specific situations. After all, if bibliography offers one kind of evidence to the textual critic, he cannot sensibly say that he desires only so much, and no more, of that kind of evidence; but if his attention to those details causes him in a particular case to neglect his search for letters or documents or other kinds of external evidence, then obviously he can be criticized in that instance for undue concentration on one type of evidence. What Thorpe tries to argue, however, is that the CEAA *Statement*, by requiring attention to bibliographical details, implies such attention to be "the efficient cause of an ideal edition" (p. 72).[84] The *Statement*, he believes, reflects "the view of a text as a system of infinitely perfectible details, by which scrupulous attention to all details will ultimately yield ideal results" (p. 57). Although he does not wish "to suggest that meticulous care is pedantry" (p. 76), he does suggest that close analysis of what seem to be unimportant variants is a waste of time (e.g., p. 74). He does not acknowledge the fact that laborious collation of texts[85] and analysis

83. I have commented in somewhat more detail on these parts of Thorpe's argument in "Bibliography and Science" (cited in footnote 70 above), pp. 78-80. Thorpe devotes an entire chapter, "The Province of Textual Criticism" (pp. 80-104), to setting forth the view that the "bibliographical orientation" of textual criticism is excessive; and his discussion of textual criticism as a "science" occupies the second section (pp. 57-68) of his chapter on "The Ideal of Textual Criticism" (this chapter was originally read on 8 February 1969 at a Clark Library Seminar and published that same year, along with a paper by Claude M. Simpson, Jr., in a pamphlet entitled *The Task of the Editor*, pp. 1-32).

84. Thorpe believes that the title *Statement of Editorial Principles* should be "Statement of Editorial Methodology"

(p. 73), and he takes the title to be indicative of a confusion between aims and techniques. Actually the CEAA pamphlet deals with both, as the title of the 1972 revised edition (*Statement of Editorial Principles and Procedures*) attempts to indicate.

85. Thorpe is correct in saying that "actual collations never provide more than some facts on which the trained intelligence can work" (p. 73); but the point he misses in the *Statement*'s remark that relevance is decided by collation is simply the fact that external evidence (e.g., an author's statement that a particular edition is a piracy) must be tested by what appears in the text itself (e.g., the presence or absence of differences that could reasonably be regarded as authorial revisions). See footnote 27 above.

of variants accomplish just as much when they demonstrate the absence of significant variants—or the presence of variants only in "the relatively trivial matters of spelling, punctuation, and capitalization" (p. 51)[86]—as when they show the existence of dramatically different readings. And no editor that I have heard of ever claimed that "scrupulous attention" to details and "meticulous care" are "a complete substitute for intelligence and common sense" (p. 78).[87] One must agree with Thorpe's later insistence (pp. 179-183) on the importance of a thorough knowledge of the author's works and period and of a diligent search for external evidence. But there is nothing inherent in the attention to bibliographical detail which prevents an editor from giving attention to other essential matters. The CEAA *Statement* does set forth the importance of accuracy in collating and proofreading, but it also points out the necessity for knowing the author's works and for searching out all relevant documents bearing on the history of a text[88]—and the CEAA editions have repeatedly been responsible for the uncovering of new documents and the assembling of comprehensive collections of reference material. An editor who neglects any part of his duty is open to criticism, and Thorpe's conclusion that editors should exploit "every kind of relevant evidence" (p. 79) is unexceptionable; but his belief that the "strongly bibliographical cast" (p. 103) of the CEAA *Statement* leads to a "glorification of method" (p. 79) rests on the fallacious assumption that attention to one kind of detail necessarily involves the neglect of other kinds. Some editors may of course be guilty of neglecting evidence, but it seems perverse to search for the cause of their incompetence in their careful attention to one kind of relevant detail.

86. If Peckham needs evidence that people still do react differently to accidentals than to substantives, Thorpe's statement here (and elsewhere, as on p. 74) provides a good illustration. Philip Young, like Thorpe, seems to judge the worth of editorial labor by how dramatically the text is altered, when he remarks that he "cannot find a single really significant difference between the new text [Ohio State *Scarlet Letter*] and that of the Riverside Edition (1883), regularly referred to in the bibliographies as Standard" ("Hawthorne and 100 Years: A Report from the Academy," *Kenyon Review*, 27 [1965], 215-232; reprinted as "Centennial, or the Hawthorne Caper," in *Three Bags Full* [1972], pp. 79-98). Young's discussion fails to recognize that what he regards as insignificant may appear significant to another critic and that the evidence, whatever it is, should be available in print for all to consult.

87. This statement occurs in a paragraph which was not present in the 1969 published version of this chapter.

88. The CEAA *Statement* does not take a great deal of space to make this point, nor does Thorpe, who says, "The sources of such information are so various that it is hardly worth mentioning any, except as examples" (p. 181).

A more consequential matter which Thorpe takes up is the treatment of accidentals (pp. 131-170).[89] After providing a sampling of
statements from authors of various periods, stressing their indifference
to accidentals, and a historical survey of printers' manuals, suggesting
that printers over the years have felt an obligation to "correct" accidentals, Thorpe concludes that "probably in most cases" the author
"expected the printer to perfect his accidentals" and that therefore
"the changes introduced by the printer can be properly thought of
as fulfilling the writer's intentions" (p. 165). It seems to me that there
are two basic difficulties with Thorpe's position. The first is that
quotations from authors and from printers' manuals are not comparable, because the former are statements of personal opinion (often
prompted by specific situations), while the latter are public announce-
ments of recommended general practice. Thus Thorpe's evidence from
the printers' manuals[90] is sufficient to show that printers have widely
regarded the alteration of accidentals in copy as part of their function;
but his evidence from individual writers by no means can be generalized upon to suggest that in any given instance the chances favor an
author's having been indifferent to the handling of accidentals. The
conclusion would seem to follow—contrary to Thorpe—that, without
convincing evidence on the other side, an author's manuscript stands
a better chance of reflecting his wishes in accidentals than does a
printed text. Here the second difficulty arises—in Thorpe's conception
of an author's "intention." In his opening chapter—his well-known
essay on "The Aesthetics of Textual Criticism"[91]—he asserts, "While
the author cannot dictate the meaning of the text, he certainly has final
authority over which words constitute the text of his literary work"
(p. 10). As a result of this distinction between "meaning" and "words,"
Thorpe tends to accept at face value an author's statement about
wording, without focusing on the fact that the motivations influencing
such a statement may be just as complex as those lying behind a statement of intended "meaning." Although he recognizes that, in the
absence of an authorial statement, the intended wording must be
arrived at through a critical analysis of all available evidence (p. 193),

89. This chapter is an expanded version
of a paper read at the University of Kansas
on 30 April 1971 and published later that
year as a pamphlet entitled *Watching the
Ps & Qs: Editorial Treatment of Accidentals.*

90. Additional evidence of the freedom
with which nineteenth-century compositors

altered accidentals is offered in two of
James B. Meriwether's contributions to the
CEAA Newsletter: "House-Styling, Vin-
tage 1856," No. 3 (June 1970), pp. 11-12;
"'On Careless Punctuation,'" No. 5 (De-
cember 1972), p. 3.

91. Originally published in *PMLA*, 80
(1965), 465-482.

at various points he implies that the existence of a statement settles the matter—as when he says that "the personal testimony by the author as to his intentions is plainly the most primary textual evidence that there can be" (p. 109).[92] This point of view leads to an uncritical acceptance of an author's remarks about his indifference to accidentals (or his preference for those in the printed text). The upshot of Thorpe's discussion is his astonishing recommendation that "the editor will do best to spend only a modest amount of his time on accidentals— mainly a losing cause—and devote himself to matters of substance" (p. 168). It is difficult to reconcile Thorpe's readiness to believe that an author preferred the printer's accidentals with his strict view of "the integrity of the work of art" (pp. 14-32); and it is hard to see how an editor whose aim is to establish the author's intended text, in accidentals as well as in substantives,[93] can justify the decision in advance to spend a "modest" amount of time on the accidentals. Like the earlier discussion of bibliographical detail, this chapter on accidentals reflects a peculiar view of scholarly endeavor: it suggests, in effect, that a scholar's sense of perspective is shown less by his ability to evaluate and integrate data than by his prior decision to limit his consideration of certain clearly relevant areas.[94]

92. Thorpe's position on this question is criticized by Peckham, who points out (p. 152) that "intention" about past events must inevitably be a reconstruction, for which an author's statement is only one piece of evidence. In an essay called "The Intentional? Fallacy?", included in *The Triumph of Romanticism* (1970), Peckham states the point more fully: "Briefly, an inference of intention is a way of accounting for or explaining the generation of an utterance; it can never be a report. The speaker of an utterance has greater authority than anybody else in his so-called intentional inference only because he is likely to have more information for framing his historical construct, *not* because he generated the utterance" (p. 441). See also footnote 81 above.

93. Although Thorpe says, "The basic principle is that the author's intentions with respect to accidentals should be carried out" (p. 198), he also asserts, at the end of the same paragraph, "Whether the text should be presented in old-spelling or in modernized accidentals is mainly a matter of convenience for the intended audience"—as if there is no contradiction involved. He surveys the arguments for and against modernizing accidentals on pp. 134-140 and pp. 169-170 and concludes, "I can say that the losses from modernization seem to me less than most textual scholars assume" (p. 170). Nevertheless, despite his reluctance to distinguish clearly the purposes and implications of the two kinds of texts, the primary focus is on the author's own wishes: "Our task is, I believe, to fulfill the intentions of the writer in these small details [accidentals] as well as in greater matters" (p. 165).

94. For Bowers's criticism of Thorpe's position, see footnote 6 in "The New Look in Editing," *South Atlantic Bulletin*, 35 (1970), 8; for Peckham's, see *Proof*, 1 (1971), 122, 135-138, 152. See also the reviews by John Feather, in *MLR*, 68 (1973), 381-382, David J. Nordloh, in *Resources for American Literary Study*, 3 (1973), 254-257, and G. R. Proudfoot, in *Library*, 5th ser., 28 (1973), 77-78.

If Thorpe's book, weakened by such contradictions, does not manage to serve the useful function of fairly surveying "the basic principles which underlie the practice of textual criticism" (p. vii), neither does Philip Gaskell's chapter on "Textual Bibliography" (pp. 336-360) in *A New Introduction to Bibliography* provide the kind of basic summary of current thinking which one might expect of an "introduction." Although his exposition of "Copy-Text" (pp. 338-343) does not specifically mention Greg's rationale, he does provide an accurate statement of its general application, with one important exception.[95] He is unwilling to push that rationale to its logical conclusion and recognize that a fair-copy manuscript, when it survives, becomes the copy-text, except when there is convincing evidence pointing toward the first (or some later) edition as the proper choice.[96] His argument rests on the same assumption as Thorpe's:

Most authors, in fact, expect their spelling, capitalization, and punctuation to be corrected or supplied by the printer, relying on the process to dress

95. Bowers, in his review of Gaskell, "McKerrow Revisited," *PBSA*, 67 (1973), 109-124, speaks of Gaskell's "rejection of Greg's classic theory of copy-text" (p. 122). But Gaskell does not reject it totally: his explanation of the difference between substantives and accidentals and of the reason for choosing an early text as authority for accidentals is obviously derived from Greg. What Gaskell rejects is the logical extension back to the manuscript of the steps that led to the choice of the first edition over a later edition as copy-text. Cf. my review in *Costerus*, n.s. 1 (1974).

96. The separate question of whether different versions of a work exist, each deserving to be edited separately from different copy-texts, is touched on by Gaskell in a somewhat confusing way. Near the beginning of the chapter he calls it "an anomaly of bibliographical scholarship today" that "much effort is expended" on editing works "of which the early texts differ from each other only in minor and frequently trivial ways," while "books of which we have texts in several widely different forms are either avoided by editors or edited in a single version" (p. 337). If "single version" means one of the author's versions, the process would seem to be what the situation probably calls for; if it means (as

the context suggests) an eclectic or "critical" text, one would have to say that such a text might be, but would not necessarily be, inappropriate—depending on the way in which the forms of the work are "widely different," whether as a result of a large number of changes or as a result of the nature of what changes there are. That Gaskell is thinking primarily in quantitative terms is shown later in the chapter. In discussing authorial revision of printed texts (p. 341), he states that the first edition remains the copy-text, provided that the author did not revise the punctuation and provided that "the revision [of substantives] is not extensive (say no more than a word or two in each paragraph)." Similarly, after describing the extensive revisions of *Pamela* (citing 8400 changes in the first two volumes of the last version), he asserts, "Here it would obviously be impossible for an editor to incorporate the first, the intermediate, and the final versions of the novel in a single critical text" (p. 342). Maybe so, but the reason is not the sheer number of changes; for only the nature of the differences, and not merely their quantity, can justify regarding two versions of a work as, in effect, separate works. I discuss this point further in my forthcoming article on "The Editorial Problem of Final Authorial Intention."

the text suitably for publication, implicitly endorsing it (with or without further amendment) when correcting proofs.   (p. 339)

He concludes that it "would normally be wrong, therefore, rigidly[97] to follow the accidentals of the manuscript, which the author would himself have been prepared—or might have preferred—to discard" and asserts that "in most cases the editor will choose as copy-text an early printed edition, not the manuscript" (p. 340). Later, he reiterates that "the manuscript if it survives, will be consulted but will not be followed in accidentals unless the compositor appears to have misrepresented the author's intentions" (p. 358). Although he allows for situations in which the manuscript is the proper choice, he places the presumption of authority with the first printed text. I have already commented on the difficulties of maintaining such a position, but I should perhaps call attention to the way in which Gaskell's wording itself reveals some of them. To say that an author is "implicitly endorsing" the accidentals of the proofs when he lets them stand is not at all the same as to say that he prefers them, and it ignores the economic (and other) factors which may have influenced his decision; similarly, to believe that an author "would himself have been prepared . . . to discard" the accidentals of his manuscript is not the same as to believe that he wished to discard them, and it surely does not give an editor license to carry out that discarding. Gaskell asserts that the accidentals of a first edition, despite "the process of normalization carried out in the printing house," will "still be closer both to the text that the author wanted, and to the reading of his manuscript, than the altered accidentals of the second and third editions" (p. 340). This statement is true, but the reference to manuscript readings undermines the general argument: if there is any desirability in having the accidentals resemble those of the manuscript, then the manuscript ought to be chosen for copy-text in the first place; on the other hand, if the author's preference is for the first-edition readings, then the manuscript is irrelevant in this context. Gaskell raises further doubts in the reader's mind by citing the example of Thomas Hardy, who, "in revising his printed texts for new editions, appears to have changed the normalized accidentals back to the forms of the original manuscript" (p. 342). Even though Hardy may not be a typical case, his revision illustrates the point that a writer may acquiesce in printing- or publishing-house styling without preferring it. Is not the more reasonable approach,

97. Of course, "rigidly" prejudices the case, since an editor who "rigidly" followed the manuscript, or any other text, without regard for the specific evidence involved would plainly be in the wrong.

then, to presume, until contrary evidence is adduced, that a manuscript reflects the author's intentions in accidentals, rather than to begin with the presumption that it does not?

A further confusion is introduced by the argument that an author's accidentals may stand in need of correction. Gaskell doubts "whether it is worth preserving thoroughly bad punctuation just because it is the author's" (p. 358) and later advises, "Let us carry out the author's intentions wherever we can, but not to the extent of taking pride in reproducing the manifest inadequacies of his accidentals" (p. 359). But punctuation which seems "bad" to the editor may have seemed appropriate to the author; and if the editor's aim is to preserve what the author wrote, rather than his own "improvements" upon it, he cannot very well say that he will pursue the author's intention only up to a point, and no farther. Gaskell's belief that "an editor may reasonably aim at consistency in his final version" (p. 358) suggests that he is thinking of a modernized text,[98] although most of his comments seem to be concerned with editions that aim to recover the author's intentions. At any rate, it is true that his discussion never focuses on the differences in purpose between modernized and unmodernized texts:

Printed accidentals are unlikely to have had more than the general approval of the author, and if they seem to be both unsatisfactory and in contravention of the author's usual practice, the editor will have to emend them. (Whether he will emend them according to the conventions of the author's period or to those of his own is something else which he will have to decide.) (p. 360)

The illogic of this passage results from the fact that two kinds of editions are being talked about simultaneously. Since "unsatisfactory" accidentals may not be "in contravention of the author's usual practice," the editor is being instructed here to emend only those "unsatisfactory" accidentals which are not characteristic of the author, thus producing a partially regularized, but not modernized, text. But when he has done that, he does not still have open to him the option of

---

98. That regularizing or normalizing amounts to modernizing has been made clear by Hershel Parker in "Regularizing Accidentals: The Latest Form of Infidelity," *Proof*, 3 (1973), 1-20. Furthermore, as he says in his cogent concluding section on the dangers of modernizing, "Normalizing to satisfy an editor's instinct for tidiness or to make smooth the way of a reader is ultimately demeaning for the editor and insulting to the reader." I have made some further comments on regularizing in "Bibliographical Problems in Melville," *Studies in American Fiction*, 2 (1974), 57-74, and in "The New Editions of Hawthorne and Crane," *Book Collector*, 23 (1974), 214-229.

emending "according to the conventions . . . of his own" period—that is, of modernizing. After all, there would be no point in selecting the readings in need of emendation on the basis of whether they are uncharacteristic of the author and then to emend them on the basis of present-day practice. Either the editor decides to establish, as accurately as he can, the author's own accidentals; or he decides to make all the accidentals conform to the practice of his own time. The fact that the former approach is necessary for scholarly (that is, historical) study does not, of course, mean that there may not be occasions on which the latter is more appropriate. But the failure to distinguish carefully between the two cannot lead to clear thinking about editorial problems. It is unfortunate that Gaskell's discussion gives the impression of describing (as one would expect an "introduction" to describe) current generally accepted practice; beginners who turn to it for guidance will be puzzled and misled.[99]

This account of the CEAA's application of Greg's rationale to American literature and of the critical reaction to it suggests several observations. To begin with, one must recognize that, when Wilson expressed surprise at the "violence and venom" of the correspondence

99. A third book of a general and introductory nature which appeared in 1972 is F. W. Bateson's *The Scholar-Critic: An Introduction to Literary Research.* Although not limited to bibliographical and textual matters, as Thorpe and Gaskell are, it contains a chapter on "Textual Criticism" (pp. 126-146) which belittles the " 'biblio-textual' school" of Greg and his followers (for supposedly attempting to eliminate literary judgment from editing) and endorses modernized texts. His argument for modernization seems strangely inconsistent with his own general position. He begins by labeling as a fallacy the view that "the ability to compose great literature necessarily carries with it the ability to spell and punctuate it correctly" (p. 139). But he later makes the sensible distinction between "good English" and "correct English," and it would seem that the attempt to enforce "correct" punctuation (by whatever standard) on an author's work would reveal as petty an attitude as to wish that he had been more "correct," and perhaps less effective, in his wording. And if printed literature is to be considered a recorded form of oral language—as Bateson describes it in "Modern Bibliography and the Literary Artifact," in *English Studies Today,* 2nd ser. (1961), pp. 67-77, from which part of this chapter is drawn—it would seem that punctuation would have to be regarded as an inextricable part of the effort to convey nuances of meaning in print. When he recommends that accidentals "should always be modernized" except when "such a process affects the meaning" (p. 142), it does not seem unreasonable to conclude that his statement amounts to saying that accidentals should never be modernized. That we can understand Shakespeare without reading him in his own pronunciation—a point cited by Bateson in support of his position—is irrelevant; for, while the pronunciation of words does not, within limits, seriously affect their meaning, the way in which we are directed to speak them by the punctuation does frequently affect it. (Bateson has also expressed his view of modernizing in a letter to the *TLS,* 1 January 1971, pp. 14-15.)

aroused by his article, he was calling attention to characteristics which have unfortunately been manifested by a number of persons in this debate, on both sides. It may be gratifying to some editors to find that people care enough about editing to become emotionally involved in theoretical discussions, but scholarship is not advanced by arguments which rest on preconceptions or vested interests or clashes of personality. There can be no doubt that some of this debate has sunk to that level, and the opponents of CEAA policy are not the only ones at fault. What is particularly unfortunate is that so much time and energy has been poured into arguments about superficial or nonexistent issues, when there are so many issues of importance that remain to be considered. The belief that bibliographical and textual work is not humanistic simply because it tries to establish facts or utilizes mechanical aids—and that those engaged in it therefore do not really care about literature—is obviously an emotional rallying cry, not a proposition to be seriously entertained. Similarly, the view that editors who follow Greg are engaged in a mysterious, complex procedure with an elaborate, arcane terminology can only be regarded as an invention of those who are temperamentally disinclined to perform editorial work, for it would be uncharitable to believe that they actually find these concepts and terms a strain on the intelligence. As emotional reactions, these attitudes are understandable, and proponents of Greg's theory have sometimes done their part to provoke them; but as intellectual arguments, there is simply nothing to them.

I am not suggesting that the entire controversy has been frivolous; but even the more serious arguments have so often resulted from a misunderstanding of what is really an uncomplicated approach that one is puzzled to account for them in any but emotional terms. Neither am I saying that Greg's theory and the CEAA application of it ought not to be criticized and analyzed, for any serious intellectual position can only benefit from thoughtful constructive criticism. The point, indeed, is that there has been too little—scarcely any—of this kind of criticism. Yet much of fundamental importance remains to be thought about. The question of what is meant by authorial intention, of how that intention affects the treatment of punctuation, of what differences may be required in working with a typescript rather than a holograph manuscript—such matters as these, when disentangled from self-serving attacks on or defenses of particular editions, need more discussion. Now that a considerable interest in editorial matters has been aroused, a great deal can be accomplished if the collective effort of those interested is expended constructively. No one pretends to have solved all the problems, but solutions can best be approached by a positive effort to understand what accomplishments have so far been achieved and to build on them. Presumably all readers are interested in seeing reliable texts of American literary works made widely available; it would be unfortunate if those who share a common goal allowed themselves to be diverted by controversy from keeping that goal at the center of their attention and working together to attain it.[100]

---

100. While the present paper was in proof, another essay critical of Greg's theory appeared. Vinton A. Dearing, in "Concepts of Copy-Text Old and New," *Library*, 5th ser., 28 (1973), 281-293, argues that Greg's procedure, by emphasizing an early text rather than a later one, "implies that a scribe or compositor regularly puts more errors into a text than the author takes out of his copy" (p. 293). Actually, of course, it implies no more than that errors do creep into a text as it is transmitted; each variant must still be given careful individual attention. Dearing's proposed solution raises many more questions than it answers: "Count the changes certainly made by the author and those certainly made by the scribe or compositor, and assign the rest to the cause with the greater total." I trust that it is unnecessary to enumerate the difficulties which such a statement involves. Still another relevant essay which appeared too late to be cited above is "The CEAA: An Interim Assessment," by Hershel Parker with Bruce Bebb, *PBSA*, 68 (1974), 129-148, which offers succinct evaluations of the CEAA editions in respect to design, arrangement of material, textual policies, and the provision of historical essays.

The Editorial Problem of Final Authorial Intention

S CHOLARLY EDITORS MAY DISAGREE ABOUT MANY THINGS, BUT THEY are in general agreement that their goal is to discover exactly what an author wrote and to determine what form of his work he wished the public to have. There may be some difference of opinion about the best way of achieving that goal; but if the edition is to be a work of scholarship—a historical reconstruction—the goal itself must involve the author's "intention." The centrality of that concept to scholarly editing can be illustrated by W. W. Greg's "The Rationale of Copy-Text,"[1] which, in the quarter century since it first appeared, has established itself as the most influential document in modern editorial theory. What Greg succeeded in accomplishing was to provide a rationale for selecting, and then emending, a basic text in those cases in which the choice was not made obvious by the histori-

* An earlier version of this essay was written in the spring of 1968 for the first volume of *Bibliographia*, a journal then proposed for publication by Oliver & Boyd of Edinburgh. The plans for that journal have now been canceled by Oliver & Boyd, who have ceased the publication of works of this nature; and I am publishing the essay here, considerably revised. I mention this background only because I have alluded in print to an article with this title as "forthcoming in *Bibliographia*"; such citations should now be taken to refer to the article printed here.

1. *SB*, 3 (1950-51), 19-36; reprinted, with a few revisions, in Greg's *Collected Papers*, ed. J. C. Maxwell (1966), pp. 374-391. Cf. Fredson Bowers, "Current Theories of Copy-Text," *Modern Philology*, 48 (1950-51), 12-20; and "McKerrow's Editorial Principles for Shakespeare Reconsidered," *Shakespeare Quarterly*, 6 (1955), 309-324. For a detailed examination of Greg's position and of the commentators upon it, see G. T. Tanselle, "Greg's Theory of Copy-Text and the Editing of American Literature," *SB*, 28 (1975), 167-229. The Center for Editions of American Authors of the Modern Language Association of America has published a manual based on Greg's approach, *Statement of Editorial Principles and Procedures* (rev. ed., 1972); an appended essay, "Relevant Textual Scholarship," pp. 17-25, conveniently draws together references to many of the discussions of Greg's theory or of editions based on it.

cal, biographical, bibliographical, and linguistic evidence available. In such instances, an editor requires some guiding principle by means of which he can maximize the chances of adopting what the author wrote and minimize the chances of incorporating unauthorized readings into his text. Greg's now celebrated solution rests on the position that, if a finished manuscript of a text does not survive, the copy-text for a scholarly edition should normally be the text of the earliest extant printed edition based on the missing manuscript, for it can be expected to reproduce more of the characteristics of the manuscript than any edition further removed; variants from later editions which are convincingly shown to be revisions by the author can then be incorporated into this copy-text. Because authors who revise their work do not always give as much attention to what Greg calls "accidentals" (matters of spelling and punctuation) as to "substantives" (the words themselves)—and because such attention is in any event extremely difficult to determine—the copy-text usually remains the authority for accidentals; and if an editor adopts as authorial certain substantive variants in a later edition, he need not adopt all the other variants in that edition. Following this plan, the editor has a rational means for deciding among indifferent variants (he retains the copy-text readings); and the resulting critical text should be closer to the author's intention than any individual surviving form of the text.

Although Greg did not address himself to the question of a precise definition of "author's intention," it is clear from such a summary that he considered the goal of an edition—and he was speaking of an "old-spelling critical edition"—to be the reconstruction of a text representing the author's final wishes about the version of his work to be presented to the public. In Fredson Bowers's words, the task is "to approximate as nearly as possible an inferential authorial fair copy, or other ultimately authoritative document";[2] or, as he put it another time, following Greg's theory will produce "the nearest approximation in every respect of the author's final intentions."[3] If an author can be shown to have gone over his work with scrupulous care for a revised edition, examining accidentals as well as substantives, the revised edition (as the closest edition to an "ultimately authoritative document") would become the copy-text. Such a situation does not arise in most

2. "Textual Criticism," in *The Aims and Methods of Scholarship in Modern Languages and Literatures,* ed. James Thorpe (rev. ed., 1970), p. 33. Cf. his *Textual and Literary Criticism* (1959), p. 120: a critical edition attempts "to approach as nearly as may be to the ideal of the authorial fair copy."

3. "Some Principles for Scholarly Editions of Nineteenth-Century American Authors," *SB,* 17 (1964), 227.

instances, but Greg recognized its importance: "The fact is," he said, "that cases of revision differ so greatly in circumstances and character that it seems impossible to lay down any hard and fast rule as to when an editor should take the original edition as his copy-text and when the revised reprint" (p. 390). In other words, an editor cannot avoid making judgments about the author's intention on the basis of the available evidence; the strength of those judgments, in turn, will depend on his historical knowledge and his literary sensitivity.[4] The job of a scholarly editor, therefore, can be stated as the exercise of critical thinking in an effort to determine the final intention of an author with respect to a particular text.[5]

Just what is meant by "author's final intention," however, has not been made entirely clear, although at first glance the concept may seem so self-evident as not to require formal definition. Its use in connection with editing suggests that an editor's task is not to "improve" upon an author's decisions, even when he believes that the author made an unwise revision, and that an editor's judgment is directed toward the recovery of what the author wrote, not toward an evaluation of the effectiveness of the author's revisions.[6] Furthermore, the concept, as a goal of editing, would seem clearly to imply that, when an editor has strong reason to attribute a revision to the author, he will accept that revision as "final" on the grounds that, coming second, it represents the author's considered and more mature judgment. Greg suggests that this procedure is equally valid for dealing with wholesale revision when he writes, "If a work has been entirely rewritten, and is printed from a new manuscript, . . . the revised edition will be a substantive one, and as such will presumably be chosen by the editor as his copy-text" (p. 389).

It is true that, in many instances, the simple interpretation of

4. I have made further comments on the role of judgment in editing in "Textual Study and Literary Judgment," *PBSA*, 65 (1971), 109-122.

5. It is convenient to use the word "author" in such statements as this. But nothing said here or elsewhere in this essay is meant to imply that scholarly editing is not also appropriate for anonymous works or works which are the product of an oral tradition. One can infer an "author" who created a given work even if a particular name is not attached to him or if "author" has to be defined as encom-passing a number of people; in such cases, it is still meaningful to set as a goal the historical reconstruction of the text which reflects the intention (as defined below) of its creator(s) at a particular time. Cf. note 68 below.

6. Sometimes the literary effectiveness of a variant reading is used as an argument that the revision is authorial; but it is fallacious to assume that an author's revisions will always result in improvements (as judged by the editor or present-day scholars) and that no one else was capable of making such improvements.

"final intention" to mean that intention reflected in the last alterations made or proposed by the author is workable enough and results in no ambiguity as to the aim of the editorial process. Nevertheless, such an interpretation does not answer certain theoretical questions which can assume practical importance in the remaining instances. Two basic kinds of situations particularly require further consideration: cases where the editor must distinguish authorial alterations from alterations made by someone else and must decide what constitutes "authorial intention" at such times; and cases where the editor faces alterations unquestionably made by the author but must still decide which readings represent the author's "final intention." In what follows I shall offer some preliminary comments on these two situations. But it is necessary to begin with at least a brief consideration of the meaning of "intention" for this purpose and with some recognition of the critical implications of attempting to discover "authorial intention."

I

The question of the meaning of "intention," both in general terms and in relation to works of art, involves many complex philosophical issues and has been widely debated.[7] Probably the best-known and most influential discussion of this subject in relation to literary works is W. K. Wimsatt and Monroe C. Beardsley's 1946 essay, "The Intentional Fallacy," which takes the point of view that the author's intention is irrelevant to the process of literary interpretation and evaluation.[8] Although the essay is not as clear as it might be in dis-

---

7. Many of the general philosophical discussions do not take up the specific case of intention in literature (or in art generally), but such discussions may nevertheless provide some useful background by showing ways of approaching the subject. Two well-known works of this kind are G. E. M. Anscombe, *Intention* (1957; 2nd ed., 1963); and Jack W. Meiland, *The Nature of Intention* (1970), which includes a checklist of related studies on pp. 131-134. A general treatment of the theoretical basis for connecting intention and art is provided in Anthony Savile's "The Place of Intention in the Concept of Art," *Proceedings of the Aristotelian Society*, 69 (1968-69), 101-124.

8. *Sewanee Review*, 54 (1946), 468-488;

reprinted in Wimsatt's *The Verbal Icon* (1954), pp. 3-18. They first set forth their position in the article on "Intention" in *Dictionary of World Literature*, ed. Joseph T. Shipley (1943), pp. 326-329; the criticism of this article by Ananda K. Coomaraswamy in "Intention," *American Bookman*, 1, no. 1 (Winter 1944), 41-48, was in part responsible for their elaborating their argument in the now famous essay. Since that time, each has restated and offered further comments upon the position. Beardsley began his *Aesthetics* (1958) with a section on "The Artist's Intention," pp. 17-29, 66-69; and more recently he has published *The Possibility of Criticism* (1970). And Wimsatt has made a "reentry into the debate" with "Genesis: A Fallacy Revisited," in *The Disciplines of Criticism*,

tinguishing among kinds of intention, it has become a classic statement of the position that the critic should not be influenced in his examination of the literary work itself by any information relating to what the author thought he was saying in that work. Other writers have argued the opposing view—notably E. D. Hirsch, Jr., whose *Validity in Interpretation* (1967) supports the position that the meaning of a work is the meaning put there by the author.[9] Discussions of this kind, however, regularly take the text as given and focus on the activity of the critic as he faces that text; they do not raise the question of the authority of the text itself, apparently assuming that the text in each case is the text as the author wished it to be.[10] Of course, a

ed. Peter Demetz, Thomas Greene, and Lowry Nelson, Jr. (1968), pp. 193-225. A great many discussions of the Wimsatt-Beardsley view have been published. Among the adverse criticisms, valuable essays are Eliseo Vivas's review of *Verbal Icon*, "Mr. Wimsatt on the Theory of Literature," *Comparative Literature*, 7 (1955), 344-361; William H. Capitan's examination of Beardsley's *Aesthetics*, "The Artist's Intention," *Revue internationale de philosophie*, 18 (1964), 323-334; and Michael Hancher's review of *The Possibility of Criticism* in *Journal of Aesthetics and Art Criticism* [*JAAC*], 30 (1971-72), 391-394. Leslie Fiedler's "Archetype and Signature: A Study of the Relationship between Biography and Poetry," *Sewanee Review*, 60 (1952), 253-273, which takes a view opposed to Wimsatt and Beardsley, led to the discussion of both essays by Emilio Roma III, "The Scope of the Intentional Fallacy," *Monist*, 50 (1966), 250-266; and Frank Cioffi's "Intention and Interpretation in Criticism," *Proceedings of the Aristotelian Society*, 64 (1963-64) 84-106, brought a rejoinder from Beardsley in a review in *JAAC*, 26 (1967-68), 144-146. Generally favorable responses are R. Jack Smith, "Intention in an Organic Theory of Poetry," *Sewanee Review*, 56 (1948), 625-633; and Rosemarie Maier, "'The Intentional Fallacy' and the Logic of Literary Criticism," *College English*, 32 (1970-71), 135-145 (with comments by Michael Hancher and Maier in the following volume, pp. 343-348).

9. Hirsch's argument had earlier appeared in "Objective Interpretation," *PMLA*, 75 (1960), 463-479, an essay included as an appendix in his book, pp. 209-244. The book, as an important and thoughtful statement of a position which has been unpopular since the advent of the New Criticism, has naturally been the subject of a great deal of discussion. Among the important reviews of the book are those by George Dickie, *JAAC*, 26 (1967-68), 550-552, and Robert Scholes, *Philological Quarterly*, 47 (1968), 280-283. The July 1968 number of *Genre* (1: 169-255) was devoted to "A Symposium" on the book, with contributions by Monroe C. Beardsley, George Dickie, Morse Peckham, Gale H. Carrithers, Jr., Leo Rockas, Arthur Efron, Merle E. Brown, and John Huntley. The following March Hirsch replied with "The Norms of Interpretation—A Brief Response," *Genre*, 2 (1969), 57-62; and he has recently offered a further elaboration of some of his ideas in "Three Dimensions of Hermeneutics," *New Literary History*, 3 (1971-72), 245-261. Morse Peckham discusses both the Wimsatt-Beardsley essay and Hirsch's book in "The Intentional? Fallacy?", *New Orleans Review*, 1 (1968-69), 116-124, reprinted in *The Triumph of Romanticism* (1970), pp. 421-444.

10. For instance, Wimsatt, recognizing that the contents of a work may be used to learn something about the author, says, "For whatever does get into a poem presumably is put there by the poet and reflects *something* in the poet's personality

corrupt text could equally well be the subject of critical analysis;[11] but the question of the bearing of authorial intention on interpretation would hardly arise unless the text is assumed to be what its author wished.

One might at first conclude, therefore, that such discussions of intention are irrelevant to editorial work, conceived of as operating at an anterior stage and providing the material for the critic to analyze. If, in other words, one could assert that the editor's task does not involve critical decisions but only the recovery of factual information about what word or mark of punctuation the author wanted to have at each point in his text, one could then say that any effort to understand or assess the "meaning" of the text is an entirely separate matter and that the possibility of an "intentional fallacy" applies only to this interpretive and evaluative activity.[12] It is immediately apparent, however, that the job of the editor cannot be so regarded. If the aim of the editor is to establish the text as the author wished to have it presented to the public (and we shall postpone any consideration of other possible editorial aims), he cannot divorce himself from the "meaning" of the text, for, however much documentary evidence he may have, he can never have enough to relieve himself of the neces-

---

and life" ("Genesis: A Fallacy Revisited," p. 199). But the role of the editor is precisely to try to remove that "presumably" and to present a text consisting of what was in fact put there by the author. Similarly, Marcia Muelder Eaton, in "Good and Correct Interpretations of Literature," *JAAC*, 29 (1970-71), 227-233, remarks, "For purposes of simplicity I am assuming that the speaker uttered the words he meant to utter, i.e., that there were no slips of the tongue. This is certainly not too much to assume, since our main interest here is literature, and we certainly make such assumptions with respect to literary works" (p. 230). But slips of the author's pen or the compositor's hand, not later caught by the author, are the equivalent of "slips of the tongue" and certainly do occur in printed matter.

11. Throughout this essay I use "critical" in the common sense of "entailing judgment"—the sense which the word carries in the term "critical edition." I am not, that is to say, using "criticism" in the spe-

cial sense which Hirsch (*Validity in Interpretation*, pp. 210-211) gives to it in his distinction between "interpretation" and "criticism," where the first means "the construction of textual meaning as such" ("the *meaning* of the text") and the second "builds on the results of interpretation," confronting "textual meaning not as such, but as a component within a larger context" ("the *significance* of the text"). I do not discuss here (except briefly near the end of section III) editions which are not critical—editions, that is, which present exact transcriptions of particular texts and which do not involve the editor's judgment in emending those texts.

12. This view is expressed by Rosemarie Maier (see note 8 above): "it is extremely unlikely that the determination of a text to criticize is actually literary criticism; textual decisions, unless they are the result of criticism of each version as an individual poem, are actually pre-critical decisions" (p. 144).

sity of reading critically. Suppose, for example, that the only extant text of a work is a fair-copy manuscript in the author's hand. The editor in such a case cannot simply reproduce the text mechanically, without thinking about its meaning: there is always the possibility that the author, through an oversight or slip of the pen, did not write down what he meant to write, and the editor who is reading critically may be able to detect and correct such errors, or at least some of them. It is an act of criticism, however elementary, for an editor to recognize that where the author wrote "the the" he actually meant "to the." In other instances it may be equally obvious that the author cannot have meant what he wrote, and yet it may be impossible to say with certainty which of several possible corrections conforms with what he had in mind. Yet the editor will probably find it necessary to make *some* correction, since the reading of the manuscript is plainly wrong. When two or more texts of a work exist and there are differences between them, there may be no conclusive evidence to show which differences are the result of the author's revisions and which are not. Yet the editor must decide which of the readings to accept at each point of variation. These decisions are based both on whatever external evidence is available and on the editor's judgment as to how the author was most likely to have expressed himself at any given point. This judgment in turn is based on the editor's familiarity with and sensitivity to the whole corpus of the author's work and on his understanding of the individual work involved. He may be specifically concerned only with the author's intended meaning in one sentence, or even one phrase, but the interpretation of that sentence or phrase may depend upon the author's intended meaning in the work as a whole.

It is clear, then, as soon as one starts to talk about "intention," that various kinds of intention need to be distinguished, and many of the recent discussions of intention in literature do attempt to subdivide the concept. Thus T. M. Gang differentiates between "practical intention" (intention "to achieve a certain result") and "literary intention" (intention to convey "a certain significance"); John Kemp distinguishes between "immediate intention" (that which a man "intends, or sets himself, to do") and "ulterior intention" ("that which he intends or hopes to achieve as a result of doing what he does"); Morse Peckham discriminates between "mediated intention" ("a statement or other sign") and "immediate intention" ("metaphorical extension of mediated intention into the area of 'mind' "); and Quentin Skinner, borrowing terms from J. L. Austin's *How to Do*

Things with Words (1962),[13] speaks of "illocutionary intention" (what a writer "may have been intending to do *in* writing what he wrote") and "perlocutionary intention" ("what he may have intended to do *by* writing in a certain way"), as well as of "intention to do x" (a writer's "plan or design to a create a certain type of work").[14]

Of such classifications of intention, one of the clearest and most useful has been set forth by Michael Hancher.[15] In his view, "author's intentions" can be divided into three types: (1) "programmatic intention"—"the author's intention to make something or other"; (2) "active intention"—"the author's intention to be (understood as) acting in some way or other"; and (3) "final intention"—"the author's intention to cause something or other to happen." The first refers to the author's general plan to write a sonnet, say, or a realistic novel;

13. This influential treatment of meaning (edited by J. O. Urmson from Austin's notes for the 1955 William James Lectures) provides a useful terminology for discussing speech acts. A "locutionary" act involves only the "performance of an act *of* saying something"; an "illocutionary" act involves the "performance of an act *in* saying something" (p. 99); and a "perlocutionary" act involves "what we bring about or achieve *by* saying something" (p. 109). Another important account of meaning, taking an intentionalist approach (based on the idea that language consists of "non-natural" signs which are given an "occasion-meaning" by a speaker), is H. P. Grice's "Meaning," *Philosophical Review*, 66 (1957), 377-388, supplemented by his "Utterer's Meaning and Intentions," *Philosophical Review*, 78 (1969), 147-177. There have been a considerable number of papers which build upon or analyze Austin's and Grice's contributions. Austin has been used by, among others, William P. Alston in *Philosophy of Language* (1964), esp. pp. 34-49 (cf. his "Linguistic Acts," *American Philosophical Quarterly*, 1 [1964], 138-146), and John R. Searle in *Speech Acts* (1969), esp. pp. 54-71; and Michael Hancher has illustrated the usefulness of the concept of illocutionary acts in analyzing literature in "Understanding Poetic Speech Acts," *College English*, 36 (1974-75), 632-639. A "largely destructive criticism" of Grice which is of particular interest to students of literature is Max Black's "Meaning and Intention: An Examination of

Grice's Views," *New Literary History*, 4 (1972-73), 257-279 (which also contains a listing of many of the previous commentaries on Grice). Marcia Eaton has contributed a checklist of material on speech-act theory to *Centrum*, 2, no. 2 (Fall 1974).

14. The essays referred to are Gang, "Intention," *Essays in Criticism*, 7 (1957), 175-186; Kemp, "The Work of Art and the Artist's Intentions," *British Journal of Aesthetics*, 4 (1964), 146-154; Peckham, "Reflections on the Foundations of Modern Textual Editing," *Proof*, 1 (1971), 122-155 (see p. 152; Peckham discusses these matters at greater length, but does not use these particular terms, in "The Intentional? Fallacy?", cited in note 9 above); Skinner, "Motives, Intentions and the Interpretation of Texts," *New Literary History*, 3 (1971-72), 393-408. See also Richard Kuhns, "Criticism and the Problem of Intention," *Journal of Philosophy*, 57 (1960), 5-23, which distinguishes "intention as aiming at a result" from "intention as the conveying of a meaning." George Whalley prefers to use the term "intension" (which he defines as "the impulsive orientation of the person [author] in a moment of awareness"), because "intention" implies "a disguised attempt to explain the contemplative in terms of the technical" (*Poetic Process* [1953], p. xxvii).

15. "Three Kinds of Intention," *Modern Language Notes*, 87 (1972), 827-851.

the third refers to his hope that his work will change the reader's viewpoint, say, or bring wealth to himself. The second is the one which concerns the meanings embodied in the work: "Active intentions characterize the actions that the author, at the time he finishes his text, understands himself to be performing in that text" (p. 830).[16] Hancher's argument is that the first and third kinds of intention—programmatic and final—are indeed irrelevant to the interpretation of a literary work but that the second—active intention—must be taken into account in the interpretation (and evaluation) of the work.

Before pursuing the implications of that argument, we should pause long enough to note that what editors in the tradition of Greg are likely to call "final intention" does not correspond to what Hancher here calls "final intention." Rather, the intention with which editors are concerned is Hancher's "active intention," the intention that the work "*mean* (and be taken to mean) something or other" (p. 831). The fact that an editor, as briefly suggested above, must examine both the author's intention to use a particular word and the author's intention to mean a particular thing in the work as a whole—indeed, must make decisions about the first in the light of the second—is adequately accommodated in Hancher's concept of "active intention." Hancher's initial illustration of the concept includes comment on Hopkins's intention in using "buckle" in "The Windhover" as well as on his intention for the meaning of "the whole action of that poem." Because an intention regarding the meaning of a work as a whole may not always seem distinct from a programmatic intention, Hancher later recognizes that a programmatic intention may "involve a kind of active intention" (p. 836) but distinguishes between such "*projected* active intention" and the "active intention that ultimately defines the meaning of the completed text" (p. 837). Therefore "active intention," as he defines it, does cover the authorial intentions with which an editor has to deal. Accordingly, whenever I speak of "intention," unless otherwise specified, I am referring to the kind of intention included in Hancher's concept of "active intention"; even when I use the term "final intention," in conformity with the common practice of editors, the word "intention" still refers to the same concept (and not to what Hancher calls "final intention")—though just what "final" may mean in the phrase remains to be examined later.

It can readily be inferred from what I have already said about Hancher's conclusion that he does not belong to that group of critics

16. Active intention thus corresponds to Austin's illocutionary act and to most of the locutionary act (Hancher, pp. 841-842).

who believe in "semantic autonomy" (to use Hirsch's phrase)—the idea that a verbal construction carries its own inherent determinate meaning regardless of what meaning was intended by the author. As Beardsley puts the idea, "texts acquire determinate meaning through the interactions of their words without the intervention of an authorial will."[17] Hancher's argument for the relevance of active intention to literary interpretation shows that he defines "the" meaning of a work as the meaning intended by its author.[18] It is difficult to refute such an argument without taking the position that the language of a literary work operates in a different way from the language of ordinary discourse; yet that position cannot convincingly be taken so long as it is impossible to draw a distinct line between works which are literary and works which are not.[19] Language, after all, consists of

17. *The Possibility of Criticism*, p. 30.

18. His emphasis on "the" in several key statements (e.g., p. 851) implies that other definitions of meaning are possible; indeed, he goes on to make explicit the point that "we may entertain other meanings that seem valuable."

19. Richard Ohmann has attempted to draw such a line in "Speech Acts and the Definition of Literature," *Philosophy and Rhetoric*, 4 (1971), 1-19; and "Speech, Literature, and the Space Between," *New Literary History*, 4 (1972-73), 47-63. His definition of a literary work is "a discourse whose sentences lack the illocutionary forces that would normally attach to them. Its illocutionary force is *mimetic*" (1971, p. 14). He insists that his dividing line is a firm one, but the result is that some utterances not usually regarded as literature (jokes, "ironic rejoinders," "fables within political speeches") fall on the literature side. "Let me simply record my belief," he replies, "that the definition is not severely at fault in admitting the wrong discourses to the category of literature" (p. 16). Cf. his earlier "Speech, Action, and Style," in *Literary Style: A Symposium*, ed. Seymour Chatman (1971), pp. 241-259: "literature can be accurately *defined* as discourse in which the seeming acts are hypothetical" (p. 254). Beardsley takes a similar approach but seems to concede that his dividing line is more sugges-

tive than precise. Literature, he says, is characterized by "its exploitation to a high degree of the illocutionary-act potential of its verbal ingredients"; it is "the complex imitation of a compound illocutionary act" (*The Possibility of Criticism*, p. 61). But he admits that what this amounts to is that a literary work has "richness and complexity of meaning"—or, earlier, that it "directs attention to itself as an object of rewarding scrutiny" (p. 60). More recently he has refined his definition, partly in response to Colin A. Lyas, who (in "The Semantic Definition of Literature," *Journal of Philosophy*, 66 [1969], 81-95) had criticized his previous definition of literature (*Aesthetics*, pp. 126-128) as "a discourse in which an important part of the meaning is implicit." Beardsley now defines "literary discourse" as "discourse that is either an imitation illocutionary act or distinctly above the norm in its ratio of implicit to explicit meaning" (both help to make a discourse "an object of attention in its own right")—see pp. 37-38 of "The Concept of Literature," in *Literary Theory and Structure: Essays in Honor of William K. Wimsatt*, ed. Frank Brady, John Palmer, and Martin Price (1973), pp. 23-39. This kind of definition, it seems to me, does not solve the problem but only shifts the terms in which it is expressed: one still has the problem of distinguishing between real illocutionary acts and imitations of illocutionary acts. Moreover, Marcia Muelder Eaton has shown that the author's inten-

symbols, which must be invested with meanings if they are to mean anything. At the same time, a reader does not have access to an author's mind, and, if he understands a text to mean something, it is (at least to begin with) as a result of certain conventions of language which both are following.[20] Yet texts (or utterances) do not have to be complex in order for the conventions involved to be capable of more than one interpretation. The possibility is raised, therefore, that the meaning or meanings a reader finds in a text do not correspond to the meaning or meanings which the author intended.[21] To reject "semantic autonomy" (or "immanent meaning") is not to deny that texts are capable of multiple interpretations. Indeed, the fact that multiple interpretations are possible is a refutation of the idea that a text embodies a determinate meaning.

How, then, is the author's intended meaning to be discovered? In answering that question, one is inevitably drawn back to the work itself as the most reliable documentary evidence as to what the author intended. If he made no statement setting forth his intention, one has

tion has just as direct a bearing on such imitations of illocutionary acts as on illocutionary acts themselves; she proposes (in an extension of Austin's terminology) that these imitations be called "translocutionary" acts. See "Art, Artifacts, and Intentions," *American Philosophical Quarterly*, 6 (1969), 165-169; and "Good and Correct Interpretations of Literature" (see note 10 above). E. D. Hirsch, in "Some Aims of Criticism" (in the Wimsatt festschrift, pp. 41-62), argues that literature has "no independent essence": "It is an arbitrary classification of linguistic works which do not exhibit common distinctive traits, and which cannot be defined as an Aristotelian species. . . . The idea of literature is not an essentialistic idea" (p. 52). Cf. also *College English*, 36 (1974-75), 453.

20. As Quentin Skinner puts it, "an understanding of conventions, however implicit, must remain a necessary condition for an understanding of all types of speech act." See p. 135 of his "Conventions and the Understanding of Speech Acts," *Philosophical Quarterly*, 20 (1970), 118-138. He later (in the article cited in note 14 above) makes a focus on conventions one of his two rules (along with focus on "the writer's mental world") for recovering in-

tention (pp. 406-407). The role of conventions in understanding is one of the concerns of Karl Aschenbrenner, in "Intention and Understanding," *University of California Publications in Philosophy*, 25 (1950), 229-270. Saussure's distinction between "langue" and "parole," summarized by Hirsch in *Validity in Interpretation*, pp. 231-235 (cf. pp. 69-71, leading into his discussion of "genre"), offers an approach to the relation between the "system of linguistic possibilities" which a language provides ("langue") and an individual utterance made in that language ("parole"). Theories of language are discussed by Morris Weitz in connection with multiple interpretations of a literary work in *Hamlet and the Philosophy of Literary Criticism* (1964), pp. 215-227. See also P. F. Strawson, "Intention and Convention in Speech Acts," *Philosophical Review*, 73 (1964), 439-460, and other discussions of Grice alluded to in note 13 above.

21. Geoffrey Payzant expresses this idea in broader terms: "Of the shapes that are imposed through skill upon stuff . . . some are devised by the maker and some are not." See p. 157 of "Intention and the Achievement of the Artist," *Dialogue*, 3 (1964-65), 153-159.

nowhere else to go for direct evidence (though of course one can take into account various historical and biographical circumstances); and if he did make a statement, it may, for a great variety of reasons, not be accurate. As Morse Peckham has pointed out, any attempt, by the author or someone else, to explain the intention of a work ("an utterance") constitutes an inference about an event which took place in the past; the author's account carries greater weight "only because he is likely to have more information for framing his historical construct, *not* because he generated the utterance."[22] Furthermore, as William H. Capitan has noted, "what an artist gives us as his intention is subject to the artist's limitations in putting his intention into words."[23] The position has been well stated by Quentin Skinner:

> To discount a writer's own statements is not to say that we have lost interest in gaining a correct statement about his intentions in our attempt to interpret his works. It is only to make the (perhaps rather dramatic, but certainly conceivable) claim that the writer himself may have been self-deceiving about recognizing his intentions, or incompetent at stating them. And this seems to be perennially possible in the case of any complex human action.[24]

Hirsch, who does not recognize as "meanings" any meanings other than the author's, decides what Wordsworth "probably" meant in "A slumber did my spirit seal" by turning to "everything we know of Wordsworth's typical attitudes during the period in which he composed the poem" (p. 239). Contemporary statements about these attitudes may of course be useful, but are not Wordsworth's poems the chief source of information about his attitudes? And if a given body of writings can provide such evidence, is it not possible that a smaller body of writings—or even the single poem—could provide it? As Hirsch

22. "The Intentional? Fallacy?" (see note 9 above), p. 441. Cf. Sidney Gendin, "The Artist's Intentions," *JAAC*, 23 (1964-65), 193-196: "We do expect, much of the time, that authorship or discovery will carry with it expert knowledge. But in such cases it is the knowledge itself which becomes the ground for being the authority; the authorship is not the ground. . . . If an artist has some peculiar knowledge of his work, it is not obvious that this is so merely because he is its creator. We must have some independent means of establishing his expertness" (p. 194). René Wellek says that an author's statements "might not even represent an accurate commentary on his work, and at their best

are not more than such a commentary," in his and Austin Warren's *Theory of Literature* (2nd ed., 1956), p. 137.

23. "The Artist's Intention" (see note 8 above), p. 328.

24. "Motives, Intentions . . ." (see note 14 above), p. 405. Of course, authors' statements may be deliberately deceiving rather than "self-deceiving." Beardsley points out that artists "are often inclined to the most whimsical and bizarre statements [about their work], and seem to enjoy being deliberately misleading"; see p. 292 of his "On the Creation of Art," *JAAC*, 23 (1964-65), 291-304.

admits, "A poet's typical attitudes do not always apply to a particular poem" (p. 240); so one is inevitably thrown back on the poem itself. I do not think it necessary to review here the various arguments for or against "semantic autonomy"[25] in order to make my point: all I am suggesting is that a rejection of the notion of "semantic autonomy" is not incompatible with the position that the work itself provides the best evidence of the author's intended meaning.

The bearing of these ideas on the task of the editor is worth making explicit. At the start, the editor has settled one important question through his definition of his goal: he is concerned with establishing the text as intended by the author, and thus he has no doubts about the relevance of the author's intention to his undertaking. But then he recognizes that the most reliable source of information about the author's intention in a given work is that work itself. He will take other information into account, but he must always measure it finally against the very text which is the subject of his inquiry. The editor may at first feel that his job is different from the critic's in that he is concerned with establishing intended *wording*, not with explicating intended *meaning*. That is, he may think (in Austin's terms) that he is dealing only with the author's locutionary act, not his illocutionary act. But he soon realizes that his discovery of textual errors or his choice among textual variants involves his understanding of the intended meaning of the text. For if either of two alternative words makes sense at a given point, the determination of which the author intended clearly involves more than his locutionary act.[26] Greg's

25. Such as that supporting the idea offered by Beardsley in *The Possibility of Criticism*, pp. 16-37; or those opposing it presented by Hirsch in *Validity in Interpretation*, pp. 10-14, by Peckham in "The Intentional? Fallacy?" (see note 9 above), and by Hancher in "Three Kinds of Intention" (see note 15 above).

26. Coomaraswamy (see note 8 above) makes a similar point: "one can so identify oneself with a subject and point of view that one can foresee what will be said next. . . . If, in fact, one cannot do this, textual emendation would be possible only on grammatical or metrical grounds" (p. 46). Isabel C. Hungerland, too, comments on this matter: "The way in which we interpret (explain and see) a whole literary work may determine our understanding of words (e.g., where there are ambiguous words), of sentences (e.g., where ironic meanings are possible), or of allusions"; see p. 742 of "The Concept of Intention in Art Criticism," *Journal of Philosophy*, 52 (1955), 733-742. Hans Zeller, in "A New Approach to the Critical Constitution of Literary Texts," *SB*, 28 (1975), 231-264, takes the "predictability" of a text as an argument against the use of the text as a key to its author's intention: "To edit the text according to the intention of the author, when the singularities of his intention are known to us only through this text, can be achieved only if the text is in a certain sense redundant, that is to say, predictable. But this condition is fulfilled, as experiments have shown, only in the case of utilitarian texts (e.g., newspaper articles), and not in the case of poetic texts" (p. 259). But this position surely takes "predictability" in too narrow a

rationale tells an editor what to do when he is at an impasse, but it does not eliminate the need for judgments; indeed, it relies on them. So the editor finds himself in the position of the critic after all. Merely because he has already decided that his concern is with the author's intention does not mean that the issue of "semantic autonomy" is irrelevant to him, for he, too, will be turning to the text itself as his primary evidence.

The key to the use of the work as evidence of its author's intended meaning must lie in the approach which the critic (editor) takes.[27] One critic may believe that he has found through internal evidence the most satisfactory explication of a work and may not be interested in whether or not this meaning was intended by the author.[28] Another critic, who wishes to find the author's intended meaning, will read the work in the light of all the historical and biographical evidence he can locate and may thereby eliminate certain meanings as ones which the author could not have intended;[29] his interpretation of the text is thus limited by certain external information, but his positive evidence still comes from the text itself. If I hastily dash off a message for someone and the recipient finds it ambiguous, he will attempt to rule out certain meanings on the basis of what he knows of me and of the circumstances which occasioned the message; what he finally concludes to be my intended meaning, however, cannot be based merely on what the external evidence suggests I would be likely to say in that situation but must rest on the words I actually did use. Furthermore,

---

sense: the fact that "artistic structures . . . themselves transgress the rules or codes which they have set up in the text" does not mean that the critical editor is prevented from seeing when such a transgression is taking place.

27. Henry David Aiken puts the matter this way: "The aesthetic relevance of a particular interpretation . . . can be established only with respect to a certain mode of appreciation, a certain way of approaching and handling the work of art." See p. 748 of "The Aesthetic Relevance of Artists' Intentions," *Journal of Philosophy*, 52 (1955), 742-753.

28. Hirsch admits, "The text sometimes seems so much better if we ignore the author's probable intention or what he probably wrote. Every interpreter has a touch of the medieval commentator look-ing for the best meaning, and every editor has a drop of Bentley's blood. It is not rare that anachronistic meaning on *some* ground or other is undoubtedly the best meaning" ("Three Dimensions of Hermeneutics" [see note 9 above], p. 259).

29. As Cioffi (see note 8 above) says, "biographical facts act as a kind of sieve which exclude certain possibilities" (p. 90); "They can serve the eliminative function of showing that certain interpretations of a work are based on mistaken beliefs about the author's state of knowledge" (p. 92). Similarly, Huw Morris Jones, in "The Relevance of the Artist's Intentions," *British Journal of Aesthetics*, 4 (1964), 138-145, comments, "We can eliminate some interpretations as being such that an artist at a certain period in a certain society could never have intended such meanings" (p. 140).

if I mistakenly wrote one word while intending another, it may be that the external evidence would cast doubt on my use of that word, but any correction of the error would have to be justified by the context. The work itself is the controlling factor in statements made about its meaning, whether or not those statements aim at elucidating the author's intended meaning.

The scholarly editor is in the same position as the critic who is concerned with the author's intended meaning. Regardless of how many meanings he finds in the text, the scholarly editor makes corrections or emendations on the basis of the one he judges most likely to have been the author's intended meaning. Hancher speaks of a *science* of interpretation, in which the critic's aim is to determine the "authorized" or intended meaning, and an *art* of interpretation, in which the critic's aim is to find the most satisfying meaning according to his own "norms of value."[30] Some critics would protest that all meanings are part of an intended complex combination of meanings, intended in the sense that the author, whether consciously or unconsciously, created a structure in which they could be discovered. But this appeal to "subconscious intention," as T. M. Gang has indicated,[31] implies a universal set of relationships between consciously produced patterns and their subconscious origins—relationships which, if they are always in operation, cannot be specifically intended and are always available for anyone to discern. One need not deny that such meanings can be found in the work and that they may be valuable (and offer revealing insights into the author's personality and motivation) in order to believe that "intention" cannot be a useful concept if it is made so broad as to cover all potentially discoverable meanings. It is certainly true that neither the author nor anyone else can construct an explanatory paraphrase which is the exact equivalent of the work itself; but

30. "The Science of Interpretation and the Art of Interpretation," *Modern Language Notes*, 85 (1970), 791-802. The first, he says, involves questions of validity, the second questions of value. A similar distinction is made by Eaton in "Good and Correct Interpretations of Literature" (see note 10 above).

31. "Intention" (see note 14 above), pp. 184-186. Hirsch's principal discussion of "Unconscious and Symptomatic Meanings," on pp. 51-57 of *Validity in Interpretation*, tries to distinguish between those unconscious meanings that are "coherent with the consciously willed type which defines the meaning as a whole" (p. 54) and those that are "symptomatic" of the author's personality, attitudes, and the like. The latter, while interesting and even important, are not part of the "verbal meaning" of a work, whereas the former are a part of it, since they are locatable in a specific "linguistic sign." This dichotomy is of course an application of Hirsch's larger distinction between meaning and significance, but it also serves to illustrate that one cannot escape the primacy of the text itself as a guide to intended meaning. Some criticism of this part of Hirsch's discussion occurs in Beardsley's *The Possibility of Criticism*, pp. 20-21.

it does not follow that the *intended* meanings of the work are inex-
haustible.

An editor could, of course, emend a text so that it would, in his
view, be a more successful expression of that meaning which he finds
most valuable in it; but his activity would have nothing to do with
the author. In Hancher's terms, he would be engaging in the "art"
of interpretation—or, rather, editing on the basis of that kind of interpretation. A scholarly editor sets as his goal the reconstruction of the
text intended by the author. In Hancher's terms, he is engaging in the
"science," not the art, of interpretation—but it is still *interpretation*
and entails critical thinking. His defined approach is what controls the
use he makes of what he finds in the work. He will probably find more
than one meaning there, but his specialized knowledge places him in
a privileged position for assessing which of them can most reasonably
be regarded as the author's.[32] The text he produces can, like any other
text, be the subject of critical speculation by those who have no
interest in the author's intention; but it can also serve the needs of
those critics who are concerned with the work as the product of a
particular mind. That an interpretation by one of the former turns
out to seem more satisfying to many readers than an interpretation
by one of the latter has no bearing on the importance or desirability
of the task which the scholarly editor has set himself.

These considerations suggest, first of all, that editing is a critical
activity and that the scholarly editor cannot avoid coming to terms
with the critical problem of authorial intention. Second, there is a
specific and clearly defined aspect of the broad concept of "intention"
which is the appropriate concern of the scholarly editor—the intention
of the author to have particular words and marks of punctuation
constitute his text and the intention that such a text carry a particular

---

32. Theodore Redpath is making roughly
the same point when he says that "the
probable intention of the poet does at least
sometimes afford a criterion by which to
judge whether a certain meaning which is
attributed to a poem is probably correct
or not." See p. 366 of "Some Problems of
Modern Aesthetics," in *British Philosophy
in the Mid-Century*, ed. C. A. Mace (1957),
pp. 361-390. In other words, the primary
emphasis is on what one finds in the
poem; one can then try to determine
whether it is a possible, and even a probable, meaning for the author, given the
circumstances he was in at the time, to

have intended. Similarly, Savile (see note
7 above) remarks, "At least in the context
of art we know that the temporal and geographical point of origin of the text, the
documents accessible to the artist, and the
cultural climate of his time are all of first
importance in assessing what interpretation
of his text is the best in the circumstances
of its production. . . . With the aid of
hindsight we may get closer to the best
possible contemporary reading than any
contemporary did. We may be helped in
this by later works, or by theories of be-
haviour that make explicit to us what the
artist only dimly intuited" (pp. 122-123).

meaning or meanings. Finally, the scholarly editor will amass all the evidence he can find bearing on each textual decision; but, whenever the factual evidence is less than incontrovertible, his judgment about each element will ultimately rest on his interpretation of the author's intended meaning as he discovers it in the whole of the text itself. What controls the editor's freedom of interpretation is his self-imposed limitation: he is concerned only with that intention which his knowledge of the author and the period allows him to attribute to the author.

II

An editor who has given some attention to such preliminary questions has at least begun to reach an understanding of "authorial intention." But there are a number of further questions which arise as he attempts to make judgments in the light of this conception of intention. Perhaps the most common editorial situation is that in which the editor must decide whether a given variant reading is a revision by the author or an alteration (conscious or inadvertent) by someone else. In these cases, at least one intermediate stage of documentary evidence is lacking, and the editor is trying to determine from the surviving material those changes which the author made in that now missing document. He must also face the question whether it is ever possible to think of changes not made by the author as nevertheless fulfilling, or contributing to, the author's intention.

The basic situation can be illustrated by Sherwood Anderson's *A Story Teller's Story* (1924). The only surviving prepublication text of this work is the typescript printer's copy, which bears revisions by three people: Anderson himself, Paul Rosenfeld, and E. T. Booth, the publisher's editor. One has direct evidence, therefore, for assigning the responsibility for each of these alterations; but the first printing of the book (Huebsch, 1924) contains additional changes, not marked on the surviving typescript and presumably entered on the now lost proofs. Deciding which of these changes were made by Anderson is the central task in editing this book.[33] What the editor has to do is to familiarize himself with all the available relevant evidence—bibliographical, historical, biographical. He may then find that some of it is

---

33. Ray Lewis White's edition (1968), though it is called a "critical text," fails to make these decisions, for it includes in brackets in the text both the passages marked for deletion on the typescript and the further passages deleted in the printed text. I have commented on the shortcomings of this volume and the other volumes in this edition in "The Case Western Reserve Edition of Sherwood Anderson: A Review Article," *Proof*, 4 (1974), 183-209.

convincing enough to dictate certain decisions. For example, on (or just before) 28 October 1924 Anderson wrote to Rosenfeld explaining why he had cut out some material about Waldo Frank.[34] Since several paragraphs about Frank are present in the typescript but not present in the first impression, one can conlude that this is the deletion referred to and that it was made by Anderson on the proofs. But for most of the alterations in the first impression there is no such compelling evidence; most of the editor's decisions must finally be critical judgments, resulting from an evaluation of what evidence there is, from an understanding of Anderson's habits of revision, and from a familiarity with and sensitivity to his style and ideas. Even the deleted Waldo Frank passage leads the editor to a related judgment, for that deletion is only a part of a considerably longer deletion made in the first impression. Because the entire passage concerns Anderson's reactions to various writers, one may conclude that he probably eliminated all of it, and not merely the part about Frank which he happened to mention to Rosenfeld. But that conclusion is a judgment, supported by a critical argument, not by verifiable facts.

The same observations can be made about situations involving variants between printed editions. In these cases the missing documents are the author's marked copy of the earlier edition (or its proofs, or whatever served as printer's copy for the edition set later) and the marked proofs of the later edition. If no document survives which antedates the proofs of the earliest setting of the text, then of course one is dealing wth texts which have already been subjected to the routine of the printing- or publishing-house. Thus the essential difference between this situation and the one described above is that here the editor is working at a greater remove from the author's faircopy manuscript or typescript; but his approach to the problem remains the same. For instance, neither the manuscript of *The Rise of Silas Lapham* nor the proofs set from it survive; and the history of the early printed texts, which vary from one another substantively at a number of points, is such that one text might contain the later readings in one part of the book and another the later readings in a different part. So for any given variant, the editor must first try to determine the order of the readings and then decide whether the later one could be an authorial revision or correction. At one point in Chapter 19 Irene's complexion is described as "snow-white" in the serialized magazine text and as "colourless" in the first book edition

34. See Walter B. Rideout's review of in *English Language Notes*, 7 (1969-70), White's edition of *A Story Teller's Story* 70-73.

(set from proofs of the magazine text); since the publication schedule for the book made it highly unlikely that the book proofs of the last part (Chapters 19-27) were given a proofreading by anyone outside the printer's or publisher's offices and since there was an opportunity for second magazine proofs of this part to be gone over later, one can reasonably conclude (barring the unlikely possibility that "colourless" is simply a compositorial error or that the book publisher's editor engaged in this kind of revision) that the magazine reading "snow-white" is the later reading here. Deciding that it was in fact Howells's alteration is of course a matter of judgment, but a judgment made within the limits imposed by the factual evidence.[35] In the case of *Moby-Dick*, those limits are wider, because it is known that the publisher's reader for the English edition made numerous substantive alterations and that Melville also had the opportunity to make revisions for that edition; distinguishing the two categories can result only from critical judgments as to which kinds of changes are likely to have been made by a somewhat pedantic reader concerned with expurgation and which are more characteristic of Melville.[36] Fredson Bowers makes the same point in connection with Fielding's *Miscellanies*, where some parts of the first edition were set from marked copies (not extant) of printed periodical texts: "This is a critical process almost exclusively, with only occasional bibliographical guidance, in which the editor shoulders his proper responsibility to separate the author's intended alterations from the verbal corruption that inevitably accompanies the transmission of a text."[37] Sometimes a statistical analysis of internal evidence can be of material assistance in making a critical choice among variants: tabulating the pattern of recurrences of unusual spellings and other features in Shakespearean texts can help to determine which characteristics of those texts derive from the compositors' preferences and which from the printer's copy itself;[38] or examining each variant in the syndicated appearances of Stephen

35. For further details, see *The Rise of Silas Lapham*, ed. Walter J. Meserve and David J. Nordloh (Selected Edition of William Dean Howells, 1971), pp. 373-388.

36. The relationship between the readings of the American and English editions is explored in detail in the "Note on the Text" to the forthcoming *Moby-Dick* volume in the Northwestern-Newberry Edition of *The Writings of Herman Melville*.

37. "Textual Introduction," in *Miscella-*

nies by Henry Fielding, Esq; Volume One, ed. Henry Knight Miller (Wesleyan Edition, 1972), pp. lii-liii.

38. Most of these techniques of bibliographical analysis are conveniently illustrated in Charlton Hinman's *The Printing and Proof-Reading of the First Folio of Shakespeare* (1963); the principles underlying the use of the techniques are explored in Fredson Bowers's *Bibliography and Textual Criticism* (1964).

Crane's stories and dispatches in the light of the quantitative evidence (how many times each reading turns up) can help to establish the reading of the syndicate's master proof. Such evidence must then be subjected to critical scrutiny: the fact that only one out of six newspaper texts of Crane's "The Pace of Youth" reads "clinched" at a point where all the others read "clenched" does not in itself dictate "clenched" as the authorial reading, for Crane invariably wrote "clinched."[39]

Once the editor has made his judgments as to which variants are attributable to the author and which to someone else, he must consider the exact status of the latter group. Are all variants for which someone other than the author is responsible to be rejected outright, or is it conceivable that the author's intention may sometimes be fulfilled by other persons? It is not only conceivable but unquestionably true that others can and do sometimes correct an author's writing and in the process fulfill his intention. An author may write down one word but be thinking of a different one, or in reading proofs he may fail to notice a printer's error which creates a new word. When these erroneous words are plausible in their contexts, they may never be recognized by anyone as erroneous; but when one of them does not make sense, and when the correct word is obvious, anyone who makes the correction is carrying out the author's intention. Frequently an editor may believe that a particular word cannot have been intended but is not certain just what the intended word should be; only his critical assessment of the whole matter can determine whether it is preferable in that case to let the questionable word stand and call attention to the problem in a note or to substitute a word which catches the apparent intended sense (again, of course, with an explanation), even though that word may not be the exact one which the author had in mind. In the typescript of *A Story Teller's Story*, then, alterations in the hand of E. T. Booth cannot simply be dismissed; they must be inspected carefully, because Booth may have noticed places where the typescript reading certainly (or almost certainly) cannot have been Anderson's intended reading, and there is always the chance that an editor might otherwise fail to detect some of them.

An examination of Booth's revisions, however, leads to a more difficult question. Since Booth was the editor for the publisher, can one

39. This example is discussed by Fredson Bowers in his edition of Crane's *Tales of Adventure* (University of Virginia Edition of *The Works of Stephen Crane*, 1970), p. 198. He takes up the general problem of "radiating texts"—the situation in which two or more extant texts are equally close to the lost manuscript, with no intervening texts surviving—in "Multiple Authority: New Problems and Concepts of Copy-Text," *Library*, 5th ser., 27 (1972), 81-115.

argue that, because Anderson expected his book to be gone over in the publisher's offices, the changes made by Booth become a part of Anderson's intended wording? Or, to put the question in more general terms: can one argue that changes made (or thought to have been made) by the publisher and passed (or presumably passed) by the author in proof constitute changes intended by the author? This question is very different from asking about an editor's alteration of obvious errors. The correction of a reading which the author cannot have intended amounts to a restoration of what was in his mind but not on paper, or of what was in his now lost manuscript but not in print. It does not involve any change of the author's intention. But revisions, as opposed to corrections of outright errors, were not previously intended by the author; if the author then explicity endorses them, he is changing his intention. He is free to do so, of course, just as he may have shifted his intention several times before his manuscript ever left his hands. What is at issue, however, is whether he can delegate someone else to carry out his intention, or part of it. If he says that he expects changes, or certain kinds of changes, to be made in the publisher's offices, can the results be regarded as representing his intention, without shifting the definition of "intention"? One might argue, for instance, that Anderson—aware of some of the shortcomings, by conventional standards, of his spelling, punctuation, and sentence structure—did not "intend" for his writings to be published exactly as he wrote them but "intended" for them to be made to conform with conventional practice. But one might also argue, on the other side, that Anderson's writing as it came from him reflects his intention more accurately than it does after being standardized, and that any intention he may have held regarding publishers' alterations amounted only to his realistic understanding of what had to be done in order to get published (and thus was not part of his active intention in the text).[40]

40. Anderson's editor, Ray Lewis White, seems to take both sides of the question. In his edition of *Tar* (1969), he says that "Anderson's loose punctuation, meant to reproduce for the reader a flowing, simple style, was standardized and 'stiffened' by the Boni and Liveright editors" (p. xvii); in *Marching Men* (1972), he reports that Anderson "learned to apologize for his untutored prose" and "continued all his life entrusting to his publishers final preparation of his writing" (pp. xxiv-xxv). Cf. note 33 above. For the view of a publisher's editor, defending publishing-house alterations as part of an author's intention, see Albert Erskine, "Authors and Editors: William Faulkner at Random House," in *The William Faulkner Collection at West Point and the Faulkner Concordances*, ed. Jack L. Capps (1974), pp. 14-19. Simon Nowell-Smith has provided a survey of author-publisher relations in respect both to punctuation and to censorship in "Authors, Editors, and Publishers," in *Editor, Author, and Publisher*, ed. William J. Howard (1969), esp. pp. 8-16.

The importance, for editorial practice, of settling this question in general terms is evident. When an editor faces a choice for copy-text between a fair-copy manuscript (or printer's copy) and a first impression, he needs to have—in the absence of convincing evidence—a general policy to fall back on, a policy based on the inherent probabilities in such situations. Of course, if the editor has convincing evidence—not merely the author's statements but detailed information about the author's methods of going over proofs—he can make his decision on that basis. But, as is more likely to be the case, if the evidence is not sufficient for making a competent decision, the editor must have further guidance. Greg's rationale, pointing out the usual deterioration of a text (particularly its accidentals) from one manuscript or edition to another, leads the editor back to the fair-copy manuscript or the earliest extant text which follows it. There has been some disagreement with this position, however, based on the view that the author's intention encompasses the actvities which take place in the step from manuscript (or typescript) to print and that the intention is not "final" until the text conforms to the standards which will make it publishable. Philip Gaskell concludes that "in most cases the editor will choose as copy-text an early printed edition, not the manuscript"; the accidentals of the manuscript, he says, "the author would himself have been prepared—or might have preferred—to discard."[41] James Thorpe agrees:

In many cases, probably in most cases, he [the author] expected the printer to perfect his accidentals; and thus the changes introduced by the printer can be properly thought of as fulfilling the writer's intentions. To return to the accidentals of the author's manuscript would, in these cases, be a puristic recovery of a text which the author himself thought of as incomplete or unperfected: thus, following his own manuscript would result in subverting his intentions.[42]

41. *A New Introduction to Bibliography* (1972), pp. 340, 339.

42. *Principles of Textual Criticism* (1972), p. 165. Paul Baender similarly believes that the Center for Editions of American Authors (following Greg's principles) "has not sufficiently recognized that a writer's acquiescence in his publisher's alterations may also be construed as self-expression"; see p. 141 of "Reflections upon the CEAA by a Departing Editor," *Resources for American Literary Study*, 4 (1974), 131-144. Zeller (see note 26 above) goes farther and says that whatever an author passes in preparing the copy for an edition (with the exception of a strictly defined category of "faults") should be regarded as authorized, regardless of its source, for the author in passing it is reacting to a different version of his work in which it plays a role: "it does not matter whether the variants are original or extraneous, misprints (as we shall see, there are misprints and misprints) or variants introduced by a publisher's editor. . . . The necessary condition for our establishment of text is only that he [the author] should have registered the

In support of his view, Thorpe offers examples of a number of writers over the years who have expressed their indifference to matters of spelling and punctuation or have asked for help in making their spelling and punctuation conform to an acceptable standard.

Such arguments for preferring the first edition to the manuscript seem to me misguided. While it is true that most authors have the intention of getting published, such an intention is of a different order from their intention to have certain words and punctuation, resulting in a certain meaning, in their text. The intention of writing something publishable is what Hancher would call a "programmatic intention"; what the editor is properly concerned with, as we have seen, is the author's "active intention" manifested in the work. There is no reason why in some instances an author's active intention might not conflict with his programmatic intention. That an author may submit to various publishing-house alterations as a routine procedure in the process of publication does not amount to his changing his active intention about what his writing is to consist of. To say that he "expects" or is prepared to have certain changes made by the printer or publisher is not the same as to say that he prefers or wishes to have them made; to take his implicit approval of these changes on the proofs (or the printer's copy) as a sign that he is now more satisfied with his text is to ignore the many external factors (Melville's "Time, Strength, Cash, and Patience") which at this stage might prevent him from restoring readings that he actively desired. It is of little help to survey what writers in the past have said on the subject of publishers' alterations of their spelling and punctuation, even if there were a valid statistical basis for concluding, as Thorpe does, that most are "of the indifferent persuasion" (p. 151). Indifference is far from suggesting intention; and the motivation for the indifference would in each case have to be examined in order to know how to interpret the statements. But if the attitudes of writers toward this question cannot be fairly generalized about, the views and practices of printers and publishers can. Printers' manuals, after all, are normative and instructional statements, offering a far more trustworthy basis for generalization than individual authors' expressions of their own attitudes. Thorpe himself, after quoting from various manuals, recognizes that, for most of the period with which he is concerned, "it has been the printers (particularly the compositors and proofreaders) who have

---

readings in question" (p. 256). Examining the author's motivation in passing certain readings which did not originate with him is futile, Zeller argues, because "the magnetic needle of the author's wishes is quivering in the field of non-aesthetic forces" (p. 245; see also note 52 below).

mainly exercised this control over the text in the process of transmitting it" (p. 152). And Gaskell admits that "printers seldom gave authors much choice in the matter" (p. 339). If printers and publishers can be assumed as a general rule to have made alterations in the accidentals of the texts which passed through their hands, and if the attitudes of authors toward those changes have been complex and uncertain, it would seem that, in the absence of additional evidence, an author's manuscript could be taken as a safer guide than the printed text to his intentions regarding accidentals.[43]

Whether there is sufficient evidence in a given case to justify taking the first edition rather than the manuscript as copy-text is a matter of judgment. What the editor must attempt to assess is whether the author genuinely preferred the changes made by the publisher's reader or whether he merely acquiesced in them. The idea that an author can actively intend in his work a revision made by someone else depends in effect on the extent to which the two can be regarded as voluntary collaborators. Since collaboration implies shared responsibility, the "author's intention" in a collaborative effort results from a merging of the separate intentions of the individual authors; the final result is thus intended by each of the authors. A work need not be signed with more than one name, of course, for it to be a collaboration. Nor is it necessary for the authors involved to perform equal shares of the work; indeed, two people may collaborate only on certain aspects of a work, and their joint intention would apply only to the words or elements involved. The facsimile edition of the revised manuscript-typescript of *The Waste Land* offers a rare opportunity to observe some of the collaboration which can underlie a great work. In certain passages Pound's revisions (such as "demobbed" in line 139) or deletions (as in "Death by Water") actually constitute collaboration, though there are other places where Eliot rejects Pound's suggestions (as in the lines on Saint Mary Woolnoth, lines 67-68). That the work is to some extent collaborative is implied by Valerie Eliot's comment, in her description of "Editorial Policy," that "It has been difficult to decide who cancelled certain lines, especially when both Eliot and Pound have worked on them together."[44] A study of this facsimile does not suggest that an editor should incorporate into the text of the poem the lines which Pound rejected and Eliot did not restore; one can argue that at those points Eliot's intention merged

43. I have offered a more detailed and direct criticism of Thorpe's and Gaskell's position in *SB*, 28 (1975), 222-227.

44. *The Waste Land: A Facsimile and Transcript of the Original Drafts Including the Annotations of Ezra Pound*, ed. Valerie Eliot (1971), p. xxxii.

with Pound's intention, even though Pound's markings are what survive on paper. The fact that Pound went over the poem as a friend and not as a publisher's editor does not alter the essential point: in either case it is possible for someone other than the "author" to make alterations which are identical with the intention of the "author," when the relationship partakes of the spirit of collaboration.

The question, posed earlier, of whether it makes sense to believe that an author can ask someone else to carry out his intention in some respect may now be answered in the negative. By definition, an author's active intention cannot include projected activity and cannot include activity of which he is not in control. The ultimate example of delegated intention in writing would be for a person to ask someone else to write an entire work for him; if he then announced that it represented his "intention," he could only mean his intention to write a certain kind of work (his programmatic intention), for his active intention would not be involved. The same is true regardless of what portion or aspect of a work is at issue, as long as the element contributed by someone other than the author must be described with such expressions as "It is what the author expected to have done" or "It is what the author would have done if he had found time." However, if an author accepts what someone else has done not in a spirit of acquiescence but of active collaboration, the result does represent his active intention. Since the scholarly editor, in establishing a text, is concerned with an author's active intention in that text, he can accept into the text what he knows (or strongly believes) to be initially the work of someone else only when it can be regarded as having been accepted by the primary author as a true collaboration. This approach does not alter the crucial role which the editor's judgment plays in evaluating evidence, but it may provide a useful framework into which that evidence can be placed. It also suggests the relative infrequency with which publishers' alterations can be taken to supersede an author's known practice in a prepublication stage of his work.

III

After the editor has separated authorial from nonauthorial alterations and has decided how to treat the nonauthorial ones, he still faces the question of how to define "final" with respect to the authorial variants. Normally, of course, when there are two authorial readings at a given point and their sequence can be determined, the later one is taken to represent the author's "final intention." However, there are in general two kinds of situations in which this view of "final intention" will prove unsatisfactory: (1) when the nature or extent of the revisions is such that the result seems, in effect, a new work, rather than a "final version" of an old work;[45] and (2) when the author allows several alternative readings to stand in his manuscript or vacillates among them in successive editions. In the first case, one may say that there is more than one "final" intention; in the second, that there is no final intention at all.

The editorial problem in both cases usually reduces itself to quantitative terms: when the authorial variants are few in number, it makes little practical difference if an editor selects one group of readings as "final" and incorporates them into his text, since the reader will be able without much difficulty to analyze the variants for himself and come to his own conclusions about the way in which these variants alter the total effect of the work; but when the number of variants is great, the system of presenting one final text with variant readings in notes is less satisfactory, and the only practical solution is to produce more than one text (perhaps arranged in parallel columns), each representing a different "intention."[46] That the recognition of more than one valid text of a given work is often forced on an editor by the practical exigencies of recording variant readings should not obscure the fact that the theoretical problem of determining "final" authorial intention has no necessary connection with the quantity of variants.

Turning to the first of the two categories—in which an author's revisions produce, in a manner of speaking, a new work—one can idenitfy several patterns. The most clear-cut involves those situations in which the author's revisions reflect motives which make it impossible for an editor to accept the later version of a work as truly representing the author's intention, even though, in temporal terms, this version is "final." If, for instance, an author deletes passages for the purpose of producing a condensation or simplifies the language to make the work appropriate for younger readers, the special motives in each case prevent the resulting revisions from being definitive. The revised version, in such cases, does not represent a refinement of the work as previously "completed" but a new work conceived for different pur-

45. One must use such qualifiers as "in effect" when calling this kind of version a "new work," since obviously there must be something similar about the two versions or they would not be regarded as "versions of a work" in the first place. At the same time, there is the implication that not every difference produces, for the practical purposes of editing, a "new work." Cf. note 54 below.

46. Bowers, in his essay "Textual Criticism" in the Thorpe pamphlet (see note 2 above), briefly refers to such cases in which "the rewriting is so extensive as to make ridiculous any attempt at synthesis of the two forms in one critical text" (p. 47; see also his footnote 32).

poses; if the new version has merit, it is as an independent work to be edited separately. This is not to deny that the author might make in the process some revisions which an editor would adopt as emendations in his copy-text, but in order to qualify for adoption they would have to be revisions unconnected with the aim of condensation or simplification.[47] In other words, two types of revision must be distinguished: that which aims at altering the purpose, direction, or character of a work, thus attempting to make a different sort of work out of it; and that which aims at intensifying, refining, or improving the work as then conceived (whether or not it succeeds in doing so), thus altering the work in degree but not in kind. If one may think of a work in terms of a spatial metaphor, the first might be labeled "vertical revision," because it moves the work to a different plane, and the second "horizontal revision," because it involves alterations within the same plane. Both produce local changes in active intention; but revisions of the first type appear to be in fulfillment of an altered programmatic intention or to reflect an altered active intention in the work as a whole, whereas those of the second do not.

A similar situation occurs when an author makes revisions, not because he wishes to, but because he is asked or compelled to. Herman Melville, after the publication of *Typee* (1846), was asked by his American publisher, Wiley & Putnam, to soften his criticism of the missionaries in the South Seas for a revised edition, and in July 1846 he complied by deleting about thirty-six pages of material and revising other passages. These changes alter the tone of the book and are not in keeping with the spirit of the original version. There is no question that Melville is responsible for the changes, and in this sense they are "final"; but they represent not so much his intention as his acquiescence. Under these circumstances, an editor is justified in rejecting the revisions and adopting the original readings as best reflecting the author's "final intention"; in fact, to accept the readings which are final in chronological terms would distort that intention. But again the two types of revision must be separated, for Melville made some revisions in July 1846 which had no connection with the expurgation of political, religious, and sexual references—and these an editor would

---

47. Of course, a revision which does not actually implement the aim of, say, simplification may have been made by the author in the belief that it does. It may be impossible for an editor to distinguish between such revisions and those which genuinely were unconnected with the motive of simplification. All he can do is to judge, on the basis of the texts in front of him and his knowledge of the author, which revisions the author can reasonably be thought to have considered simplifications (whether or not they seem such to the editor himself).

adopt.[48] In other words, the "vertical" revisions are rejected, and the "horizontal" revisions are accepted.[49] Just as accidental and substantive variants are, in Greg's rationale, to be treated separately, so, too, known authorial revisions must be divided into categories for editorial decision according to the motives or conceptions they reflect.

A further related problem—the weight to be attached to an author's statement about his revisions—can also be illustrated by the *Typee* case. After removing the passages on the missionaries from the American edition, Melville wrote to John Murray, his English publisher, "Such passages are altogether foreign to the adventure, & altho' they may possess a temporary interest *now*, to some, yet so far as the wide & permanent popularity of the work is conserned [*sic*], their exclusion will certainly be beneficial." One could argue that Melville is simply making the best of the situation, that he is rationalizing the changes and trying to convince himself that they are for the better; on the other side, one could say that here is a strong statement from the author about his "intention" and that the author's wishes, so stated, must be respected. However, in the same way that an author may make revisions which do not reflect his ultimate wishes about his work, he may also make statements which, for various reasons, are less than completely candid. In the end, one cannot automatically accept such statements at face value; as in any historical research, statements can only be interpreted by placing them in their context, by reconstructing as fully as possible the course of events which led up to them. The publisher, in the case of *Typee*, and not the author, initiated the revisions, and there is no evidence, internal or external, to suggest that they are the kinds of changes Melville would have made without pressure from someone else; even his statement implies that the revised work is in a sense a different work, stemming from a different set of programmatic intentions—aimed at producing a permanently popular work, not dated by discussions of current issues. After these considerations, an editor need not feel that Melville's statement makes the case for rejecting the expurgations any less strong.[50] Such state-

---

48. For a more detailed discussion of these revisions and the editorial problems they pose, see *Typee*, ed. Harrison Hayford, Hershel Parker, and G. Thomas Tanselle (Northwestern-Newberry Edition, 1968), pp. 288-291, 315-318.

49. Whether or not one might wish to produce a separate text incorporating vertical revisions generally depends on how

much historical or aesthetic interest such a text would have. In the case of revisions made because of outside pressure to expurgate, there would presumably be little interest in having a separately edited text of such a version.

50. Further examples of Melville's revisions of *Typee*, along with a discussion of the possibility of editorial rejection of

ments by authors should always be carefully evaluated, like any other evidence, but they cannot be binding on an editor. Only the circumstances of each case can dictate the weight to be accorded to these statements, just as the author's actual revisions cannot be indiscriminately adopted without reference to the entire historical situation surrounding them.

This treatment of authors' statements has certain further implications. The essential issue, stated baldly, is whether an editor can presume to reverse an author's decision. Even if Melville did not want to revise *Typee*, the fact remains that he did so and even asserted decisively that the result was an improvement. Is it not the author's prerogative to determine the ultimate form of his work? Suppose that Melville meant what he said and that, even though he would not have made the revisions without external influence, he was sincerely convinced that he had done the right thing. Most editors would disagree with him, but they would also say that it is not an editor's place to determine what the author *should* have done. If the author has a lapse in taste, the argument goes, that lapse is a historical fact which scholarly research cannot undertake to repair. There is no answer to this argument, of course, so long as the revision was definitely an attempt to improve the work in terms of its original conception (horizontal revision). But when the revision shifts that conception and thereby produces a different work (vertical revision), the editor may only confuse matters by presenting the revised version as the basic text: if he finds the original version a more faithful representation of the author's vision, he is not abdicating his scholarly responsibility in favor of an undisciplined subjectivity if he edits that version on its own terms as a separate work (and goes on to include the variant readings of the revised edition in notes). It is one thing for an editor to impose his taste upon an author's work by choosing among variant readings solely on the basis of their appeal to him; it is quite another for him to put that taste to the service of historical understanding by allowing it to guide him in distinguishing among the levels of authorial revision and discriminating among the various artistic conceptions they represent.

The most familiar situation in which more than one "final" intention can be said to exist occurs when an author, at a later stage in his career, extensively revises a work completed years before—not because

---

authorial revisions in this and other works of Melville, are given by Hershel Parker in "Melville and the Concept of 'Author's Final Intentions,'" *Proof,* 1 (1971), 156-168.

he is compelled to, nor because he wants to condense it, expand it, or adjust it to a different audience, but because he feels he can improve it artistically. The classic case of such revision is the New York Edition (1907-09) of Henry James. It seems to be generally agreed that an attempt to record in textual notes the variant readings between the original and revised versions of the novels and stories included in that edition would be of questionable utility, since the revisions are so pervasive that they create substantially new works. Both versions of a given work deserve to be read in their own right, and an essay generalizing upon and categorizing the differences between them may be more useful than a list of variants appended to one of the texts. Many essays of this kind have appeared, and a fairly recent one, on "Pandora," sums up the situation: "the net result is neither striking improvement nor fatal tampering. The story is better in some ways, worse in others. But it is different—one cannot assert that the changes really add up to nothing."[51] The revised version, because it is essentially "different," manifests a "final intention" which does not supersede the "final intention" of the earlier version. Merely because the revision came at the end of a long career, when James's artistry and insight were presumably more mature, it cannot invalidate the intrinsic merits of the original version. The two are discrete works.

If this point of view has been readily accepted in extreme cases of revision, it has scarcely been considered at all in instances of slight revision. But why should the *quantity* of alterations affect one's theoretical position? If one treats a heavily revised text as an independent work simply because the difficulties of handling the variants in any other way are overwhelming and then edits a less heavily revised work as a single text with notes because it is possible to do so, the theoretical basis of the whole operation is questionable. The idea that a revised version can be considered a separate work is sometimes said to rest on the concept of organic form—the view that form and content in a work of art are so integrated that any alteration produces a new entity. Of course, it is not necessary to adduce this concept in order to make the point: changing a word in any utterance results technically in a different utterance. Although the change of one word in a novel

---

51. Charles Vandersee, "James's 'Pandora': The Mixed Consequences of Revision," *SB*, 21 (1968), 93-108 (see p. 107). The same kind of comment can be made in regard to revisions in a lyric poem. Thomas Clayton, for instance, writing on "Some Versions, Texts, and Readings of 'To Althea, from Prison,'" in *PBSA*, 68 (1974), 225- 235, says of two readings that "it is pointless to argue which is 'better'; the readings are different, and the versions of the poem are significantly different depending upon the presence of 'birds' or 'gods,' respectively: the dialectic of the whole depends upon the part" (p. 234).

makes less practical difference than the change of one word in a brief lyric poem, strictly speaking each version (both of the novel and of the poem) is a "separate work." Maintaining this position would not quite put an end to all scholarly editing, because editors would still have the task of detecting nonauthorial readings (emendations of publishers' readers, compositors' errors, and the like) and purifying the text of them;[52] but they could not choose among authorial variants, for they would have to consider each group of them, for each successive impression or edition, as resulting in a new work to be edited separately.[53] Clearly such a situation would be intolerable from a practical point of view; in the majority of instances editorial choice among authorial variants does not deprive readers of the opportunity for reconstructing other forms of the text on the basis of the material presented in the apparatus, and a list of variants has the positive advantage of drawing together the evidence from various versions into a form where it is conveniently comparable.

52. Even a nonauthorial variant, of course, produces a separate work which could be made the subject of critical analysis, but the scholarly editor's aim, as it has been defined, is to reconstruct the text (or texts) in conformity with the author's intention. As to whether his aim should be so defined, see below in section IV. Zeller (see note 26 above) does hold the position that "a new version comes into existence through a single variant," because "a text, as text, does not in fact consist of elements but of the relationships between them" and therefore "variation at one point has an effect on invariant sections of the text" (p. 241). He believes that each authorized text has an integrity of its own and that the editor's duty is to intervene in a text only to correct "textual faults" (readings which contradict "the internal text structure" [p. 260] and which are confirmed as corrupt by bibliographical analysis). To judge variants individually and to emend one text with authorial variants from another is, in his view, to produce a "contaminated" text. Zeller has focused clearly on the problem, and certain parts of his discussion are similar to what I am saying here. The central difference between his position and the one I set forth below is that for him a "new version implies a new intention" (p. 241), whereas I believe that a critical distinction can be made between versions resulting from different intentions for the work as a whole and those resulting from the same intention. Furthermore, Zeller does not think that intention can be defined to exclude the nonliterary forces which affect authorial decisions: "What is termed the intention of the author is an undetachable part of these forces. . . . Only the textual history is within the editor's reach" (p. 244). But if it makes sense to speak of artistic and nonartistic elements in intention (that is, to speak of active intention and certain programmatic intentions), then there is surely a dividing line between them (however concealed) which critical intelligence can attempt to discover. Zeller's procedure does produce what can be called a critical text, because errors are corrected; but emendations of authorial variants are ruled out, and the issue finally becomes the question of the value of a critical approach to editing.

53. If they considered the variants singly rather than in groups, even a relatively small number of variants would result in an astronomical number of separate works; it is true, however, that any group of authorial revisions may contain some which seem to move in a different direction from the others and which thus demand separate consideration.

If, in practice, editors are not going to regard each version as necessarily a separate work, then some rationale is required for distinguishing those instances of revision which are to be edited as separate works from those which are not. A quantitative dividing line is not logical: it would be impossible to set up a particular number of revisions, or words involved in revisions, as the test for defining a separate work in this sense.[54] What is more meaningful than the extent of the revisions is their nature. One author might make 3000 changes in his selection of adjectives and adverbs, for instance—and perhaps improve his book stylistically—without altering his original conception of the work at all; another might make only ten revisions in key passages and change the whole direction of the book. Whether or not two versions of a book are treated by an editor as independent works should depend on a qualitative, not quantitative, distinction. If revisions do not spring from the same conception of an organic whole as the original version manifested (what I have called vertical revisions), then they produce a new work, even though the actual number of new readings is small; if revisions are attempts to develop and improve the original conception (what I have called horizontal revisions), then they do not produce a separate work for practical purposes, regardless of the number of changes involved.[55] Generally, large numbers of alterations do follow from a changed conception or programmatic intention, but the point is that there is no necessary connection between the two.

In making decisions about authorial intention, an editor may be inclined to take into account a related factor, the timing of the changes. When an author, late in his life, makes revisions in an early work, one could argue that the result will almost surely constitute an effectively different work, since it is unlikely that the author will have the same conception of his work in mind as he had during the process of its original composition. James's revisions are a case in point, but the argument can be applied to other instances in which neither the extent of the changes nor the shift in intent is so pronounced. When

54. From here on I use "separate work"—as I trust the context indicates—in the practical sense of "a work to be edited separately."

55. Richard Kuhns (see note 14 above) is getting at this same question when he says, "Within limits changes can be made without altering the basic organization and fundamental meaning of the work; but if we go outside those limits the work is seriously affected. . . . There is a difference between the values of the parts of a work which if changed would not alter the over-all effect of the work, and the values of the elements of a work which if changed would alter the over-all effect of the work" (p. 18). The key, in his terms, is whether or not the "style" is affected, "style" being defined as "a kind of organization of elements capable of sustaining a constant 'focal effect.'"

Arthur Stedman edited *Typee* in 1892, he claimed to have made alterations "by written direction of the author" (who died in 1891). The only presently known evidence of any authorial direction is a note in Mrs. Melville's hand listing four changes which her husband requested.[56] Even assuming that this note accurately represents Melville's final wishes, how much weight is to be given to a few isolated changes suggested nearly fifty years after the original composition of the work? Two of the changes represent the same kind of expurgation which Melville was required to make for the earlier revised edition and are not consistent with the spirit of the work. These revisions are different from James's not merely in quantity but in the fact that they are not part of a sustained and coherent reshaping of an early work. Instead, they are simply instances of sporadic tinkering; such tinkering, when performed during or soon after the composition of a work, can be expected to fit the general tone and spirit of the whole, but when it occurs much later the results may well seem out of place. A systematic job of revision, even if it does not result in many changes, may have a coherence of its own, but isolated changes frequently clash with the larger context. Nevertheless, it is obviously possible for authors to make consistent sporadic revisions late in life, and the timing of revisions is therefore not in itself the key. Just as a quantitative measure of revision will not serve to distinguish what versions are to be edited as separate works, so a time limit is similarly unrealistic: one cannot say that all revisions made within a week, or a month, or a year of the original composition are to be accepted as part of the same conception, while those made after that time either result in different works or represent random thoughts not consistent with any coherent plan. What is important, once again, is the nature of the changes, and no mechanical rule—about their extent or their timing— can produce meaningful distinctions among them with respect to underlying conceptions or motives.

The role which these considerations play in editing and the critical nature of the decisions they imply are well illustrated in Bowers's edition of Stephen Crane's *Maggie*.[57] Crane's book was first printed privately in 1893; three years later, in order to secure publication by D. Appleton & Co., he agreed to make revisions, particularly the elimination of profanity. But, as Bowers points out, Crane's alterations were not limited to bowdlerizing: "It is clear from many examples

56. For a fuller discussion of this document and its editorial implications, see *Typee* (cited in note 48 above), pp. 312-313.

57. In *Bowery Tales* (University of Virginia Edition, 1969).

that he took the opportunity to make stylistic revisions as well as literary improvements" (p. lxviii). As in the case of *Typee*, an editor will reject the enforced expurgations and will accept the stylistic revisions made at the same time. But *Maggie* offers in addition a difficult intermediate category: the removal of various sordid details, culminating in the cancellation of a 96-word paragraph describing a "huge fat man," which had appeared in the 1893 edition at a strategic point, just before Maggie's death at the end of Chapter 17. The first critical question is obviously to decide whether these alterations were among those which Crane made under duress or whether he made them independently, judging them to be artistic improvements. Answering that question, as Bowers recognizes, involves literary judgment, and he provides a long interpretive discussion (pp. lxxvii-xci) of the implications of the removal of that paragraph, concluding with the view that Crane did delete it for artisic reasons. Once that decision is made, there is a second critical question to be faced: does this revision (and the scattered lesser ones similar to it) produce an essentially different work? Bowers clearly states the possibiliy:

> In some literary works it is generally recognized that a revision may be so thoroughgoing—so motivated throughout by the author's altered political, social, or artistic concepts—as to require complete acceptance on its own terms as the final intention in every respect both of accidentals and of substantives. . . . Under such conditions there is nothing for it but to treat the early and late texts as quite independent units and to establish each separately, perhaps in parallel form, with no attempt to merge the two in terms of the divided authority of accidentals and substantives. Divided authority does not exist and no synthetic text is possible for the early and revised editions of such works as Jonson's *Every Man in His Humour*, Wordsworth's *Prelude*, or Whitman's *Leaves of Grass*. (pp. xciii-xciv)

He then concludes that "*Maggie* does not bear comparison with these examples," arguing that Crane "was operating from a strong literary conviction about the integrity of a text once written and published" (p. xcv). It is possible, then, by incorporating the 1896 revisions which Crane "made for his own purposes and satisfaction" (p. xcvii), to produce a single " 'ideal' text of *Maggie* as a literary fact, not a limited 'ideal' text either of the 1893 or of the 1896 edition" (p. xcv). Obviously this conclusion is reached through critical analysis, and another editor might analyze the situation differently and come to the opposing view—that there are two distinct *Maggies* which it would be improper to merge.[58] No incontrovertible answer is to be expected to a question like this, dependent on judgment; but every editor in his own work must recognize that the question exists and reach an answer to it.[59]

With some authors the possibility of multiple "final" intentions is further intensified. Instead of making one systematic revision of a work at some point later in life, they revise their work continually throughout their careers. An extreme example of this method, referred to by Bowers in the passage quoted above, is Whitman's *Leaves of Grass*, which was extensively revised eight times between 1855 and 1892. When an author works in this way, successive editions constitute a printed record of a developing mind. The fact that Whitman said of his final "deathbed" edition (1891-92) that any future edition should be "a copy and facsimile, indeed, of the text of these . . . pages" does not mean that critics and scholars must reject all earlier editions as works in their own right.[60] Even if Whitman came to think of the earlier editions as preliminary drafts for his final version, each of those editions was published and at the time of its publication represented a final version that he was willing to present to the public and thus his final intention as of that moment.[61] If one decides that the revisions at each stage are the kind which spring from an altered conception of the whole, one can argue that each edition of *Leaves* is a separate work with its own final intention. (The situation would differ from that of Henry James only in the greater number of separate works, resulting from the greater number of stages of revision.) In that case, Whitman's last text is not—as an intended work—any more "final" than his earlier texts; it merely comes later. To one taking this position, Whitman's own judgment should of course be no embarrassment; it is only a critical pronouncement about his work, not an element within the work.

58. I have discussed this case in connection with Greg's theory, on pp. 221-223 of "The New Editions of Hawthorne and Crane," *Book Collector*, 23 (1974), 214-229.

59. Bowers has made further comments on the relationships between editions offering "eclectic" texts and those offering texts of particular stages of revision, in "Remarks on Eclectic Texts," *Proof*, 4 (1974), 31-76.

60. Some of the earlier versions have been edited separately: see, for example, *Whitman's Manuscripts: Leaves of Grass (1860)*, ed. Fredson Bowers (1955), which prints as parallel texts the manuscript versions of certain poems and their first published versions (in 1860); and *Leaves of Grass: The First (1855) Edition*, ed. Malcolm Cowley (1959). Cf. Bowers, "The Walt Whitman Manuscripts of 'Leaves of Grass' (1860)," in his *Textual and Literary Criticism* (1959), pp. 35-65.

61. As John Kemp (see note 14 above) says, "a published work of art has been, as it were, detached from the artist, and he has sent it out into the world, with the result that later versions do not necessarily cancel earlier published ones as later cancel earlier in the working-out stage before publication" (p. 152).

These issues are raised in an acute form in connection with the poetry of W. H. Auden. Joseph Warren Beach, in *The Making of the Auden Canon* (1957), describes in great detail the way in which Auden continually omitted or revised passages to bring his poems into conformity with his current ideological preoccupations. In 1945, for example, he gave the poems from "In Time of War," in Beach's words, "a more distinctively religious cast than they had when first written in 1938 and published in 1939" (p. 10). Throughout his career, according to Beach, Auden displayed a faculty for "domesticating, within the frame of mind that at any moment possesses him, work conceived in some quite different frame of mind" (p. 15). In preparing a collected edition, he not only revised poems to make them "reasonably acceptable to him at a time when he was concerned that his work should be as edifying spiritually as it was imaginatively arresting" (p. 242); he also arranged the poems in alphabetical order so that their connections with previous volumes or particular stages in his career would be obscured. The situation is reminiscent of Whitman's preparation of an authorized final edition, but in Auden's case the emphasis is more clearly on ideological content than on artistic form. As with Whitman, Auden's final text can be regarded as only another text, reflecting a different conception of his work.

Beach's analysis presents, in effect, the apparatus for a critical edition in essay form—a method which, for this kind of author, is perhaps more useful than a list of variant readings, since such a list tends to suggest that the versions compared are essentially the same work. At the end of his book Beach takes up—in one of the few discussions of the subject in print—some of the editorial implications of multiple authorial intention. One can concur with his feeling of dissatisfaction about Auden's collected text and yet find a curious logic in his conclusion:

[Auden's] alternative would have been to range his poems in chronological order and leave them, as far as was consistent with his artistic standards, just as they were originally written. We should then be able to read them in their original context and to follow the course of an interesting mind in its progress through successive periods in the pursuit of truth. This manner of presentation would have done better justice to many fine poems as intelligible and organic creations of poetic art. It would have involved the candid admission on the author's part that, by his present lights, he had occasionally been subject to error and confusion. But such candor would only have reflected credit on the poet, and it could not in the end have been a disservice to the truth as he later came to see it. (p. 243)

In these comments Beach is explaining what he wishes Auden had done but in the process confuses the roles of author and scholarly editor. The particular revision and arrangement which Auden decided upon for his collected poems represent, in themselves, one of the "successive periods" in the "course of an interesting mind." The fact that he did not arrange his poems in chronological order or leave them unaltered does not prevent the editor from making the earlier texts available. Many of Auden's decisions may not please an editor, but, whatever they are, they constitute the only material the editor has to work with. One can criticize an author's lapses, but one cannot expect him to treat his own work as if he were a scholarly editor.

Pursuing the nature of Auden's "identity," Beach sensibly asks, "And how . . . can we question the right of an author to be his own judge as to the intent of a.piece of writing, or to make it over so as to give it a new direction?" (p. 251). This, after all, is the central issue. But the answer again proves troublesome: "What I have suggested is that such a making over of a work of literary art is not to be accomplished by cutting out a few offensive passages, or by merely hanging the work in a different gallery in different company; and that it is vain to suppose that now it means something essentially different from what it did." In other words, as he goes on to say, a work of art should have "a wholeness, or integrality, that underlies all the diverse and even conflicting elements" (p. 253). It is precisely because of its "integrality," however, that any adjustments made in a work of art may turn it into a different, if no less integral, work. To say that an author's last version of a work means the same thing as his earliest is to abandon all criticism; but to find that a late version fails to supersede an early one is not to deny the author's right to do with his work as he pleases. In the end, whenever there are authorial revisions, an editor is not fulfilling his responsibility to the work of literature if he does not assess the nature of those revisions, in order to determine whether he is really dealing with only a single work.

Before glancing at the argument that this approach to editing gives the editor too much freedom to be eclectic, let us turn to the second major category in which "final intention" is problematical—those instances in which there is literally no final intention, either because the author never prepared his manuscript for publication or because he wavered in his revisions for successive printings.[62] Perhaps the most

---

62. If finality is defined in terms of publication, one could say that the latter case involves multiple intentions. The whole pattern of revisions in such a case, however, separates it from the usual instances of continual revision and suggests that the author had not really come to a decision when he was forced to select one reading or the other for publication at a particular time.

common instances of this situation occur in the editing of letters. Although letters, generally full of abbreviations and elliptical remarks, can be described as manuscripts not prepared for publication, they have one peculiar feature: they were not (in most cases) intended for publication. Whatever form the manuscript is in, therefore, if the letter was sent, represents "final intention"; the posting of a letter is equivalent to the publication of a literary work, for each activity serves as the means by which a particular kind of communication is directed to its audience. When letters are published, do they automatically become a different genre, subject to different conventions, or is their intention distorted if they are not reproduced exactly as they arrived in the recipient's hands? If the author prepares his own letters for publication, he will almost certainly alter them (at least with respect to accidentals, but possibly also to substantives), and he will probably expect them to be subjected to the same processes of copy-editing and house-styling as any other work. But when letters are published posthumously, does the fact that the author would have expected them to be adjusted to conform with the conventions of published writing justify an editor's attempt to perform those adjustments? Clearly it does not, because, as we have seen, what an author expects is different from what he actively intends. In any case, an editor cannot possibly put himself in the frame of mind of a publisher's house-stylist of some previous period, and the changes he would introduce, however knowledgeable he may be, could carry no authority. Additionally, the abbreviations and other unconventional features of a letter may be its most revealing characteristics; if they are removed or normalized, the substance of the letter and the nuances conveyed to the recipient may be obscured, if not substantially altered. Naturally, some adjustments are inevitable, since complete fidelity to the original would mean photographic reproduction on the same quality of paper. But alterations—even in such matters as the misspelling of words—should be made with extreme caution if the effect of a letter as a private document is to be retained. This procedure comes closer to the author's intention, as revealed in the finished text of each letter, than following any directions the author may have pronounced when he was thinking of his letters more as literary property than as private expression.[63]

A similar situation exists in connection with journals, notebooks, and other personal papers, except that for these classes of material

63. For a fuller discussion of these problems (with somewhat different conclusions), see Robert Halsband, "Editing the Letters of Letter-Writers," *SB*, 11 (1958), 25-37; and Simon Nowell-Smith (see note 40 above), esp. pp. 16-27.

there is not even that degree of finality accorded to letters by the act of posting. If the writer made no final selection among alternative words or phrases, an editor has no basis—nor justification—for doing so; to prepare a "clear text" which reads smoothly is to change the essential nature of the document. Such works, though they may turn out to be literature, form a special genre in which the necessity for final choice (forced upon an author in the case of published works by the act of publication) does not apply. From a practical point of view, some of these works gain little from the preservation of their formal texture, and it may be that the group of readers who will be turning to a particular document may find the loss of such fidelity a price worth paying for a conveniently readable text. The nature of the document and the uses to which it may be put will in each instance determine the degree of compromise which can be tolerated. In some cases a full transcription may be accompanied by a separate "reading text."[64] But the theoretical point remains: altering private papers to conform to conventional standards of publication makes different works of them and thus is bound to distort their meaning.

When writers leave unfinished, or unprepared for publication, literary works of other genres—those which are normally circulated in published form—the problem is somewhat different. In these cases the rejected readings, false starts, and uncanceled variants are of interest in showing the writer's manner of working and stylistic development, just as they are when found in the surviving manuscripts of a published work; but they do not reflect the essential nature of the work itself, as they do in a letter or a journal. An editor who completes the author's job by preparing such works for conventional publication (correcting errors, choosing among uncanceled variants, and the like) is not obscuring the final effect or meaning of the work but rather clarifying it. When a poem, left in manuscript, is posthumously published in the form of an exact transcript, it is being treated like a his-

---

64. A good example of this method is the Harvard University Press edition of *The Journals and Miscellaneous Notebooks of Ralph Waldo Emerson*, ed. William H. Gilman *et al.* (1960-   ). The volumes of detailed transcription currently in progress are to be followed by selections in clear text. Whenever a text is likely to be quoted or reprinted frequently in standard typographical contexts where symbols and multiple readings seem (by tradition) out of place, it becomes particularly important to provide such additional clear texts, de-spite the theoretical difficulties they entail. For a discussion of some of the problems of editing journals, see William H. Gilman, "How Should Journals Be Edited?", *Early American Literature*, 6 (1971), 73-83. Cf. also G. T. Tanselle, "Some Principles for Editorial Apparatus," *SB*, 25 (1972), 41-88 (esp. pp. 46-47); and Eleanor D. Kewer, "Case Histories in the Craft of the Publisher's Editor, Culminating in a Justification of Barbed Wire," in *Editor, Author, and Publisher*, ed. William J. Howard (1969), pp. 65-73.

torical document; when it is published in a clear reading text, it is being treated like a work of literary art. Both forms may have their uses, but only the second can represent (or attempt to represent) the author's intention.[65]

The poems of Emily Dickinson present a special situation: they are clearly poems (not journal entries or letters), but they were not intended for publication. They contain both eccentric punctuation (often impossible to reproduce in type) and uncanceled alternative readings. If an editor decides to publish as exact transcriptions as possible of these poems (or even photographs of the manuscripts), he is doing what normally is most sensible for works not intended for publication. But in this case he would be doing less than full justice to the material, which belongs to a genre conventionally circulated in some kind of published form and with decisions among alternative readings already made. The fact that Emily Dickinson did not "intend" publication does not alter the basic nature of the material and automatically convert into notebook jottings what would have been called poetry if published. Her distrust of publication does not obligate an editor to leave her poems unpublished (or to edit them as if they were private papers) any more than an author's "deathbed" edition obligates an editor to regard previous editions as superseded. In either case the work has an existence distinct from the wishes (expressed or implied) of its creator, and "intention" regarding publication is different from the active intention embodied in the work. Whether or not Emily Dickinson's manuscripts were specifically "intended" for publication is really beside the point; the important matter is that they are manuscripts of poems not prepared for publication. Although an editor will rightly feel an obligation to present as fully as possible the evidence available in those manuscripts (as documents in the history of American literature), he should feel equally obliged to make decisions among the author's alternative readings and produce a clear text of the poems (as literature).[66] An editor who

---

65. E. A. J. Honigmann, in *The Stability of Shakespeare's Text* (1965), argues that Shakespeare perhaps made revisions in the process of copying, so that some of the variants we now have may represent authorial "second thoughts." The editor, therefore, must "screw his courage to the sticking place and choose between each pair of variants"; what he is doing is "to attempt a feat left undone by Shakespeare, to finalise an unfinalised text" (p. 168).

66. Thomas H. Johnson's Harvard edition of Emily Dickinson's poems (1955) presents a clear text, with variant readings in notes; but the decisions as to which readings were to be included in the main text were not generally made on the basis of literary judgment. Cf. Johnson's "Establishing a Text: The Emily Dickinson Papers," *SB*, 5 (1952-53), 21-32.

thus "completes" unfinished poems is not being presumptuous but is simply facing his responsibility. One editor's choice among alternatives may of course differ from another's, but the excellence of any critical edition—whether based on unprepared manuscripts or not—is directly related to the critical powers of its editor.

IV

Some of the implications of the Dickinson problem for editorial theory are discussed by R. W. Franklin at the end of his important book *The Editing of Emily Dickinson: A Reconsideration* (1967). Franklin correctly asserts that "from the variant fair copies of a single poem we should choose its best" (p. 133), and he objects to any nonliterary or mechanical basis of selection among alternatives in unfinished manuscripts as resulting merely in "a worksheet without all the work" (p. 134). Since an uncompleted manuscript obviously lacks finality, he concludes, "The principle of editing that a text exactly represent the author's intention is inadequate." He therefore calls for "a new editorial procedure for material unprepared by the author for publication"—a procedure which would be "a compromise between the demands of authorial intention and the demands of the poems" (pp. 142-143). One might carry the argument a step further, however, and note that since authorial intention is ultimately ascertainable only through the poems, no compromise is necessary except in the sense that two kinds of edition, rather than a single one, may be desirable: a complete transcription, faithful to the demands of the document, and a reading text (or more than one), faithful to the demands of the work of art.

Generalizing upon the specific situation, Franklin points to the "conflicting bases of criticism and editing"—conflicting because the modern critical position upholds "criticism divorced from authorial intention." Is there an inconsistency, he is asking, within the discipline of literary study, if a text, presented to the literary critic for analysis in the light of one set of principles, is prepared for him by the editor under a different set of principles? An author's final intention, he believes,

is like a Platonic archetype, unchanging, complete, and perfect in its own way, against which any one of its appearances in print can be corrected. Unfortunately, an author's intentions are not necessarily eternal and may exist as precariously as do any of their appearances: destroying a manuscript may destroy all trace of intention. Moreover, the separate appearances, even as an altered poem, have an existence as real as the archetype. (p. 142)

Readers of literature, he says, are not accustomed to dealing with multiple wordings in a final text nor with composite authorship. Yet one Dickinson "poem," "Those fair—fictitious People," has twenty-six variants that fit eleven places, amounting to 7680 possible poems; and other poems, as traditionally printed and studied, would have to be called "Dickinson-Todd-Higginson's," since editors were responsible for some of the words. In the end, Franklin observes, "the fact that we are not organized to talk about an altered poem as a poem shows how little the subject of our pursuit is poetry" (p. 141).

Two issues are involved in these considerations, and they are basic to all kinds of editing, whether the copy-text is an uncompleted manuscript or a printed edition: (1) What does "intention" signify, and when is it final? (2) Does it matter whether the *author's* wording is recovered, particularly when emendations by others are improvements? These questions ask for definitions of the three words "final authorial intention" and for justification of them as an expression of the goal of editing. I hope that what I have said up to now has provided some answers to them and will serve as background for the following brief replies, specifically directed at Franklin's conclusions.

The second of the questions is easier to answer than the first. No one presumably would deny that any alteration in a literary work could be regarded as producing a different work and that the new work could be made the subject of critical analysis. Neither would anyone deny that nonauthorial revisions could produce a work superior to the original and more rewarding for study.[67] Nevertheless, if an editor sets out to edit the works of a particular writer, he has under-

---

67. James Thorpe, however, does not seem to me to give adequate recognition to this possibility in the opening chapter ("The Aesthetics of Textual Criticism," originally published in *PMLA*, 80 [1965], 465-482) of his *Principles of Textual Criticism* (1972). He grants that "status as a work of art is not affected by whether [the work's] intentions all belong to the titular author"; but he immediately adds that "the integrity of the work of art depends very much on the work being limited to those intentions which are the author's," and he then insists that it is this "final integrity which should be the object of the critic's chief attention" (p. 31). Of course, his book is concerned with editing which seeks to establish what the author wrote; but the nature of that activity might have been more helpfully defined in relation to other possi-

ble editorial goals. Instead, there is the implication (which contradicts the first statement quoted above) that the work of art can only be preserved through the efforts of editors who purge it of the nonauthorial features that it continually attracts. We are told that "forces are always at work thwarting or modifying the author's intentions" and that the work "is thus always tending toward a collaborative status" (p. 48); therefore, "aesthetic objects . . . must be protected in order to preserve the work from becoming a collaborative enterprise" (p. 49). The scholarly editor is not so much "protecting" the work as restoring a particular form of it which has historical (and perhaps also aesthetic) interest; purely as an aesthetic object the work might well be better off without protection.

taken a task of historical research, and his goal must necessarily be the recovery of the words which the author actually wrote. That the bulk of scholarly editorial work has been of this sort does not imply that all critics will find this kind of edition appropriate for their purposes or that no other approach to editing is legitimate. A critic may choose to discuss a series of poems on death, say, rather than a series of poems by Milton, Shelley, Tennyson, and Dickinson; so long as he operates outside of a historical framework and makes no references to the authors or their times, he need not be concerned with whether he has the precise words of a particular author but only with whether he has the "best" version of each poem from an aesthetic point of view. Similarly, an editor could edit a collection of poems on death, letting his own aesthetic judgments guide him in improving upon any previously known version of each poem; the editor would become a self-invited collaborator of the original author, and the editorial process would be creatively, rather than historically, oriented. This kind of editing occurs regularly in publishing houses, and many books normally attributed to a single author are already the work of more than one person by the time of their first publication (one thinks immediately of the editorial labors of Maxwell Perkins at Scribner's).[68] The crucial point

68. See A. Walton Litz, "Maxwell Perkins: The Editor as Critic," in *Editor, Author, and Publisher*, ed. William J. Howard (1969), pp. 96-112. The author's attitude toward such changes is of course a separate matter, taken up in section II above. Morse Peckham has questioned whether it is meaningful to think of the "author" as distinguishable from others who work on the same text, and thus whether the recovery of authorial intention is a possible goal, in "Reflections on the Foundations of Modern Textual Editing" (see note 14 above). Whenever an author revises his work, Peckham argues, he is looking at something already created and is no longer in the position of the creator (or the "initiator" of the "discourse"); he may be the first to revise the work, but his activity is no different from that of publishers' readers or editors who come along later. Peckham's point is similar to the one I am making here, because it recognizes that the activity of "editing" need not have any connection with a concept of "author." I would go on, however, as Peckham does not, and claim that the initiator of a dis-

course can be identified as a historical figure (whether or not his name is known —cf. note 5 above), distinct from others because he is the initiator; that an interest may attach to this initiator; and that the task of attempting to segregate his contributions to the discourse from those of others is therefore one legitimate scholarly pursuit. I have commented in somewhat more detail on this argument of Peckham's in *SB*, 28 (1975), 215-219. Cf. also the remark by Anthony Savile (see note 7 above): "If art conveys value through intentional means it is entirely natural that we should single out for attention the agent whose intentions these are" (p. 106). Zeller's position (see notes 26, 42, and 52 above) is similar to Peckham's in stressing "the difficulty, indeed the impossibility, of obtaining a text attributable exclusively to the author" (p. 249). But, unlike Peckham, he does not reach the point of questioning the individuality of the "author"; indeed, he distinguishes between the attitude of the author toward his text and the attitude of "the reader, the exegete or the editor" (p. 258). Baender (see note 42 above) also

is that once a critic refers to two poems *because they are by the same author,* he has introduced a consideration extrinsic to the poems, and he must thereafter be concerned with the words which the author wrote. Studying poems by particular authors or representative of particular historical periods, therefore, requires a knowledge of what the authors themselves wrote; studying poems by theme or type, without regard for biographical and historical contexts, requires only poems, and the number of hands through which a poem has passed to reach its present state of excellence is irrelevant. Academic departments are usually organized to study the historical development of literature, and it is not surprising that scholars in those departments produce editions which attempt to recover authorial wording. That they do so, however, is not indicative of a split between editorial and critical theory.

The other question—the meaning of "intention"—is too complicated a philosophical issue to be settled here; but we can at least agree that authorial intention in literature cannot simply be equated with an explicit statement by the author explaining his motives, purposes, aims, wishes, or meaning, for intention must surely exist even if no such statements were made or are extant, and any available statements may be inadequate or misleading. The only direct evidence one has for what was in the author's mind is not what he says was there but what one finds in his work. An editor, only through his analysis and understanding of the meaning of the work in the light of his knowledge of the author and the times, will be in a position to use authorial active intention as a basis for editorial choice. That is to say, of the meanings which the editor sees in the work, he will determine, through a weighing of all the information at his command, the one which he regards as most likely to have been the author's; and that determination will influence his decisions regarding variant readings. Recognizing "finality" of intention, in turn, depends on his ability to distinguish revisions which develop an intention in the same direction from those which push it in another direction: the former represent final intentions, the latter new intentions. Whether the editor rejects such "new" intentions or edits a separate text embodying them will vary with the particular situation. But so long as he is producing an edition of an author's writings, he must choose among the author's uncanceled

---

agrees with some parts of Peckham's discussion; but he is opposing Peckham when he affirms his belief "that human beings are discrete, that an individal has the power and privilege of self-expression and of changing his mind, and that other individuals do not have the privilege of altering that self-expression or of forcing that change of mind" (p. 141) .

variants or published revisions in the light of his total understanding of the work and its author.

If it is objected that this conception of the editorial process gives an editor excessive freedom and substitutes subjectivism for rigorous discipline, two answers may be made. In the first place, a scholarly editor (as opposed to a creative one) is still pledged to print only the author's words. He may select readings on the basis of his own literary judgment only when the alternatives are authorial variants; when he chooses an authorial reading previous to the author's last one (or what he judges to be the last one), his justification is that the reading is "final" in terms of his view of the work as an organic whole and that the later reading either creates a new work or is an isolated alteration at odds with the spirit of the work. Beyond that, one may observe that critical perception is necessarily crucial to any act of historical reconstruction, any evaluation of evidence, and thus any edition labeled "critical"; therefore, as Greg says, "it would be disastrous to curb the liberty of competent editors in the hope of preventing fools from behaving after their kind." Perhaps the principal source of difficulty lies in thinking of the editorial and the critical functions as essentially distinct. When one recognizes that justice can be done to an author only by doing justice to his text, one also understands that the editor and the critic must be inseparable.

External Fact as an Editorial Problem

WHEN KEATS IN HIS SONNET ON CHAPMAN'S HOMER WROTE of "stout Cortez," rather than Balboa, staring at the Pacific with eagle eyes, he created what has become the classic instance of a factual error in a work of imaginative literature. Yet few readers have been bothered by the error or felt that it detracts from the power of the sonnet, and editors have not regarded it as a crux calling for emendation. Amy Lowell, after mentioning the possibility that Keats was thinking of Titian's painting of Cortez, dismisses the matter: "at any rate he put Cortez, probably by accident. It is no matter."[1] Classroom editions of Keats have often included some similar comment, such as Clarence DeWitt Thorpe's note that begins, "Historically, 'Cortez' should be read 'Balboa,'" and ends, "Poetically, it does not matter; the poem is true and magnificent."[2] Scarcely anyone would dispute Thorpe's conclusion that the poem is "true and magnificent," as it stands, or would advocate the substitution of "Balboa" in it. But the consensus of opinion on the question does not mean that no significant issues are raised by it. The view that an historical error does not detract from the greatness of a poem is of course grounded on the argument that an imaginative work creates its own internal world for the communication of truth: the work can express a "truth" relevant to the outside world without being faithful to that world in the details out of which the work is constructed. No one is surprised by the expression of this principle, which is, after all, central to an understanding of literature as metaphorical statement. What is less often considered, however, is the complexity of its editorial implications.

Certainly a critical editor cannot take as a general rule Thorpe's comment that "Poetically, it does not matter." Whether or not a particular error matters depends on more than whether or not it occurs in a poem or a "creative" work: sometimes a factual error in a poem may indeed call for correction, while at other times it may not, and the editor

---

1. *John Keats* (1925), p. 181.
2. In the Odyssey Press edition of the *Complete Poems and Selected Letters* (1935), p. 45.

must decide which is the case in any given instance, and why. If "Cortez" need not be or should not be corrected, the reason is not simply that factual inaccuracies are necessarily irrelevant to the artistic success of poems; the reason must instead focus on why it is either impractical or unwise to make a change in this particular case. Is "Cortez" so much a part of the pattern of versification as to rule out an alteration to a word of so different a sound as "Balboa"? Does "Cortez," calling up in the reader's mind the early days of the Spanish in Central America, manage to convey the meaning that was intended—or, at least, is it not too far off the mark to prevent the reader from grasping that meaning? (If the word, through some error of transmission, had been misspelled in such a way as not to be recognizable as "Cortez"—resulting perhaps in a name with no allusive significance or one with an inappropriate association—what would the editor do?) Or, on another level, does the long familiarity of the "Cortez" reading have any bearing on the editor's feeling that a change cannot now be contemplated? If so, does it make a difference whether the traditional, if unfactual, reading is one (like "Cortez") known to have been written down by the author or whether it is one whose origins are less certain? However simple or obvious it may seem at first to say that the "Cortez" reading should not be disturbed, questions of this kind are inevitably involved.

The editor of a critical text sets out to eliminate from a particular copy-text what can be regarded as errors in it; defining what constitutes an "error" is therefore basic to the editorial procedure. Any concept of error involves the recognition of a standard: an editor can label certain readings of a text erroneous only by finding that they fail to conform to a certain standard. Determining appropriate standards for editorial judgment must take into account the nature of the piece of writing as a whole and the nature of each individual passage in it as well as the nature of the edition that is to result, and it must recognize that errors may fall into discrete classes, each demanding different treatment. One may feel that errors of historical fact, for instance, should be corrected in some kinds of works (or passages) and not in other kinds, but that decision involves some consideration of authorial intention and will thus be affected by the attitude that the edition is to take toward questions of intention. If the goal of an edition—as with most scholarly critical editions —is to attempt to establish the text intended by the author at a particular time, one's decisions about what constitutes errors will be affected accordingly. Intention and error are inseparable concepts, because errors are by definition unintended deviations (unintended on a conscious level, that is, whatever unconscious motivation for them there may be). If a writer intentionally distorts historical fact for the purposes of a work, that distortion is not an error in terms of the work, nor is it a textual error from the editor's point of view.

An editor must distinguish, however, between accepting factual errors because they are intended features of a literary work and accepting them because they reveal the mental processes of the author. The latter interest is a legitimate and important one, but it may conflict with the aim of establishing the intended text of a work. Both interests can be accommodated through the use of textual notes, but one of those interests must be chosen as the rationale for the editor's treatment of the text itself. If one's aim is to reproduce the text of a particular document, then obviously one reproduces it errors and all, for the errors may be revealing characteristics of the author's direction of thought and in any case are part of the historical record to be preserved. But if one's aim is to offer a critical edition of that text as a finished literary work, one can no more follow a policy of retaining all factual errors than pursue a course of correcting all such errors. In a critical edition the treatment of factual errors can be no mechanical matter, covered by a blanket rule; instead, the editor must give serious thought to the circumstances surrounding each one, thought that will involve settling basic questions about the nature of the editing being undertaken.

Errors of external fact are of course only one category of the larger class of discrepancies in general. Many discrepancies in texts are internal: that is, certain readings are identifiable as errors not because they fail to agree with recognized facts but because they are inconsistent with points established elsewhere within the text. When, for example, Minnie Mavering is referred to as "Molly" in Howells's *April Hopes* or Tashtego is called "Daggoo" in *Moby-Dick*,[3] the discrepancies are matters of internal, rather than external, fact. The authors in these cases cannot have intended to refer to their characters by the wrong names, and the editor of a critical text will rectify such errors. Not all internal errors can be corrected by the simple substitution of a name, however. As alert readers have long noticed, the *Pequod* is described early in *Moby-Dick* (Chapter 16) as having a tiller ("Scorning a turnstile wheel at her reverend helm") but later in the book is given a wheel helm with spokes (Chapters 61, 118—in which the helmsman is said to "handle the spokes" and "ostentatiously handle his spokes"). Similarly, Pip is referred to as an "Alabama boy" (Chapter 27) and is told that a whale would sell for thirty times what he would in Alabama (Chapter 93); but there is also a reference to his "native Tolland County in Connecticut" (Chapter 93) and his father "in old Tolland county" (Chapter 99). Melville evidently did not intend

3. See the Indiana edition of *April Hopes*, ed. Don L. Cook *et al.* (1974), pp. 221–222; and *Moby-Dick*, Chapter 61.

these discrepancies, but a scholarly editor who attempts to eliminate them faces the difficult problem of guessing how Melville would have rewritten the passages. In some instances of this kind the editor's educated guess may be the best solution, but often the wiser course is to let the discrepancies stand.

It should be clear, however, that the editor who allows such errors to remain does so only in the belief that nothing better can be done and not because they are regarded as part of the author's intended text. Internal errors resemble external errors in the sense that they are recognizable by reference to something outside the immediate context: a reading in one sentence (or phrase) is erroneous or discrepant because it fails to match what is said in another sentence (or phrase) elsewhere in the work. But the "external" facts in such instances are still within the limits of the piece of writing, and the author's intention with respect to the internal consistency of the work is made clear to the reader in the work itself. The editor is normally in a position to know, in other words, whether the world of the work is a realistic one, in which a person named Minnie cannot suddenly become Molly and a wheel cannot change into a tiller, or a surrealistic one, in which such "facts" are not stable. In the case of allusions that extend outside the limits of the work, however, the editor is in a more difficult position. Because the reference is to something with an independent existence, one is faced with the question whether the author is attempting to be accurate in citing an external fact or is adapting it so as to give it a new existence within the work. Errors of external fact, therefore, pose quite a different problem from internal discrepancies. They are worth investigating in their own right and because they lead one to consider the fundamental assumptions of editing.

I

One of the most common situations involving external allusion occurs when a writer quotes from an earlier piece of writing. Insofar as the emphasis of the reference is on a verifiable independent source, the quotation should be exact. But insofar as the writer's intention is to adapt the quotation, it becomes a created element in the new work and cannot then be deemed incorrect merely because it fails to correspond with an external source. In many cases the motivation is mixed: the writer wishes to call on the authority of a previous author (expecting readers to recognize the author or the work cited) but at the same time wishes to alter the quotation to serve a particular purpose in the new context. Of course, a writer sometimes simply misquotes without intending to, and if no consequences follow from the misquotation, it is merely an error and nothing more; but if the misquotation becomes the basis for discussion or implication, then it has become an integral part of the new work, whether the misquotation was consciously intended or not.[4]

Many of the possible editorial problems involving quotations can be illustrated by a single famous instance, the section of "Extracts" prefixed to *Moby-Dick*. In this section Melville draws together eighty quotations, ranging from the Bible to mid-nineteenth-century fiction, constituting a massive epigraph to the book. One might at first feel that epigraphs are not part of the text they introduce and that there would thus be no legitimate reason for their not being accurate; but a moment's reflection reminds one that an author selects an epigraph in order to set up a relationship between its implications and those of the text to follow and that one should not be surprised, therefore, if the epigraph were intentionally slanted to make the relationship clearer. Epigraphs are as much a part of a text as the quotations embedded in it. In the case of Melville's "Extracts," the creative nature of epigraphs is evident: the sweep of the assembled material is intended to suggest the greatness and universality of the subject of whales and whaling.[5] Melville furthermore places his quotations in a dramatic framework: they are said to be "Supplied by a Sub-Sub-Librarian," who has "gone through the long Vaticans and street-stalls of the earth" in search of them. The fact that supposedly they have been prepared by a created character does not, of course, mean that any errors in them must necessarily be accepted as contributing to the characterization, but it does strengthen the point that misquotations may at times be functional, and intentionally so. Whether misquotations are in fact intended as part of a characterization can only be determined by the context, and in this instance there is nothing to indicate that Melville wished the reader to regard any errors as lapses on the Sub-Sub-Librarian's part; on the other hand, he may well have wished to alter certain quotations to make them more appropriate as epigraphs to the work that follows, and misquotations in the "Extracts" must be judged critically with this possibility in mind.[6] A survey of some of the editorial

4. This point is taken up in more detail below, in Part II.

5. The two-paragraph prefatory note to the "Extracts" warns the reader not to take the "whale statements, however authentic, in these extracts, for veritable gospel cetology" and claims for them only that they provide "a glancing bird's eye view of what has been promiscuously said, thought, fancied, and sung of Leviathan, by many nations and generations, including our own."

6. Some critics, such as Viola Sachs in *La Contre-Bible de Melville* (1975), assume that all readings of the American first edition were intended by Melville, and they erect their interpretations on that assumption. This approach is uncritical and unrealistic in that it does not admit the possibility that the American text might contain transmissional errors or other unintended readings. But it does draw attention to the fact that the critical editor, in deciding what constitutes an error in the text, may be called upon to assess the soundness of various critics' commentaries.

questions raised by the "Extracts" can provide a convenient introduction to the issues involved in dealing with external references in general.

Perhaps the most straightforward situations are those in which misquotations result from obviously intended alterations by Melville. In the second extract, for example, from Job 41:32, the wording of the printed text[7] (the manuscript does not survive) exactly matches that of the King James Bible except that "Leviathan" is substituted for "He" in "Leviathan maketh a path to shine after him." Clearly no one, in the process of transmission from manuscript to print, could have misread Melville's "He" as "Leviathan"; furthermore, the indefinite reference of "He" calls for some explanation when the passage is quoted out of context. It seems certain that Melville wrote "Leviathan," intentionally altering the wording of his source. Similarly, the extract from Montaigne contains the clause "the sea-gudgeon retires into it in great security," whereas the passage in Hazlitt's Montaigne (Melville's source) reads "this little fish" instead of "the sea-gudgeon." Again, the change cannot have resulted from a misreading of handwriting. Although it is perhaps conceivable that Melville wrote "sea-gudgeon" as a result of losing his place momentarily—since "sea-gudgeon" occurs in an earlier (unquoted) part of Montaigne's sentence—it is much more likely that he wished not to lose this term and substituted it in what is otherwise essentially an accurate quotation. Even undistinctive words can sometimes be recognized as Melville's alterations: the extract from Waller consists of two couplets, separated by a row of asterisks indicating ellipsis; in the second couplet "his" (twice) and "he" appear, rather than Waller's "her" and "she"— substitutions obviously made so that the gender of the pronouns would match that in the first couplet, now that the two couplets are juxtaposed (in the original, forty lines separate them).[8] In instances of this kind the

---

7. References such as this to the text of *Moby-Dick* are to the text of the original American edition (Harper & Brothers, 1851), which was set from the manuscript furnished by Melville and which must serve (in the absence of that manuscript) as the copy-text for a scholarly critical edition. The attention only to wording—and generally not to punctuation and spelling—is commented on below. In the examples to follow, I draw on information turned up by various members of the editorial staff of the Northwestern-Newberry Edition of Melville. The problems in the "Extracts" will be more fully and systematically dealt with in the forthcoming *Moby-Dick* volume in that edition. For valuable comments on an earlier version of this essay—both the part on Melville and the more general part—I am indebted to Fredson Bowers, Harrison Hayford, and Richard Colles Johnson.

8. In the passage from William Tooke's edition of Lucian (1820), Melville's alterations seem clearly to result from his wishing to change the diction: "sea" replaces "deep" and "monstrous" replaces "enormous" (though this second change could involve a misreading of handwriting). In the extract from William Scoresby, the distance at which one can hear the shaking of the whale's tail is said to be "three or four miles" rather than the "two or three miles" of the original, an obvious change for exaggeration. And in the quotation from Thomas Beale "Sperm Whale" is substituted for "sea beast," a change making more explicit the reference to whales.

editor of a critical edition will retain what are in fact misquotations, recognizing that the aim is to reproduce Melville's intended form of the quotations. (The accompanying apparatus should of course inform the reader in each case of the relation between the source passage and the passage of text being edited, for the retention, as well as the alteration, of an "error" in a quotation constitutes an editorial decision that must be put on record.)

Thinking about these examples leads one to see some of the conditions under which emendations in the "Extracts" would have to be made. Unintended slips—authorial, scribal, compositorial—can be present in the text of the "Extracts" just as in the body of the book, and a critical approach to the text demands that all "misquotations" be evaluated and not automatically accepted as intended alterations. When, in the quotation from Blackstone, "caught near the coast" appears instead of "caught near the coasts," and, in the extract from Frederick Debell Bennett, "these weapons" replaces "those weapons"—or when the passage from Uno von Troil contains "lime-stone" instead of "brim-stone"—the substituted word in each case could easily have resulted from a simple transmissional error (such as a memorial lapse or a misreading of handwriting), and in none of these cases does there seem to be any reason for an authorial change. A number of such examples occur in poetic quotations from prominent sources: in the second extract from *Paradise Lost*, Leviathan is said to be stretched like a promontory "in," rather than "on," the deep and to spout out a sea "at his breath," rather than "at his trunk"; and in the extract from Cowper we read that "rockets blew [rather than 'flew'] self driven, / To hang their momentary fire [not 'fires'] / Around [not 'Amid'] the vault of heaven." All these misquotations are conceivable misreadings of handwriting or slips in copying, and it is difficult to see why Melville (or anyone else) would wish to make them intentionally ("fire" for "fires" is a clear instance of error, because the word is supposed to rhyme with "spires" two lines earlier). Slips of this kind, which probably occurred in the process of transmission from authorial manuscript to printed book, call for emendation by the critical editor.

Of course, some of these erroneous readings may have been present in Melville's manuscript, but as long as they can be argued to be unintentional slips the case for emendation is not altered.[9] When the printed

9. Some evidence suggesting that Melville intended to quote accurately in certain instances is available at those points where the original English edition (set from Melville's revised proofs of the American edition) corrects the American, since no one other than Melville would have been likely to bother making such changes. One example is the correction in the English edition of the reading "stuffed with hoops" to "stiff with hoops" in a line from *The Rape of the Lock*; for other examples, see note 10 and the discussion of the

text reads "Hosmannus" at a point where the name in Browne's *Pseudo-doxia Epidemica* is "Hofmannus," the error may well have been Melville's own: since he was probably using his copy of the 1686 edition and was accustomed to transcribing long *s* as "s," he may have mistaken the "f" in this proper name for a long *s*. Some instances are less clear-cut but still make the same point. A line from Elizabeth Oakes Smith is printed in the "Extracts" as "A mariner sat in the shrouds one night," although the original reads "on the shrouds." The reading "in" could simply be a scribal or compositorial misreading of Melville's "on"; but it is also possible that Melville wrote "in," not because he wished to alter the wording but because he was not copying carefully, the "in" perhaps coming naturally to him as the more idiomatic wording. Unless there is reason to believe that Melville intended to revise the quotation—which seems unlikely here—the possible presence of the "in" in his manuscript should not deter the editor from emending to "on."[10] In other words, whenever the possibility of a misreading of handwriting or of an authorial slip outweighs the possibility that the misquotation is an intended one, the editor seeking to establish what the author wished will emend to correct the quotation. Whatever interest there may be in Melville's writing "Hosmannus" and "in the shrouds"—if indeed he did so—belongs to a different level of concern; such evidence will be preserved in the notes but does not belong in a text aimed to satisfy another concern.

An additional example or two may serve further to clarify the role of arguments based on possible slips or misreadings of handwriting. In the Smith quotation, four lines after "in the shrouds," there is the clause "it floundered in the sea," where "it" refers to "whale"; in the original the subject is "he," not "it," but here the conservative editor is likely to feel that the possibility of an intentional change is enough stronger to war-

---

Bunyan citation below. (Of course, some literate person in the English printing- or publishing-house could conceivably have been responsible for certain corrections of this kind; but the pattern of the corrections and the nature of some of the sources involved suggest a greater likelihood that the corrections are Melville's.)

10. Another example possibly involving an idiom could result in a different decision, because of differing circumstances. The quotation from Charles Wilkes's *Narrative of the United States Exploring Expedition* (1844) contains the phrase "with look-outs at the mast-heads," although Wilkes uses the singular "mast-head." To employ the plural when more look-outs than one are involved is an idiom Melville uses repeatedly (as in "the business of standing mast-heads," "the earliest standers of mast-heads," and "modern standers-of-mast-heads" in Chapter 35); furthermore, he apparently gave close attention to this extract in preparing the proofs to send to England, because the reading "her near appearance" in the American edition is altered to the correct one, "her mere appearance," in the English, and it is unlikely that anyone other than Melville would have made such a correction from this kind of source. Under these circumstances, then, there seems stronger reason to leave "mast-heads" than to change it, even though the possibility always remains that it results from a slip or a misreading of handwriting.

rant the retention of the "it." This misquotation could of course have been a mere slip, but at least a misreading of handwriting does not seem to be involved in this case, and that in itself lends some weight to the argument against emendation—though it cannot be the decisive factor. The opening line of the extract from Waller reads "Like Spenser's Talus with his modern flail," but the adjective in Waller is actually "iron," not "modern." There would seem little possibility that "modern" could result from a misreading of handwriting (or from a slip of the pen, for that matter); but "modern" makes no sense, and the editor may well take the position that the word cannot have been intended (even if its presence as an error cannot be explained) and that an emendation is in order. The argument is somewhat strengthened by the fact that Melville a few years later, in "The Bell-Tower," referred to Talus as an "iron slave." But this information is fortuitous: the point is that the editor's critical judgment carries more weight than inconclusive speculation about the transmissional process. That "modern" cannot be explained as arising from a particular kind of error of transmission does not mean that it must therefore be retained by a conservative editor, if that editor considers the change unlikely to have been intended by the author. The critical editing of a text must extend to the quotations that are a part of the text. Because quotations have external sources, the editor has access to one more stage of antecedent document at these points than elsewhere in the text and thus is in a more informed position for detecting erroneous readings.

The process of locating those external sources, however, raises some important questions of editorial procedure. First is the problem of deciding what particular edition of a source text is the proper one to use for comparison. If the text of a quotation in the "Extracts" matches the text of the corresponding passage in the first edition of the work quoted from, the problem does not exist, for it does not matter whether Melville used the first edition or some other edition, as long as the resulting quotation is accurate.[11] But when the text in the "Extracts" does not correspond with that of the first edition, one cannot assume that the difference necessarily results from a transmissional error in the process of writing and printing *Moby-Dick* or from a deliberate change on Melville's part; it may be that Melville copied accurately, but from a different edition. If

11. The possibility that Melville used either a revised or a corrupt text and misquoted from it in such a way as to produce the reading of the first edition is hardly worth the editor's while to think about in most instances. It is conceivable, however, that such a situation could occasionally be of some importance, if an author were attempting to reproduce a passage from a revised edition of a work and through an unlucky slip managed to recreate the reading of the unrevised text; but this occurrence would of course depend on an extreme coincidence.

so, the editor's thinking about the passage will be affected, and it is therefore important to know, if possible, the immediate source of each quotation. Yet in the case of many classics that have gone through numerous editions and have been excerpted and quoted even more often the editor cannot be expected to have searched through all possible sources. It is conceivable, for example, that Melville happened to take the Waller passage from a secondary source that misquoted "iron" as "modern"; but an editor cannot begin to find all the places where Waller's lines may have been quoted and has no choice but to proceed on the basis of the available knowledge. Frequently, however, an editor will know some of the favorite sources that an author is likely to use and may even have some information about the particular copies read. That Melville's ninth extract—identified only as *"Other or Octher's verbal narrative taken down from his mouth by King Alfred. A.D. 890"*—comes from Robert Henry's *The History of Great Britain* (1771) is not difficult to learn when one knows that J. Ross Browne's *Etchings from a Whaling Cruise* (1846), one of Melville's principal sources, also quotes this passage; furthermore, it is clear that Melville took the passage directly from Browne, and did not go back to Henry, because his extract agrees with Browne in reading "this country" at a point where the first edition of 1771 reads "these parts." A similar instance is the extract from Bunyan, which does not reproduce the relevant passage from the 1682 edition of *The Holy War* but instead follows the wording (except for a sixteen-word ellipsis) of a paraphrase of this passage in Henry T. Cheever's *The Whale and His Captors* (1849).[12]

The question that all this leads to is how the editor should handle errors or alterations that were already present in the immediate source of the quotations. If Melville quotes a corrupt text under the impression that he is providing the reader with another author's words, is it part of an editor's duty to replace that corrupt text with an accurate text? Answering this question goes to the heart of the concept of scholarly critical editing. Expecting editors to make such "corrections" of quotations is in effect asking them to establish the text of each quoted passage so as to fulfill its author's intentions. Such a procedure would mean treating each quotation as if it were an individual item in an anthology, not a part of a context created by another writer. The reader comes to Melville's "Extracts" not to seek established texts of Waller and Bunyan but

---

12. In some cases another extract may provide a clue to the source. The quotation from John Hunter is a paraphrase of the original wording in the *Philosophical Transactions* of the Royal Society for 1787; but it matches exactly (except for the omission of "an") the wording quoted by William Paley in his *Natural Theology* (1802)—which is the work Melville cites for the immediately following extract.

to see what Melville does with those authors; the editor's job is to establish Melville's versions of Waller and Bunyan, which may turn out to be considerably different from the texts that would appear in scholarly editions of them. If a corrupt text of a quotation is the one that Melville knew, responded to, and wished to set before his readers, then that text is the intended one under these circumstances. Emendation may be necessary if it is clear that the copy-text version of a quotation contains readings unintended by Melville, but the test for emendation is not whether the readings were unintended by the original writer. In order to be in a position to make intelligent decisions on this question, an editor is obviously required to perform some textual research among editions of the quoted work: if the copy-text version of a quotation does not match the text of the first edition of the quoted work, the editor must attempt to locate another edition that does match, for otherwise there is no basis for judging whether the variants were present in Melville's immediate source or originated at a later point (either in his own copying—intentionally or inadvertently—or in the succeeding steps of transmission). The scholarly editor must be able to draw the line between restoring an author's intended wording of a quotation and collaborating with the author by pushing the process of "correcting" the quotation to a point never contemplated by the author. To claim that Melville intended to quote accurately is not to the purpose: aside from the historical question of the degree of accuracy implied at a given time in the past by the act of "quoting" (discussed below), this claim mixes up different kinds of intention. That Melville may have "intended" in advance to quote accurately the sentiments of various writers does not alter the fact that the scholarly editor's concern is with Melville's active intention as he wrote, reflected in the quotations themselves.[13] The immediate sources he accepted and used become the authoritative sources for the quotations in this context.

Thus the extract from Thomas Fuller's *The Holy State, and the Profane State* reads "mighty whales which swim" at a point where the first edition of 1642 and the "second edition enlarged" of 1648 read "mighty whales who swim"; but because "which" is the reading of the London 1841 edition—the edition borrowed by Melville, according to Merton M. Sealts's *Melville's Reading* (1966)—there would seem to be no reason

13. These different kinds of intention are discussed in more detail in G. T. Tanselle, "The Editorial Problem of Final Authorial Intention," *Studies in Bibliography*, 29 (1976), 167–211 (which includes references to many other treatments of the subject). An important and still more recent discussion, containing some useful criticism of that essay, is Steven Mailloux's "Authorial Intention and Conventional Reader Response," Chapter 7 (pp. 171–206) of his University of Southern California dissertation, "Interpretive Conventions and Recent Anglo-American Literary Theory" (1977).

to emend. The editor is not called upon to investigate whether any authority could attach to "which" as a reading in Fuller's text, for Melville evidently copied accurately the wording of the passage that struck him in the 1841 edition; whether or not that wording corresponds exactly to Fuller's intention is irrelevant, because it is the wording that Melville encountered and used. In the case of the Waller extract, if an edition or secondary source available to Melville could indeed be found containing the phrase "modern flail," no emendation would be required, however peculiar the reading seems, because the passage with that reading in it would be the one that Melville reacted to and found appropriate for inclusion in the "Extracts." Until such a source is found, however, the inherent unlikelihood of the reading will weigh more heavily with an editor than the theoretical possibility that Melville came upon the reading somewhere; the editor is acting responsibly if, after a reasonable search in Waller editions and books known to have been used by Melville, the reading is regarded as an error to be emended. Some textual research is nevertheless clearly necessary. An editor who looked only at the original 1645 edition of Waller's *Poems* would find that the line reads "Like fairy Talus with his iron flail" and might conclude that "Spenser's Talus," as well as "modern flail," is an erroneous reading (though possibly one intended by Melville to identify the allusion). But a little further research would reveal that "fairy" was changed to "Spenser's" in the 1664 edition and would thus place "Spenser's" in a different class of readings from "modern." Without such textual investigation, editors are not in a position to make informed judgments; but pursuing that research by no means implies that they are shifting their focus from the intentions of the quoter to those of the quoted.[14]

14. Melvyn New has encountered a situation in which he believes that an editor should employ as the copy-text for a long quotation the first edition of the work quoted from. In *Tristram Shandy* Sterne quotes the entire "Memoire" from Heinrich van Deventer's *Observations importantes sur le Manuel des accouchemens* (1734); New argues that "Much of the wit of the 'Memoire's' inclusion in *Tristram* lies in the fact that Sterne could use it verbatim," that "it is not a fiction but an historical record of an actual deliberation." One can guess, New says, that "had Sterne had photoreproductive processes available to him, he would have used them for providing a printer's copy of the 'Memoire'" and that one "comes closest to Sterne's intention" by using the 1734 Deventer text. New recognizes, however, that this text would have to be emended with what seem to be Sterne's intended alterations and that punctuation "remains a difficult problem, whichever text is used as copy text"— thus in fact reopening the question of how much is gained by adopting the earlier copy-text. Whether or not one is persuaded by New that presumptive authority here should be given to the 1734 text, one can agree that the problem is to separate Sterne's "function as copyist" from his "function as artist" (due allowance, of course, being made for contemporary conventions of "copying") and that "in the text underlying any borrowed material there is the possibility of a wealth of bibliographical and critical information." See "*Tristram Shandy* and Heinrich van Deventer's *Observations*," *PBSA*, 69 (1975), 84–90; and "The Sterne Edi-

A related element in considering a writer's intentions in making a quotation is an understanding of the contemporary conventions of quoting. Generally before the twentieth century (and in some cases even into the century) quotations were not thought of as "inaccurate" or "incorrect" if they occasionally departed from the wording—to say nothing of the punctuation and spelling—of the source, as long as they did not distort the gist of its meaning. It was not considered wrong, even in expository writing (that is to say, writing not usually classed as "imaginative" or belletristic), to place between quotation marks what we would now think of as a paraphrase or an adaptation. For an editor to make such "quotations" conform to modern standards of accuracy, therefore, would be to modernize (that is, to employ a modern approach—for the corrected quotation would often be less "modern" in form); and the scholarly editor will not wish to engage in modernizing here any more than with the punctuation and spelling of the rest of the text. In checking Melville's extracts against their sources, then, an editor need not be concerned with spelling, punctuation, capitalization, or other formal matters except to the extent that discrepancies markedly affect meaning (or obviously result from slips or nonauthorial styling) or that agreements point to Melville's immediate sources. It clearly never occurred to Melville to be troubled about taking a twenty-word middle section out of a long sentence of Davenant's and beginning it with a capital letter; or juxtaposing, without ellipsis marks (and actually in reverse order), two sentences from Bacon's *History Naturall and Experimentall of Life and Death* (1638) that are in fact separated by six of Bacon's "Items"; or running together two lines of verse without indicating the line break, as in the extracts from Bacon's version of Psalm 104 and from *1 Henry IV*. When Melville inserts "Fife" in parentheses after "this coast" in his quotation from Robert Sibbald and "whales" in parentheses after "these monsters" in his extract from Darwin, he is using parentheses to mark explanatory insertions in the way that we would now use square brackets.[15] An editor who injects ellipsis dots, virgules, and brackets into these quotations is modernizing, by requiring Melville's quotations—and each of the extracts is in fact printed in quotation marks—to conform to present-day standards. The place for showing these relationships between the

---

tion: The Text of *Tristram Shandy*," in *Editing Eighteenth Century Novels*, ed. G. E. Bentley, Jr. (1975), pp. 86–87.

15. The extract from Darwin in fact illustrates two practices: the insertion of "(whales)" occurs within the quotation, whereas the quotation is interrupted—by the use of closing and then opening quotation marks—for the insertion of "(Terra Del Fuego)" after "the shore."

quotations and their sources is the textual apparatus or other editorial end-matter; in the text itself the scholarly editor will wish to respect nineteenth-century customs in the use of quotation marks (and what they imply about the enclosed material) just as much as nineteenth-century practices in placing apostrophes, commas, and other punctuation.

This custom of allusive quotation is represented among Melville's extracts by a wide diversity of situations, which thus help further to define the nature of the accuracy that is attempted. In addition to substitutions, which often could be the result of a slip of the pen or a misreading of handwriting, there are instances of insertion, omission, and paraphrase that cannot reasonably be considered inadvertent. For example, the extract from the account of Schouten's sixth circumnavigation in John Harris's *Navigantium atque Itinerantium Bibliotheca* (1705) begins, "Here they saw such huge shoals of whales," whereas the passage in Harris reads "saw an incredible number of Penguins, and such huge shoals of whales." Obviously Melville wished to omit the six words after "saw" as irrelevant to his purpose; deleting the reference to penguins focuses more attention on the whales, but Melville saw no reason to note his ellipsis.[16] Similarly, in the quotation from Jefferson there is an unmarked omission of fifty-one words between the subject and the verb; the sentence from Daniel Tyerman and George Bennet's *Journal* (1831) silently omits eleven words; and five are left out of the sentence from James Colnett's *Voyage* (1798).[17] Sometimes omissions and substitutions occur together, as when four words are omitted and four other alterations are made in the sentence from Richard Stafford, causing it to refer only to one man and one whale instead of to a group of each. The motivation for some of these changes is not always as obvious as in the omission of the reference to penguins or the insertion of "Whale-" in "The Whaleship Globe" (the extract from William Lay and Cyrus Hussey), but there can be no doubt that such alterations are intentional and that they did not, in Melville's view, prevent the results from being regarded as "extracts" from the works named. Indeed, passages placed in quotation marks could depart even further from the originals and consist entirely of paraphrase: the sentences from Stowe, Boswell, and James Cook are far enough from the original wording that they have to be considered paraphrases made by Melville (unless he was following secondary sources

16. The same situation occurs in the quotation from Margaret Fuller's translation of Eckermann's *Conversations with Goethe*, where Melville has silently omitted "and sea-monsters" following "whales."

17. Transitional words in source passages form another obviously intended class of omissions. The omission of "other" from "what other thing" in the extract from Philemon Holland's edition of Plutarch and of "on the other hand" from a quotation from Frederick Debell Bennett are necessary adjustments when the passages are taken out of context.

that have not yet been located). And the first sentence of the extract from Uno von Troil was apparently constructed by Melville's rearranging parts of the original sentence. It is impossible to analyze precisely the various reasons underlying these changes; but it is clear that the desire to alter passages so as to emphasize their connection with whaling is not the sole explanation. The pattern of the extracts as a whole shows that the concept of what constitutes "quotation" here is a much looser one than present-day writers are accustomed to. As in any other piece of writing, intention is ultimately defined by the work itself, and the extracts, as a group, establish their own standards. When Melville's departures from his sources result simply from his practice of approximate quotation, they cannot be thought of as "unintended." Errors, to be emended editorially, can certainly be located in the extracts, but the process of identifying them must be founded on an understanding of the level of accuracy attempted in the first place. (And in a scholarly edition the information used by the editor for determining this level will be available to the reader in the notes that record or explain the differences between the extracts and their sources.)

Melville's twisting of quotations for his own purposes—beyond any customary casualness in quoting—does, however, play a significant role in producing the wording found in the "Extracts." When Melville paraphrases a passage, places the result in quotation marks, and labels the source, he is engaging in allusive quotation but is approaching the border line—even by nineteenth-century standards—between quotation and fresh composition. He apparently crosses that line in the passage that purports to be from Antonio de Ulloa, describing the breath of the whale "attended with such an insupportable smell, as to bring on a disorder of the brain"; these words seem in fact to be Melville's own elaboration of the three-word phrase "an insupportable smell," which refers in Ulloa to a fish called "cope." The next step is to create an entirely new passage and provide it with a fictitious source: the extract following the one from John Ramsay McCulloch is labeled *From 'Something' unpublished* and is presumably Melville's own extension of a point raised by the McCulloch quotation, for it is clearly designed to follow McCulloch's statement but does not occur there in the original. Melville does not engage in this practice often, but the presence of one or two examples further strengthens the view of the "Extracts" section as a creative work and not a mere anthology.

Suggesting that something created on the spot has an independent existence outside the work tends to break down any rigid boundary between what is external and what is internal, and references to "real" sources can sometimes partake more of the internal world of the work than of external reality. One extract, which describes some white crew members returning from the pursuit of a whale to find "their ship in bloody possession of the savages enrolled among the crew," is credited to a *"Newspaper Account of the Taking and Retaking of the Whale-ship Hobomack."* In fact, however, no such mutiny took place on board the Falmouth ship *Hobomok*. Melville's recollection of stories he must have heard probably resulted in the mixing together of details of two different events: the 1835 fight between some Namorik Islanders and the crew of the Falmouth ship *Awashonks*, and the 1842 mutiny by some Kingsmill Islanders on board the Fairhaven ship *Sharon*. The details of the *Sharon* mutiny fit more closely with those described in the extract; but one of the officers of the *Awashonks* in 1835 was captain of the *Hobomok* in 1841, when Melville's ship encountered it, and Melville may therefore have been thinking partly of his account. After investigating this tangle, Wilson Heflin decided that this extract must be "a piece of Melville's invention."[18] If so, no substantive emendation would be appropriate. To replace *"Hobomack"* with *"Awashonks"* or *"Sharon"* (which one?) would probably not restore what Melville intended to write; and, while either one would fit the facts somewhat better, there is no reason why Melville should be required to follow facts here. Whether or not the spelling of the ship should be corrected to *"Hobomok"* is a separate question. Because Melville did know of the actual *Hobomok* and because "o" and "a" are sometimes difficult to distinguish in his handwriting, it may be that he wrote "Hobomock" rather than "Hobomack," and one could defend an emendation to *"Hobomock"* (as a permissible variant of the correct spelling) or possibly to *"Hobomok."* Recognizing that what the extract describes never took place aboard the real *Hobomok* does not prevent one from correcting the spelling of the ship's name on the assumption that the actual ship *Hobomok* is being referred to in the citation—for the likelihood is that Melville was thinking of the real ship but confusing what happened on it.[19] The supposed quotation is thus

18. "Herman Melville's Whaling Years" (Vanderbilt diss., 1952), p. 224.

19. Knowledge of the range of variant spellings recorded in the *DAE* for the Indian evil deity—including "Hobomoko," "Abamacho," and "Hobbamock"—might cause one to argue that "Hobomack" falls within the range of permissible deviation, but presumably such a range did not exist for the ship's name. A different kind of argument against emending the spelling would be to say that the correction does not make the citation fit the extract better than it did before and that under the circumstances the *Hobomack* becomes in effect a fictitious ship of Melville's invention. The great similarity between "Hobomack" and "Hobomok," however, makes it difficult to believe that Melville did not have the real ship in mind. And an editor's intervention to correct Melville's intended reference in the citation carries no implication that the extract and the citation are being brought into closer agreement: there is no reason why Melville cannot be allowed to place on board a real ship events that never occurred there, and no reason why an editor cannot make a local correction of a spelling error without being obligated to produce factual accuracy in the larger context.

inspired by real events and refers to a real ship; but the *"Newspaper Account,"* and the *Hobomok* mutiny it reports, exist only within Melville's "Extracts."

Discussion of *"Hobomack,"* which occurs in a citation rather than an extract, calls attention to the fact that problems of external reference are just as likely to occur in the citations. Some of the questions they raise are the same as those connected with quotations in general. Thus the citations of Darwin's *"Voyage of a Naturalist"* and Lay and Hussey's *"Narrative of the Globe Mutiny"* should not be considered errors simply because these are not the actual titles of the two books; the works alluded to are easily identifiable from such references, which are examples of the widespread nineteenth-century custom of allusive citation.[20] And when Robert P. Gillies's *Tales of a Voyager to the Arctic Ocean* (1826) is reported as *"Tales of a Whale Voyager to the Arctic Ocean,"* one knows that the inaccurate citation, with *"Whale"* inserted, is intended by Melville. Or when *"Most Extraordinary and Distressing"* is omitted and *"Spermaceti-Whale"* becomes *"Sperm Whale"* in the long title of Owen Chase's *Narrative* (1821), one can allow the altered wording to stand on the grounds that it seems more likely to have resulted from intentional alteration than inadvertent slip. But another long title, for Henry T. Cheever's *The Whale and His Captors* (1849), is transcribed so precisely as to suggest that exact quotation is intended, and the one slight omission —an "as" introducing the last phrase—should therefore probably be rectified.

Citation of an altogether wrong title raises a more interesting issue. The extract from James Montgomery is credited to *"World before the Flood"* but actually comes from his "The Pelican Island"; the error is one that Melville takes from a secondary source, because Cheever's book quotes the same lines from Montgomery and provides the same citation. The question, raised earlier, whether an editor is called upon to correct the errors of a secondary source, requires further thought in a case of this kind. Misquotations in the text derived from a secondary source— and there are two in the Montgomery passage deriving from Cheever— generally do not require emendation because they constitute part of the passages as the quoter knew them.[21] But allowing an erroneous citation of this sort to stand is a different matter. It is true that Melville was equal-

---

20. A related kind of approximate citation occurs in the reference to *"Opening sentence of Hobbes's Leviathan."* The sentence quoted is actually the fifth, but *"Opening"* should not therefore be called an error: *"Opening sentence"* is apparently what Melville wrote, meaning "a sentence that is part of the opening," "an early sentence."

21. A third error in the Montgomery extract, "instincts" for "instinct," should be corrected because the word is correct in Cheever and because the misreading could easily have resulted from a slip.

ly trusting of Cheever here and accepted the title as *"World before the Flood"*; but surely his intention in writing it down, judging from his practice in the "Extracts" as a whole, was simply to provide a factual reference. Of course, one can also argue, as with the misquotations in the text, that he may have responded to the wording of the title he found in his source and that the title should similarly not be corrected. Another extract (although the situation is not quite parallel) may provide some relevant evidence: *"Pilgrim's Progress"* is corrected in the first English edition to *"Holy War,"* a correction that was evidently among those made by Melville on the proofs sent abroad and one that reflects a concern for correct citations. In any case, the decision on the Montgomery citation is a difficult one. Editors could argue either way; but there would seem to be enough difference in function and effect between a citation of source and a quotation to justify differing treatments, and a case can be made for correcting the Montgomery reference. (Even if no emendation is made, a note should of course call attention to the correct title and explain Melville's source of the incorrect one.) Other corrections of factual errors in citations are less debatable: the man who wrote on the Bermudas in the *Philosophical Transactions* of the Royal Society in 1668 was named Stafford, not "Strafford," and the date of Jefferson's *"Whale Memorial to the French minister"* was 1788, not "1778."[22] There is no pattern in the "Extracts" suggesting the deliberate alteration of facts of this kind: although the "Extracts" section can be called an imaginative work, it maintains a firm link with external reality.

Another, much shorter, preliminary section precedes the "Extracts" at the front of *Moby-Dick*, and it raises similar problems because it, too, is made up of material having an existence outside the work and is assigned a fictional compiler, a "Late Consumptive Usher to a Grammar School." Called "Etymology," this section consists of three quotations, followed by a list of the words for "whale" in thirteen languages. Such a list would appear to be purely a factual matter, but the critical editor, interested in Melville's intention, will find that it raises some intricate questions. One of them can serve as a kind of conspectus of the considerations involved in dealing with external fact in a literary work. Just before the English word "WHALE" in the list appears the entry for the Icelandic, and the word given in the original edition is "WHALE," identical with the English. Because this is not the Icelandic for "whale"

---

22. On another occasion, a date in a citation identifies the actual edition used. The citation *"Captain Cowley's Voyage around the Globe. A.D. 1729"* is not an error, even though Cowley's voyage took place in 1683–86 and an account of it appeared in William Hacke's *A Collection of Voyages* in 1699, because another edition of Hacke appeared in 1729. Melville's date, therefore, refers to his source and not to the actual voyage.

and because it seems unlikely that Melville would have wished to have two identical words in his short list (one of the purposes of which appears to be to display a variety of words)[23] it would at first seem reasonable to regard the Icelandic "WHALE" as a scribal or compositorial error (influenced by the word in the next line), or as an authorial slip. But the situation is not that simple: Melville himself may very well have intended to write the word "whale," because in Uno von Troil's *Letters on Iceland* (1780), in the paragraph just preceding the one from which Melville took one of his extracts, there occurs the expression "*illwhale* (bad whales)," in which the first word is offered as the Icelandic and the parenthesis as the English translation. From this Melville may have concluded that if he dropped the "ill" from "illwhale" he would be left with the Icelandic for "whale." If so, he was doubly wrong: in the first place, "illwhale" is not an Icelandic word, and the second edition of Troil (1780) corrects it to "*Illhwele*"; in the second place, removing the "Ill," even from this corrected form, does not produce the word for "whale." What is the editor to do? If Melville is misled by an error in a source and bases a discussion on the error, nothing can be done; but here there is no discussion, only a simple listing in which Melville apparently intended to give the correct word. But if one applies to Troil's corrected text the operation Melville seemingly performed on the first text, one still has an incorrect word; the editor would be in the position of making an emendation no more correct than the original reading. If one decides to correct the text, then, one must bypass Melville's presumed source entirely and insert the modern Icelandic word "hvalur."[24] One could reasonably defend this action by arguing—as with certain facts in the citations of sources for the extracts—that Melville's intention, evident in the text, to provide correct facts justifies the editor's going beyond Melville's knowledge to make the correction, so long as the error does not achieve a possible significance of its own within the text. On the other hand, one could argue against the emendation by saying that, if Melville did indeed, on the basis of consulting an outside source, regard "whale" as the correct Icelandic word, "whale" is thus his intended form and should

23. The last two words in the list differ by one letter: "pekee-nuee-nuee" for Fegee, and "pehee-nuee-nuee" for Erromangoan. Whereas "pehee" is an acceptable rendering of the word for "fish" usually transcribed as "pihi," "pekee" is not; yet an editor must be cautious about emending it, for Melville's desire to show different words may have taken precedence here over any desire to offer precisely accurate information. (Using this argument here would not prevent an editor from correcting a factual error elsewhere in the list where the circumstances were different.)

24. Assuming that Melville would not have intended to give the Old Icelandic "hvalr." (If "whalr" were a variant of "hvalr," it might be a tempting possibility, differing from "whale" by only one letter; but it is a highly improbable form.) The Northwestern-Newberry editors are grateful to Richard N. Ringler for help with this problem.

remain. But Melville's use of Troil's erroneous *"illwhale,"* while highly likely, is after all conjectural and should not be elevated to the status of fact. One cannot dismiss entirely the possibility that first suggested itself: "whale" as a scribal or compositorial error for the correct word (presumably "hvalur") in Melville's manuscript, or even Melville's own lapse (with "hvalur" as what he meant to write). Even if one finally emends on this basis, the speculation about Melville's possible use of Troil is not wasted effort, for in suggesting one explanation for the appearance of "WHALE" in the text it focuses attention on a crucial issue: the degree to which Melville wished to respect external fact in this instance. Besides, the critical editor cannot be in a position to make informed judgments at such points without investigating all available leads to external sources. This illustration draws together a remarkable number of basic editorial questions and shows how references to external fact can provide peculiarly effective test cases for revealing how thoroughly an editorial approach has been thought through.

II

If the "Extracts" and the "Etymology" in *Moby-Dick* are unusual in providing such a concentrated array of editorial questions, the questions themselves are not at all extraordinary but are in fact the characteristic ones that arise whenever external references are involved. Sampling the thinking that goes into answering those questions in this particular instance should serve as preparation for considering the general problem in a larger framework. To begin with, determining what is "external" to a piece of writing—and what in it should therefore be expected to correspond with a standard outside itself—is a difficult task of definition. As soon as one starts to check quotations, titles of books, dates, and names of persons and places against external sources, one begins to ask how these elements differ from the spellings of all the ordinary words of the text and whether there is actually anything in the text that does not have to be measured against an external standard. On one level, of course, any communication has to be regarded as made up largely of external elements: a writer or speaker would not be able to communicate without utilizing a set of conventional symbols that are interpreted in the same way by other persons. The words and grammar of a language are external in this sense, for writers must in some degree conform to linguistic conventions that are a social product and are not their own personal inventions. Editors are concerned with such matters, and in attempting to establish unmodernized texts they take pains to see that the spelling and punctuation, for instance, conform to the standards of the writer's time or fall within the range of possibilities conventionally tolerated at that time. But editors will feel that they are not quite doing the same thing when they "correct" a date or a quotation or the spelling of an historical figure's name; they will feel, in other words, that specific historical facts constitute a different category from the medium—words and grammar—employed for communication and are external to the communication in a different sense.

In thinking about these matters, Ferdinand de Saussure's seminal distinction between *langue* and *parole* is basic, for it separates language, with its infinite possibilities for expression, from each particular act of speaking—it separates "what is social from what is individual." *Langue* is "a product that is passively assimilated by the individual," whereas *parole*, the individual act of execution, is "wilful and intellectual" and is "never carried out by the collectivity."[25] This distinction can, by extension, help to explain the editor's role. Editors, of course, deal with individual acts of expression, and their task, in reconstructing an author's intention, is to determine just what in the expression, as it has come down to them, is "wilful"; they constantly examine the characteristics of the preserved *parole* in the light of the *langue*, as it were. When a word is not spelled conventionally or a singular verb follows a plural subject, are these "wilful" deviations by the author or are they simply errors of transmission (including authorial slips) at points where the author was passively following (or intending to follow) the conventions of the language? An author may, for the purposes of the immediate act of expression, decide to violate the rules of the language, and that violation can become an effective part of the communication; but if such violation proceeds too far it can prevent communication and turn the utterance into a purely private one.[26] The act of critical editing is a constant weighing of the extent to which a work can be autonomous. At each point of possible deviation from the norm, the editor is called upon to adjudicate the claims of idiosyncrasy against those of convention. In most instances, all there is to go on is the intention manifested in the work itself; the editor's decisions are based on an understanding of the internal workings of a particular act of expression.[27] For this reason one can think of these

25. *Course in General Linguistics*, ed. Charles Bally, Albert Sechehaye, and Albert Reidlinger, and trans. Wade Baskin (1959), pp. 13–14.

26. No distinct line separates the two. What may seem nonsense in one context may become concrete poetry in another.

27. Archibald A. Hill, in "The Locus of the Literary Work," *English Studies Today*, 3rd ser. (1964), pp. 41–50, after discussing the bearing of Saussure's distinction on literary study, defines "intention" as a "structural hypothesis derived from analysis of the text" (p. 50). A fuller discussion of this point occurs in G. T. Tanselle's "The Editorial Problem of Final Authorial Intention" (see note 13 above).

matters as internal, even though in handling them one must naturally refer to the external conventions of the medium.

The difference at points where quotations, dates, and the like occur is that in these instances there is something external to be taken into account in addition to the potentialities of the language itself. These parts of the expression make external reference in a way that the rest of the words do not; they are second-hand elements, so to speak, because they are taken over from a previous *parole*, a previous specific use. The situation is most obvious in the case of quotations: words quoted (or even paraphrased) from a particular passage by another writer have lying behind them, when placed in a new context, an external standard of reference besides that of the words and grammar involved—namely, the specific configuration of words and syntax that constituted the other writer's communication. This additional standard poses for editors an additional problem: at such points they have to consider not only words, punctuation, and grammar—as they would anywhere—but also what relation the passage is meant to bear to the original (or some other earlier) occurrence of the same passage. Determining what makes it in fact the "same" passage (when the two are not identical) is analogous to deciding when authors' revisions of their own works produce new works and when they do not. Indeed, authors returning to work they have previously written stand in much the same relationship to it as they would to the work of other authors. The central question faced by editors whenever they are confronted with a piece of writing that contains within it fragments from earlier pieces of writing is the one formulated by E. D. Hirsch, Jr., in his summary of Saussure: "should we assume that sentences from varied provenances retain their original meanings or that these heterogeneous elements have become integral components of a new total meaning?" Put another way, "should we consider the text to represent a compilation of divers *paroles* or a new unitary *parole* 'respoken' by the new author or editor?" Hirsch replies that "there can be no definitive answer to the question, except in relation to a specific scholarly or aesthetic purpose."[28]

28. *Validity in Interpretation* (1967), p. 233. The role of literary sensitivity in determining the function of misquotation in an author's writing is well illustrated by Christopher Ricks in "Pater, Arnold and Misquotation," *Times Literary Supplement*, 25 Nov. 1977, pp. 1383–85. Ricks concludes that Pater reads "what he wishes to have been said": he creates a "'world within' . . . only by a violation of a world without, another man's 'world within' as it had become embodied . . . in the inter-subjective world which is the words of a poem." Whereas "Pater's misquotations are the rewriting of his authors so that they say special Paterian things," Arnold's "are the rewriting of his authors so that they say unspecial things," reducing "something individual to something commonplace." Another discussion of the creative use of quotations, pointing a parallel with the developing text of a ballad through oral tradition, is M. J. C. Hodgart's "Misquotation as Re-creation," *Essays in Criticism*, 3 (1953), 28–38. Misquotations that become integral parts of the works in which

In scholarly editing, the editor aims to conform to the desires of the author and must therefore attempt to understand the author's aesthetic purpose in quoting. There may be times when an author intends to be factually accurate in making a quotation and other times (even within the same work) when the author is less concerned with the quotation as a quotation than with making it a supporting element in the new context. The editor of a critical text cannot escape the responsibility of judging which is the case at any given point.

If quotations are perhaps the most immediately obvious examples of second-hand, or repeated, *paroles*, they are by no means the only elements of a discourse that can be so classified. References to actual geographical locations, specific historical figures, dates of real events, and so on are also instances where words are taken over from a prior use. Ordinary concrete nouns, like "chair" and "table," refer to any member of a given class and not to individual objects until employed by a writer or speaker to do so; spelling or pronouncing "chair" correctly is a function of the conventions of the language, not of the particular use in referring to one specific actual or imagined chair. The same can frequently be said of words like "Jefferson" and "1788": a writer can create an Oliver Jefferson, spell his name "Jeffarson," and have him participate in a fictitious battle at a fictitious location in 1788. To do this is to pin "Jefferson" (as well as "1788") down to one among the infinite possibilities of denotation it contains. But if the context shows that the reference is to Thomas Jefferson's whale memorial of 1788, the writer is using a "Jefferson" and a "1788" for which precise denotations have already been established. If indeed the reference is to the real Thomas Jefferson and to the whale memorial actually issued in 1788—and that is a crucial editorial question—the writer is not assigning the denotations to the words but is in effect quoting an earlier specific assignment, one that many readers may already be familiar with and will recognize without explanation. Although it is not customary in written material to place quotation marks around a proper name whenever a previous use of the name is meant, the similarity between such references and quoted passages of writing is obvious. In either case the writer is employing words over which there is an external control beyond the ordinary conventions of the language. These words, then, are the ones that can be said to involve "external fact" and to add thereby an additional dimension to the editorial problem.

That dimension can be illustrated by the treatment of the spelling of proper names as well as by the handling of quotations. When the edi-

they occur are to be distinguished, of course, from incidental slips, even when those slips may have some kind of psychological significance (this point is discussed further below).

tors of the Centenary Edition of Hawthorne emend a governor's name from "Burnett" to "Burnet" and another one from "Phipps" to "Phips" in "The Prophetic Pictures," "Smollet" to "Smollett" in "Old News," and "Glumdalea" to "Glumdalca" in *Fanshawe*,[29] they are acting in each case on the judgment that the reference is to a figure (whether real or fictitious) with an existence independent of Hawthorne's work and that the name therefore has an externally verifiable spelling. Whereas the "correct" spelling of ordinary words is determined by the usage of the people who employ those words and continually evolves along with the language, the spelling of an individual's name, it would seem, is fixed:[30] departures from that spelling, no matter how common, are errors. The matter cannot simply be left there, however. To do so would be analogous to saying that quoted passages must conform to the original and that all misquotations are errors requiring emendation. Two factors complicate decisions about emending personal names. One is the attitude toward spelling during the lifetimes of the individuals concerned and their own attitudes toward the spellings of their names; many Elizabethans, for instance, spelled their own names in different ways—in keeping with the approach to spelling in general at the time—and as a result more than one "correct" spelling can exist, just as more than one authorized form of a quotation may be possible, at points where its author has revised it. Even in periods when spellings in general are less flexible, it is not unknown for certain people to spell their names differently at different times in their lives, and various traditions of using one or another of such "correct" forms to refer to these people may grow up, just as one of the authorized versions of a passage may be more widely cited than the others at certain periods. There may be some range of possibilities, in other words, all of which are "correct." A second factor influencing editorial decisions is the possibility of legitimate motives for utilizing "unauthorized" spellings. A spelling that is in fact incorrect may become part of an established literary tradition, and writers using such a spelling are merely drawing on that tradition; or, alternatively, writers may alter a spelling on their own for its effect in the context where they are using it. The former possibility is not the same as saying—as one can with ordinary words—that the correct spelling changes with time, for the ways in which people spell their own names are historical facts that cannot be altered, even though a writer may choose to make refer-

29. *Twice-Told Tales*, ed. J. Donald Crowley, Fredson Bowers, *et al.* (1974), pp. 169–170; *The Snow-Image and Uncollected Tales* (1974), p. 142; *The Blithedale Romance and Fanshawe*, ed. Fredson Bowers *et al.* (1964), p. 408.

30. Within a given language, that is, for the spelling is sometimes altered for representation in other languages.

ence to a tradition of spelling certain names differently. The editor who allows such spellings to stand has gone through a process of finding defensible support for historical errors—a process unnecessary in the case of ordinary words whose conventional spellings at the time a writer used them were no longer what they had been at an earlier time.

When Melville refers in the "Etymology" section to "Hackluyt,"[31] one can argue that the spelling is not simply an error for "Hakluyt," both on the grounds that greater latitude was permitted in spellings in Hakluyt's time and on the grounds that Melville was drawing on (or assumed he was drawing on) an established tradition represented by the occurrence of "Hackluyt" in Charles Richardson's *Dictionary*, his source at this point. But when George Bennet's name appears as "Bennett" at the end of the sixty-fifth extract, the likelihood that the spelling is a mere slip outweighs other possibilities, for the man is a nineteenth-century figure, there is no established tradition of referring to him as "Bennett," and there seems no plausible reason for Melville to have introduced such a change intentionally; the spelling should therefore be corrected. And Melville's repeated spelling of Owen Chase's name as "Chace" (in the "Extracts," in Chapter 45, and in other places outside of *Moby-Dick*) is also an error, no matter how consistently Melville used it, for he had Chase's 1821 book in front of him, he was clearly referring to that particular writer, and there is no other acceptable spelling for that writer's name. The same line of reasoning applies to geographical names as well as personal names, although the continuing existence of places means that traditions of "unofficial" spellings of place names may be stronger than in the case of personal names. When "Nuremburgh" turns up in Hawthorne's "Ethan Brand," the Centenary editors correct it, as an outright error, to "Nuremberg."[32] But when "Heidelburgh" appears consistently in *Moby-Dick* (Chapter 77), one can argue that what is actually an incorrect spelling conveys for Melville a certain flavor and that in any case the presence of this spelling in one of Melville's important source books (John Harris's *Navigantium atque Itinerantium Bibliotheca*) suggests that Melville was aligning himself with whatever tradition that book represents in this matter. "Heidelburgh" remains an erroneous spelling, but the editor may decide, with good reason, that it is not an erroneous reading in this particular text. These arguments, of course, are based on the prior assumption that the references are to the "real" Hakluyt, Bennet, Chase, Nuremberg, and Heidelberg and not to invented people and places with similar names. But the question must al-

31. This spelling also occurs in Chapter 75.
32. *The Snow-Image and Uncollected Tales* (1974), p. 96.

ways be considered, for a change of spelling in a proper name can be said to produce a new name, not just a different form of the old one,[33] in the same way that an altered quotation can be regarded as a different piece of writing. Therefore, in dealing with proper names that are identical with, or closely resemble, those of real people and places, editors must first determine from the context whether the reference is indeed to those people and places and then decide, again from the context, the extent to which a departure from the external facts can be justified as a part of the writer's active intention—an intention either to draw on a tradition or to introduce something new. The issues raised by the spelling of the names of real people and places do resemble in some respects those associated with any questions of spelling. But the crucial difference is the additional level of external reference involved in employing words whose individualized denotations have been established outside the context in which those words are now placed. It is true that only through the context can one finally decide which words these are; but once they are located, they fall into a different class from the other words by virtue of their reference to external facts. In thinking about them, editors need to go beyond the preparation they bring to other words, for they need to be acquainted with the forms these words have taken in their historical association with particular people and places. Like quotations, proper names force editors to ask themselves what status a "fact" has when it is moved from one context to another.

The issues involved show themselves clearly when a fact is moved into a work of fiction. Within a fictional world, facts can be altered in any way the author sees fit; yet to the extent that the author wishes a fact to be recognized it retains some connection with the outside world. These proportions—and their implications, both in the immediate passage and in the novel or story as a whole—are what the editor has to think about in order to decide whether or not to correct an error of external fact. One of the most pervasive questions has to do with setting. If a novelist places the action in real locations at a particular time, how much accuracy is intended in the details referring to that setting? Or, put another way, if certain datable events are employed, do all the other details have to be consistent with the date thus suggested? In Howells's *A Hazard of New Fortunes* an adverbial variant in one sentence alters the time-setting of the entire novel. The *Harper's Weekly* text reads, in a reference to Washington Square, "The *primo tenore* statue of Garibaldi had not yet taken possession of the place"; in the other texts "not yet" is replaced with "already," shifting the action to some time between the erection of

33. For some additional comment on this point, see G. T. Tanselle, "Textual Study and Literary Judgment," *PBSA*, 65 (1971), 120–121.

that statue in 1888 and the completion of the novel in 1889. The editors of the Indiana Howells, recognizing that this variant involves "a question of the historical perspective of the novel," argue for the "already" reading on the grounds that Howells finished the novel in 1889 and that his "choice of detail" suggests a fictional setting at the same time.[34] There is at least one detail, however, pointing to an earlier date: Lindau refers to his wife's death "Right after I got home from the war—twenty years ago," placing the action in the middle 1880s.[35] If one adopts the "already" reading as Howells's final intention, the question is whether this discrepancy makes any difference. It is not, after all, an internal discrepancy, for neither the date of the end of the Civil War nor that of the erection of the Garibaldi statue is given in the novel, and there is no reason why, for fictional purposes, the two sentences need to be regarded as inconsistent. On the other hand, these references are in fact externally verifiable, and Howells's intentions as to factual accuracy can only be gauged by his methods as revealed in the text itself. Since this novel is essentially "realistic," one could argue that inconsistencies involving external fact do matter and that the two sentences should be brought into alignment. Whether the authority attaching to the "already" reading carries enough weight to require the editor to add a word altering Lindau's statement or whether the earlier "not yet" reading (presumably authorial at least, even if superseded) is preferable so as to obviate further editorial intrusion is a delicate editorial question. Even if one believes that the "already" must be adopted as Howells's intention and that consistency in external fact is also intended, one may feel that the addition of even a single word to the other sentence goes beyond an editor's prerogative and that the inconsistency must stand, even though contrary to the spirit of the work. Certainly a great amount of rewriting cannot be undertaken, but deciding whether the insertion of a single word (what word? "over" or "about" before "twenty"?)[36] is excessive constitutes another question of

34. This is what I take to be the meaning of the sentence reading "Howells' choice of detail seems to place the fiction at roughly the same time as the historical events upon which it draws." See *A Hazard of New Fortunes*, ed. David J. Nordloh *et al.* (1976), pp. 55, 537–538.

35. As Harold H. Kolb, Jr., points out in his review of this volume of the Howells edition in *American Literary Realism 1870–1910*, 10 (1977), 314–317. Another possible detail suggesting a pre-1888 date for the early part of the novel is the streetcar strike described late in the book, if it is to be identified with the New York strike of early 1889 (certainly it was inspired by that strike.

36. Of course, if "twenty years ago" can be taken to mean "roughly twenty years ago," there would be no inconsistency with either version of the other sentence. But the theoretical question remains, even if the present illustration, in that case, were not particularly apt; and there would still be the problem, in this illustration, of choosing between "not yet" and "already," even though one difficulty in making the choice would have been removed. (Determining how exact the reference to twenty years was intended to be involves some consideration of linguistic customs and traditions: the vagueness about round numbers prevalent

editorial judgment. The crucial issue for present purposes is not how the inconsistency is rectified but the considerations involved in deciding whether it can be and needs to be rectified—whether, first of all, the editor can reasonably do anything about it and then, if so, whether it is actually an inconsistency in the fictional world.[37]

More often a factual problem in a novel involves only a local context and does not affect the entire time-scheme or setting of the work. But even so, sensitivity to the nature of the whole, as well as to the local context, is necessary for deciding when factual accuracy is in order. Frequently an historical figure becomes a character in a novel and engages at times in events that actually took place and at other times in events that are fictitious; in assessing any particular "factual" error, therefore, the editor must consider both the historicity of the immediate context and the methods of weaving together fact and fiction used throughout the book. Even in a *roman à clef*, where the historical figures are given new names, the relation of the depicted characteristics and events to actual ones (or traditional ideas of the "actual" ones) cannot be ignored, for an editor may be able to decide among variants or detect corrupt readings by knowing those external facts. The elusive nature of fact in fiction[38] is a fascinating subject for speculation and has been much written about,

---

in Elizabethan times, for instance, seems to be of a different order from the attitude toward such figures in Howells's time.)

37. A similar instance, involving the dating of the narration of a novel, occurs in *Moby-Dick*. A speculative passage in Chapter 85 refers to "this blessed minute" and then defines it (in the first American edition) as "fifteen and a quarter minutes past one o'clock P.M. of this sixteenth day of December, A.D. 1851." Because the book was published in London in October 1851 and in New York in November 1851, the year in this passage is probably a compositorial error for "1850" (the reading in the first English edition, set from proofs of the first American). As far as internal consistency is concerned, of course, "1851" would cause a problem only if there is another historical reference in the book with which it would come in conflict. But it seems most likely that Melville's intention at this point was to make the internal world of the book and the external world of reality coincide and to refer to a date that was realistically conceivable as the actual date of composition of this passage (if not in fact the actual date). John Harmon McElroy, in "The Dating of the Action in *Moby Dick*," *Papers on Language & Literature*, 13 (1977), 420–423, comments on the 1850 date of narration and on other historical references that date the *Pequod*'s voyage in 1840–41.

38. I am not suggesting that fact is ever anything but elusive, even outside of fiction; but this is not the place to raise the philosophical question of what is real. By "fact" here, as I have tried to define it earlier, I mean specific people, places, things, and events with an existence independent of the work under consideration. Saul Bellow has interestingly discussed the role of facts in fiction in "Facts That Put Fancy to Flight," New York *Times Book Review*, 11 Feb. 1962, pp. 1, 28. Many readers, he says, are concerned with the accuracy of the realistic surface, and publishers' editors will therefore wish to check on such questions as "How many stories does the Ansonia Hotel really have; and can one see its television antennae from the corner of West End Avenue and Seventy-second Street?" He proceeds to contrast writers who are "satisfied with an art of externals" (and who produce "a journalistic sort of novel") with those "masters of realism" in whose work "the realistic externals were intended to lead inward."

particularly by literary critics and biographers seeking correlations between authors' lives and their works; the subject also turns up in the popular press, discussions in recent years having been stimulated by Truman Capote's concept of the "nonfiction novel" and by television dramatizations based loosely on real events. These commentaries—some of which are concerned with the ethics of placing real people in compromising situations they are not known to have found themselves in[39]— generally deal with different questions from those the editor must think about. The editor's interest is not basically in whether a real person has been slandered by a fictional representation or whether a real event has been misrepresented but whether the details present in the text are those that the writer intended to be there. In order to be in a position to make an informed judgment on that matter, however, the editor has to learn, as far as possible, what the external facts are and to analyze—like the critic and biographer that the editor must in part be—the nature of the transmutation of those facts into fiction.

The border lines between external fact and fictional fact are constantly shifting, as Melville demonstrates when in Chapter 72 of *Moby-Dick*, after describing the "monkey-rope" tying together the harpooneer (on the whale's slippery back) and the bowsman (on deck), he appends a footnote beginning, "The monkey-rope is found in all whalers; but it was only in the Pequod that the monkey and his holder were ever tied together. This improvement upon the original usage was introduced by no less a man than Stubb." A fictional fact—a usage invented by a fictional character on a fictional ship—is here thrust out into the real world as the *Pequod* is compared with all other ships; or, rather, the real world is pulled into the novel, for the external truthfulness of the statement about all ships is irrelevant to the fictional world, in which it becomes a fact that the *Pequod* differs from all other ships in its use of the monkey-rope. Yet external facts may have to be called on when there is an internal discrepancy. In the American first edition of *Moby-Dick*, a passage discussing some famous whales (Chapter 45) refers to "Timor Tom" and "New Zealand Jack," but the next paragraph cites "New Zealand Tom"; in the English edition the discrepancy was evidently noted, for "Tom" in the third instance is changed to "Jack," thus producing consistency. It is clear that the American text must be emended, but the change selected in the English edition is not the only one that would make the names consistent, and the editor must decide which way to do it. Knowing that Melville's source, Thomas Beale's *The Natural History*

39. See, for instance, the comments on "Washington: Behind Closed Doors" in *Time*, 19 Sept. 1977, pp. 92–93, and in Michael J. Arlen's "The Air" department in *The New Yorker*, 3 Oct. 1977, pp. 115–124.

of the Sperm Whale, gives the names as "Timor Jack" and "New Zealand Tom" should settle the matter. Melville was of course free to alter these names if he wished; but since the editor has to make some emendation and since there is no evidence in this passage to suggest that Melville wanted to change the names, the obvious course is to emend them in conformity with the external source. At another point (Chapter 99) Flask figures that a doubloon worth sixteen dollars will buy him 960 two-cent cigars. At first this discrepancy seems purely an internal one, a matter of incorrect arithmetic. But of course the idea that it is a discrepancy rests on the assumption that American dollars of one hundred cents are meant or that no bulk rate was customary for two-cent cigars. If one argued that the "dollars" were Spanish-American dollars, freely circulating among American seamen as the equivalent of a British crown or $1.20, the discrepancy would vanish, as it would if one were to establish that two-cent cigars sold for 20¢ a dozen. External facts are relevant, in other words, to determining whether or not Melville could have intended the figures in the printed text.

Many references to external facts in novels do not involve such internal discrepancies (or seeming ones) that call attention to themselves but rather are discrepant only when compared with an outside source. *Moby-Dick*, again, can conveniently illustrate how the treatment of these "errors" must vary with the immediate context. At one point (Chapter 101) the narrator presents some statistics about the stocks of food on a whaling ship, statistics said to be taken from a book called "Dan Coopman." A check of Melville's source for this passage, William Scoresby's *An Account of the Arctic Regions* (1820), shows that a double "error" is present: the book, according to Scoresby, is "Den Koopman," and he actually cites the statistics from a different work. But the playful nature of Melville's passage makes any "correction" out of the question. First of all, he takes "Dan Coopman" to be "the invaluable memoirs of some Amsterdam cooper in the fishery, as every whale ship must carry its cooper." This use of the name would in itself prevent an editor from altering the spelling or substituting another name. In addition, the spirit of the passage is suggested by the reference to "Dr. Snodhead, a very learned man, professor of Low Dutch and High German in the college of Santa Claus and St. Pott's, to whom I handed the work for translation." Within such a context the misattribution of the statistics is of no moment, for Melville is not expecting the reader to think of "Dan Coopman" as any more or less real than "Dr. Snodhead." An earlier passage, near the reference to "New Zealand Tom" (Chapter 45), offers a contrast. There the captains who insistently search for particular celebrated whales are said to have "heaved up their anchors with that express object as much

in view, as in setting out through the Narragansett Woods, Captain Butler of old had it in his mind to capture that notorious murderous savage
Annawon, the headmost warrior of the Indian King Philip." In fact it
was Captain Benjamin Church who pursued Annawon in Rhode Island
in 1676; Colonel William Butler's expedition was against the Indian
leader Brant in upstate New York in 1778. The sentence could be made
factually correct by substituting "Church" for "Butler," and an editor
could persuasively argue in favor of this emendation: the reference seems
to be a simple factual allusion, in a context stressing facts, and there
seems to be no literary reason for Melville's wishing to alter the name.
"Butler" is probably a mere slip (since Melville knew the story of Brant
also) for the intended word "Church"; and because no further discussion
in the text depends on the word "Butler" (that is, the error is confined to
this one clause), it is feasible for an editor to make the change. *Moby-
Dick* may be more extreme than many works of fiction in its oscillation
between the imaginative and the factual, but it illustrates a point applicable to all fiction: that a fictional framework does not preclude the existence within it of passages (of whatever length, whether a chapter or
only part of a sentence) that aim to be factually accurate. An editor,
therefore, can justifiably make factual corrections in a work of fiction;
deciding when they are justified entails literary sensitivity and is one of
the responsibilities of the critical editor.

The editing of another of Melville's works has occasioned some debate over this principle, and the argument put forth can be instructive.
Harrison Hayford and Merton M. Sealts, Jr., in preparing their reading
text (1962) of *Billy Budd, Sailor*, follow the reasoning just outlined and
correct errors of fact when in their judgment the context shows that Melville was trying to be factually accurate.[40] Thus when Melville refers to
the execution of "a midshipman and two petty officers" aboard the actual ship *Somers*, Hayford and Sealts alter "petty officers" to "sailors,"
since only one was in fact a petty officer. Peter Shaw has attacked this decision and, with a notable lack of restraint, calls it "Possibly the most
stunning liberty with an author's text in the twentieth century."[41] Shaw's
objection is based on the argument that errors are revealing. "Freud's
doctrine in *The Psychopathology of Everyday Life*," he says, "offers the
definitive argument against unconsidered editorial corrections." Naturally editorial emendations should never be "unconsidered," but he
seems to be saying that corrections of factual error should probably never
be undertaken in the first place: "Freud's book made it a matter of com-

40. They discuss this category of emendations on pp. 215–216.
41. "The American Heritage and Its Guardians," *American Scholar*, 45 (1975–76), 733–
751 [i.e., 37–55]; quotation from p. 742.

mon sense that an error usually reveals more than does a controlled statement of intention." Shaw unnecessarily confuses the issue here, for statements of intention are beside the point: obviously a statement of intention does not necessarily match the actual realized intention, and editors are not concerned with statements of intention but authors' intentions as manifested in their works. At any rate Shaw is correct to observe that errors can be revealing, and his application of the point here is to say that, because Melville's cousin had been a first lieutenant on the *Somers,* "Any unconscious exaggeration by Melville of the rank of those executed has possible significance for the astute reader." The question he does not go on to address, however, is why this kind of significance is appropriate to be preserved in the *critical text* of a literary work like *Billy Budd* (that the original reading should be preserved in the notes goes without saying).

What Shaw fails to take into account in his discussion is the difference between working papers or private documents and finished literary products intended for an audience. When editors prepare private papers for publication, there is no doubt that they should not smooth out the text by eliminating factual errors, misspellings, deleted phrases, and the like.[42] All these features are part of the essential nature of such documents, and their psychological significance is one of the reasons for the importance of the documents. When Sir Walter Scott in his journal refers to an acquaintance whose real name was Durham Calderwood as "Calderwood Durham" or speaks of a marriage that actually took place in 1825 as occurring "in the beginning of 1826," these slips are integral parts of the text of the document, and one would be losing part of what the document has to offer if they were corrected; W. E. K. Anderson is right to leave them in the text in his Clarendon edition and merely to point out the errors in footnotes.[43] There is no question, in other words, that Shaw's point is correct in regard to the texts of private documents. Literary works and other works intended for publication, however, open up additional possibilities. They, too, can be treated as documents, and editors can prepare *literatim* transcriptions of any extant manuscripts, or facsimiles of particular copies of printed editions. Such work is valuable in making important evidence more widely available. But works intended for publication also demand to be edited in another way, which results in texts incorporating their authors' final intentions about what was to be placed before the public. Such works—by virtue of the fact they

---

42. The rationale for this position is set forth by G. T. Tanselle in "The Editing of Historical Documents," *SB*, 31 (1978), 1–56.

43. *The Journal of Sir Walter Scott* (1972), pp. 425, 412.

are intended for publication—have a public as well as a private aspect. When one is concerned to retain in the edited text all the readings of a particular document, one is focusing on a single stage in the growth of the work. The document is of historical significance because it preserves that stage; but usually no single extant document preserves a text that is free of error, in the sense that it contains all the readings finally intended by the author.[44] Therefore it is important, in approaching these intellectual products as *works* and not simply as specific *documents*, that editors use their informed judgment to produce eclectic texts, drawing critically on the available evidence and on their own sense of what constitutes an error in a given text. The evidence present in the extant documents can (and should) be recorded as notes to the critical text, but the text itself does not attempt to reproduce exactly any particular document.

In the case of *Billy Budd*, the preserved papers are clearly a private document, a working draft; but they contain a work of fiction, a work of the kind normally intended for a public audience, and not a diary or notebook entries. Recognizing this dual interest in the papers, Hayford and Sealts have prepared two edited texts. One of them, a "genetic" text, attempts to provide an accurate transcription of the textual features of the document, showing in the process the order of Melville's deletions, insertions, and alterations; the other, a "reading" text, attempts to offer a critical text representing Melville's intentions for the work as discernible from the document. The former aims to do justice to the manuscript as a document of Melville's biography and of American literary history; the latter aims to do justice to its text as a work of fiction. In the former, Melville's phrase "a midshipman and two petty officers" naturally appears, for there is no question here of emending what Melville actually put on paper, even if it was not what he intended to write. But in the latter, critical judgment must be employed to decide whether that factual error is one that Melville intended to make for the purposes of his fiction; Hayford and Sealts conclude that it is not, and they correct it. To believe that in doing so they have exercised an unwarranted liberty is to fail to understand the nature and the value of critical editing. Obviously another critic may disagree with them and argue that there are reasons for thinking that Melville particularly wished to say "petty officers" here; the issue involves literary judgment, and differences of opinion about it are bound to exist. But criticizing Hayford and Sealts's decision

44. This is not to suggest that a critical text cannot be undertaken to represent any particular stage in the history of a work, for the same point can be made about the relation of the surviving documents to the author's final intention at any specific time. Producing a critical text of some version of a work that was later revised further by the author is not the same thing as editing a transcription of one document.

on this basis is not to object to the *process* of emending a text in conformity with the editor's view of the author's intention.

Shaw's criticism, on the other hand, in effect questions the validity of critical editing: Shaw disapproves of the Hayford-Sealts emendation because the original reading may provide psychological insight into Melville's motivation, and he is thus objecting to a critical text for not being a transcription. The confusion in his thinking is suggested by the two possible interpretations that he offers of "Any unconscious exaggeration by Melville of the rank of those executed": Melville may have exaggerated "to increase the importance of the parallel with the *Somers*" or "out of a vaguely shared guilt over his cousin's complicity in the matter." The first, which would not have been unconscious, has to do with the literary effect of the comparison and could presumably be a reason for retaining the original reading in a critical text; the second, insofar as it is conceivable, is a reason for being interested in the error but not a reason for leaving it in the critical text of a literary work.[45] When Shaw concludes that the Hayford-Sealts emendation is "as significant as a nineteenth-century editor's excision of an entire paragraph of sexually explicit or politically dangerous material," he reveals his failure to understand that editorial alteration of a text can ever be anything other than a kind of censorship, something standing in the way of the author's expression rather than promoting it. This episode illustrates in dramatic fashion how the discussion of a factual error in a work of fiction demands a clear understanding of the different editorial approaches that can productively be employed. The essential prerequisite to clear thinking on the matter is recognizing the difference between a transcription, in which the editor must faithfully reproduce the errors of a particular document, and a critical text, in which the editor is not bound to retain a factual error simply because it is present in an authoritative document. A critical editor may finally decide to retain such an error on critical grounds but not because the error is a revealing Freudian slip, suggestive of the author's state of mind at the time of the preparation of a given document. The two approaches are distinct, and neither can be carried out competently if considerations applicable to one are allowed to intrude into the other. Errors of external fact often seem to provide the test cases for determining how well an editor has learned that lesson.[46]

45. In a footnote, Shaw gives another, and more far-fetched, example of a slip "useful to the critic": the appearance of F. R. Leavis's name as "F. L. Leavis" in an essay of Fredson Bowers. Shaw believes that "Leavis evidently has been confused with the older English critic F. L. Lucas" and that this slip reveals a "slightly old-fashioned" cast of mind. Surely such tenuous speculation offers no real grounds for preserving what is clearly an unintended reading, very likely a compositor's error.

46. Another Hayford-Sealts emendation in *Billy Budd* has been questioned by another

If factual errors in fiction need not always be corrected in a critical text, one might at first assume that the situation would be different with "nonfiction" writing—any writing that is expository in nature, attempting to deal with the real world directly, not through the creation of an imagined world. Surely, one might think, factual errors and misquotations cannot be a legitimate part of the intended texts of such works. Everyone senses the distinction that René Wellek speaks of when he says, "There is a central and important difference between a statement, even in a historical novel or a novel by Balzac which seems to convey 'information' about actual happenings, and the same information appearing in a book of history or sociology."[47] The difference is undeniable, and yet there seem to be intermediate shadings. One reads a "book of history" like Gibbon or Macaulay as a work of literary creativity, and not merely because it is from the past and limited in its information by what was known at the time. Or one reads an essay of sociological or philosophical analysis for its mastery of exposition, recognizing that some of its points may be half-truths or distortions employed to advance a particular argument. Of course, the truth or falsity of the information conveyed does not alter the fact that in such works the author is speaking directly to the reader, not through a fictional persona or a created world. Any author, whether producing novels and poems or writing essays, may undertake to alter facts for the purposes of the work, and what we think of as "creative literature" does not exclude so-called "nonfiction."[48] Many attempts have been made to distinguish writing that is "literature" from writing that is not,[49] but no satisfactory dividing line has ever been established. The implication of all this for the editor of a critical text is to suggest that a blanket rule regarding the correction of factual errors in nonfiction would be just as shortsighted as such a rule for more obviously "literary" works. Since deciding whether a given work can be regarded as "literature" is itself an act of critical judgment, no such classification

---

critic in a different way. In his Bobbs-Merrill edition (1975), Milton Stern differs from Hayford and Sealts on the necessity of correcting Nelson's rank, from "Vice Admiral" (as it appears on leaf 70 of the manuscript) to "Rear Admiral" (as Hayford and Sealts correct it). Stern does not rule out all corrections of fact and believes in making critical distinctions between one situation and another. His argument in this case is that Melville "makes a point of Nelson's rank more than once"; therefore "he might have attached significance to the ranks he assigned" (p. 165). This argument, however, is not critical: the fact that the error appears more than once is no guarantee that it was intended; the crucial question, not taken up, is whether there is reason to believe that Melville did attach significance to "Vice Admiral."

47. *Theory of Literature* (1949), p. 15.

48. See, for instance, Stanley Edgar Hyman's *The Tangled Bank: Darwin, Marx, Frazer and Freud as Imaginative Writers* (1962).

49. A number of them are listed by G. T. Tanselle in *SB*, 29 (1976), 176, footnote 19.

can serve to delimit for the editor certain writing to be treated in a different way from other writing. Instead, the critical editor must approach so-called "nonfiction" in the same way as fiction: the author is just as capable of altering facts intentionally, just as likely to develop a point based on an error, and just as much bound by the customs of the time; and the editor therefore has the same responsibility to assess each factual error in the light of the evidence offered by its context.

Perhaps even more than with fiction, a common situation in nonfiction is the occurrence of quotations from other works. Several philosophers have now been accorded careful critical editions, and the problem of quotations has been confronted in them. In the first volume (1969) of Jo Ann Boydston's edition of *The Early Works* of John Dewey, Fredson Bowers contributes a statement of textual policy that records a central point: "In Dewey's texts," he says, "all quotations have been retained just as he wrote them even though not always strictly accurate, since that was the form on which he was founding his ideas" (p. xvii). A basic reason for allowing inaccurate quotations to stand, in fiction as well as nonfiction, is that the quotations in that form may have ramifications that are unemendable—they may be the subject of a discussion in the text or may have influenced the author's thinking. Retaining Dewey's quotations "just as he wrote them," however, raises another problem, for it is conceivable that what he wrote at times contained mere slips and did not always reflect what he intended to write (whether or not what he intended to write was accurate), and it is also possible that some errors in quotations in printed texts or in nonauthorial manuscripts or typescripts are slips by people other than Dewey. Bowers does not go into this question because no emendations in quotations are in fact made in this volume; but the relevance of the issue is clearly recognized by Jo Ann Boydston, who, in her introduction to the appendix that prints the correct wording of the inaccurate quotations,[50] says, "It should be noted that specific changes, both in substantives and in accidentals, may have been instituted in the transmission rather than by Dewey himself. The variable form of quoting does suggest that Dewey, like many scholars of the period, was not overly concerned about precision in accidentals, but many of the changes in cited materials may well have arisen in the printing process" (p. lxxxix). Recognition of that fact underscores the necessity for a critical approach to each quotation, an attempt to judge on the

50. Bowers suggests that one of the uses of this appendix is to help the reader decide "whether Dewey had the source open before him or was relying on his memory" (p. xvii)—a problem the editor will already have thought about in determining whether any emendations are justifiable, for certain kinds of slips are more common when one is copying (intending to copy accurately) than when one is remembering (intending perhaps only to paraphrase).

basis of the available evidence—including the editor's understanding of the author's methods in general and aims in the particular passage—just which inaccuracies of quotation were probably slips. It is also worth observing that Boydston's statement calls attention to the importance of knowing contemporary standards: in an unmodernized edition it would clearly be wrong to hold Dewey to stricter standards of accuracy in quotation than were customary among his colleagues.

In later volumes of the Dewey edition some emendations in quotations are made, and the critical approach implicit in Boydston's comments in the first volume is more explicitly remarked upon. Bowers adds to his essay the point that sometimes "special circumstances in a specific text require the correction of quotations within the text itself" (IV, xlix; V, cxxviii); and Boydston notes that some house-styling of Dewey's periodical pieces encompassed the quotations as well, giving the editor a reason for restoring certain punctuation to those quotations (V, clxxvi). Sometimes an internal contradiction calls attention to what was intended in the quotation: Dewey quotes a sentence from Paul Bourget, but the text omits a clause on Stendhal, leaving four writers mentioned; because Dewey refers to the "five" writers in the quotation, it is clear that he intended for that clause to be present, and it is of course restored (III, 37). In other cases, the internal contradiction may be less mechanical but no less forceful: when a quotation from Alexander Bain reads, "a mental association is rapidly formed between his [the child's] obedience and apprehended pain," it is clear that Dewey could not have intended to substitute "obedience" for the "disobedience" of the original and could not have believed that the original read that way, and an emendation is rightly made (IV, 330). Generally, however, misquotations pose more debatable questions for an editor. The Dewey edition does not emend a misquotation from F. H. Bradley that reads "it is here the intellect alone which is [instead of "has"] to be satisfied" (*Middle Works*, IV [1977], 58) or one from F. J. E. Woodbridge that reads "by insisting that by [instead of "from"] the nature of mind" (p. 224). It is unlikely that Dewey made these changes intentionally, but one could argue that they are so insignificant as to be allowable in the tradition of approximate quotation;[51] on the other hand one could argue that the "is" and "by" are slips induced in each case by the presence of the same word earlier in the line and that they are simply mistakes that ought to be corrected. Even though approximate quotation is justifiable as a contemporary convention, any

51. Boydston points out in the first volume of *The Early Works* that "Dewey used source material in the whole range of possible ways, from paraphrase recall to verbatim copying out. . . . quotation marks do not necessarily signal a direct, precise quotation" (p. lxxxix).

misquotation can be expected to alter the meaning slightly, and one must therefore give thought to whether or not the change was intentional. If it appears not to be, then at least where substantives are involved the arguments for retention of the error as an example of the tolerated imprecision of the time would seem in many instances to carry less force than the arguments for emendation.[52] In the Dewey edition a phrase from William James appears as "any one part of experience" (p. 99), whereas the original contains "our" before "experience." How does one draw the line here between allowable imprecision of quotation and a slip that violates the author's intention? Considering the shade of difference in emphasis produced by the omission, one might feel that Dewey could not have regarded the shorter version as an acceptable paraphrase or approximation of the longer and that—unless the shift in nuance can itself be seen as intentional—the omitted word should be restored. These are difficult critical questions, and it should be clear that they are no less difficult because the piece of writing happens to be "nonfiction."[53]

Since decisions on such matters must grow out of the immediate context of the passage and the larger context of the author's times and general practice, they will vary from situation to situation; they will also

52. The same cannot necessarily be said about accidentals: because it is more difficult to reason about which discrepancies in accidentals are intentional and which inadvertent, the decision whether or not to correct the accidentals of a quotation falls back more heavily on a consideration of contemporary attitudes toward accuracy in quotations. (For works in which some looseness of quotation is tolerated, there is the companion question of the extent to which readers need to be informed about the accidentals of the original; whereas discrepancies in substantives between copy-text and source should always be reported in the apparatus, one can argue that the desirability of reporting such discrepancies in accidentals varies with the situation—perhaps, for instance, being more important for some expository works or passages than for some "creative" ones.)

53. Some debate over editing quotations in such works has recently occurred in connection with the omission of a "not" in a quotation from Joseph Spence as it appears in the first edition of Johnson's *Life of Pope* (1781). Colin J. Horne's proposal that the word be restored ("An Emendation to Johnson's *Life of Pope*," *Library*, 5th ser., 28 [1973], 156–157) has been objected to by J. P. Hardy, who argues that "surely the modern editor's prime duty is to reproduce the most authoritative text that can, on all available evidence, be attributed to Johnson" (29 [1974], 226). Horne's reply (30 [1975], 249–250) tries to clarify the nature of critical editing, especially in regard to quotations: such an editor, Horne recognizes, does not simply reproduce an authoritative text but corrects it so that it can be printed "as the author *intended* it to be and not as what, by some oversight, he actually wrote in error"; and this principle, he makes clear, must apply to the entire text, quotations and all (he underscores the illogic of holding "that one principle should apply to quotations and quite another to the main body of the text"). That certain misquotations in "nonfiction" or expository works must, however, be allowed to stand is effectively stated by Horne: "No editor, I think, would correct the habitual misquotations in Hazlitt's writings because, it may fairly be claimed, they are, in that form, what Hazlitt intended. They are authentic as being precisely how he remembered them and as such they are evidence of his adaptive memory of his extensive reading and his partly deliberate adaptation of the quotation to what he was himself writing."

inevitably vary, as with any question involving judgment, according to the person making the decision. Thus Fredson Bowers, editing another late nineteenth-century American philosopher, William James, reverses in his statement of procedure the relative emphasis on retention and correction of misquotation announced in the Dewey edition. In the James edition, he says, "an attempt has been made to identify the exact edition used by James for his quotations from other authors and ordinarily to emend his carelessness of transcription so that the quotation will reproduce exactly what the author wrote." But at some points, he adds, "James altered quotations for his own purposes in such a manner that his version should be respected" (*Pragmatism* [1975], p. 182). Correction of misquotation is here the general rule, and retention the exception; and many emendations in quotations, often to correct punctuation or small differences of substantives, are in fact made.[54] There is no question that the approach is critical, and some misquotations are not emended; but there is a bias toward the correction of misquotations, just as there is one toward the retention of them in the Dewey. This difference in emphasis ought to spring from a difference in the evaluation of these authors' intentions in quoting, seen against a background of the conventions of quoting in their time. If in practice it also springs to some extent from the fact that two different editors are performing the work, there can be no objection, so long as all the factors have been taken into account and the evidence is recorded. Critical editing depends on individual judgments, made by people intimately acquainted with the authors and their methods of working; the treatment of quotations can never rest on a mechanical rule, for it must always involve an understanding of the authors' intended use of the quotations as well as of the conventions for quoting within which they are operating.[55]

If those conventions even in scholarly writing in the late nineteenth and early twentieth centuries allowed more flexibility than we are now accustomed to, it hardly needs to be stated that the situation was still freer in earlier periods. The point has been well put in the Yale edition

54. The list of emendations in this edition is designed as the place to record all differences in the texts of quotations, even those that are not emended. The principle of providing readers with this information (handled in the Dewey by the section called "Correction of Quotations") is important, for without it readers are not in a position adequately to evaluate the editors' treatment of quotations; readers need to know where misquotations have been allowed to stand as well as where they have been emended.

55. James's preface to *The Meaning of Truth* illustrates the delicacy of judgment involved, because James there quotes from his own earlier *Pragmatism*. The editor is faced not only with the usual questions that quotations raise but with the additional consideration that James may be taking this occasion to revise what he had previously written. Bowers's text (1975) allows James to make unmarked omissions but generally restores the punctuation and italicization of the original.

of Jonathan Edwards, where in the second volume (*Religious Affections,* 1959), John E. Smith explains how the difficulty in the eighteenth century of conveniently consulting all the books one might need made it "necessary to rely upon memory and extracts copied somewhat hastily and stored up for use at a later time" (p. 81). He goes on to describe the kinds of misquotations that occur, in a passage that could apply equally well to many earlier and later writers:

> Very few of the direct quotations in the *Affections* are to be found in exactly the same form in the original editions, even though most changes are minor and do not materially affect the meaning involved. Edwards often paraphrased his source, and some of this paraphrased material appears within inverted commas along with direct quotation; the result is that the line between the two is difficult to draw. Edwards also made minor modifications, such as the changing of tenses or the dropping of an article or pronoun, and he often strung together passages from different parts of a book, omitting material in between without use of ellipsis dots. What appears in some cases to be a sentence or paragraph from one page of a work is actually a construction from several pages, and it is identified by him in the citation only by the first page (or the last) from which the quotation is taken.

The sentence that follows, however, concludes the paragraph on a questionable note: "The quotations in this edition are left as they appeared in the first edition, so that the interested student might be enabled to examine Edwards' own practice." This approach is an uncritical one, taking for granted that the first edition accurately represents "Edwards' own practice" and not inquiring into the possibility that some readings of the first edition might be errors introduced in the printing process. The editor is right not to make all quotations conform to their sources, but he should not therefore go to the opposite extreme and assume that the quotations as they appear in print are necessarily what the writer intended. The earlier volume of the Edwards edition, Paul Ramsey's text of *Freedom of the Will* (1957), exhibits the same problem, though the policy is defended somewhat differently. After pointing out the varieties of "quotation" that Edwards engaged in, Ramsey says that in no instance is Edwards "unfaithful to the original author's meaning, or, between the quotation marks, unfair to him" (p. 122). He then adds, rather irrelevantly, "To correct his quotations so as to make them formally quite exact would mutilate the text with bracketed insertions, and to repeat the quotation accurately in a footnote would needlessly burden the page." The basic argument here is that editorial emendation of the quotations is unnecessary because they accurately reflect the gist of the original authors' statements. Such a position does not question whether Edwards intended to represent those statements in exactly the way they appear in the first edition. The Yale Edwards edition, in other words, admirably describes the nature of Edwards's quoting but does not take a critical approach to the treatment of his quotations as they are found in the printed texts.[56]

If quotations in nonfiction works should be treated in a critical spirit, it is equally true that bibliographical citations and other references to external facts in them must also be so treated. In Bowers's edition of James's *Essays in Radical Empiricism* (1976), James's citation of A. S. Pringle-Pattison's book as *"Man and the Cosmos"* instead of *Man's Place in the Cosmos* (p. 53) is not emended (though of course the correct title is recorded in the notes), for there is no question about what James wrote, which is a characteristic example of nineteenth-century allusive citation. On the other hand, when Washington Irving, in *Mahomet and His Successors*, begins a sentence with "The Arabs, says Lane," and ends the paragraph with a correct reference to *"Sale's Koran,"* it is clear that "Lane" is merely a slip for "Sale," and Henry A. Pochmann and E. N. Feltskog make the emendation (p. 374) in their Wisconsin edition (1970). Joseph J. Moldenhauer and Edwin Moser, in their volume of *Early Essays and Miscellanies* (1975) in the Princeton edition of Thoreau, attempt to distinguish between erroneous information and typographical errors in Thoreau's sources: when Thoreau gives James Hogg's birthdate as 1772 instead of 1770, they do not correct it, because his source also gives 1772 as the year; but when he follows that source in citing "Madoc of the Moor," they emend "Madoc" to "Mador" on the grounds that the source reading was merely a typographical error. Other editors might disagree with this distinction and argue the case differently; but one cannot quarrel with the Thoreau editors' recognition of the necessity for applying critical judgment to each factual error and not handling all errors by a ready-made rule. In some cases, as the Thoreau edition illustrates, the basis for correcting a factual error in a copy-text may be provided by an author's earlier draft. In Thoreau's fair-copy manuscript of his early essay on "Sir Walter Raleigh," the year 1592 is said to be eight years before Raleigh's imprisonment, but the correct year, 1595, is present in two previous drafts (p. 188); and in *The Maine Woods* (ed. Moldenhauer, 1972) the copy-text statement that "our party of three paid two dollars" (p. 160) can be corrected by reference to the first draft, where the fare is recorded as three dollars per person (Thoreau's "2" and "9" resemble one another). Factual errors can of course be corrected without such documents, but their existence helps to confirm the author's inten-

56. And this edition, it should be added, is not one that excludes all editorial emendation; in fact, it is a modernized edition. (Ramsey's point that the text is not "put forth in completely modern form" refers only to the fact that idioms and other matters of wording are not modernized.) But the inappropriateness of modernization for a scholarly edition of this kind is an entirely different point from the one I am concerned with here.

tion. And that intention is what is crucial: the fact that a piece of writing is "nonfiction" cannot relieve the scholarly editor of the obligation to investigate the author's intention (as perhaps influenced by the customs of the time) before deciding to "correct" what is technically a factual error.

These considerations call attention to the fine line that an editor must draw between correcting in the sense of emending a text in the light of the author's intention and correcting in the sense of revising. Henry Pochmann, in the *Mahomet* edition, is well aware of the problem when he notes that he cannot correct Irving's grammar or syntax "short of making the transition from editing to revising Irving's text" (p. 602). After he describes Irving's methods of constructing approximate quotations, he adds, "Because the primary concern is to reproduce what Irving wrote, or intended to write, the editor has concentrated on what Irving's text shows and has noted or corrected Irving's alterations [of quotations] only when it can be shown that his modifications are erroneous or unintentional, or both." Although the inclusion of the word "erroneous" makes the sentence less clear (since from the editor's point of view the only things that can be erroneous within the text are those that are unintended), this statement is useful both because it sets forth a sensible point of view for handling quotations (and, by extension, other matters involving external fact) and because its seeming ambiguity forces one to focus on the vexing problems of intention. To say that an editor reproduces what an author "wrote, or intended to write" is obviously meant to allow the editor to correct the author's slips of the pen. It is not meant to imply that all factual errors are necessarily slips and are to be corrected by the editor; but the difficulty of constructing a sentence making that distinction explicit suggests the difficulties of the distinction itself. A factual error is not a slip, of course, if an author intentionally alters the facts; but neither is it a slip if the author has copied accurately from an inaccurate source. That the author in the latter case intended to get the facts right does not give the editor license to correct them if there is a reasonable possibility that the erroneous facts have had some influence on the author's thinking and thus have ramifications elsewhere in the text. One is dealing, in other words, with the author's immediate intention in the act of writing; basing editorial decisions on some more programmatic intention to be "accurate" would frequently mean becoming a collaborator of the author and undertaking a new stage of revision which that author never got around to.

The editing of Thoreau's college papers, though rather a special case, illustrates the point. Thoreau made some revisions in his papers before submitting them to Edward T. Channing; when Channing marked those papers he was carrying the process of revision—or indicating how to carry it—one stage further. Moldenhauer and Moser, in their *Early Essays* volume, accept into the text Thoreau's revisions before he submitted the papers but not those made as a result of Channing's directives—"unless," they add, "the original reading is an error that the editors would have emended had Thoreau himself not corrected it" (p. 311). Thus one can correct slips of Thoreau's pen, for to do so is to act in accordance with his intention at the moment of writing; but to adopt revisions prompted by a schoolmaster's markings is to accept an altered intention imposed from outside. The reader is interested in what Thoreau wanted to write, not in what someone else wished him to do. In the same way, any editor who corrects factual errors in texts merely because they are factual errors, without carefully considering the relation of those errors to the author's active intention, is playing the role of the schoolmaster, concerned more with maintaining an *a priori* standard than with understanding the internal demands of a particular situation. The critical editor is pledged to use judgment: deciding in advance to reproduce the copy-text exactly is not appropriate, for the goal is not a facsimile or diplomatic text; but neither can the critical editor decide in advance to correct all errors of external fact, for the goal is not to carry forward the authorial process of revision. Editorial emendations in a critical text that aims to respect the author's intention must be made in the light of the intention manifested in the version of the work being edited. Whether the work is "fiction" or "nonfiction," the editor must strive to make emendations that are faithful to the spirit of the historical document under consideration and that do not move on into the area of prescriptive correcting.

This point of view, particularly when applied to "nonfiction," is bound to raise a question in many readers' minds. Surely, they would say, writers of "nonfiction" set out to be informative, and if one does not correct all their errors one is caring more about the writers as individuals of interest in their own right than about the subjects they are discussing. Where, in other words, do we draw the line between an interest in a piece of writing for the information it conveys and an interest in it as the expression of a particular individual at a specific time? Irving's historical works were intended to be informative, but today we turn to them more to experience Irving's prose and to observe his handling of the material; if we wish to learn the "facts" about the historical events he dealt with, we feel that more recent accounts, based on further research, have superseded his treatments. Similarly, we are not indignant over James's and Dewey's misquotations, because we are interested in the versions that influenced their thought; but if we read current scholarly treatments of the same subjects we regard misquotations and factual errors as faults. The reason is not merely that conventional standards may have become more rigorous; it is that in the former case our interest is historical and in the latter it is not. But what is read today for its "truth" is read tomorrow for its "historical interest"; the same pieces of "nonfiction" move from one status to the other, and the editor is not faced with two discrete bodies of material, but only one, which in fact comprises all writing. The distinction to be made is between kinds of editing, not kinds of writing. What is called editing in a magazine- or book-publisher's office is not historically oriented, and publishers' editors hope to find and eliminate factual errors—that is, what can be regarded as errors in the light of current knowledge—in the manuscripts they prepare for publication. When a scholarly editor undertakes to edit a text, however, the task is retrospective and the interest historical, no matter how recent the piece of writing happens to be.

If a publisher's editor had informed F. O. Matthiessen that he was quoting a corrupt text of *White-Jacket* with the reading "soiled fish" for "coiled fish," he would have revised his discussion accordingly, for it was not his aim to analyze a phrase Melville never wrote. But if a scholarly editor were to prepare an edition of Matthiessen's book, nothing could be done about rectifying the erroneous "soiled," which forms the basis for an analysis of "the unexpected linking of the medium of cleanliness with filth."[57] Even if Matthiessen had not made a point of the word "soiled," the scholarly editor would have to think very carefully before correcting it in the quotation, for Matthiessen quoted accurately the Constable text, assuming it to be correct, and that text is the one lying behind his commentary. The critical activity of the scholarly editor is directed toward recovering what an author intended at a particular time, whether that time was yesterday, four decades ago, or four centuries ago.[58] This principle applies to matters of external fact just as much as to any other feature of the work, although editors sometimes seem more tempted to abandon their historical orientation when dealing with those matters.

Reference to Matthiessen's discussion of "soiled" is a reminder that on many occasions an author's elaboration of an erroneous point makes any emendation out of the question: it is fruitless to consider—except as an exercise—whether or not one would emend "soiled" if Matthiessen

57. *American Renaissance* (1941), p. 392. The error was originally pointed out by John W. Nichol in "Melville's '"Soiled" Fish of the Sea,'" *American Literature*, 21 (1949–50), 338–339.

58. The result may be a "new" version in the sense that the text never existed physically in this form before, but the aim is still historical reconstruction, not the application of critical ability to the further "revision" or "improvement" of the work beyond the point where the author left it.

had not discussed the word, because in fact he did discuss it, and one cannot rewrite the passage for him. Quite apart from questions of intention, then, there is always the practical question of whether or not any alteration is feasible. Presumably Yeats did not intend to misquote two lines from Burns so that they contain the phrase "white moon" rather than "wan moon," but his penetrating analysis of the use of "white" in the passage eliminates any possibility of editorial correction.[59] Situations involving internal contradiction as well as external fact may be such that an editor has no alternative but to leave them alone. When Ahab appears in "his slouched hat" (Chapter 132) just two chapters after a hawk has flown off with it (and we are told that it "was never restored"), an editor is powerless to make a change that will produce consistency. Similarly, when Melville describes the baleen of the right whale (Chapter 75), he has a sentence pointing out that "One voyager in Purchas" calls these bones one thing, "another" calls them something else, and "a third old gentleman in Hackluyt" speaks of them in a still different way. The fact is that the third quotation is a paraphrase of Purchas, not Hakluyt; but if "Purchas" were to be substituted for "Hackluyt," Purchas would be named twice, and the rhetorical effect of the sentence would be changed. What is a factual error must be allowed to stand (whether or not Melville meant to be accurate here) because the error plays a role in the rhetoric of the passage as he wrote it, and correcting the error would amount to stylistic revision.[60]

There are thus two considerations that need to be kept in mind in dealing with factual errors. First one must consider whether a correction can realistically be undertaken. If a correction involves only a simple substitution, then it can be seriously considered; but if the erroneous information has been referred to repeatedly or been made the basis of further comment, there is no way to make the correction, short of more extensive rewriting and alteration than a scholarly editor can contemplate. This consideration is purely a practical one and has nothing to do with authorial intention: some errors can be considered for correction, others cannot. In the latter case, there is no point debating what the author intended, for no alteration can be attempted; besides, the use to which the error has been put makes it in effect an intended part of the

59. This example, and other similar ones, are discussed in Hodgart's "Misquotation as Re-creation" (see note 28 above), pp. 36–37. The creative nature of Yeats's misquotations is also taken up in Jon Lanham's "Some Further Textual Problems in Yeats: *Ideas of Good and Evil*," PBSA, 71 (1977), esp. 455–457, 467.

60. The situation is somewhat more complicated, since the first reference has not been found in Purchas, and it may be erroneous also. But neither has it been located in Hakluyt, so there is no basis for switching the two names. These difficulties may support the view that Melville was more concerned here with rhetorical effect than with factual accuracy.

text, even if it originated as a slip. But in the case of errors that can feasibly be corrected, the editor must take up the second, and more difficult, kind of consideration, to determine whether or not they *ought* to be corrected. It is here that the editor's critical assessment of all relevant factors is crucial—an assessment of the nature of the sentence and passage where the error occurs, the observed habits of the author, the conventions of the time. Decisions to emend must rest on informed critical judgment, and no less so where questions of external fact are concerned. Clear thinking about emendations of factual errors requires that these two levels of consideration be thoroughly understood: the recognition, first of all, that some errors by their nature are unemendable; and, second, the awareness that any mechanical rule of thumb for handling the emendable errors involves an abandonment of the editor's critical function.

The reasons for leaving Keats's "Cortez" alone are therefore somewhat more complicated than those Amy Lowell seems to imply when she says that Keats used the name "probably by accident" but that "It is no matter." To say that what an author puts into a text "by accident" is "no matter" suggests an uncritical approach to the text; it implies an acceptance of whatever is present in a particular text, as if one were approaching the text of a working document, where one is interested in preserving false starts and errors for their psychological significance. But the sonnet is a finished work of art, not merely a literary document, and it demands to be edited critically, with attention to possible emendations to restore the author's intention. Whether Keats intended to disregard historical fact or confused the historical Balboa with Cortez, however, need not be pondered, for there is no question that "Cortez" is the word he put into the poem at this point, and the role which that word plays in the patterns of sound and rhythm in the poem makes it an integral element of the work. Furthermore, the connotations of "Cortez" are such that it is able to serve as a vehicle to carry the intended tenor of the figure. This is one of those situations where an "error" is unemendable because the use made of it within the work rules out any editorial attempt to rectify it. "Cortez" must remain, not because author's accidents do not matter, but because it—accident or not in origin—became, as Keats wrote, an inextricable part of the work. Probably Amy Lowell had such points in mind, but her elliptical statement does not make them clear and even seems to encourage the view that the accuracy of external references in literary works need not be seriously investigated.

References to external fact, as in this instance, raise textual questions because they call attention to a second "text" (the historical fact) with which the text under consideration can be compared. Editorial attention is necessarily drawn to variants between two or more texts of a work; but a critical editor's duty is also to try to identify any errors in a text at points where variants do not exist or in cases where there is only one text. If quotations or other references to external fact or uses of external documents are involved, the editor has assistance in this task that is not otherwise available, for a point of comparison outside the immediate text can be established. At many other places in a text one has no basis for speculating about whether a reading is erroneous, but when words are quoted from another writer or a date is cited, for example, one can compare the text with the outside source or fact. Even in cases of paraphrase (or translation), where a passage is loosely based on an external source, knowledge of the wording of that source is relevant. Differences found in the text are not necessarily to be regarded as errors, but in many cases familiarity with the external facts enables one to recognize a slip of the pen or a misreading of handwriting that could not have been detected any other way. And in instances where only printed texts or late manuscripts are available, such knowledge allows one to speculate about certain readings in now lost anterior documents, for one can know the sources that underlie parts of those documents. Recognizing that writers need not be held to strict accuracy in their historical allusions does not eliminate the critical editor's responsibility for checking each allusion and making a textual decision about it. The presence in a text of quotations, paraphrases, or references to historical fact undoubtedly raises some perplexing editorial questions; but it also provides editors with a splendid opportunity of demonstrating what critical editing at its most effective can accomplish.

Some Principles for Editorial Apparatus

NYONE WHO UNDERTAKES TO EDIT A TEXT MUST NECESSARILY make some basic decisions about the kind of editorial apparatus that is to accompany that text. Sometimes these decisions are so thoughtless that they are hardly recognized as decisions at all — as when a publisher's editor selects a particular early edition to be photographically reproduced, without commentary of any kind, in a cheap paperback series. At other times they are the result of careful deliberation — as when a scholarly editor who has constructed a critical text sets forth in several lists the data he had at his disposal in examining variants and making emendations. In between, the spectrum includes a wide variety of kinds of apparatus: one edition may be entirely unannotated except for a prefatory note explaining the source of the text and perhaps generalizing about certain changes made in it; another may record variant readings (or the more important of them) in brackets within the text or at the foot of the page; another may limit its annotation, at the foot of the page or at the end of the volume, to definition of obscure words and identification of historical allusions; and still another may be principally concerned with citing previous critics' remarks about individual passages. But whatever form the apparatus takes — from the rudimentary to the elaborate — it represents some sort of thought about the extent to which the editor should make himself visible to the audience at which he is aiming.

Some kinds of apparatus, of course, are in part determined by the purposes of the edition: thus a variorum edition must by definition include apparatus which records variant readings. But an editor's basic job is to produce a text, and normally neither the exact form nor the extent of the apparatus is automatically determined by that job. A careful and reliable text obviously could be published without any accompanying apparatus, while an irresponsible text could be offered with extensive notes and tables. Such is not usually the case; but the fact remains that the precise nature of the apparatus is determined by a different set of decisions from that which lies behind the establishment of the text. It is true that most of the recent editions based on Greg's rationale for choosing a copy-text[1] have similar categories of lists in the apparatus. But there is nothing in his theory itself which requires such lists; rather, it could be said that these lists provide the most important kinds of information which ought to be supplied in any scholarly edition, regardless of the principles followed in constructing the text. Decisions affecting the text involve questions of authorial intent; decisions affecting the apparatus involve questions of editorial responsibility. When an editor prepares a text for a scholarly audience, it is his responsibility to furnish all the information required for evaluating and rethinking his textual decisions; in a popular edition, on the other hand, he may feel with some justification that his primary responsibility is to provide explanatory annotation rather than textual evidence — but of course the care with which the text itself is prepared would not be less merely because the apparatus is simpler.[2] It should be clear, therefore, that a general rationale for editorial apparatus can be discussed independently of any rationale for editing. And equally obvious is the basic principle to be borne in mind in making decisions about apparatus: that the kind of apparatus presented is an indication less of the nature of the text than of the type of audience for which the edition is intended.

Just what apparatus is appropriate for a particular audience is a matter about which opinion naturally changes over the course of time, as scholarly techniques develop and bibliographical knowledge accumulates. In the nineteenth century, conventional practice for scholarly editions was to list variant readings (usually a selection of those considered most significant) in footnotes, with more discursive notes placed either at the end (as in William Aldis Wright's Cambridge Shakespeare, which began in 1863) or in a second set of footnotes, below the first (as in Horace Howard Furness's Variorum Shakespeare, which began in 1874). A new standard was set in 1904, when the first volume of R. B. McKerrow's edition of Nashe appeared; though in arrangement it was similar to earlier editions (variants in footnotes, with discursive notes in a supplementary volume), it marked a turning point

---

1. "The Rationale of Copy-Text," *SB*, 3 (1950-51), 19-36; reprinted in Greg's *Collected Papers*, ed. J. C. Maxwell (1966), pp. 374-91.

2. The ground rules might be different—

if this were what Fredson Bowers calls a "practical edition"—so that less research would be expected. But the *care* devoted to establishing the text on the basis of the available evidence would be no less, for this is the editor's essential task.

in its discussions of the bibliographical history of each work, leading to a careful choice of "copy-text" (the term was first used here) — which in turn lent an added sense of objectivity and control to the record of variant readings, for it was defined to include *all* departures (with a few minor exceptions) from that copy-text, as well as other significant variants. McKerrow went on, in his *Prolegomena for the Oxford Shakespeare* (1939), not only to refine and elaborate his editorial procedure but also to discuss in detail the form which he believed editorial apparatus should take; although in general arrangement he advocated the old system of two sets of footnotes (one of variant readings, one of historical and linguistic information), his discussion of the symbols and form to be employed in each entry for a variant reading (pp. 73-98) was by far the most extensive that had ever appeared, and its influence is still present today.

But the event which has been most important in influencing the form of the apparatus in many of the more recent scholarly editions was the publication in 1953 of the first volume of Fredson Bowers's Cambridge edition of Dekker. What Bowers did to make the apparatus more conveniently usable was to break down the listing of variants into several parts: only the substantive departures from the copy-text were recorded in footnotes; the departures in accidentals were then gathered into a separate list at the end of the text; and two more lists at the end dealt with press-variant formes and with substantive variants in other pre-1700 editions ("historical collation"). Since that time many editions have employed some variety of Bowers's plan, most notably the series of editions now in progress under the auspices of the MLA Center for Editions of American Authors. These editions maintain Bowers's distinction between lists of emendations and historical collation; but since they are "clear-text" editions, no apparatus appears on the pages of text, and all the emendations of the copy-text — both substantives and accidentals — are usually joined in one list. The adoption of this approach to editorial apparatus by the CEAA editions of Clemens, Stephen Crane, John Dewey, Hawthorne, Howells, Irving, Melville, and Simms[3] suggests that a new pattern for the treatment of

3. Informal citations of these editions throughout this essay refer to the following: *The Mark Twain Papers*, ed. Frederick Anderson *et al.* (Berkeley: University of California Press, 1966-   ), esp. *Hannibal, Huck & Tom*, ed. Walter Blair (1969), and *Mysterious Stranger Manuscripts*, ed. William M. Gibson (1969); *The University of Virginia Edition of the Works of Stephen* *Crane*, ed. Fredson Bowers (Charlottesville: University Press of Virginia, 1969-   ); *The Early Works of John Dewey, 1882-1898*, ed. Jo Ann Boydston, in consultation with Fredson Bowers (Carbondale: Southern Illinois University Press, 1969-   ); *The Centenary Edition of the Works of Nathaniel Hawthorne*, text ed. Fredson Bowers, with Matthew J. Bruccoli (Colum-

apparatus in scholarly editions seems to be emerging—at least for works of the sixteenth century and later. The elements in this pattern are basically four: a set of discursive textual notes, a list of emendations in the copy-text, a record of line-end hyphenation, and a historical collation. Other lists are sometimes added to cover special problems, but these four, along with an essay setting forth the textual situation which accounts for the particular choice of copy-text, have come in recent years to represent one established kind of scholarly apparatus.[4]

Although the form of the apparatus in a large number of scholarly editions from the last twenty years is therefore similar, it is by no means identical, even in those which follow the same basic plan. There is no reason, of course, to insist on such identity in outward appearance, so long as the approach to the material is sound, since different circumstances naturally entail somewhat different treatments. Never-

bus: Ohio State University Press, 1962-   ) ; *A Selected Edition of W. D. Howells*, ed. Edwin H. Cady, Don Cook, Ronald Gottesman, David J. Nordloh *et al.* (Bloomington: Indiana University Press, 1968-   ); *The Complete Works of Washington Irving*, ed. Henry A. Pochmann *et al.* (Madison: University of Wisconsin Press, 1969-   ) , esp. *Mahomet and His Successors* (1970); *The Writings of Herman Melville: The Northwestern-Newberry Edition*, ed. Harrison Hayford, Hershel Parker, and G. Thomas Tanselle, with Richard Colles Johnson (Evanston and Chicago: Northwestern University Press and The Newberry Library, 1968-   ); *The Writings of William Gilmore Simms: Centennial Edition*, ed. John Caldwell Guilds and James B. Meriwether (Columbia: University of South Carolina Press, 1969-   ). In addition, the following are referred to allusively throughout: *The Dramatic Works in the Beaumont and Fletcher Canon*, ed. Fredson Bowers *et al.* (Cambridge: Cambridge University Press, 1966-   ) ; *The Dramatic Works of Thomas Dekker*, ed. Fredson Bowers (Cambridge: Cambridge University Press, 1953-61) ; *The Journals and Miscellaneous Notebooks of Ralph Waldo Emerson*, ed. William H. Gilman *et al.* (Cambridge: Belknap Press of Harvard University Press, 1960-   ) ; *The Wesleyan Edition of the Works of Henry Fielding*, ed. W. B. Coley, Fredson Bowers, *et al.* (Mid-

letown, Conn.: Wesleyan University Press, 1967-   ) , esp. *Joseph Andrews*, ed. Martin C. Battestin (1967) .

4. Standard brief descriptions of this kind of apparatus appear in two essays by Fredson Bowers: "Textual Criticism," in *The Aims and Methods of Scholarship in Modern Languages and Literatures*, ed. James Thorpe (1963; rev. ed., 1970) , esp. pp. 53-54; and "Some Principles for Scholarly Editions of Nineteenth-Century American Authors," *SB*, 17 (1964), esp. 227-28. See also *Statement of Editorial Principles: A Working Manual for Editing Nineteenth Century American Texts* (CEAA, 1967) , pp. 9-10. During the same years there have, of course, been proponents of other approaches to editing and to apparatus. Among the best known are Edmund Wilson (represented by his essays in the *New York Review of Books* on 26 Sept. and 10 Oct. 1968, reprinted the same year in pamphlet form as *The Fruits of the MLA*) and F. W. Bateson (represented by his editorial plan for "Longman's Annotated English Poets" and reflected in his letter in the *TLS* on 1 Jan. 1971, pp. 14-15). Some discussion of Wilson's views can be found in *Professional Stndards and American Editions: A Response to Edmund Wilson* (MLA, 1969) and of Bateson's in Thomas Clayton's letter in the *TLS* on 18 Dec. 1970, p. 1493.

theless, if a standard form exists and if there is no special reason to depart from it, following that form can be a positive advantage: it makes the apparatus easier to use, since readers acquainted with other editions will already know the system and will not be distracted from the content by trying to keep in mind a new plan or new symbols. Because one possible standard of this kind has been developing in recent years, it seems worthwhile to give further thought to the rationale of apparatus and to the implications of certain differences in form. The comments which I offer in the following pages are not intended as an attempt to establish "rules" but simply as a discussion of some of the considerations involved in thinking through the details of an editorial apparatus. Although I shall be mainly concerned with scholarly editions, many of the principles apply equally to more popular editions. Some remarks on the general arrangement of the apparatus and on the symbols to be employed will be followed by discussions of the four main divisions of modern apparatus enumerated above: textual notes, emendations, line-end hyphenation, and historical collation.

i. Arrangement

The first decision to be made about the arrangement of apparatus is its location. Are variant readings or editorial symbols to appear within the text itself? Or is the annotation to be provided at the foot of each page? Or at the end of the text? Or in some combination of these places? The tendency in recent years has been toward "clear text" — that is, no editorial intrusions of any kind on the pages of the text itself — and there are at least two important reasons for encouraging this practice. In the first place, an editor's primary responsibility is to establish a text; whether his goal is to reconstruct that form of the text which represents the author's final intention or some other form of the text, his essential task is to produce a reliable text according to some set of principles. Relegating all editorial matter to an appendix and allowing the text to stand by itself serves to emphasize the primacy of the text and permits the reader to confront the literary work without the distraction of editorial comment and to read the work with ease. A second advantage of a clear text is that it is easier to quote from or to reprint. Although no device can insure accuracy of quotation, the insertion of symbols (or even footnote numbers) into a text places additional difficulties in the way of the quoter. Furthermore, most quotations appear in contexts where symbols are inappropriate; thus when it is necessary to quote from a text which has not been kept clear of apparatus, the burden of producing a clear text of the passage is placed on the quoter. Even footnotes at the bottom of the text pages are open to the same objection, when the question of a photographic reprint arises. Once a scholarly text of a work has been established, every effort should be made to encourage publishers who plan to issue classroom or other practical[5] editions of the work to lease that text and reproduce it photographically, thus assuring wider circulation of a reliable text.[6] But in such cases it is the text which is leased, not the apparatus; and while the apparatus, like any other published research, is available for all to draw upon, it would not necessarily be appropriate for inclusion in such leased editions, which might more usefully carry an apparatus emphasizing explanatory rather than textual annotation. The presence of any apparatus on the pages of the text, therefore, may prove in the long run a hindrance to the dissemination of a responsible text.

Arguments can of course be advanced for inserting editorial apparatus into a text, and it is true that on certain occasions this arrangement is desirable. For instance, the nature of such materials as letters, notebooks, and journals — works never intended for publication — may not always be accurately reflected in clear text, which requires a choice among alternative readings that is often alien to the spirit of a private document. In these cases a text which includes editorial insertions and symbols recognizes that canceled readings and uncanceled variants are in fact integral parts of such works and comes as close as possible (short of a facsimile) to reproducing their essential character.[7] In

5. The term "practical edition" is used here in the sense established by Fredson Bowers in "Practical Texts and Definitive Editions," in *Two Lectures on Editing* (1969), pp. 21-70. Further comment on the relation between definitive editions and widely disseminated reading editions appears in his "The New Look in Editing," *South Atlantic Bulletin*, 35 (1970), 3-10.

6. Encouraging such reproduction does not imply that only one reliable text of a work can exist. Obviously more than one text can be prepared following sound scholarly procedures, for there may legitimately be differences of opinion about certain emendations which rest on critical evaluation. (For discussion of this point, see G. T. Tanselle, "Textual Study and Literary Judgment," *PBSA*, 2nd Quarter 1971.) The point is that a practical edition should

embody *some* reliable text, and, if such a text exists, the publisher of a practical edition should be encouraged to lease it rather than reprint, with no rationale, whatever previous text comes most readily to hand.

7. Some works of this kind may be of such importance that they will be frequently quoted; in these cases it may be more convenient to have a clear text (with variant readings recorded at the end), even at the sacrifice of the basic texture of the original. This sort of decision, involving a weighing of what is gained against what is lost, has to be made separately for each individual case. For further comment on this problem, see G. T. Tanselle, "The Editorial Problem of Final Authorial Intention," forthcoming in *Bibliographia*.

addition, manuscripts of works which conform to genres ordinarily intended for publication — whether or not they were so prepared — may be of interest in their own right as revealing steps in the author's creative process. Such manuscripts may appropriately be edited in the form of a "genetic text," which through symbols (often, necessarily, elaborate ones) makes clear the various stages of alteration and revision. The document being edited is still a private one (like letters and journals), even though it happens to embody a text intended for eventual publication. An outstanding example of a genetic text is the one prepared by Harrison Hayford and Merton M. Sealts, Jr., from Melville's *Billy Budd* manuscript (1962); because a genetic text is not easily readable, however, and because *Billy Budd* is a work of fiction rather than a private journal, the editors have also established a "reading text," free of all apparatus on the pages of the text. (Another method of dealing with this sort of manuscript — footnotes describing the revisions — is discussed below.) Thus it can be said that clear text may often be inappropriate when the material to be edited is a working document of a private nature; but when a work of the kind normally intended for publication is being edited as a finished piece of writing[8] rather than as a semifinal document, any intrusion into the text works against the editor's ultimate goal of presenting a text as the author intended (or would have intended) it to be presented.[9]

Notes at the foot of pages of text also can be defended at times. There is no denying the argument that the location is more convenient for reference than the end of the text, and editors may wish to place the most important apparatus there, even when they reserve the bulk of it for the end. Fredson Bowers, in his move to make apparatus less cumbersome, took the view that scholarly editions "should be made more attractive to the general user, first by removing all but the most immediately pertinent of the apparatus to appendices in the rear, thus freeing the text page from all information that is only of reference value and so of no immediate concern to the reader."[10] In his edition

8. I use the term "finished piece of writing" rather than "literary work" in order to include historical, technical, and scientific writings or any other work completed for publication or of a type usually intended for publication.

9. Another use of symbols in the text, convenient in certain situations in practical editions, is to draw the student's attention to important revised passages. In the Signet *Typee* (ed. Harrison Hayford, 1964), passages which Melville deleted in the revised American edition of 1846 are enclosed in square brackets, and those which he revised are both bracketed and numbered, with the revised wording given at the end of the volume according to the reference numbers.

10. "Old-Spelling Editions of Dramatic Texts," in *Studies in Honor of T. W. Baldwin,* ed. D. C. Allen (1958), p. 14.

of Dekker, only substantive emendations are given at the foot of the page, and other editions have followed a similar plan — the California *Works of John Dryden* (first volume, 1956), for example, which records only the emendations (substantive and accidental) in footnotes. Once the decision has been made, however, not to clutter the text pages with the entire apparatus, it is a difficult question to decide just how much of the apparatus is of such immediate importance that it should be retained on those pages, separated from the rest of the apparatus. What the issue comes to in the end is whether the advantages of having some data available without turning any pages outweigh the decided disadvantages of having the text pages encumbered with visible signs of the editorial process. And the advantages of the former are less strong when related information must be turned to at the back anyway, while the disadvantages of the latter are strong enough to have dictated this shift of at least some of the material in the first place.[11] Of course, footnote apparatus is not objectionable in editions of manuscript drafts or journals, for the same reason that genetic texts are appropriate there. Sometimes footnotes, rather than symbols in the text, are used in such editions to record manuscript alterations: a good example is Bowers's parallel-text edition[12] of *Whitman's Manuscripts* (1955), in which footnotes to the manuscript texts describe in words rather than symbols the exact nature of the manuscript alterations (footnotes, that is, without reference symbols in the text, so that the text remains clear). At other times footnotes are used in addition to symbols in the text, as

11. The question takes a slightly different form for practical editions, since it may be felt that a classroom edition with little apparatus except explanatory notes should offer those notes as easily accessible footnotes. It is perhaps true that more students will read them as footnotes, but the price paid for this attention is a high one: not simply the distraction from the text (which is after all more important for the students to read), but the cumulative psychological effect of always (or nearly always) encountering classic works encased in an obtrusive editorial framework which sets them apart from other books read outside of class. Sometimes it is objected that references to line numbers are awkward and inconvenient when side-numbers counting the lines do not appear on the text pages. Side-numbers have been so widely used in connection with poetry that they probably constitute little distraction there (and thus do not prevent a poetic text from being "clear"); but their presence on a page of prose remains an intrusion and lends the page a "textbook" air. The psychological advantages of clear text, therefore, can be said to compensate for the minor inconvenience of having to count lines.

12. The use of parallel texts is often a more sensible way of exhibiting complicated revisions than to present one established text with the revisions recorded in apparatus; besides, some complex revisions result in what amounts to a different work, so that both forms of the work deserve to be presented as texts in their own right. Placing two texts in parallel columns or on facing pages is in itself a kind of apparatus; but, except for that, the comments made here about the texts of other editions would also apply to the individual texts of a parallel-text edition.

in the Harvard edition of Emerson's journals, where the footnotes (keyed to numbers in the text) provide both textual and historical information in discursive form. In neither case are the footnotes intrusions as they would be on the pages of the finished text of a novel or poem. But whenever footnotes do appear on any kind of text pages, the proximity of note to text should not lead an editor into thinking that his decisions about the readings of the text itself are less important. H. H. Furness, in the first volume of his Variorum Shakespeare, declared that, "in such an edition as the present, it makes very little difference what text is printed in extenso, since every other text is also printed with it on the same page" (p. viii). To take such a point of view is practically to abandon editing a text in favor of constructing an apparatus, for the text then exists largely as a frame of reference for the apparatus. A record of variants presented as a work of scholarship in its own right can be useful,[13] but there should be no illusion about its being an edition.[14] In the end, a decision to use or not to use footnotes reflects an editor's critical judgment about the nature of the text he is editing combined with his evaluation of the relative importance, in terms of psychological effect on the reader, of clear text as opposed to text with simultaneously visible apparatus.[15]

If an editor decides to place his apparatus at the end rather than on the text pages, several questions of arrangement still remain. One of the first is whether, if a volume contains more than one work, the apparatus pertaining to a given work should come immediately after the text of that work or whether the entire apparatus should be gathered at the end of the volume. Practice has varied in the CEAA editions: the Ohio State Hawthorne and some volumes of the Virginia Crane have apparatus following each work, whereas the Southern Illinois Dewey has apparatus at the back of each volume. Of course,

---

13. Indeed, sometimes the apparatus appended to a text is more important to scholars than the text itself, since, if it is well done, it provides the evidence on which other editions can be constructed by editors who do not agree with the interpretation of the evidence represented in that particular edition. A good example of an apparatus presented as a piece of research in its own right is Matthew J. Bruccoli's "Material for a Centenary Edi-.tion of Tender is the Night," SB, 17 (1964), 177-93.

14. Even a facsimile or a diplomatic edition of one particular impression of a work or one particular copy of an impression is based on a decision to present a given text and cannot be approached with the attitude that "it makes very little difference what text is printed in extenso."

15. Since the basic goal of an edition is to establish a text rather than to present an apparatus, the effect which the text makes would apparently—if it comes to a choice—be given somewhat more weight than the convenience with which the apparatus can be located.

the number of separate works involved has some bearing on the decision: the first volume of the Dewey edition contains many individual essays never before collected, whereas the first volume of the Crane edition and the third of the Hawthorne each contain the texts of only two separately published books. In the case of the Dewey, therefore, apparatus after each work would have produced a cumbersome volume in which editorial material continually alternated with the text and in which reference to the apparatus was inconvenient since the reader would never know just which pages contained the apparatus to any given work; in the case of volumes made up of only two or three works, on the other hand, it could be argued that the proximity of the apparatus following each work is an advantage and further that this arrangement emphasizes the discreteness of the texts which happen to be published in the same volume. Nevertheless, even when the number of separate works is small, the act of consulting the apparatus seems more difficult when the apparatus is placed at the ends of the works rather than all together at the end of the volume;[16] in addition, the occurrence of apparatus at scattered points throughout a volume, though it does not violate the idea of clear text, is undeniably a greater editorial intrusion than would exist if all the editor's data were collected at one location. Essentially the difficulty arises out of the fact that, from the textual point of view, one is concerned with two or more "books," while from the point of view of design one is dealing with a single physical volume. Since the placement of apparatus does not affect an editor's principles for establishing a text but does affect the design of the finished volume, and since the volume, as the smallest separate physical unit in an edition — and not the literary work or "book" — is the unit which the reader must manipulate, it seems reasonable to suggest that the apparatus (once the decision has been reached to place it at the "end" rather than on text pages) should probably in most circumstances be gathered in one section at the end of each physical volume.[17]

16. Both because one knows less readily where to turn to find the apparatus and because comparative study involving several works requires more extensive page-turning. In addition, the editor may have practical reasons for preferring a single block of apparatus at the end, since it enables him to key all his apparatus to page proof at one time. If sections of apparatus are scattered through a volume, the process is inevitably less efficient; for if the editor gets galleys first, he must wait to key the apparatus for his second text until the apparatus for his first has been made into pages, so that the pagination of the second text is known, and so on through the volume; and if the editor receives pages directly, then the apparatus must be set up with blank references ("oo.oo") and all the figures later altered.

17. Considerations of the ease with which

A related question is the precise arrangement of the material at the end of the volume. Just as it seems easier to turn to the apparatus if it is all at one location, so is it simpler to refer to the information about a particular work if it is presented at one spot within that section of apparatus. Normally when a reader consults the apparatus he is studying a single work, and he finds the apparatus more convenient if all the lists pertaining to that work occur together, so that he does not have to turn back and forth from the relevant part of a long list of emendations for the whole volume to the relevant part of a full historical collation, and so on. One might argue, of course, that to have only one list of each type for the whole volume — as in the Dewey edition — consolidates the information more economically and is in conformity with the view of the volume as a single physical entity. The difficulty, however, is that the volume is still composed of individual works, each with its own textual history and each requiring separate editorial consideration; any apparatus which does not segregate the material relating to each work is likely to obscure the variations in copy-texts and in numbers of authoritative editions involved and to suggest a greater uniformity than in fact exists. Obviously this is not to say that the true situation cannot be perceived by a careful reader — after all, neither system, in the hands of responsible editors, conceals relevant information. The whole point is whether one system is clearer and easier to use than the other, and the advantage in this regard would seem to lie with the system which presents separate blocks of data for each individual work. The greater ease with which, under this system, one can move from one category of data to another and gain an overview of the kinds of editorial decisions involved (even without remembering which pages the work covers) surely outweighs the slightly greater expenditure of space entailed.[18]

individual texts and apparatus can be reproduced photographically have little relevance here, for even when the apparatus immediately follows the work the pagination would be appropriate for separate issue only for the first work in the volume; and when pagination must be altered in any case, there would be no additional problem in taking the apparatus from the end of the volume and altering its page numbers also. A real problem might arise, of course, if the apparatus for a given work were not presented as a unit and if apparatus pertaining to other works appeared on some of the same pages; but

there is no reason why apparatus at the end of a volume cannot be so arranged as to avoid this problem. (See the following paragraph and footnote 18.)

18. Some extra space is required, of course, for the additional headings which would be needed. Further space would generally be used if one always began the section for a given work on a new page, in an attempt to facilitate photoreproduction of an individual text with its apparatus (see footnote 17). But if only a few long texts were involved, little space would be wasted in this way, while for shorter texts,

Whether or not a volume contains more than one work or has apparatus arranged by work, another question which an editor must decide is the order in which the various parts of the apparatus are to be presented. Although the record of emendations in the copy-text generally precedes the historical collation, there is otherwise little consensus on this matter. Some editions place the discursive textual notes after the list of emendations, while others give them first; some put the list of line-end hyphenation last, while others insert it immediately after the record of emendations. The issue is not one of major importance: what is important is that these kinds of information be present, not that they be present in a particular order. Still, they have to appear in some order; and the editor, if he does not settle the question by flipping a coin, must have some rationale for selecting one order over another. If an advantage, however slight, does exist favoring one arrangement, that arrangement is preferable to a purely random order hit upon by an individual editor — preferable not only because there is some reason for it but also because its adoption would result in greater uniformity among editions. At any rate, the editor should be aware of the various considerations involved in the ordering of the lists.

One common arrangement is to place the list of emendations first (if it does not appear as footnotes), since it could be considered of most immediate importance, recording as it does the editorial alterations in the copy-text. Generally this list is followed (as in the Ohio State *Scarlet Letter*, the California Mark Twain, and the Dewey edition) by the discursive textual notes; because a common practice now (following Bowers's Dekker) is to mark with an asterisk those emendations which are discussed in the notes, the section of notes can in a sense be regarded as an appendage to the list of emendations. On the other hand, most editors find it necessary occasionally to comment on readings they have not emended, giving their reasons for not altering what might at first seem to be incorrect. Notes of this kind obviously do not relate to the list of emendations, since no emendations are recorded at these points. One way of solving this awkwardness is to insert asterisked entries in the list of emendations calling attention to

---

such as essays, stories, and poems (where more space might be wasted, since more of these works could be included in a volume), there would be less reason to accommodate photoreproduction, because less demand exists for separate reprints of individual short works. There would be little reason, in other words, for beginning the apparatus to each work on a new page except when a volume contains only two or three long works.

these notes, simply by citing the reading involved and adding *"stet"* to show that the reading was the same in the copy-text.[19] The result is that every discursive note can be located by means of the asterisks in the list of emendations; but the price paid for this convenience is that the list of emendations is no longer, strictly speaking, a list of emendations, because it also contains certain instances where emendations have not been made. This list is then less easy to use for surveying the emendations as a whole or compiling statistics about them, since one would have to be alert for those items which are not emendations at all. The function of such a list would be less clear-cut and less easy for the reader to comprehend; and the convenience of having asterisk references to all the notes (if, indeed, it really is a convenience) is probably not worth so high a price. An alternative, and more satisfactory, solution is simply to reverse the order of the two sections, placing the textual notes before the list of emendations. One effect of this change is to remove any implication that the notes are tied to the list of emendations; asterisks can still be used in the list of emendations to call attention to notes, but no awkwardness results from the fact that some of the notes take up readings not entered in the list. This arrangement emphasizes the real function of the notes: to comment on any readings — whether emendations or not — which raise some problem from a textual point of view and which thus require some explanation. Many readers not interested in rejected variants will be reading carefully enough to wonder about certain peculiar expressions and will turn directly to the textual notes to see what explanation is offered for the adoption (whether through emendation or retention) of these expressions. Placing these notes nearest the text is both suggestive and convenient: suggestive of the fact that the notes make direct comments on readings in the established text, and convenient because it allows all the sections of the apparatus in tabular, rather than discursive, form to fall together.[20] In recent years this position for the textual notes has

19. Bowers's Dekker employs this system, though the situation is somewhat different since the record of substantive emendations appears as footnotes. It is also used by Matthew J. Bruccoli in "Material for a Centenary Edition of *Tender is the Night*," *SB*, 17 (1964), 177-93, but again there are special circumstances since here the apparatus is presented independently of the text. And the Virginia Crane edition uses the *"stet"* system even though the list of emendations follows the textual notes.

20. Still another arrangement is employed in the first volume of the Simms edition, where the list of emendations and the textual notes are merged: that is, whenever a reading requires comment, the comment is inserted at the appropriate point in the list of emendations. The advantage, of course, is a reduction in the number of separate sections of apparatus, so that the reader is involved in less cross reference between sections. But, as usually happens when notes are tied to a list of emenda-

been gaining favor and has been employed in the Crane, Howells, Irving, and Melville editions and in the Hawthorne edition beginning with the second volume.[21]

Once it is decided to make the textual notes the first of the four main divisions of the apparatus,[22] it is not difficult to settle on the list of emendations as the second. Of the standard lists, it is the one most directly connected with the edited text, since it records the editorial changes which that text embodies and enables the reader to reconstruct the basic document, the copy-text. The question that remains, then, is the order of the other two basic lists — the historical collation and the record of line-end hyphenation. The hyphenation list is often put in last position (as in the Dewey, Howells, and Irving editions, in certain volumes of *The Mark Twain Papers*, and in the first volume of the Hawthorne edition); apparently the reason is that hyphenation seems in some intangible sense less "significant" than the instances of substantive variation in the authorized editions. Yet if one of the reasons for giving precedence, among the lists, to the record of emendations is that it is concerned with editorial decisions, consistency would suggest that the hyphenation list should follow immediately, since it too records editorial decisions — that is, one half of it does, the half that lists line-end hyphens in the copy-text. And the other half — noting the established forms of compounds divided at line-ends in the edited text — is of direct use to any reader who wishes to make a quotation from the text. The historical collation, on the other hand, is simply a factual register of the variations (usually only the substantive ones) present in a given group of editions; although it is valuable in setting forth much of the textual evidence at the editor's disposal, its purpose is not pri-

tions, some entries for unemended readings have to be included in the list. Furthermore, there is the danger that the insertion of blocks of discursive material into the list will make the list less easy to follow; in the case of the first Simms volume, the number of notes is small enough that this difficulty does not arise to any significant extent, but it remains a possibility when there is a considerable number of notes—and when the number is small, the notes may actually prove less readily accessible if imbedded in a list. Finally, difficulties of design in joining paragraphs and lists (as when lengthy notes must be accommodated to a double-column page designed primarily for listed items) provide an additional argument against using this system under ordinary circumstances.

21. The Cambridge Dekker and Beaumont-Fletcher editions also place the textual notes immediately after the text, but in effect these notes follow the substantive emendations, since the substantive emendations are recorded in footnotes on text pages.

22. The positions of various other special lists which may be required are commented on below, at the points where these lists are discussed.

marily to list editorial decisions,[23] and it is thus set apart from the other main sections of the apparatus in this regard. If the principle of arrangement is to be — as seems sensible — a movement from what is most directly associated with the final edited text to what is least directly connected with it, there is little doubt that the hyphenation list should precede the historical collation (as it does in the Crane, Fielding, and Melville editions and in the Hawthorne beginning with the second volume).

A suggested standard order, therefore, for the four basic parts of the apparatus is as follows: (1) textual notes; (2) emendations; (3) line-end hyphenation; and (4) historical collation. Another essential part of the editorial matter is an essay describing the editorial principles followed in the edition, the textual history of the individual work, and any special problems emerging from the application of those principles to that particular historical situation. This kind of essay is frequently labeled as an "introduction" and placed at the beginning of the volume, preceding the text. Although such a location does not contradict the notion of clear text (since it obviously does not affect what appears on the text pages), it does result in the editor intruding himself at a very prominent place in the volume; what is probably more in keeping with the spirit of the clear-text principle and with the decision to place apparatus at the end is to think of the textual essay not as an introduction to the entire volume but only as an introduction to the apparatus — and thus to be placed at the end, though preceding the other parts of the editorial matter dealing with textual concerns (a plan followed by a number of editions, such as the Howells, Irving, Melville, and Simms).[24] In cases where related documents of textual interest exist (a manuscript fragment from an early draft, a published preface differing from the one in the copy-text edition, a map or other nontextual appurtenance of the copy-text edition, and the like), they can properly be printed or discussed as another section of the editorial apparatus — a section which should probably come last, since such material often is not keyed directly to the established text and in any case is only peripherally related to it. Finally, the editorial apparatus

23. Though incidentally it does list the substantive ones, since each entry has to be keyed to the reading which appears in the edited text.

24. In the Dewey edition, both a textual introduction and a historical introduction precede the text; but the pages on which they appear are numbered with small roman numerals, and this sequence of pagination is resumed at the back of the volume for the remainder of the apparatus. This arrangement thus makes it simple, in other printings or photographically reproduced sub-editions, to bring all the editorial matter together.

in some instances may include explanatory, as opposed to textual, annotation: many editions provide a historical essay on the background, composition, publication, and reception of the work, and some —especially those of nonfiction — also offer notes identifying allusions and an index. The historical essay is sometimes placed at the beginning of the volume, even when the textual essay follows the text (as in the Howells and Simms editions), and at other times it is put in the end matter, preceding the textual essay (as in the Irving and Melville editions); the argument for the latter position is the same as in the case of the textual essay — to allow the edited work to have the opening place in the volume. The explanatory notes — if they are not treated as footnotes[25] — might reasonably be the first section to follow the text, preceding any of the textual apparatus (as in the Howells edition), though they might logically follow the historical essay, if that essay were in the end matter; and an index, whether or not it covers the editorial contributions, should retain its conventional position at the very end of the physical volume (as in the Dewey edition). Since the nontextual annotation is discursive in form or is set up in forms (such as indexes) about which much has already been written, and since the related documents by their nature usually present special situations which must be treated on an individual basis, the remarks on form in the pages which follow will be limited to the strictly textual apparatus.

ii. Symbols

Practically every edition makes some use of symbols or abbreviations; indeed, they are almost unavoidable unless one is dealing with a text so uncomplicated that scarcely any apparatus results. The primary motive behind most (but not all) symbols and abbreviations is economy, for if an editor is going to refer dozens (or even hundreds) of times to a particular impression, published at a given time by a given publisher and identifiable perhaps only by certain typographical peculiarities, it is merely common sense that he devise some concise way of making the reference. But he must also realize that, beyond a point, the interests of economy work in the opposite direction from those of clarity. In 1863 William Aldis Wright recognized (as every editor must) this dilemma: "We will now proceed," he said in the introduction to the Cambridge Shakespeare, "to explain the notation employed in the foot-notes, which, in some cases, the necessity of com-

---

25. In the Wesleyan Fielding, though the textual apparatus is at the end of the volume, the explanatory notes are placed at the bottom of the text pages (keyed to footnote numbers in the text).

pressing may have rendered obscure" (p. xxii). When symbols are multiplied to the point where it is difficult for the reader to keep them in mind, so that he must constantly consult a key to decipher what is being said, the time has come to rethink the whole system. In some fields, such as mathematics or chemistry, symbolic statements, however complex, are admirably suited to the purposes they are intended to serve; but the apparatus to a literary text is generally directed toward the readers and students of that text, for whom a knowledge of special symbols is not necessary in their principal work of understanding the text. It is not reasonable, therefore, to ask the users of a textual apparatus to become acquainted with an elaborate symbolic structure, since that apparatus is only a reference tool, rather than the central focus of their attention. Nineteenth-century editors tended to make excessive demands along these lines; and even McKerrow's *Prolegomena*, though its thoughtful treatment of symbols is important and though the symbols it advocates are individually sensible, sets up too many of them, with the result that in combination they can be bewildering. Fortunately, the recent trend, since Bowers's Dekker, has been toward the simplification of symbols. In thinking about editorial symbols, the essential principle to be kept in mind is that for this purpose the value of a symbol ought to be judged on the basis of convenience rather than economy (though economy is often a prime element in convenience): if a symbol, both in itself and in combination with others, makes the apparatus easier to refer to and understand, it is a good one; if it does not, it should be abandoned.

Perhaps a distinction should be made between symbols which stand for particular editions or impressions and those which stand for concepts. One cannot object to a multiplicity of symbols representing editions, if there happens to be a large number of editions involved, for the symbols are still easier to manipulate than cumbersome identifications of the editions in words; but further symbols to be used in conjunction with the edition-symbols for making comments about particular situations may easily proliferate to the point where they are less easy to follow than the same concepts expressed in words. Thus when McKerrow uses parentheses to indicate "a reading which is not *identical* with the one given but which is *substantially* the same in meaning or intention so far as the purpose of the note is concerned" (p. 82) and then inserts two parallel vertical lines within the parentheses "as a warning that, although the editions thus indicated support the reading in question, the *context* in which their reading occurs is not identical with that of the other texts" (p. 85), one may begin to feel that the goal of the apparatus has become compression rather than ease of comprehension.[26] Yet no one would be likely to have strong objection to the many abbreviations and symbols — such as "Theo.," "Johns.," "Cap.," "Camb.," "Fl," "Q1"—which McKerrow employs as shorthand designations for individuals editions. Indeed, these abbreviations, though numerous, are largely self-evident and rarely would need to be looked up more than once; even aside from their economy and ease of transcription, therefore, they have the positive advantage of being recognizable at a glance (whereas a fuller identification in words normally would take somewhat longer to read).

If it can be agreed, then, that the use of symbols is desirable for reference to editions and impressions, the practical question which arises is what system to use in establishing the symbols. There are two basic approaches: one is to arrange the editions in chronological order and then to assign them arbitrary sequential designations, such as the letters of the alphabet or numbers; the other is to construct each symbol so that it contains enough rational content connecting it with its referent to serve as a mnemonic. The choice of system depends on what kind of information is deemed most useful in connection with a given text, since each system, in order to make certain facts obvious, sacrifices other facts. In the first system, one can tell immediately that a particular reading is, for example, from the third edition (by means of a "C" or "3") but cannot tell (and may not be able to remember without checking) the year of that edition and whether it was English or American. The second system, conversely, might provide in the symbol the information that the edition was an 1856 American one (through some such symbol as "A1856" or "A56") but would not at the same time reveal its position in the sequence of editions. A variety of the first system has conventionally been used for pre-nineteenth-century books: a letter designating format (such as "F" for folio and "Q" for quarto), followed by numbers indicating the succession of editions within each format. Thus "Q4" would identify the fourth quarto but would not indicate the year of publication nor whether the edition came before or after the second folio. Attempts to combine the two approaches have not been successful because forcing too much significance into a symbol renders the symbol more cumbersome and to some extent defeats the purpose of establishing symbols as simple and easily recognizable designations. An edition reference like "3A56" is,

26. McKerrow was clearly aware of this feeling and admits that compression was his principal consideration: "I may say here that the conventions, which at first sight may appear somewhat complicated and even perverse, have only been adopted after careful thought and experiment, and actually do—at least in my deliberate opinion—make it possible to give all necessary facts in the minimum of space" (p. 77).

on the fact of it, not simple, particularly when it occurs in a table full of similar references; furthermore, it contains a possible ambiguity (whether the 1856 American edition is the third edition or the third American edition) which may cause its meaning to be less easy to remember and may keep one turning to the key for reassurance. If it is also necessary to take impressions into account, the symbol becomes even more unwieldly, whether it is "3A2 (56)," "3Ab56," "AIIIii56," or whatever. It is clearly a mistake to try to construct symbols which reveal edition, impression, year, and country of publication at the same time; if a symbol is to serve efficiently its basic function of providing a convenient and unambiguous reference, it cannot bear the weight of so much information, and the editor must decide which pieces of information will produce the most useful symbols in a given situation.

For earlier periods (before the beginnings of machine-printed books), the bibliographical and textual information conveyed by reference to format makes such symbols as F_1, F_2, Q_1, etc., more revealing than reference to years of publication would be — and simpler as well, since the common situation in which more than one quarto appeared in a single year would have to be reflected in letters or other marks appended to the year designations. This system is one of the few well-established conventions in reference notation, and, with usefulness and simplicity on its side, there is little reason to oppose its popularity. For later books, however, format cannot always be determined and in any case is a less useful fact for incorporation in the symbol, since the variants to be reported are likely to be between impressions as well as editions. The most obvious adjustment would be merely to eliminate the format designation and use consecutive numbers (or letters) to refer to successive editions, with attached letters (or numbers) to indicate impressions within any edition. The Hawthorne edition assigns capital roman numerals to editions, with superscript lower-case letters for impressions (e.g., "III^c"), while the Howells edition employs capital letters for editions, with arabic numerals for impressions (e.g., "$B2$").[27] Such a system is simple and neat; but, if a large number of editions and impressions are involved, it is difficult, even

27. In both cases, however, some of the symbols do not follow the same system. In *The Scarlet Letter*, the first two editions are designated not by roman numerals but by "1850^1" and "1850^2"; and in *Their Wedding Journey* the serial publications are referred to as "S_1" and "S_2" (chronologically S_1 would precede A, and S_2 would follow C). Both editions use the mnemonic symbol "MS" for manuscript texts, and the Hawthorne uses "E" to distinguish English editions. In the Wesleyan *Joseph Andrews*, the five editions published during Fielding's lifetime are designated by simple arabic numerals, 1 through 5.

with repeated use, to remember with certainty what many of the symbols stand for, and continual reference to the key is unavoidable. A mnemonic system, on the other hand, may generally be somewhat less simple; but, so long as it is not a great deal more cumbersome, the fact that the user can remember numerous symbols without difficulty may be regarded as an offsetting advantage. (Besides being easier to use, brief symbols may be preferable for practical reasons of economy, especially if the apparatus is set in double column, where longer symbols might produce additional run-over lines.) Probably the most workable and adaptable mnemonic system is to identify editions by letters and to attach years for particular impressions. Thus if only one English and one American edition are involved, the letters "E" and "A" are sufficient, with a given impression referred to as "E1855" or "E55." When more editions are involved, letters representing the name of the publisher or the city of publication could be used; and when more than one impression occurs in a particular year, appended lower-case letters could indicate the sequence within the year. References to manuscript, typescript, and proof could employ the usual symbols "MS," "TS," and "P," as in the Howells edition. Obviously other adjustments would be required in certain situations. If, for example, there is more than one edition from the same publisher, a prefixed number could indicate the fact (as "2H," where "H" stands for the publisher's name), unless year-designations are going to appear so often as to make the symbol cumbersome. In that case the technique of consecutive lettering could be applied, though with some lessening of the mnemonic value of the system, which would then be evident principally in designations of later impressions ("C75" would be the 1875 impression of the third edition).

Regardless of the variations in the basic system, an extremely useful convention which emerges is that a letter by itself stands for all impressions of an edition and a year is attached only when a particular impression is meant. But even this convention is best modified in certain situations: in the case of Irving's *Mahomet* there is only one English impression but nine American printings, all from the same publisher; the sensible way in which the Wisconsin edition assigns symbols here is to use "E" for the English impression and simple year designations without attached letters ("50" for "1850") for the Putnam impressions.[28] This arrangement is perfectly clear and is

28. The system referred to in *Mahomet*, p. 584, note 17, as the standard system for the Irving edition uses such symbols as "1A1," "1A2," etc. It is difficult to decide whether the mnemonic value of these symbols is greater than that of symbols

simpler than if a superfluous "A" or "P" were prefixed to the numbers. In another kind of situation, a letter may even be made to stand for more than one edition. Some volumes of the Crane edition, for example, involve syndicated newspaper pieces, for which the text in one newspaper is no closer to the syndicate's master proof and no more authoritative than the text in many other newspapers. In these instances of "radiating texts," Fredson Bowers introduces (in the fifth volume of the Crane) the symbol "N" to stand for all the located newspaper texts, attaching superscript figures when necessary to identify specific newspapers. The generic letter suggests the essential equality of the various newspaper editions, and the superscript figures distinguish themselves from the regular figures used in other symbols to indicate chronological sequence. The basic principle in each situation is to make the symbols as simple as the textual situation will allow, so long as they retain enough substance to be easily remembered. (Certain symbols which are sometimes used to stand for groups of edition-symbols are commented on below in the discussion of the historical collation.)

In regard to symbols which stand for abstract concepts or relationships rather than concrete documents or impressions, the most prudent course of action is to keep their number as small as possible. Only two such symbols (both suggested in McKerrow's *Prolegomena*) have gained any currency in recent editions, and the reasons for their importance will suggest the kinds of circumstances in which symbols are desirable. Both symbols are used in reporting variants in punctuation: one, the centered tilde or wavy dash ($\sim$), stands for the word previously cited, when the variant is not in the word but in the punctuation associated with it; the other, the caret ($_\wedge$), calls attention to the absence of punctuation at a given point. The justification for the first is not simply that it saves the effort of repeating the identical word, for the small amount of effort saved would be no justification at all if the repetition of the word would be clearer; the fact is, however, that the information is conveyed more clearly with the symbol than without it:

218.4 indefatigable,] A; $\sim$;
218.4 indefatigable,] A; indefatigable;

In the second example, the reader may see the difference in punctua-

incorporating references to years; but under most circumstances of any complexity, symbols which employ the last two digits of the year (instead of the second figure here) and initials of publishers (when more than one publisher in a given country is involved) are probably easier to remember.

tion immediately, but he cannot be sure that no other difference is involved until he examines the two words closely to see that they are identical;[29] in the first, the curved dash tells him instantly that the only variant reported here is that of punctuation. Furthermore, using the curved dash eliminates the possibility of introducing a typographical error into the word the second time it is set; hopefully such an error would be caught in proofreading, but there is no point in needlessly setting up situations in which errors of this kind can enter. The caret is similarly useful in providing a clearer statement than is possible without it:

> 188.23 approaching,] 57; ∼∧
> 188.23 approaching,] 57; approaching
> 188.23 approaching,] 57; ∼

The difficulty with the last two examples is that in them empty space is made to carry the burden of significance for the entry. It is true, of course, that no foolproof way exists to guarantee the accuracy of what appears in print, and it may be that in proofreading the danger of overlooking an unintentional omission of punctuation is no greater than that of failing to notice an incorrect mark of punctuation. Nevertheless, it is reassuring to the reader to find a caret calling attention to an intended lack of punctuation. In any case, the whole point of the entry is to inform the reader that punctuation is absent at a given spot in a particular text, and it is more straightforward to make this point positively by actually noting the lack than to imply it by simply printing nothing. As these two symbols illustrate, therefore, conceptual symbols are justified when they reduce the chances of error in proofreading, when they are clearer in the context than their referents would be, or when they eliminate the necessity of regarding the absence of something as significant. The wavy dash and the caret may take a few seconds to learn, but the importance of what they contribute easily outweighs whatever unfamiliarity they may at first present to some readers. When a symbol fails to meet these tests — that is, when it is merely a shorthand device and makes no positive contribution to clarity — it is better not adopted, for only a slight proliferation of such symbols can render an apparatus needlessly forbidding. Except in certain editions of manuscripts,[30] there is rarely any need to have more

---

29. Of course, if a variant in punctuation were not involved, the punctuation would not be included in the reading at all; but the fact that it is included does not rule out the possibility that a spelling variant also exists at this point.

30. As stated above, editions of manuscript material which attempt to show stages of composition may require more

symbols than the curved dash and the caret, along with the symbols for individual documents.

iii. Textual Notes

The section of discursive notes on textual matters is generally entitled "Textual Notes" but sometimes (as in the Irving and Melville editions) is called "Discussions of Adopted Readings." Both titles suggest an important point about the content of these notes: they are comments on individual problematical readings in the text which has been established, and any reading which appears there is the "adopted reading," whether it results from emendation or retention of the copy-text reading. The notes, in other words, discuss not simply emendations but also places where emendations might have been expected and yet, after careful consideration, have not been made. (The principal reason for putting the textual notes before the list of emendations, of course, is to emphasize the fact that they refer to the text itself and not to the emendations.) Since these notes deal with individual readings, it is important to keep general matters out of them and to limit them to cases which raise special problems. Any textual problem which recurs a number of times ought to be taken up in the textual essay, since it then constitutes a general textual problem and since a repetition of the same explanation several times in the notes or extensive cross-references between the notes would be more awkward and, indeed, less clear than one coherent discussion in which all the evidence is brought together.

The most convenient form which the textual notes can take is a citation of page and line number (or act, scene, and line),[31] then the reading under discussion (shortened by an indication of ellipsis if

---

elaborate sets of symbols (including perhaps angle brackets for canceled matter and vertical arrows for insertions, both of which have been fairly widely used); but the general principles for evaluating symbols outlined here would still apply. (Useful examples of symbols for editing manuscripts are found in the Hayford and Sealts *Billy Budd* and in the Emerson and the Irving journals.) It should be noted that complicated alterations in a manuscript can also be set forth in verbal descriptions, without any symbols at all, as in the Ohio State *House of the Seven Gables* and in the California *Hannibal, Huck & Tom* and *Mysterious Stranger Manuscripts*. Fredson Bowers, in his review of the New York

Public Library edition of *Walt Whitman's Blue Book* (ed. Arthur Golden), makes some comments on the relative merits of the two approaches and finds Golden's method an uneconomical mixture of the two—see *JEGP*, 68 (1969), 316-20.

31. A sensible convention which has become well established is to use periods to separate the elements of these reference numbers (e.g., "240.17" or "III.ii.75"). All references in the apparatus should obviously be to the edited text (though in the textual essay a discussion of type damage or defective inking in an early edition might well involve page-line references to that edition).

necessary), followed in turn by the discussion itself. Generally a square bracket, the conventional sign to distinguish a lemma, separates the reading from the discussion but is of course not essential.[32] The note itself need not say what has been substituted or retained, because the reading of the edited text is the one fact which the reader inevitably knows at the time he consults the note, and if, in addition, it is cited at the head of the note, he has that reading before him on the same page. It is superfluous and uneconomical, therefore, to begin a note by saying, "We retain x at this point because . . ." or "This text adopts the reading y here owing to the fact that . . . ." Instead, all that is required is a direct statement, as simple as possible, of the facts which led to the decision which is already obvious. Thus a note might begin, "X, though unidiomatic, appears in a similar context at 384.27 . . ."; or, "No evidence has been discovered which would support z, the copy-text reading, as standard usage at the time, and the phraseology at 412.16 suggests that z is probably a compositorial error for y . . . ." The notes should be kept as few as possible: there is no point explaining matters easily checked in standard dictionaries or encyclopedias, nor is there any reason to refer to those general problems more cogently handled in the textual essay. Annotation which is unnecessary for either of these reasons only wastes the reader's time[33] and reveals the editor's failure to give sufficient thought to the rationale for textual discussions.

iv. List of Emendations

The purpose of the list of emendations is to provide a convenient record of all the changes of textual interest[34] — both substantive and

---

32. A space, for example, would suffice; or, as in the Howells edition, the reading itself need not be cited, since the discussion can be constructed so as to make clear what word or words in the cited line are in question.

33. It might not literally waste a particular reader's time if a given fact, though easily ascertainable in the dictionary, were not already known to him. But an editor cannot pitch his annotation at his text's least informed reader, even if he could discover who that is; some minimum level must be recognized, and it seems reasonable to say that spellings or usages readily discoverable in standard dictionaries fall below that level. (Explanatory, as opposed

to textual, annotation is of course a different matter; in an explanatory note it may well be useful to have a brief identification of a historical figure, even though he is listed in the basic biographical reference works. The essential difference is that historical allusions, however numerous, are manageable in number and affect one's understanding of the meaning of the text, whereas the kind of textual notes ruled out here might logically involve half or more of the individual words of a text and by definition would not raise such special problems as interpretation or meaning.)

34. As opposed to those which may be classed, for one reason or another, as nontextual—about which more is said below.

accidental — made in the copy-text by the editor(s) of a given edition. The essential parts of each entry are simply the page and line citation, the reading of the edited text, the symbol representing the source of that reading, and the rejected copy-text reading. The general form which these items usually take includes a square bracket to signify the lemma and a semicolon to separate the source of that reading from the copy-text reading which follows:[35]

10.31 whom] W; who

Another possibility, employed in the Melville edition, eliminates the bracket and the semicolon and places the two readings in separate columns. It could perhaps be argued that this scheme makes the list slightly easier to use for purposes of surveying the nature of the emendations as a whole or constructing various kinds of statistics about them, since the source symbols would more readily show up along the right side of the first column and the copy-text readings would have a common margin in the second column. In any case, if the list is limited strictly to those readings of the copy-text which do not appear in the edited text, no symbol is required after the second reading, since in each case it is by definition the copy-text reading. (In those unusual instances in which a deficient copy-text is rectified by intercalations from another text, so that the copy-text is in effect composite, symbols following the second reading are helpful, even though a separate list of the intercalations would presumably be available.) It is important, however, to understand the reason for setting up a list restricted in this way. So long as a historical collation is to be included in the apparatus, the readings of the copy-text could be ascertained from it and would not necessarily have to be presented in a separate list. But this arrangement would be awkward and inconvenient in two ways: first, since the historical collation is normally limited to substantive variants and since the reader may legitimately wish to know all emendations, including accidentals, the absence of a separate list of emendations would cause the historical collation to become an uneven mixture, combining a complete record of substantive variants with an incomplete record of variants in accidentals; second, discovering what emendations had been made would be somewhat less easy if notation of them were imbedded in the larger historical collation. There is no question about the necessity of having at hand a record of all editorial

---

35. Often each of these entries is placed on a separate line, but sometimes, to save space, they are run on in paragraph form (a form which makes individual entries somewhat less easy to locate).

alterations in the basic authoritative document chosen to provide copy-text; and the greater convenience of having that record as a discrete unit, along with the resulting greater consistency of the historical collation, provides compelling reason for what might otherwise seem a superfluous or repetitive list. The situation is a good illustration of the principle that some sacrifice of economy is more than justified if the result is truly greater clarity and usefulness.

In the light of this summary of the general rationale behind the idea of a separate list of emendations, two common variations in the basic form outlined above are worth examining. One is the segregation of substantives and accidentals into two different lists. This system is used in Bowers's Dekker and the Cambridge Beaumont and Fletcher (where emendations in substantives are listed at the foot of the page and emendations in accidentals at the end of the text), as well as in the Virginia edition of Crane's *Maggie* and the Wesleyan edition of Fielding's *Joseph Andrews* (where both lists come at the end of the text). Since the purpose of a list of emendations is to make the whole range of emendations easier to examine and analyze, it follows that under certain circumstances — particularly when there is an especially large number of emendations in accidentals — the separation of substantives and accidentals will make such examination easier still. In other words, if the total number of emendations is small or even moderate, little is gained by exchanging the simplicity of one list for the complication of two; but when there are a great many emendations, with the possible result that the emendations in substantives would be obscured by being included in the same list as a large number of emendations in accidentals, the data may be much easier to use if the two categories are listed separately. To do so is only to extend the principle of convenience and clarity on which the whole list is founded in the first place. And, by a further extension, certain large categories of automatic alterations within the list of accidentals itself may be separated so as not to overwhelm the other individual alterations of probably greater significance. For example, in the Northwestern-Newberry *Typee* 224 words ending in "-our" in the British copy-text are changed to the American "-or"; once the policy of making this category of changes is adopted, the changes themselves are automatic, and to list all 224 instances in a list of emendations would place an unnecessary impediment in the way of using the list to trace the more important alterations. Yet it is unwise to make any textual changes silently;[36] so these

---

36. Nontextual changes—those affecting the design of the document embodying the copy-text but not the text itself—may of course be made silently. But to make tex-

224 alterations of spelling are recorded in a footnote to the textual essay. In the Dewey edition many emendations are made in the capitalization of words standing for concepts, and these emendations are gathered into a separate list of "concept capitalization."[37] Whenever there is a large separable category of emendations, this practice is a useful way to avoid, on the one hand, overburdening the main list and, on the other, risking the dangers of silent emendation.

A second variation from the most basic form of an emendations list is the inclusion of at least some of the further history of the rejected copy-text readings. That is, instead of providing simply the copy-text reading at those points where the copy-text has been emended, the entry includes the sigla for certain other editions which agree with the copy-text and sometimes includes the full history of the reading in the collated editions. One often-used plan,[38] following Bowers's Dekker, is to trace, at each point of emendation, the readings of all collated editions (that is, all which might contain textual authority) down to the earliest which can serve as the source of the emendation. Thus in the entry

$$\text{IV.iii.19} \quad \text{we] } Q_3; \text{ me } Q_{1-2}$$

the earliest edition to contain the adopted emendation is Q_3, and the history of the reading down to that point is given (Q_1 and Q_2), rather than just the copy-text (Q_1) reading; what the history of the reading in any collated editions after Q_3 may have been is not revealed here

tual changes silently, even though the categories of such changes are announced and discussed in the textual essay, is to deny the principle that it is risky to allow the absence of a positive designation to be significant (cf. the comments on the caret above). Thus, in the Melville example, merely informing the reader that "-our" spellings are changed to "-or" does not allow him to reconstruct the copy-text with the certainty he would have if he could follow an actual list of changes; for he could not be sure that every "-or" word in the edited text was originally "-our," whereas with a list he would know explicitly just where the changes were made. Furthermore, the specific instances of any type of textual alteration, however trivial they may seem, may be of particular concern to some linguistic, literary, or historical scholar, and the burden of locating these instances should not be placed on the user of the text but is rather the editor's responsibility.

37. The same principle is followed in the Ohio State *Fanshawe* and the California *Mysterious Stranger Manuscripts*, where a number of groupings of identical changes in accidentals are made; here, however, the references are cited in paragraph form in the list of emendations at the point of first occurrence of each type. To some extent this arrangement disrupts the smooth sequential flow of the list of emendations and makes it somewhat less easy to follow; but there is no doubt that it is an advantage to the reader to have these groups of identical emendations brought together somewhere.

38. It is used, for example, in the Fielding, Hawthorne, and Crane editions.

but can be ascertained from the historical collation. In other editions (such as the Howells and the Irving), the complete history (in the collated editions) of the readings at certain points of emendation is given, either explicitly or through a specified system of implication; when this plan is followed, none of these entries reappears in the historical collation, which is then limited to rejected substantives. In both of these arrangements, the distinction between the historical collation and the list of emendations has been blurred to some extent; as a result, the functions of these lists are less clear-cut, and therefore more cumbersome for the editor to explain and less easy for the reader to comprehend. Including in the emendations list the history of the readings down to the point of emendation means that the emendations list becomes partly historical in function and repeats part of the material from the historical collation; but the presence of some historical information in the emendations list does not obviate the need for turning to the historical collation, since anyone wishing to examine the evidence available to the editor at a given point of substantive emendation must look at the historical collation in any case to see if there were variants in editions later than the one from which the emendation is drawn.[39] In the other system, the emendations list takes over even more of the function of the historical collation — indeed, it becomes the historical collation for certain emended readings.[40] And though none of this material is repeated in the other historical list (now containing only rejected substantives), there is no one place where the reader can go to survey all the evidence at the editor's disposal relating to substantive variants. So long as it is agreed in the first place that there is value in having a separate list of emendations, the simplest way of dividing the data is to make one list strictly a record of emendations and the other strictly a historical record. The functions of the two lists are then easier to understand, and the lists are correspondingly easier to refer to and work with.

The question of distinguishing between substantives and accidentals is often not an easy one, because some alterations of punctuation, for instance, do have an effect on meaning; but unless the substantives and accidentals are to be placed in separate lists, the question does not arise in constructing the record of emendations. Two other basic

39. Only if the source of the emendation were the editor himself or the last of the collated editions could the reader know that no additional information would be found in the historical collation.

40. In the Howells edition, when editions later than the one from which an emendation is taken agree with that edition, the complete history is implied in the entry. But when a later edition reverts to the reading of the copy-text, that further history is not offered in the emendations list. See footnote 66.

problems of definition always have to be faced, however: since the list aims to enumerate emendations in the copy-text, the editor must have precise definitions of what constitutes an "emendation" and what is meant by "copy-text" if he is to have a firm basis for deciding what to include in the list and what to leave out. In practice, defining the two concepts becomes a single problem, for however one is defined affects the definition of the other. Editors of critical editions[41] generally agree that there is no point listing as emendations such changes as those in the display capitals at the opening of chapters, in the typographical layout of chapter headings, in the length of lines, or in the wording of running titles. Whether an editor defines "emendation" so as to exclude changes concerned with styling or design, or whether he defines "copy-text" to exclude purely typographical features of the text, the result comes to the same thing in the end. Technically, of course, an "emendation" is simply a correction or alteration, and it is the qualifying phrase "in the copy-text" which through precise definition serves to delimit the kinds of alterations to be listed. There should be no difficulty in defining "copy-text," if the distinction between "text" and "edition" is observed: "text" is an abstract term, referring to a particular combination of words, spelled and punctuated a particular way; "edition" is a concrete term referring to all copies of a given printed form of a text. Thus a "copy-text" is that authoritative text chosen as the basic text to be followed by an editor in preparing his own text, and it does not include the formal or typographical design of the document which embodies that text.[42] The type-face, the width and height of the type-page, the arrangement of headings and ornaments, and the like, are all parts of the design of an edition but are not elements of the text which is contained in that edition; similarly, the formation of letters, the spacing between words, the color of the ink, and the like, are not parts of the text embodied in a manuscript. It does no harm for an editor to enumerate certain features of design which he regards as nontextual, but it is not actually necessary for him to do so if he has defined "copy-text" carefully, for his definition will have excluded such details as external to the text.[43] Omission of any

41. Of course, editors of facsimile or diplomatic editions are necessarily concerned with formal and typographical matters and must take them into account.

42. See G. T. Tanselle, "The Meaning of Copy-Text: A Further Note," *SB*, 23 (1970), 191-96.

43. Nontextual details often play a great role in the bibliographical analysis which leads to the establishment of the text (as when wrong-font types allow a bibliographer to learn something about the timing of the distribution of type from preceding formes or about the order of formes through the press), but they are nevertheless not a part of the text.

notice of alterations in design does not constitute a category of silent emendations in the copy-text, since the design is not a part of that text at all.

One problem in the specification of copy-text is raised by the existence of variations within an impression. Such variations may be caused by stop-press corrections or by type which slipped or shifted during the course of printing. The precise definition of copy-text in terms of particular states of the variations obviously determines which of these readings qualify for inclusion in the list of emendations: thus if uncorrected formes are taken as copy-text, the only press-variants which would turn up in the emendations would be those adopted from corrected formes; and if the correct spacings at points where letters shift around are regarded as characteristics of the copy-text, the only variants of this kind which would be reported in the emendations list would be those for which no copy with correct spacings had been found. The decision as to whether correct or incorrect states are taken as copy-text may vary in individual circumstances, but the point is that the copy-text must be defined in terms of the specific variants within the impression which embodies it; for this abstract "text" must have one and only one reading at any given point,[44] and to define a copy-text merely in terms of an impression is not sufficiently rigorous, since more than one reading may exist at many points within various copies of that impression.[45] Because sheets embodying corrected states of some formes (or correct spacings of letters) will be bound with sheets embodying uncorrected states of other formes (or incorrect spacings of other letters), it is unlikely — when more than a few press-variants occur — that any single physical copy can be found which contains the entire copy-text.[46] Emendations in the copy-text, therefore, are not simply emendations in the text of a particular copy; and the copy-text remains an authoritative documentary form of the text, even though no one existing physical entity (or even no one physical entity that ever existed)

---

44. With the exception that, when all variants are manifestly incorrect and their order is indeterminate (as in the example cited in footnote 48), designating only one of them as the copy-text reading becomes a pointless exercise. (In the case of a manuscript copy-text, of course, alternative uncanceled readings may well exist at individual points.)

45. Thus Bowers, in the general textual introduction to the Cambridge Beaumont and Fletcher, defines the copy-texts as

embodying the readings of corrected formes: "The normal assumption is that the present edited text reproduces the corrected readings when press-variation is present if no contrary record is made" (I,xix).

46. Since a photographic reproduction of a single copy is often used as printer's copy for a critical edition, it follows that not every textual alteration marked on that copy is an emendation in the copy-text, for some may bring the printer's copy into conformity with the copy-text.

happens to preserve it. The exigencies of producing a book — the fact that the forme is the unit in printing and the sheet the unit in gathering a copy of a book together for binding[47] — makes it natural that the finished product may contain a mixture of states. One may have to examine a large number of copies of a given impression to discover the press-variants in it, and one can never be sure that any copies left unexamined do not contain additional variants. In the Ohio State *Scarlet Letter*, for instance, collation of eight copies of the first impression produced five variants, all examples of loosened type which either shifted position or failed to print. At four of the points of variance, some copies carried the correct reading; but in the remaining case one copy read "t obelieve," and the others read "tobelieve." Since the correct spacing in this one instance did not occur in any of the examined copies, it had to be listed as an emendation, whereas the other four variants do not enter the emendations list at all, since the correct form of each did appear in at least one copy.[48] If, however, another copy were to be collated in which "to believe" appeared correctly, that form would no longer be an emendation and should not appear on the emendations list. As with any other research, the conclusions must be based on the evidence at hand; and that evidence, in any inductive investigation, is probably incomplete. If the number of surviving copies is small, one can examine all the available evidence and still be far from the truth; if the number is large, one may reasonably wish to set some practical limits on the extent of the investigation. But in either case the results are liable to modification by the next copy which turns up. The danger is unavoidable; but at least one can operate with precision and rigor within the limits of the located evidence. Part of what that entails is defining the copy-text in terms of press-variants (saying, for example, "the text in a copy of the 1850 impression with x at 172.15, y at 234.21, and z 278.11"), for only in this way can one know what constitutes an emendation and belongs in the list.

There are some variations among copies of a given impression which are nontextual and need not be reported, any more than differences in design between the copy-text print and the critical edition

47. Some further discussion of this point appears in G. T. Tanselle, "The Use of Type Damage as Evidence in Bibliographical Description," *Library*, 5th ser., 23 (1968), esp. 347-48.

48. When neither form is correct, as in "t obelieve"/"tobelieve," it makes little difference which is considered the copy-text form, since an emendation is required in either case; in such instances, especially when the order of the variants is not clear, there is no point in choosing among incorrect forms, and both readings might as well be listed as the rejected copy-text readings.

need be specified. Usually it is not difficult to distinguish between these nontextual press-variants and the press-variants of textual significance just discussed. They are frequently due to differences in inking or in the amount of damage which a particular piece of type (or letter in a plate) has suffered. Variations in inking need not be reported if all the letters are visible, but if the inking is so poor that some letters do not show up at all in any copy examined, the variation is in effect a textual one of the kind described above. Battered letters or marks of punctuation — whether or not the batter varies from copy to copy — can be silently corrected without involving textual emendation, so long as there is no question what letters or marks are intended. But if the damage is great enough to raise possible doubt about their identity, any attempt at correction becomes a textual emendation and must be listed. Thus if a dot appears in the middle of a sentence at a place where it could be the upper half of either a colon or a semicolon, and if no examined copy shows enough of the lower half for identification, a textual decision is required to correct the punctuation; or if a small mark appears between two words where it could perhaps be a hyphen, and if no examined copy clears up the matter, the editor's decision to consider it a hyphen rather than, say, a part of the damaged preceding letter is a textual one; or if a letter which ought to be "e" appears to be a "c" in every examined copy, the correction is a textual emendation. The importance of having access to a large number of copies for this kind of checking is obvious. Most editors rightly feel that it is unfortunate if their lists of emendations have to be overburdened with entries which are probably not really emendations at all and which might be eliminated if more copies were available for examination. But without those copies, there is no alternative to recording them as emendations, since there is no documentary proof that the copy-text contained the correct readings.

Finally, a few minor points about form should be noted. (1) First, the list will be clearer in the end if each lemma consists simply of the word or words which constitute the emendation, without any of the surrounding words.[49] Occasionally an editor will feel that it would be helpful to the reader to have an additional word or two of the context, to enable him to see more clearly the nature of the alteration involved, while he is looking at the list. It is difficult to say, however, what would be sufficient context for this purpose, but generally a few words would not be enough; and as the cited readings become longer, the actual

---

49. Similarly, punctuation following (or preceding) a word need not be cited when only the word, and not the punctuation, is at issue.

emendations become less easy to pick out, with the result that this approach makes the list more difficult to use (as well as less consistent, since there would be no way of defining objectively how much should be cited). The only times when a word in addition to the actual emendation should be reported are when the same word as the emendation appears elsewhere in the same line (so that one of the two words adjacent to the emendation is required to identify it), when a mark of punctuation is emended (so that the word preceding the punctuation—or after it, in the case of opening quotation marks — is convenient, and sometimes essential, for locating the emendation), and when something is deleted from the copy-text (so that the point of deletion can be located). (Even the first of these can be eliminated if one adopts Greg's device of using prefixed superscript numbers to indicate which of two or more identical words is at issue, but this system is perhaps somewhat less easy for the reader to follow.) (2) A second formal matter which might cause difficulty is the notation of a missing letter (or letters). When loosened type causes letters to shift, without any letters failing to print, there is of course no problem because the usual between-word spacing can be used (as in "t obelieve"); but when loosened type or a damaged plate results in the complete disappearance of letters, it is important to show that space for these letters exists. It clearly makes a difference whether a reading is reported as "race" or as "[ ]race," for the second shows that a letter has dropped out and that the original word was "brace," "grace," or "trace." These empty spaces can be noted in various ways. The Hawthorne edition simply uses a blank space, which works well enough between words but is less clear if the missing letter is at the beginning or end of a word; Kable's edition of *The Power of Sympathy*[50] employs a caret to mark the space, creating an ambiguity since the caret is also used to signify the absence of punctuation; and the Melville edition uses square brackets, which may be somewhat cumbersome but are fairly suggestive and do not conflict with another symbol. (3) Another question of notation concerns those emendations which are in fact additions to the copy-text — that is, words or passages for which there is no counterpart in the copy-text. One common editorial device is to use the abbreviation "*Om.*" or "*om.*" to signify the lack of corresponding text at a given point in the copy-text. If the abbreviation is specifically defined in this way, it is clear enough; but if it is not explicitly defined and is allowed to suggest "omitted," it can be misleading, since the omission of anything implies

50. William Hill Brown, *The Power of Sympathy*, ed. William S. Kable (Columbus: Ohio State University Press, 1969).

that something was available to be omitted, whereas the additions to a copy-text are often passages not yet written at the time the copy-text was completed. A phrase like "[*not present*]," which suggests no direction of change, would avoid the problem and would require no explanation.[51] (4) There remains the question of adjusting the symbols for editions and impressions to take variant states into account. If one of the uncorrected formes of a particular sheet is taken as copy-text but requires emendation at several points from the corresponding corrected forme, the symbol indicating the source of the emendations must note the state involved. For hand-printed books the conventional method is to attach a "u" or "c" in parentheses to the symbol for the edition — "Q1 (u)," "F2 (c)" — though of course superscript letters could also be employed. For later books, if the symbol for a given impression ends with figures, states can be represented by suffixed letters ("A55a," "A55b") or — regardless of the makeup of the symbol — by superscript letters ("A55^a"); these letters signify the sequence of presently known states of individual readings within an impression (not necessarily "uncorrected" and "corrected" states of formes).[52] Because no single copy of a book may contain all the uncorrected or corrected formes, or all the earliest or latest states of variants, these attached letters — for books of any period — must be understood to refer, not to physical "books" (that is, not to entire copies of a given impression), but to readings that may or may not be present in any individual copy of the proper impression. A copy containing one Q1 (u) reading may contain other Q1 (c) readings, or a copy containing some A55^a readings may have other A55^b readings. For this reason the superscript letter may have an advantage over the suffixed one in emphasizing the fact that it is essentially a different kind of symbol — referring to a stage of variation at a particular point within an impression, not to the whole impression (or edition), as does the basic symbol to which it is attached. Many formal matters such as these may seem of minor consequence in themselves, but, taken together, the decisions regarding them may make the diffrence between a list of emendations

51. Editorial comments of this kind should of course be enclosed in square brackets to show that they are not actual readings; italicizing them is usually not sufficient, since italic words could appear in the text.

52. In other words, the letters do not stand for general stages of revision or alter-

ation but refer only to the sequence at a given point. Thus there is no reason to suppose that one reading labeled "A55b" occurred at the same time or in the same process of revision as another with the same label; all that the symbol implies is that these are the second readings at each of these points.

which is cumbersome and perhaps misleading and one which is convenient, logical, and easily understood.

v. List of Ambiguous Line-End Hyphenation

Until Fredson Bowers called attention to the matter in 1962,[53] no consideration (to my knowledge) had been given to the editorial problems raised by possible compound words hyphenated at the ends of lines. Such hyphenation clearly presents problems in two ways: first, when a possible compound is hyphenated at the end of a line in the copy-text, the editor must decide whether to print the word in his edition as a hyphenated word or as a single unhyphenated word; second, when a possible compound is hyphenated at the end of a line in a scholarly critical edition, the editor must have some means for informing his readers whether this word should be reproduced, in any quotation from the text, as a hyphenated word or as a single unhyphenated word. As a result, the necessity of including two hyphenation lists in the apparatus of critical editions cannot be denied. The first of these lists, recording line-end hyphenation in the copy-text, is essential to complete the record of editorial decisions. The editor's decision whether or not to retain a line-end hyphen in a given word can be more difficult than some of his decisions reported in the list of emendations. Yet it does not really produce an emendation, for if he prints the hyphen he is only retaining what, after all, is already present in the copy-text; and if he eliminates the hyphen he is only treating it as the printer's convention for marking a run-over word. Obviously some line-end hyphens present no problems: those simply breaking a word which cannot possibly be a compound (as "criti-|cism"), where the hyphen is only a typographical convention, not to be retained when the word will fit within a line; and those dividing compounds in which the second element is capitalized (as "Do-|Nothing"), where the hyphen is to be retained whenever the word is printed. But in between is a large area of possible compounds where no automatic answers can be given; the treatment of these hyphens depends on various factors (the author's characteristic usage, the conventions of the time, and the like), and the editor is not providing readers with a full record of his textual decisions unless he specifies these cases. The second list, recording line-end hyphenation in the editor's own text, is necessary if the editor is to complete his task of establishing a text — for if there are places in a text where a reader does not know precisely what reading

---

53. In the Ohio State edition of *The Scarlet Letter* and in his paper before the South Atlantic Modern Language Asociation (cited in its 1964 published form in footnote 4 above).

the editor has adopted, the text cannot be considered established. An editor has failed in part of his responsibility if he produces a text in which the reader, quoting a particular passage, has to make decisions on his own about the hyphenation of certain possible compounds.[54] Both these hyphenation lists, then, are indispensable parts of an editorial apparatus. (For convenience, I shall refer to the first kind of list described here as the "copy-text list" and the second as the "critical-text list.")

Because the Center for Editions of American Authors has required editions prepared under its auspices to include the two hyphenation lists (as specified in its 1967 *Statement of Editorial Principles*), the value and importance of these lists are becoming more widely recognized. Among the CEAA editions themselves, however, there are some variations in form, arrangement, and approach; and a glance at the principal variations will suggest some of the factors which need to be considered in setting up these lists. Probably the most noticeable difference among editions is in the order of the two lists. One may feel that it makes little difference about the order, so long as the two lists are there; but if an editor is trying to follow some consistent rationale in the overall arrangement of the entire apparatus, then surely one arrangement of the hyphenation lists fits that scheme better than another. Several editions (the Crane, Fielding, Hawthorne, and Simms and *The Mark Twain Papers*) place the critical-text list before the copy-text list, while several others (the Dewey, Howells, Irving, and Melville) reverse this order. The general rationale outlined above suggests placing nearest the text those parts of the apparatus taking up decisions affecting the edited text. Following this plan, the copy-text list should precede the critical-text list, for the copy-text list does record editorial decisions and in this sense is an appendage to the list of emendations (the immediately preceding section, according to this arrangement); the critical-text list, on the other hand, does not involve editorial decisions in establishing the text[55] but only printer's decisions

---

54. And obviously, if the reader is accurately to reconstruct the copy-text from the critical text, he must have this information for interpreting the critical text.

55. If a possible compound coincidentally hyphenated at the end of a line in both the copy-text and the critical text is not recorded in a separate list, then it would appear in both these lists, and to that extent words involving editorial decisions might appear in the critical-text list. But their presence there has nothing to do with the fact that their established forms result from editorial decisions; they are there only because they are hyphenated at the ends of lines in the critical text. The fact that editorial decisions are involved can be learned only by noting the reappearance of the same words in the copy-text list.

in setting the text (decisions necessitated by the exigencies of right-margin justification).

Indeed, the functions of the two lists are so different that it is somewhat artificial to place them side by side; only the superficial fact that both deal with hyphenation has caused them to be grouped together. The copy-text list fits logically into the textual apparatus because it is historically oriented: that is, it records certain words in a historical document about which the editor of a critical text has to make decisions. But the critical-text list is merely a guide to the proper interpretation of certain fortuitous typographical features (hyphens) of a given edition of that critical text; its usefulness is not in studying textual problems but simply in *reading* the edited text. In other words, the edited text is not really complete without the critical-text list, for without it certain hyphens in that text would be ambiguous. The other parts of the apparatus are important to certain audiences, but the edited text could of course be printed without them; the critical-text list, on the other hand, is essential to all audiences, and the edited text should never be printed without it. If, for example, a publisher leases a CEAA text and reproduces it photographically, he should include the critical-text list, whether or not he is including any other apparatus; if, instead, he sets the CEAA text in type anew, he should prepare a new critical-text list which applies to his own edition. It is extremely unfortunate that the copy-editors' convention for indicating to the printer which hyphens are to be retained (one hyphen above another, resembling an equals sign) has never become a generally accepted convention for use on the printed page; if an editor could utilize such a double system of line-end hyphens, the printed form of his edited text would be self-contained, without any typographical ambiguity requiring a separate list to elucidate.[56] As matters stand, however, to do so would violate the notion of clear text, since the double hyphen would strike the reader as an unfamiliar symbol. It will not be possible, therefore, in the foreseeable future to eliminate the critical-text list, and yet it presents something of an anomaly in the textual apparatus. Logically it should be separated from the rest of the apparatus and placed as an independent entity immediately following the text. Yet it is unrealistic to think that the easy grouping together of all matters connected with hyphens will be readily superseded; and

---

56. Of course, an editor could insist that the lines of the text be reset until no hyphen which should be retained in quotation fell at the end of a line; in practice, this approach is often prohibitively expensive and, in some cases, virtually impossible of achievement.

one can only hope that this arrangement does not obscure the widely different purposes of the two lists nor cause reprint publishers to overlook the relevance of the critical-text list to their concerns.

Some editions contain more than two lists in the section on line-end hyphenation. For instance, a third list that sometimes appears (as in the Crane, Dewey, Fielding, Hawthorne, and Simms editions) is a short one recording those instances in which a line-end hyphen occurs in a possible compound in the critical text at the very point where a line-end hyphen also falls in the copy-text. The function of a separate list of these words is to show that the established forms in these cases result from editorial decisions. Nevertheless, these words do not logically constitute a third category; they merely belong to both the preceding categories. A simpler arrangement, therefore, would be to have only the two lists — the copy-text list and the critical-text list — with certain words appearing in both. The introductory note to the critical-text list could not then say — as these notes do in some editions — that the words occurred with hyphens (or without hyphens) in the middle of lines in the copy-text; it would have to say that for each word the "established copy-text form" is listed. If the reader wishes to know which forms were established through editorial decision, he can quickly check the appropriate spot in the copy-text list to see if the word also turns up there.[57] Still another hyphenation list which has been employed (as in *The House of the Seven Gables* and *The Marble Faun*) records line-end hyphens in the critical text which are true emendations (that is, hyphens at points where none are present in the copy-text). Again, such words do not form a separate category but, rather, readings that belong in two categories — in this case the critical-text hyphenation list and the list of emendations. The simplicity of an arrangement which keeps the number of word-division lists down to the basic two is not merely an advantage to the bewildered reader who may never have encountered any hyphenation lists before; it also dramatizes the logical division between the two functions which hyphenation lists serve.[58] Furthermore, it sets as few obstacles as

57. And if the editor feels that it is of some help to the reader to have such words noted, a symbol can be placed beside those words which appear in both lists. (The Melville edition uses a dagger for this purpose.)

58. And emphasizing this division helps to make clear—as removing the critical-text list to another location would make still clearer—why some words turn up in two lists: since the critical-text list has nothing to do with editorial decisions, any word in it which in fact results from an editorial decision must naturally be found also in one of the two lists which record editorial decisions—the list of emendations or the copy-text hyphenation list.

possible in the way of the quoter or reprint publisher by presenting one, and only one, consolidated list of ambiguous hyphens in the critical edition.

The matter of deciding just which line-end hyphens are to appear in these lists can be approached in two ways. One method is to list all compound words and all words which might be regarded as compound, if they are hyphenated at a line-end, recording the forms they should take when they fall within the line; such a list would contain both hyphenated and unhyphenated words. Another method is to list only those words whose line-end hyphens are to be retained when the words come within a line and to say that all other line-end hyphens can be ignored as compositorial word-division; such a list would contain only hyphenated words.[59] Each method has its advantages and disadvantages. The first system has the advantage of being explicit (listing all words about which a question might arise), whereas the second proceeds by implication (making the absence of a word assume positive significance); on the other hand, the second system has the advantage of covering in condensed fashion — through its combination of direct statement and implication — every instance of line-end hyphenation in an entire work, whereas the first may result in an extremely long list and still omit words that some readers would consider "possible compounds." Presumably one could infer, even in the first type of list, that omitted instances of line-end hyphens are not significant (that is, that those hyphens should not be retained in transcription), but the fact remains that the actual content of the list is not precisely defined, since the question of what constitutes a "possible compound" is a subjective one. It might never occur to one person to think that the line-end hyphens in "cup-|board" or "inter-|view," for example, should be retained, while another person might expect to find them in the list for explicit guidance. The first kind of list, in other words, is somewhat inefficient, because for all its length it may always fail to note words considered "possible compounds" by some people; the second type of list, in contrast, can in shorter space be positively complete, because

59. It should be clear that the opposite possibility (employed in the first volume of the Simms edition)—that is, recording only those instances of possible compounds hyphenated at line-ends in the critical text which should be transcribed as single unhyphenated words—leaves ambiguities unresolved, for the reader still has to distinguish between purely compositorial hyphens, dividing unhyphenated words at line-ends, and the hyphens which should in fact be retained. (Of course, listing *every* line-end hyphen which should be eliminated in transcription—the only way to make this approach unambiguous—would be foolishly inefficient, since the majority of line-end hyphens in any printed work normally fall into this category, and the list would be extended inordinately.)

the criterion for inclusion does not involve any attempt to define "possible compounds."

This second type of approach, then, might seem preferable for the hyphenation lists in a scholarly edition, were it not for two further considerations. In the first place, this approach, for full effectiveness, requires that one have at hand the edition referred to. That is, if an editor says that all line-end hyphens, other than those listed, are merely compositorial, the reader who wishes to look over those allegedly compositorial hyphens must consult the edition under discussion and run his eye down the right margin of the pages. Furthermore, if the policy of an apparatus is to record all the editor's textual decisions, those instances in which a line-end hyphen in a possible compound has been dropped are just as significant for inclusion as those instances in which it has been retained; to define the first category by a process of elimination (as what remains after the second category is specified)[60] is as unfair to the reader as to make silent emendations, for it requires him to search through a text himself to locate the individual instances. It becomes obvious, therefore, that one of these methods is more appropriate for one of the hyphenation lists, and the other method is more appropriate for the other list. The copy-text list should follow the method of noting all possible line-end compounds and showing the editorially established form of each, with or without hyphens — for this list refers to a document outside the volume which the reader has in his hands at the moment, and it records editorial decisions necessary for the reader to know about in evaluating the editorial process or in reconstructing the copy-text. The critical-text list, on the other hand, more appropriately follows the system which notes only those line-end hyphens to be retained in transcription — for this list refers to the printed form of the text in the volume already in the reader's hands, and it has nothing to do with editorial decisions. In other words, the more explicit system is necessary for a full recording of editorial decisions, whereas the more concise system is preferable for elucidating purely typographical ambiguities of the new edition. Once again, the differences in the purposes of the two lists are reflected in differences in method. If the hyphenation lists are set up in this way, and if their introductory comment[61] and their form[62] are kept as simple as possible,

---

60. Of course, what remains is actually made up of two categories: possible compounds which, by editorial decision, should not contain hyphens, and words which are not possible compounds and which naturally do not contain hyphens.

61. Because the functions of these lists are not always grasped at first by the general reader, it is important that the headnote to each list not make the lists sound more complicated than they are. For the copy-text list, nothing more is needed

the reader should have no difficulty following them or understanding why, in their different ways, they are important.

vi. Historical Collation

The remaining principal division of the apparatus is the one which records the variant readings that have occurred in significant editions of the text. Its emphasis is historical, as distinguished from the list of emendations, where the emphasis is on the changes made by the present editor in the basic text he is following. Some of those changes were probably adopted from (or noted in) other editions, but the primary function of the entries in the list of emendations is not to provide the history of the variant readings at those points;[63] such history, as well as the history of other variants (where no emendation of the copy-text occurred), is reserved for this "historical collation," as it is often called. Two limitations are normally imposed on the historical collation. In the first place, it does not usually survey (at least in the case of nineteenth- and twentieth-century works) every edition of the text which has ever appeared, but only those of possible textual significance; thus all authorized editions which were published during the author's lifetime are included (since any changes present in them could have resulted from his revision), as well as any posthumous editions which purport to utilize newly available authoritative documents or which could conceivably have utilized such evidence.[64]

---

than a statement of this kind: "The following are the editorially established forms of possible compounds which were hyphenated at the ends of lines in the copy-text." And for the critical-text list: "In quotations from the present edition, no line-end hyphens are to be retained except the following."

62. The simplest form is merely to list, following the appropriate page-line number, the word in its established form. Since the place where line-end division occurred is obvious in most cases, there is usually no need to mark it with a vertical line. Of course, when the point of division is not obvious—as in a compound with three elements and two hyphens—a vertical line can be used; but even then the vertical line is useful only in the copy-text list, not in the critical-text list. (The Dewey edition, in the critical-text list, gives the word first as a lemma, showing the line-ending with a vertical stroke, and then the established hyphenated form; such repetition does not make the function of the list clearer and indeed would seem to add a needless complication.) Furthermore, in the critical-text list, where every page-line citation would technically contain two line numbers (since each cited word runs over a line-end in the critical text, to which all citations are keyed), the awkwardness of the double-line reference serves no real purpose, and each page-line citation might as well refer simply to the line on which the word begins.

63. Sometimes certain of these entries do in fact provide histories of the readings involved, but that is not their primary function.

64. Certain other editions which, because of their wide popularity or impressive

Second, the historical collation is generally limited to substantive variants, on the grounds that variants in accidentals from edition to edition are of so little significance (particularly in light of Greg's rationale for selecting a copy-text) as not to justify the great amount of space and labor which a record of them would entail.[65] This limitation obviously necessitates distinguishing substantives from accidentals, not always an easy task; but if the distinction is to be meaningful, one should guard against admitting variants in punctuation into the historical collation as "semisubstantives" unless they clearly involve substantial alterations of meaning.

Some editions (such as the Howells and the Irving) limit the historical collation in one further way: by entitling it "Rejected Substantives" and listing in it only those substantive variants which are not adopted as emendations in the copy-text. Under the basic form of this system, each entry in the list of emendations must provide the full history of the readings at that spot, because none of these entries will reappear later in the historical collation. In effect, the historical collation is split into two lists, one containing entries involving emendation of the copy-text and another covering the remaining substantive variants, where no emendation is involved. (In another version of this system, any agreements with the rejected copy-text reading in editions later than the one from which the emendation is drawn — or any additional post-copy-text readings — would appear in the list of rejected substantives, and thus in these cases the list of emendations would not provide the entire history of the variants.) [66] The obvious motive for this arrangement is economy, and there is no doubt that in many cases the apparatus can be considerably shortened by the procedure; how much it is shortened depends on the number of substantive emendations (exclusive of those initiated by the editor at points where no

---

scholarship, have been influential in the history and study of the text may also be included in the historical collation, even though the variant readings present in them can carry no authorial sanction; indeed, editions of Elizabethan works often include practically every previous edition in their historical collations and thus provide the complete history of the treatment of the text with regard to substantives.

65. In the Melville edition the historical collation is entitled "List of Substantive Variants."

66. This plan is followed in the Howells edition (note the entries in *Their Wedding Journey* for 102.28 or in *Literary Friends and Acquaintance* for 223.23). As a result of the overlapping function of the two lists under this plan, the reader cannot know, when looking at the list of emendations, whether or not any given substantive entry contains the complete history of the variants at that point and must turn to the list of rejected substantives to see if any additional history is recorded there.

other variants exist), since under this system none of them would have to be repeated in the historical collation. If a particular text requires an extremely large number of substantive emendations, it is possible that so much space might be saved as to justify this method on grounds of economy alone; but in most situations it is perhaps questionable whether the saving of a few pages is the most important consideration. The price paid for the economy, after all, is some loss of clarity and convenience. For one thing, the functions of the two lists become less clear-cut and distinct and therefore less easy to explain to the reader and less easy for him to comprehend: one list serves both as a record of editorial emendations (substantives and accidentals) in the copy-text and as a partial historical collation, and the other completes the historical collation (for substantive variants only). In addition, the reader making a serious study of the variants may be somewhat inconvenienced by not having the full range of historical evidence regarding substantive variants brought together in a single list or at a single place,[67] necessitating a search through the emendations list. Of course, if the emendations are divided into two lists, one for substantives and one for accidentals (as they probably should be whenever a list of "rejected substantives" replaces a full historical collation), this objection carries less force. But the fact remains that an emendations list is predicated on the idea that it is important to have a concise and readily accessible record of all textual changes made in the copy-text; if that list is made to carry part of the burden of the historical collation as well, then it becomes in effect a segment of the historical collation, and the logic of having two lists becomes less clear. In most cases, it would seem that the slightly greater space required for a full historical collation (that is, one which includes adopted as well as rejected substantive variants) is offset by the advantages of keeping the historical evidence intact — and separate from the record of the editor's conclusions based on that evidence.

The form of the entry in a historical collation is essentially the same as in a list of emendations, except that the sources of the rejected readings must be specified (whereas in a list of emendations the rejected readings are by definition from the copy-text and thus do not have to be individually identified as such). In addition, since the reading from the edited text provides the lemma in each case, there is strictly speaking no necessity to identify its source, since if it is not from the copy-text its source is recorded in the list of emendations.

---

67. There might be more than one list with historical emphasis, as discussed below.

Even in a simple entry, therefore, these differences reflect the differing functions of the two lists:

> 10.31   whom] W; who   [*list of emendations*]
> 10.31   whom] who 50-60,E   [*historical collation*]

Although it is not necessary in the historical collation to specify the source(s) of the lemmata, it does no harm, particularly in the cases of those which are emendations. Furthermore, the list of emendations names only the immediate source of an emendation, and if the historical collation does not specify later editions in which this reading occurs, the history of the variant is provided only by implication:

> 127.4   moan] moon 37-42; mean 60-70
> 127.4   moan] 45-57; moon 37-42; mean 60-70

Both these entries convey the same information, but in the first the reader has to be told that any of the collated editions not specified agree with the lemma, while in the second the history of the lemma is provided explicitly. It is a common practice to say that editions not listed agree with the reading to the left of the bracket; when a great many editions and variants are involved, the economy of this system no doubt makes it a sensible one, but it does require that the reader be familiar enough with the editions collated to remember which ones are not specified (or else he has to turn to the list of collated editions to see which ones they are). Although the entries can be run on in paragraph form, they are generally presented on separate lines, and specifying the history of the lemma does not usually cause an entry to spill over into a second line; under these circumstances, there seems little reason not to aid the reader by naming explicitly (or in inclusive form, as "45-57") all the editions covered.[68] One of McKerrow's symbols, the plus sign, has frequently been used to signify all collated editions later than the one indicated; using the plus sign is preferable to allowing this information to be implied by the absence of certain

---

68. However, impressions of an edition need not be specified when there are no variants in them. Thus if "A" stands for the only American edition, that symbol alone could signify all the collated impressions of the American edition. But if a variant first shows up in, say, "A1847" (or "A47"), its history will be represented more clearly by "A47-76" than by defining "A47" to include all subsequent collated impressions. The use of inclusive notation, of course, does not result in the appearance of every siglum in each entry, but, when the symbols include mnemonic allusions to years or sequences, the grouping which would include any given siglum is obvious. For convenient reference, a list of all collated editions (or impressions) with their sigla should be included in the headnote to the historical collation (as well as in the headnote to any other sections in which the sigla are used).

sigla, but unless the number of editions is very large it would be still better to specify them individually.[69] When they are so specified, the reader can study the variants of any given edition by running his eye down the page and noting the appearances of the proper siglum (or the groupings which include it), without having to remember or figure out where that siglum would fall in entries which do not list it (or clearly refer to it). Finally, the form of the entire list may be further modified by leaving out the brackets and semicolons and arranging the readings in columns. The advantages are the same as when the column form is used in the emendations list, but the limitation of this arrangement is that it is awkward if more than two or three variants are involved in individual entries. When, for example, there is only one American and one English edition — as in the case of Melville — a two-column historical collation is feasible;[70] but when a work went through more than two editions, with the resulting possibility of more variant readings (but not the same number in each instance), the conventional form, with brackets following lemmata and semicolons following sigla, is to be preferred.[71]

69. A related symbol of McKerrow's, the plus-and-minus sign ($\pm$), is put to good use in Bowers's Dekker to stand for a general but not exact agreement among several editions, where the minor variations are irrelevant to the main fact which the entry is recording The same method could be applied to the specification of individual editions by enclosing in parentheses those sigla which refer to editions containing the slightly variant readings. (Such a practice would conform to McKerrow's use of parentheses, referred to above, to indicate "a reading which is not *identical* with one which is given but which is *substantially* the same in meaning or intention so far as the purpose of the note is concerned" [p. 82].) Sometimes earlier editions went too far in multiplying symbols of this sort: in the opening volume of the Variorum Shakespeare (1874), for example, Furness employs "&c," "*et cet.*," and "*the rest*" to stand for different groups of editions.

Another symbol relevant to the matter of inclusive notation is the dollar sign, which has been borrowed from descriptive bibliography and introduced into textual apparatus by Bowers in the fifth volume of the Crane edition; it is used there to mean "all" or "every" when attached to symbols which subsume a number of documents (such as "N," the syndicated newspaper texts of a given work). The symbol is useful in "$N" to emphasize the fact that all the examined N texts agree and "$N (—N4)" to reinforce the statement that all but one agree; but since "N" is already a generic symbol, defined as all the examined newspaper texts, the dollar sign is essentially a device for adding emphasis rather than for condensing the statement.

70. Even in such a case, a variant at a point of emendation is somewhat awkward, since the reading in the edited text must be cited as the key for the entry, and it is different in these instances from the first-column (copy-text) reading.

71. It would be highly undesirable to have a situation in which a reading from a third edition had to be placed in a third column, even though it agreed with the reading in one of the other two editions; such an arrangement would make it more difficult for the reader to note agreements among editions and would open up more possibilities for typographical errors in the list.

Variants within impressions raise special problems for the historical collation, just as they do for the list of emendations. Since a knowledge of such variants in the copy-text edition is necessary for the precise specification of copy-text, they should certainly be recorded (at least those which involve more than variations in inking or slight type damage) ; but since these variations are likely to be in accidentals as well as substantives, not all of them would be appropriate for recording in the historical collation (if, as usual, that collation is limited to substantives). It seems sensible, therefore, to set up a special list to record such variants[72] (examples are the lists of press-variants in the Dekker and Beaumont-Fletcher editions and the lists of variants within the first and within the second editions in the Ohio State *Scarlet Letter*); alternatively — or additionally — these variants can be discussed in the textual essay as part of the definition of copy-text or of the bibliographical comment on other editions (as in the Melville edition). If any of the variants do turn out to be substantives, they should also be reported in the regular historical collation, since they form a part of the full history of the readings at these points. But determining which ones are substantives sometimes turns — as information about variants within impressions necessarily turns — on the particular group of copies collated or examined. In Chapter 70 of Melville's *White-Jacket*, for instance, the American edition (copy-text) reads "President" at a point where many copies of the English edition read "[ ]resident"; the space suggests that a "P" failed to print, but what did print — "resident" — is a different word, and, if no copies of the English edition could be found with the "P," the word would technically be a substantive variant. Copies reading "President" were eventually located, however, and this variant — though it deserves mention in the textual essay (or in a special list) — need not be entered in the historical collation. Once again, the intimate connection between descriptive bibliography and editing is evident: the greater the number of copies which are examined, the more reliable the evidence on which the edition is based.

The idea of separating certain categories of historical information for presentation in special lists can be applied to other situations as well. Two kinds of special lists may result. One kind merely repeats data present in the full historical collation — data which the reader may find useful to have brought together in one spot. In the Hawthorne edition, for example, there are sometimes (as in *The*

---

72. Sigla in these lists would refer to particular copies of books, not just to particular impressions.

Blithedale Romance and *The Marble Faun*) lists of rejected first-edition substantive variants (rejected in favor of manuscript readings). The entries in these lists are included in the full historical collation, but because of their importance for critical study they are made more easily accessible by this additional listing as a separate group.[73] This type of list is purely for the reader's convenience and can be a great help when there is an important category of variants difficult to survey as a whole in the regular historical collation. The other kind of special list (like the list of variants within an impression) records information which should be made available to the reader but which, though historical in nature, does not readily fit into the historical collation. This situation often arises in treating pre-copy-text variants (such as alterations in a manuscript), especially if variants in accidentals as well as substantives are to be reported. Of course, if only substantive pre-copy-text variants are recorded, and if they are not of such quantity as to overwhelm all the later substantive variants, they can simply be included in the regular historical collation (as in the Wisconsin *Mahomet*), and no separate list is required. But when either of these conditions does not apply, a special list is advisable. In the Hawthorne edition, both accidental and substantive alterations in the manuscripts of *The Blithedale Romance* and *The Marble Faun* are listed, and the number of substantive alterations alone is far greater than the total number of substantive variants in the later editions; under these circumstances, the wisest course, adopted by the Ohio State edition, is to provide separate lists entitled "Alterations in the Manuscript."[74] These special historical lists including both substantives and accidentals are also appropriate on occasion for post-copy-text variants, as when a particular later edition is of enough importance in the history of the text to warrant recording all its textual variants. An example, in the Ohio State *Scarlet Letter*, is the list of variants between the first and second editions; any substantive variants in this list naturally occur in the regular historical collation as well, but they are repeated here along with the variants in accidentals to facilitate study of the precise relationship between the two texts. The basic historical collation, there-

---

73. These lists do not record the complete history of the variants listed, for their function is only to note that the variants were present in a particular edition and are not adopted in the critical text. (Strictly speaking, therefore, no sigla at all would be required in such lists.)

74. When only a brief manuscript fragment survives, it can be treated either in a separate list (as "The Ohio State University Leaf" in *The Blithedale Romance*) or in a complete transcription with accompanying apparatus (as in the Northwestern-Newberry *Typee*, *Mardi*, and *White-Jacket*).

fore, will often be buttressed by additional lists, sometimes regrouping information for the reader's convenience and sometimes reporting supplementary information.[75]

Any consideration of editorial apparatus is misguided if it loses sight of the convenience of the reader. For some audiences, the apparatus may be irrelevant and need not accompany the edited text; but for most scholarly audiences an edition without apparatus resembles any other work that lacks documentation — it may be brilliantly done, but it provides no aids for facilitating the scholar's independent investigation of the evidence. The apparatus (as the word itself suggests) is a tool for expediting further study, and a tool, to be effective, must be as simple and as easy to use as the circumstances allow. Fredson Bowers — through his connections with editions of Dekker, Beaumont and Fletcher, Fielding, Hawthorne, Crane, and Dewey — has done more than anyone else to set the course of modern apparatus along these lines. As a result of his efforts, there is now not only a widespread acceptance of an efficient basic approach to apparatus but also an increased awareness of the significance of apparatus. Though just a tool appended to a text, the apparatus may well be the only part of an edition that can meaningfully be called "definitive": there may legitimately be differences of opinion about certain emendations which an editor makes, but a responsible apparatus is a definitive statement of the textual situation (within the limits of the copies examined). What constitutes an apparatus responsible in both form and content is therefore a matter worth serious consideration. Only by being fully cognizant of the issues and problems involved in setting up an apparatus can an editor make those decisions which will establish his apparatus as a lasting contribution to literary study.

---

75. Placing all such lists immediately after the basic historical collation helps to make clear that they are parts of the historical record, appendixes in a sense to the historical collation. (The attempt to make the list of emendations serve as a partial historical collation is not an extension of the principle that certain categories within the historical collation can be conveniently separated, for it mixes the functions of the lists; all these special supplementary lists are purely historical in function.) Some-times certain of these lists—especially those dealing with variants within an impression—are placed first in the apparatus, since they often deal with material which chronologically precedes that taken up in other lists; but chronology is not the general basis for the organization of the apparatus as a whole, and readers can probably find their way around in an extensive apparatus more easily if the arrangement is based on the distinct functions of the several lists.

The Editing of Historical Documents

I F THE THIRD QUARTER OF THE TWENTIETH CENTURY CAN BE CON-
sidered—as it often is—an age of editing, one of the principal reasons is the existence and influence of two American organizations:
the National Historical Publications Commission (NHPC), re-
named in late 1974 the National Historical Publications and Records
Commission (NHPRC); and the Center for Editions of American Authors (CEAA), succeeded in 1976 by the Center for Scholarly Editions
(CSE). The NHPC (NHPRC)[1] has since 1950 given encouragement and
assistance to a large number of multi-volume editions (more than four
dozen) of the papers of American statesmen, especially those of the late
eighteenth and nineteenth centuries; the CEAA, from 1963 through
1976, gave its official approval to volumes in fourteen editions, pre-
dominantly of the works of nineteenth-century American literary figures.[2] As a result, massive scholarly editions have been produced in an
unprecedented quantity during these years; hundreds of scholars have
been connected with these projects, and widespread discussion and
awareness of the problems and aims of editing have been engendered.
The presence of these editions has dramatically altered the scholarly
landscape in American history and literature within a generation.[3]

1. In what follows I shall use "NHPRC" when referring in general to the editions
produced with the assistance of the Commission from 1950 on; but for historical accuracy
"NHPC" will be used in those instances where the reference is clearly to events preceding
late 1974.

2. A comprehensive list of "Documentary Works Planned, in Progress, and Completed
in Association with the National Historical Publications Commission" appears in Oliver W.
Holmes, *Shall Stagecoaches Carry the Mail?* (1972), pp. 93–105; many of the editions are
also listed in the Brubaker and Monroe articles mentioned in note 10 below. Earlier lists
form the appendix to *"Let every sluice of knowledge be open'd and set a flowing": A Tribute to Philip May Hamer . . .* (1960) and Appendix B to the NHPC's 1963 *Report* (see note
8 below). Most of the CEAA editions are mentioned in the CEAA's *Statement of Editorial
Principles and Procedures* (rev. ed., 1972), pp. 22–23, and in *Studies in Bibliography*, 25
(1972), 43–44; all of them are listed in *The Center for Scholarly Editions: An Introductory
Statement* (1977), pp. 7–8.

3. Bernard Bailyn, for instance, states that the Jefferson edition "introduces a new
era in the history of American documentary publications" ("Boyd's Jefferson: Notes for a

When there is so much editorial activity directed toward material from a single country and, for the most part, a single century, one would expect a great deal of communication among the editors involved; indeed, the creation of coordinating organizations like the NHPC and the CEAA suggests a recognition of the need for such communication. However, the fact that two organizations have seemed necessary indicates that the communication has not very readily crossed the boundary lines between academic disciplines. Regrettably, but undeniably, editors of "literary" material and editors of "historical" material[4] have gone their separate ways; members of each group have discussed common problems among themselves but have remained remarkably uninformed about what was taking place in the other group. One does not have to examine many volumes to recognize a central difference between the historical and the literary editions: the historical editions in general give more attention to explanatory annotation than to the detailed recording of textual data, whereas the literary editions reverse this emphasis. It is a fact that most of the historical editions do not meet the standards for reporting textual information established by the CEAA and would therefore not qualify for the award of the CEAA emblem. Whether those particular standards are justifiable is a separate question; what is disturbing is that such different standards should prevail in the two fields. If one could argue that the material edited by historians is different in kind from that edited by literary scholars, there might be some reason to expect different approaches. Indeed, the NHPRC editors do have more occasion to deal with manuscript letters and journals than with texts which were published by their authors, and for CEAA editors the opposite situation prevails. No doubt these relationships are largely responsible for the lesser concern of historians with questions of copy-

Sketch," *New England Quarterly*, 33 [1960], 380–400 [p. 380]). He also refers to the "series of massive documentary publications launched since World War II" and calls it "a remarkable movement in modern American letters" ("Butterfield's Adams: Notes for a Sketch," *William and Mary Quarterly*, 3rd ser., 19 [1962], 238–256 [pp. 239–240]). Edmund S. Morgan proclaimed in a 1961 review of the Adams edition that "a new kind of scholarship has begun in the United States" ("John Adams and the Puritan Tradition," *New England Quarterly*, 34 [1961], 518–529 [p. 518]); and Esmond Wright, in another review of the Adams project, declared that this "age of the editor" is "transforming the methodology and character of American history" ("The Papers of Great Men," *History Today*, 12 [1962], 197, 213).

4. I shall not continue to place "literary" and "historical" in quotation marks but wish to make clear that these adjectives are used here only to refer to the fact that some persons are generally thought of as literary figures and some as historical figures; the adjectives are not meant to imply that there is any firm dividing line between material of literary interest and material of historical interest or that material cannot be of interest in both ways simultaneously. (In fact, all documents are of historical interest; and I trust that it will be clear when—as in the title—I use "historical" in this more basic sense. See also note 18 below.)

text and textual variants and for the greater concern of literary scholars with these matters. Nevertheless, literary editors frequently must edit letters and journals, and historical editors must handle statesmen's published, as well as unpublished, works. The editing of literary and of historical material should have many more points of similarity than of difference; and a greater understanding of mutual problems, between the two groups of editors, is bound to have a salutary effect on the editing produced by both groups.

There have recently been some encouraging signs to suggest that the dangers of editorial parochialism are perhaps becoming more widely recognized. Most notable is the broadening of the scope of the Modern Language Association's committee on editions: no longer limited to editions of American authors, it now provides simply a "Center for Scholarly Editions"—editions of any kind of material from any time and place—and it has shown itself to be concerned with promoting greater contact between editors in different fields. A similar development is the careful editorial attention which has lately been given to certain philosophers: Jo Ann Boydston's edition of John Dewey (1967–   ), Fredson Bowers's of William James (1975–   ), and Peter H. Nidditch's of John Locke (1975–   )—the first two are CEAA editions—manifest an approach to textual matters which had previously been limited almost exclusively to more clearly bellettristic or "literary" writing.[5] In 1972 Edwin Wolf, 2nd, published a timely and well-considered appeal for historians to begin applying to historical works the techniques of analytical bibliography which have long been associated with literary studies, particularly with the editing of English Renaissance drama.[6] He calls attention to the historian's lack of sophistication in dealing with printed texts by pointing out that two of the most respected editors of historical manuscripts, Julian P. Boyd and Leonard W. Labaree, "never questioned the validity of the text of only a single copy of any printed work" (p. 29). After citing some examples of variants in American printed works of the eighteenth century, he again laments the "tradition of a wall separating bibliography as applied to literary works from bibliography as

---

5. Interest in editing scientific manuscripts is increasing also, as evidenced by a Conference on Science Manuscripts in Washington on 5–6 May 1960; one of the papers presented was Whitfield J. Bell, Jr., "Editing a Scientist's Papers," *Isis*, 53 (1962), 14–19, which takes Benjamin Franklin as its principal example.

6. "Historical Grist for the Bibliographical Mill," *Studies in Bibliography*, 25 (1972), 29–40. Cf. the way P. M. Zall begins his article on "The Manuscript and Early Texts of Franklin's *Autobiography*," *Huntington Library Quarterly*, 39 (1976), 375–384: "How odd it is that even in this bicentennial year we should know more about the texts of Shakespeare's plays than we do about the text of Franklin's *Autobiography*—especially since Shakespeare's manuscripts are nowhere to be found, while the original manuscript of the *Autobiography* lies open to the public in the gallery of the Huntington Library."

applied to historical or political works" (p. 37). Nicolas Barker has also found occasion recently to comment on this point: in one of his editorials for the *Book Collector* he rightly says, "Historians, even more than literary scholars, have been apt to neglect the physical form in which the evidence on which they subsist has been preserved."[7]

In many other respects, the situation in which historical editors find themselves is similar to that of literary editors. In each field there was increased recognition, in the years following World War II, of the need for new editions of basic writings. In each field there was one man whose work provided the impetus and model for further work: the first volume of Julian P. Boyd's edition of Jefferson in 1950 set the pattern for many later historical editions, and the publication of that volume was the occasion for President Truman's reactivating the NHPC (which had originally been established in 1934);[8] the first volume of Fredson Bowers's edition of Hawthorne in 1962 was influential among literary editors in showing how the editorial techniques developed for Renaissance plays were applicable to nineteenth-century literature, and soon after its publication the CEAA was formally constituted (1963).[9] In each field there is thus an agency which serves as coordinator and clearinghouse, though with some differences: the NHPRC[10] is a government

7. "Morgan & Brown," *Book Collector*, 25 (1976), 168.

8. The principal official statements of the position of the new NHPC are *A National Program for the Publication of the Papers of American Leaders: A Preliminary Report* ... (1951); *A National Program ... A Report* ... (1954); and *A Report to the President* ... (1963). See also Philip M. Hamer, *The Program of the National Historical Publications Commission* (1952). The 1954 report states that the NHPC's "primary responsibility, in addition to that of planning, is to cooperate with and assist other organizations or individuals in their work on parts of the national program" (p. 30); the brief section on "Editorial Policies" (pp. 32–33) stresses the importance of presenting uncensored texts of both sides of a correspondence.

9. The CEAA's position was officially set forth in 1967 in a *Statement of Editorial Principles*; this booklet was revised in 1972 as *Statement of Editorial Principles and Procedures*.

10. The history of the NHPRC—and of previous historical editing in America as background to it—has been expertly recounted in a number of essays (which also inevitably express opinions on what standards are desirable in editing). See, for example, Clarence E. Carter, "The United States and Documentary Historical Publication," *Mississippi Valley Historical Review*, 25 (1938–39), 3–24; L. H. Butterfield, "Archival and Editorial Enterprise in 1850 and in 1950: Some Comparisons and Contrasts," *Proceedings of the American Philosophical Society*, 98 (1954), 159–170; Waldo G. Leland, "Remarks," *Daedalus*, 86 (1955–57), 77–79; Julian P. Boyd, " 'God's Altar Needs Not Our Pollishings,' " *New York History*, 39 (1958), 3–21; Butterfield, "Historical Editing in the United States: The Recent Past," *Proceedings of the American Antiquarian Society*, 72 (1962), 283–308; Philip M. Hamer, " '... authentic Documents tending to elucidate our History,' " *American Archivist*, 25 (1962), 3–13; Leland, "The Prehistory and Origins of the National Historical Publications Commission," *American Archivist*, 27 (1964), 187–194 (reprinted, revised, as "J. Franklin Jameson and the Origin of the National Historical Publications Commission," in *J. Franklin Jameson: A Tribute*, ed. Ruth Anna Fisher and William Lloyd Fox [1965],

agency (part of the General Services Administration and housed in the National Archives building), which undertakes to do some research (such as locating relevant manuscripts in archives) for editors; the CEAA[11] was, and the CSE is, a committee of the Modern Language As-

---

pp. 27–36); Lester J. Cappon, "A Rationale for Historical Editing Past and Present," *William and Mary Quarterly*, 3rd ser., 23 (1966), 56–75; Butterfield, "Editing American Historical Documents," *Proceedings of the Massachusetts Historical Society*, 78 (1966), 81–104; Robert L. Brubaker, "The Publication of Historical Sources: Recent Projects in the United States," *Library Quarterly*, 37 (1967), 193–225; H. G. Jones, "The Publication of Documentary Sources, 1934–1968," in *The Records of a Nation: Their Management, Preservation, and Use* (1969), pp. 117–133; Haskell Monroe, "Some Thoughts for an Aspiring Historical Editor," *American Archivist*, 32 (1969), 147–159; Walter Rundell, Jr., "Documentary Editing," in *In Pursuit of American History: Research and Training in the United States* (1970), pp. 260–283; E. Berkeley Tompkins, "The NHPRC in Perspective," in the proceedings of the Iowa conference on *The Publication of American Historical Manuscripts*, ed. Leslie W. Dunlap and Fred Shelley (1976), pp. 89–96. The Brubaker and Monroe essays include detailed surveys of the critical reception of NHPRC editions. Historical accounts also appear in the NHPC's 1951, 1954, and 1963 reports (see note 8 above); more recent developments can be followed in the NHPRC's newsletter, *Annotation* (1973–).

Earlier discussions are J. Franklin Jameson, "Gaps in the Published Records of United States History," *American Historical Review*, 11 (1905–6), 817–831; and Worthington Chauncey Ford, "The Editorial Function in United States History," *ibid.*, 23 (1917–18), 273–286. Some analyses of earlier American editing are Fred Shelley, "Ebenezer Hazard: America's First Historical Editor," *William and Mary Quarterly*, 3rd ser., 12 (1955), 44–73; Lee Nathaniel Newcomer, "Manasseh Cutler's Writings: A Note on Editorial Practice," *Mississippi Valley Historical Review*, 47 (1960–61), 88–101; L. H. Butterfield, "Worthington Chauncey Ford, Editor," *Proceedings of the Massachusetts Historical Society*, 83 (1971), 46–82; and Lester J. Cappon, "American Historical Editors before Jared Sparks: 'they will plant a forest . . .,'" *William and Mary Quarterly*, 3rd ser., 30 (1973), 375–400.

A few other general comments on the NHPRC or recent documentary editing are worth mentioning: Dumas Malone, "Tapping the Wisdom of the Founding Fathers," *New York Times Magazine*, 27 May 1956, pp. 25, 32, 34, 37, 39; Whitfield J. Bell, Jr., "Editors and Great Men," *Aspects of Librarianship*, No. 23 (Winter 1960), pp. 1–8; Adrienne Koch, "Men Who Made Our Nation What It Is," *New York Times Book Review*, 21 February 1960, pp. 1, 22; David L. Norton, "The Elders of Our Tribe," *Nation*, 192 (1961), 148–150; Koch, "The Historian as Scholar," *Nation*, 195 (1962), 357–361; John Tebbel, "Safeguarding U.S. History," *Saturday Review*, 45, no. 25 (23 June 1962), 24–25, 52; Leslie H. Fishel, Jr., "The Federal Government and History," *Wisconsin Magazine of History*, 47 (1963–64), 47–49; [John F. Kennedy and Julian P. Boyd], "A White House Luncheon, June 17, 1963," *New York History*, 45 (1964), 151–160; James C. Olson, "The Scholar and Documentary Publication," *American Archivist*, 28 (1965), 187–193; Richard B. Morris, "The Current Statesmen's Papers Publication Program: An Appraisal from the Point of View of the Legal Historian," *American Journal of Legal History*, 11 (1967), 95–106.

11. For the history and background of the CEAA, see William M. Gibson and Edwin H. Cady, "Editions of American Writers, 1963: A Preliminary Survey," *PMLA*, 78 (1963), 1–8 (September supp.); Willard Thorp, "Exodus: Four Decades of American Literary Scholarship," *Modern Language Quarterly*, 26 (1965), 40–61; Gibson, "The Center for Editions of American Authors," *Scholarly Books in America*, 10 (January 1969), 7–11; John H. Fisher, "The MLA Editions of Major American Authors," in the MLA's *Professional Standards and American Editions: A Response to Edmund Wilson* (1969), pp. 20–26 (cf. "A Calendar," pp. 27–28, and a reprinting of Gibson's 1969 article, pp. 1–6); and Don L. Cook, "Afterword: The CEAA Program," in *American Literary Scholarship: An Annual*, 1972, pp. 415–417.

sociation of America, which draws some funds from the National Endowment for the Humanities[12] and which calls attention to excellence in editing by awarding an emblem to volumes that qualify (after being requested to inspect printer's copy for those volumes by their editors). In each field there has been some controversy surrounding the new editions, though for characteristically different reasons: criticism of the literary editions has been concerned principally with textual matters, whereas the main questions raised about the historical editions have had to do with the quantity of annotation, the justification for letterpress rather than microform publication, and the choice of material to be edited in the first place.[13] And in each field the editors have found that a great many of their colleagues neither understand nor respect editorial work;[14] in both fields an attempt has been made to improve graduate training in editing and to bring about a greater interest in and

12. The CEAA allocated NEH funds to the individual associated editions; the CSE draws NEH funds only for its own operation, and the award of NEH grants to particular editions is made directly by the NEH.

13. A history and analysis of the controversy over the CEAA editions is provided by G. T. Tanselle in "Greg's Theory of Copy-Text and the Editing of American Literature," *SB*, 28 (1975), 167–229; some of the criticism of the NHPRC editions is found in the articles cited in notes 81, 82, 83, and 84 below, and some commentary on that criticism in the paragraph to which those notes are attached.

14. For example, Julian P. Boyd has said, "I deplore the fact that these [editorial] enterprises, despite the labors of J. Franklin Jameson and others, arose on the edge of the profession, beyond it, or even on occasion, in spite of some obstacles thrown up from within it"; see "Some Animadversions on Being Struck by Lightning," *Daedalus*, 86 (1955–57), 49–56 (p. 50). He also has stated, "That a mastery of the techniques and uses of scholarly editing is not now regarded as part of the indispensable equipment of the academic historian and as being a recognizable aspect of his duty is beyond question," and he points out that many people regard "the editorial presentation of documents as being almost mechanical in nature"; see "Historical Editing in the United States: The Next Stage?", *Proceedings of the American Antiquarian Society*, 72 (1962), 309–328 (pp. 314–315). Lester Cappon, in "A Rationale" (see note 10 above), also speaks of "the academic historian's prejudice against editing as a second-class pursuit"—a view in which the editor "appears to be a lone wolf, a kind of 'sport' detached from the mainstream of teaching, engaged in a task that is useful but nevertheless expendable" (pp. 58–59). Walter Rundell, in *In Pursuit of American History* (see note 10 above), summarizes, "Traditionally, academic historians have not held the function of documentary editing in especially high regard" (pp. 262–263). And Paul H. Bergeron—in "True Valor Seen: Historical Editing," *American Archivist*, 34 (1971), 259–264—says, "Only occasional efforts are made to breach the wall of prejudice that separates historians and editors" (p. 259). Cf. Stanley Idzerda, "The Editor's Training and Status in the Historical Profession," in the Dunlap and Shelley volume (see note 10 above), pp. 11–29. Such comments as these could be applied to the literary field as well; on the general lack of understanding of editing, see also note 80 below. Occasionally one hears the opposite point of view: Leo Marx, in "The American Scholar Today," *Commentary*, 32 (1961), 48–53, is bothered by "a suspicion that the scholar-editor is in fact the type we encourage and reward beyond all others" (p. 49); but his misunderstanding of editing is revealed by his labeling the editor a "humanist-as-technician" (p. 50). In the historical field, it may be noted, there has been a greater tradition of the full-time editor, independent of academic responsibilities, than in the literary field.

acceptance of editorial projects for dissertations—though the historical field, with the various NHPRC conferences, institutes, and fellowships in editing, has been more active in this regard that the literary.[15]

Despite some differences, editors in the two fields are in similar enough positions and face similar enough problems that one would expect them not only to be conversant with each other's work but to approach each other's concerns in an understanding and constructive spirit. In fact, however, there is, in the extensive editorial literature in the two fields,[16] practically no discussion which takes up the NHPRC and CEAA editions together or which examines the textual policies of the NHPRC editions in the way those of the CEAA editions have often been examined. The most publicized article of this sort is unfortunately one which confuses the issues more than it clarifies them. Peter Shaw, writing for a general audience in the *American Scholar* and interested in exploring textual matters,[17] was in a position to inaugurate a period of productive interdisciplinary discussion; but the regrettable tone of some of his remarks, as well as the fact that they are sometimes uninformed and incoherent, results in an essay which cannot command respect or offer a fruitful basis for further discussion. Shaw believes that the historical editors "unquestionably have had far greater success than their literary counterparts" (p. 739) and finds the literary editors' "tragic flaw" to be "their respect for language" (p. 740). But when he then praises the historical editors' "respect for historical fact," since for them "both the text and its variants qualify as historical facts" (p. 743), one

15. Editing has also perhaps been the subject of scholarly meetings more often in the historical field. Examples are the "Symposium on the Manuscript Sources of American History: Problems of Their Control, Use, and Publication" at the American Philosophical Society in November 1953 (see its *Proceedings*, 98 [1954], 159–188, 273–278); the session on "Publishing the Papers of Great Men" at the 1954 meeting of the American Historical Association (see *Daedalus*, 86 [1955–57], 47–79); the discussion of "Historical Editing in the United States" at the 150th annual meeting of the American Antiquarian Society in October 1962 (see its *Proceedings*, 72 [1962], 283–328); the session on the "Publication of Historical Source Materials" at the AHA meeting in December 1964; the series of "Special Evening Gatherings on the Writing, Editing, and Publishing of American History" at the Massachusetts Historical Society in 1964–65; and the session on "Historical Editing" at the 1974 AHA meeting.

16. The literature of the NHPC has been recorded by Oliver W. Holmes in "Recent Writings Relevant to Documentary Publication Programs," *American Archivist*, 26 (1963), 137–142—supplemented by an October 1971 typewritten list prepared by NHPC. Relevant materials can also be located in the checklists of archival scholarship which have appeared annually in the *American Archivist* since 1943. The literature of the CEAA (and related editions) is surveyed in an essay, "Relevant Textual Scholarship," appended to the CEAA's *Statement* (see note 2 above), pp. 17–25, and in *The Center for Scholarly Editions: An Introductory Statement* (1977), pp. 5–19. A few checklists of material also appeared in the *CEAA Newsletter* (1968–75).

17. "The American Heritage and Its Guardians," *American Scholar*, 45 (1975–76), 733–751 [i.e., 37–55].

becomes lost. His point lacks any real substance because it is based on the superficial view that a modern literary editor produces an "eclectic text" and a historical editor a "faithful transcription of a single text" (p. 739)—without examining, for instance, what kinds of texts and textual histories may lead to a literary editor's decision to be "eclectic" or what kinds of textual facts are not recoverable from many historical editors' "faithful" transcriptions. It is naïve to suggest that "the historical editor requires a literary appreciation of nuance, while the literary editor needs the historian's respect for fact" (p. 740); but one can nevertheless agree with Shaw that "each set of editors might usefully have advised the other"—though not because they have "opposite kinds of problems."

What is needed is mutual discussion of common problems, and in this spirit I should like to raise a few questions about the textual policies of some of the historical editions, in the light of what has been learned about editing by the literary editors. In order fairly to assess Shaw's assertion that the historical editors have been more successful, one must examine carefully the editorial rationale and procedures followed by those editors. A survey of the differing practices of a number of editions of letters and journals—both historical and literary—will lead, I think, to a consideration of some underlying issues—issues basic not merely to the editing of the papers of American statesmen but to documentary[18] editing in general.

I

Three statements of editorial policy for historical editions appeared within the space of five years in the early 1950s; all three have been influential, and an understanding of modern American documentary editing must begin with them. The first, and the most influential, was Julian P. Boyd's account of his "Editorial Method" (pp. xxv–xxxviii) in the first volume of *The Papers of Thomas Jefferson*, published by Princeton University Press in 1950.[19] Boyd states that his general aim is "rigidly to

18. Although all written and printed artifacts are documents of historical interest (as pointed out in part III below), I am using "documentary" and "document" to refer particularly to private papers, such as letters, diaries, notebooks, rough drafts, and the like.

19. The method was also summarized by Lyman H. Butterfield in "The Papers of Thomas Jefferson: Progress and Procedures in the Enterprise at Princeton," *American Archivist*, 12 (1949), 131–145. The early planning of the edition is reflected in Boyd's *Report to the Thomas Jefferson Bicentennial Commission on the Need, Scope, Proposed Method of Preparation, Probable Cost, and Possible Means of Publishing a Comprehensive Edition of the Writings of Thomas Jefferson* (1943).

adhere to scrupulous exactness in the presentation of the texts as Jefferson wrote them" (p. xxviii), but he recognizes that "complete exactitude is impossible in transmuting handwriting into print"; he has therefore worked out a "standard methodology which, though sometimes consciously inconsistent, is nevertheless precise" (p. xxix). From this, one assumes that the only changes to be introduced are those necessitated by the typography. As soon as he starts to explain the methodology, however, one begins to wonder how it supports his aim of adhering to the text with "scrupulous exactness." He says that he is going to follow a "middle course" between "facsimile reproduction" and "complete modernization," except in the case of business papers and of certain important documents (like the Declaration of Independence), which are to be "presented literally." There are thus two categories of material, accorded different treatment: letters and ordinary documents, presented with some degree of "conventionalization";[20] and business papers and important documents, presented as literally as print allows. Only the treatment of the second category would seem to fulfill the goal of presenting with "scrupulous exactness" the texts "as Jefferson wrote them" or of providing "as accurate a text as possible" which preserves "as many of Jefferson's distinctive mannerisms of writing as can be done" (p. xxix).

In the first, and larger, category, spelling, grammar, and capitalization remain unchanged, except that each sentence is made to begin with a capital letter (in contrast to Jefferson's practice). As for punctuation, however, "for the sake of clarity this literal policy will be less rigorously applied" (p. xxx): periods are supplied, when lacking at the ends of sentences, and unnecessary dashes, such as those which follow periods, are deleted.[21] Although this alteration of punctuation is minimal, one may well ask what is gained by eliminating these dashes; they could not cause a modern reader to misinterpret the sense, and, if they are a characteristic of Jefferson's style, to delete them is at best to modernize and at worst to risk losing a nuance of meaning. More troublesome is the treatment of abbreviations and contractions. They are "normally" ex-

20. Except that the "place and date-line, the salutation, and the complimentary close in letters will also be retained in literal form," though "the date-line is uniformly placed at the head of a letter" (p. xxx). It is somewhat surprising that these features of letters are singled out to be rendered with greater fidelity than the bodies of the letters.

21. More liberties are taken with "documents not in Jefferson's handwriting" if the punctuation makes a passage "misleading or obscure"; but if more than one meaning is possible, the punctuation is not altered and the problem is discussed in a note (p. xxx). The trouble with such an approach is that if only one meaning is possible the reader does not really need the editor's intervention in the punctuation in order to find it.

panded, with the exception of those designating money or units of measure and weight, those standing for proper names, and a miscellaneous group containing such forms as "wou'd," "do." (for "ditto"), and "&c." (though "&" alone is altered to "and"). The rationale for this arbitrary list of abbreviated forms to be retained is not clear, especially since Boyd recognizes that some of them will require editorial expansion in brackets. If there is a value in preserving these contractions, why should others be expanded silently? Boyd gives an example to show Jefferson's extensive use of abbreviations in hurried jottings: "wd hve retird immedly hd h. nt bn infmd" is expanded into "would have retired immediately had he not been informed" (p. xxxi). The expanded text, Boyd argues, "represents the kind of clear and readable form that Jefferson himself would have used for a document intended for formal presentation in print. It makes for clarity and readability and yet sacrifices nothing of Jefferson's words or meaning." But the document was not in fact intended for formal presentation, and to smooth its text out silently is to conceal the essential nature of the preserved document. And if the nature of a document is misrepresented, even if the literal "meaning" is preserved, can one say absolutely that the meaning has in no way been sacrificed? It is true that a long passage full of such abbreviations would slow the reader down, but the reader's convenience is surely not the primary consideration here. The argument presented for expanding contractions like "wd" and "hd" could just as well be applied to "Wmsbgh," yet contractions of geographical names are allowed to stand. Perhaps this distinction is one of the conscious inconsistencies Boyd alludes to, but the reason for it remains unclear. It is disturbing because it would seem to reflect a wavering between two editorial approaches—an indecisiveness whether to transcribe or to normalize.

Three basic decisions about the nature of the edition are implicit in what has been said up to this point. One is that the text is to be critical, in the sense that it incorporates certain kinds of changes dictated by the editor's judgment. A second is that the original text will not be fully recoverable from the data provided; some editorial changes, in other words, will not be recorded. And the third is that the edited text will not be "clear text"—that is, it will incorporate bracketed editorial insertions. These decisions also evidently underlie the treatment of substantive matters, which Boyd turns to next. Conjectured readings are placed in roman type in square brackets and editorial comments (such as *"In the margin"*) appear in italics in square brackets. Such intrusions suggest precision, and it is therefore unfortunate that a bracketed reading in roman type followed by a question mark can mean two different things: either a conjecture at a point where the manuscript is mutilated and part of the text is missing or else an attempt to read a faded passage or one that is "too illegible to be deciphered with certainty" (p. xxxii).[22] Obvious errors in the original texts are corrected, again indicating that the edited text is a critical one. In writings by Jefferson, the original readings in these instances are provided in notes; in writintgs by others (such as letters to Jefferson), the original readings are not reported— "though," Boyd adds, "if an error has psychological significance it will be allowed to stand, with a note when required." Once it is recognized, however, that errors can have psychological significance, it becomes hard to justify a policy that conceals any of them. And this treatment of errors —emending the text and recording the original readings in notes—is a further reflection of editorial indecisiveness, for it represents a third approach in contrast to the treatment of conjectured readings and of some contractions. In the case of errors, the text is emended but is kept free of editorial symbols; conjectured readings are also placed in the text but are marked there as such; and certain contractions remain un-emended but are explained by an editorial insertion in the text. Finally, if two or more copies or drafts of a document exist, variant or canceled readings are reported in notes only when they are "significant." (The variants in fact may not always be known, for it is stated a few pages later that "The editorial policy does not call for full collation of every document extant in more than one version" [p. xxxvi].)[23] Nothing is said about the possibility that a variant reading could call attention to an error in the copy-text, which might then be emended with that variant reading. Of course, if the editorial policy regards each edited text as an edition of a single copy of a document, emendations from other copies would not be allowed. But emendation to correct "obvious errors" is permitted here, and such a category is naturally a subjective one. Can a policy be logically defended which allows the correction of errors that a given editor discovers without recourse to another copy of the text but does not permit the correction of errors that he locates only through examination of another copy? Any procedure that might be called "eclectic" is automatically rejected by some editors. But if a text is not to be presented literally, then the editor's judgment is involved in determining at each point what ought to be in the text;[24] and it is

22. When such passages are not conjecturable, they are indicated by spaced periods within brackets if "one or two words or parts thereof" are missing; if a larger amount is missing, "a note to this effect will be subjoined."

23. There may of course be some versions with no claim to authority. But a distinction should be made between those copies which it is essential to collate—even for an "ordinary" document—and those which can safely be dismissed. (In a later article ["Some Animadversions"—see note 14 above], Boyd says, "We insist upon collating every text available" [p. 52].)

24. Of course, judgment is involved, even in a literal presentation, in deciding what

hard to draw a line between being critical (using one's judgment) and being eclectic (considering readings which come from outside a given copy of a text, whether from the editor's head or from another copy of the text). Perhaps such a line could, with careful definition, be worked out; but Boyd's discussion does not acknowledge the existence of this problem, though it implicitly raises the issue.

All these points, one must remember, relate to the treatment of letters and "ordinary documents." The other category of texts, "documents of major importance," are handled very differently. They are presented literally, exactly as found in the document supplying the copy-text—though with bracketed editorial insertions when required for clarification. Variant readings, as before, appear in notes; but all of them, not just the "significant" ones, are recorded. Canceled passages, however, are now given in the text, in italics within angle brackets, placed before the revised wording. Aside from the fact that it is unclear why canceled matter should be reported within the text for major documents and in notes for ordinary documents, the approach employed for the major documents is far simpler and more satisfactory than that for the ordinary documents. With the major documents, no complicated rules are necessary, and yet the reader knows exactly what he is using (with one exception to be noted below); with the ordinary documents, in spite of the complex guidelines, he cannot always know the reading of the original or what evidence is available in other copies or drafts. It may be true that fewer people will be interested in textual details about the ordinary documents; but, if those documents are less important, why should considerable editorial effort be expended to make them more conveniently readable, especially when that effort serves to conceal some evidence that could conceivably be of use? The juxtaposition of the two kinds of texts is in itself somewhat awkward; and the straightforward handling of the major documents makes the compromises involved in the treatment of the ordinary documents appear all the more unsatisfactory by contrast.

There is, however, one serious weakness in the presentation of the major documents: the system used for recording canceled passages. The simple insertion of canceled matter in angle brackets cannot possibly inform the reader in many cases of the true textual situation, especially when no provision is made for labeling which words or syllables are entered above the line. For instance, in the edited text of Jefferson's first draft of the Virginia constitution of 1776, the following appears:

is in fact present in the original text; but that is a different application of judgment from the one which results in altering what is in the text. (This distinction is commented on further in part III below.)

"unless suspended in their operation for his <*con*> assent" (p. 338, lines 4–5). One would naturally assume that Jefferson had started to write "consent," changed his mind after writing the first syllable, then marked it out and wrote "assent." But a check of the manuscript (reproduced facing p. 414) shows that Jefferson actually wrote "consent" and at some time after that crossed out the first syllable and inserted "as" above it.[25] The printed transcription not only misrepresents the manuscript but fails to show that the revision may have occurred at a time later than that of the original inscription. A few lines later occurs the phrase "endeavoring to prevent the population of our country <*by*> & for that purpose obstructing the laws" (338.16–17); Jefferson's revision becomes clear only when one knows that "& for that purpose" was inserted above the line at the time when "by" was deleted. Beginning in the next line the edited text contains a phrase that is bound to leave readers even more puzzled: "raising the conditions of new appropriati<*ng*>ons <*new*> of lands" (338.18–19). One can of course read the final text here; but if one wishes to know how it read earlier, one cannot simply add the bracketed letters, because no indication has been given of what words or letters were added at the time when the bracketed material was canceled. The manuscript shows that Jefferson first wrote "conditions of appropriating lands." After this "of" the word "new" is careted in; "on" is written over the "ng" and followed by "s"; and after that another caret points to "new of" with the "new" marked out. Thus Jefferson first revised his wording to "conditions of appropriating new lands"; then he further altered it to "conditions of new appropriations of lands." These examples are enough to show that the system is inadequate; reporting cancellations in this way serves little purpose because it does not provide enough information to allow one to reconstruct the stages of revision.[26]

What I have been saying about the textual policy of the Jefferson edition is not meant to cast doubt on the accomplishment of this edition in other respects. It is surely a great achievement in its assemblage and arrangement of material, its exemplary historical annotation, and its generally efficient physical presentation (with each document followed by concise descriptive, explanatory, and—in some cases—textual notes). And it deserves to be praised for the role it has played in causing serious scholarly attention to be turned to the full-scale editing of important statesmen's papers—it has eloquently demonstrated why the scholarly

25. The identical situation occurs again at 338.25.
26. Some further remarks on Boyd's method in such texts are made by St. George L. Sioussat in *American Historical Review*, 56 (1950–51), 118–122—in one of the few reviews of an NHPRC edition to pay close attention to textual matters.

editor must place "the exacting claims of history" above "the amenities and a respect for the privacy and feelings of individuals" (p. xxviii). What is to be regretted is that an edition in such a strategic position of influence is so unsophisticated in its handling of the actual text. There is no single right way to edit a text, but the editorial policy of the Jefferson edition does not suggest that the alternatives have been clearly thought through. As a result, there is indecision as to whether the text is to be literal or critical, whether it is to be modernized or unmodernized, and whether it is to incorporate apparatus or have the apparatus appended. The reason given for retaining "&c." is that "it was widely used in eighteenth-century printing" (p. xxxi), but Jefferson's "&" is expanded in ordinary documents to "and," presumably because it would not have appeared in an eighteenth-century printed version. Yet, as Boyd recognizes, an editor cannot undertake to capitalize various nouns for Jefferson, even though Jefferson's "extreme economy" in the use of capitals was a matter in which he "differed from his contemporaries" (p. xxx). Is the question of how a given letter or private note would have appeared in print in the eighteenth century even a relevant one, when such documents were not intended for print? The way Jefferson wrote them, however unconventional it may have been, is what the reader is interested in. This view prevails part of the time, since the editor has thought it worthwhile to transcribe the major documents literally. But at other times there seems to be a feeling that formal matters are really not important and that a partially "conventionalized" rendering is all the reader needs. The statement of editorial method, in short, reflects no coherent textual rationale.

Two years later Clarence E. Carter published *Historical Editing* (1952), a 51-page pamphlet which in some ways is the counterpart, for the historical field, of the CEAA's *Statement of Editorial Principles and Procedures* (1967, 1972). Although it was not meant to be an official statement of the NHPC (as the CEAA's pamphlet was a committee position paper), it was published as Bulletin No. 7 of the National Archives and was written by a man with extensive editorial experience in connection with a government project, *The Territorial Papers of the United States* (1934–). Unlike the CEAA's pamphlet, which emphasizes printed texts and devotes most of its space to discussion of textual matters, Carter's booklet deals with manuscript texts and spends only ten pages on textual questions. Carter refers favorably to Boyd's work early in his discussion (pp. 10–11), but it is clear that Carter's position is more conservative than Boyd's and that he places a higher value on the formal aspects of a text.

Carter begins his account of "Textual Criticism" (pp. 20–25) with the problem of establishing the authenticity of a document, and then he turns to "the operation designed to clear up such corruptions as may have entered it" (p. 23). This statement suggests that the kind of edited text which Carter envisions is a critical one, not an exact transcription. The matter soon becomes less clear, however. Although he admits that originals may contain errors, he discusses emendations only in regard to copies. He implies that originals are not to be emended, because even in the copy retained by the writer "no editorial emendations are permissible": "it is an official record, and the only resort is to call attention to the presence of specific errors" (p. 24). A copy made by someone else, in contrast, may be emended—but whether silently or not is uncertain. "Conjectural emendations," he says, "are recommended only when it is clear that the errors are due to the inadvertence of the scribe." But, he goes on, "such emendations should be plainly identified as such in footnotes or by editorial brackets in the text" (p. 23). Yet on the next page he says that "slips of the pen" by the copyist can be corrected by "unidentified emendations." Apparently the second category is meant to consist of obvious errors, such as "the transposition of letters in words, or the repetition of words or lines," and the first of less obvious errors. But such a distinction is not definite enough to provide a workable basis for deciding which emendations are to be silent. There is a curious mixture here of strictness and leniency: nothing, not even errors, can be altered in a text from a document in the author's hand; but scribal copies can be emended, sometimes silently. This mixture also reflects an indecision similar to Boyd's about the nature of the editor's task—whether it is to produce an exact transcription of a surviving document or a critical text not identical with the text in any single extant document. The issue emerges squarely in Carter's paragraph on "the occasional needs to reconstruct a document when two or more textual versions are encountered, each of which possesses attributes which stamp it as authentic" (p. 24). The word "reconstruct" suggests the production of an emended text; but his "harmonizing of the various versions" amounts to "the choice of the one which seems to be the most complete one of chronological priority," with readings from the other versions placed in brackets or in footnotes.[27]

Carter says nothing further about emendation but instead turns to "Transcription" (pp. 25–30), where the emphasis is clearly on what he calls "exact copy." His comments are based on a thorough understanding of the value of retaining the original punctuation and spelling; he cites some useful examples illustrating the importance of punctuation

27. Carter had earlier made the same points in his article, "The Territorial Papers of the United States," *American Archivist*, 8 (1945), 122–135.

in official documents (p. 26) and notes that the "interest in bad spelling lies partially in that it indicates the current pronunciation" (p. 28).[28] He believes that superscript letters, ligatures, abbreviations, date-lines, addresses, signatures, and the like should all be reproduced exactly.[29] Canceled matter, he says, can be inserted into the text, appropriately marked, or reported in notes—but not simply ignored. To eliminate these passages, as he rightly points out, "omits an element that often indicates what was actually passing through the mind of the writer which he concluded not to set down, and of course it also represents carelessness in many instances—a not unimportant facet of a writer's character" (p. 29). Carter's discussion of "Transcription," taken by itself, sets forth an intelligent and well-considered approach, which is admirably put in practice in his own work on *The Territorial Papers* (commented on further below).

Although he stresses objectivity here and throughout, he is aware that subjective judgment enters into transcription. When a mark of punctuation is not clearly identifiable, for instance, "it becomes the editor's responsibility to determine from the sense of the passage what was probably intended, and to proceed accordingly" (p. 26). This view is more realistic than the one expressed at the end of the preceding section, where he says that "the editor must eschew any and all forms of interpretation; he cannot deal with his documents in a subjective manner" (p. 25). What he is primarily getting at in this earlier statement is that the editor should not interpret the facts presented in his text, leaving that task for "the historian who uses the edited documents as a basis of historical composition." He is adamant on this point: "It cannot be too strongly emphasized that the editor's sole responsibility, after having established the purity of the documents, is to reproduce them with meticulous accuracy." Despite his insistence, the issue is not so easily settled, for it can be argued that the editor, having thought deeply about the text, is in the best position to suggest interpretations of it in his

---

28. A few years later, Carter made the case even more forcefully, in "The Territorial Papers of the United States: A Review and a Commentary," *Mississippi Valley Historical Review*, 42 (1955–56), 510–524. Every aspect of a document, he says there, is "part and parcel of the intellectual climate of an era. Editorial tampering with punctuation, spelling, paragraphing, and the like, which means the introduction of textual corruptions, is anathema" (p. 516).

29. The only departure he condones is in regard to spacing: "unusual spacing should not be reproduced" (p. 27), he says, and all paragraphs should begin with indentions and (surprisingly) all salutations run in with the first lines of texts. It would be more in keeping with Carter's respect for documentary evidence not even to allow these alterations. Spacing can of course be regarded as a nontextual matter; but Carter's desire to "avoid undue expanses of blank paper" seems a trivial justification for changing the way a writer sets off a salutation or complimentary close.

annotation. In any case, this question does not affect texual policy. But Carter does not perhaps sufficiently recognize the extent to which judgment inevitably enters the editorial process, especially when emendation is allowed. His discussion, like many others in the historical field, neglects printed texts and (perhaps partly for that reason) fails to confront adequately the issues involved in an editor's decision to produce a critical text; the issues are present even when the only choice for copy-text is a holograph letter, but they may call themselves more forcibly to the editor's attention when he has more occasion to deal with multiple versions of a text. Nevertheless, Carter's comments are generally sensible, as far as they go, and he at least takes notice of—if he does not fully pursue—the problems of choosing a copy-text when one is faced with several copies, none of which is in the author's hand, or with multiple possibly authoritative texts. Certainly his views on punctuation and spelling and on the necessity for recording variants deserve to be heeded more than they have been.

A third influential statement on historical editing was published two years after Carter's, in the *Harvard Guide to American History* (ed. Oscar Handlin *et al.*, 1954)—which contained a short section on "The Editing and Printing of Manuscripts" (pp. 95–104), prepared primarily by Samuel Eliot Morison. Because of the wide circulation which the *Guide* has achieved, a great many people have been exposed to this discussion, and it has often been referred to in historical literature as a standard account of editing. When the *Guide* was revised in 1974 (ed. Frank Freidel *et al.*), the editors apparently saw no need to alter this section, for it was retained in practically identical form ("Editing and Printing," pp. 27–36).[30] Yet it is a superficial treatment of editing which, like Boyd's and Carter's, oversimplifies or fails to touch basic questions which any editor must consider.

The discussion attempts "to set forth general principles of editing American documents" and begins with the usual point that "printing is unable to reproduce a longhand manuscript exactly." But from there on, difficulties arise. Three methods of preparing texts are announced—called the Literal, the Expanded, and the Modernized—and a preliminary section offers directions that apply to all three. Some of these directions are overly precise and unnecessary—such as specifying that a salutation should be printed in small capitals or that the date line, regardless

30. Citations below are to subsection and paragraph numbers of the 1954 edition; the identical passages can easily be located in the 1974 edition, where the paragraph numbers remain the same (the subsections are not numbered but readily identified). The only significant revision in 1974 is the alteration of the opening paragraph to include references to five more recent discussions of editing, including Carter's.

of where it appears in the original, should consistently be "printed either in *italics* under the heading, or at the end" (I.2). What such directions do reveal is that some silent alterations of the original are to be allowed—even in the Literal Method, since these directions apply to all the methods. Three other preliminary directions indicate further— and more objectionable—silent alterations. When a manuscript is torn or illegible, editorial comments are to be inserted in italics within brackets and conjectured readings in roman type within brackets, as Boyd recommended; but, unlike Boyd, the *Guide* claims that "if only one to four letters [of a long word] are missing, brackets are unnecessary and pedantic" (I.3)—on the grounds that the editor can be sure in those cases of what had originally been written. Yet obviously one cannot really be certain what spelling was used; not to indicate in some way what the editor has done misrepresents the surviving evidence by offering as a fact what is actually an inference.[31] Another direction calls for inserting "[*sic*]" after "a very strange spelling or mistake of the original writer" (I.5), implying that mistakes are not to be emended. Yet the same direction states, "One may correct, without notice, obvious slips of the writer's pen such as 'an an hour ago.' " As in Carter's discussion, nothing explicit is said about what distinguishes errors to be silently corrected from those to be retained. The two categories in fact represent very different approaches to editing, and their juxtaposition here requires further explanation. Still another direction, dealing with manuscript alterations, asserts that "canceled passages are omitted unless they contain something of particular interest, when they may be inserted in a footnote" (I.7). No discussion of what value canceled passages may have is given, nor of what might cause some to be of particular interest; if the point had been taken up and analyzed, the difficulty of regarding any cancellations in a letter or journal as insignificant would have become apparent.[32]

The subsection on the Literal Method begins with the statement, "Follow the manuscript absolutely in spelling, capitalization, and punctuation"—unaccompanied by an explanation of how this directive is consistent with such earlier rules, applicable to all methods, as the one permitting silent corrections of slips of the pen. And it is immediately followed by a troublesome exception: "in very illiterate manuscripts,

---

31. Besides, the arbitrary limit of four letters is illogical, since there could well be instances of more missing letters in which the intended word was equally obvious.

32. The final sentence of this rule makes the odd suggestion that a clerk's marginal glosses in "court and similar records" may "either be omitted, or used as subheadings to save expense." If they are so unimportant that they can be omitted entirely, it seems strange that an alternative is to give them a prominent place in the text itself—so prominent as to impose upon the text the sense of its structure envisioned by the clerk.

where little or no punctuation is used, a minimum necessary to understand the text may be supplied; and in documents where the writer begins practically every word with a capital, the editor may use his discretion " (II.1). Although the editor is told that he should state "the practice followed" in a preliminary note, there is no requirement for him to record his alterations. Obviously the point of a literal method is to reproduce the text of a document exactly as it stands; if a manuscript is "illiterate," the reader of a literal text of it will expect to see the characteristics that make it illiterate. There is no logic in setting up a category called "Literal Method" and then saying that an editor can, in extreme cases, make changes for the convenience of the reader and still produce a literal text. Even if there were really much difficulty in reading a text in which most words are capitalized, the ease of readibility is not a criterion for a literal text. A few changes, of purely typographic significance, can be defended in a literal text, such as the elimination of the long "s"—a literal text, after all, is to be distinguished from a type-facsimile. Manuscript abbreviations, however, constitute a difficult category: one would expect an abbreviation to be reproduced, not expanded, in a literal text, and yet some abbreviations would require specially cast types to be printed. The rule given here is to print abbreviations and contractions "exactly as written *within the limitations of available type*" (II.4) and otherwise to expand them without brackets (II.5). This procedure is defensible as a practical compromise; but unfortunately the impression is given that an editor need not explain exactly what he has altered in this respect.

For the so-called Expanded Method, taken up next, the *Guide* recommends Boyd's practice, though it prefers more expansion of abbreviations and more standardization of designations for money, weights, and measures. In fact, most of the discussion is concerned with the treatment of abbreviations, the general policy being to "spell out all abbreviations except those still used today . . . and those of months, proper names, and titles" (III.2). No rationale is given for the aims of the Expanded Method, but since the goal is not to produce a modernized text (that is the subject of the third method) it is not clear why the present-day currency of an abbreviation is relevant. Nor is it clear just what changes are to be made silently. All sentences are to begin with a capital and end with a period, "no matter what the writer does" (III.1); these changes and most expansions of abbreviations are apparently to be made without comment, but supplied letters which follow the last one in a superscript abbreviation are, inexplicably, to be enclosed in brackets ("m^o" becomes "mo[nth]"). Except for the treatment of the opening and closing of sentences, the original capitalization and punctuation are to be retained

(III.1), and the spelling as well, even if inconsistent (III.5); the point in standardizing the money, weight, and measure designations, therefore, becomes less clear by contrast.[33] Indeed, the point of the Expanded Method as a whole is puzzling. It is not, as one might at first suppose of an emended but unmodernized text, to correct errors, nor is it to produce consistency, except in a few minor respects; it is simply, as the name indicates, to expand some of the abbreviations. But this expansion does not really constitute a separate "method"; it is more accurately regarded as a form of annotation. One could just as well have a literal text with the explanations of the abbreviations in brackets or notes; indeed, such a procedure would be preferable to the uncertainties suggested here. If the Expanded Method were truly a different method of editing, it would have to involve a basically different approach to the text—a critical approach, for instance, in which the text is emended to correct errors and resolve cruxes. Despite the confusions of the section on the Expanded Method, it ends with a salutary caution:

Some editors begin every new sentence with a capital letter, even if the writer does not. This is unobjectionable if it is clear where the writer intended a new sentence to begin; but often it is not clear. Punctuation in all manuscripts before the nineteenth century is highly irregular; and if you once start replacing dashes by commas, semicolons, or periods, as the sense may seem to warrant, you are asking for trouble. (III.6)

Ironically this closing statement, which contradicts the opening point of the section ("always capitalize the first word and put a period at the end of the sentence no matter what the writer does"), is the most sensible one in the whole discussion.[34]

The subsection on the Modernized Method requires little comment. Modernization is said to be for "the average reader who is put off by obsolete spelling and erratic punctuation." The extent to which the average reader is "put off" by such features of a text is probably not so great as many editors seem to think. In any case, the modernization

33. Incidentally, the rule on such designations (III.3) states, "Points after monetary abbreviations are superfluous." But a previous rule (III.2b) tells what to do if an abbreviation is "still obscure after superior letters are brought down and a point added," as if the addition of the point is a factor in producing clarity. Whether abbreviations are written with or without periods is a matter of convention; determining whether or not a period is "superfluous" does not normally involve considerations of meaning.

34. Another statement which offers valuable advice occurs in the preliminary subsection: "In reprinting a document it is better to prepare a fresh text from the manuscript or photostat; for if an earlier printed edition is used as the basis, one is apt to repeat some of the former editor's errors, or maybe add others of one's own" (I.9). The last seven words should of course be eliminated: an editor can naturally make mistakes of his own, but this danger is present whether he is working from the original or a printed edition.

recommended here is a confused concept. The first direction is the expected one: "Modernize the spelling, capitalization, and punctuation, but pay scrupulous respect to the language" (IV.1)—although one might not expect the additional statement, "Paragraphs and sentences that are too long may be broken up." What is confusing, however, is that the same instruction also contains this sentence: "Where the original writer has obviously omitted a word like *not*, or, for instance, has written *east* when you know he means *west*, the editor may add or correct a word; but he should place it within square brackets." The correction of errors is an entirely separate matter from modernization, and the two should not be linked together here as aspects of the same "method." One can modernize a text without correcting errors, and one can emend without modernizing. An introduction to editorial method which does not make this distinction will only encourage illogical thinking.

The confusions which underlie the *Guide*'s whole discussion are epitomized in the concluding remarks on "Choice of Method" (VI). The choice is said to depend "partly on the kind of document in question, but mainly on practical considerations, especially on the purpose of the publication." The nature of the document does determine whether expansion of abbreviations or modernization is required, once it has been decided that the edition is aimed at an audience which would require such alterations; but that decision comes first, since for some purposes only the literal approach will suffice, regardless of the complexities of the document. To say that documents of the sixteenth and seventeenth centuries "full of contractions" should be printed literally "in a publication destined for scholarly readers only" is both to underestimate the capacities of a wider audience and to ignore completely the possibility of accompanying a literal text with textual annotation. But why anyone, scholar or not, needs an unmodernized text does not seem to be fully grasped: an expanded text is said to be better for the student than a modernized one "because the wording, spelling, and punctuation of the original give it a certain flavor"—a statement suggesting only a trivial interest in these matters (and again including "wording" as one of the concerns of modernization). The assertion that "for a new edition of some classic such as the Virginia 'Lament for Mr. Nathaniel Bacon,' or the poetry of Edward Taylor, the Modernized Method is best" shows a complete failure to understand the serious reasons for being interested in spelling and punctuation and implies that those features are of less concern in "literary" than in "historical" documents. (An earlier similar comment claims that the "texts of recent editions of Shakespeare, Dryden, and the King James Bible have been established by this [modernized] method"—as if modernizing could "establish" a text, instead of being a way of altering a text, once established.)[35] The motto offered at the end of the section is in the spirit of the rest of the discussion: "Accuracy without Pedantry. / Consistency first, last, and always." The accuracy required for establishing a text may be regarded as pedantry by some, without affecting its desirability, and what excessive accuracy might be is not defined. If consistency of editorial treatment is the prime virtue, then surely a logical consistency of editorial rationale is a necessity; the *Guide* in this respect sets a poor example.[36]

These three statements of editorial method were not the only ones available to historical editors of the 1950s and 1960s. Thirty years earlier, for instance, the Anglo-American Historical Committee produced a two-part "Report"[37]—the first dealing with medieval and the second with modern documents—which was in many ways an intelligent and carefully considered statement. Unfortunately it recommended modernizing punctuation for all documents;[38] but, unlike some later treatments, it recognized the importance of recording cancellations and revisions and of providing a detailed account of the practice of the manuscript text in any respect in which the editor alters it.[39] Boyd, Carter,

35. A superficial reason is also given for not being literal in quotations cited in secondary works: in these cases "the Expanded Method is far preferable to the literal, since the latter clashes unnecessarily with a modern text and makes readers pause to puzzle over odd spellings and abbreviations." (The Expanded Method here sounds very similar to the Modernized.) For some reason bracketed explanations are disapproved of in such quotations, though appended footnotes are not.

36. Just before the end it is stated that every text "should be compared word for word with the original, or with a microfilm or photographic copy," as if comparison against a photocopy could be substituted for comparison against the original. Many later historical editors do in fact comment on having taken their texts from photostats, microfilms, and the like, seemingly unaware of the dangers involved; literary editors more frequently remark on the necessity for the collation of transcriptions against the original manuscripts. For an excellent statement explaining why photographic reproduction can be "the most dangerous thing of all" for persons who have "a touching faith in the notion that 'the camera does not lie,'" see pp. 70–72 of Arthur Brown's article cited in note 97 below.

37. "Report on Editing Historical Documents," *Bulletin of the Institute of Historical Research* [University of London], 1 (1923–24), 6–25; 3 (1925–26), 13–26.

38. "It is customary to adopt modern methods of punctuation, and cases are few in which departure from this procedure is advisable. The editor should, however, be careful not to alter the sense of a passage in altering the punctuation" (3, 22).

39. Two still earlier statements have much in common with the later ones. Charles Francis Adams, Jr., in "The Printing of Old Manuscripts," *Proceedings of the Massachusetts Historical Society*, 20 (1882–83), 175–182, complains about the practice of reproducing manuscript abbreviations in print and believes that fidelity to a manuscript text "can be carried to fanaticism" (p. 182), though he does recognize that at least "the scholarly few" may wish to preserve the "complexion, as it were, of the period to which the book belongs." In "Suggestions for the Printing of Documents Relating to American History," *Annual Report of the American Historical Association*, 1905, 1:45–48, the position is taken that a

and the *Harvard Guide*, however, are more important for anyone examining the NHPRC editions. Boyd's edition led the way for the later editions and was taken as a model, and the other two discussions followed in quick succession at a time when some of the later editions were being organized. The first and third especially have had a considerable influence on a large number of American editions, which either refer to them explicitly or are modeled on other editions that follow their recommendations. If that were not the case, they would hardly deserve the attention given them here; but their deficiencies have apparently not been regarded as obvious. The discussion in the *Guide* is the least satisfactory, as Carter's is the best, of the group; all three have serious shortcomings, but the one with the most merit ironically has been cited the least often. A recognition of the indecisiveness of these discussions—particularly the two most influential ones—in regard to editorial theory and procedure suggests what a weak foundation they provide for the massive superstructure later erected.

II

A brief survey of some of the historical editions which followed, beginning in 1959 with the Franklin, Calhoun, and Clay editions, will illustrate how similar their characteristic position is to that of one or more of the three statements of the early 1950s.[40] Leonard W. Labaree, in *The Papers of Benjamin Franklin* (Yale University Press, 1959-   ),[41]

manuscript should be printed "in the form which it would have borne if the author had contemporaneously put it into print" (p. 47), with obvious mistakes corrected, abbreviations expanded, and some punctuation clarified—though with certain cancellations recorded, as offering "some indication of the mental process of the writer." A more recent discussion by Edith G. Firth, "The Editing and Publishing of Documents," *Canadian Archivist Newsletter*, No. 1 (1963), 3-12, makes clearer the reasons for not modernizing and recognizes that much modernization in any case results from "underestimating Everyman's ability" (p. 4). A similar point of view was cogently set forth thirty years earlier by Hilary Jenkinson, in "The Representation of Manuscripts in Print," *London Mercury*, 30 (1934), 429-438 (which also comments on the relation between historical and literary editing).

40. My brief comments on the editorial policies of these editions are not meant to be comprehensive; many other features, both praiseworthy and regrettable, could be discussed in addition to those I select as relevant illustrations here. Most of the editions, for instance, place in brackets editorial conjectures for illegible or missing words or letters, and most report variants or canceled readings on a selective basis, but these practices are generally not referred to. Citation of page numbers in each case, unless otherwise specified, refers to the first volume of an edition.

41. On the history and editing of Franklin's papers, see Francis S. Philbrick, "Notes on Early Editions and Editors of Franklin," *Proceedings of the American Philosophical Society*, 97 (1953), 525-564; William E. Lingelbach, "Benjamin Franklin's Papers and the American Philosophical Society," *ibid.*, 99 (1955), 359-380; Leonard W. Labaree and Whitfield J. Bell, Jr., "The Papers of Benjamin Franklin: A Progress Report," *ibid.*, 101 (1957),

sets out to follow "a middle course between exact reproduction . . . and complete modernization" (p. xl)[42] and cites the *Harvard Guide* for "a discussion of principles which the editors have in general followed." The aim is "to preserve as faithfully as possible the form and spirit in which the authors composed their documents, and at the same time to reproduce their words in a manner intelligible to the present-day reader." Insofar as the second aim involves alteration of the original, it would seem to be incompatible with the first. Labaree distinguishes his treatment of printed copy-texts from that of manuscript copy-texts. The former, he says, are "considered as having been edited once from an original manuscript" and therefore are presented as originally printed, except for the silent alteration of certain typographic conventions (italic proper names are made roman and words in full capitals are made lower case) and the silent correction of "obvious" errors (otherwise, "no attempt will be made to reconstruct the original version"). In manuscript copy-texts, however, contractions are expanded, periods are placed at the ends of sentences, and punctuation is altered in various other ways: "A dash used in place of a period, comma, or semicolon will be replaced by the appropriate mark of punctuation . . . . Commas scattered meaninglessly through a sentence will be silently omitted" (p. xlii). These procedures leave the editor in the ironic position of treating printed texts—which are at least one step removed from the author's manuscript and may contain compositors' alterations—with greater respect than authorial manuscript texts, in which there is direct evidence of the author's practice. Furthermore, there is no recognition of the fact that printed texts may vary from copy to copy or that manuscript texts may be of a kind that were never intended for publication. The idea that a printed copy-text has already "been edited once" and thus requires less alteration implies that the scholarly editor's function, like that of the printing- or publishing-house editor, is to put a text—regardless of its nature—in "publishable" shape. But, as Labaree knows, a scholar is interested in the "form and spirit" of Franklin himself; and most of the silent changes described here can only take one farther away from him. Part of the texture of contemporary detail is sacrificed for the sake of a

532–534; Labaree, "The Papers of Benjamin Franklin," *Daedalus*, 86 (1955–57), 57–62, and "The Benjamin Franklin Papers," *Williams Alumni Review*, 59 (February 1967), 11. P. M. Zall's article (see note 6 above) illustrates the kind of work which remains to be done on the textual history of Franklin's *Autobiography*, even after the appearance of the Yale edition.

42. Cf. his generalization, in "Scholarly Editing in Our Times," *Ventures*, 3 (Winter 1964), 28–31, that recent editors "may make concessions . . . to modern usage in such matters as spelling, capitalization, and punctuation, but they reproduce to the utmost of their ability the phraseology of the original" (p. 29).

supposedly more readable text, though many of the deleted features would not have caused a reader any real difficulties in the first place. One must wonder why, if a partially modernized text of Franklin had to be produced, it could not have been accompanied by a record of editorial alterations.[43]

The same year, in *The Papers of John C. Calhoun* (University of South Carolina Press, 1959–), Robert L. Meriwether took a different position from Labaree, arguing that printed texts could be treated more freely than manuscript texts because Calhoun was not responsible for printed reports of speeches and the like; yet the freedom employed— involving the silent revision of capitalization and punctuation and the breaking up of paragraphs—seems excessive, especially in view of the fact that Calhoun probably revised the reporter's accounts in some cases (p. xxxv). In manuscript texts, the editor does not allow Calhoun to employ two marks of punctuation together (one is chosen), and dashes at the ends of sentences are silently changed to periods. The most confusing device in this edition is the use of roman type in square brackets to represent both editorial restorations and authorial cancellations. W. Edwin Hemphill, taking over with the second volume (1963), makes explicit reference to the Expanded Method of the *Harvard Guide* (p. xxvii). By contrast, *The Papers of Henry Clay* (University of Kentucky Press, 1959–), edited by James F. Hopkins,[44] says little about editorial method and nothing about punctuation, except that the lowering of superscript letters sometimes affects the punctuation. Presumably punctuation is otherwise unaltered, and the "original spelling and capitalization have been retained" (p. ix), so that this edition may come closer to offering a literal treatment than the others of 1959—although "typographical errors" in printed texts are silently corrected. The problem of variant texts, frequently slighted in historical editions, is at least commented on here: "When several contemporary copies, but not the original letter of delivery, have been discovered, that which most closely approximates the form identified with the sender has been used. When there are several versions of a manuscript in the inscriber's hand, that which most closely represents his final intent has been accepted." This statement shows no awareness of the intricacies of textual criticism. The first sentence does not recognize the possibility of constructing an "eclec-

43. Labaree follows Boyd's system of printing significant canceled passages in footnotes for ordinary documents and recording cancellations within the text for important documents. A few criticisms of the textual policy of the Franklin edition appear in J. A. Leo Lemay's review of the eighteenth volume in *American Historical Review*, 81 (1976), 1223–24.

44. See also his "Editing the Henry Clay Papers," *American Archivist*, 20 (1957), 231–238.

tic" text; it assumes that the task is to edit a single document, not the text which is found embodied in several documents. Yet when errors in a printed copy are silently corrected, the editor is concerning himself with an idealized text rather than with the reproduction of a specific embodiment of the text; the principle that is recognized in handling a printed text is not extended to situations involving scribal copies, though both may obviously contain departures from the author's manuscript. And the second sentence does not suggest the difficulties of determining "final intent" or the importance of variant readings among the holograph drafts.

In 1961 two more large editions began publication. One was *The Adams Papers* (Belknap Press of Harvard University Press)—which, like the Jefferson and Franklin editions, had been designated a priority project by the NHPC.[45] Lyman H. Butterfield, describing his editorial method in the first volume of *The Diary and Autobiography of John Adams*, praises those other two editions, and it is clear that his procedures closely resemble those of the Jefferson edition (with which he had earlier been associated).[46] He aims at a "middle ground between pedantic fidelity and readability" (p. lvi) and adds that scholars who are "concerned with the ultimate niceties of a critical passage" can "resort" to the microfilm edition of the Adams papers.[47] It is true that the availability of the papers on microfilm makes it easier for a scholar to check readings in the manuscripts, but that fact has no bearing on the editor's responsibility for producing a sound text in a letterpress edition. The reason for undertaking a letterpress edition of material available on

45. For general accounts of the papers, see L. H. Butterfield, "The Papers of the Adams Family: Some Account of Their History," *Proceedings of the Massachusetts Historical Society*, 71 (1953–57), 328–356 (abridged as "Whatever You Write Preserve" in *American Heritage*, 10 [April 1959], 26–33, 88–93); Butterfield, "The Adams Papers," *Daedalus*, 86 (1955–57), 62–71; and Wendell D. Garrett, "The Papers of the Adams Family: 'A Natural Resource of History,'" *Historical New Hampshire*, 21, no. 3 (Autumn 1966), 28–37. All three include some historical comments on the editing of the papers. See also *Butterfield in Holland: A Record of L. H. Butterfield's Pursuit of the Adamses Abroad in 1959* (1961), with comments by Julian P. Boyd and Walter Muir Whitehill; and *The Adams Papers: Remarks by Julian P. Boyd, Thomas B. Adams, L. H. Butterfield, the President of the United States* (1962).

46. There is thus the same difficulty here with interpreting canceled matter placed in angle brackets, when there is no symbol for interlineations: one cannot always tell whether the cancellation was made at the time of inscription or possibly later.

47. This edition (1954–59), in some 600 reels, has been influential in the movement to make manuscript collections available in microfilm form. For historical and evaluative comments on it, see L. H. Butterfield, "'Vita sine literis, mors est': The Microfilm Edition of the Adams Papers," *Quarterly Journal of the Library of Congress*, 18 (1960–61), 53–58; Merrill Jensen, Samuel Flagg Bemis, and David Donald, "'The Life and Soul of History,'" *New England Quarterly*, 34 (1961), 96–105; and Wendell D. Garrett, "Opportunities for Study: The Microfilm Edition of The Adams Papers," *Dartmouth College Library Bulletin*, n.s., 5 (1962), 26–33.

microfilm is not simply to offer a more readable (that is, partly modernized) text; it is to furnish readers with a text which has benefited from the editor's critical thinking about what the writer meant to have in that text.[48] Of course, a scholar under any circumstances may wish to consult the original manuscripts (just as he might wish to check on any other documentation); but to justify silent alterations in a printed text on the grounds that a scholar can always look at the manuscripts is to conceive of editing as little more than styling for present-day readability. In addition, the discussion suggests that only a few scholars will be interested in such matters as punctuation and even takes a disparaging tone toward anyone concerned with them. Rather than counting on the reader's agreement that it is "pedantic" to be interested in the "ultimate niceties" of a text, it would be more positive and productive to assume that readers will want to understand the text as fully as they can and will not wish to slight any aspect of it in the process.

As with many other historical editions, the determination here not to emend from a variant text is in odd contrast to the leniency with which the selected text is handled. Relevant texts are collated and "significant" differences are recorded; however, Butterfield says, "Whatever version is found *in the manuscripts being edited* has perforce been considered the 'basic' text in the present volume" (p. lix). Two years later, in the opening volume of *Adams Family Correspondence*, a supplementary editorial discussion marks a notable departure from this practice: the comparison of copies, it is said, can call attention to clarifications of grammar, corrections of spelling, and the like, and such changes are adopted silently (p. xlv). The fact that their immediate source is another document makes this an "eclectic" procedure, and the statement is a welcome recognition of the possibility of editing a text rather than a document. The Adams edition, unlike many of the literary editions of published works, does not fully carry this approach through; but it has gone farther than most of the historical editions in enunciating the principle on which the establishment of critical texts rests.[49]

The other edition beginning in 1961, *The Papers of Alexander Hamilton* (Columbia University Press), edited by Harold C. Syrett,[50] places even more stress on modernization: not only are punctuation and capitalization altered "where it seemed necessary to make clear the sense

48. And, on the nontextual side, to provide historical annotation.
49. Whether critical texts are more appropriate for some kinds of material than others is a separate question, as is the desirability of a record of all emendations in critical texts.
50. In an earlier article on "The Papers of Alexander Hamilton," in the *Historian*, 19 (1956–57), 168–181, Syrett and Jacob E. Cooke say that the Hamilton editors "expect to rely heavily on the precedent set by the Jefferson papers." See also Syrett, "Alexander Hamilton Collected," *Columbia University Forum*, 5, no. 2 (Spring 1962), 24–28.

of the writer" but a "special effort has been made to eliminate the dash, which was such a popular eighteenth-century device" (p. xvii). The reader is at more of a loss than usual to know what the editor has done, because "unintentional slips" are handled in one of four ways (they are allowed to stand, explained in a note, corrected with bracketed insertions, or corrected silently), but there is no discussion of the circumstances for choosing one method over another. Deletions are reported only when "the significance of a manuscript seems to warrant it," as is also the case in *The Papers of James Madison* (University of Chicago Press, 1962–), edited by William T. Hutchinson and William M. E. Rachal (and, later, Robert A. Rutland).[51] Because Madison made some revisions in his papers long after they were written, the editors rightly feel that these later alterations should be distinguished from the earlier ones: "Changes which the editors believe that Madison made in later life, when looking back over his papers, are given in footnotes" (p. xxxvii). But since the determination of which revisions fall into this class rests on editorial judgment and since cancellations are not reported ordinarily, there is the possibility that in some instances Madison's later revisions have been incorporated into the text, with no record of canceled readings to call attention to the potential problem. Donald Jackson's edition, the same year, of the *Letters of the Lewis and Clark Expedition, with Related Documents, 1783–1854* (University of Illinois Press, 1962), is again a partly modernized edition: "When in doubt as to how to proceed in a trivial matter I silently follow modern practice." He employs identical policies in two later editions, *The Journals of Zebulon Montgomery Pike* (University of Oklahoma Press, 1966–) and *The Expeditions of John Charles Frémont* (edited with Mary Lee Spence; University of Illinois Press, 1970–). Like many of his fellow editors, he insists on normalizing the end-punctuation of sentences and eliminating superfluous dashes.[52] He is also characteristic in neglecting the possibility of authoritative variants in printed texts; as he says in the *Frémont*, "Material taken from printed texts is so indicated . . . but no attempt is made to record other printed versions." His departures from his copy-texts are in general said to be "based on common sense and the current practice of scholars." Whether that current practice is in turn based on a coherent and defensible editorial rationale is not in-

51. For a history of the early work on this edition, see William H. Runge, "The Madison Papers," *American Archivist*, 20 (1957), 313–317.

52. One troublesome aspect of the punctuation in the *Frémont* is the treatment of the accent in Frémont's name. The editors have decided that the name can appear both with and without the accent; but they will not then allow it to appear both ways within a single document.

quired into; practices which are current tend to become self-perpetuating by inspiring uncritical acceptance.[53]

Some of the other editions of the late 1960s follow the same path. The goal of *The Papers of Henry Laurens* (University of South Carolina Press, 1968–), edited by Philip M. Hamer (and, later, George C. Rogers, Jr.),[54] is to follow "with some deviations" the Expanded Method of the *Harvard Guide*. Although the object is "not only an accurate but a readable text," the word "accurate" here cannot refer to punctuation, and modernization seems to take first place: "The flavor of the eighteenth century . . . has been maintained where clarity would not be sacrificed" (p. xxxi). The editorial function is conceived of as the accurate conveyance of "meaning" rather than of a text: "Superfluous commas may be omitted or reduced in number, and commas will be added when they will assist the reader, but no punctuation will be changed unless it is clear to the editors that no change of meaning will result." What is clear to one informed person, of course, may not be so to another, and it is debatable whether the "readability" gained is worth the price of not knowing what is in the original; reporting the evidence would not settle the question whether modernization is desirable, but it would make the situation more tolerable. The *Correspondence of James K. Polk* (Vanderbilt University Press, 1969–), edited by Herbert Weaver, also modernizes for "clarity," including grammar in what can be altered. "These changes have generally been made silently," Weaver says, "rather than risk cluttering the pages with editorial props that divert attention from the meaning or spirit of the writers" (p. xii)[55] —though the alterations themselves have already done that to some extent.

Not all the editions of the late 1960s, however, conform to the prevailing pattern. One is pleasantly surprised to find that Arthur S. Link's edition of *The Papers of Woodrow Wilson* (Princeton University Press, 1966–)[56] makes very few—and clearly defined—silent emendations

53. Jackson has described the process of getting an edition underway (drawing on his experiences with his more recent edition of George Washington's papers) in "Starting in the Papers Game," *Scholarly Publishing*, 3 (1971–72), 28–38. (He also comments on "The Papers of George Washington" in *Manuscripts*, 22 [1970], 2–11.)

54. See also Rogers's "The Papers of Henry Laurens," *University of South Carolina Magazine*, 1 (1965), 5–8.

55. The next sentence reads, "In the few instances where excessive editorial license was practiced, that fact has been noted." Surely the editor does not find his own alterations excessive; what is presumably meant is that some alterations are too great to go unnoted. But the reader has no way of knowing where the line has been drawn between silent and reported emendations.

56. See also Burl Noggle, "A Note on Historical Editing: The Wilson *Papers* in Perspective," *Louisiana History*, 8 (1967), 281–297.

(such as lowering superscript letters and replacing dashes with periods at the ends of sentences); otherwise, each document is "reproduced *exactly* as it appears in the original" (p. xvi), with any change marked by brackets (and deleted matter reported in angle brackets). It is true that the changes are made "for the sake of clarity," as in the other editions, but here the reader knows where they occur. Similarly, LeRoy P. Graf and Ralph W. Haskins, in *The Papers of Andrew Johnson* (University of Tennessee Press, 1967–),[57] make no changes of spelling or punctuation without using brackets (and apparently the only alteration of punctuation is the insertion of bracketed periods), although they add in the second volume (1970) that slips of the pen are eliminated. A third edition of these years, John Y. Simon's edition of *The Papers of Ulysses S. Grant* (Southern Illinois University Press, 1967–),[58] is particularly commendable. It can state flatly that "None of Grant's spelling, grammar, or punctuation has been altered" (p. xxxi), and it reports deletions in canceled type.

Most of the historical editions which followed in the 1970s unfortunately did not imitate these three editions but continued in the familiar pattern of partial modernization and selective recording of evidence. Robert A. Rutland's edition of *The Papers of George Mason* (University of North Carolina Press, 1970) states that it is following Boyd's *Jefferson*; while it retains inconsistent spellings, it silently regularizes the punctuation of sentence-endings, reduces Mason's capitalized pronouns to lower case, and inserts periods "in place of many a semicolon or colon that the writer obviously intended to function as a break rather than a pause" (p. xxii). Haskell M. Monroe, Jr., and James T. McIntosh, in *The Papers of Jefferson Davis* (Louisiana State University Press, 1971–) also silently emend punctuation according to modern standards, sometimes "correcting" a colon to a comma or a period; but, oddly, they do not insert what they regard as needed punctuation where no punctuation is present in the manuscript, representing the lack instead by an extended space. *The Papers of Joseph Henry* (Smithsonian Institution Press, 1972–), edited by Nathan Reingold, takes the Adams edition as its model and incorporates canceled matter in angle brackets if of "historical, psychological, or stylistic significance" (it is hard to

57. See also Graf, "Editing the Andrew Johnson Papers," *Mississippi Quarterly*, 15 (1962), 113–118.

58. For a survey of the history and reception of this edition, see Haskell Monroe, "The Grant Papers: A Review Article," *Journal of the Illinois State Historical Society*, 61 (1968), 463–472. In connection with the editorial archives amassed by the staff of the Grant edition, Simon has discussed the interesting question of the policy that should be established regarding access to such material, in "Editorial Projects as Derivative Archives," *College and Research Libraries*, 35 (1974), 291–294.

see how any canceled matter could be eliminated on these grounds). Although punctuation and spelling are said to be "usually faithfully preserved," "ubiquitous dashes are converted to modern commas and periods, and a few commas and periods are inserted silently where absolutely necessary for clear understanding" (p. xxxv).

Louis R. Harlan, in the second volume (1972) of *The Booker T. Washington Papers* (University of Illinois Press, 1972–),[59] describes his policy of silently correcting "typed and printed errors" and regularizing some punctuation, "except in semi-literate letters, which are reproduced exactly as written in order to avoid an inordinate amount of editorial intrusion into the document." A more valid reason for printing them as written is that the documents are more revealing unemended —an argument which could be applied to a much wider range of material. The first volume of this edition, containing Washington's published autobiographical writings, illustrates the way in which editors who primarily work with single manuscript texts sometimes fail to report adequately on multiple printed texts. Harlan's brief textual comment on *Up from Slavery*, for instance, merely says that the first book edition is used as copy-text in preference to the serialization in the *Outlook* because the magazine "did not include all that later appeared in the book version" and because "Negro" is spelled with a capital, as Washington wanted it, in the book but not in the magazine. Nothing is said to characterize the material added to the book or to explain the relation of the book text in other respects to that of the magazine, and no lising of variants is provided. The two texts do differ occasionally in punctuation and spelling ("coloured" in the book vs. "colored" in the magazine, for example), but the question of which text better reflects Washington's practice in these respects is never addressed.

In E. James Ferguson's *The Papers of Robert Morris* (University of Pittsburgh Press, 1973–), slips of the pen and "casual or incorrect punctuation" (p. xxxiv) are corrected: "Dashes and commas randomly distributed in the manuscripts are silently removed." Herbert A. Johnson's *The Papers of John Marshall* (University of North Carolina Press, 1974–) also silently emends some punctuation but interestingly confuses the author's intention with standards of correctness for a published work: sentences are supplied with opening capitals and closing periods "as necessary to preserve the original intention of the writer" (p. xxxvi). Apparently printed texts are reproduced with greater fidelity than manuscript texts, if that is what is meant by saying that dashes at the

---

59. See also Pete Daniel and Stuart Kaufman, "The Booker T. Washington Papers and Historical Editing at Maryland," *Maryland Historian*, 1 (1970), 23–29; and Harlan and Raymond W. Smock, "The Booker T. Washington Papers," *ibid.*, 6 (1975), 55–59.

ends of sentences are "silently omitted from documents other than those that reproduce a previous imprint." In other respects punctuation is not emended silently, for Johnson recognizes "the uncertainties involved in correcting any given writer's use of the comma." He very sensibly continues, "Should considerations of clarity dictate some explanatory insertion, the editors have added punctuation in square brackets, thereby permitting the reader to reach his own decision concerning the propriety of the editorial decision."[60] *The Papers of Daniel Webster* (University Press of New England, 1974–   ), edited by Charles M. Wiltse,[61] is similarly cautious about silent changes and makes none except to replace the dashes "intended" as periods; it is careful to retain misspellings and abbreviations or to alter them only in brackets. Merrill Jensen's two recent editions, however, go to the opposite extreme: both *The Documentary History of the First Federal Elections, 1788–1790* (with Robert A. Becker; University of Wisconsin Press, 1976–   ) and *The Documentary History of the Ratification of the Constitution* (State Historical Society of Wisconsin, 1976–   )[62] remove capitals and italics "except when they are evidently used by the author for emphasis," add punctuation "if needed to clarify meaning," and modernize spelling except for personal names (p. xvi); although official documents and a few others are given in a literal text, other printed texts are emended to eliminate certain eighteenth-century practices, "except when capital letters and italics were evidently used for emphasis by the author or the printer."

Enough has been said to show the characteristic textual practices of the NHPRC editions and other editions modeled on them. But I do not wish to imply that "historical" editions are the only ones which have indulged in partial modernization and selective reporting of emendations and have in general taken a superficial view of textual matters. A number of editions of the letters of literary figures—not particularly influenced by the modern practice of historians—are equally unsatisfactory. The influence, in fact, may go the other way, because *The Yale Edition of Horace Walpole's Correspondence* (Yale University Press, 1937–   ), edited by Wilmarth S. Lewis,[63] was the first of the modern

60. Johnson, incidentally, exactly reverses Boyd's practice regarding "&" and "&c.": the former he retains and the latter he changes to "etc."—"to conform to modern usage and typography."

61. See also his "The Papers of Daniel Webster," *Source*, 1 (1971), 6–8.

62. Cf. Robert E. Cushman, "A Documentary History of the Ratification of the Constitution and the First Ten Amendments," *Quarterly Legal Historian*, 1 (March 1962), 3–6.

63. Lewis has commented on "Editing Familiar Letters" in the *Listener*, 49 (1953), 597–598—reprinted in *Daedalus*, 86 (1955–57), 71–77—and on "Editing Private Correspondence" in *Proceedings of the American Philosophical Society*, 107 (1963), 289–293 (where he confuses the issue by asserting that any editor who favors literal transcriptions of eighteenth-

large-scale editions of a single figure and has been cited as an influential force in some of the historical accounts of the NHPRC editions.[64] Lewis did set a good example in his thorough explanatory annotation and in his careful headnote to each letter giving details about the manuscript. His treatment of the text, however, raises some questions. Although he indicates, with brackets, emendations of words, he makes numerous silent emendations of punctuation and spelling. The policy is to retain Walpole's punctuation (but not that of his correspondents) and his spelling of proper names, but "to normalize other spellings and capitalization." One of the justifications offered is "a considerable gain in readability and appearance." The "considerable" is debatable, but readability is at any rate the standard argument for modernization—although the question remains why thorough modernization is not therefore undertaken to make the text even more readable. Another justification is more troublesome: "What is amusing and 'flavoursome' in small doses becomes wearisome in large, and it imparts an air of quaintness to a text which was not apparent to the correspondents themselves" (p. xxxvi). Surely no serious reader will regard any characteristics of a particular time in history as merely quaint; all characteristics are part of the evidence for historical understanding, and it is an insult to the reader to suggest that he can better perceive the intended tone of a letter if certain features of it have been altered for him.

Similar problems arise in many other literary editions. Theodore Besterman's edition of *Voltaire's Correspondence* (Institut et Musée Voltaire, 1953–65)[65] is famous because of its enormous size; the completion of an edition of 21,000 letters is indeed an accomplishment, to say nothing of bringing it out a second time in a revised "definitive edition" (*Correspondence and Related Documents*, 1968–76). Although Voltaire's alterations are recorded in notes, the treatment of the main text is disappointing: the first edition reports that apostrophes are inserted and "a minimum of capital letters and punctuation, where lacking" (p. xiii), and the revised edition follows the same policy (pp. xvii–xviii; Besterman says, "without attempting to modernize, I have introduced a measure of regularity"). The edition offers an example of the kind of inconsistency which partial modernization almost invariably leads to: "When Voltaire used an accent it has been reproduced even if

century documents should also "wear a wig while at work and give up cigarettes for snuff").

64. As in Butterfield's "Historical Editing . . . The Recent Past," in Rundell's "Documentary Editing" (see note 10 above), or in Labaree's "Scholarly Editing" (see note 42 above). See also Butterfield's comments in *The Letters of Benjamin Rush* (American Philosophical Society, 1951), p. lxxvii.

65. See also his "Twenty Thousand Voltaire Letters," in *Editing Eighteenth-Century Texts*, ed. D. I. B. Smith (1968), pp. 7–24.

it now looks wrong, but when he omitted one it has been supplied."[66] Gordon S. Haight, in *The George Eliot Letters* (Yale University Press, 1954–55), says that his "principal concern has been the reader's convenience" (p. xxxv); though he retains spelling, he treats punctuation "a little more freely, adding or deleting an occasional mark to save rereading." In the same year Allan Wade, in *The Letters of W. B. Yeats* (Hart-Davis, 1954), argues for "correcting" both spelling and punctuation on the grounds that Yeats was poor at both. To retain Yeats's spelling would "in the long run appear merely tediously pedantic" (p. 16); Yeats's "faults" in punctuation, he says, "I have silently corrected, and I have not hesitated to introduce commas into sentences which, without them, are either ambiguous or almost meaningless" (p. 17)—obviously running the risk of giving those sentences meanings which Yeats did not intend. E. S. de Beer does not attempt to normalize punctuation in *The Diary of John Evelyn* (Clarendon Press, 1955) but does supply "without note a certain amount of punctuation" aimed "solely at intelligibility," arguing that for "strict linguistic study" one must consult the manuscripts (p. 68). In *The Swinburne Letters* (Yale University Press, 1959–62), Cecil Y. Lang says, "I have always tried to make readability my first concern" (p. xlix), and he follows the practice of reproducing printed texts "faithfully" but making some alterations in manuscript texts.

The same approach continues to appear in literary editions of the 1960s and 1970s. Harry T. Moore, in *The Collected Letters of D. H. Lawrence* (Heinemann, 1962), comments on some of Lawrence's seeming deficiencies of punctuation and states, "rather than belabour the reader by calling attention to these peccadilloes I have quietly done what was needed" (p. xxi). Rupert Hart-Davis silently emends spelling, capitalization, punctuation, and paragraphing in *The Letters of Oscar Wilde* (Hart-Davis, 1962). Wilde's habitual dashes, he says, "make the letters difficult to read, and I have re-punctuated normally as the sense seems to demand" (p. xi). Wilde also liked to capitalize words beginning with "t" and "h," "presumably because he enjoyed making those particular capitals more than their lower-case equivalents." Hart-Davis believes that "to perpetuate this whim would only irritate the reader," and he has "followed the standard usage wherever the capital clearly has no significance." But he has just told us what significance those two capitals have. Why should a writer not be allowed to indulge his

---

66. Precisely the opposite policy (correcting any accents present according to modern practice, but not supplying accents when they are omitted) is applied to the French in the sixth volume (1967) of *The Correspondence of Edmund Burke*, ed. Thomas W. Copeland *et al.* (Cambridge University Press and University of Chicago Press, 1958–).

"whims" in a letter? It is a perfect place for him to do so, because the text will not have to go through the hands of a publisher or a printer before reaching the intended audience. *The Letters of Henry Wadsworth Longfellow* (Belknap Press of Harvard University Press, 1966–   ), edited by Andrew Hilen, is like some of the NHPRC editions in silently correcting "mere slips" but not altering errors or variations in proper names. "Occasionally," Hilen says, "I have silently provided punctuation, or deleted it, in order to clarify meaning" (p. 13). Leon Edel, in the *Henry James Letters* (Belknap Press of Harvard University Press, 1974–   ), makes silent corrections "where they were obviously called for" (p. xxxv), but in the letters of the young James he retains "relevant misspellings" because "they are a part of the flavor of the letters." Unfortunately he does not extend this argument to the later letters.

I do not wish to prolong this litany unnecessarily. I have merely tried to cite a sufficient number of examples to show that there is a considerable body of editors whose approach to the editing of letters and journals is in the spirit of the policies set forth in Boyd's *Jefferson* and the *Harvard Guide*. And it is by no means only the historians who fall into this group. While it is true that most of the NHPRC editions—with only a few exceptions—are of this type, there are certainly a great many literary editors whose practice coincides with that of the NHPRC editors.[67] Most of the editions mentioned are praiseworthy in many respects: most of them reflect thorough research and exemplary annotation. But their treatment of the actual texts is relatively casual and unsophisticated by comparison. It is clear, from this survey, that one widely followed approach to editing documents assumes that some modernization is essential and that a silently modernized or corrected text can serve most purposes of historical study. The assumption is made, however, without adequate consideration of the role which such features as spelling and punctuation play in private documents and the extent to which they constitute part of the total body of evidence that the historian needs to have at his disposal. What I have said about these editions can perhaps begin to indicate why their textual policies are bound to seem unsatisfactory to anyone who has given careful thought to textual matters and the nature of written communication.

III

At the time when Boyd's *Jefferson* was about to come out and the NHPC to be revitalized, there were some editions other than the Wal-

---

67. Although, it is fair to add, none of the editions with a CEAA or CSE emblem can be classed in this category.

pole which might have been turned to as models, and it is unfortunate that they did not have more influence at that strategic moment. The Walpole edition, because of the enormous size of the undertaking, may have seemed a closer parallel to the large editions which were projected to accommodate the masses of papers accumulated by statesmen; but certain smaller editions could have offered a sounder textual policy. Paget Toynbee and Leonard Whibley's three-volume edition of *Correspondence of Thomas Gray* (Clarendon Press, 1935), for instance, states, "The text is printed as Gray or his correspondents wrote it, with the spelling, punctuation, use of capitals, and abbreviations of the originals" (p. xxiii); and Ralph L. Rusk's six-volume edition of *The Letters of Ralph Waldo Emerson* (Columbia University Press, 1939) requires little space for an explanation of editorial policy, for Rusk says simply, "I have tried to print a literal text, with no interpolated corrections or apologies" (p. v). Gordon N. Ray's four-volume edition of *The Letters and Private Papers of William Makepeace Thackeray* (Harvard University Press, 1945–46) is a model edition. Ray presents "a literal text" and is not bothered, as so many editors seem to be, by sentences which end with dashes rather than periods. In an admirable statement, he sums up why it is important to preserve in print the spelling and punctuation of the manuscripts:

Thackeray, the most informal of letter writers, was a past master at shaping his sentences in the precise contour of his thoughts by oddities of punctuation and orthography and by whimsical distortions of words not unlike Swift's "little language" in the *Journal to Stella*. Not to reproduce these peculiarities faithfully would be to falsify the tone and blur the meaning of the letters. (p. lxxiii)

Although the details which lead to this conclusion might have to be altered somewhat in the case of other writers, it is difficult to see how the conclusion itself could be improved upon as a guiding statement for all editors of letters.

Another notable edition, which began to appear just after the first volume of the Jefferson but early enough that it could have been influential in the formative days of the new NHPC, is Elting E. Morison's eight-volume edition of *The Letters of Theodore Roosevelt* (Harvard University Press, 1951–54). The letters are "printed as written without further indication of Roosevelt's frequent and startling departures from the norm of accepted usage in spelling." Morison, like Ray, has given careful thought to the rationale for such a policy, and he makes an intelligent statement of the case:

No doubt this will strike the readers, as it has from time to time struck the editors, as a piece of unnecessarily solemn scholarship. But it seemed simpler, and safer on the whole, to leave Roosevelt's own text untouched rather than to interfere from time to time to correct or alter words or phrases to conform to what must be, in some cases, assumed meanings. Also these letters may serve as interesting documents on causation, since they were written by the President to whom the mission of simplified spelling commended itself. (p. xix)

Also during these years historical editors in particular should have been aware of the excellent example being set by Clarence E. Carter in his major project, *The Territorial Papers of the United States* (Government Printing Office, 1934–); it was in 1956, in the introduction to the twenty-second volume, that he made an important statement of his aim of "literal reproduction."[68] Even more persuasively than in his *Historical Editing*, he pleads the case for an unmodernized text:

in brief, the idiosyncrasies of both the writer and the age are preserved. To proceed otherwise would be to bypass certain significant facets of the cultural status of an earlier era as glimpsed in the character of the written record, which, it is submitted, equates with the bare facts of politics and wars as historical grist. (pp. viii–ix)

Modernization, he rightly concludes, "tends to obscure rather than to clarify." Some literary editors, too, were commenting in the 1950s on the importance of exact transcription of letters and journals. R. W. Chapman, reproducing the manuscripts "as closely as typography admits" in his three-volume edition of *The Letters of Samuel Johnson* (Clarendon Press, 1952), points out the value of errors:

I have preserved Johnson's occasional inadvertences, such as the omission or repetition of small words, partly because they furnish some indication of his state of health or his state of mind, partly because they show the sort of error to which he was prone and may therefore help us in judging the text of those letters of which the originals are lost. (p. viii)[69]

Kathleen Coburn, at the beginning of *The Notebooks of Samuel Taylor Coleridge* (Pantheon Books [later Princeton University Press],

68. For references to two similar statements of his, see notes 27 and 28 above. His earlier edition of *The Correspondence of General Thomas Gage* (Yale University Press, 1931–33) is characteristically careful but does not contain an analogous announcement of textual policy.

69. Johnson's spelling is of particular interest, too: "I have respected Johnson's spelling. It was worth while to show that the great systematic lexicographer did not in his own practice achieve a consistent orthography, and was conspicuously careless about proper names" (p. x). See also Chapman's "Proposals for a New Edition of Johnson's Letters," *Essays and Studies*, 12 (1926), 47–62.

1957–   ),[70] agrees, stating that "Slips of the pen are respected, in conformity with the argument of Dr. Chapman in editing Johnson, that such things have their own interest and significance" (p. xxx), and she adds that Coleridge himself remarked on this point.[71] Howard Horsford, editing Melville's *Journal of a Visit to Europe and the Levant* (Princeton University Press, 1955), suggests the importance of precision in his careful descriptions of cancellations and his thorough discussion of the difficulties of Melville's handwriting. Hyder Edward Rollins, in *The Letters of John Keats* (Harvard University Press, 1958), notes that "Keats penned his sentences rapidly and spontaneously, not carefully and artfully" (p. 17), and therefore his "queer punctuation" and "occasional grammatical slips" are indicative and should not be rectified. And Thomas H. Johnson's edition of *The Letters of Emily Dickinson* (Belknap Press of Harvard University Press, 1958) presents all holograph letters "in their verbatim form" (p. xxv), which involves many dashes.[72] With editions of this kind available to point the way, the NHPC editors of the late 1950s were unwise to turn in a different direction.

In 1960 four editions appeared which, in their somewhat differing ways, represent the approaches followed by the best of the literary editions of the 1960s and 1970s. All are characterized by scrupulous reporting of details of the manuscripts, but what distinguishes a number of them from most earlier careful editions of manuscripts is a system—not unlike that long in use for printed copy-texts—whereby certain categories of emendation can be allowed in the text, with the original readings preserved in notes or lists. Henry Nash Smith and William M. Gibson's edition of *Mark Twain-Howells Letters* (Belknap Press of Harvard University Press, 1960) involves no normalizing of punctuation or spelling, and it records significant cancellations. James Franklin Beard, in *The Letters and Journals of James Fenimore Cooper* (Belknap Press of Harvard University Press, 1960–68), does alter some punctua-

70. Cf. her "Editing the Coleridge Notebooks," in *Editing Texts of the Romantic Period*, ed. John D. Baird (1972), pp. 7–25.

71. It is surprising, however, given this policy, that she regularizes Coleridge's "careless apostrophes" (p. xxxii)—especially in view of the variable placement of apostrophes which occurs even in printed matter in the nineteenth century.

72. Examples of editions in these years which present manuscript texts almost, but not entirely, in "verbatim" or "literal" form are *The Letters of William Gilmore Simms*, ed. Mary C. Simms Oliphant, Alfred Taylor Odell, and T. C. Duncan Eaves (University of South Carolina Press, 1952–56); and *Collected Letters of Samuel Taylor Coleridge*, ed. Earl Leslie Griggs (Clarendon Press, 1956–71). Both these retain the original spelling and punctuation but silently eliminate such slips as repetitions. *The Collected Works of Abraham Lincoln*, ed. Roy P. Basler *et al.* (Rutgers University Press, 1953), silently corrects typographical errors in printed texts but brackets all emendations in manuscripts; Basler feels, however, that Lincoln's "habitual dash at the end of a sentence or following an abbreviation" must be altered to a period.

tion for clarity and amend some spellings, but these editorial alterations are recorded in footnotes (except for a few specific categories),[73] while "legible cancellations" are incorporated into the text within angle brackets. The text of Merrell R. Davis and William H. Gilman's edition of *The Letters of Herman Melville* (Yale University Press, 1960) also incorporates a few emendations of punctuation for clarity, but they are all listed in the meticulous textual notes at the end. These notes additionally include such details as foreshortened (hastily written) words: one can learn from them that what appears in the edited text as "thing," for example, resembles "thng" in the manuscript (merely misspelled words, of course, are not altered). Cancellations are all transcribed, either in the text (in angle brackets, along with braces for insertions) or in the textual notes. *The Journals and Miscellaneous Notebooks of Ralph Waldo Emerson* (Belknap·Press of Harvard University Press, 1960–   ), edited by William H. Gilman *et al.*, goes farther in the use of symbols to record as much textual information as possible within the text. It aims to come "as close to a *literatim* transcription" as is feasible in print (p. xxxviii) and does indicate the stages of Emerson's revision with great precision; some categories of editorial alteration, here too, are not labeled in the text but are reported in textual notes at the end. The volumes of Emerson *Journals* which appeared after the CEAA emblem was instituted have received the emblem, and later CEAA editions of journals further illustrate the modern practice of the full recording of manuscript characteristics. Washington Irving's *Journals and Notebooks* (University of Wisconsin Press, 1969–   ), as edited by Henry A. Pochmann *et al.*,[74] is uncompromisingly literal (it respects Irving's lower-case sentence openings, for example) and contains one of the most thorough discussions in print (pp. xix–xxvi) of the problems involved in exact transcription (amply demonstrating that the process is not mechanical). Claude M. Simpson's edition of *The American Notebooks* of Nathaniel Hawthorne (Ohio State University Press, 1972), as is usual with CEAA volumes, makes some emendations in the text but records them, as well as authorial alterations of the manuscript, in lists at the end. And Mark Twain's *Notebooks & Journals* (University of California Press, 1975–   ), as edited by Frederick Anderson *et al.*, offers an

73. Such as closing parentheses and quotation marks. Although Cooper's use of a dash for a period is respected, sentences are nevertheless made to begin with capital letters.

74. Pochmann, as general editor of the Irving edition, was instrumental in formulating the policy for editing the journals; the volume editor for the first volume (1969) is Nathalia Wright and for the third (1970) Walter A. Reichart. William H. Gilman has said that the Irving editors "have spelled out their answers to problems [of journal editing] in more detail than any other conscientious and sophisticated editors I know of" (see his important review, cited in note 105 below).

excellent discussion of editorial procedures (pp. 575–84) and is a model of how to combine the emendation of certain obvious errors (always listed at the end, accompanied by "doubtful readings") with the preservation of "the texture of autograph documents" (which contain "irregularities, inconsistencies, errors, and cancellations").[75]

These are not the only praiseworthy editions of letter and journals in the 1960s and 1970s,[76] and a few others deserve mention not simply for their high standards of literal transcription but for the cogency of their statements justifying that approach. *Shelley and His Circle* (Harvard University Press, 1961–), edited from the holdings of the Carl H. Pforzheimer Library by Kenneth Neill Cameron (later by Donald H. Reiman),[77] surpasses all these other editions in its efforts to reproduce in type the features of manuscripts—printing careted material, for example, above the line and in smaller type. The aim is "the traditional one" of producing "a foundational text . . . from which other editors may depart as they wish," and the rationale is stated with great effectiveness:

75. Cancellations are thus included in the text, but there is also a list of "Details of Inscription" at the end, making clear the stages of revision at each point.

76. Harold Williams's edition of *The Correspondence of Jonathan Swift* (Clarendon Press, 1963–65) also prints the texts with "exact care," preserving "variants in spelling, capitalization, and punctuation" (p. xviii), including the period-dash combination at the ends of sentences; and Elvan Kintner's edition of *The Letters of Robert Browning and Elizabeth Barrett Barrett, 1845–1846* (Belknap Press of Harvard University Press, 1969) similarly presents a literal text, indicating insertions with arrows and allowing sentences to end with dashes and without periods. Some generally successful editions of these years do, however, include a small amount of modernization or normalizing. A. Rupert Hall and Marie Boas Hall's edition of *The Correspondence of Henry Oldenburg* (University of Wisconsin Press, 1965–) follows the spelling and punctuation of the original but expands some abbreviations. Chester L. Shaver's *The Early Years* (Clarendon Press, 1967) and Mary Moorman's *The Middle Years* (1969) in the revised edition of *The Letters of William and Dorothy Wordsworth* preserve the spelling and punctuation of the originals, but they inexplicably expand ampersands. Sentences are allowed to end with a dash and no period, but the "frequent ampersands have been changed to 'and' for the convenience of the reader" (Moorman, p. ix); it is difficult to see how ampersands constitute a sufficient inconvenience to warrant alteration in any case, but particularly when other potentially more troublesome practices are not altered. M. R. D. Foot and H. C. G. Matthew's edition of *The Gladstone Diaries* (Clarendon Press, 1968–) follows the original punctuation and spelling "as closely as can be" (p. xxxviii) but expands some abbreviations and alters dashes to periods or commas "as the sense requires." The policy of the second volume of the "Research Edition" of *The Yale Edition of The Private Papers of James Boswell* is to normalize capitals and periods for sentence openings and closings and to ignore insignificant deletions, but to report any alterations of punctuation to "relieve ambiguities" and any corrections of "patent inadvertencies" in spelling; see Marshall Waingrow's edition of *The Correspondence and Other Papers of James Boswell Relating to the Making of the "Life of Johnson"* (McGraw-Hill, 1969), pp. lxxix–lxxxiii. (Cf. Frederick A. Pottle, "The Yale Editions of the Private Papers of James Boswell," *Ventures*, 2 [Winter 1963], 11–15.)

77. See also Reiman's "Editing Shelley," in *Editing Texts of the Romantic Period*, ed. John D. Baird (1972), pp. 27–45.

There is, moreover, it seems to us, aside from the question of accuracy of representation a positive value in this traditional method which is insufficiently stressed. Changes, no matter how trivial, take the reader one remove from the author. An author's own punctuation, his cancellations and interlineations, even his misspellings, play a part in expressing mood or personality. Retained, they make a text no more difficult to read than an everyday letter from a friend. And even if an occasional passage could be made clearer by changing it, such exceptions are not, in our opinion, balanced by the total loss. (p. xxxiv)

Herbert M. Schueller and Robert L. Peters, in their edition of *The Letters of John Addington Symonds* (Wayne State University Press, 1967–69), give some additional reasons for offering a literal text:

We know that sometimes a quiet changing of manuscripts meets with approval; this practice, however, seems indefensible with respect to Symonds because, 1) the letters were not edited by *him* for publication, 2) they extend over his whole lifetime and show the influences of maturity on his personal expression, 3) the continuing characteristics are often Victorian practices rather than personal idiosyncrasies, and 4) to make deliberate changes in the originals is to go beyond the prerogatives even of editors. (p. 14)

In *The Journals and Letters of Fanny Burney* (Clarendon Press, 1972–), Joyce Hemlow[78] allows errors to stand "as the normal hazards of hasty or spontaneous writing" and believes that "the twentieth-century reader probably needs few such props" as modernization (p. lviii). Leslie A. Marchand, in his editorial introduction to *"In my hot youth": Byron's Letters and Journals* (Murray, 1973–), adds further to the strength of the case:

Byron's punctuation follows no rules of his own or others' making. He used dashes and commas freely, but for no apparent reason, other than possibly for natural pause between phrases, or sometimes for emphasis. He is guilty of the "comma splice", and one can seldom be sure where he intended to end a sentence, or whether he recognized the sentence as a unit of expression. . . . Byron himself recognized his lack of knowledge of the logic or the rules of punctuation. . . . It is not without reason then that most editors, including R. E. Prothero, have imposed sentences and paragraphs on him in line with their interpretation of his intended meaning. It is my feeling, however, that this detracts from the impression of Byronic spontaneity and the onrush of ideas in his letters, without a compensating gain in clarity. In fact, it may often arbitrarily impose a meaning or an emphasis not intended by the writer. I feel that there is less danger of distortion if the reader may see

78. See also her "Letters and Journals of Fanny Burney: Establishing the Text," in *Editing Eighteenth-Century Texts*, ed. D. I. B. Smith (1968), pp. 25–43.

exactly how he punctuated and then determine whether a phrase between commas or dashes belongs to one sentence or another. (p. 28)

Marchand, like most of the other advocates of this point of view, adds that the unmodernized text is not difficult to read; but the reasons for not modernizing, it is clear, are of sufficient weight that the question of whether the resulting text is somewhat difficult to read is of secondary importance.[79]

The statements quoted here, which make a number of different points and refer to a variety of periods and kinds of material, add up to an impressive argument and are no doubt sufficient in themselves as a criticism of the partially modernized and silently emended editions described earlier. Merely to juxtapose comments on editorial policy from the two kinds of edition is to show up the weaknesses of attempting to justify modernization and silent alterations in scholarly editions of historical documents. But it will perhaps be useful to try to sort out more clearly the issues involved, especially since there has been so little discussion of the matter, at least in connection with the editions of statesmen's papers. Although a voluminous literature has grown up around the NHPRC editions, it contains very little commentary on textual procedures, and what there is seldom touches on fundamental questions. The NHPRC editions have probably been more extensively reviewed than the CEAA editions; but in both fields it is difficult to find reviewers who can adequately analyze textual policies, and the reviews of NHPRC volumes in particular have almost consistently slighted—or ignored completely, except for a perfunctory word of praise—the textual aspects of the editions.[80] The historical significance of the contents of these edi-

---

79. Another example of the kind of significance which punctuation can have is offered by Desmond Pacey, in "On Editing the Letters of Frederick Philip Grove," in *Editing Canadian Texts*, ed. Francess G. Halpenny (1975), pp. 49–73; Grove placed slang words in quotation marks, and Pacey retains them "since they indicate something of his stiffness of character" (p. 72). (Pacey, however, favors silent emendation of spelling errors, expansion of abbreviations, and regular italicization of titles.)

80. Reiman (see note 77 above) comments on the "dearth of knowledge and standards of judgment of editing . . . among those who review such publications [editions] in learned journals" (p. 37). And L. H. Butterfield, in "Editing American Historical Documents" (see note 10 above), says, "It is in fact shocking to find how low the threshold of tolerance sometimes is for poorly edited materials among those who should know better" (p. 98). Examples of the praise bestowed on the editorial practices of some of the historical editions, without a serious analysis of those practices, are the following: the Jefferson edition is said to be provided "with every ingenuity of typographical suggestion of the state of the manuscripts" (*Times Literary Supplement*, 6 April 1951, p. 206); the Jefferson practices are called "so satisfactory as to require only minor modifications to adapt them to each later project" (*American Archivist*, 25 [1962], 449); the Clay edition reflects "the precision that has come to distinguish the science of historical editing at its mid-twentieth century peak of perfection" (*Journal of Southern History*, 26 [1960], 238); "Boyd and his fellow editors have per-

tions and the quality of the explanatory annotation—on which the reviews concentrate—are important matters, but the way in which the text has been established and presented is surely of first importance in evaluating an edition.

Considerable criticism has been directed at the NHPRC editions but for essentially irrelevant or trivial reasons. One objection, raised by Leonard W. Levy, for example, in his reviews of the Madison edition, is that the explanatory annotation is carried to excessive lengths.[81] Another criticism questions the choice of material to be edited. J. H. Plumb, among others, believes that too much attention is paid to unimportant documents,[82] and Jesse Lemisch argues that the pattern of figures chosen to be edited reflects a bias "in the direction of white male political leaders."[83] Whatever justice there may be to these opinions, they have nothing to do with the quality of the editions themselves. If the annotation is accurate and helpful, it will be of use, and there is little point in wishing there were less of it; and any document or figure is of some historical interest. Individual tastes regarding what material is worth spending time on, and judgments about priorities, will naturally vary; one may deplore another's choice of subject, but it is unrealistic to criticize accomplished work for having usurped time better spent on something else. Still another frequent complaint is that letterpress edi-

---

fected techniques of research, skills of analysis, and modes of presentation" (*Louisiana History*, 8 [1967], 282).

81. *Mississippi Valley Historical Review*, 49 (1962–63), 504–6; *Journal of American History*, 51 (1964–65), 299–301. The first refers to "the editorial imperialism and compulsiveness that characterize these volumes"; the second comments on "monumentally trifling footnotes" and "fantastically detailed annotations" and finds the editors "making the profession of editing look purely pedantic."

82. Writing on "Horace Walpole at Yale" in the *New York Review of Books*, 5, no. 4 (30 September 1965), 9–10, Plumb objects to publishing "every scrap of writing committed to paper by one man" (which demands "little more than industry and accuracy") and asserts that Wilmarth Lewis started "a new and dangerous form of historical activity" which has "spread among historical and literary scholars like measles among the Aztecs, and as disastrously." Similarly Esmond Wright, in "Making History," *Listener*, 68 (1962), 803–804, names five ways in which the editions threaten the historian; one of them is the scale of the editions, for all the facts "blur rather than reveal."

83. In "The American Revolution Bicentennial and the Papers of Great White Men: A Preliminary Critique of Current Documentary Publication Programs," *AHA Newsletter*, 9, no. 5 (November 1971), 7–21 (p. 9). "The present publications program," Lemisch believes, "should be seen in part as a vestige of the arrogant nationalism and elitism of the 'fifties" (p. 11), and he suggests other kinds of papers worthy of attention, such as the records of ordinary and "inarticulate" people which would provide materials for studying popular protest, racism, sexism, and so on. Some correspondence relating to his article appeared in the same journal in May 1972 (10, no. 3, 25–28). The article was later excerpted in the *Maryland Historian*, 6 (1975), 43–50, followed by a new article in which Lemisch states that little progress has been made since 1971 in editing the papers of undistinguished persons: "The Papers of a Few Great Black Men and a Few Great White Women," pp. 60–66.

tions are too expensive and time-consuming to produce and that microfilm publication of the documents would be cheaper, faster, and more appropriate.[84] Certainly the well-established microfilm publication programs of the NHPRC, the National Archives, the Library of Congress, and various state historical societies are to be praised;[85] but making photographic reproductions of document collections widely available is by no means a substitute for editing those documents,[86] as Julian Boyd and Lester Cappon, among others, have effectively pointed out.[87] The skilled editor, employing his critical intelligence and fund of historical detail, establishes a text which marks an advance in knowledge over the mere existence of the document itself. Microfilm editions of unedited documents do not obviate true editions; but editing takes time, and one is back at the earlier question of individual priorities for spending time.

These controversies are really peripheral to the main business of editing. Since individual priorities do differ, anyone may decide not to become an editor; but for those who elect to undertake editorial projects, surely the first priority is the text itself, its treatment and presentation. And when one considers the divergences of textual policy which

84. For example, Gerald Gunther, reviewing the Adams papers in the *Harvard Law Review*, 75 (1961–62), 1669–80, argues that "the present emphasis on multi-volume publication projects" is the "slowest and costliest" way to make manuscripts accessible; he believes that the NHPC has inadequately identified "the purposes of publishing manuscript collections," confusing publication with printing, and that more use should be made of microfilm (esp. pp. 1670–76). Steven R. Boyd, in "Form of Publication: A Key to the Widespread Availability of Documents," *AHA Newsletter*, 10, no. 4 (September 1972), 24–26, also favors microfilm, asserting that the NHPC letterpress program "is failing to make documentary sources generally available" and that "no new letterpress projects should be begun at this time." General discussions of alternatives are Charles E. Lee, "Documentary Reproduction: Letterpress Publication—Why? What? How?", *American Archivist*, 28 (1965), 351–365; and Robert L. Zangrando, "Alternatives to Publication," *Maryland Historian*, 7 (1976), 71–76 (which suggests that historians in general should give more consideration to forms of publication other than letterpress).

85. Some accounts of these programs can be found in Fred Shelley, "The Presidential Papers Program of the Library of Congress," *American Archivist*, 25 (1962), 429–433; Wayne C. Grover, "Toward Equal Opportunities for Scholarship," *Journal of American History*, 52 (1965–66), 715–724; L. H. Butterfield, "The Scholar's One World," *American Archivist*, 29 (1966), 343–361; Frank B. Evans, "American Personal Papers," *Quarterly Journal of the Library of Congress*, 24 (1967), 147–151; and Shelley, "The Choice of a Medium for Documentary Publication," *American Archivist*, 32 (1969), 363–368.

86. It should also be recognized that even photographic reproductions can distort the originals. Cf. note 36 above.

87. For example, see Boyd, "Some Animadversions" (see note 14 above), p. 51, and " 'God's Altar . . .' " (see note 10 above), p. 21; Cappon, "The Historian as Editor," in *In Support of Clio: Essays in Memory of Herbert A. Kellar*, ed. William B. Hesseltine and Donald R. McNeil (1958), pp. 173–193, and "A Rationale" (see note 10 above), pp. 72–73. The debate over the role of the editor as an interpretive historian is further examined by Cappon in "Antecedents of the Rolls Series: Issues in Historical Editing," *Journal of the Society of Archivists*, 4 (1970–73), 358–369.

distinguish most NHPRC editions from the CEAA and CSE editions, the first question to ask is whether there is an essential difference between the materials of historical interest and those of literary interest that would necessitate differing treatments. Nathan Reingold, in a letter to the *American Scholar* (45 [1976], 319) commenting on Peter Shaw's article, suggests such an explanation, pointing out that the CEAA editors work with printed texts, whereas the historical editors for the most part deal with thousands of "scrappy and informal" bits of manuscript. It is true that the bulk of the CEAA and CSE editions are of works which have previously appeared in print,[88] but those editions do include numerous volumes of manuscript letters and journals, and of course in the literary field in general many editions of such material exist. It may also be true that letters predominate in editions of statesmen's papers, but the comprehensive editions do include speeches, reports, and other works of a public nature normally intended for distribution in printed form. Is a letter written by a literary figure in some way fundamentally different from a letter written by a statesman? Both are historical documents: literary history is still history, and all letters offer historical evidence. And either letter may be regarded as "literature": a statesman may produce masterly letters, and a literary figure may write pedestrian ones. Is a novel or a poem fundamentally different from a work which a statesman prepares for publication? At their extremes, imaginative literature and factual reporting seem to be different kinds of communication, but in between there is a large area in which they overlap. No clear line can be drawn between writing which is "literature" and writing which is not. Certainly the editor of an individual's whole corpus of papers is likely to encounter writings which can be regarded either way: some of Franklin's and Jefferson's best-known writings have often been classified and analyzed as literary works, whereas Hawthorne's *Life of Franklin Pierce* and Whitman's journalism are not always considered literature. There sometimes seems to be an assumption that close attention to textual nuances—and thus the need for recording textual details—is more vital to the study of literary works and other writings by literary figures.[89] Apparently that is part of Fred-

---

88. Even in these cases, however, a manuscript rather than a printed edition may be chosen as the proper copy-text.

89. Robert Halsband, editor of *The Complete Letters of Lady Mary Wortley Montagu* (Clarendon Press, 1965–67), remarks, "It seems paradoxical that political and social historians—who, one would think, are sticklers for exactness—should prefer normalized texts, whereas literary historians strive for exact transcription"; and he conjectures that to the former "the facts are paramount," whereas the latter are concerned also with "nuances of style" (pp. 30–31). See his discussion of "Editing the Letters of Letter-Writers," *SB*, 11 (1958), 25–37—a useful survey of the problems involved (although it favors partial normalization and selective recording of deletions). Another general survey is James Sutherland's

erick B. Tolles's point when he criticizes the "zeal" of the editor of George Mercer's papers for her "reverent handling" of the texts: "it seems important to remind ourselves," he says, "that they are not sacred codices of Holy Writ or variant quartos of *Hamlet*."[90] He also means, of course, that Mercer's papers are not as important as *Hamlet*. But neither the importance nor the literary quality of a piece of writing determines the amount of attention that must be paid to nuances of expression; if one seriously wishes to understand a text, whatever it is, no aspect of it can be slighted.[91] There is no fundamental distinction, then, from a textual point of view, between the materials edited by the historian and those edited by the literary scholar. Letters, journals, published works, and manuscripts of unpublished works fall into both fields; all of them are historical documents, and any of them can be "literary."[92]

A distinction does need to be made, but not between literary and historical materials. Rather, the important distinction is between two kinds of writings which both historians and literary scholars have to deal with: works intended for publication and private papers.[93] Works intended for publication are generally expected to conform to certain conventions not applicable to private documents. For example, a finished work is expected to incorporate the author's latest decisions about what word he wishes to stand at each spot; in a private notebook jotting, however, or even in a letter to a friend, he can suggest alternative words and is under no obligation to come to a decision among them.[94] Simi-

---

"Dealing with Correspondences," *Times Literary Supplement*, 26 January 1973, pp. 79–80 (in a special issue on "Letters as Literature").

90. In his review of Lois Mulkearn's edition of the *George Mercer Papers Relating to the Ohio Company of Virginia* (University of Pittsburgh Press, 1954), *Pennsylvania Magazine of History and Biography*, 74 (1955), 113–114. Cf. Julian Boyd's reply in "Some Animadversions" (see note 14 above), p. 50.

91. Reuben Gold Thwaites, early in the century, recognized the literary interest in essentially nonliterary materials in his edition of the *Original Journals of the Lewis and Clark Expedition, 1804–1806* (Dodd, Mead, 1904–5); he prints the texts of successive drafts because "in a publication of original records it appears advisable to exhibit the literary methods of the explorers" (p. lvii).

92. The 1951 and 1954 reports of the NHPC (see note 8 above) include the names of literary figures in the lists of papers which need to be edited; the 1963 report comments, "American literature also presents a picture of compelling need. With few exceptions, no scholarly and acceptable texts of the works of any national figure in the field of American letters are available" (p. 28), and adds that it is prepared to give to literary editions "such assistance and encouragement as may be within its power."

93. Reingold approaches this point in his letter to the *American Scholar* when he acknowledges that occasionally "historical editors may reprint publications or present the texts of unpublished writings intended for print."

94. One of the best assessments of the importance of this practice is made by Timothy L. S. Sprigge in his edition of *The Correspondence of Jeremy Bentham* (University of London Athlone Press, 1968–): "Special mention must be made of Bentham's habit, even in his letters, of writing alternative words and phrases above the line without deleting the

larly, he can spell and punctuate as he pleases in a private document, but he will have difficulty getting a work published if it does not conform, at least to some extent, to current standards. Whether or not a writer really wishes to have his manuscript altered by a publisher's editor or a printer to bring it into such conformity is a complex question of intention, and editorial debate on this issue is likely to continue. Some editors feel that a surviving completed manuscript of a published work is the proper choice for copy-text because it reflects the author's characteristics more accurately, while others feel that the published text should be the copy-text because the author expected his manuscript to be subjected to the normal routines of publishing. No doubt the answer will vary in different situations, but this is not the place to explore the question.[95] The point here is to contrast that situation with the very different one which exists for private documents. In the case of notebooks, diaries, letters, and the like, whatever state they are in constitutes their finished form, and the question of whether the writer "intended" something else is irrelevant. One still sometimes hears the argument that an editor must make alterations in such documents because the writer would have expected to make changes in them for publication. If the writer had in fact prepared them for publication, they would then no longer be private documents but works intended for the public; they would have passed through the usual steps leading to publication, as any other work would, and the author probably would have made alterations in them, since the original documents would be parallel with the rough or semifinal drafts of other kinds of works. But when the writer did not prepare his own letters or diaries for publication, they remain private papers. The scholarly editor who later wishes to make them public is not in the same position as the writer or the writer's contemporary publisher. Not only is it impossible for him to know what the writer or his publisher would have done to them; but if he presents them as anything more polished or finished than they were left by the writer, he is falsifying their nature. A journal, as a piece of writing for one's own use, is in its final form whenever one stops adding to it; a letter, as a communication to a private audience of one or two, is in its

original. In draft letters his intention was presumably to make a final choice at a later stage. But when writing to intimates he often left these alternatives standing; and this is at times a literary device of a distinctive character, the effect of which is that the sense of the passage arises from an amalgam of the two (or more) readings" (p. xxi). (After this admirable statement, it comes as a surprise to learn that Sprigge does not always print these alternative readings; to do so, he says, "would seriously imperil the readability of the text." And the ones he includes are marked in such a way as to be indistinguishable from interlinear insertions that replaced canceled matter.)

95. I have commented on this matter in "The Editorial Problem of Final Authorial Intention," *SB*, 29 (1976), 167–211 (esp. pp. 183–191); cf. *SB*, 28 (1975), 222–227.

final form whenever it is posted. The writer is under no constraint to conform to any particular convention in these writings, except to the extent that he hopes a letter will be comprehensible to its recipient. Any idiosyncrasies in them—however contrary to the standards for published works—are an essential part of their character.

These considerations lead to the conclusion that a scholarly edition of letters or journals should not contain a text which has editorially been corrected, made consistent, or otherwise smoothed out. Errors and inconsistencies are part of the total texture of the document and are part of the evidence which the document preserves relating to the writer's habits, temperament, and mood. Modernization, too, is obviously out of place. While it is not the same thing as the correction of errors or inconsistencies, the line between the two is often difficult to establish. Even in many published works the spelling, punctuation, and capitalization are inconsistent, and to assume that the writers or publishers intended them to be consistent or cared whether they were consistent or not is to read into the situation a point of view held by many people today but one that has apparently not always been held. Correcting errors is somewhat different, since by definition an error is not intended; but it is frequently difficult to avoid a modern bias in deciding what constitutes an error. Editors of published works are increasingly recognizing that to regularize or to make certain supposed corrections is to modernize.[96]

In the case of private documents, then, where errors and inconsistencies are an integral part of the text, the argument against modernization is doubly strong. Indeed, the position that the text of a *scholarly* edition of any material can ever be modernized is indefensible. Many editors of literary works have long understood this fact,[97] and it is difficult to explain why such a large number of editors of private documents have, during the same period, neglected it. They are not always cognizant of a distinction between correcting and modernizing; but to sub-

96. A cogent statement of this position is Hershel Parker's "Regularizing Accidentals: The Latest Form of Infidelity," *Proof*, 3 (1973), 1–20, which also contains an excellent summary of the arguments against "full" or "partial" modernization. See also Joseph Moldenhauer's comments in his edition of Thoreau's *The Maine Woods* (Princeton University Press, 1972), pp. 399–400.

97. See, for example, W. W. Greg's strong statement of the position in *The Editorial Problem in Shakespeare* (2nd ed., 1951), pp. l–liii; and Fredson Bowers, "Old-Spelling Editions of Dramatic Texts," in *Studies in Honor of T. W. Baldwin*, ed. D. C. Allen (1958), pp. 9–15 (reprinted in his *Essays in Bibliography, Text, and Editing* [1975], pp. 289–295 [esp. pp. 291–293]). A standard exposition of many of the arguments for and against modernization is found in two essays of 1960: John Russell Brown (favoring modernization), "The Rationale of Old-Spelling Editions of the Plays of Shakespeare and His Contemporaries," *SB*, 13 (1960), 49–67; and Arthur Brown (opposing modernization), ". . . A Rejoinder," *ibid.*, 69–76.

ject such documents to either is to violate their integrity. Ultimately the position of these editors rests on a failure to grasp the significance of punctuation, capitalization, and spelling as functional elements of written expression. They think, as a result, that they can make alterations "for clarity" and "for the reader's convenience" without affecting the content of the document in any important way. In most instances, they greatly exaggerate the difficulty of reading the original text, and it is hard to see how the reader's "convenience" is really served by changing a dash to a period, an ampersand to "and," or an upper-case letter to lower case.[98] What, in the end, do they accomplish, other than depriving the reader of the experience of reading the original text? Is the text "clearer" as a result of their labors? Frequently it is less clear, because documentary editors rarely modernize more than a few features, leaving the text with a confused and unhistorical mixture of elements that clash with each other.[99] What is intended as a help becomes a barrier between the reader and the text he is interested in reading. Anyone who has examined a number of the partially modernized editions of letters can only react with incredulity at the things which editors seem to think readers need to have done for them. The modernizing editor is both condescending and officious: he assumes that the reader is not serious enough to persevere in reading a work if the punctuation, capitalization, and spelling do not conform to present-day practice, and his belief in the necessity of making changes blinds him to the triviality and senselessness of many of his alterations.[100] Modernization, or partial modernization, is clearly incompatible with the goals of the scholarly editing

98. As Samuel Schoenbaum says, "Surely the illusion of quaintness fades very quickly as the reader settles down to the material at hand" (p. 23); see "Editing English Dramatic Texts," in *Editing Sixteenth Century Texts*, ed. R. J. Schoeck (1966), pp. 12–24. A curious fact is that the feature of manuscript letters most frequently discussed and altered by editors is a dash (with or without other punctuation) at the end of a sentence (or even within sentences). Changing the dash to a period (or, within sentences, to some other appropriate mark) is usually regarded not as modernization but as the correction of an error; any practice that has been so widespread in private writing over so many years, however, is more sensibly regarded as a standard custom than as an error. (Of course, even if it were an idiosyncrasy—"error"—of a particular writer, that fact would not be a reason to alter it.)

99. The case against partial modernization of a published work has been most effectively stated by Fredson Bowers (who calls it "basically useless and always inconsistent") in his review of the second volume (1963) of *The Yale Edition of the Works of Samuel Johnson*, which modernizes capitalization (and the italicization of quotations) but not spelling and punctuation; see "The Text of Johnson," *Modern Philology*, 61 (1964), 298–309, reprinted in his collected *Essays*, pp. 375–391 (esp. pp. 378–381). Hershel Parker (see note 96 above), surveying a number of comments, says that partial modernization "has been all but hooted out of textual circles" (p. 1).

100. The point has been succinctly put by Hershel Parker (see note 96 above): "Normalizing to satisfy an editor's instinct for tidiness or to make smooth the way of a reader is ultimately demeaning for the editor and insulting to the reader" (p. 19).

of private documents—a fact which points to the most tragic weakness of many of the NHPRC editions.

Once it is settled that letters and journals are not to be presented in a corrected or modernized text, there still remains the question of whether editorial symbols are to be employed within the text or whether the text is to be free of such symbols ("clear text"). Even though no corrections are made,[101] there will be occasions when the editor needs to introduce a comment, such as "word illegible," "edge of paper torn, eliminating several words," or "written in the margin." Whether these explanations are entered in brackets in the text or printed as appended notes is to some extent merely a mechanical matter. But there is a theoretical aspect to the question. It is often argued that novels, essays, poems, and other works intended for publication should be edited in clear text, because such works are finished products, and the intrusion of editorial apparatus into the text (recording emendations or variants, for example) would be alien to the spirit of the work. For this reason the CEAA editions of this kind of material are in clear text, with the textual data relegated to lists at the ends of the volumes.[102] Private documents are different, however, in that they are often characterized by not being smooth—by containing, that is, false starts, deletions, insertions, and so on. The problem of how to handle deletions gets to the heart of the matter. Simply to leave them out, as is often done (or done on a selective basis), is indefensible, since they are essential characteristics of private documents.[103] One solution would be to leave them out of the text and report them in notes. But to do so would make the text appear smoother than it is; no evidence would be lost, but the reader would have to reconstruct the text of the document, which is after all of primary interest. If, on the other hand, the deletion is kept in the text but clearly marked as a deletion (with angle brackets or some other device),

---

101. Some responsible editions, as noted earlier, do incorporate certain minor categories of correction—not modernization—into the text and indicate exactly what has been done in notes. If these categories are carefully defined, their presence in the text may not seriously interfere with the aim of maintaining the texture of the original. It is dangerous to argue, however, that nothing is lost just because all the evidence is available in the notes; there is an important difference in emphasis between a reading which is chosen to stand in the text and one which is relegated to a note or a list.

102. There are practical advantages to this system, also, in the case of works likely to be reproduced photographically for widespread distribution by commercial publishers. For further discussion, see G. T. Tanselle, "Some Principles for Editorial Apparatus," *SB*, 25 (1972), 41–88 (esp. pp. 45–49).

103. One of the reasons for their importance is suggested by Boyd when he refers to "those revealing deletions and first thoughts that so often unmask the writer's true feelings or motives" ("Some Animadversions" [see note 14 above], p. 52). Even when they are not revealing in this way, they are still part of the characterizing roughness of the document and are indicative of the writer's process of composition.

the nature of the original is more accurately rendered in print. In reading the original, one would see a phrase with a line through it, for instance, and then read the phrase which replaced it; by keeping the deleted matter in the text, the editor allows the reader to have the same experience. But when canceled matter is recorded, it is essential at the same time to indicate whether the replacement (if any) occurs on the same line or is inserted above the line, so that the reader can tell whether the revision was made in the process of writing the words or perhaps at a later time.[104] A number of the NHPRC editions devote some attention to cancellations, but their frequent failure to specify interlinear insertions makes it impossible for the reader to use properly the texts of the cancellations which they do provide. Some situations can become very complex and may require an editorial description of what has happened as well as editorial symbols. This description might well be placed in a note rather than in the text; but since the text will contain editorial symbols in any case, one could decide to include editorial comments—at least the brief ones, like "illegible"—within the text.[105] The crucial point is that if a private document is presented in clear text it loses part of its texture.[106]

The argument thus far has assumed that for any given text the evidence available to the editor is a single document in the hand of the author. In those cases the editor's goal is to reproduce in print as many of the characteristics of the document as he can. The goal is not, in other words, to produce a critical text, except to the extent that judgment is involved in determining precisely what is in the manuscript. And judgment is inevitably involved: the editor of *Shelley and His Circle* points out that if a word clearly intended to be "even" looks more like "ever" it is still transcribed as "even." Distinguishing between

104. Methods of transcribing manuscripts in clear text (with apparatus) or in descriptive form (with symbols in the text) are carefully described by Fredson Bowers in "Transcription of Manuscripts: The Record of Variants," *SB*, 29 (1976), 212–264.

105. Of course, a text with several kinds of brackets in it (and other symbols such as arrows) will be more awkward to quote in secondary works, and this practical consideration may, in the case of a few important texts likely to be widely quoted, cause the editor to choose clear text and record all deletions in notes; it is questionable, however, whether what is gained from a practical point of view really justifies the loss incurred. Generally, in any case, there is no more reason to regularize or modernize a quoted excerpt than the complete text itself. The problem of the quoter as his own editor, along with many other considerations affecting the extent of editorial intrusion in private documents, is taken up by William H. Gilman in an excellent and thorough discussion (occasioned by the appearance of the first volume of the Irving *Journals*), "How Should Journals Be Edited?", *Early American Literature*, 6 (1971), 73–83.

106. This point was not recognized by Lewis Mumford in his famous review of the Emerson *Journals*, "Emerson Behind Barbed Wire," *New York Review of Books*, 18 January 1968, pp. 3–5, which objects to the inclusion of cancellations and editorial symbols. (See also the related correspondence in the issues of 14 March, pp. 35–36, and 23 May, p. 43.)

an actual misspelling or slip of the pen and merely indistinct or hasty handwriting requires careful judgment. The editor, even in presenting an "exact" transcription of the text of a document, must keep the writer's habits and intention in mind, if he is to be successful in discovering what that text actually says at difficult spots. If, for instance, a manuscript clearly reads "seperate," there is no doubt that the author wrote the word with a middle "e"; whether or not the author intended to misspell is irrelevant, so long as one agrees that an author's errors in private documents are of interest and should be preserved. But if the word only looks like "seperate" because the author has been careless in forming an "a" in the second syllable, the editor who prints "seperate" is neither transcribing accurately nor respecting the author's intention. In a case like "even"/"ever," the intention as determined by the context plays a greater role: deciphering handwriting and understanding the content are inseparable.[107] It is frequently necessary, therefore, even in connection with a so-called "literal" transcription, for an editor to append notes recording editorial decisions, if the reader is to be fully apprised of the state of the manuscript. But these decisions, it should be clearly understood, result from the effort to determine what the text of the document actually says, not what the editor believes it ought to say.

The situation is different, however, when the textual evidence is not limited to a single holograph document; there may be several drafts, versions, or copies, and they may be in the hand of a copyist or in printed form. In such cases the editor has a fundamental decision to make about the nature of his edited text: is it still to be a transcription of the text of a single document (with evidence from related documents given in notes), or is it to be a critical text which attempts through emendation (based on a study of all the documents) to represent the writer's intentions more fully than any single surviving document can? This decision will rest on the nature of the surviving documents—on their relative authority and completeness. When there are various versions or drafts of a letter in the author's hand, the editor would normally choose the one actually posted, if it survives, or the retained copy or latest surviving draft if it does not, as the document to be edited; variant readings and canceled matter in the other documents might then be added in notes, but—in line with the reasoning suggested above—they would not be emended into the text itself. If, on the other hand, the extant version or versions of a text are not in the author's hand—as when a letter

107. Shaw (see note 17 above) objects to the "essentially subjective basis for editorial revisions" (p. 741) in the critical-text policies of the CEAA editions and regards the attempt to "recapture 'the author's intention'" as opening "the door to chaos" (p. 740). He fails to acknowledge the subjectivity and concern for "intention" which are a part of all editing, even the transcription of a single manuscript text.

survives only in several scribal copies or in print—the editor is faced with the problem of distinguishing those features which reflect the author's intention from those which result from the habits and errors of another person (the copyist, the compositor, the printer's or publisher's reader, and so on). Since the interest is in the characteristics of the author's expression, not in those of a copyist or compositor, this problem is worth solving. For if an editor presents the text of a nonholograph document in an exact transcription, as he would that of a holograph document, he is respecting equally its authorial and its nonauthorial features; but if he attempts, so far as his evidence allows, to remove some of the nonauthorial features, he comes that much closer to offering what was present in the author's manuscript.

Editors of works which were intended to be made public commonly have this problem to deal with. When confronted with a printed text or texts, or with a printed text which differs from the author's manuscript, or with a scribal copy or copies, these editors frequently take it as their responsibility to evaluate the evidence (on the basis of their specialized knowledge of the author, his time, and the textual history of the work) and then to choose and emend a copy-text so as to obtain a maximum number of authorial readings and characteristics and a minimum number of nonauthorial ones.[108] The CEAA editions of works intended for publication have taken this approach, on the ground that more is to be gained by encouraging a qualified editor to apply what judgment and sensitivity he has to the problem of determining the author's intended text than by requiring him to reproduce the text present in a particular surviving document. Some mistakes are bound to result, but in general a text produced in this way is likely to come closer to what the author intended than a single documentary text could possibly do. (An accompanying record of emendations and variant readings is naturally important, so that the reader can reconstruct the copy-text and reconsider the evidence for emending it.) Editors of letters and journals will perhaps less frequently encounter similar situations, but when they do they should remember that preparing a critical text of nonholograph materials is not inconsistent with a policy of presenting a literal text of holograph manuscripts. Rather, it is an intelligent way of recognizing that a consistency of purpose may require different approaches for handling different situations. The aim of an edition of a person's letters and journals is to make available an accurate text

108. This "eclectic" approach is thoroughly discussed in Fredson Bowers's "Remarks on Eclectic Texts," *Proof*, 4 (1975), 31–76 (reprinted in his collected *Essays*, pp. 488–528). See also the various writings on Greg's rationale of copy-text; many are mentioned by G. T. Tanselle in *SB*, 28 (1975), 167–229.

of what he wrote; that goal cannot be achieved as fully for nonholograph documents as for holograph ones, but it is the editor's responsibility to come as close as he can in either case.[109]

When Peter Shaw claims that the NHPRC editions show more respect for historical fact than do the CEAA editions, he fails to recognize that an edition with a critical or "eclectic" text does not necessarily conceal historical facts and that an edition of a single documentary text does not necessarily reveal all relevant facts. Whether they do so or not depends on their policies for recording textual data.[110] CEAA editions are required to include textual apparatuses which contain records of all editorial emendations as well as several other categories of textual information;[111] most of the NHPRC editions, on the other hand, incorporate several kinds of silent emendations.[112] Readers of the former are able to reconstruct the original copy-texts and are in possession of much of the textual evidence which the editor had at his disposal; readers of the latter cannot reconstruct to the same degree the details of the original documents and are not provided with carefully defined categories of textual evidence on a systematic basis. The CEAA editors fulfill an essential editorial obligation: they inform their readers explicitly

109. A difficult category consists of semifinished manuscripts of the kinds of works normally intended for publication: the manuscripts of some of Emily Dickinson's poems and of Melville's *Billy Budd* are prominent examples. From one point of view they are private documents, and their nature can best be represented by a literal transcription showing cancellations and insertions in the text; from another point of view they are simply unfinished literary works and ought therefore to be printed in a critically established clear text, the form in which one normally expects to read poems and fiction. The solution which Harrison Hayford and Merton M. Sealts, Jr., reach in their edition of *Billy Budd* (University of Chicago Press, 1962) is to print a "genetic text" accompanied by a "reading text." For some comments on the general problem and on Dickinson's poems in particular, see Tanselle's "The Editorial Problem of Final Authorial Intention" (see note 95 above), esp. pp. 205–207.

110. Shaw says, "With an eclectic text, the problem of variants is solved at the expense of making them disappear from view" (p. 739)—as if there is something about an eclectic text which prohibits the recording of variant readings.

111. Including at least the substantive variants in post-copy-text editions and the treatment of ambiguous line-end hyphens, along with a textual essay and discussions of problematical readings. For further explanation of the CEAA requirements, see the CEAA *Statement of Editorial Principles and Procedures* (rev. ed., 1972).

112. Shaw's argument for the Freudian significance of errors (pp. 742–743) is actually a more telling criticism of most of the NHPRC editions than of the CEAA editions; when a CEAA editor does correct an error, he reports that fact in a list of emendations, whereas NHPRC editors often make corrections without notifying the reader where these corrections occur. Shaw objects to the CEAA editor who "rewrites usage, punctuation, spelling, capitalization, and hyphenation" (p. 741) and misleadingly implies that this practice is in contrast to that of NHPRC editors; actually, changes of this kind occur with greater frequency in the NHPRC editions—and are often not recorded in any way. At another point Shaw seems to take a different position on the question of errors: "It would be unfair to the author literally to transcribe his manuscript without correcting his obvious oversights" (p. 740).

of what textual information can and what cannot be found in their pages.[113] The truth is, therefore, that the CEAA editions are actually more respectful of documentary fact, and at the same time they recognize more fully that fidelity to a writer's intention demands, under certain circumstances, an eclectic approach to the documents. Comparing a CEAA edition of a novel with an NHPRC edition of letters creates a false opposition; but when CEAA and NHPRC editions of similar materials—two volumes of letters[114] or two volumes of works intended for publication—are compared, the CEAA volumes characteristically exhibit a more profound understanding of the problems involved in textual study and a greater responsibility in treating textual details. The NHPRC editors have undeniably been successful in the nontextual aspects of their work, and the CEAA editors could learn from them in regard to explanatory annotation. But in textual matters the CEAA editors are far in the lead. ⌐

This state of affairs is a depressing reminder of how little communication sometimes exists between fields with overlapping interests. In 1949, the year before the first volume of the Jefferson edition appeared, Fredson Bowers commented on the importance of textual study for all fields of endeavor:

No matter what the field of study, the basis lies in the analysis of the records in printed or in manuscript form, frequently the ill-ordered and incomplete records of the past. When factual or critical investigation is made of these records, there must be—it seems to me—the same care, no matter what the field, in establishing the purity and accuracy of the materials under exami-

113. One of the reasons the CEAA editions are not "definitive," Shaw says, is "the physical impossibility of comparing and recording all the variants as demanded by copy-text theory" (p. 748). Presumably any respectable theory would require an editor to compare texts and locate variants; the CEAA policy for recording variants, however, has nothing to do with theory—obviously a text edited according to Greg's theory of copy-text would remain so edited whether or not it were accompanied by any apparatus. It is true that CEAA editions do not always record all variants (neither do the NHPRC editions); but the important point is that CEAA editions clearly define what categories of variants are to be recorded and record all that fall within those categories, whereas NHPRC editions normally record variants selectively on the vague basis of "significance." Therefore, if the word "definitive" must be used, it would seem to fit CEAA apparatus but generally not NHPRC apparatus. The objection has been well put by Bowers, who says of the Johnson edition (see note 99 above) that the reader "has no way of knowing whether he is or is not accepting in ignorance any of the extensive editorial silent departures from the copy-text features" (p. 379).

114. Shaw is incorrect in saying that CEAA editions "include no plans to publish authors' letters" (p. 748). The opening of the same sentence is also incorrect: "Unlike the historical editions, most of them are selected, not complete, editions." It would be more accurate to say that most of the CEAA editions are planned to be complete, not selective, and that many of the NHPRC editions are in fact selective (leaving out the texts of certain less important documents and instead summarizing them or mentioning their existence in a calendar of manuscripts).

nation, which is perhaps just another way of saying that one must establish the text on which one's far-reaching analysis is to be based.[115]

In the twentieth century scholars of English literature—especially of Elizabethan drama—have taken over from the Biblical scholars and classicists as leaders in the development of textual theory and practice; and in the last generation the editing of nineteenth-century American literature has been a focal point in this continuing tradition. But the principles that have been emerging are not limited in their applicability to the field of literature. Students in all fields have occasion to work with written or printed documents, and they all need to have the habit of mind which inquires into the "purity and accuracy" of any document they consult. The NHPRC volumes have been singled out here because they constitute a prominent block of modern editions and can serve as an instructive example: the difference between the way American statesmen and American literary figures have recently been edited is a striking illustration of how two closely related fields can approach the basic scholarly task of establishing dependable texts in two very different ways, one of which seems superficial and naïve in comparison to the other. But history and literature are not the only fields that would mutually profit from a more encompassing discussion of textual problems; many editorial projects are now under way in philosophy and the sciences, and the fundamental questions which editors must ask are the same in those fields also. Editing is of course more than a matter of technique; a text can be satisfactorily edited only by a person with a thorough understanding of the content and historical and biographical setting of that text. Nevertheless, there is a common ground for discussion among editors in all fields. The time for closer communication of this kind is overdue; not only editors but all who study the written heritage of the past will benefit from it.

115. "Bibliography and the University," *University of Pennsylvania Library Chronicle,* 15 (1949), 37–51 (p. 37); reprinted in his collected *Essays,* pp. 3–14.